Asian/Oceanian Historical Dictionaries
Edited by Jon Woronoff

Asia
1. *Vietnam*, by William J. Duiker. 1989. *Out of print. See No. 27.*
2. *Bangladesh*, 2nd ed., by Craig Baxter and Syedur Rahman. 1996
3. *Pakistan*, by Shahid Javed Burki. 1991. *Out of print. See No. 33.*
4. *Jordan*, by Peter Gubser. 1991
5. *Afghanistan*, by Ludwig W. Adamec. 1991. *Out of print. See No. 29.*
6. *Laos*, by Martin Stuart-Fox and Mary Kooyman. 1992. *Out of print. See No. 35.*
7. *Singapore*, by K. Mulliner and Lian The-Mulliner. 1991
8. *Israel*, by Bernard Reich. 1992
9. *Indonesia*, by Robert Cribb. 1992
10. *Hong Kong and Macau*, by Elfed Vaughan Roberts, Sum Ngai Ling, and Peter Bradshaw. 1992
11. *Korea*, by Andrew C. Nahm. 1993
12. *Taiwan*, by John F. Copper. 1993. *Out of print. See No. 34.*
13. *Malaysia*, by Amarjit Kaur. 1993. *Out of print. See No. 36.*
14. *Saudi Arabia*, by J. E. Peterson. 1993. *Out of print. See No. 45.*
15. *Myanmar*, by Jan Becka. 1995
16. *Iran*, by John H. Lorentz. 1995
17. *Yemen*, by Robert D. Burrowes. 1995
18. *Thailand*, by May Kyi Win and Harold Smith. 1995
19. *Mongolia*, by Alan J. K. Sanders. 1996. *Out of print. See No. 42.*
20. *India*, by Surjit Mansingh. 1996
21. *Gulf Arab States*, by Malcolm C. Peck. 1996
22. *Syria*, by David Commins. 1996
23. *Palestine*, by Nafez Y. Nazzal and Laila A. Nazzal. 1997
24. *Philippines*, by Artemio R. Guillermo and May Kyi Win. 1997

Oceania
1. *Australia*, by James C. Docherty. 1992. *Out of print. See No. 32.*
2. *Polynesia*, by Robert D. Craig. 1993. *Out of print. See No. 39.*
3. *Guam and Micronesia*, by William Wuerch and Dirk Ballendorf. 1994
4. *Papua New Guinea*, by Ann Turner. 1994. *Out of print. See No. 37.*
5. *New Zealand*, by Keith Jackson and Alan McRobie. 1996

New Combined Series
25. *Brunei Darussalam*, by D. S. Ranjit Singh and Jatswan S. Sidhu. 1997
26. *Sri Lanka*, by S. W. R. de A. Samarasinghe and Vidyamali Samarasinghe. 1998
27. *Vietnam*, 2nd ed., by William J. Duiker. 1998
28. *People's Republic of China: 1949–1997*, by Lawrence R. Sullivan, with the assistance of Nancy Hearst. 1998
29. *Afghanistan*, 2nd ed., by Ludwig W. Adamec. 1997
30. *Lebanon*, by As'ad AbuKhalil. 1998
31. *Azerbaijan*, by Tadeusz Swietochowski and Brian C. Collins. 1999
32. *Australia*, 2nd ed., by James C. Docherty. 1999
33. *Pakistan*, 2nd ed., by Shahid Javed Burki. 1999
34. *Taiwan (Republic of China)*, 2nd ed., by John F. Copper. 2000
35. *Laos*, 2nd ed., by Martin Stuart-Fox. 2001
36. *Malaysia*, 2nd ed., by Amarjit Kaur. 2001
37. *Papua New Guinea*, 2nd ed., by Ann Turner. 2001
38. *Tajikistan*, by Kamoludin Abdullaev and Shahram Akbarzedeh. 2002
39. *Polynesia*, 2nd ed., by Robert D. Craig. 2002
40. *North Korea*, by Ilpyong J. Kim. 2003
41. *Armenia*, by Rouben Paul Adalian. 2002
42. *Mongolia*, 2nd ed., by Alan J. K. Sanders. 2003
43. *Cambodia*, by Justin Corfield and Laura Summers. 2003
44. *Iraq*, by Edmund A. Ghareeb. 2003
45. *Saudi Arabia*, 2nd ed., by J. E. Peterson. 2003
46. *Nepal*, by Nanda R. Shrestha and Keshav Bhattarai. 2003

Historical Dictionary of Nepal

Nanda R. Shrestha
Keshav Bhattarai

Asian/Oceanian Historical Dictionaries, No. 46

The Scarecrow Press, Inc.
Lanham, Maryland, and Oxford
2003

SCARECROW PRESS, INC.

Published in the United States of America
by Scarecrow Press, Inc.
A wholly owned subsidiary of the Rowman & Littlefield Publishing Group, Inc.
4501 Forbes Boulevard, Suite 200, Lanham, Maryland 20706
www.scarecrowpress.com

PO Box 317
Oxford
OX2 9RU, UK

Copyright © 2003 by Nanda R. Shrestha

All rights reserved. No part of this publication may be reproduced, stored in a retrieval system, or transmitted in any form or by any means, electronic, mechanical, photocopying, recording, or otherwise, without the prior permission of the publisher.

British Library Cataloguing-in-Publication Information Available

Library of Congress Cataloging-in-Publication Data

Shrestha, Nanda R.
  Historical dictionary of Nepal / Nanda R. Shrestha, Keshav Bhattarai.
    p. cm. — (Asian/Oceanian historical dictionaries ; no. 46)
  Includes bibliographical references.
  ISBN 0-8108-4797-3 (hardcover : alk. paper)
  1. Nepal—History—Dictionaries. I. Bhattarai, Keshav, 1955– II. Title. III. Series.
DS494.5.S58 2003
954.96'003—dc21

2003006882

©™ The paper used in this publication meets the minimum requirements of American National Standard for Information Sciences—Permanence of Paper for Printed Library Materials, ANSI/NISO Z39.48-1992.
Manufactured in the United States of America.

Contents

Maps	vii
Tables	xi
Editor's Foreword (Jon Woronoff)	xxiii
Acknowledgments	xxv
Acronyms and Abbreviations	xxvii
Notes to the Reader	xxxi
Chronology	xxxvii
Introduction	1
THE DICTIONARY	35
Appendix: Prime Ministers and Council Chairmen, 1951–2003	337
Glossary	341
Bibliography	347
About the Authors	411

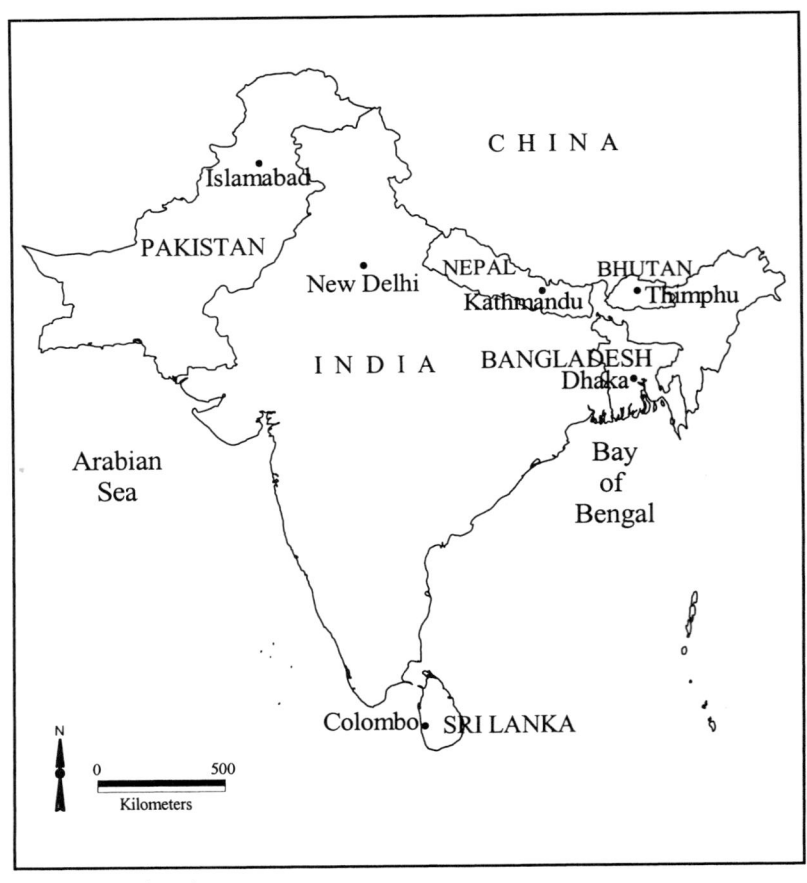

Figure 1. South Asia.

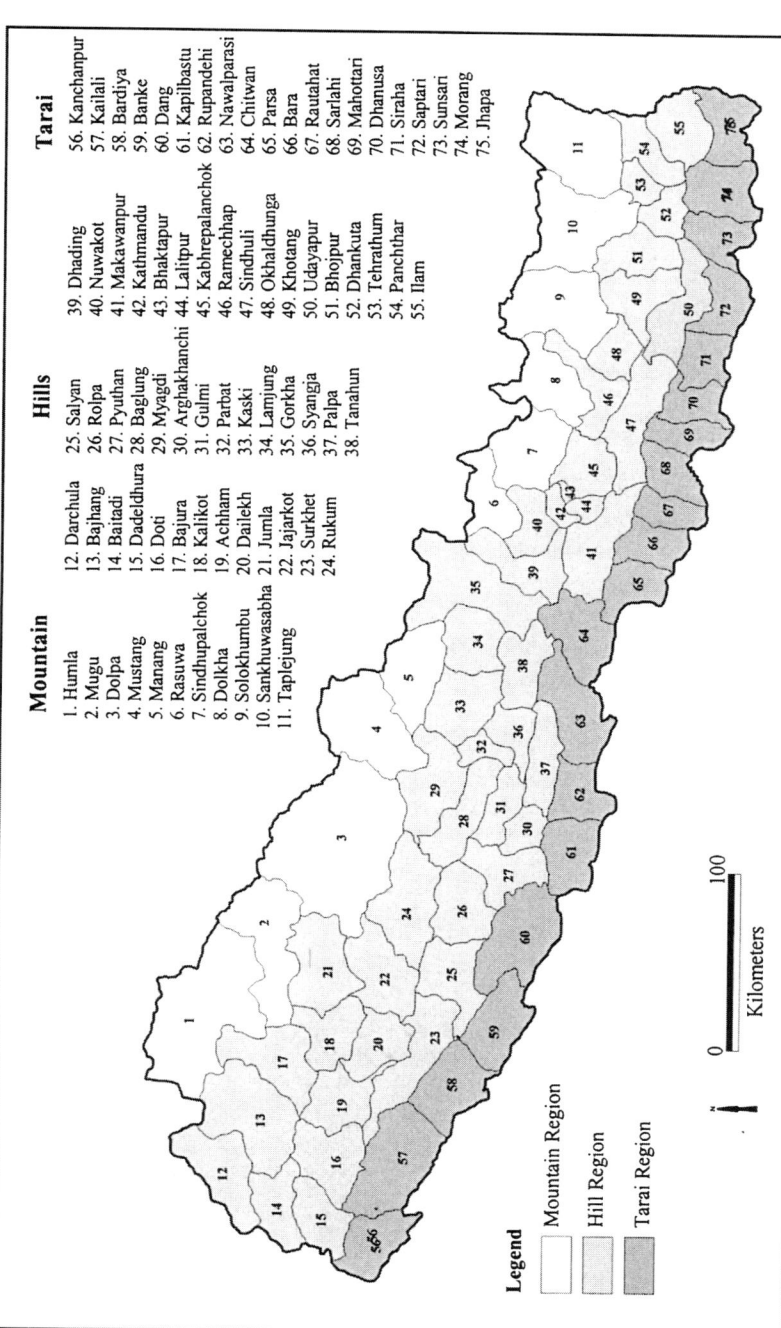

Figure 2. Physiographic Regions and Administrative Districts of Nepal.

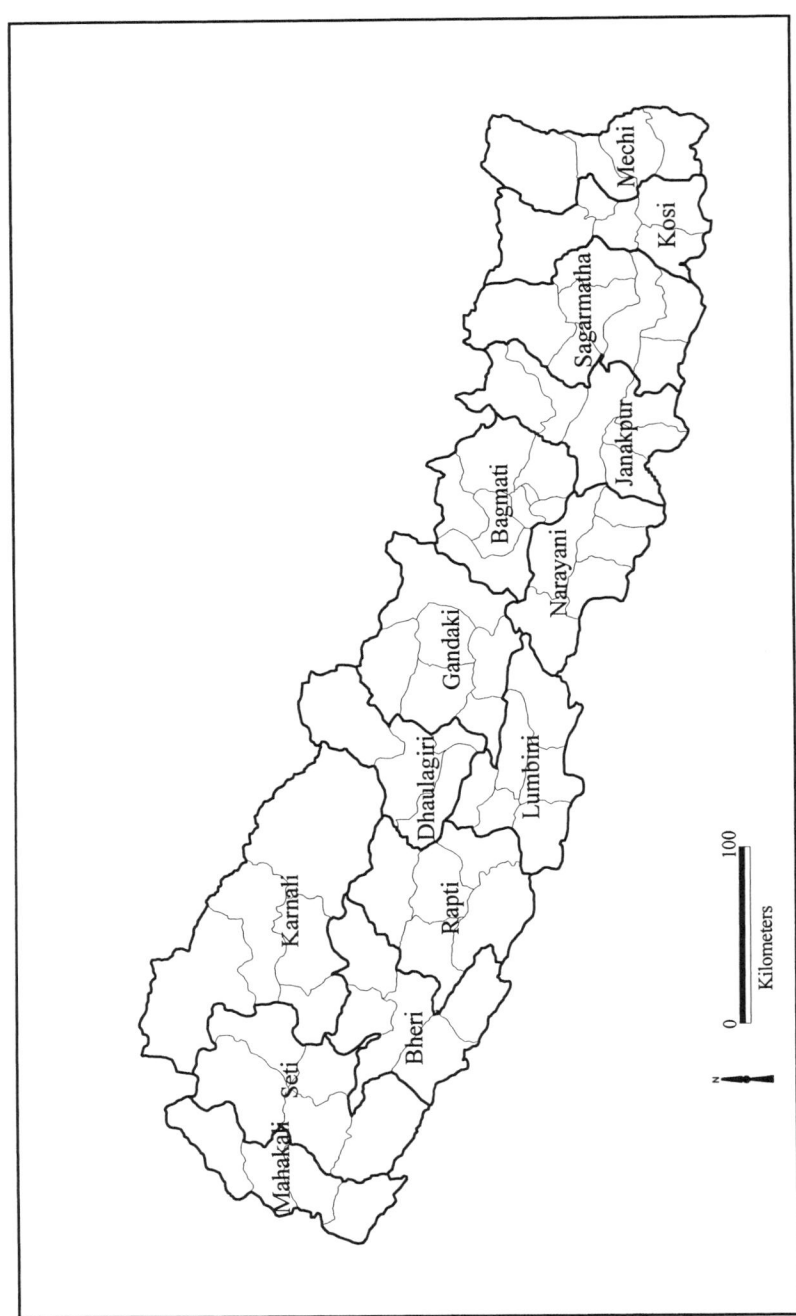

Figure 3. Administrative Zones of Nepal.

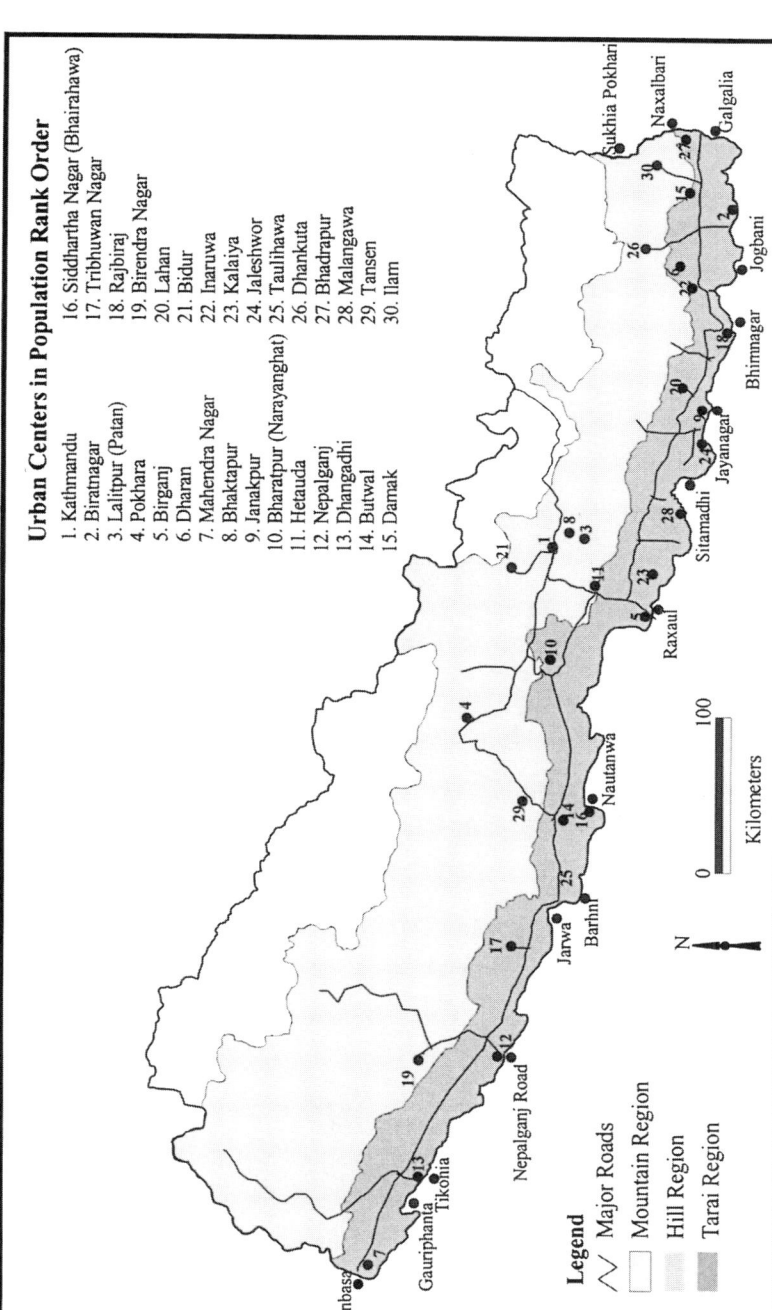

Figure 4. Major Urban Centers of Nepal and Indian Railheads.

Table 1: Structural Data, 1961–2001

Category	1961	1971	1981	1991	2001
Population (million)	9.4	11.6	15.0	18.5	23.2
Population growth (%)	1.6	2.1	2.6	2.4	2.4
Urban population (000)	338	464	959	1,698	3,303
Rural employment (%)					76.0
Industrial employment (%)					6.0
Literacy (%)	8.9	14.0	23.3	39.6	52.6*
Male	16.3	23.6	34.0	54.4	69.0*
Female	1.8	3.9	12.0	25.0	39.0*
Life expectancy (years)	38.5	41.0	49.5	54.5	59.0
Male	37.0	42.1	50.9	55.0	60.0*
Female	39.9	40.0	48.1	53.5	58.0*
Birth rate/1,000 people	47.0	42.0	43.5	41.6	34.0*
Death rate/1,000 people	22.0	21.4	13.5	13.1	10.1*
Infant mortality/1,000 live births	193.0	172.0	117.0	97.0	64.0
Male	200.0		136.0	94.0	63.0*
Female	186.0		111.0	101.0	65.0*

* Estimates

Source: Population Projection for Nepal, 1996–2016. Kathmandu: Ministry of Population and Environment, 1998, and additional demographic data on its website: www.mope.gov.np; *Nepal: Key Indicators.* Asian Development Bank, website: www.adb.org

Table 2: Regional Population Distribution, 1961–2001

Region (population in million)	1961	1971	1981	1991	2001
Mountain + Hill Regions	6.0				
(% of total population)	(63.6)				
Mountain Region		1.1	1.3	1.4	1.7
(% of total population)		(9.9)	(8.7)	(7.8)	(7.3)
Hill Region		6.1	7.1	8.4	10.3
(% of total population)		(52.5)	(47.7)	(45.5)	(44.2)
Tarai Region	3.4	4.4	6.6	8.7	11.2
(% of total population)	(36.4)	(37.6)	(43.6)	(46.7)	(48.5)
Nepal	9.4	11.6	15.0	18.5	23.2
(% of total population)	(100)	(100)	(100)	(100)	(100)

Source: Population Projection for Nepal, 1996–2016. Kathmandu: Ministry of Population and Environment, 1998; *Statistical Year Book of Nepal, 2001.* Kathmandu: Central Bureau of Statistics, 2001.

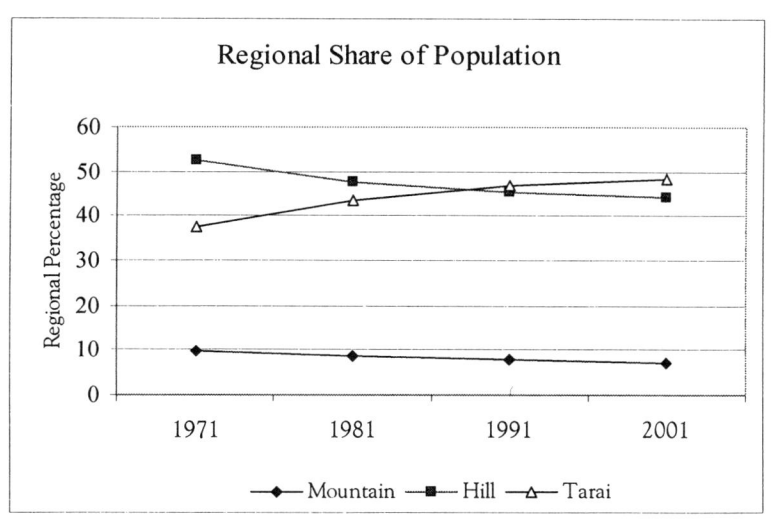

Table 3: Gross Domestic Product, 1985–2000

Economic Activity (production value in million Rupees)	1985	1990	1995	2000
Agriculture, fisheries & forestry	22,761	50,470	85,569	142,908
Mining and quarrying	193	449	1,117	1,815
Manufacturing	2,511	5,956	19,555	35,387
Electricity, gas & water	184	523	2,862	5,895
Construction	3,761	8,943	23,093	36,127
Trade, restaurant & hotel	4,561	10,507	24,326	43,109
Transport and communication	2,679	5,724	13,995	29,281
Finance and real estate	3,987	9,269	20,533	36,919
Community and social service	3,803	7,861	18,924	37,922
Imputed bank service charge	(425)	(1,954)	(5,060)	(10,708)
Indirect taxes less subsidies	2,571	5,668	14,261	24,898
GDP at current market prices	46,586	103,416	219,175	383,553
Net factor income from abroad	661	1,934	4,817	13,125
GNP at current market prices	47,247	105,350	223,992	396,678
Exchange rates: Nepali Rupees per 1 US dollar				
End of year	20.7	30.4	56.0	74.3
Average for the year	18.3	29.4	51.9	71.1

Source: Statistical Year Book of Nepal, 2001. Kathmandu: Central Bureau of Statistics, 2001; *Nepal: Key Indicators.* Asian Development Bank, website: www.adb.org

Table 4: Domestic Production, 1985–2000

Production (in metric tons)	1985	1990	1995	2000
Agriculture				
Rice (paddy)	2,837	3,409	2,928	4,030
Sugarcane	425	997	1,500	2,103
Maize	1,024	1,201	1,273	1,445
Wheat	625	855	914	1,184
Potatoes	504	677	840	1,183
Millet	179	230	268	295
Barley	25	27	30	31
Jute	33	16	11	15
Total	5,652	7,412	7,764	10,286
Manufacturing				
Cement	32	101	327	248
Iron goods	15	36	95	145
Sugar	11	32	49	77
Soap	8	12	24	74
Jute goods	20	8	20	50
Tea	1	1	2	4
Strawboard	1	1	1	1
Fertilizer	43	67		
Total	131	258	518	599

Source: Statistical Year Book of Nepal, 2001. Kathmandu: Central Bureau of Statistics, 2001; *Nepal: Key Indicators.* Asian Development Bank, website: www.adb.org

Table 5: Import-Export Structure and Trend, 1990–2000

Import-Export Categories	1990			2000		
	Import	Export	Deficit	Import	Export	Deficit
Food and Live Animals	1,608	616	− 990	10,893	4,240	− 6,653
Crude Materials	1,571	239	− 1,332	7,012	561	− 6,451
Animal/Vegetable Oil/Fat	476	20	− 456	4,446	3,230	− 1,216
Chemicals	2,824	11	− 2,813	14,474	3,933	− 10,541
Basic Manufactures	5,065	2,693	− 2,372	34,420	15,839	− 18,581
Misc. Manufactures	1,248	1,573	325	6,683	21,509	14,826
Mineral Fuels	1,516		− 1,516	9,098		− 9,098
Machine/Transport Equip.	3,790		− 3,790	20,546		− 20,546
Others	228	4	− 224	985	510	− 475
Total	18,326	5,156	−13,170	108,557	49,822	− 58,735

Source: Nepal: Key Indicators. Asian Development Bank, website: www.adb.org

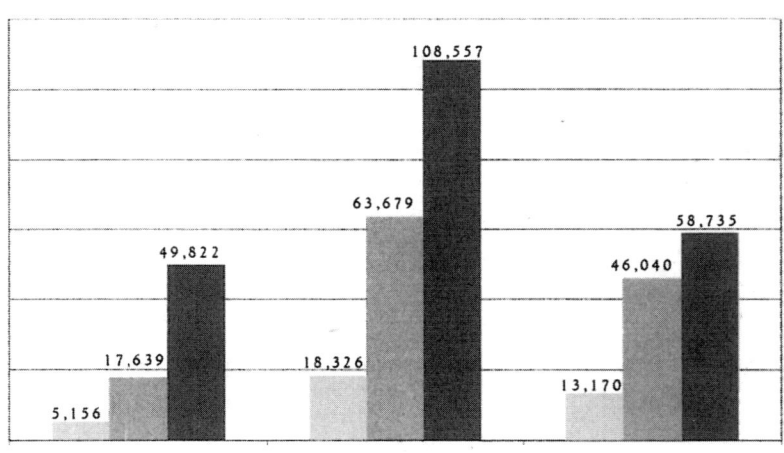

Table 6: Direction of Imports and Exports, 1990–2000

Major Import-Export Countries (value in million US dollars)	1990 Import	1990 Export	2000 Import	2000 Export
India	58.5	14.8	522.3	172.8
China (Hong Kong)	25.9		115.8	
Singapore	86.4		102.6	
China (People's Republic)	43.1		191.6	
Argentina			220.7	42.5
United Arab Emirates			74.4	
Japan	109.9	1.7	37.7	
Saudi Arabia			32.7	
New Zealand	30.1		19.1	
Thailand	39.8		31.9	
United States		49.5		220.2
Germany		76.6		90.2
United Kingdom		12.2		19.4
France		5.5		14.2
Bangladesh		0.6		1.9
Italy		3.3		8.4
Switzerland		12.7		21.0
Subtotal	393.7	176.9	1,348.8	590.6
Others	35.5	34.4	270.7	80.2
Total	429.2	211.3	1,619.5	670.8

Source: Nepal: Key Indicators. Asian Development Bank, website: www.adb.org

Table 7: Major Exports, 1990–2000

Major Exports (in (million Rupees)	1990	1995	2000
Carpets	2,319	7,718	9,842
Garments	1,399	5,139	13,942
Pulses	212	457	1,057
Jute goods	5	231	1,104
Total	3,935	13,545	25,945

Source: Nepal: Key Indicators. Asian Development Bank, website: www.adb.org

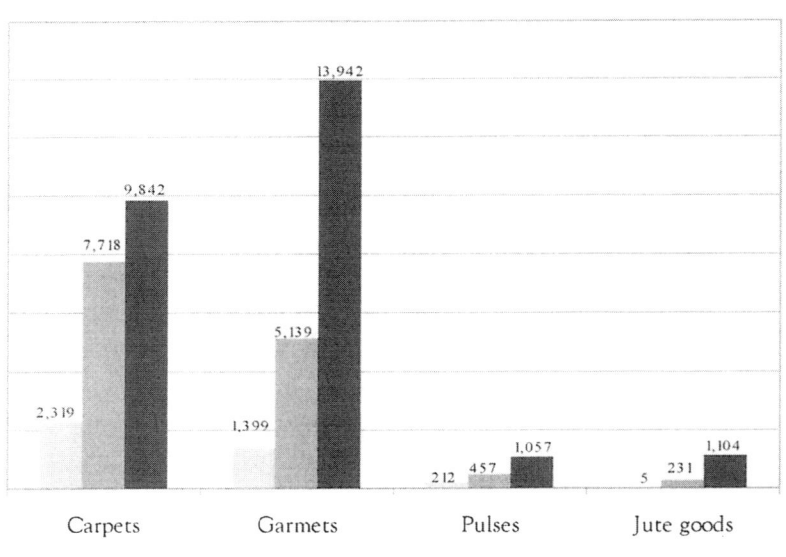

1990 ▓ 1995 ■ 2000

Table 8: Number of Tourists by Major Nationality, 1990–1999

Country of Origin	1990	1995	1999
Australia	10,249	9,201	11,873
Austria	2,624	3,852	6,377
Canada	4,917	5,047	7,578
Denmark	2,840	4,629	4,577
France	19,909	19,208	24,490
Germany	18,565	33,971	26,378
India	59,764	117,260	140,661
Italy	11,952	10,267	12,870
Japan	15,021	25,360	38,893
Netherlands	5,972	8,681	17,198
Spain	8,515	7,129	9,370
Switzerland	5,278	5,981	8,431
United States	21,426	24,655	39,332
United Kingdom	23,877	26,768	36,852
Others	43,976	61,386	106,624
Total	254,885	363,395	491,504

Source: *Statistical Year Book of Nepal, 2001*. Kathmandu: Central Bureau of Statistics, 2001.

Table 9: Zonal Population Distribution by Religion, 1991

Zone	Hindu	Buddhist	Muslim	Christian	Others	Total
Mechi	831,999	91,462	15,644	2,394	176,711	1,118,210
Kosi	1,270,724	74,823	72,793	4,476	106,647	1,529,463
Sagarmatha	1,560,184	100,224	67,979	1,765	68,915	1,799,076
Janakpur	1,749,559	181,785	127,898	772	1,904	2,061,816
Bagmati	1,639,772	588,165	6,757	9,533	6,578	2,251,805
Narayani	1,490,710	205,802	169,188	3,091	2,543	1,871,334
Gandaki	1,126,116	127,816	7,571	3,389	1,236	1,266,128
Dhaulagiri	467,897	21,491	671	193	625	490,877
Lumbini	1,869,676	17,523	122,851	2,030	1,593	2,012,673
Rapti	1,010,311	888	4,364	555	724	1,046,842
Bheri	1,043,641	3,262	53,983	1,016	1,141	1,103,043
Karnali	241,702	18,668	27	62	70	260,529
Seti	1,006,131	3,333	3,037	504	1,317	1,014,349
Mahakali	658,533	3,873	446	1,600	500	664,952
Nepal	15,966,955	1,439,115	653,209	31,380	370,504	18,491,097
Percent	86.4	7.9	3.5	0.2	2.0	100.0

Source: *Statistical Year Book of Nepal, 2001*. Kathmandu: Central Bureau of Statistics, 2001.

Table 10: Population Distribution by Age and Sex, 1991

Age Group	Male	Female	Total
0 to 4	1,371,225	1,336,127	2,707,352
5 to 9	1,430,265	1,375,868	2,806,133
10 to 14	1,209,803	1,117,483	2,327,286
15 to 19	878,035	914,492	1,792,527
20 to 24	729,279	857,484	1,586,763
25 to 29	648,268	726,141	1,374,409
30 to 34	552,339	601,962	1,154,301
35 to 39	516,229	511,018	1,027,247
40 to 44	409,992	432,727	842,719
45 to 49	374,362	359,800	734,162
50 to 54	307,446	291,038	598,484
55 to 59	250,040	215,917	465,957
60 to 64	215,479	216,166	431,645
65 to 69	141,707	128,765	270,472
70 to 74	94,230	89,722	183,952
75 +	92,275	95,413	187,688
Total	9,220,974	9,270,123	18,491,097

Source: *Statistical Year Book of Nepal, 2001*. Kathmandu: Central Bureau of Statistics, 2001.

Table 11: Age and Sex Composition, 1991

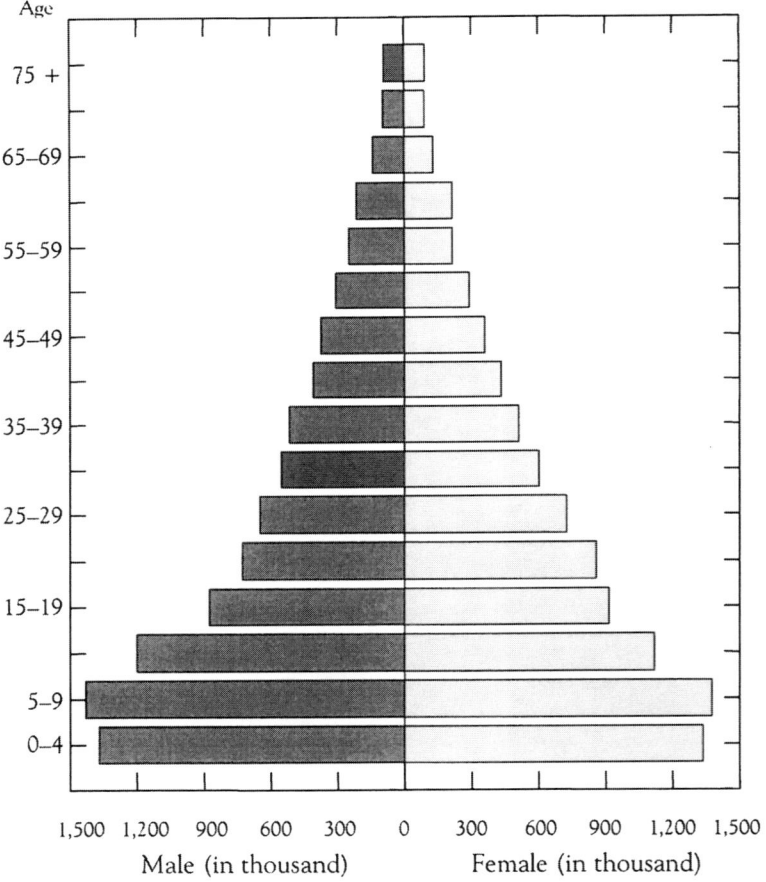

Table 12: Zonal Population Distribution by Sex, 2001

Zone	Male	Female	Total	Sex Ratio
Mechi	654,999	660,144	1,315,143	0.992
Kosi	953,494	957,938	1,911,432	0.995
Sagarmatha	1,072,166	1,067,654	2,139,820	1.004
Janakpur	1,320,263	1,259,733	2,579,996	1.048
Bagmati	1,539,416	1,479,442	3,018,858	1.041
Narayani	1,258,980	1,200,216	2,459,196	1.049
Gandaki	699,223	790,256	1,489,479	0.885
Dhaulagiri	267,153	298,290	565,443	0.896
Lumbini	1,239,358	1,283,785	2,523,143	0.965
Rapti	631,282	656,814	1,288,096	0.961
Bheri	716,006	708,319	1,424,325	1.011
Karnali	157,367	152,420	309,787	1.032
Seti	662,387	675,066	1,337,453	0.981
Mahakali	427,453	437,055	864,508	0.978
Nepal	11,599,547	11,627,132	23,226,679	0.997

Source: *Statistical Year Book of Nepal, 2001*. Kathmandu: Central Bureau of Statistics, 2001, and "Preliminary results of census 2001" loose sheets enclosed.

Editor's Foreword

We know little about some countries, indeed, close to nothing in the general public. About others, we seem to actually know less than nothing. Nepal may fit in that category. Too much of what the public "knows" derives from brief and usually pleasant vacations or idyllic descriptions, which make the place look like Shangri-La. Shangri-La it is not—and probably never was. Instead, as this book shows, it is just an ordinary country with an extraordinary number of problems. These include standard ones like inadequate economic development and social infrastructure, poverty and corruption, plus worsening pollution, but now also a Maoist uprising, which shows that it never quite provided alternative means of expression or more than superficial democratization. This will make it even harder for Nepal to progress; it might well regress instead.

    This book, thank goodness, does not engage in clichés or indulge illusions. It describes Nepal's history, politics, economy, society, and religion in fairly straightforward terms and in a reasonably balanced manner. It focuses on significant rulers of the past and present as well as lesser beings who have risen from among the people in what is still a kingdom strongly permeated with traditional religion. The broad historical background can be found in the introduction, with numerous details in the dictionary section. The chronology shows where Nepal comes from and, alas, where it has gone wrong several times and is wandering aimlessly at present. The bibliography makes it possible to learn even more about the real Nepal, and serves as an antidote to the often deceptive travel guides and travelers' tales.

    The *Historical Dictionary of Nepal* was written not by historians or political scientists, like most of the books in this series, but geographers of all things. That is hardly a drawback. Geographers, more than other academics, have to see things from the ground up and cover a lot of territory. This comes in handy for a country like Nepal. Moreover, both authors were born in Nepal, raised in Nepal, and began their studies in Nepal. Both then emigrated. Keshav Bhattarai, the younger of the two, actually worked as a district forest officer in Nepal before coming to the United States, where he is now associate professor of geography at Central Missouri State University. Nanda R. Shrestha, who came to the United States in 1972, is currently professor of resources and cultural management in the School of Business and Industry at Florida A&M University. Over the years, he has visited Nepal frequently and written on its geography and economic development extensively. This includes several books, namely, *Landlessness and Migration in Nepal*, *In the Name of Development: A Reflection on Nepal*, and *Nepal and Bangladesh: A Global Studies Handbook*. Together they are a knowledgeable pair of guides with whom to explore the country.

Jon Woronoff
Series Editor

Acknowledgments

First of all, we would like to thank Jon Woronoff for asking us to do this book and for his many insightful comments and editorial suggestions on its earlier draft. In addition, we are very grateful to Florida A&M University and to Dean Sybil C. Mobley for granting Nanda R. Shrestha a sabbatical leave to work on this book. Without their support, it would have been very difficult for us to complete it in a timely manner. Dinesh Bhattarai of the Nepali Embassy in Washington, D.C., provided information on some of the recent developments concerning Nepali politics and society. We would also like to extend our sincere thanks to Kim Tabor and Niki Averill for their meticulous help in the production and copyediting of this book. Often forgotten in such an endeavor are the silent and invisible contributors who endure the most but get the least credit for their critical role in bringing it to fruition. They are the family members, the anchors of what we do, both in the personal and professional domains of our lives. We owe much to our respective families for their endless support and understanding, without which it would not have been possible to finish this volume. They are our silent warriors and eternal inspiration.

Nanda R. Shrestha
Florida A&M University
and
Keshav Bhattarai
Central Missouri State University

Acronyms and Abbreviations

ADB	Asian Development Bank
ADB-N	Agricultural Development Bank of Nepal
AFP	Agence France-Presse
AIC	Agriculture Inputs Corporation
APROSC	Agriculture Projects Services Centre
ARTEP	Asian Regional Team for Employment Production
ASD	Agricultural Statistics Division
BBC	British Broadcasting Corporation
BS	Bikram Sambat (Nepal's calendar system)
CBS	Central Bureau of Statistics (Nepal)
CDG	Centre for Development and Governance
CEDA	Centre for Economic Development and Administration
CGDS	Centre for Governance and Development Studies
CNAS	Centre for Nepal and Asian Studies
CPFD	Community and Private Forestry Development
CPN	Communist Party of Nepal
CREST	Centre for Resources and Environmental Studies
CWIN	Child Workers in Nepal
CWS	Child Welfare Society
DANIDA	Danish International Development Agency
DFO	District Forest Officer
DFRS	Department of Forest Research and Survey
DHM	Department of Hydrology and Meteorology
DMP	Department of Medicinal Plant
DOA	Department of Agriculture
DOHS	Department of Health Services
ENPHO	Environment and Public Health Organization

ESCAP	Economic and Social Commission for Asia and the Pacific
FAO	Food and Agriculture Organization
FES	Friedrich Ebert Stiftung
FINNIDA	Finnish International Development Agency
FMUDP	Forest Management, Utilization and Development Project
FNCCI	Federation of Nepalese Chambers of Commerce and Industry
FOPHUR	Forum for Protection of Human Rights
FPDC	Forest Products Distribution Committee
GDP	Gross Domestic Product
GNP	Gross National Product
GTZ	German Agency for Technical Cooperation
GWRDB	Ground Water Resources Development Board
HMG	His Majesty's Government
HPL	Himal Power Limited
ICIMOD	International Centre for Integrated Mountain Development
IDS	Integrated Development Systems
IIDS	Institute of Integrated Development Systems
ILO	International Labour Organisation
INGO	International Nongovernmental Organization
IUCN	International Union for Conservation of Nature (World Conservation Union)
LDC	Least Developed Country
LRMP	Land Resource Mapping Project
MLD	Ministry of Local Development
MOA	Ministry of Agriculture
MOF	Ministry of Finance
MOFASC	Ministry of Forest and Soil Conservation
MOH	Ministry of Health
MOHA	Ministry of Home Affairs
MOPE	Ministry of Population and Environment
MOWAR	Ministry of Water Resources
MP	Member of Parliament
MRD	Movement for the Restoration of Democracy
NARC	Nepal Agriculture Research Centre
NCC	Nepal Chamber of Commerce
NCP (NC)	Nepali Congress Party
NDC	Nepal Development Council
NDP	National Democratic Party (*see* RPP)
NIDC	Nepal Industrial Development Corporation

Acronyms and Abbreviations

NEFAS	Nepal Foundation for Advanced Studies
NESAC	Nepal South Asia Centre
NGO	Nongovernmental Organization
NHRC	National Human Rights Commission
NOC	Nepal Oil Corporation
NORAD	Norwegian Agency for Cooperation and Development
NPC or NC	Nepali Congress Party
NPC	National Planning Commission
NRB	Nepal Rastra Bank
NSP	Nepal Sadbhavana Party
POLSAN	Political Science Association of Nepal
RNAC	Royal Nepal Airlines Corporation
RONAST	Royal Nepal Academy of Science and Technology
RPP	Rastriya Prajatantra Party (*see* NDP)
RVDP	Rapti Valley Development Project
SAARC	South Asian Association for Regional Cooperation
SAP	South Asia Partnership
SLC	School Leaving Certificate
TADO	Terrorist and Disruptive Activities Ordinance
TCN	Timber Corporation of Nepal
TU	Tribhuvan University (Nepal)
UCEP	Underprivileged Children's Educational Programme
UFL	United Left Front
UML	Unified (United) Marxist-Leninist (*see* CPN)
UNCDF	United Nations Capital Development Fund
UNDP	United Nations Development Programme
UNEP	United Nations Environment Programme
UNESCO	United Nations Educational, Scientific and Cultural Organization
UNFPA	United Nations Population Fund
UNICEF	United Nations Children's Fund
USAID	United States Agency for International Development
USEF	United States Educational Foundation
USIA	United States Information Agency
USOM	United States Operations Mission (predecessor to USAID)
VDC	Village Development Committee
WHO	World Health Organization
WWF	World Wildlife Fund

Notes to the Reader

NEPALI LANGUAGE

Is it "Nepali" or "Nepalese?" This is the question one may ask. The quick answer is both are common in vernacular use, but no "Nepalian," please. Throughout this volume, we use "Nepali." Its variation—some might say deviation—is "Nepalese." In some corners, the latter is more common than "Nepali." We, however, use "Nepali" in this volume because it is far more appropriate and reflective of the Nepali system than the term "Nepalese." Furthermore, the word "Nepali" is historically embedded. That is why the vast majority of Nepalis use it rather than its variant form, i.e., "Nepalese." Common use of "Nepalese" among most Nepali elite and foreigners is mainly attributed to the anglicization of "Nepali." Regardless, the word "Nepali" refers to the people of Nepal as well as anything pertaining to Nepal. And it is the country's national language.

Written in Devanagari script, Nepali is similar to, but not identical with, Hindi. There are many words used in these languages that are similar. They carry the same meaning and are generally pronounced the same way. Those who can read Nepali can read Hindi and vice versa. The grammar structure is quite similar. All of this is directly attributed to the fact that they are both derived from Sanskrit—the language of original Hindu texts and epics and of Vedic or religious studies in the past, monopolized by the upper crust of the Brahman caste.

Nepali has 31 consonants and 16 vowels (including both long and short vowels). In spite of its elaborate structure and sound system, most of the Nepali sounds are not difficult to master. Many are very similar to English. That is, unlike in some other languages, Nepali entails no contradiction between the way it is written and the way it is pronounced. For instance, in Spanish, the letter "j" in its written form often has the sound of the letter "h" in its spoken form (e.g., Jose). But Nepali is straightforward in this respect in that the letter "j" is pronounced with a "j" sound. That is true with virtually every English alphabet, with the possible exception of the letter "v" which sometimes carries the sound of the letter "b" (e.g., Vishnu for Bishnu). This is an unnatural deviation, resulting from the influence of the Indian pronunciation and romanization system adopted in Nepal. If one happens to deploy a "v" sound as opposed to a "b" sound in such cases, there is no harm in that most will readily understand the deviation.

There is, however, one specific Nepali sound that poses a challenge for many Westerners. This sound is associated with the seventh consonant and can be written in Roman alphabets as "chh." This is basically the aspirated and slightly elongated version of the English sound "ch" as in "*ch*urch." This sound comes more from the throat region than from a single flap of the tongue against the front part of its roof. This is one sound that gives most Westerners, including those who are linguistically versatile, some consternation as they have difficulty mastering it even after a long stay in the country. Although both sounds appear to have the same base, the "chh" sound is definitely distinct, for instance, "*Chh*etri," one of the caste groups. Nepali has a separate consonant for the "ch" sound which is non-aspirated. The "jh" sound (e.g., *jhakri* meaning a shaman) which, too, is aspirated in contrast to the "j" sound is also somewhat difficult, but nothing like what one faces with the "chh" sound. The "th" sound is also problematic, for it can be either aspirated or non-aspirated. Nepali has two distinct alphabets with the "th" sound. In its aspirated form, the letter "h" in the "th" sound is almost silent as in "Ka*th*mandu" or "Shres*th*a." In its non-aspirated form, it is pronounced with a dental sound as in the word, "*th*ink."

Similar to Japanese, the word structure or sound system usually follows an alternate consonant-vowel-consonant pattern, for example, "tapai kahile Nepal pharkane pheri?" (When are you returning to Nepal again?). If one observes each word in the Nepali sentence, it is clear that each consonant (or what one may call a consonant unit as in "ph") is followed by a vowel. The "a" vowel when used to romanize Nepali words can have both the long and short "a" sounds, thus causing some confusion as to how one should pronounce a given Nepali word. Take "K*a*thm*a*ndu." In this instance, both "a" sounds—K*a* and m*a*—are long as in "c*a*rtoon." On the other hand, take the word "k*a*rm*a*." Here both "a" sounds are short as in "b*a*lloon."

The vowel "e" in Nepali is phonetically pronounced in most cases like the "e" sound in the English word "cherry" or "day." The "I" in Nepali can sound like either the English word "h*i*d" or "h*ee*d." This may be confusing to most Westerners, but most Nepalis make little distinctions between the long and short "e" sounds generated by the vowel "I" (as in h*i*d vs. h*ee*d). This shortcoming is not based on the lack of two distinct sounds in Nepali. The language indeed has both the long and short "e" vowels and, hence, sounds, and most Nepalis do make such distinctions in Nepali writing. But the distinction is invariably blurred during conversations. This holds true even among the educated Nepalis and when Nepali words are romanized. On the other hand, the "o" vowel sound in Nepali almost always carry the "o" sound as in "h*o*pe." Not too many exceptions exist to this norm. But it is different with the "u" sound. Similar to its sound system in English, it can take on both the short "a" sound like "d*u*rbar"(palace; some do spell this word as "d*a*rbar") close to "*u*rban" or a "u" sound like "Kathmand*u*" as in "p*u*t." The Nepali "k" sound is almost always written with the letter "k" unlike in English, which has several variations of the general "k" sound, e.g., "*c*omic," "*k*ernal," "*ch*arisma," and "ba*ck*."

Noticeable variations may be observed when some Nepali names and words are written in Roman letters. For instance, the family name Pande, could be spelled as Panday or Pandey. It can get even more complicated for a name like Poudel, another family name, as some may write it as Paudel, Poudyal, or Paudyal. One can find many other cases. This tendency is more common with family names than with first and second names.

Unlike in English in which the sentence (grammar) order is subject-verb-object, in Nepali the sequence is subject-object-verb. For instance, "I go home" in English would be "I home go" in Nepali. It is, nonetheless, important to keep in mind that there is enough flexibility in the sentence formation both in speaking and writing. Casual conversational Nepali or colloquial Nepali can be even more flexible. It is common for people to converse in single words rather than in complete sentences, yet be quite clear in communicating messages and meanings. One thing that is critical to remember about Nepali is that it is very hierarchical with a social class connotation when it comes to addressing others. For instance, the pronoun "you" has at least three different words in Nepali to differentiate social status: "*ta*"(pronounced with a dental "t" sound and nasal accent; used for those with low social status, ranks, and for children), "*timi*" (for medium status or amongst close friends), "*ta-pai*" (for high status, higher ranks, seniors, etc.). The hierarchical variations for the pronouns "she, he, they" are not as severe as they are for the "you." Foreigners who are not well versed in the social hierarchical system of Nepal are advised to avoid using the first two versions of the "you" just to play it safe.

NEPALI PROPER NAMES

Most Nepalis have three names, including the family name or surname. In the case of women's names, their family names change upon marriage as they, unlike in the Chinese tradition, adopt their husbands' family names. Again unlike in China or Korea, but similar to Western countries, Nepalis write their given names first and family names last. It is precisely the family names that invariably serve as their caste or ethnic identity, something that seldom happens in the West. One may, however, occasionally come across Nepali last names that may not provide any immediate caste identity. Take, for example, Madhav Kumar *Nepal*, one of the dictionary entries in this volume. In this case, *Nepal* is the last name of Madhav Kumar, but it offers no clear indication of his caste or ethnic affiliation. Obviously, it is a name that was adopted or invented; it does not exist in any of the historical caste or ethnic groups. Many Nepalis tend to form the impression that when people change their last or family names, those people belong to low caste groups. They believe such a family name change is a way to hide their true caste or ethnic identity. But there are few reliable mechanisms to ascertain the veracity of such assertions.

The first and second names are given names. In Nepal, as in India—or for that matter among Hindu (Sanskritic) names in general—one can observe what may be described as a two-pronged tradition. That is to say, some write first and second names separately as two different names, whereas others combine them into one name. Take two entries from the dictionary, for example, to illustrate the point: *Ganeshman* Singh and *Baburam* Bhattarai. In both cases, their given names actually have two names: *Ganesh Man* and *Babu Ram*. So one may write their given names both ways, unless they have already established a specific precedence. In fact, it is common to see their names written both ways. In this volume, we have tried to adhere to the pattern that appears to be most common, at least more common. In the dictionary entries, we have avoided hereditary or titular affixes to certain names, namely Rana and Shah names. Many Ranas have an inherent tendency to attach Jang Bahadur (J. B.) to their names to delineate their distinct Jang Bahadur lineage, that is, to indicate their superior status even among the Ranas themselves. After all, they have created three different classes of Ranas: A, B, and C. "A" is, of course, the highest class, the direct descendants of Jang Bahadur, or "pure blood" as they prefer to call it. So the full name is written as Juddha Shamsher *J. B.* Rana. Similarly, the later Shah kings have added *Dev* (divine or god) to their names to signify that they are Lord Vishnu's incarnations. Therefore, they project this divine or god image of themselves by affixing *Dev* (god or divine) to their names, e.g., King Mahendra Bir Bikram Shah *Dev*. In this volume, we have removed such aggrandizements from their names in order to maintain consistency with other biographical entries and to capture the basic core of the Nepali name system and structure.

Finally, we offer a word of caution regarding biographical dates reported in this volume. Since the Nepali calendar is different from the Western calendar, conversion of Nepali years into Western years can be tricky and sometimes slightly off, especially when exact dates (date and month) are missing. In preparing this volume, we have done our best to be as accurate as possible in converting Nepali dates which we obtained from different sources. For any inadvertent errors that might have occurred in this endeavor, we sincerely apologize.

CURRENCY

The Nepali currency is called the Rupee as in India, but the two currencies do not weigh the same in term of monetary value. Over the years, the value of the Nepali Rupee has been depreciating vis-à-vis the U.S. dollar as well as other international currencies (*also see* table 3).

Rupees per 1 US dollar	1985	1990	1995	2000
End of year	20.7	30.4	56.0	74.3
Average for the year	18.3	29.4	51.9	71.1

HOW TO READ THE DICTIONARY SECTION

The *Historical Dictionary of Nepal* is arranged alphabetically in order to make it user friendly. Depending on the topical or biographical importance in the national context, some entries are discussed at greater lengths than others. The reader can more fully explore certain topics by using cross-references provided for many entries, and they are printed in boldface type. In addition, more or related information available on certain matters is given at the end of an entry under *see also*.

Chronology

EARLY HISTORY

563 B.C. (Birth of Buddha) The Buddha (Siddhartha Gautama) was born in Lumbini, located in the Tarai district of Kapilvastu, which was then ruled by the Sakya (Shakya) dynasty. Siddhartha was a Sakya prince.

Before 400 A.D. Various pastoral dynasties ruled Nepal which included the Kathmandu Valley and its surrounding areas. The Valley was later ruled by the Kirata dynasty, founded by Yellung Kirata from the eastern hills. The Kirata dynasty's rule spanned at least 1,500 years, until it was dislodged in 400 A.D. by what came to be known as the Licchavi period.

THE LICCHAVI RULE

400–879 With the inception of the Licchavi period, Nepal slowly moved onto the terra firma of history. This period is often regarded as the "Golden Age" in Nepali history. The era began with the rule of Vrasadeva (400–425) and concluded with Mandeva IV (875–879). Raghavadeva, whose rule began in 879, seemed to be the transitional ruler separating the end of the Licchavi period and the advent of the Medieval period.

THE MEDIEVAL PERIOD

879–1200 Advent of the Medieval period ushered in a dark phase in the history of Nepal as the country was completely shrouded in chaos and confusion. The eclipse cast by the Medieval period lasted for more than 300 years until the onset of the Malla regime with the rule of Ari Malla (Arimalla) in 1200 A.D.

THE MALLA RULE

1200–1482 (The Early Malla Period) This was the period when the Kathmandu Valley was maintained and ruled as one kingdom. While this phase of the Malla rule continued to expand the foundation built during the Licchavi period, the kingdom embarked on a self-destructive course following the death of Jayasthiti Malla in 1395.

1200–1216 Reign of Ari Malla (Arimalla), the founder of the Malla period.

1345–1346 Sultan Shams ud-din Ilyas of Bengal raided Kathmandu.

1382–1395 Reign of Jayasthiti Malla, perhaps the most farsighted of all the Malla rulers, who was responsible for instituting many social codes, including the classification of castes and subcastes. The lasting impact of his social and institutional codes is still felt in many aspects of social life in Nepal.

1428–1482 Reign of Yaksha Malla, the last Malla ruler of the unified Malla kingdom of the Kathmandu Valley.

1482–1769 (Breakup of the Malla Kingdom) Following the death of Yaksha Malla in 1482, the Malla Kingdom of the Kathmandu Valley was split into three separate kingdoms of Kathmandu, Bhadgaun (Bhaktapur), and Patan (Lalitpur). This division signaled the breakdown and eventual downfall of the Malla rule.

1559 Gorkha principality established in the central hills.

1743 Prithvi Narayan Shah was crowned king of Gorkha. Soon after his coronation, Prithvi Narayan embarked on a long military campaign of territorial conquests, consolidation, and national unification.

1769 Prithvi Narayan Shah completed the conquest of all three Malla kingdoms, setting the stage for the unification of fragmented Nepal. The city of Kathmandu was declared the capital of the new Nepal. He was also the founder of the Shah dynasty.

THE EARLY SHAH RULE

1769–1846 (The Shah Period) With the unification of Nepal began what can be loosely described as the country's Modern period. Many events took place during this period.

1769–1816 Continued territorial expansion and annexation.

1770–1775 Restriction on trade with Tibet and dispute over the circulation of Nepal-minted coins in Tibet.

1775 Death of King Prithvi Narayan Shah; Treaty between Nepal and Tibet.

1775–1777 Reign of King Pratap Singh Shah.

1777–1799 Reign of King Rana Bahadur Shah after King Pratap's death.

1788 First Nepal-Tibet War.

1789 Nepal-Tibet Treaty.

1791 Second Nepal-Tibet War.

1792 Treaty of Commerce between Nepal and the East India Company; China-Nepal War.

1793 The Kirkpatrick Mission to Kathmandu.

1799 Abdication of Rana Bahadur Shah and accession of his infant son, King Girvana Yuddha Bikram, at the age of one and a half. Following that event, Rana Bahadur went to live in Varanasi, India, a place often considered to be a Hindu sanctuary.

1799–1816 Reign of King Girvana Yuddha Bikram Shah.

1801 Treaty with the East India Company's government.

1803 Amar Singh Thapa led Nepal's westward expansion, pushing its boundary all the way to the Satlej (Sutlej) River in India.

1804 The 1801 treaty with the East India Company nullified.

1806–1837 Bhimsen (Bhim Sen) Thapa took office as *Mukhtiyar* (prime minister) and held it until 1837.

1814–1816 War with the British in India (Anglo-Nepal War).

1816 The Treaty of Sagauli (Sugauli) ratified in March. As part of the treaty, Nepal ceded roughly one-half of its territory to British India.

1816–1847 Reign of King Rajendra Bikram following King Girvana Yuddha's death.

1837 Dismissal of *Mukhtiyar* General Bhimsen Thapa.

1839 Rearrest and most gruesome death of Bhimsen Thapa.

1845 Mathbar Singh Thapa was appointed prime minister for life in January. A few months later in May, he was assassinated by his own nephew Jang Bahadur Kunwar.

1846 (Kot Parba) Nepal witnessed its bloodiest courtyard massacre in which 29 leading *bhardars* (court nobles) were slaughtered by Jang Bahadur Kunwar and his brothers. After the massacre, Jang became prime minister and commander in chief.

THE RANA RULE

1846–1951 The sudden rise of Jang Bahadur Kunwar in 1846 began what a few years later came to be known as the Rana rule, rooted in hereditary and autocratic prime ministership. As Rana prime ministers usurped power, they turned the Shah kings into figurehead with little authority or power.

1846–1877 Rule of Prime Minister Jang Bahadur Rana.

1846 King Rajendra was compelled by Crown Prince Surendra to vacate the throne, and then went to Varanasi, India, with his junior queen and two sons.

1847–1881 Occupation of the throne by King Surendra Shah.

1847 In July, ex-King Rajendra was brought back to the country but kept under house arrest until his death in July 1881.

1850–1851 Prime Minister Jang Bahadur Kunwar traveled to Britain and other European countries. He departed from Calcutta, India, in April 1850 and returned to Nepal in February 1851. Such a trip by a prime minister was unprecedented in Nepal's history.

1854 Promulgation of the Muluki Ain (administrative procedures, legal frameworks, or national civil codes regarding various matters) by Prime Minister Jang Bahadur Kunwar.

1857 Prime Minister Jang Bahadur Kunwar led a Nepali battalion to India to help the East India Company suppress the Sepoy Mutiny. His support proved critical for British victory and continued rule of India.

1858 King Surendra bestowed upon Jang Bahadur Kunwar the honorific title of "Rana," an old title used in northern India to denote martial glory. As a result, Jang Bahadur removed his surname "Kunwar" and replaced it with "Rana," thus initiating the Rana clan and premiership in Nepal.

1877–1885 Rule of Prime Minister Ranoddip Singh Rana.

1878 Death of Crown Prince Trailokya Bikram Shah and the devolution of his royal rights to his infant son Prithvi Bir Bikram Shah.

1881–1911 At the age of six, Prithvi Bir Bikram was crowned king upon his grandfather's death.

1885–1901 Rule of Prime Minister Bir Shamsher Rana, following the assassination of Prime Minister Ranoddip Singh.

1901 Rule of Prime Minister Dev Shamsher Rana, following the death of Bir Shamsher. In a month, Dev Shamsher was deposed from his office in a bloodless coup and was replaced by Chandra Shamsher.

1901–1929 Rule of Chandra Shamsher Rana.

1911–1955 Tribhuvan Bir Bikram ascended to the throne after King Prithvi Bir Bikram's death.

1914–1918 (World War I) More than 200,000 Gorkha (Gurkha) soldiers placed at the disposal of the British Empire. In addition, almost 17,000 Nepali soldiers sent to India for garrison duties.

1918 Tri-Chandra College founded, the first college in the nation.

1923 A new treaty signed with British India.

1924 Slavery (*das pratha*) abolished by Chandra Shamsher.

1929–1932 Rule of Prime Minister Bhim Shamsher Rana, following the death of Chandra Shamsher Rana.

1932–1945 Rule of Prime Minister Juddha Shamsher Rana, following the death of Bhim Shamsher Rana.

1934 A massive earthquake caused enormous damage in Kathmandu.

1936 Nepal Praja Parishad—or Praja Parishad (People's Council)—was founded under the leadership of Tanka Prasad Acharya. It was the first political party in Nepal, created to overthrow Rana autocracy and establish democracy. In Bihar, India, the party published a periodical called *Janata* (The People) to promote its political position and policy, advocating a multicaste, democratic government and the overthrow of the Ranas.

1939–1945 (World War II) Once again, Nepal's hill villages sent forth their young lads to fight and die for the British Empire. Over 160,000 recruited. Altogether more than 24,000 were killed and 40,000 incapacitated while serving the imperial cause of the global British army.

1940   Arrest of 43 Nepal Praja Parishad leaders and workers for plotting to dismantle the Rana rule. King Tribhuvan was found to be involved in the plot.

1941   Of the 43 arrested in 1940, three of the primary leaders were given capital punishment and executed. **24 January:** On the order of Prime Minister Juddha Shamsher, Dharma Bhakta Mathema, who gave King Tribhuvan lessons in wrestling, was hanged to death. Also hanged on the same day was Shukra Raj Shastri, an anti-Rana activist who had been jailed since 1938. **27 January:** Three days later, Juddha Shamsher had Dasarath Chand and Ganga Lal Shrestha executed by shooting. These four executed leaders are recognized as *shahid* (martyrs). Every year, Nepal celebrates Shahid Dibas (Martyrs' Day).

1945   Return of the last nine units of the Nepali troops to Kathmandu.

1945–1948   Padma Shamsher Rana's climb to prime ministership, when Juddha Shamsher voluntarily relinquished his office.

1947   **24 January:** All-India Nepali National Congress set up by Nepali political exiles and Nepalis domiciled in Varanasi and Darjeeling, India. **4–27 March:** Jute mill workers' strike at Biratnagar and arrest of several leaders, including Bishweswar Prasad (B. P.) Koirala and Man Mohan Adhikari. **25 April:** A friendship and commerce agreement signed with the United States. **30 April–4 May:** Mass anti-Rana demonstration and processions in the Kathmandu Valley. **11 July:** The status of British and Nepali legations in London and Kathmandu elevated to embassies. **15 August:** Independence of India. The end of the British Raj proved to be a deadly blow to the Rana rule as it fell four years later.

1948–1951   Rule of Prime Minister Mohan Shamsher Rana, following Padma Shamsher's resignation.

1949   **22 April:** The Communist Party of Nepal (CPN) was established, with Puspa Lal Shrestha leading it as its founding general secretary. **1 May:**

Mohan Shamsher imprisoned B. P. Koirala who went on a 27-day hunger strike (*annasan*).

1950 (Setting the Stage for Rana Demise) **9 April:** The Nepali Congress Party born out of a merger between Nepali National Congress and Nepal Democratic Congress parties. **31 July:** Treaties of Peace and Friendship and of Trade and Commerce signed with India. **24 September:** Arrest of Nepali Congress armed volunteers. **6 November:** King Tribhuvan Bir Bikram Shah, who fled the palace with his queens and Crown Prince Mahendra Bir Bikram Shah, sought asylum in the Indian Embassy in Kathmandu. But his younger son, Prince Gyanendra Bir Bikram Shah, happened to be left behind. **7 November:** Prince Gyanendra was crowned king. **11 November:** The Indian Embassy flew King Tribhuvan and his family to Delhi on two Indian Air Force planes. **11 November:** Birganj, a key gateway town along the Nepal-India border, captured by Nepali Congress armed freedom fighters. **24 December:** Prime Minister Mohan Shamsher unilaterally proposed his own internal reforms.

RETURN OF THE SHAH RULE

1951 During this year several key events occurred, culminating in the demise of the Rana rule and the revival of the Shah rule. **8 January:** Prime Minister Mohan Shamsher Rana announced more reforms and reversed Prince Gyanendra's succession to the throne. **10 January:** In India, self-exiled King Tribhuvan welcomed Mohan Shamsher's reversal of Prince Gyanendra's illegitimate crowning. **7 February:** Agreement known as "Delhi compromise" was reached to form a joint government with equal representation from the Rana and Nepali Congress sides, with Mohan Shamsher as prime minister. B. P. Koirala appointed as home minister (security and defense portfolio). **15–17 June:** Indian Prime Minister Jawaharlal Nehru's visit to Nepal. **6 November:** Police firing killed Chiniya Kaji, a student protester. **10 November:** Following Chiniya Kaji's death, Home Minister Koirala tendered his resignation, along with his Congress ministers, thus undercutting the Ranas' tenuous hold on the government. **12 November:** Prime Minister Mohan Shamsher and his Rana cabinet members resigned, thereby handing the power to the king to appoint a new government. **16 November:** Tribhuvan selected Matrika Prasad Koirala as prime minister and appointed a new non-Rana government, thus bringing finality to the end of the Rana rule.

1952 **March:** First Lady Eleanor Roosevelt of the United States visited Nepal during a world tour. **June:** The U.S. Information Service opened a library called the American Library in Kathmandu.

1953 Edmund Hillary and Tenzing Norgay became the first two climbers to ever reach the summit Sagarmatha (Mt. Everest) on 29 May.

1954 **June:** U.S. Ambassador George Allen visited Nepal. During the summer monsoon season, Nepal experienced a series of devastating floods and landslides as a result of torrential rains that lasted several days. The natural disaster caused enormous damage in the central hills as houses were swept away, properties destroyed, and farm land lost. Approximately 1,000 people were killed, over 130,000 rendered homeless, and domestic animals washed away. **October:** The U.S. Operations Missions (USOM) in Nepal signed an agreement to assist in reconstruction.

1955–1972 Reign of King Mahendra Bir Bikram Shah. After the death of King Tribhuvan on 13 March 1955, Mahendra was crowned king.

1956 USOM announced in February a $2 million grant of economic aid to Nepal, focused on malaria eradication, community development (land reclamation and settlement), and road construction in the Rapti Valley of the central Tarai district of Chitwan. That is, the Tarai frontier in Chitwan was opened for hill migrants to move in, reclaim land, and resettle in the area. Known as the Rapti Valley Development Project (RVDP), it was Nepal's first systematically planned Tarai land settlement and agricultural development project—all designed to rehabilitate the hill victims of the 1954 natural disaster.

1957 King Mahendra announced in December his plan to hold elections on 18 February 1959 to form a parliamentary government.

1958 Election Commission constituted in May.

1959 **12 February:** Announcement of the new constitution accepting a parliamentary government but vesting the Crown with sovereign authority over all three branches: executive, judicial, and legislative, including the army. **18 February:** National parliamentary elections got underway. **3 April:** National elections completed. **10 May:** Announcement of national election results. Nepali Congress led by B. P. Koirala won 74 out of 109 seats in the House of Representatives. **27 May (Dawn of Democracy in Nepal):** Formation of the first nationally elected democratic government headed by Nepali Congress. Its leader B. P. Koirala became the first elected prime minister of Nepal.

1960 (Palace Coup, Revival of the Absolute Shah Rule, and Infanticide of Democracy) King Mahendra launched a palace coup on 15 December against Prime Minister Koirala's infant government. He jailed Koirala, along with many party leaders and prematurely aborted nascent democracy. Mahendra usurped all the power and restored his direct rule.

1962 King Mahendra promulgated on 16 December a new constitution and formalized a four-tier Panchayat system. Even though it was heralded as partyless, Panchayat was essentially a one-party political system grafted to bolster Mahendra's absolute rule and wishes.

1972 King Mahendra died in January during a hunting trip to Chitwan in the central Tarai. His son Birendra Bir Bikram Shah succeeded him.

1972–1990 King Birendra's absolute rule between 1972 and 1990.

1979 In early 1979, nationwide pro-democracy agitation and protests against the Panchayat system. As the protest movement heated up and spread, it posed a serious threat to the system. In response, the king announced on 24 May that he would hold a national referendum on Panchayat within a year.

1980 The national referendum was held on 2 May, and the king and Panchayat declared victorious in a referendum which was believed to have been rigged. As a result of the referendum, Panchayat gained a semblance of popular legitimacy. Subsequently, some cosmetic amendments to the constitution were made in December.

1981 Elections to the National Panchayat held in May. Political parties rejected the amended constitution and boycotted the elections.

1982 B. P. Koirala passed away on 21 July.

1983 Founding of the South Asian Association for Regional Cooperation (SAARC) on 2 August, during the Delhi meeting of Bangladesh, Bhutan, India, the Maldives, Nepal, Pakistan, and Sri Lanka. However, it took four years before the association was inaugurated on 7 December 1986, at its Dhaka meeting. Established to promote regional cooperation and growth, SAARC is headquartered in Kathmandu.

1986 Second elections held to the National Panchayat. Again, Nepali Congress and most other parties boycotted the elections.

1989 India imposed an economic embargo on Nepal in March, with the declaration of the expiry of the trade and transit treaties between the two countries and closing of all but two border entry points. Nepal suffered a debilitating blow as its economic conditions deteriorated, particularly in the Kathmandu Valley. In fact, it proved to be a prelude to the downfall of the Panchayat system.

DEMOCRACY AND CONSTITUTIONAL MONARCHY

1990 (**Second Coming of Democracy, End of the Panchayat System, and Constitutional Monarchy**) Though seemingly legitimized by the referendum, Panchayat's longevity was never secure due to its internal decay and dysfunctionality. A new pro-democracy movement ensued to disarm the Panchayat system. The movement unfolded as follows: **15 January:** Six different factions of the Communist Party of Nepal joined together to form a united front: United Left Front (ULF). **18–20 January:** Defying its banned status, the Nepali Congress Party (NCP) held a national conference within the country and announced 18 February as the launching date of its nonviolent, pro-democracy movement against Panchayat. ULF decided to join NCP to fulfill the mission of the movement. **18 February:** As planned, NCP and ULF jointly launched the pro-democracy movement known as the Movement for the Restoration of Democracy. **19 February:** The Movement organized nonviolent protests, including a national call for Nepal Band (Nepal shutdown, i.e., closing shops, grounding transportation, and so forth). In Bhaktapur, police fired on protesters, causing some deaths and many injuries. **24 February:** A protest at Bir

Hospital by several hundred nurses and health workers. **25 February:** Black day observed in Kathmandu and other cities. Later, the Nepal Engineering and Medical associations issued statements of support. **2 March:** Successful second Nepal Band throughout the country, followed by various other types of protests and anti-Panchayat statements from several professional groups. **14 March:** Third successful Nepal Band observed across the country, and other forms of protests continued. Students, intellectuals, shopkeepers, professionals, workers, and masses of other people swelled the ranks of protesters. **16 March:** Government-organized pro-Panchayat rally in Pokhara. King Birendra addressed the crowd and took a defiant stance against the Movement. **23 March:** National People's Unity Day observed. **29 March:** Planned-blackout in the Kathmandu Valley as people turned off their electricity as a form of protest. **30 March:** Some people killed and many injured by police firings in Patan. **4 April:** Massive demonstrations in the Valley. Police firing killed some demonstrators in Kirtipur. **6 April:** King Birendra removed Prime Minister Marich Man Shrestha and appointed Lokendra Bahadur Chand prime minister with a promise to reform. His seemingly palliative move and promise of reforms failed to sway the Movement as the people had lost faith. Thousands of protesters filled the streets and marched toward the palace, chanting anti-Panchayat and anti-king slogans. Police fired, killing some and injuring many. That was the largest demonstration that Kathmandu had ever witnessed in its political history. In a separate police firing in Butwal, there were some fatal casualties. **7 April:** Continued police brutality and killing provoked more and larger demonstrations across the nation. **8 April:** The shaken king lifted the ban on all political parties. **16 April (End of the Panchayat System):** Prime Minister Lokendra Chand resigned. King Birendra dissolved the National Panchayat, thus sounding Panchayat's death knell. **19 April (Revival of Parliamentary Democracy):** King Birendra grudgingly called on Krishna Prasad Bhattarai, a senior NCP and Movement leader, to form an interim coalition government to draft a new constitution and to hold national parliamentary elections. **11 May:** Birendra appointed a Constitution Commission without consulting with the interim government, thus revealing his deep-seated aversion toward the Movement for eroding his absolute monarchy. But this commission was rejected. **31 May:** Birendra was compelled to consult with the interim government and announced the formation of another Constitution Commission. **10 September:** First draft of the new constitution submitted to the king, who forwarded it to the interim cabinet. **11 October:** The cabinet finalized the constitution and submitted it to Birendra for his review and approval. **21 October:** In a stunningly insidious and defiant move—that revealed, once again, his continued resistance to democracy—King Birendra shelved the constitution finalized by the cabinet. In its place, he released his own draft vastly different from the one the cabinet had submitted. The king was publicly criticized for his open attempt to thwart the people's will with his antidemocratic moves and his obvious motive behind them. **5 November:** However, the cabinet did incorporate some features of the palace draft into its final draft and resubmitted the revised constitution. **11 November (End of the Absolute Shah Rule and the Emergence of Constitutional Monarchy):** Birendra promulgated a new constitution which constitutionalized the Crown and legitimized a multiparty democratic system.

1991 **8 January:** With the elections looming on the horizon, the United Left Front (ULF) and another communist faction merged to create a new Communist Party of Nepal called Unified Marxist-Leninist (CPN–UML), thus becoming the largest communist faction and a formidable electoral force. **5 May:** Elections held. Nepali Congress won the majority of the contested parliamentary seats. **29 May:** Nepali Congress formed the government with Girija Prasad Koirala as prime minister. This was the second elected government in Nepali history.

1994 **10 July:** Prime Minister Koirala resigned after losing the vote of confidence. With the Parliament dissolved, the date was set for new elections. **15 November:** Elections held and no party won a clear majority. The Communist Party of Nepal–Unified Marxist-Leninist won the plurality of seats and NCP came second. **29 November (First Communist Government in Nepal):** CPN–UML managed to form a minority government led by Man Mohan Adhikari, the second popularly elected Marxist government in the world.

1995 **March:** U.S. First Lady Hillary Rodham Clinton went to Nepal on a three-day visit. During her visit, she toured various health and education service organizations and Chitwan's national park and wildlife reserve. **10 September:** Prime Minister Man Mohan Adhikari's minority government collapsed. **11 September:** A coalition government of NCP, National Democratic Party (NDP), and Nepal Sadbhavana Party (NSP) led by NCP leader Sher Bahadur Deuba was formed.

1996 **13 February:** "People's War" declared by the Maoist faction of the Communist Party of Nepal (CPN–Maoist), led by Puspa Kamal Dahal (alias Prachanda), Baburam Bhattarai, and Mohan Vaidya (alias Kiran). A nationwide guerila revolution was launched from their power base in the western hills (namely around the districts of Pyuthan, Rolpa, Rukum, and Salyan). It is pertinent to point out that it is the very region where, since the early 1980s, the American government agency called the United States Agency for International Development (USAID) has implemented the biggest integrated rural development project in Nepal's economic history. Commonly known as the People's War, the ongoing revolution spread throughout the country.

1997 **6 March:** The Deuba government dissolved. **10 March:** A new coalition government of NDP, CPN–UML, and NSP formed under NDP leader Lokendra Bahadur Chand. **8 September:** Death of Ganesh Man Singh, NCP's supreme leader and the national statesman. **3 October:** The Chand government fell. **6 October:** A new three-party coalition government of NDP, NCP, and NSP constituted with another NDP leader Surya Bahadur Thapa as prime minister.

1998 (The Endless Game of Governmental Shuffle) **11 April:** Prime Minister Thapa resigned. **12 April:** Girija Koirala formed a minority NCP government. **21 December:** Prime Minister Koirala resigned, but managed to form a new coalition government with CPN–UML and NSP two days later on 23 December.

1999 (Fresh General Elections) **26 April:** Death of CPN–UML leader and former Prime Minister Man Mohan Adhikari. **3, 5 May:** Third parliamentary elections were held in two phases. NCP won the majority of seats in the House of Representatives—111 out of 205—whereas CPN–UML won 71 seats. **31 May:** Headed by Krishna Prasad Bhattarai as prime minister, NCP formed a new government.

2000 **18 March:** Prime Minister Bhattarai was ousted by his own party member and former Prime Minister Girija Koirala who replaced him.

2001 (Palace Massacre, More Governmental Shuffle, and the Year of Chaos and Volatility) **1 June:** In a bizarre and bloody palace massacre, King Birendra Bir Bikram Shah and his immediate family members were gunned down by Crown Prince Dipendra Bir Bikram Shah, who is believed to have later shot himself. Dipendra was placed on life support. **2 June:** Dying Dipendra was declared king. **4 June:** King Dipendra pronounced dead. With no heirs surviving from Birendra's lineage, Dipendra's uncle Gyanendra Bir Bikram Shah (Birendra's brother) was crowned king. **22 July:** Ongoing internal power struggles within NCP drove Prime Minister Koirala out of power. He was replaced by another NCP leader and former Prime Minister Sher Bahadur Deuba, who espoused a plan to hold negotiations with the Maoists in order to end the People's War that had already cost hundreds of lives across the nation. **23 November:** Following the breakdown of peace talks with the Deuba government, Maoists ended a four-month-old cease-fire with a wave of attacks on police posts and army barracks. The attacks continued. Scores of police and army personnel were killed. It was also reported that the army had killed several hundred Maoist fighters during its assaults on them. **26 November (State of Emergency Declared):** In response to growing Maoist actions across the country, King Gyanendra declared a state of emergency, thus suspending decade-old and hard-won civil liberties, including freedom of the press as well as freedom of assembly, expression, and movement. Nepal's nascent democratic experiment was, once again, severely strained in the name of weeding out the Maoist movement which controlled almost 30 percent of the national territory.

2002 (Continued Conflicts between the Nepali Army and the Maoist Forces, Swelling Death Tolls, and Political Uncertainties) 4 January: SAARC meeting held in Nepal. **17 January:** The government announced new taxes on industrial products and additional import-export duties to fund military offensive against the Maoists. **18 January:** U.S. Secretary of State Colin Powell's visit to Nepal. In addition to holding talks with the king and prime minister, Powell was briefed by the army chief on the military offensive against the Maoists. Subsequent to his visit, American military advisors/personnel were sent to Nepal to advise and train Nepal's armed forces in their fight against the Maoists. **16–17 February:** At midnight, Maoist rebels launched the deadliest ever attack of their six-year-old movement. According to news reports provided by *The Kathmandu Post* and BBC online, 142 people were killed. The Maoists, seeking to overthrow Nepal's monarchy and establish a socialist republic, mounted attacks on a local airport, government buildings, a military barracks and armory in Mangalsen, and the district headquarters of Achham in far western Nepal.

Buildings were blown up and banks looted. Gun battles between rebels and the security forces went on for many hours from midnight until well after dawn. Among the dead during the offensive were 57 out of 58 soldiers, 49 policemen, the chief district officer Mohan Singh Khatri, the district intelligence officer Lok Raj Upreti and his wife, a postman, and a local photographer. The casualties also included some rebels. In addition, many were injured. **2 March:** The state of emergency was extended. **29 March:** A bomb explosion destroyed a bridge in Kathmandu, wounding 27 people. **12 April:** Maoist revolutionaries killed almost 90 policemen in four separate and almost simultaneous attacks in the district of Dang in western Nepal, about 190 miles west of Kathmandu. Also killed during the attacks and counter military assaults were scores of rebels. Over 300 were feared dead, including both policemen and rebels. **13 April:** A land mine blast in the far western district of Bajura killed 3 people. This was believed to be the first land mine explosion in Nepal. **16 April:** Maoists ambushed a police patrol and killed at least 9 policemen in the Gorkha district, about 70 miles west of Kathmandu. **18 April:** Two bomb explosions shook the capital city of Kathmandu. This was a clear indication that the raging People's War had extended its frontier from the rural fringes to urban trenches. The intensification of the confrontations between the military and Maoists has besieged the nation and claimed more than 3,500 lives since the Maoist revolution was set in motion in early 1996, and the number of casualties continues to climb everyday. Of the current total, 1,700 have been killed since the declaration of the state of emergency in November 2001 and subsequent military mobilization against the Maoists and those suspected of supporting the People's War. Many more have been jailed. Although the number of military and police casualties have been quite small relative to innocent and rebel body counts, the Maoists have so far gained a psychological edge over the Nepali army and police forces despite their massive military disadvantage. **23 April:** In response to a Maoist call for a nationwide strike, Nepal was shut down as everything came to a halt. Businesses, schools, and offices were closed across the country. **24 April:** The nation remained paralyzed. The total shut down was most noticeable in the bustling twin cities of Patan and Kathmandu. In the meantime, the Bush administration asked Congress for a supplemental appropriation of $20 million in military aid for Nepal. This is in addition to sending U.S. military advisers who have been actively scouring parts of Nepal currently controlled by the Maoist revolutionaries. For the first time, the Nepali government floated bounty offers of $64,000 for the capture or murder of Maoist supremo: Baburam Bhattarai, Prachanda (Puspa Kamal Dahal), and Kiran (Mohan Vaidya). **27 April:** According to the Nepal government press release, a total of 35 Maoists were murdered by its army in several clashes. **2 May:** Maoists proposed to resume peace talks with the government, but the prime minister rejected the offer. **3 May:** Just days ahead of Nepali Prime Minister Sher Bahadur Deuba's visit to the United States to plead for more aid, the government of Nepal claimed to have killed a total of 90 rebels—50 in Rolpa and 40 in Doti. **4 May:** As the prime minister prepared for his eagerly awaited U.S. visit to meet with President George W. Bush, the government dramatically raised the body count of the Maoist fighters reported killed by the army on 3 May—from 90 to 396. There was no independent confirmation of this claim. **6 May:** Nepal's Supreme Court ruled that marital sex without a wife's consent should be considered rape, along with forced sex with sex workers. Viewed as alien until a few years ago, the subject of marital rape emerged as an important social issue. This ruling nullified the current law which failed to recognize marital rape as a crime. **7 May:** Nepali Prime Minister Sher Bahadur Deuba arrived in the United States and met with President Bush to extract additional military and financial assistance to fight against what he called "Maoist terrorism in the country," while atrocities raged on at the domestic front. According to the Associated Press, "Army helicopters fitted with night-vision devices carried out the air strikes in the remote western districts of Rolpa and Pyuthan." Relentless aerial bombardments of the Maoist bases and camps in the western hills were reported. In the meantime, despite the lack of any independent verification, the government continued to raise, almost on a daily basis, the number of rebels its army claimed to have killed. The number stood at more than 560 since the previous Thursday. In its news report, the Associate Press mentioned that Amnesty International was gravely concerned that civilians were being killed by the Nepali army in the name of eliminating the Maoist rebels. Regarding the U.S. role in Nepal's ongoing war, AFP reported that at least a dozen U.S. military experts had in recent weeks toured far western parts of Nepal. There was a team out there from U.S. Pacific Command to see where military assistance could be best allocated. **11 May:** After a ferocious battle against waves of Maoist forces, Nepal's army was short of men and weapons. They retreated from two positions in the western hills to regroup and brace for another major attack by the Maoists. **13 May:** From the United States, Prime Minister Deuba flew to London and met with British Prime Minister Tony Blair to seek aid, including weapons and logistical training. **22 May (Parliament Disbanded):** King Gyanendra dissolved the lower house of Parliament—the House of Representatives—as the majority of the representatives appeared unwilling to renew the state of emergency that the king had imposed. **23 May:** The ruling Congress party suspended Prime Minister Deuba because he had asked the king to dissolve Parliament without consulting with the party. **26 May:** The ruling Congress party expelled Prime Minister Deuba from the party, but his post of prime ministership was not affected due to the fact that Parliament had already been dissolved. **27 May (State of Emergency Reimposed):** The king reimposed the state of emergency, thus continuing to suspend all civil or constitutional rights in the country, two days after it lapsed amid a bitter row over moves to extend it. **19 June:** A two-day international conference was held in London to discuss ways to help the government of Nepal to root out the Maoist revolution raging in the country. In addition to the United Kingdom, the conference was attended by the United States, Russia, China, India, Australia, and several European countries. British Foreign Office Minister Mike O'Brien mentioned the British military aid to Nepal was boosted from $1 million to almost $10 million this year. **25 June:** India offered to help Nepal to fight the Maoists. **27 June:** As part of its push for privatization, the government of Nepal prepared to sell up to 49 percent of its Royal Nepal Airlines to private companies or joint ventures. A human rights group called Reporters without Borders (Reporters sans Frontières) reported that Krishna Sen, editor of the pro-Maoist newspaper *Janadisha*, was tortured to death by the national security forces the previous week after being taken into detention in May. **16 July:** Journalists in Nepal began a boycott of all government functions. In addition, the Nepali Journalists' Federation called for a blackout of news and pictures of the prime minister, his cabinet, and other government officials. Massive flooding and landslides resulting from the torrential monsoon rains caused enormous damage in the eastern hills, especially the Khotang district, 300 kilometers away from Kathmandu. **19 July:** Maoist revolutionaries renewed their call for a resumption of dialogue with the government to end the People's War that has been waged since 1996. **20 July:** Emboldened by huge amounts of military aid from the United States and India to destroy the Maoists, the government hardened its position. It rejected the offer of peace talks from Prachanda, the Maoist leader. **23 July:** The United Kingdom agreed to provide almost $5 million worth of military hardware. **13 August:** It was reported that a total of 422 people had been killed and another 173 still missing after weeks of floods and landslides in Nepal. Over a quarter of a million people have been badly affected by the floods caused by torrential monsoon rains in 47 of Nepal's 75 districts. **8 September:** Hundreds of

Maoist rebels attacked a remote police post in Sindhuli district, 160 kilometers southeast of Kathmandu, killing at least 48 officers. **9 September:** A fierce battle occurred between security forces and Maoist rebels in the west of Nepal after two rebel attacks in as many days left more than 100 people dead. **11 September:** The government lifted a nine-month-old state of emergency ahead of parliamentary elections scheduled to begin in November 2002. **16 September:** Normal life was brought to a halt by a general strike called by the Maoist rebels. Two people, including a policeman, were killed in separate incidents during the day. **18 September:** The Election Commission granted permission to more than 100 political parties to contest the parliamentary elections to be held in November. **27 September:** Women won abortion rights as a new law was passed to decriminalize abortion and broaden women's property rights. **3 October:** Prime Minister Sher Bahadur Deuba asked King Gyanendra to postpone the elections scheduled to be held in November by a year due to security concerns caused by the long-running Maoist insurgency. **4 October (Dismissal of Prime Minister Deuba and King's Direct Rule):** King Gyanendra unexpectedly sacked the entire cabinet headed by Sher Bahadur Deuba and assumed executive powers. In addition, the king indefinitely postponed parliamentary polls, scheduled to be held in November. **11 October:** King Gyanendra appointed Lokendra Bahadur Chand—a diehard monarchist and leader of the right-wing National Democratic Party—to be Nepal's new prime minister, who later proposed peace talks with the Maoist revolutionaries. Representatives from donor countries held talks with the government of Nepal to discuss the Maoist rebel uprising in the country. The meeting was organized by the British government to consider Nepal's military needs to fight the rebels, including sophisticated arms and training. **12 October:** A bomb blast destroyed a statue of the late King Mahendra, the father of the present monarch. **19 October:** Prime Minister Chand vowed to resolve peacefully the long-running Maoist insurgency. The rebels had not responded yet to Chand's offer to hold talks, but they earlier condemned King Gyanendra's move to assume executive powers. **21 October:** The army claimed to have killed nine Maoist rebels in clashes with the security forces in the southwestern Tarai district of Bardiya. In a separate incident, soldiers were injured in a booby trap laid by the rebels in the northwestern hill district of Kalikot. **25 October:** Maoist rebels announced that they were ready for peace talks to end an increasingly deadly insurgency. **12 November:** Because of a three-day general strike, locally known as a *band* (closure), almost everything, shops, offices, restaurants and bars, were all shut. The strike was called by the Maoist rebel movement. **15 November:**

Upsurge of violence in which 23 policemen died in a rebel attack on a police station at Tarkukot in the Gorkha district, about 150 kilometers west of Kathmandu. In a separate incident, at least 37 security personnel and 55 rebels were said to have died in a clash in the remote mountain town of Khalanga in the Jumla district, about 600 kilometers west of Kathmandu. **27 November:** A group of Gurkha soldiers taken prisoner by the Japanese in World War II won a victory over the British government as a court ruled they were wrongly excluded from a special compensation payment. In a trenchant judgment, High Court judge Justice McCombe said the decision to exclude the Gurkhas was racist. **4 December:** Prachanda, a top Maoist rebel leader, renewed a call for peace talks to resolve the long-running insurgency. **6 December:** Nepal's ousted Prime Minister Sher Bahadur Deuba led thousands of supporters in a march through Kathmandu to protest against his dismissal by King Gyanendra, and demanded to be reinstated. **8 December:** Five people were killed and more than 30 were injured when Maoist rebels blew up a bus at Karkare in the Sindhuli district, roughly 100 km east of Kathmandu. **14 December:** A senior U.S. official urged Maoist rebels to stop fighting and start peace talks to end the conflict. **15 December:** Tens of thousands of people demonstrated against King Gyanendra's assumption of executive powers. The largest left-wing party, the Unified Marxist-Leninist (CPN–UML), organized the rally in what was seen as a sequel to similar demonstrations by other parties. **28 December:** Suspected Maoist rebels set off a bomb in a hostel on the outskirts of Kathmandu, wounding seven people. **29 December:** A general strike called by Maoist rebels paralyzed Kathmandu as most shops were closed and streets were deserted. **30 December:** Nepal's government, fighting an increasingly violent revolt against the constitutional monarchy, hinted it was prepared to release information about detained Maoist rebels as a prelude to peace talks. But the government expected the rebels to offer something in return.

2003 (Increased Political Chaos and Volatility) 3 January: Amid a widening rift with major political parties over his assumption of executive powers three months ago and the continuing conflict with Maoist rebels, King Gyanendra issued a plea for national unity to resolve the country's on-going political crisis. **11 January:** Police rescued 14 children, aged between 14 and 17. They were forced to work as bonded laborers at a weaving factory in Kathmandu; they worked as wool spinners within the dark, cold rooms of the secretly run factory. **26 January:** Police Chief Krishna Mohan Shrestha was killed outright while walking near his house on the outskirts of Kathmandu. His wife and bodyguard were also gunned down, presumably by Maoist rebels. Shrestha became the head of Nepal's armed police force when it was formed about two years ago to combat the Maoist movement. **29 January:** The Maoist revolutionaries declared a cease-fire vowing to sit for renewed peace negotiations. Shortly afterwards, the Nepali government said it would also observe a suspension of hostilities. **27 February:** In the High Court in London, former Gorkhas, who served with the British army, lost their fight for equal pay with British servicemen and women. **29 March:** Baburam Bhattarai, the number two in the Maoist rebel hierarchy, emerged out of hiding and was designated to lead the Maoist team at the peace talks with the government. **31 March:** Baburam Bhattarai shared a public forum with Prime Minister Lokendra Bahadur Chand and said the rebels were ready to sit for the talks as soon as the government created a conducive atmosphere. He also met leaders of the Nepali Congress, the Unified Marxist-Leninist party, and other parties ahead of the proposed talks. **1 April:** A government negotiator said the peace talks with the Maoist camp, due to begin on Tuesday, had been delayed by two days. **4 May (Launching of the Joint People's Movement):** Five out of six national political parties with seats in the dismissed House of Representatives—the Communist Party of Nepal–Unified Marxist-Leninist, Janamorcha Nepal, Nepali Congress Party, Nepal Sadbhavana Party, and Nepal Peasants and Workers Party—joined forces, declaring to launch what they called the Joint People's Movement against the king. Notably absent from this coalition was the right-wing, pro-Panchayat National Democratic Party led by Lokendra Bahadur Chand and Surya Bahadur Thapa. **9 May:** The Joint People's Movement began with a large parade of black flags to protest the king and his executive power. The Nepali government accepted two key Maoist demands by agreeing to free three jailed rebel leaders and limit army patrols at the end of a second round of talks aimed at stopping a seven-year revolt that had killed 7,200 people. One of the rebel negotiators told reporters that the decision would have a significant impact in terms of creating an atmosphere of confidence for talks. He also said they were ready for another round of talks with the government side to discuss their political agenda. **30 May:** Ongoing protests against the king and his executive power took a new turn, demonstrating their strength and vigor. As part of the Joint People's Movement, there were huge marches across the country, with some openly calling for the abolition of the monarchy and establishment of Nepal as a republic. The Nepali government unleashed its police forces across the nation to attack protesters, killing some and wounding many. Following these developments,

Prime Minister Lokendra Bahadur Chand announced his resignation. **31 May:** More protests swept Nepal as the opposition parties engaged in the joint movement kept up their pressure on the king to form a new government of national unity. They proposed Madhav Kumar Nepal, general secretary of CPN–UML, as their choice to head the new government. **4 June:** In defiance of the Joint People's Movement and its leaders' demand and reconciliatory proposal, King Gyanendra named Surya Bahadur Thapa, an unapologetic royalist and rival leader of the right-wing National Democratic Party, to be the new prime minister of Nepal. **5 June:** Less than 24 hours after the king's announcement of Thapa's appointment, the Joint People's Movement rejected the king's action, launching mass protest demonstrations throughout the nation with more calls to dismantle the institution of monarchy. Opposition party leaders vowed to step up their pressure until their demand to restore the constitution and democratic rule were met. **13 June:** The joint movement continued to display its political resolve and muscle by organizing more mass demonstrations throughout the country, with protesters demanding that the king restore the parliament that was disbanded last year or form a national unity government of nominees from the country's five main political parties. **20 June:** More protest marches against the government were organized; thousands of participating demonstrators chanted anti-king slogans. A separate rally was launched in Kathmandu by a pro-Maoist group, calling for the resumption of peace talks that have been stalled since the resignation of Prime Minister Lokendra Bahadur Chand in late May. **30 June:** Student protests shut down about 10,000 private schools in the country. They were closed down indefinitely, affecting nearly 1.5 million students across Nepal. Affiliated with mainstream political parties, seven student unions jointly demanded lower fees for education.

Introduction

Nepal is a living example of contradictions. Caught in the vortex of its tortured past and uncertain future, it is undergoing a period of chaos. It is a country that was born in medieval times, grew up in the sixteenth century, and now finds itself engulfed in the high-tech gadgets and material marvels of the twenty-first century—all three phases wrapped into one. Personally speaking, our parents grew up believing—and telling us—that the earth was flat, although we learned otherwise at school. And, now, our children are surrounded by techno-gadgets that we could not even imagine when we were attending high school only decades ago. Children can now watch, right in their own room, blasting rockets pierce through heavenly bodies like flying arrows, the same bodies that our parents worshiped as distant gods with cosmic power. It was those bodies that were the centerpieces of their astrological belief system that guided their life from birth to death and beyond. The daily cycle of the sunrise and sunset seemed amazingly synchronized with our parents' own daily routine: wake up with the morning dawn and go to bed when the day ended with the fall of the darkness. With material choices limited to bare minimum, life was simple. Time was frozen and distance was meaningless, for the world revolved around the axis of their immediate surroundings. It was a pretty confined world as it was bounded within their own cosmic view; not much existed beyond that little world of their own. At least such was the case for the vast majority. But all this has changed dramatically. Within the span of a mere four decades—one generation, that is—we have traversed the whole distance from the flat-world view to the space age.

Today, electricity has reached many corners of Nepal and satellite TV has arrived. And with electricity have come TV and VCR. As satellite dishes and TV antennas compete with temple turrets to rule the urban skylines, the whole notion of cultural landscape takes on a new meaning. Then there is TV time. Once the TV is turned on, family rituals compete with TV shows which have themselves become integral parts of family rituals and routine. As people's eyes are glued to CNN or busy watching Hollywood shows imbued with sexually explicit scenes, shows that are broadcast from halfway across the world, they are suddenly oblivious to the world around them. What is amusing about this display of Hollywood sex scenes right in the family living room is the mindless societal transition and cultural hypocrisy it represents. While families have little qualm about taking a deep plunge into such shows right in their living rooms—and frequently with their teenage children—parents literally freak out if they see their daughters holding hands with their boyfriends in public places. Kissing is a social taboo. As such a behavior is interpreted as a sign of sexual promiscuity and social immorality, it is quite common for the "violators" to be harshly chastised or even physically punished. A mere mention of the word "sex" has to be whispered. Such is the living reality of life in this prudish society bound to Hindu codes and values. It is, therefore, hardly surprising that even a simple expression of pure love between the opposite sexes often requires subtleties and discreetness.

Now, with the information age shattering national boundaries and physical barriers, the Internet has arrived with a bang. While nearly 90 percent of the country still relies on the centuries old technology of oxendrawn plows to till their lands and lack easy access to drinking water, some can readily tap the fountain called the Internet and watch the whole world spin right on their monitor. One does not even need to possess a computer; there are Internet cafes where the world can be accessed for a fee. While there is no longer any shortage of information for those who have access to the Internet, not too many have much clue about the nature and content of the information they are actually receiving, how to use it, or whether they even need it, beyond its visual message and meaning which, of course, can be greatly distorted or selectively filtered. And all this is occurring in a society where, until not too long ago, people's worldview was confined to their immediate environment. Times have changed.

Given the galloping pace of change, there has been very little time for Nepal to make gradual adjustments to the demands of its present, to grow step by step along the trajectory of time and technology. There is a huge gulf between its growth capacity and the imposition of the contemporary global economy. Every step it takes appears premature and out of sync with the leap of time and compression of distance. As Nepal has been forced to learn how to run even before it knows how to crawl, it has constantly staggered like a senseless drunkard during its march to modernity, with little knowledge as to where it is going and how it plans to reach its destination safely. It is no wonder, therefore, that the country finds itself endlessly mired in confusion and floating in chaos. And such chaos and confusion touch every facet of contemporary life in Nepal: political, social, economic, and cultural.

Entrenched in a feudalistic social structure framed in traditionalism, Nepal is being overwhelmed by an onslaught of Western material values and artifacts. Simply expressed, what is emerging as a result is a climate of intergenerational clash along what can be described as the cultural fault line. While the older generation clings to traditional values, the young generation is mesmerized by everything Western, by every aspect of Western pop culture. This deepening juxtaposition between these generations is increasingly manifested in work places as well as in school hallways and public spaces. Slowly disappearing are the days when the respect for authority and for seniority used to be the hallmark of social values. Today, students have a lot less respect for teachers than in the past, and the whole educational value system is completely distorted. While everybody seems to want to go to school, only a handful of students strive to be educated. Not a day passes without some violent incident. Student protests and strikes are routine, usually for no reason. Classes are regularly disrupted and cancelled. And fights are waged. Schools are turning into a contested terrain as students increasingly see them more as a training ground for hoodlums than as a learning ground for educational enrichment and advancement.

Compounding this intergenerational tension is the fact that the country is faced with a massive growth of material consumerism, on the one hand, and population and poverty, on the other. History testifies that nothing breeds more social tension than economic malaise and social oppression. Rarely in the past did Nepal witness as many social ills—and definitely not to the same degree—as it currently faces. Today the problems range from mounting impoverishment to sociocultural breakdowns to pollution and prostitution. The more Nepal fails to cope with its problems, the more eager Western donor agencies are to propose solutions and pour in foreign aid. But what is deeply disconcerting about this rapidly unfolding drama is the parallel growth of foreign aid and domestic problems. There is, in other words, something fundamentally incongruent about foreign aid as a remedy to deepening domestic problems, for it seems to only aggravate them. This raises a renewed question about the purpose and value of Western aid. Is it simply a policy of international welfarism, a form of rewards—or what some may call bribes—to the members of the domestic ruling elite for their support of the Western global policy and plan, while keeping the masses pacified under the tantalizing spell of foreign aid. Even the persistent use of the phrase "foreign aid" sounds like a cruel joke these days because it disguises its true meaning. For a country like Nepal, what is often peddled as foreign aid for public consumption is mostly foreign debt, i.e., interest-bearing loans that must be paid back.

GEOGRAPHY AND ENVIRONMENT

Geography

Compactly squeezed in 147,181 square kilometers of territory, Nepal is a small landlocked country, stretching from east to west like Tennessee in the United States. Sandwiched between China and India, its geographical position is hardly enviable from the point of view of economic security and independence. It is precisely because of this entrapment that Nepal has been historically characterized as "a yam caught between two rocks."

Situated between 26 degrees to 30 degrees north latitude, a narrow band of land barely 150 kilometers wide, Nepal represents an unparalleled diversity of landforms. From its southern lowland belt that extends to the Gangetic Plain in India, its landforms rise in successive hill and mountain ranges, eventually reaching the towering heights of the majestic Himalayas and then sloping downward to embrace the Tibetan (Xizang) Plateau to the north. This rise in elevation is punctuated by many valleys and river basins nestled in between these ranges. However, within the maze of these mountains and valleys can be discerned some amazing ecological and physiographical order. To be specific, the country is divided into three distinct but continuous segments based on elevation and ecological variations: the Mountain, Hill, and Tarai regions.

The Mountain Region

The Mountain (*parbat*) region is situated 4,850 meters above sea level and lies to the north of the Hill region. Beyond this region, on the north side, lies the Trans-Himalayan zone of Tibet. Naturally, the landscape of the Mountain region includes some of the world's most famous peaks including Mount Everest, popularly known as Sagarmatha (the roof of the world). Its high altitude keeps the regional temperature very cold and the growing season short. Extensive human habitation and economic activities are extremely arduous because of the climate and difficult topography. As a result, it is sparsely populated and agriculture is limited. Whatever farming activity is carried out in this region is mostly confined to the low valleys and river basins. Pastoralism is a common economic activity among most mountain dwellers.

The Hill Region

Hills, commonly called *pahar* in Nepali, are found mostly between 600 and 4,850 meters in altitude and include the Kathmandu Valley, the most fertile and urbanized area in the country. In addition, there are many other smaller intermontane valleys. From the climatic perspective, this is the temperate zone of Nepal. Although the amount of land available for cultivation is limited, its mild temperature represents an ideal growing condition except in higher altitude areas. That is why agriculture is intensive in the hills, a region which has historically contained the largest population. Despite heavy outmigration, the hills still comprise around 45 percent of the total population. The higher elevation areas (above 2,500 meters) are sparsely populated, but the lower hills and valleys are densely settled. The hill landscape is both a natural and cultural mosaic, shaped by geological forces and human activity. Sculptured into a massive complex of terraces, the hills demonstrate centuries of human impacts on their environment. Nonetheless, the hills suffer from a situation of chronic food deficit. Despite its relative isolation and limited economic potential, the region has always been the political and cultural hearth of Nepal, with its decision-making power tightly centralized in Kathmandu, the nation's capital city. The central government's authority has further been consolidated since the mid-1950s when the development process was initiated with the formulation and implementation of the country's first Five-Year Plan in 1956.

The Tarai Region

In complete topographic and climatic contrast to the Mountain and Hill regions, the Tarai region is a lowland subtropical belt stretched along the Nepal-India border. Except during the months of December and January, the temperature is hot. Its altitude rises gradually from about 100 to 600 meters at the foot of the Siwalik Hills. Formed and fed by many mountain rivers, the region is rich in agricultural land. Occupying more than 60 percent of the total farmland, the Tarai is often heralded as the "granary" of Nepal. Once covered with vast amounts of malaria-infested forests, the region today suffers from forest depletion due to commercial and illegal logging as well as frontier resettlement. It is the most important internal destination for hill peasants in search of land. In light of its notable agricultural potential and remaining forest resources, the Tarai is definitely the richest economic region in the nation. Moreover, thanks to its proximity to several Indian railheads and market centers, the Tarai region enjoys the largest number of urban areas in the country, with several of them featuring some industrial base.

PEOPLE AND SOCIETY

Population

The population is a national metaphor as it tells a story about where the nation stands on the trajectory of societal development. The logic is that because people are both a national asset and liability, their overall socioeconomic conditions provide a sound reflection of their nation's standing on the vast canvas of world development. In view of this premise, the economic outlook of Nepal and its people vis-à-vis its national resource base cannot be considered too bright.

Inhabited by more than 23 million people, it is one of the most densely populated countries in the world. Relative to its total land area, Nepal's population density is nearly 160 persons per square kilometer. But this figure does not reveal the whole reality. The degree of population pressure is much heavier than this because over 70 percent of the land is unavailable for cultivation due to its rugged terrain and harsh climate. In other words, if one were to assess this situation in relation to the amount of land that is available for farming, the population density would be much higher.

Introduction 7

What exacerbates the problem of population pressure is the fact that economic or employment opportunities outside the agricultural sector are scarce. This is clearly evident from Nepal's employment structure, which reveals that over 85 percent of the people depend on farming for their livelihood and live in rural areas. Then there is the low land-productivity factor. For a country overwhelmingly dependent on agriculture, it has done very little to enhance its per unit land yields, which are about one-third of what Japan has achieved. Except in the Kathmandu Valley, where Newar peasants have managed to attain some of the highest level of land and crop productivity in the world, Nepal's agricultural technology remains stranded in the mold built in the sixteenth century.

Nowhere in the country is this predicament more acute than in the Hill and Mountain regions, which together share 53 percent of the total national population, but only 38 percent of the cultivated land. So it is obvious that compared to these regions, the Tarai fares better. With its share of 47 percent of the population on 62 percent of the arable land, it is much better positioned to tackle the population pressure problem than its sister regions. Augmenting the Tarai's regional economy is its gradually growing urban-industrial base. What is not taken into account in the national calculation, however, are two critical demographic phenomena: the population growth rate and the dependent population, particularly those who are 15 years old or below. Currently, the population of Nepal is growing at an annual rate of 2.4 percent, which is quite high. Even with more than 30 years of family planning, it has achieved little success in curtailing the rate of growth to a manageable level, somewhere around 1.0 to 1.5 percent per annum.

Given that the current annual growth rate is nearly 2.4 percent and that over 40 percent of the population is below the age of 15, the prospect for Nepal's population growth to slow down any time soon is slim. As this dependent population enters the child-bearing phase, the population is bound to swell, thus further accentuating its grim demographic problems. Historically, urbanization has served as a safety valve for rural population pressure in two distinct ways. First, since urban growth and urbanization were invariably associated with industrial growth—at least such was the case in Western Europe, North America, and Japan—cities acted as centers of off-farm employment for excess farm hands, thus bringing relief to rural areas in terms of reduced population and increased income. Second, growing urbanization led to reduced rates of population growth, partly because, unlike in rural-agricultural settings, children were no longer seen as an economic asset. But Nepal has not been able to benefit from this historical process. With barely 11 percent of the country's population living in urban areas and its industrial process in its infancy, it is one of the least urbanized and industrialized countries in the world.

For over a century, therefore, outmigration, mainly from the hills, has become an important survival and population management strategy for countless households. As adult males leave their hill villages in search of seasonal or long-term employment in India and in cities within Nepal, the pressure of population takes a slight sigh of relief in terms of daily food requirements. In addition, most migrants return with some cash incomes or send remittances to supplement family resources. As the hard times continue to haunt countless households and migration is seen as a source of income, outmigration intensifies. It is an enduring family tradition in the hills that sons not only follow the footsteps of their migrant fathers, but also pave the trails for their sons, as they tap into well-established migration networks that are now referred to as social capital. So, for a land chained to immobile mountains, Nepal has become a nation of peripatetic people, all in response to their survival instincts and imperatives.

Beyond the confines of the above demographic concerns, the question of population is intrinsically intertwined with many societal issues such as ethnicity, caste, and religious affiliations. As ingrained social institutions with specified boundaries and standards, they have historically shaped the system of governance as well as defined people's positions, status, and roles in society. Given this, it is pertinent to mention some of these social institutions and elements.

Ethnicity

Nepal is an ethnically diverse and complex society. Except for the sizable population of those of Indian birth or ancestry concentrated in the Tarai bordering India, the varied ethnic groups have evolved over time into distinct cultural patterns and groups.

The people of Nepal can be classified into three broad ethnic groups in terms of their origin. In addition to those whose origins can be traced to India and Tibet, there is a pool of indigenous people. While the Indo-Nepali group inhabits the more fertile lower hills, river valleys, and Tarai plains, the Tibeto-Nepali people generally occupy the higher hills from the west to the east. The indigenous people, on the other hand, are geographically scattered and comprise a number of tribal communities such as the Tharu and the Dhimal of the Tarai. Also included among the indigenous people are the original inhabitants of the Kathmandu Valley: the Newar. The Newars are historically recognized as the early urbanites of Nepal because they created in the Kathmandu Valley what is known as the urban culture that is imbued with elaborate social institutions, customs, commerce, and ornate arts and crafts, along with its distinct architectural heritage. The world famous pagoda style of architecture, used primarily for building temples, is historically associated with the Newars. Even their cuisines are quite distinct from other groups and more elaborate in terms of both preparation and variety. The Newars and other indigenous people and communities of Nepal predate the advent of migrants from both India (Indo-Nepali) and Tibet (Tibeto-Nepali).

Within the Indo-Nepali group, two distinct categories can be discerned. The first category includes those who fled India and moved to the safe sanctuaries of the Nepal hills several hundred years ago, in the wake of the Muslim invasions of northern India. The hill group of Indian origin includes descendants of high-caste Hindus, mostly Brahmans (Bahuns) and Kshatriyas (Chhetris). They have spread throughout Nepal except along the northern border with Tibet. They usually constitute local elites and are frequently the largest landowners in their local communities. This does not mean that they are all rich and powerful. Also included among them are many poor and less well-off Bahuns and Chhetris. The Indo-Nepali population of the hills, at the apex of which stands the royal family, has played the most dominant role in local and national politics and governance. Because of their dominance, they are the ones who claim to be most acculturated to the Nepali soil, equating their identity with that of Nepal; they see themselves as the bearers of Nepali nationalism. Other ethnic groups, with the exception of some Newars, have been peripheral to Nepal's political power structure controlled by the nexus of high-caste and dominant-class elites, namely Bahuns and Chhetris. They have not only adopted Nepali as the national and vernacular language, but also used it as an instrument of cultural, political, and social control. Nepali has been imposed as the medium of instruction in public schools and colleges. In addition to emphasizing the role of Nepali as a vernacular language for national consolidation, it has been systematically deployed to foster and fortify Nepali nationalism (mainly loyalty to the Crown). However, despite its growing use throughout Nepal, there are still pockets of people in remote areas, mainly across the Trans-Himalayan belts, where it is spoken very little, if at all.

The second group of Indo-Nepali people are primarily those inhabitants who relocated to the Tarai from northern India. They were actually encouraged by the Nepali government or its agents to move into the Tarai for land settlement during the nineteenth and early twentieth centuries when the country was attempting to expand its revenue base by bringing more forest land under cultivation. While some of those migrants later became large landowners in the Tarai, most of them remain peasants with small tracts of land or no land at all. They belong to different subethnic groups with their own respective dialects and customs. Although their facility with Nepali has greatly improved over the years, they use it sparingly.

Unlike the Indo-Nepali population, the Tibeto-Nepali people are generally found in higher altitudes. This discernable altitudinal pattern of their spatial distribution is mainly attributed to the directional origins of their early migrations. Since they originally moved into Nepal from the north, they populated the higher reaches of the hills, whereas the Indo-Nepalis with their origin in India naturally gravitated toward the lower hills and valleys. It is believed that the migrants from India brought with them a relatively more advanced form of farming technology which allowed them to exploit land intensively, thus enhancing its productive capacity to support a larger population.

The Tibeto-Nepali population includes several subethnic groups, e.g., the Gurung, Magar, Thakali, Tamang, Sherpa, Rai, and Limbu tribes. One notable feature of their cultural landscape is the communal settlement patterns. Unlike the Indo-Nepali people who are scattered throughout the country and widely mixed, these subethnic groups are concentrated in their own specific geographic pockets across the hills from east to west, i.e., each within the domain of its own communal space that is relatively self-contained. The Gurungs, Rais, Limbus, and Magars are perhaps the most renowned martial tribes of Nepal whose roles as Gorkha (Gurkha) mercenaries have been highlighted in the British military lore. They have shed their blood and sacrificed their lives to serve the British Empire from the jungles of Borneo to the islands of Malvinas (Falkland Islands).

The Caste System

One integral aspect of the Nepali society is the Hindu caste system, modeled after the ancient and orthodox Brahmanic system of the Indian plains. Like religion, the caste system is a fundamental feature of Nepal as it plays a central role in one's life from birth to death. For example, it has direct bearings on who one marries, on one's social status and mobility, and on educational opportunities and access. Although its influence has gradually waned over time, especially in cities, its undercurrent still runs deep.

To be sure, no single, universally acceptable definition can be advanced for the caste system. It is, nevertheless, commonly viewed as a multifaceted status hierarchy, with each individual ranked within the fourfold Hindu caste (*varna* or color) divisions. The word *varna* is often equated with caste, primarily because, in all likelihood, the initial caste groupings of the population within the subcontinent were based on one's complexion. The fairer the complexion the higher the caste ranking. Some extend the traditional four-tiered hierarchy to add the untouchables—namely the outcastes and socially polluted. Within this preordained construct, the caste is an indelible imprint of one's identity and status. Like a birthmark, one is born with it and lives with it.

The four castes in Nepal are the Bahun (regarded as priests), Chhetri (presumed to be rulers and warriors), Vaisya (merchants and traders), and Sudra (menial laborers). And each group has subcastes. Based on the Hindu ethos, the caste system finds its immediate application among Nepal's Indo-Nepali people, the primary adherents of Hinduism. Although the Newars have adopted the caste system, they do not strictly uphold the four Hindu divisions specified above. They technically fall in the Vaisya group, but they have their own parallel hierarchy of castes with a distinct priestly group. Since each caste is endogamous, caste membership is both hereditary and permanent. One way to change one's caste status is to undergo Sanskritization, a process which can be achieved by migrating to a new area and assuming a new caste or via marriage across the caste line. Although wealth can normally act to mitigate some of this caste-based status dilution, individual caste status is essentially rooted in one's blood purity. It is no surprise, therefore, that intercaste marriage carries a social stigma and is frowned upon by society, especially when it takes place between two castes at the extreme ends of the social spectrum.

At the core of the caste structure is a rank order of values bound up in concepts of ritual status, purity, and pollution. Consequently, caste is used to determine individual behavior, obligations, and expectations. All the social, economic, religious, legal, and political activities are prescribed by sanctions that determine access to land, position of political power, and command of human labor. It is no wonder that within this constrictive system, wealth, political power, high rank, and privilege tend to converge.

Hereditary occupational specialization is a common feature of the caste system in Nepal. Yet it is pertinent to bear in mind that caste is functionally significant only when viewed in a regional or local context and at a particular time. The assumed correlation between the caste hierarchy and the class hierarchy does not always hold, as many poor high-caste and rich low-caste households can be found throughout Nepal.

Although the footprint of the caste system is evident in almost every facet of life, compared to the Indo-Nepali population, the question of caste is less ingrained in Tibeto-Nepali communities. Insofar as they accept the caste-based notions of social ranks, the Tibeto-Nepalis tend not only to see themselves at a higher level than do the Indo-Nepalis and Newars, but also differ as to ranking among themselves. The Rai tribe's assumption of their caste superiority over the Magar and Gurung tribes is not accepted by the latter groups. Moreover, the status of a particular group is apt to vary from place to place, depending on its relative number, wealth, and local power.

Rural Society and Kinship

Nepal is predominantly a rural-agricultural society. Even in settlements designated as urban, the rural-urban distinction is easily blurred, for a large portion of the urban population tends to be engaged in farming activities. In this sense, most urban areas can be treated as spatial extensions of rural areas, but often with a commercial bent. Simply put, farming is the dominant order of society and the mainstay of the economy, a situation that is highly unlikely to change in the foreseeable future.

The basic social unit in a village is the family or *paribar*, consisting of a patrilineally extended household. The extended family system should not, however, be construed as a necessarily harmonious form of village life. Many extended families break apart as married sons tend to separate from both parents and brothers. At the time of separation, the family property is equally divided among the sons; daughters are granted no property rights (shares) unless they remain unmarried beyond the age of 35, at which point they are eligible for equal shares. If parents are alive, they each receive a share. Family separation generally occurs in cases where the head of the household is less assertive and domineering, when the father dies, or when all the sons are married. Unmarried sons normally do not separate from their parents; if the parents are deceased, then unmarried sons usually stay with their older brothers. Because family separation results in a division of

Introduction

family properties, land holdings are extremely fragmented. Sometimes separation and resulting land fragmentation turn into a bitter source of family feud, often leading to legal disputes and court battles.

Beyond the immediate family, there exists a larger kinship network that occasionally involves sharing food. This network also is an important means of meeting farm labor needs, especially during the planting and harvesting seasons, when labor shortages are quite common. Above the kinship network is the village, which functions as a broader unit of social existence. Some villages are no more than hamlets made up of just a few households, whereas others are sizable communities of several adjacent hamlets. It is not uncommon for villagers to pool their resources on certain occasions and labor together to implement village-level projects such as building irrigation ditches and channels, facilities for drinking water, or schools. If a household cannot afford to hire labor, it usually relies on the mutual labor-sharing system called *parma*, which allows villagers to exchange labor for labor at times of need.

Social Classes and Stratification

Although caste and class tend to converge, they are not the same. As already noted, there are plenty of poor high-caste people who rank quite low on the totem pole of social class hierarchy and vice versa. In terms of differences in wealth and access to political power, Nepal can be divided into: a small ruling elite class; government officials, big landholders, and merchants; and peasants and workers who together form the largest group, perhaps over 75 percent of the total population. These divisions are, of course, descriptive, functional class categories rather than social class entities based on the Marxist concept of production relations. In a way, these classes are a long continuum in Nepal's social structure because most members of the ruling elite and government functionaries have their direct roots in the rural landed class that often controls the leverage of both political power and economic structure. In short, these class divisions are largely determined by ones' socioeconomic roles and positions; they are fluid categories as individuals can move in and out of their respective class brackets.

Religion

Religion occupies center stage in Nepali life and society. Life is like a chain of religious events. From the time of birth till death, people undergo many religious ceremonies and rituals. Almost everything is ritualized within a specific religious context. In addition to birth, death, wedding, planting, and harvesting rituals and ceremonies, there are many other religious festivities in which people participate. Virtually every occasion requires a religious sanction or blessing. Some ceremonies are strictly family matters, whereas others are performed collectively and in public settings. Throughout the year Nepal celebrates numerous festivals which are nicely paced to capture various seasonal occasions and events. In a way, these festivals symbolize the rhythm of life as they are routine and predictable. They also indicate change in the pace of life from one season to another, depending on the annual cycle of farming. The two biggest Hindu festivals are the Dashain and Tihar, both of which are celebrated less than a month apart, usually in October and November. These festivals follow the rice harvest—the most joyous time for Nepali farmers and peasants. Aside from observing these events, people go to temples routinely to worship their favorite gods or goddesses.

Religion is also manifested in institutional settings and codes, primarily molded within the Hindu framework. This is not surprising because Nepal is a constitutionally declared Hindu state. Nonetheless, there is a great deal of intermingling of Hindu and Buddhist beliefs as their devotees worship at both Hindu and Buddhist temples. This mutual respect is, in fact, one of the principal reasons why adherents of these two dominant religions of Nepal have never engaged in any overt religious clashes. Differences between Hindus and Buddhists are, in practice, very subtle and academic in nature. However, nearly 90 percent of the Nepali people officially identify themselves as Hindus. This is believed to be a distorted figure as it has a great deal to do with the fact that Hinduism is the national religion. In terms of census data, Buddhists and Muslims comprise 6 and 3 percent, respectively. Although Christianity has a visible and active presence, the followers of this faith are small in number.

Hinduism is polytheistic. It incorporates many gods and goddesses with different functions and powers. But they are considered merely different manifestations of a single underlying divinity that is expressed as a Hindu triad comprising the religion's three major gods: Brahma, Vishnu, and Shiva, respectively, personifying creation, preservation, and destruction.

Vishnu and Shiva, or some of their numerous avatars (incarnations), are most widely followed and their prescribed roles are often interchangeable as they can function as both the protector and destroyer, depending on the context and the demand of time.

No less prominent in Nepali life is Buddhism, a leading world religion that is native to Nepal in terms of its origin. Its influence is profound and widespread as it transcends both ethnic and regional boundaries. Hindus, in general, regard Buddha as one of the avatars of Vishnu. The concept of avatar is a powerful one; it is believed to descend upon earth from time to time to restore peace, order, and justice, to save humanity from injustice and miseries. Time in this context is conceived in epochal terms or what the Hindus call yuga. According to the Hindu belief system and its division of cosmic time span into yugas (aeons or ages), every yuga is associated with a particular avatar, charged with the mission of rescuing humanity. In the universal cycle of creation, destruction, and preservation, it is the avatar, in other words, that keeps this cycle going as it saves humanity from total destruction, restores justice, and recreates a new order. In this sense, the arrival of the Buddha symbolized the Buddha yuga, i.e., his time to right the wrongs of the world.

Education

Historically, education was a privilege confined to members of the royalty, the nobility, and high caste and wealthy citizens. Due to both social control and the lack of schools, the general masses had little access to educational opportunities. During the Rana rule that lasted more than a hundred years, Nepal's public education infrastructure was basically non-existent. Since the Ranas feared that an educated public would rise against their oppressive rule—a fear that, indeed, proved prophetic—they denied the general masses their fundamental right to education. Those who wanted to educate their children had to send them to India.

When the Rana rule ended in 1951, Nepal had merely 310 primary and middle schools, 11 high schools, two colleges, one normal school, and one special technical school, but no university for graduate education. In the early 1950s, the national literacy rate was 5 percent: 10 percent among males and 1 percent among females. Since then, Nepal has come a long way in terms of making education available to the general public. Schools and colleges are presently open to all, and enrollment figures are rising. The long-standing prejudice against the education of girls is breaking down as verified by their increasing enrollments in schools and colleges. Yet there is no denying that quality education still remains a social preserve of the wealthy and powerful, namely landlords, businessmen, government leaders, and other elite members of the society. This is largely attributed to the fact that they are the only ones who can easily afford and are likely to pursue higher education for their children.

Despite some numerical improvements, Nepal has a long way to go. Its current average literacy rate is around 50 percent. Female literacy is much lower. What is even more dismaying is that the quality of education seems to be on the decline. The pool of qualified teachers and professors is shrinking, and those who are well qualified exhibit signs of suffering from low morale. On the one hand, the level of respect that they receive from students and society has reached its lowest point. The pay scale is so low that many professors are forced to engage in other income-generating activities, thereby treating their teaching profession as a supplementary source of income. The research focus or tradition is virtually absent, mainly because there are few research facilities available for professors. Moreover, schools and colleges are frequently closed due to strikes. And cheating is rampant at all levels and everywhere. In short, the education system of Nepal is broken and is in dire need of fundamental repairs.

While the poor and less wealthy families are entrapped in this degrading system with few alternatives, the wealthy and powerful send their children overseas—to the United States, Britain, and other advanced countries—for quality education. Consequently, Nepal's educational system is polarized along the class divide. What is even more lamentable is that under such circumstances it is very difficult to envision any tangible turnaround any time soon. Its future is bleak.

HISTORY AND POLITICS

Early Nepal

Although small in its size and economic composition, Nepal has quite a long history. Much of its early history is shrouded because of the absence of records. With this caveat in mind, Nepal's political evolution as a state is divided into: early history, the Licchavi period, the Malla period, and the Shah period which includes the Rana rule and the multiparty system. It is

Introduction   17

only after the onset of the Shah dynasty that Nepal evolved into a definable territorial and national entity. Prior to that, it was basically a constellation of many principalities. Engaged in periodic internecine wars, those principalities did little to thrust Nepal onto the stage of progress and prosperity.

Early History

Political scientist cum historian Rishikesh Shaha remarks that accounts of Nepal's early history are based on chronicles that are more literary than historical. They suggest that the Kathmandu Valley was once a lake, surrounded by lush hills. It was this valley that embodied early Nepal. This name was derived from Ne Muni (or Nemuni), a sage (*muni*) named Ne, who was regarded to be the *pala* (protector) of the Valley and the founder of the Pala dynasty. This nation, if it could be defined as such, was then called *Nepala*, the land protected by Ne. Subsequently, the name was vernacularly shortened to *Nepal*.

The Pala (Mahisapala) dynasty was a dynasty of pastoralists. As the word *mahisapala* suggests, it was a dynasty founded by mainly buffalo (*mahisa*) herders or protectors (*pala*). It was overthrown by the army of Yellung Kirata from the eastern hills, the domain of the Rais and Limbus who are, to this day, collectively known as Kiratis (Kiratas) in Nepal. Yellung subsequently established what is known as the Kirata dynasty. The Kiratas were the only Mongoloid (Tibeto-Nepali) group to ever rule Nepal. Their rule lasted for at least 1,500 years, until the rise of the Licchavis.

The Licchavi Rule

According to historians, the Licchavis started their reign some time in the first or second century. Only with the rise of a prominent Licchavi king named Mandeva I, who ruled from 464 to 508 A.D., did Nepal move on to the terra firma of history supported by epigraphic records. As Mandeva's inscriptions provided a reliable glimpse of recorded history, the veil of brackish history afflicting early Nepal was finally lifted.

In many respects, the Licchavi period brought significant social change and development with lasting effects. The Kathmandu Valley made an apparent transition from the pastoral mode to the agricultural mode of production. As the Valley increasingly developed urban characteristics, artisan activities, along with trade and commerce, flourished. Nepal's long-distance trade was intimately associated with the spread of Buddhism and religious pilgrimages to distant places. For example, during the Licchavi period, merchants and missionaries served as the primary conduit of the diffusion of Buddhism to Tibet and central Asia. In return, Nepal managed to gain money from customs duties and goods that helped to support the Licchavi state as well as the Valley's continued urban growth in terms of trade, commerce, and crafts.

King Mandeva I was the principal agent of change in the country's social system, laying the foundation of its architectural and artistic renaissance or heritage. In the many successive ruling dynastic lineages of Nepal, chained together by an entourage of corrupt, self-serving kings and rulers, Mandeva I was a rare beacon of light, a truly benevolent king. Perhaps the most significant change that Mandeva I instituted was to put into circulation coins, thus introducing a monetary basis for commercial transactions, a bedrock of social and economic transformation. In addition to his advanced economic thinking, he held a liberal outlook on religion. This Hindu king was instrumental in building Buddhist monasteries.

Following Mandeva's death, the veil of political instability returned to the Valley because of the absence of a strong ruler. What can be described as a crisis of authority marked this period, and it lasted until the ascendence to the throne of Amsuvarman (reign: 605 to 621 A.D.). Amsuvarman was a learned and enlightened ruler with a broad-minded religious and philosophical outlook. Like Mandeva, he was very generous and liberal, always concerned about the well-being of his people and about the Valley's continued architectural and sculptural advancements.

In addition to Mandeva I and Amsuvarman, the Licchavi dynasty saw a powerful monarch in Narendradeva. When his father was ousted from the throne, he escaped to Tibet. With the help of Tibet, he managed to reclaim his father's throne in 643 A.D. and ruled until 679 A.D. It was indicated that during his rule, Tibet wielded influence over Nepal. Narendradeva was the first Nepali ruler to initiate formal diplomatic relations with China by sending a mission with lavish gifts to the emperor. Subsequently, the friendship between the two countries solidified.

Narendradeva had turned Nepal into a prosperous nation. Few would dispute that Nepal's prosperity during Narendradeva's rule was directly attributed to growing trade and commerce. The country had turned into a thriving center of entrepot trade, acting as a gateway from India to China. As Nepal learned from China the art of papermaking, handmade paper of the finest quality was added to Nepal's traditional exports of musk, orpiment, and blankets and other woolen goods to India. The heyday of the Licchavi dynasty reached its climax during Narendradeva's rule. From that point on, it underwent a gradual decline. Ultimately, it collapsed in 879, during the rule of Raghavadeva. Irrespective of its unceremonious end, the Licchavi period is generally characterized as the "Golden Age" of Nepal. By the time it was replaced by the Malla dynasty, the Licchavi rule had set Nepal on a sound footing in many respects, including diplomacy.

The Malla Rule

With the end of the Licchavi rule in 879 began a dark age for the next 300 years, until 1200 A.D. The solid foundation laid by the Licchavi rulers was severely undercut, plunging Nepal into a state of retrenchment. It is the least understood period, with only a few inscriptional sources left to guide history. Then came the rise of the Malla rule, with the appearance of leading notables starting in 1200. As the dark age gradually subsided, Nepal emerged from a state of historical malaise.

Ari Malla (Arimalla) was the first Malla king of the Kathmandu Valley. His rule began in 1200 and lasted until 1216. The early Malla period in the Valley, a period which generally denotes a time frame until the breakup of the Valley kingdom into three different kingdoms—Kathmandu, Patan (Lalitpur), and Bhadgaun (Bhaktapur)—was subjected to several external attacks from the Indian side, suggesting that Nepal was a relatively weak kingdom during that period. It is, therefore, no surprise that the overall progress of the country was hardly noticeable, although trade and urban growth continued and Nepal's relations with China and Tibet remained warm and friendly. This was evident in the fact that at the request of the Emperor Kublai Khan's teacher Saskyapa Lama of Tibet, Nepal sent a group of artisans to Lhasa to construct a golden stupa under the leadership of Aniko (or Arniko), who played an important role in the diffusion of Nepali architectural styles to Tibet and China.

Nepal embarked on the path of recovery from these early setbacks and drawbacks of the Malla dynasty, following the rise of Jayasthiti Malla in the 1370s, perhaps the first distinguished figure of the Malla dynasty. He was officially crowned in 1382 and ruled until 1395 with great foresight and fortitude. Like Mandeva I, he was forward looking and instituted many legal and social codes to consolidate the country under one set of rules. The fact that his codes still form the general basis for the way the Newar society in the Valley operates clearly indicates that it has passed the test of time. In addition, he adhered to a liberal outlook on matters of religion. But the code system he instituted regarding the classification of people into subcastes as well as rules concerning caste marriage, dining, and drinking water still haunts Nepali society, mainly the Newars.

After his death, his three sons ruled the Valley. But the kingdom was effectively divided into three units, one for each son. Eventually, it was fragmented into three separate kingdoms in 1482, exactly 100 years after Jayasthiti's coronation. The same Valley that Jayasthiti commanded so skillfully as one united kingdom turned into rival kingdoms —Kathmandu, Patan, and Bhadgaun—following the death of his grandson Yaksha Malla, whose career marked the zenith of the Malla glory. The breakup of the Malla kingdom signaled the beginning of the end of the Malla era in Nepal.

Apparently, the breakup and consequent political rivalries and intrigues did not affect the Valley's status as an entrepot trade center as it was able to maintain its economic vitality. The Valley's citizens demonstrated their remarkable resiliency, steadfastly remaining faithful to their industriousness even when there were few constructive policies forthcoming from their respective rulers to support them. But the political and moral decay was already under way, and the pomp and glitter of the three competing royal courts continued in the midst of this deepening disintegration. The inevitable fall of the Mallas finally came when the territorially and politically ambitious Gorkha king named Prithvi Narayan (Prithvinarayana) Shah managed to defeat all three kingdoms in the Valley and consolidate them and his other territorial possessions into a unified Nepal in 1769.

Modern Nepal

The Early Shah Rule and Absolute Monarchy (1743–1846)

Prithvi Narayan Shah is the founder of the Shah dynasty that continues to serve as the head of the state. Before unification, he occupied the throne of the Gorkha principality located in the central hills. Driven by his imperialistic vision, this Gorkha ruler embarked on a warpath to unify Nepal. His campaign was successful. By 1769, he had conquered all three Malla kingdoms in the Valley. He then moved his national capital from Gorkha to Kathmandu, thus laying the foundation of today's Nepal.

Introduction

The sweeping victory over the Valley kingdoms proved to be more than a symbol of territorial acquisition and foundation for national unification. With his stature greatly bolstered by his military triumphs, the victory gave Prithvi Narayan an unparalleled opportunity to cement his Shah dynasty and consolidate his absolute authority. Consequently, his power base was vastly enhanced from the political and territorial perspective. Few dared to question his absolute monarchy. Nor was there any reason to question it, for what he had undertaken during his reign had proven its worth for the greater good of both Nepal and its citizens. If historical accounts serve as a marker of his role as a national leader, his rule was relatively unscarred.

Even after Prithvi's death, the Shah rulers and their administrative heads (and military generals) continued to carry out the imperial vision charted by their founder. So successful were their military campaigns that by 1814, they had managed to extend Nepal's territorial reach to the Tista River in the east (including Sikkim) and beyond India's Kumaon and Garhwal areas in the west. Its historical glory was succinctly captured in a popular nationalistic song that every schoolkid had to read in the 1950s and 1960s. The song said, "We had erected a boundary post at Kangra on the western front and extended it to Tista to the east." In other words, Nepal's total territorial span was almost twice as big as its current size. General Bhimsen Thapa, who assumed the role of prime minister, was a powerful political actor and architect during this period. But Nepal's territorial ambition obviously went too far, especially in light of its limited man (military) power and resource base vis-à-vis British India. It finally reached a breaking point as it eventually encountered the British resistance. Bhimsen Thapa's blind ambitions or utter failure to recognize Nepal's inherent limitations resulted in the Anglo-Nepal War (1814–1816). The war proved to be a total disaster for Nepal. As the loser, Nepal was forced to sign in 1816 what is called the Treaty of Sagauli. In accordance with the terms of the treaty, Nepal was compelled to give up roughly one-half of its territorial control on both the eastern and western fronts to British India.

Factional Politics

Notwithstanding all those historical territorial highs and lows described above, Nepal plunged into a period of bitter factional politics following Prithvi Narayan's death. The nation experienced a big void in monarchical leadership. Although each successive Shah ruler remained an absolute monarch, there was no leadership emanating from the crown. The vacuum of palace leadership created a political environment in which various *bhardar* (courtier) clans were engaged in intense battles for political favors and power at the expense of national interests and citizens' welfare. Most prominent of those factions were the Thapa and Pande clans. Until the ascendency of Bhimsen Thapa to prime ministership in 1806, the administrative apparatus was shrouded in tremendous political instability. Factionalism dominated the political landscape of that period. Palace plots were endlessly hatched and intrigues were common as were murders of factional leaders. Since no ruling nobility ever felt secure, *bhardars* were busier watching their backs than taking care of the nation's business. Consequently, national growth and development was severely undercut. Yet, despite his absolute power and authority, no Shah king emerged to command and demonstrate the quality of leadership required to lead the nation in a progressive direction. Then, abruptly in 1846, the prevailing factional politics of governance came to an end with one deadly strike by Jang Bahadur Kunwar, a second-tier *bhardar* clan member at that time.

The Rana Rule: 1846–1951

Although factional politics went into dormancy, national politics saw little progress. It is, in fact, plausible to argue that with the rise of the Rana rule in 1846, Nepal entered a darker phase in its political development and dynamics. While the Shah dynasty was retained as a titular head, the Ranas ruled the nation with their autocratic grip on the leverage of power.

The Rana rule began with Jang Bahadur Kunwar who later changed his last name to Rana, thus setting his own Rana dynasty in motion. Jang Bahadur came to power through a coup called the Kot Parba (courtyard massacre) and declared himself prime minister with absolute power. The Kot Parba is one of Nepal's most violent and defining events, as it changed the course of history from which the nation has yet to recover. The entire Council of State was wiped out by Jang Bahadur and his brothers during the Kot massacre. Jang had achieved a feat that no previous *bhardar* clan (ruling political faction) leader had: to render all competing factions of the ruling class hapless in one bloody palace massacre. As a result, the Ranas became the sole axis of social, economic, and political power in Nepal.

Rana rule proved to be most damaging as the country was bled white. It also undercut the nation's self-reliant path of progress. Since the Ranas were dependent on British support for survival, they subordinated Nepal's national interest and integrity to the British Empire. They openly allowed Nepal to be a semi-colony, a primary supplier of the most vital resources for the British army: the hill youth—the dubiously renowned Gorkhas —willing to sacrifice themselves on the altar of England's imperial glory. Although they were the law of the land and masters of the Nepali masses, the Ranas essentially acted as lackeys in their relations with the British. They were more concerned about being decorated with meaningless honorary British medals for their servitude than serving the country. They copied their British masters in many respects, thus laying the foundation for the emulation of Western values among the rest of the elites. In return, the British supported them and kept them in power. It is no surprise that when the British left India in 1947, the stage was set for the Ranas' downfall.

The Rana rule saw its demise during the reign (1948–1951) of Prime Minister Mohan Shamsher, one of the most conservative Ranas to rule the country. When King Tribhuvan Bir Bikram Shah fled the palace with his family in protest of the autocratic Rana rule and went to the Indian Embassy to seek asylum, his younger son Gyanendra, the current king of Nepal, happened to be left behind with his Rana relatives. At that point, Mohan Shamsher stripped King Tribhuvan of his kingship and crown and named Gyanendra king in his place. Both of these events, however, gave a moral boost to the popular anti-Rana democratic revolution that had already been galvanized by Mohan Shamsher's increasingly oppressive measures. Mobilized by Nepali Congress and other political activists, the anti-Rana revolution made decisive gains in early 1951, forcing the Rana prime minister to yield. First Mohan Shamsher reversed his decision about Gyanendra's crowning and then agreed to head a transitional coalition government with the Nepali Congress Party (NCP) led by Bishweswar Prasad (B. P.) Koirala. But the government fell apart when Koirala decided to pull out of the incompatible coalition on 10 November. Two days later, Mohan Shamsher resigned, thereby ending his own prime ministership as well as the Rana rule 104 years after its unholy genesis.

Return of the Absolute Shah Rule: 1951–1990

The only beneficiary of the revolution that ended the Rana rule seemed to be the Shah dynasty as it was able to reestablish its rule. King Tribhuvan reclaimed his absolute power. Although, in the aftermath of the popular revolution, he had promised to hold general elections to form a democratic government, he never held one, leaving the revolutionaries and citizens dangling under his broken promise. Democracy was frozen. Four years later in 1955, he died. His son, King Mahendra Bir Bikram Shah, also kept postponing the promised election. Furthermore, he revived factional politics from its hibernation to serve his own political agenda rather than fulfill national aspirations and citizens' needs. He shuffled his self-appointed government like a deck of cards, changing the prime minister and other ministers every few months. Mahendra was in total control of power with little respect for the wishes of the people.

Finally in 1959, under mounting pressure from those who had fought hard to overthrow the Rana regime and institute a democratic system in its place, Mahendra agreed grudgingly to hold national elections to form a parliamentary government. As expected, the Nepali Congress Party won the electoral contests. The party's leader, B. P. Koirala, became the first elected prime minister of Nepal. Since King Mahendra saw democracy as a threat to his own design of absolute Shah rule, he had no intention to let the newly elected government last much longer than any of his own self-appointed prime ministers. So he launched a palace coup in December 1960. He arrested and jailed Prime Minister Koirala. The parliament was dissolved. The king declared the party system illegal; democracy was assassinated during its infancy. Later, he formed the Panchayat system, basically a one-party political setup firmly under his control, once again deploying factional politics as a time-honored instrument of divide and rule. Political repression continued under King Mahendra with a renewed zeal not seen since the overthrow of the Rana a decade earlier.

From a leadership perspective, few doubted King Mahendra's ability and acumen. It is widely believed to this day that he was endowed with the leadership qualities necessary to guide Nepal down the path of progress and prosperity. But he suffered from two egregious shortcomings that often mar leadership: a sharp tendency to be power-hungry and power-blind and a sense of insecurity. He was so power-hungry that he was blinded by it. He used power as a vehicle of personal aggrandizement rather than to fuel national growth and development. Nowhere was this more clearly demonstrated than in school textbooks that government agencies produced and that were used across the nation. Even technical textbooks such as science and math were devoted to glorifying Mahendra and his royal family although it had little relevance to the subject matters. Moreover, feeling constantly overshadowed by B. P. Koirala, Mahendra routinely explored various ways to undermine him and anything he represented. He lost track of what his monarchical authority and power could achieve for the nation. Instead, he exercised power with the mindset of controlling it rather than sharing it with those who had gained it legitimately. So the king launched a swift palace coup against Koirala's elected government simply to keep him from sharing power. As a result, his rhetoric of national development proved to be little more than hollow words.

When King Mahendra died in early 1972 during a hunting trip, his son Birendra Bir Bikram Shah assumed the throne. For 18 more years, Birendra continued to march down the road that his father had charted. But the times were changing and the masses were getting agitated not only because of the general deprivation of some basic rights, but because his rule had failed to set the country on the path of progress that the masses wanted and needed to improve their living conditions. In the midst of rising frustration, a new popular revolution erupted, this time somewhat suddenly. As the masses joined the movement, it spread rapidly. But the most intense battle was being fought in the heart of Nepal, the Kathmandu Valley, often right in front of the palace or nearby. Plenty of blood was shed. Many died. Streets were littered. Shops were closed in support of the movement. The demand for democracy was intensifying. King Birendra basically had two choices at his disposal: either to continue to suppress the fiery movement, kill more citizens, and risk the demise of his dynastic monarchy under his own watch, or give up his absolute power and accept constitutional monarchy. He chose the latter. He announced the dissolution of the much-despised Panchayat system and the establishment of multiparty democracy in 1990.

Democracy and Constitutional Monarchy: 1990–Present

Thirty years after King Mahendra choked the life out of Nepal's infant democracy, it was reborn in 1990. To be sure, Birendra saved the Shah dynasty from extinction, but the form of governance was no longer under his absolute control. Initially, an interim coalition government was formed under the prime ministership of Krishna Prasad Bhattarai, the veteran leader of the Nepali Congress Party. The new constitution was drafted and a national election was held to form the new democratic government. The NCP won 110 out of 205 seats in the House of Representatives and formed the government with Girija Prasad Koirala as its prime minister. As the second largest, the Communist Party of Nepal (Unified Marxist-Leninist or CPN–UML) became the main opposition party in the House of Representatives.

When Prime Minister Girija Prasad Koirala lost a vote of confidence three years later, a general election was held. Girija's party lost. Although the election gave CPN–UML measurable gains in the Parliament, it fell short of the majority. However, with the plurality of seats in the House, CPN–UML was able to form a popularly elected communist government in 1994. It was the first time a democratic communist government was formed since President Salvador Allende established his popularly elected Marxist government in Chile in 1970. This was quite remarkable in that communism was reeling from global setbacks in the wake of the Soviet Union's sudden disintegration. In 1995, the Nepali communist government was also dissolved as it was unable to muster enough support from its coalition partners. Since the formation of the interim government in 1990, Nepal has seen nine different governments in one decade, a clear sign that democracy is undergoing some noticeable difficulty in its early stages.

In the midst of this periodic governmental flux, the Maoist faction of the Communist Party of Nepal (CPN–Maoist) launched a peasant-based revolution called the "People's War" in February 1996. Since then, this guerilla war has disrupted the nation, with the Maoists expanding their operations from their stronghold in the western hills to many other areas. It is estimated that they currently exercise control in almost 30 percent of the national territory. In some of those areas, they have instituted a parallel administration and courts to provide quick justice. There is little denying that they have established defining markers on the political landscape of Nepal, a country which now suffers from a crisis of confidence.

Then came 1 June 2001, the day when the nation witnessed a tragic and bizarre royal massacre that took place in the royal dining room of the palace. During the dinner time, King Birendra and his entire family were violently murdered by his own son, Crown Prince Dipendra Bir Bikram Shah, who, by most accounts, later shot himself. In critical condition, he was hospitalized and declared the new king. Dipendra died on 4 June. Since King Birendra's whole family lineage was wiped out and Dipendra had no heir, the Shah dynastic lineage shifted from the father-son nexus to the nephew (Dipendra)-uncle (Gyanendra) nexus.

Immediately after Dipendra was pronounced dead, the royal crown was handed over to Birendra's brother Gyanendra Bir Bikram Shah, who is now the head of the state. Prime Minister Sher Bahadur Deuba (NCP) had espoused prior to assuming prime ministership that he was going to bring an end to the surging Maoist movement through negotiations. His attempt to negotiate a settlement with the Maoists revolutionaries was, however, deadlocked in late November 2001 as he refused to meet their demands. In addition, in the aftermath of the terrorist attacks on New York and Washington, D.C., on 11 September 2001, the George W. Bush administration apparently decided to offer necessary military aid to Nepal to suppress the Maoist movement. As a result, the government of Nepal stiffened its position and, subsequently, the Maoists withdrew from any further negotiations and broke off a four-month cease-fire with a series of attacks on army and police posts, killing dozens of policemen and soldiers. In response, King Gyanendra declared a state of emergency on 26 November, thus suspending civil liberties, including freedom of the press and freedom of assembly, expression, and movement. Once again, Nepal's nascent democracy has come under severe stress and human rights under increasing pressure.

The Nepali army has been unleashed against the Maoist revolutionaries. The armed clashes have become almost a daily event, turning this land of the Buddha into a killing field. Hardly a day passes without some news of killings. Under the cover of the state-of-emergency rule, the Nepal government has routinely arrested many citizens and jailed them without charges or trials. The army has also killed many innocent people in the name of law and order and rooting out the rebels. Whether justified or not, most of those killed in the military assaults are accused of either being Maoist rebels or collaborating with them to overthrow the monarchy. And the Maoists are hardly any more innocent than the military in this rapidly unfolding drama of endless attacks and counterattacks—a drama that has already consumed about 7,200 lives since early 1996, about 5,400 being killed since the end of November 2001.

Since February 2002, following the sixth anniversary of the People's War, the battles have intensified and become ever deadlier in terms of both the frequency and body counts. Since Secretary of State Colin Powell's visit to Nepal in mid-January 2002 to pledge U.S. support to the country, Washington has been visibly involved in the country's effort to suppress the Maoist revolution. As an extension of the Bush administration's global war on terrorism, the United States has boosted its aid, sending military hardware and personnel to advise and train the Nepali army. According to an AFP news report, the U.S. State Department confirmed that at least a dozen U.S. military experts from the Pacific Command toured the countryside where the Maoists have established their control. In addition, President Bush authorized $20 million in supplemental military aid for Nepal.

On 7 May, Prime Minister Sher Bahadur Deuba met with President Bush to extract additional anti-terror military and financial support from Washington. However, both the open U.S. military involvement in Nepal and Deuba's use of the terrorism card to garner increased foreign aid in order to keep his government afloat have not gone unnoticed. They have engendered heavy criticism and deep suspicion in certain Nepali political quarters. They see the whole scenario as an integral part of the Bush administration's terrorism-guided, heavy-handed global policy and as a form of direct U.S. interference in Nepal's internal affairs. In their eyes, this new development represents a potential threat to Nepal's national sovereignty.

Since November 2001, the state of emergency has been renewed twice. Just prior to the latest imposition of the state of emergency in late May 2002, the king dissolved Parliament upon the request of Prime Minister Sher Bahadur Deuba. Because of Deuba's unilateral move to dissolve Parliament in order to avoid the vote of no confidence and save his own prime ministership, the ruling Nepali Congress Party has split between the Deuba and Girija Prasad Koirala factions—a development which is very likely to undermine the NCP's ability to win an outright majority of seats in the House of Representatives in future elections.

In view of the upcoming November elections, on 11 September 2002 the government lifted the state of emergency. However, concerned about the impact of the deepening military confrontations with the Maoists on parliamentary polls, Prime Minister Deuba asked King Gyanendra on 3 October to postpone the elections. The following day on 4 October, the king stunned the nation. Reminiscent of how his father, King Mahendra, ended democracy by launching a palace coup in 1960 against the Nepali Congress government headed by Prime Minister B. P. Koirala, in one swift move King Gyanendra dismissed Prime Minister Deuba, along with his Nepali Congress government. One major difference between the two actions was that, unlike his father, Gyanendra did not immediately abolish the political parties by banning them. King Gyanendra then assumed executive powers and indefinitely postponed the elections. The 12-year-old democratic experiment was suddenly brought to a screeching halt. Exercising his executive powers, on 11 October the king appointed former Prime Minister Lokendra Bahadur Chand of the right-wing National Democratic Party—a staunch monarchist—to be Nepal's prime minister. Soon after the appointment, Prime Minister Chand vowed to resolve peacefully the ongoing war with the Maoists.

In a surprise development, the Maoist leader, Prachanda, declared an immediate cease-fire on 29 January 2003 after the government announced that it would stop calling the Maoists terrorists, lift rewards offered for their capture (dead or alive), and withdraw international police warrants issued for the rebel leaders. The government immediately reciprocated the Maoist cease-fire by suspending its military offensive against them. The following day both the government and Maoists agreed to engage in peace negotiations. Although no date or venue was set for talks, the cease-fire instantly spurred hopes that the bloody uprising would come to an end and peace would finally prevail in this impoverished mountainous country.

Yet Nepal's ever brittle democracy remains a huge question mark. Once again, Nepal's political fate is in limbo. Even though the king promised to hold parliamentary elections, no dates were given. Nor did he offer any indication that they would be held any time soon. In the midst of all this, a new and curious scenario has surfaced. That is, will the suspension of the People's War and peace negotiations with the Maoists finally put Nepal back on track for a more promising and peaceful future, or will they only embolden King Gyanendra to defy the current of time and resurrect absolute monarchy, thus quashing the dreams of enduring democracy in this tiny nation of 23 million people? This is the question that now confronts Nepal.

The question has gained greater weight in light of the uncertainties that loom heavy in the rapidly shifting political landscape of Nepal. There have been huge protest marches against the king because of his antidemocratic actions and refusal to follow the constitution. In early May 2003, five out of six national political parties with seats in the dissolved House of Representatives (i.e., the Communist Party of Nepal–Unified Marxist-Leninist, Janamorcha Nepal [People's Front Nepal], Nepali Congress Party, Nepal Peasants and Workers Party, and Nepal Sadbhavana Party) joined forces to embark on what they call the Joint People's Movement against the king and to restore the constitution. This movement's initial phase got underway with a large parade of black flags. Throughout the month of May protests continued across the country in various forms and in growing numbers. In support of the movement, students staged mass demonstrations against the king. As police forces attacked protesters in various cities across the nation, violence erupted, causing some deaths and numerous injuries. The first political casualty of these new, rapid developments was Prime Minister

Lokendra Bahadur Chand who resigned on 30 May. In order to restore order in the nation's volatile political climate, the five political parties engaged in the joint movement asked the king to form a new government of national unity under the prime ministership of Madhav Kumar Nepal, general secretary of the CPN–UML. But, in defiance of their reconciliatory proposal and their growing movement, King Gyanendra appointed Surya Bahadur Thapa to be Nepal's new prime minister. Widely recognized as a staunch royalist, Thapa is a prominent member of the right-wing, pro-Panchayat National Democratic Party that refused to lend support to the Joint People's Movement. Less than 24 hours after Thapa's ascension to prime ministership, the joint movement unleashed massive demonstrations, vowing to step up protests against the king, with some openly calling for the abolition of the institution of monarchy and the establishment of Nepal as a democratic republic. As the king and the frustrated opposition parties intensify their fight for political supremacy in terms of power relations, the cursed land of Nepal becomes increasingly mired in a seemingly endless crisis. What will happen next is difficult to predict.

ECONOMY

Political Economy and Development

Buried in the furrows of poverty, this land of Buddha is anything but peaceful from a socioeconomic perspective. The vast majority of people live hand to mouth, constantly swinging between the vulnerable space of hunger and starvation, despair and destitution. For many, life is a daily struggle. There is no certainty of where the next meal will come from, and such is the fact of life in Nepal whether one lives in the rural fringes or urban trenches.

With an annual per capita income of $220, the World Bank has labeled Nepal as one of the poorest countries in the world. Nearly 45 percent of the households live below the poverty line as defined by the World Bank. There are several factors that account for the country's abject poverty: its landlocked position, limited resource base, low agricultural growth and productivity, minimal industrial development, high population growth rates, increasing institutional breakdowns, and endless administrative corruption. To this list must be added *leadership*—the foundation of all. Roughly defined, leadership constitutes total political commitment to national well-being and progress rather than to personal bank accounts and vested class interests, as well as the fundamental political ability to lead the civil servants and general populace on the path of institutional integrity and openness, justice, fairness, and democracy. While there is no dearth of leaders, or at least those who freely claim to be leaders, leadership is constantly and conspicuously missing from Nepal's political scene.

Few would doubt that India's monopoly over Nepal's access to the sea leaves it vulnerable, with little bargaining leverage for securing unrestricted transit facilities and trade with other nations. This is one of the requirements of economic growth and development. Furthermore, India has a choke hold on the Nepali economy, a fact that was sufficiently demonstrated during the embargo of 1989. As the embargo went into effect, India closed most of the transit points along the border, allowing only limited amounts of basic goods and commodities to enter Nepal. The gravity of the embargo was further magnified by the fact that India supplies most of the basic goods consumed in the country.

Socioeconomic Evolution

Despite such locational disadvantage and heavy dependency on India, Nepal once had a relatively self-sufficient, though subsistence, economy. Historically, Nepal, like most other societies, has evolved through many technological phases of socioeconomic formation—from the hunting and gathering mode of production technology to the pastoral and then agrarian modes. In recent years, the country has witnessed its nascent entry into the industrial and service modes where carpet production and tourism occupy center court. To be sure, it is difficult to pin down a specific time frame for the hunting and gathering phase of Nepal's socioeconomic formation due to the absence of necessary historical records. Nonetheless, there is evidence to suggest that by the time the Pala dynasty was established in the lush Kathmandu Valley, Nepal's socioeconomic formation was no longer dominated by hunting and gathering; it had already evolved into pastoralism as a primary form of production technology and development. The very self-descriptive word *mahisapala* makes it clear that the Pala dynasty was indeed founded in the Valley by buffalo (*mahisa*) herders or protectors (*pala*). It was a dynasty of pastoralist rulers: Mahisapalas.

Although some agriculture was practiced, the pastoral form of production technology remained dominant at least until the emergence of the Licchavi period. With the rise of the Licchavis came a new transition in Nepal's socioeconomic formation. The Kathmandu Valley developed its agricultural base thanks to its highly fertile soil, including many traits typical of an urban civilization such as commerce. As a result, the economic foundation expanded, allowing the Valley and its Newar population to engage in long-distance trade and to exercise a wider economic influence. Yet pastoral practices were common outside of the Valley, particularly among the nomadic immigrants from the north (Tibet) who crossed into the hills during the unrecorded period of Nepali history. As previously noted, the migrant communities of that time constituted Tibeto-Nepali groups who occupied the hills where they combined their pastoral practices with some farming. It appeared that farming gained increased popularity with the decreasing hill altitude. The Gurungs and Magars occupying lower hills practiced farming to a much higher degree than those Tibeto-Nepalis who inhabited higher hills, e.g., the Sherpas and Thakalis. The farming system among the Tibeto-Nepali groups was mostly organized around what can be described as the communal mode of production, that is, the communal ownership of land known as the *kipat* system.

With the arrival of the massive waves of Hindu migrants from the south, the pastoral technology and the communal mode of production underwent gradual declines as they were progressively overshadowed by a higher form of technology and socioeconomic formation: the agrarian mode of production. To be more specific, those Hindu migrants, who fled Muslim invasions of northern India less than a thousand years ago and who later flooded the hills of Nepal, brought with them a relatively advanced form of farming technology and class-structured social institution. As they (now Indo-Nepalis) embarked on the path of asserting their institutional and economic domination over local populations (Tibeto-Nepalis), the pastoral technology and communal mode of production naturally yielded to the more productive agrarian mode of production. As the land occupied center stage in the agrarian system controlled by Hindu migrants from India, farming emerged as the principal economic activity or source of livelihood.

Also characterized as the domestic mode of production, most people under the agrarian mode produced for household consumption rather than for market exchange. Since the country produced enough goods and most of its daily necessities, the external dependence was limited to such items as salt, kerosene, and spices. Today, the economic situation is different. The country is grossly dependent on external development resources, that is, foreign aid. As it appears, no economic development project can get off the ground without some foreign assistance, in the form of either loans or grants. For a country with a gross national product (GNP) of $5 billion, its external debt totals over $2.6 billion or more than 50 percent of GNP. This clearly shows the gravity of Nepal's external dependency.

FUTURE PROSPECTS

No matter how one analyzes Nepal's economy, its present condition is mired in poverty and its future uncertain. Its problems are too varied and too entrenched to have sustained solutions. Despite this generally gloomy outlook, its agricultural and tourism sectors hold some tangible prospect for future progress. One might ask: how could Nepal expect to achieve agricultural development under the condition of limited land resources? The simple fact that Nepal's crop yields per unit of land are so low means there is tremendous room for raising land productivity through technological improvements and carefully balanced shifts from low-value to high-value crops, e.g., vegetables and potatoes. In addition, as the breadbasket of Nepal, the Tarai enjoys substantial potential for agricultural development in terms of increased land productivity.

Currently, however, tourism is perhaps the only sector to have posted continuous growth and expansion over the past 40 years. There is enough evidence to be hopeful about tourism's continued march for the next few years. To be sure, this will require its geographical diversification from its current gravitational axis based in the Kathmandu Valley to other parts of the country. Failure to attain such diversification will most likely strain its growth potential. Tourism in the Valley is already approaching a point of saturation in terms of its pending environmental crisis due to heavy air pollution. One additional problem facing Nepal's tourist industry is the People's War that has been raging since 1996. This internal atmosphere of fear was further aggravated by the event of 11 September 2001, and ongoing concerns about international travel. Nepal normally receives an estimated half-a-million tourists annually. But, in 2001, it experienced a 17 percent drop. The worst impact was felt in November, usually the busiest month for the tourist industry; tourist arrivals in Nepal fell by 43 percent during that month. Most hotels, restaurants, and stores catering to tourists were generally empty. In addition, key exports such as garments and carpets which are strongly tied to tourism went down.

Some may argue that, in light of Nepal's determined push for privatization of state-owned enterprises and relatively liberal foreign investment policies, its industrial horizon is quite bright. While it is always hazardous to project too far into the future, no amount of neoliberalism or privatization is likely to suddenly rectify the country's deep-seated, multidimensional industrial woes. These extend from total dependency on imported raw materials to the limitations imposed by a small domestic market and the paucity of convenient international transit facilities. Neoliberal policies certainly seem to have injected some temporary vigor into this sector, but they are fraught with expectations that defy the macroeconomic realities of Nepal. In addition, the advocates of neoliberal policies are tainted with a one-sided view that greatly inflates their benefits while completely ignoring their detrimental effects.

In the final analysis, unless the country achieves dynamic agricultural development relatively fast and at a furious pace, the specter of poverty will continue to haunt the country for the foreseeable future. This is not a pleasant prospect, but it is a reality that Nepal can hardly afford to ignore or treat lightly. The problem of festering poverty and the consequent plight of the poor is compounded by the fact that the country has consistently suffered from the lack of genuine leadership, one that is truly committed to national progress and uplifting the masses. It is no exaggeration that the history of Nepal is chained to the shackles of factional and patrimonial politics. Even after the dawn of democracy a decade ago, the nation has failed to break free from these shackles. Political leaders are concerned more about their own personal, clan, and party gains than about national welfare. The fact that there have been 10 different governments since 1990—almost one every year—is quite revealing of the direction in which Nepal is headed. It is clear that political parties and their leaders exercise the whole notion of democracy mostly as an electoral game rather than as a tool of national consolidation and reconciliation, much needed institutional reforms in bureaucracy and civil service, development of civil society, and sustained economic progress. Corruption is out of control. Under such circumstances, the likelihood of a historical upswing in the national economy and reduction in pervasive poverty remains dim.

The Dictionary

A

ABAL. A traditional category of arable land based on productivity or soil quality and irrigation. Such a system of land categories was mainly instituted for the purpose of levying land taxes. According to this system, *abal* is the best quality of cultivable land because it is fertile and contains good quality soil. As such, it carries the highest rate of land taxes. At least two different seasonal crops can be grown on this type of land, paddy rice being the primary crop. Unirrigated *abal* lands are ideal for dry rice, maize, and a variety of vegetable crops. Assuming that every production input (and condition) remains the same, *abal* lands show the highest level of crop productivity per unit of land relative to other types of land. It is followed by *doyam*, *sim*, and *chahar*, with a decreasing level of soil fertility. *Doyam* is second grade as it contains sandy materials with a lower ability to retain moisture. However, two crops can be produced on it as long as it is regularly fertilized. Ranked third on the quality scale, *sim* land generally lacks irrigation facility except for rainfalls. As a result, its yield level is naturally lower than the first two types of land. Compounding its problem is its relatively steep land gradient in some cases. Not surprisingly, therefore, it is usually confined to hilly areas and river banks commonly called *tar* or *tadi* (generally dry and barren fields). While in the past this type of land was usually used as a pasture field for grazing animals, it is being increasingly brought under cultivation because of growing land shortages. The lowest grade of land is called *chahar* which contains significant amounts of sand and gravel. Again because of land shortages, even this type of land is now being increasingly used for growing crops. It is, however, cautioned that such land categories are strictly based on their natural conditions. The categories could change in that they could go up or down the grade hierarchy, depending on sustained land improvements or degradation. *See also* AGRICULTURE.

ABIR. Vermillion powder generally put on the forehead to mark victory or celebration. It is one of the required ingredients for worshiping and during festivals. It is invariably mixed with **rice** and yogurt when it is placed on one's forehead. Because it is red, it is considered to be a joyful color. Therefore, it is never used during times of mourning or other sorrowful events. In fact, on sorrowful occasions, no red color is used or worn. In Nepal those who are undergoing a period of ritual mourning wear plain white clothes. Widows, even after the prescribed period of mourning is over, rarely wear anything red, at least not in public.

ACHARYA, BABURAM (1887–1972). Famous historian, scholar, and literary critic. It is believed that he is the one who named **Mount Everest** Sagarmatha, which means "the roof of the world." For his enormous contributions to the study of Nepali history, he was decorated with the title of Itihas Shiromani (a crown jewel among Nepali historians).

ACHARYA, BHANU BHAKTA (1814–1868). Regarded as the founder of Nepali poetry or Adhikabi. Born in the central hill district of Tanahun, his adaptation of the **Ramayana**, a highly popular **Hindu** epic, into Nepali earned him the reputation of being Nepal's first literary giant. What was important about his *Ramayana* work was that it was composed in simple, idiomatic, rhythmic Nepali. It was the first piece of Indian or **Sanskrit literature** that, Michael Hutt notes, was not only translated into Nepali, but was truly "Nepali-ized." It served as a model of Nepali poetry for many decades. His *Ramayana* is still one of the most significant achievements and certainly among the best-loved works of Nepali literature. Bhanu Bhakta composed it in the late 1840s, but it was not published until 1887. It was **Motiram Bhatta** who was instrumental in its first publication. There is no doubt that Bhanu Bhakta played a foundational role in the development of Nepali as a literary language and in the subsequent evolution of Nepali literature. It is no surprise, therefore, that Nepal celebrates Bhanu Jayanti (anniversary) every year.

ACHARYA, HARIBANSA (1958–). A comedian who is popular for his satirical depiction of Nepali politics and society. His pieces are sometimes broadcast on **Radio Nepal** and are available on tape for commercial consumption. In addition, he occasionally does stage performances.

ACHARYA, MEENA (1941–). She is an economist and scholar who is associated with **Nepal Rastra Bank** (the central bank of Nepal) since 1996 and several other social institutions. She has authored and co-authored several studies on **women**'s status and roles in development.

ACHARYA, SHAILAJA (1944–). Active leader of the **Nepali Congress Party.** Her emergence on the Nepali political scene coincided with her rebellious act of hoisting a black flag against King **Mahendra Bir Bikram Shah** in 1960. For that act, she was kept in prison for three years (1960–1963). As an elected member of the **Parliament**, she served as minister of **agriculture** in 1991–1992. She is considered to be a rapidly rising star within her party.

ACHARYA, TANKA PRASAD (1912–1992). Founder of Nepal's first political party, **Praja Parishad** or Nepal Praja Parishad (People's Council) in 1936. He was arrested in October 1940 for anti-**Rana** activities, but escaped the death penalty because of his **Bahun** caste (it was considered a heinous sin to kill a Bahun). In early 1956, he was appointed prime minister (1956–1957) by King **Mahendra Bir Bikram Shah.**

ADHIKARAN. Administrative offices during the **Licchavi period**, for example, Purbadhikaran (of the east region), Paschimadhikaran (of the west region), Kuther Adhikaran (for collection of revenue and issuance of warrants), and Bhattadhikaran (of the army). It is a form of authority or control over a geographical entity or some administrative process.

ADHIKARI, BHARAT MOHAN (1936–). A politburo member of the **Communist Party of Nepal** (Unified Marxist-Leninist or UML) who actively participated in the pro-democracy movement. He served as finance minister in 1994. He is one of the few members of the **House of Representatives** who won all three general **elections** (1991, 1994, and 1999) held since the second coming of democracy in 1990.

ADHIKARI, KRISHNA LAL. Revolutionary writer. His book *Makaiko Kheti* (Corn Farming) published in 1918 was a literary attack on the

Rana regime. Imprisoned for that book, he died in prison, an episode that was later known as the Makai Parba.

ADHIKARI, MAN MOHAN (1920–1999). A renowned leftist political leader, Adhikari received his higher education in **India**. Along with **Puspa Lal Shrestha**, he was instrumental in the formation of Nepal's first communist party, the **Communist Party of Nepal**. He was later elected the party's general secretary. He played a paramount role in the pro-democracy movement of 1990. When his party, the Communist Party of Nepal–Unified Marxist-Leninist (CPN–ULM), came to power in 1994, he became the first Marxist prime minister of Nepal. This development made Nepal the second country in the world to feature a popularly elected Marxist government (the first being Chile in the early 1970s under President Salvador Allende). He passed away on 26 April 1999.

ADHIKARI, SUBHADRA (1947–). A movie actress who has been cast in several Nepali feature films since the early 1970s. She is generally considered to be a pioneer in her field within Nepal. In her capacity as a movie actress, she was seen by many young **women** as a source of inspiration in the 1970s.

ADHIRAJYA. Kingdom. It is a nation-state, much larger in territorial coverage, political organization, and administrative setup than what is often called a principality which, in Nepali, is referred to as a *rajya*. In this sense, Nepal became an *adhirajya* after 1769, following the conquest of the **Kathmandu Valley** and consolidation of the rest of the principalities scattered throughout the hills. *See also* BAISE RAJYA; CHAUBISE RAJYA; SHAH, PRITHVI NARAYAN.

ADHIVASI (ADHIBASI). **Sanskritic** neologism which means "aboriginal or indigenous inhabitants," for example, the **Tharus** of the **Tarai** region.

ADHIYA. Sharecropping. It is a traditional form of **land tenure**, widely practiced in Nepal. The tenant normally shares 50 percent of the crop with the landlord. Historically, it has impeded agricultural development as it gives little incentive to tenants to take measures necessary to improve land and apply innovations. While the landlord keeps at least 50 percent of what is produced, the tenant has to provide labor and incur every aspect of production costs, including the cost of land improvements and agricultural inputs. Several land reforms have been implemented over the years, presumably to rectify the embedded problem of tenancy in order to induce agricultural development, but they have all failed to bring about any significant reform in tenancy. The general consensus is that land reforms, especially the 1964 Land Reform Act, have actually undercut tenants' tenancy rights as well as their overall socioeconomic conditions. See also AGRICULTURE; LAND REFORM.

AGNI. Hindu god of fire. As a **Sanskrit** word, it simply means "fire." Fire represents powerful ritualistic symbolism as it is seen as a purifier and a deterrent against malevolent spirits (*see also* **Bhut**). In many respects, its symbolic role is identical to that of water, the opposite elemental force of fire. They are both used as indispensable elements in virtually every ritual and religious ceremony from birth to death.

AGRAWAL, GOVINDA RAM (1942–). As a research scholar, he has authored several studies on business management and economics. He also served as advisor to the **Nepal Industrial Development Corporation** (1969–1971).

AGRICULTURE. A predominantly agrarian society, Nepal is deeply embedded in crop production and animal rearing. Agriculture is the single most important economic activity; it is the backbone of the whole economic system. The **World Bank** notes that over 40 percent of Nepal's gross domestic product (GDP) is directly tied to agriculture and employs over 76 percent of the total labor force which, in 1999, was estimated to be roughly 9.5 million. Technically, however, this agricultural employment figure is lower than the actual situation because significant numbers of those employed in nonagricultural activities are also engaged in farming. It is, therefore, fair to assume that the number of people dependent on agriculture for overall family survival is closer to the percentage of the national population living in rural areas, that is, over 85 percent.

No matter how the employment structure is analyzed in the dualistic **economy** of Nepal, the agricultural sector still plays the most dominant role as the economic fate of the vast majority of Nepalis is directly anchored to its success or failure. Unfortunately, unless the **monsoon** cooperates, allowing farmers to collect bountiful harvests, Nepal no longer enjoys an agricultural surplus. Food deficits have become a chronic problem, especially in the hills. For instance, during the five-year period between 1995 and 1999, Nepal's annual agricultural growth rate averaged 2.3 percent, about the same as the population growth rate. When only the production of food crops—namely paddy (**rice**), maize, millet, wheat, and barley—was taken into account, the annual agricultural growth rate dropped to less than 1.5 percent. In simple terms, food production failed to keep pace with population growth over the same period. The **Tarai** is the only region that has a food surplus. It is no wonder, therefore, that this region is called the "granary" of Nepal.

The question of agricultural growth (or stagnation) is particularly significant for an agrarian country like Nepal where the population is growing rapidly in the face of extremely limited land resources. While the socioeconomic survival of the vast majority of peasants is intrinsically tied to agriculture, the per capita holding of cultivable land has been going down. At the national level, it currently stands at merely 0.1 hectare per capita. Nationally, 51 percent of the population owns less than 0.5 hectare of land per household, consisting of about six persons on average. Another 16 percent owns 0.5–1.0 hectare per household. In total, 67 percent of the households occupy only 17 percent of Nepal's farmland, many being entirely landless. Generally speaking, therefore, such a small amount of land is hardly sufficient to adequately support a family of six for a year. The situation is particularly precarious in the hills where land deficits are quite high.

As seen from the following table based on the 1999 data, rice is by far the most dominant crop in Nepal in terms of production volume:

Crops (1999)	**Percent**
Rice	55.7
Maize and Millet	24.7
Wheat	6.5
Potato	4.9
Oil Seeds	3.4
Tobacco	2.4
Jute	0.8
Others	1.6
Total	**100.0**

See also ABAL; ADHIYA; LAND REFORM; LAND TENURE.

AGRICULTURAL PROJECTS SERVICES CENTRE (APROSC). Set up in 1974, APROSC is a research firm that provides consultancy service and conducts contract research in the field of **agriculture** and development. During its early period, this firm played an important role in terms of agricultural and rural development policy formulation. It is based in **Kathmandu.**

AGRICULTURE DEVELOPMENT BANK OF NEPAL (ADB-N). Created in 1968, the main objective of this bank is to mobilize agricultural savings and investments to promote development. Headquartered in **Kathmandu**, it has an extensive network of local branch offices to facilitate loans for commercial agricultural development.

AGRICULTURE INPUTS CORPORATION (AIC). Public enterprise. It was established for the purpose of producing and supplying agricultural inputs such as chemical fertilizers, high yielding seeds, and insecticides. Initially formed in 1965 as the Agriculture Supply Corporation, it is also engaged in agricultural research. *See also* AGRICULTURE.

AGRICULTURE TOOLS FACTORY. Public enterprise set up in 1968 with the help of the former Soviet Union. The factory produces various agricultural tools, mostly for the domestic market. It is based in the **Tarai** district of **Birganj**, a city along the Indian border.

AHIMSA. Nonviolence. A **Buddhist** concept, it espouses the principle of no killing of any living beings; not even intentional injury to them. While some Buddhists practice it as a religious principle, in Nepal it has little history or precedence of being deployed as a political tool in a manner that is similar to a Gandhian movement in **India**.

AILANI. Refers to common or public lands within the de facto jurisdiction of a community. They sometimes become targets of squatter settlement. In cities, where the land value has soared, wealthy and powerful citizens have illegally absorbed many patches of such lands. In some cases government officials sell or lease them for private use.

AIN. Laws, statutes or **civil codes**.

AIRLINES AND INTERNATIONAL AIR SERVICE. Currently, 15 different airlines fly in and out of **Kathmandu**, linking Nepal to various cities and countries. Some of these destinations are: Bahrain, Bangkok, Calcutta, Delhi, Dhaka, Frankfurt, London, Munich, Osaka, Paris, Rangoon, Shanghai, and Singapore. Among the international airlines serving Nepal are: Biman Bangladesh Airlines, Druk Airlines, Gulf Air, Indian Airlines, Lufthansa, Singapore Airlines, and Thai International. The **Royal Nepal Airlines Corporation**, which is a public enterprise, has the most extensive flight links to foreign destinations. It also provides extensive domestic flights to different parts of the country. Until the private domestic airlines companies were allowed to enter the air **transportation** market a little over a decade ago, the RNAC had a total monopoly over all domestic flights. Its flight schedules were extremely unreliable and routinely delayed for hours. Since the **privatization** of the domestic market, however, its overall service has dramatically improved. Nonetheless, it has constantly experienced losses over the years.

AIR SERVICE WITHIN NEPAL. Until fairly recently, many parts of the country were accessible only by foot. The situation has definitely improved in the past few years for two reasons. First, more domestic airfields have been established, including some in very remote areas, thus creating a wider network of airfields. Second, the **Royal Nepal Airlines Corporation** (RNAC) no longer has a monopoly over domestic flights. Several private **airlines** now provide service, leading to vast improvements in the reliability and frequency of flights in the country. In addition to regular flights, some of these airlines offer "**mountain** view" (e.g., **Mount Everest**) charter flights for tourists.

AKASH BHAIRAV. A **Hindu** god, Bhairav represents fierce power and destruction of demonic forces. It is housed in a three-roofed **pagoda** temple at **Asan Tol**, a busy and lively neighborhood in **Kathmandu**.

ALL NEPAL NATIONAL FREE STUDENTS' UNION. As a student union supporting leftist activities, it played an active role during the pro-democracy movement of 1990. It is one of the oldest students' unions in the country, normally associated with university and college campuses throughout the country.

ALMODA (ALMORA), BATTLE OF. During the **Anglo-Nepal War**, a major battle was waged in Almoda (now in **India**) by the Nepali troops commandeered by **Amar Singh Thapa** against the British forces (British East India Company). Eventually, Amar Singh agreed to a truce.

AMADABLAM. One of the peaks (6,812m) in the Khumbu Range of the **Himalaya**. Regarded as one of the most beautiful peaks, it attracts many **mountain** climbing expeditions every year.

AMALI. Local magistrate or tax collector with certain judicial duties, appointed and assigned to particular administrative territories. This is an old practice that used to be common prior to 1951, that is, before the demise of the **Rana** regime.

AMANAT. System of revenue collection and management by a government office, or by an agency empowered by the government on a contractual basis. It used to be commonly practiced prior to 1951.

AMATYA, PIYUSH BAHADUR (1943–). Industrial entrepreneur in **Kathmandu**. He founded several industrial and business concerns, e.g., the Nepal Power Engineering Company and Everest Ice Creams. He is a founding member of the Public Youth College.

AMATYA, SURYA LAL (1936–). A professor of geography, he is an authority on Nepal's physical and cultural geography. Once affiliated with **Tribhuvan University**, he has, over the years, played a significant role in elevating the status of geography and geographical studies in the country. He is now retired.

AMLEKHGANJ. Settlement north of the border town of **Birganj** in the central **Tarai**. The name means "a place of freed **slaves**" because it was actually set up to resettle some 52,000 slaves freed in the early 1900s by Prime Minister **Chandra Shamsher Rana**. It is linked to a small Indian city called Raxaul, across the border from Birganj, by a narrow gauge and poorly maintained railway line that is about 40 kilometers long.

AMSA. Share of family inheritance or properties. Due to family discords and numerical growth, family members—particularly brothers—tend to break up and establish their own separate families. Although the family system in Nepal normally involves an extended unit, it offers little immunity against family separation and breakup. Such breakups usually occur after brothers get married, especially if the head of the family fails to assert and exert authority. Once the separation decision is finalized, the family landholding (and other properties) is divided among the father, mother, and brothers, each receiving an equal amount of *amsa*. Daughters are allocated no *amsa* unless they remain unmarried beyond the age of 35. No daughter-in-law in the family is entitled to her own *amsa* unless her husband is dead. See also WOMEN'S STATUS.

AMSUVARMAN (reign: 605–621). One of the most highly respected rulers during the **Licchavi period.** He was well known for his intelligence, leadership, liberal outlook on religious faiths, and deep concern for the welfare of his citizens. He wrote *Shabdabidhya*, a treaty on rhetoric and sounds. He left behind several inscriptions and had many water tanks, wells, spouts, and rest houses built. Chinese traveler **Wang Huen-Tsang** provided a description of Amsuvarman as a distinguished king for his learning and ingenuity.

ANAND, MINAKSHI. A Nepali movie actress, she played lead roles in several Nepali feature films in the early 1980s. During the early years of her film career, she was a popular actress.

ANANTA NAG. Cosmic serpent; king of serpents in **Hindu** mythology. Regarded as the ancestor of all the snakes. It is also known as Shesh Nag. According to the belief system prevalent in Nepal, snakes are divided into good (with divine qualities) and bad snakes. See also NAG.

ANCHAL. Zone. It is a administrative unit. There are 14 *anchals* in Nepal (*see* figure 3) each of which is composed of several districts (*zilla*). Although this administrative division was created during the **Panchayat** period, it was retained ensuing the restoration of democracy in 1990.

ANDOLANKARI. Term used generically to denote agitators, activists, or those who participate in antigovernment protests or subversive activities (*andolan*). It takes on a revolutionary tone when there is mass participation in a political movement or when it involves a mass movement (*jana andolan*), for example, the pro-democracy revolution of 1990.

The Dictionary   45

ANGLO-NEPAL WAR (1814–1816). As Nepal forged ahead with its territorial expansion campaign after national unification in 1769, it encountered British resistance. Eventually, a war broke out between the British and Nepali forces in 1814. The war, which lasted almost two years, later came to be commonly known as the Anglo-Nepal War. After two years of intense battles, the British prevailed. That was the most humiliating defeat that Nepal ever suffered at the hands of a foreign army, a defeat that still haunts Nepal. *See also* SAGAULI, TREATY OF.

ANIKO (ARNIKO) (1245–1306). Famous architect, sculptor, and bronze caster from the **Kathmandu Valley**. At the request of Chinese (Mongolian) Emperor Kublai Khan's teacher Saskyapa Lama of **Tibet**, Nepal commissioned Aniko to lead a group of artisans to Lhasa to construct a golden stupa. Beijing's White **Pagoda** or Pai Ta Sze stands today as a monument to the artistic contribution of Aniko. He evidently had over 200 apprentices and pupils and his influence through these artists may be seen in the temple **art and architecture** of East and Southeast Asia. He died in **China** in 1306.

ANNAPURNA. (*Anna* = grains + *purna* = full, filled.) In Nepali, it means "the **mountain** filled with grains." The front view of Annapurna (IV) as seen from the city of **Pokhara** looks like a cap at its summit. The folklore of Annapurna has it that if the cap is full of snow in the winter, then the peasants and farmers down in the valleys will have a good year. If the cap is not filled with snow, that is a bad omen as it was believed to usher in a year of hardship. What was entailed in the folklore, in other words, was a meteorological message. A cap full of snow meant the level of winter precipitation was good. As a result, there would be enough water from the melting snow flowing down those mountains to nourish the spring crops down in the valleys, thus allowing farmers to produce good spring harvests. And, conversely, Annapurna's empty cap would result in poor harvests. In a society reliant on experiential knowledge, such a folkloric meteorological read of the local climatic condition was a proven method to prepare for the oncoming cycle of farming and fortune (or misfortune).

The Annapurna **Himalayan** Range has four Annapurna peaks: I, II, III, and IV. It is highly revered by those who live around it and is one of the favorite peaks among Western mountaineers.

APHNO MANCHHE. Someone in one's kin or clique group who offers favors, often without merit. In essence, it means: "It depends on who you know, not what you know." As a very popular phrase, it is widely used throughout Nepal, especially in the context of employment or job search. See also CHAKARI.

ARCHEOLOGY. Paradoxically, Nepal is both an archeological treasure and enigma. There is a conspicuous archeological void insofar as scientific investigation is concerned. Archaeological studies to date have been conducted by only a handful of Nepali scientists, largely in cooperation with Indian professionals, with much of the excavation work being centered in the **Kathmandu Valley** and at **Lumbini**, the birthplace of the **Buddha**.

ARCHITECTURE. See ART AND ARCHITECTURE.

ARNA. Endangered wild buffalo (*Bubalus arnee*) found in the Kosi Tappu Wildlife Reserve. It is included in Nepal's protected species group.

ARNIKO HIGHWAY. Almost 120 kilometers long, this paved road links the **Kathmandu Valley** to Kodari at the border with the **Tibetan** autonomous region of **China**. It was completed and opened in May 1967 with Chinese assistance and later named Arniko Highway in honor of **Aniko** (Arniko) who is regarded as a symbol of the enduring cultural relationship between Nepal and **Tibet**.

ART AND ARCHITECTURE. It is widely recognized that despite being a small, landlocked, and isolated country, Nepal has a long history of artistic tradition and architecture. It is veritable museum of artistic richness complimented by its natural beauty. While a rich variety of its exquisite handicrafts testifies to its artistic heritage, countless temples scattered throughout the **Kathmandu Valley** stand as monuments to its architectural achievements. Given the close association between Nepal's artistic tradition and architecture, as manifested in numerous temple structures, they go hand in hand. And they are both directly traced to the Valley's **Newars** in terms of origin, originality, internal growth, and external expansion.

The art of Nepal has been heavily influenced by its two dominant religious traditions: **Buddhism** and **Hinduism**. One may observe their influences in the elaborate and intricate decorative ornamentation of many houses and palaces, especially those in the Valley, and, of course, in the enrichment of many shrines and **pagodas**, the towering embodiment of Nepal's most indigenous architecture and artistic tradition. While the pagoda style is intimately linked to the influence of Hinduism, the **stupa** architecture, which stands in stark contrast to pagodas, is a product of Buddhism. Although the initial roots of the stupa architectural style extend to northern India, it has found its greatest and most pronounced manifestation in the soils of Nepal as exemplified by the inviting presence of the most renowned stupas in the world: **Swayambhu** and **Baudhanath**.

Beyond these two dominant examples, the manifestation of Nepali architecture can be seen in an array of traditional dwelling styles that vary from one ecological region to another and, in some cases, from one group to another. In the **Tarai** region, the traditional dwellings are mainly tied to the **Tharu** population. These houses mediate the physical and supernatural worlds of the Tharu. They are relatively small, one-story structures with a courtyard area that fulfills several functions: as a playground for children, a grain threshing and drying ground, and a ritual space to celebrate festivities and conduct funeral gatherings or purification rituals. These houses are also clustered together in relatively open, small patches of land surrounded by **forests**, a pattern of settlement that was most common until the 1960s.

Since the Tharu belief system is deeply framed by what can be generically described as shamanism in which malevolent spirits called *bhut* are centrally featured, the Tharu dwelling designs reflect their attempt to ward off or minimize *bhut* attacks at night. Since windows and doors are regarded as *bhut* entryways, their houses have few windows and usually only one door. Moreover, such designs help to reduce the chances of entries into the houses of wild creatures, for instance, deadly snakes that were omnipresent in the dense jungle environment that typified the Tarai until the 1960s. Their design also keeps the interior space relatively cool, thereby minimizing the climatic effect of the Tarai's blistering hot and humid condition.

Most of the houses in the hills where the **Bahuns** and **Chhetris** dominate numerically, along with the clusters of **Gurung** and **Magar** settlements, have a rectangular shape and an open veranda-like space right outside the entryway. This space spans the whole length of the house and is used for a variety of purposes, especially for greeting guests and socializing with family members and neighbors. They normally have a little annex on the side or right next to the house that is used as a domestic animal shelter or for storing firewood. They are usually one- to two-storied structures set on raised foundations, with stone walls plastered with regular mud and painted with red or white clay on both sides. The roofs are constructed out of either thatch, slate, or corrugated tin. Most houses have only a few small windows and one entryway, which is narrow and short. This makes the interior space quite dark and tends to preserve the heat (and smoke) generated inside from cooking. They face south, east, or west. While the scientific explanation for such directional orientation may lie in the advantage of solar exposure, which supplies much needed heat and energy during winter months, the folk belief prevalent in the hills is that northern exposure is inauspicious. There is one major distinction between Bahun and Chhetri houses and Gurung and Magar houses in terms of their settlement patterns. The former is generally dispersed with their individual houses surrounded by grain and vegetable fields, whereas the latter tend to be dense, clustered together along narrow paths or around a common open space.

Although most of the materials used for house construction are locally available, except for corrugated tin, one can see substantial variations not so much in their shapes and designs as in their sizes and the materials used. Basically, what distinguishes house types is wealth. Vernacular architecture provides, in other words, a good sense of how village society is stratified, economically as well as socially. As a general rule, while poor peasant houses are small, one-storied and show a thatch roof, those of the rich and well-off are large with slate or tin roofs.

On the other hand, Newar homes exhibit a distinct urban flavor and cultural landscape that closely correspond to their urban origin in the Kathmandu Valley. Their houses are more substantial and are often larger than those found among other hill cultures. They exude a commercial aura as they are mostly found in market centers in the hills such as **Baglung**, Bandipur, **Pokhara**, and Tansen (**Palpa**), in addition to those in the Kathmandu Valley. Most have two to three stories—or even four in some cases—and are built along both sides of commercial streets in the town. They are constructed out of brick and stone for walls and slate or corrugated tin for roofs. They also have more windows and doors with substantial wood frames. While the street-level floor is generally consigned to commercial use, e.g., to set up a clothing or general store, upper floors are set aside for residential purposes.

The high mountain and **Trans-Himalayan** region represents yet another architectural style in Nepal. In this generally arid region, the most prevalent vernacular architecture reveals flat-roof houses made of dry-laid stone walls and stone roofs plastered with mud, similar in some respects to those found further north on the **Tibetan** Plateau. They tend to be several stories high and appear to scramble up the southern slopes of hillsides, with the entire settlement looking like a honeycomb of structures linked together by shared walls and layered roof lines. Movement from floor to floor is accomplished by using hand-hewn ladders propped against the outer walls of the building. The flat roofs are used to store firewood and in winter the blanket of snow that collects on the roofs helps to insulate the structures. Livestock commonly kept inside the homes on the ground floor below the sleeping areas generate some heat and humidity, thus helping to warm the air as well as infuse some moisture in the house.

Over the years, Nepali art has evolved. Its manifestation can be viewed through four primary mediums that define the country's artistic heritage. They are: bronze craftsmanship, wood carving, stone sculpturing, and **Tanka** painting (which, although said to be borrowed from **Tibet**, has long been indigenized). It is fair to say that the Newar artists have truly mastered the art and science of bronze craftsmanship. It is mostly expressed in the form of statues of various divine entities and certain kings, together with the famous Golden Gate of **Bhaktapur**, which displays a marvelous quality of technical skill and harmonious beauty. European scholars of Nepali bronze art believe that it will stand every test virtually in all respects, especially in light of the time in which it developed.

No less refined and attractive are wood carvings and a multitude of stone sculptures found throughout the Kathmandu Valley. All major temples, royal palaces, and prominent public buildings—and now major hotels—in the country are decorated with exquisitely carved doors, windows, and window sills. The lattice work in the **Bhaktapur Durbar Square** and the peacock window situated just a short walk away from the square are two of the finest examples. Stone sculptures are even more visible as they are everywhere. For example, some of the stone carvings found in and around the **Patan Durbar Square** are not only elaborate and delicate, but also truly beautiful. **Krishna Mandir** which is constructed entirely of stone, from the foundation to the top, represents another fine specimen of how advanced Nepal's artistic tradition was in the early 1600s, a time period that preceded the industrial revolution by almost 150 years. Perceval Landon, a British visitor to Nepal, whose book is still widely referenced, wrote that "The domestic architecture of Nepal is picturesque beyond that of any other country. . . the patterns in the windows of Newar houses are considerably more elaborate than those designed by the Arab or the Sikh."

ARTHASHASTRA (ARTHA SHASTRA). (*Artha* = money; wealth + *shastra* = principle; treatise.) It is an elaborate treatise on polity, statecraft, and economics whose authorship is traditionally attributed to Kautilya, who was the famous minister of Chandragupta Maurya (324–313 B.C.). From its very inception, the *Arthashastra* has served as a valuable guide to administrative organization as it offers detailed instructions on the management of the state, the organization of national economic system, and the conduct of war.

ARUN RIVER (ARUN KOSI). Major tributary of the **Kosi River System** (seven Kosi rivers that constitute the principal drainage system in eastern Nepal). Originating in **Tibet**, it enters Nepal via the Kumbhakarna Himal Range. It is the site of the much disputed Arun III, a hydroelectric project with a proposed capacity of 402 megawatts, whose fate has yet to be decided. It was supposed to have been initially funded by the **World Bank**.

ARUN VALLEY. Deep valley formed by the **Arun River**. It is believed to be the world's biggest valley in terms of its elevation range.

ARYAGHAT. Religious bathing and cremation site on the bank of the **Bagmati**, a holy river, flowing by the temple of **Pashupati** and right through the city of **Kathmandu**.

ARYAL, ISHWOR RAJ (1921–1992). Fully committed to **education**, he was the founding headmaster (1946) of Padmodaya High School, one of the earliest secondary schools in **Kathmandu**. He will be remembered for his tireless contribution to the field of education in Nepal.

ASAN TOL. Very busy and crowded neighborhood with narrow streets, located right in the heart of **Kathmandu**. It is a highly popular center of small shops selling all types of goods, including top quality **Tanka** paintings by local artists. For Western tourists who are interested in catching an authentic glimpse of life and **Newari** traditions in the **Kathmandu Valley**, it is a must-see part of the city.

ASHOK, EMPEROR (reign: 290–232 B.C.). Maurya emperor of the second century B.C., Ashok was the principal apostle of **Buddhism**, which he spread across the region with a missionary zeal. Purportedly a tyrant as a young man, he converted to Buddhism and began to preach the gospel of universal love in various countries. Ashok sent emissaries, including his daughter, son, and younger brother, for the purpose of advancing Buddhism and its message. During his visit to **Lumbini,** he erected a famous stone pillar. Later, he had four **stupas** built at four corners of **Patan** (Tyata, Lagankhel, Pulchok and Eebahi). They were all built around 250 B.C. Although an ardent devotee of Buddhism, Ashok maintained a liberal religious outlook, insisting upon peaceful coexistence amongst religions and religious sects.

ASHOK VINAYAK. Famous temple of **Ganesh** in the **Kathmandu Durbar Square** behind Kasthamandap (*see* **Kathmandu**). Also called Maru Ganesh, it is visited by the ruling monarch during the Indrajatra festival.

ASHTA DHATU. (*Ashta* = eight; *Dhatu* = minerals.) Amalgamation of eight minerals (normally gold, silver, iron, tin, mercury, lead, brass, and copper), it is often used in traditional Nepali sculpture.

ASHTA MANGAL. Eight auspicious symbols or emblems associated with **Buddhism**. It is applied widely in temples, monasteries, jewelry, and **Tanka** paintings, mainly in the **Kathmandu Valley**.

ASHTA MATRIKA. Eight mother goddesses. Included among them are: Bramhayani, Chamunda, Kumari, Indrayani, Mahalaxmi, Maheswori, Vaishnavi, and Varahi.

ASURA. Marauding demonic character in **Hindu** mythology that causes sufferings for humanity.

ATWARI. This is one of the festivals of **Tharu** communities of western Nepal. It is usually the male members of the community who take part in this festival.

AVALOKITESWARA. Bodhisattwa (Bodhisattva) who directs his gaze downward or "The Glancing Eye." Avalokiteswara, as Lokeswara, is considered to be a **Buddhist** deity on the same level as **Shiva** in **Hinduism**.

AVATAR. Ingrained **Hindu** concept which means divine incarnation, an earthly manifestation of a given god or goddess. Hindus believe that a particular avatar descends to the earth at a particular moment in history in order to solve particular problems or miseries tormenting humanity. Accordingly, divine figures such as **Buddha** or Jesus are seen as avatars whose mission is to rescue humanity, leaving behind their epochal marks. *See also* HINDUISM.

AWAJ. "Voice" or "call" in a literal sense. It has the distinction of being Nepal's first daily newspaper published in **Kathmandu** in 1951. Its editors were **Siddhi Charan Shrestha** and Govinda Bahadur Malla. In a sociopolitical context, it implies the voice of the people. And it was precisely in this context that the *Awaj* newspaper was published.

B

BACK-TO-THE-VILLAGE NATIONAL CAMPAIGN. Known in Nepal as the Gaun Pharka Rastriya Abhiyan, it was launched with great enthusiasm in 1967 by King **Mahendra Bir Bikram Shah** as a fundamental part of his **Panchayat** initiatives. Patterned after Mao's back-to-the-village campaign in **China** during which the elite and educated members of society were required to return to villages and live and work with peasants and workers, Nepal's campaign instituted a policy whereby university students were required to return to villages for a predetermined amount of time prior to graduation, working as school teachers. It was an essential part of the graduation requirements.

Appointed by King Mahendra to lead the campaign, **Bishwa Bandhu Thapa** was instrumental in terms of giving it a concrete framework. The Back-to-the-Village National Campaign was highly heralded as a patriotic social service act, a unique opportunity for the educated to play a foundational role in contributing to the national development process. In principle, it was, indeed, a noble as well as novel idea which had the potential to elevate the quality of rural **education**, a cornerstone of national development. Some protested it as undemocratic and others participated in it willingly. Many of those who participated in it actually turned it into a viable and effective avenue to carefully spread their anti-**Panchayat** gospel. Seeing how the campaign had turned into a political weapon by anti-Panchayat forces and sensing its profound threat, it was discontinued in 1979. It is completely defunct now.

BAGH BHAIRAV. One of 64 forms of the god **Bhairav**. It is also known as Bag Bisa. Represented by a tiger (*bagh*) mask, this Bhairav has a three-tiered **pagoda** temple in the city of **Kirtipur**. Built by King Sadasiva (reign: 1574–1578) of the Kingdom of **Kathmandu**, the spacious courtyard of this temple contains several images. It has a rectangular canopy and gilded spires.

BAGHCHAL. Unique Nepali chess game. Once a very popular game, not too many people play it nowadays. It is played by two players on a square board with crisscrossed lines, with one side representing four tigers and another twenty goats. The contest is between tigers trying to kill the goats and goats trying to trap all of the tigers. Despite its declining popularity, largely due to new sources of entertainment, recreation, and socialization, national *baghchal* championship contests are held to keep the tradition alive.

BAGHJATRA. Fair observed in **Pokhara** around the festival of Krishna Ashtami. Its celebration involves men dressed as kings riding on horses and chasing a pair of men dressed as tigers, which they pretend to kill. This tradition has seen a dramatic decline; it is rarely celebrated nowadays.

BAGLUNG. District in the **Dhaulagiri Zone**. It also refers to the western hill town of Baglung, the district headquarters. It includes a wildlife reserve (Dhorpatan) and a domestic airstrip at a nearby place called Balewa. Its total area of 1,784 sq. km. is inhabited by almost 233,000 people (1991). The town of Baglung is a popular urban center where the **Newars** have historically dominated the commercial sector. The district as a whole is quite well-known for the production of high quality hashish or *charesh* (extracts of marijuana or **ganja** plant resin) as it is called in Nepali and for an indigenous variety of beans. Dark brown in color and slightly bigger than black-eyed peas in size, this local variety called *thulo* (big) *bhatta* (bean) is very popular throughout Nepal.

BAGMATI RIVER. Considered to be a sacred river originating at Bagh Dwar, Shivapuri **Mountain**, it flows right by the temple of **Pashupati** and through **Kathmandu**. It joins the Bishnumati River at Teku. The adherents of **Hinduism** believe that taking ritualistic baths and being cremated at the Bagmati are important acts of religious devotion. As a result, the river has many bathing and cremation ghats (stalls) such as **Aryaghat** and **Gaurighat**. The **Bagmati Zone** is named after the river. Roughly 163 kilometers in length, it eventually joins the Ganges in India.

BAGMATI ZONE. One of the 14 zones (*anchals*); administrative unit of Nepal (*see* figure 3). Flanked by the **Kathmandu Valley** with a huge population concentration, it is the most populous zone in the country. It covers a total area of 9,428 sq. km. and contains eight districts: **Bhaktapur**, Dhading, Kabhre, **Kathmandu**, **Lalitpur**, Nuwakot, Rasuwa, and Sindhupalchok (*see* figure 2).

BAHRA (BARHA). (*Bahra* = 12.) It is a **Newar** custom of hiding a young woman for 12 days in a secluded place, immediately following the first menstruation or, in some cases, prior to its occurrence. In essence, the *bahra* ceremony is symbolic of the emergence of womanhood: the girl becomes a woman. As such, it is the female version of ***bartaman***, a traditional ceremony which applies to boys. Sometimes *bahra* is performed as a communal affair in which case several girls/women are isolated in one place. During this period, *bahra* girls/women are prohibited from seeing males. That is why they are isolated. It is also invariably called *gupha*, which literally means "cave." *Gupha* is practiced among non-Newar population groups as well. Since menstruation is regarded as a form of female pollution, menstruating women are not allowed to touch men, water, and cooked food except their own portion. Under the glare of modernization, the practice of this old tradition has been slowly declining, mainly in urban areas.

BAHUN/BAHUNI. Nepali variation of the term Brahman (highest **Hindu caste**). Males are characteristically called Bahun, whereas Bahuni is used for females. When applied in a certain context and with a certain tone, the term can convey a derogatory connotation.

BAHUNBAD. Brahmanism, which is used as a pejorative term to suggest **Brahman** nepotism. It is like an unwritten code system or policy designed by the **Bahuns** for the Bahuns. It tends to perpetuate the dominant position of Brahmans in the institutional and political establishments of Nepal.

BAHU, SINHA SARTHA. Legendary traveler from **Kathmandu** who went to **Tibet**. Legend has it that he was visited by Karunamaya, a goddess, who told him to return home with his men but to leave their mistresses behind. His men disobeyed the goddess and were subsequently eaten by their mistresses. Unlike his men, Sinha Sartha Bahu returned, but his mistress followed him to Nepal where she asked the king to help her. When the king took her into his palace, she devoured him—and Sinha later became king.

BAIDHANIK KANUN. First planned **constitution** drafted in 1947 by Prime Minister **Padma Shamsher Rana**, but it was never passed and implemented. It had provisions for civil rights, court of justice, bicameral legislature, village, town and district **Panchayat**, public service commission, auditor general, and adult franchise.

BAISE. (*Bais* = 22.) Used in the context of the 22 principalities—*Baise Rajya*—that ruled the Karnali basin in the west prior to national unification that began after **Prithvi Narayan Shah**'s conquest of the three **Malla** kingdoms of the **Kathmandu Valley** in 1769.

BAISE RAJYA. Collective term applied to describe the 22 principalities in the Karnali basin in the west that operated like local fiefdoms. They were all annexed to Nepal between 1786 and 1809, some through negotiations and others as a result of their military defeat at the hands of Nepal's unification campaign forces. Because of the paucity of specific historical records regarding their territorial boundaries, rules, and names, there are no fixed or permanent lists of those ministates. The following names have often been mentioned at different times and by different Nepali historians in the annals of Nepal: Achham, Bajhang, Chilli, Dailekh, **Dang**, **Doti**, Garbhakot, Gautam, Jahari, Jajarkot, Jumla, Kalagaon, Malneta, Musikot, Phalebang, Rolpa, Rukumkot (now Rukum), and Thalahara. Also mentioned are: Bampi, Bilaspur, Biskot, Chhana, Darmaka, Darna, Dullu, Durayal, Gajur, Galkot, Goriakot,

Majal, Malebam, and others. There is, however, some consensus among historians that the principalities of Doti, Jumla, and Bajhang, which today are separate administrative districts, were quite influential and relatively powerful. See also CHAUBISE RAJYA.

BAJA SANGRAHALAYA. (*Baja* = musical instrument; musical sound; *sangrahalaya* = museum; collection.) National museum of musical instruments in **Kathmandu**. It was founded in 1977 by the **Royal Nepal Academy**.

BAJRACHARYA (VAJRACHARYA). Priestly **caste** group among the **Buddhist Newar** population that has its own caste hierarchy, separate from the **Hindu** caste system. They are also known as Gubhaju. **Kathmandu, Patan, Pokhara**, and Tansen represent some of their major concentration centers.

BALI. Fixed share of crops given to a professional (low) **caste** service provider on an annual basis, chiefly to **Damai** (tailor caste), **Kami** (blacksmith caste), or **Sarki** (leather worker caste that also serves as land plowers) households in return for their service. Crop shares are given in lieu of wages or monetary costs of their service. When used in a routine sense, the term also means "harvests" or "crops." See also ADHIYA; AGRICULTURE; LAND TENURE.

BALAJU. Scenic water garden situated northwest of **Kathmandu**. It is famous for *Baisdhara*, i.e., 22 (*bais*) crocodile-mouthed waterspouts (*dhara*), of which 21 were built by King **Jayaprakash Malla** (reign: 1734–1768) before Kathmandu was conquered by **Prithvi Narayan Shah**, whose grandson **Rana Bahadur Shah** added the twenty-second spout. All these spouts are tapped into an unknown underground (natural) water system. It has historically been regarded as one of the most scenic sites in the Valley. It includes the statue of Bala Narayana, a replica of **Budha Nilkantha** that was established by King **Pratap Malla**. It is popular as a picnic site, especially among Kathmandu's romantic young lovers and couples.

BALAJU INDUSTRIAL DISTRICT. Founded in 1960 with American aid and located near **Balaju**, it is the first industrial center of the country.

It produces biscuits, cattle food, plastic utensils, clothes, polythene, and dairy products. *See also* INDUSTRY.

BALAJU TEXTILE INDUSTRY. One of the manufacturing enterprises within the **Balaju Industrial District** engaged in the production of cotton cloths. Much of what it produces is consumed locally. Some of the cloths are used to make items that are exported overseas. *See also* INDUSTRY.

BALLABH, ISHWAR (1937–). Modern poet, essayist, and critic. He is also a founding member of the Nepali literary movement, Tesro Ayam (third dimension), and has received many awards for literary contributions. His poems are often characterized by intellectuality, depth, and spontaneity. He is a very well-known name within the literary circle of Nepal.

BANDAKI. Form of mortgage or collateral. Historically, the term has been used in the context of land collateral or agrarian indebtedness, which is one of the most debilitating problems of the rural **economy**. Peasants often mortgage their lands to moneylenders in lieu of interest payments, thus losing their rights to cultivate them.

BANDHUDATTA. Buddhist priest in "The Story of Karunamaya" who was sent to find Karunamaya to aid Nepal. *See also* BAHU, SINHA SARTHA.

BANEPA. Urban center or municipality in Kabhre district founded by King Ananda Deva (reign: 1147–1167). It emerged as a separate kingdom after Yaksha Malla (reign: 1428–1482), the last **Malla** king of the united **Kathmandu Valley**, allocated it to his son Rana Malla. According to the 1991 census, it had a population of 12,622.

BANGDEL, LAIN SINGH (1925–2002). Nepali artist and novelist born in **Darjeeling, India**. His literary works include a 1947 novel entitled *Muluk Bahira* (outside the country or in a foreign land) and *Rembrandt* (1965). He is, however, mostly recognized as a leading artist of Nepal.

BANKING. It is fair to assert that the notion of banking as a formal and organized financial institution was quite foreign to most Nepalis until the

1960s, although the first commercial bank of Nepal—**Nepal Bank Limited**—was founded as early as the 1930s. The number of people and formal businesses depositing money in the bank constituted a tiny minority. It was not until about three decades ago that banking as a medium of financial and commercial transactions began to gain some traction. To this day, using checks for routine purchases remains alien and unacceptable, mainly because many businesses, which are quite small in scale, are not equipped or prepared to handle them, even though most businesses catering to foreign tourists readily accept most major credit cards. Despite this fundamental resistance, banking in Nepal has significantly changed and improved in recent years. Currently, the banking system consists of the **Nepal Rastra Bank** (the central bank), about 15 commercial banks, and 2 development financing banks.

The Nepal Rastra Bank is solely responsible for regulating and supervising the country's banking institutions. It issues currency as well as determines the daily buying and selling rates of most foreign currencies. In short, it is solely in charge of implementing the national monetary policy in order to maintain the financial stability and health of the **economy**. On the other hand, commercial and development banks are responsible for providing industrial, agricultural, and commercial loans to individuals as well as businesses. They offer both industrial term (long-term) credits and short-term working capital loans. The Nepal Bank, **Rastriya Banijya Bank** (commercial bank of Nepal), and Agricultural Development Bank are quite active in the credit lending area and mostly operate through their branches, which are scattered in different parts of the country.

There are about a dozen foreign joint venture banks, e.g., the Bank of Kathmandu, Everest Bank, Himalayan Bank, Nepal Arab Bank, Nepal Bangladesh Bank, Nepal Bank of Ceylon, Nepal Grindlays Bank, Nepal Indo-Suez Bank, and Nepal SBI Bank. Additionally, the American Express, Citibank, Standard Chartered Bank, and Union Europeean de CIC have representatives in **Kathmandu**. In recent years, there has been a noticeable increase in both the number and size of banks, financial institutions, and insurance companies, all due to the government's push for **privatization** or market liberalization. As a result of this increasing competition within the banking sector, the cumbersome system of foreign currency exchange and transfer has greatly improved.

BANSBARI LEATHER AND SHOE FACTORY. Founded in 1965 in **Kathmandu** with Chinese assistance. Initially established as a public enterprise, it was **privatized** in 1992. The market for its products are mostly confined to Nepal; they have difficulty competing in foreign markets because of their relatively poor quality. When it was founded and began to market its products, the factory had an adverse effect on the **Sarkis** of the **Kathmandu Valley** and surrounding areas. In terms of their **caste** roles, one of the primary professions of the Sarkis is to makes shoes to meet the local demand. As an increasing number of consumers began to develop a preference for factory-made shoes, the Sarkis found themselves out of work. This situation forced many to migrate to urban areas where they became sidewalk shoe-polish and shoe-repair vendors. Some of them were employed in the factory as shoemakers.

BANSKOTA, SHAMBHUJIT (1956–). A popular musician, comedian, and singer, he is associated with **Radio Nepal**. He has performed as a playback musician and **music** director for several Nepali movies produced in the 1990s.

BARAL, ISHWAR (1923–). Nepali essayist, critic, and professor. He has edited several books and two literary magazines: *Indreni* (rainbow) and *Dharti* (earth). He also served as a professor of Nepali Studies at **India**'s Jawaharlal Nehru University from 1978 to 1988.

BARAL, LOK RAJ (1941–). A professor of political science and opinion leader, he has authored *Oppositional Politics in Nepal* (1977) and *The Politics of Balanced Independence: Nepal and SAARC* (1988). He was president of the University Teachers' Association (1969–1970) and Political Science Association of Nepal (1963–1964 and 1992).

BARGIYA SANGATHAN. Class (*bargiya*) organizations (*sangathan*). Following the introduction of the **Panchayat** system, the government formed several *bargiya sangathans* to represent various social groups loosely defined as classes, e.g., youth, peasants, workers, **women**, and ex-soldiers. The concept of class in this context is primarily based on functional categories rather than defined in a Marxist sense, i.e., in terms of class or production relations.

BARI. Usually used as a generic term to mean "unirrigated land." When the word is used in the context of crops being grown, it simply means "cultivated land" or "a garden plot."

BARKHI. Period of mourning which usually lasts one year and during which time the mourner must be dressed in white (symbolic of the color of death). Those observing *barkhi* do not wear anything red which, in Nepal, is the color of joyous celebration. Furthermore, it is generally observed by sons and wives upon the death of their parents and husbands, respectively. It is believed that *barkhi* observance paves the way for the dead to enter heaven.

BARTA. Ritualistic fasting that is quite common among the **Hindus**. It is widely practiced and observed on religious and ceremonial occasions several times a year. It is plausible to argue that it was first introduced as a religious tradition or act in order to minimize the annual intake of food without causing nutritional harm to the body. After all, most of South Asia, including Nepal where Hinduism was dominant prior to Muslim invasions, suffered—and still suffers—from chronic food shortage. *Barta* could also have been instituted as a system of periodic bodily cleansing for health purposes.

BARTAMAN (BRATAMAN). Rite of passage for boys; variation of *Bratabandha*, which technically means "tying the loincloth." In many respects, it is the male (boy) version of **bahra**. What *bartaman* essentially signifies is the emergence of the boy into manhood. No longer free to run around naked as an innocent child, he is now supposed (required) to cover his sexual organ (hence the use of loincloth), a phallic symbol of the reproductive ability of manhood. As he is technically burdened with the responsibility of life or manhood, he becomes a full member of his **caste** with all the ritual obligations that a man is supposed to perform. Similar to *bahra*, the tradition of *bartaman* is mainly confined to the high-caste **Hindu** and **Newar** groups. *See also* SANYAS.

BARUN-MAKALU NATIONAL PARK. National park covering 1,500 sq. km. excluding the conservation area of 830 sq. km. Gazetted in 1992, it is located in the Barun Valley around Mount Makalu and its areal coverage is primarily confined to the Sankhuwasabha district. It is rich in orchids, medicinal plants, oaks, bamboos, and many other plants. Its fauna include over 400 species of birds, endangered red panda, musk deer, clouded leopard, ghoral, wild boar, and barking deer.

BASANTAPUR DURBAR. Nine-storied palace which is the centerpiece of the **Kathmandu Durbar Square**. It was built by **Prithvi Narayan Shah**, following his conquest of the Kingdom of **Kathmandu**. It is situated at the core of Kathmandu.

BASNET, KHAGENDRA BAHADUR (1930–). Founding president of the Nepal Association for the Blind and Disabled (1972). He also founded in 1977 the Khagendra Navajeevan Kendra for the rehabilitation of disabled people.

BASNET, KUMAR (1943–). He is a well-recognized Nepali singer who is responsible for the popularity of **Bhote** *selo*, a particular genre of folk **music** in Nepal. It is mainly the folk music of the **Bhote, Tamang**, and **Sherpa** tribes, but also practiced by some other **Tibeto-Nepali** groups. He is credited with developing the Tunga, a musical instrument that is used with Bhote *selo* whose origin may be traced to **Tibet**. To many, Kumar Basnet is a household name.

BASUKI NAG. Cosmic serpent guarding treasures of **Shiva**, worshiped especially during the Nag Panchami festival. Its temple, called *Basuki Mandir*, is found inside the **Pashupati** complex. *See also* NAG.

BATSALA TEMPLE. Stone temple with a bronze bell called the "bell of the barking dogs." The sound of this is said to be a duplication of the sound of death. It was hung by King Bhupatindra Malla (reign: 1696–1722) in the **Bhaktapur Durbar Square**.

BAUDHANATH (BOUDHANATH). It is a **Buddhist stupa** in Baudha (Boudha) east of **Kathmandu**. Held in great veneration by **Buddhists** as well as **Hindus**, it is perhaps the largest spherical stupa constructed in honor of Lord **Buddha**. Legend has it that a Hindu king in ancient time built a pond with stone waterspouts. Since no water came out of the waterspouts, the king became concerned and began meditating. Following the meditation, it dawned upon the king that water would not flow out of the spouts unless a person endowed with all 32 virtues was sacrificed to the waterspouts. There was none save himself endowed with 32 virtues. Determined as he was to make the water flow out of the waterspouts, he asked his son to go to the pond at midnight and chop off the head of a person lying there wrapped in white cloth. The prince did as his father ordered him. And the water began to flow out of the spouts. As the prince discovered what he had done, he stood aghast at the sight. With his soul smitten, the prince went to the shrine of Goddess Bajrajogini at Shankhu east of **Kathmandu**, where he lived an austere life praying to her for several years. Pleased with his prayer, the goddess asked the prince to build a temple of the Buddha to atone for his sin. The stupa that the prince built is what is called Baudhanath. It is now surrounded by compact houses where many Lamas and **Tibetan** refugees reside.

BEL. Wood apple (*Aegele marmelos*), which holds religious significance for **Hindus**. It is believed to represent a form of Lord **Vishnu**. Bel plant leaves are widely used during Hindu worships and ceremonies. During the **Inhi** ritual, which is practiced in the **Newar** communities, young and unmarried girls are first symbolically married to bel fruits. In the past when manufactured glue was rare in Nepal, the inside content of this fruit was widely used as glue to seal papers and envelopes. As a result, virtually every government office used to have split bel fruits. As they are edible, some people eat them when they are fully ripe.

BHABAR. Narrow strip of land between the **Churia** Hills and the **Tarai**. Its forests include some commercially valuable trees, e.g., sal, sisso, simal, and khayar, and serve as a habitat for deer, tigers, elephants, and rhinoceroses. *See also* CHAR KOSE JHADI.

BHADGAUN. Old name of **Bhaktapur**; Kingdom of Bhadgaun during the second phase of the **Malla period**. *See* BHAKTAPUR.

BHAILO. The custom of collection of charitable donations amidst singing of typical melodies by groups of men, women, or children who go from household to household in the community. Practiced only during the **Tihar** festival, it has some entertainment value.

BHAIRAHAWA. *See* SIDDHARTHA NAGAR.

BHAIRAV. Famous **Tantric** deity. It is a fierce personification of Lord **Shiva**, and comes in many different forms, e.g., **Akash Bhairav, Kal Bhairav, Unmatta Bhairav, Bagh Bhairav,** and Mahankala Bhairav that represents mass deaths or cataclysmic events. They are invariably depicted in statues, carvings, or paintings with a fierce look wearing a garland of slain human heads—presumably those of evil-doers. Bhairav is worshiped, feared, and propitiated, mainly in the **Kathmandu Valley**.

BHAKTAPUR. Previously called **Bhadgaun**, it is the smallest and most densely populated district in the **Bagmati Zone**. According to the *Gopalraj Vamsavali* (Chronicles), it was founded by Anandadeva (reign: 1147–1167). King **Amsuvarman**'s inscription indicates that its name was Khopring during the **Licchavi period**. The same name is used for its district capital and medieval city, whose urban population totaled slightly over 61,000 in 1991. With its rich architectural history, the city of Bhaktapur is a major tourist center in the **Kathmandu Valley**; it is well known for its arts and crafts, vegetable production, and yogurt. The Bhaktapur yogurt, popularly known as *juju dhau* in **Newari** is highly acclaimed and prized throughout the Valley for its delicious taste as well as texture. Spread over an area of 119 sq. km., the district of Bhaktapur had nearly 173,000 people in 1991.

BHAKTAPUR DURBAR SQUARE. Famous complex comprising a palace (*durbar*), temples, and courtyards in **Bhaktapur**. The palace is known as the Pachpanna Jhyale Durbar, which means it has 55 (*pachpanna*) windows (*jhyal*). The complex includes four religious pilgrimage sites called Tirtha (Jagannath, Rameswora, Kedarnath, and Badarinath), along with a bronze bell and a golden fountain. The Golden Gate built in 1753 by **Ranajit Malla** (reign: 1722 to 1769), **Bhadgaun**'s last king, is an important attraction of the square, which is included in the World Heritage List (1979).

BHAKTAPUR INDUSTRIAL DISTRICT. Industrial manufacturing center in **Bhaktapur**. Founded in 1978, the center includes mostly small industries. Handicraft and pottery production is a principal feature.

BHAKTAPUR MUSEUM. Museum of woodcrafts charged with the conservation and preservation of the fine woodworks of days past. Based in a former palace, there are many fine examples of woodcrafts and other artifacts that made **Bhaktapur** famous. Due to the lack of adequate funding for its day-to-day operation and maintenance, the museum is in poor condition.

BHANDARI, DHUNDI RAJ (1930–). Professor and historian. He has written history books and actively participated in the 1950–1951 anti-**Rana** revolution. He is one of the leading scholars of Nepal.

BHANDARI, GANESH (1914–). A traditional musician who specializes in the sitar (a tradition Indian string musical instrument). He once taught **music** at Padma Kanya Campus (women's college). He is a very well-known sitarist of Nepal.

BHANDARI, MADAN KUMAR (1952–1993). Leftist politician and revolutionary born in the Taplejung district. As a political activist, he remained underground until 1989. From 1989 until his accidental death in 1993, he served as secretary general of the Unified Marxist-Leninist faction of the **Communist Party of Nepal**. During the 1991 **election** for the **House of Representatives**—the first such election following the second coming of democracy in 1990—he ran against incumbent Prime Minister **Krishna Prasad Bhattarai** of the **Nepali Congress Party** and defeated him. Widely viewed as a highly charismatic leader who helped shape the Unified Marxist-Leninist's new policy toward democratization, Bhandari died in a road accident in 1993. It is commonly believed that the accident that took his life was premeditated.

BHANDARKHAL PARBA. Historical massacre at Bhandarkhal located in **Kathmandu**. Reacting to **Jang Bahadur Rana**'s murderous act during the **Kot Parba**, King Rajendra Bikram Shah's junior queen, Rajya Laxmi Devi Shah, quickly hatched a plot to kill Jang Bahadur Rana. She organized a feast on 31 October 1846 at the Bhandarkhal garden and invited Jang Bahadur. Having been tipped off about the queen's plan, Jang Bahadur came prepared with his men. The event culminated in a massacre of Jang's enemies, except for the queen. As a consequence, the junior queen left Nepal in November for Banaras, **India**, with her sons and King Rajendra. Subsequently, Jang's power base was further consolidated.

BHARATI, NARA BAHADUR (1937–1966). Scientist who is known for his invention of artificial rubber from mustard oil in 1960. He was given the first Tribhuvan Puraskar (award) in 1959 for contributions in the field of science and technology.

BHARDARI SABHA. Assembly of *bhardars* (courtiers) during the **Malla period** and early **Shah dynast** rule. Directly nominated by the king, its members acted as advisors to the king on state affairs as well as civil administrators. It was essentially equivalent to a ministerial council. The two most powerful and invariably antagonistic *bhardari* clans during the pre-**Rana** Shah period were the Thapa and Pandey. *See also* THAPA, BHIMSEN.

BHATTA, ANANDA DEV (1936–). A literary critic and writer who has authored several literary works and who teaches English at **Tribhuvan University.** He is also a political activist who was responsible for coordinating the communist unity promotion forum in 1990.

BHATTA, DIBYA DEO (1930–). Highly regarded professor of botany at **Tribhuvan University** and author of a book entitled *Natural History and Economic Botany of Nepal* (1970). In his diplomatic role, he served as Nepal's ambassador to Myanmar from 1985 to 1989.

BHATTA, MOTIRAM (1866–1896). Writer and poet who spent about 25 years of his short life in Banaras, **India.** He is regarded as a great writer in the history of Nepali **literature.** Inspired by Indian writers and literary activists, he organized literary groups of contemporaries to engage in Nepali literary debate and publishing projects. It was Motiram who first recognized the significance of **Bhanu Bhakta Acharya**'s unpublished *Ramayana* as a groundbreaking work in the field of nascent Nepali literature. Due to his efforts, it was first published in 1887, some 40 years after its composition. After his return to **Kathmandu**, he set up a publishing business, seeing publication as a fundamental necessity to prepare the groundwork for the growth and development of Nepali literature. It is no wonder why Motiram Bhatta is regarded as one of the founding fathers of Nepali literature.

BHATTARAI, BABURAM (1954–). A leftist politician and activist who is one of the prominent leaders of the Maoist movement known as the **People's War.** He began his political career as founding president of the All India Nepali Students' Association (1977–1980). Prior to his active involvement in the Maoist movement, he edited a left-oriented monthly magazine called *Jhilko* (Sparks). Irrespective of his political views, he is commonly regarded as a bright scholar of Nepal. In May 2002, the Nepal government announced a bounty award of $64,000 to catch him dead or alive. In February 2003, he was designated by the Maoists to lead a five-member negotiation team in peace talks with the government team to end the ongoing People's War. Bhattarai remained underground for almost eight years, finally emerging out of hiding in late March 2003.

BHATTARAI, KRISHNA PRASAD (1924–). Politician and activist. A founding member of the **Nepali Congress Party**, Bhattarai was active in the anti-**Rana** revolution that culminated in the overthrow of Rana autocracy in early 1951. Along with another Congress leader, **Ganeshman Singh**, Bhattarai played a paramount role in the 1990 pro-democracy movement, which led to the dismantling of the **Panchayat** system and reduction of the king's status to constitutional monarch. Upon the dismissal of the Panchayat system, he was appointed prime minister of the interim government (1990–1991), which was responsible for drafting a new **constitution** and for holding a parliamentary **election** in 1991 to establish a democratic government. Although his Congress party won the majority of the seats in the **House of Representatives**, he failed to win his own seat. However, he won his contested seat during the 1999 parliamentary election. As a result, he was able to form a Congress government under his prime ministership. About a year later, on 18 March 2000, Bhattarai was ousted from the office of prime minister by his own party and former Prime Minister **Girija Prasad Koirala**.

BHATTARAI, TULSI PRASAD (1949–). Professor and literary critic. He has served as general manager of Sajha Prakashan, a book publishing enterprise in **Kathmandu**. He was instrumental in elevating the status of Sajha Prakashan as a leading publisher in Nepal.

BHATTI. Temporary roadside inns that serve food and drinks and provide shelter for travelers. They are usually operated by female members of **Thakali** tribe households that move to lower hills and valleys during winter months from their permanent settlements in the **Trans-Himalayan** zone close to the border with **Tibet**. While **women** set up *bhattis* as part of their winter commercial activities, adult males engage in long-distance trade during these months. A unique feature of Nepal's cultural landscape, this charming tradition of temporary Thakali *bhatti* settlement is being increasingly replaced by more permanent inns that mostly cater to low-budget foreign trekkers and tourists.

BHERI ZONE. One of the 14 administrative zones which is situated in the western hills of Nepal (*see* figure 3). It consists of five districts: Banke, Bardiya, Dailekh, Jajarkot, and Surkhet. It is named after the Bheri River which is a tributary of the **Karnali River**. Bheri covers 10,945 sq. km. of area and is inhabited by 1,101,653 people (1991).

BHIKSU, AMRITRANANDA MAHASTHABIR (1918–1988). Monk and activist. In addition to founding a **Buddhist** organization named Dharmodya Sabha in 1944, he established **Kathmandu**'s Anandakuti School in 1952, which now is a leading school in the city.

BHIKSHU, BHAVANI (1914–1981). As a novelist and story writer, he contributed significantly to Nepali **literature**. In 1951, he edited *Sharada*, a prominent literary magazine. A leading literary figure in Nepal, Bhavani Bhikshu received several awards for his contributions to Nepali literature.

BHIMSEN STAMBHA. *See* DHARAHARA.

BHOJPUR. District in the **Kosi Zone**. The town of Bhojpur, which is also the district capital, is famous for producing handcrafted ***Khukri*** (a slightly curved Nepali knife that is usually associated with **Gorkha** soldiers). In 1991, it had more than 198,000 people, distributed over an area of 1,507 sq. km. (*see* figure 2).

BHOTE (BHOTIA). Generic term for the inhabitants of the highland or **Trans-Himalayan** region that straddles along the border with **Tibet** (the autonomous region of the People's Republic of China). It is this general region that used to be referred to as Bhot. The term "Bhote" is derived from Bhot, meaning "the people of Bhot." At times, the term is uttered in a derogatory manner to imply uncivilized or dirty.

BHOTE *SELO*. Popular folk song and **music** of Nepal's highland people, namely the **Bhote, Tamang**, and **Sherpa** tribes. It is accompanied by dancing that resembles a typical **Tibetan** style.

BHOTO JATRA. Popular festival of the **Kathmandu Valley** during which the diamond-studded vest (*bhoto*) of Rato Machhendranath is displayed from the chariot of the deity. Held in a large group setting with a procession, it is a very popular festival in the ancient city of **Patan.**

BHRIKUTI. According to a popular Tibetan legend, there was a Nepali king called Go Cha who had a daughter by the name of Bhrikuti. She was married to Song-tsen Gampo, the famous seventh-century king of **Tibet.** Although some historians have found no historical basis for this legend, it remains deeply etched in the annals of Nepal. Whether she was a historical figure or simply a heroine of a beautiful legend, to most Nepalis, it matters little. Her place in the popular historical accounts of Nepal is secure. Bhrikuti and her husband's Chinese wife are given credit for introducing and spreading **Buddhism** in Tibet. It is also believed that many Buddhist scholars, painters, and teachers from Nepal followed her to Tibet. In addition to the construction of monasteries in Tibet, Buddhist scriptures were translated into Tibetan. Her marriage led to increased commercial and cultural interactions between the two countries. Hers is indeed a legendary name in Nepal as many things are named after her, including the **Bhrikuti Paper Mills.**

BHRIKUTI PAPER MILLS. Built with Chinese assistance, it is Nepal's biggest paper factory located in the central **Tarai** district of Nawalparasi (*see* figure 2). Founded in 1979 as a public enterprise, it was privatized in 1992. It has the capacity to produce 15,000 metric tons of paper per year.

BHUMI SUDHAR. See LAND REFORM.

BHUSAL, BASUNDHARA (1951–). She is a movie actress and dancer whose film career started with a role in *Aama*, one of the earliest Nepali cinemas, produced in 1965. Since then she has appeared in several movies.

BHUT. Malevolent spirit. It is a very popular concept and belief system throughout Nepal. According to the shamanistic belief system, a *bhut* can be a creation of witchcraft or can have its origin in a dead person whose soul (*atma*) was not released from the earth. It is believed that the soul of a person who dies a violent death or who was tortured when alive turns into a wandering soul ready to torment the living relatives until it is fully satisfied through ritual offerings. The term is gender neutral as it can be either a male or female. See also BOKSI.

BIGHA. Land measurement unit in the **Tarai**. One *bigha* is roughly equal to 1.6 acres or 0.68 hectare.

BIJAYA (VIJAYA) DASHAMI. *See* DASHAIN.

BIJUKCHHE, NARAYAN MAN (1939–). A leftist politician who was jailed during the **Panchayat** regime. He played an active role in the pro-democracy movement of 1990. In the 1991 general **election**, he was elected to the **House of Representatives** from **Bhaktapur**.

BIKAL, RAMESH (1932–). Novelist, essayist, and short story writer. Associated with **Tribhuvan University** as a professor of Nepali, he has penned several literary publications, including collections of short stories and novels. Two of his novels are: *Sunauli* and *Indrawati*. He has also authored children's books. He was awarded Madan Puraskar in 1961 for his literary contributions.

BIKAS. Very popular term in Nepal, which literally means "development."

BIKRAM SAMBAT (B.S.). Lunar calendar era used in Nepal. It is about 56 years ahead of the Christian era, e.g., 2000 A.D. is roughly equal to 2056 B.S.

BIRATNAGAR. Located close to the **Indian** border, it is the largest city in **Morang** and the second largest in the country (*see* figure 4). It is also Nepal's second-largest industrial city that features jute, match, stainless steel, textile, and many other factories. It is no exaggeration that Biratnagar has been at the forefront of industrialization in Nepal since the late 1930s when the process got underway, largely in response to the demands created by World War II. Some of those demands included products made out of jute, which grows well in this part of Nepal. Because of its raw material potential and proximity to the Indian market, it was able to attract Indian capital for establishing industrial enterprises. In other words, Indian capital investment has historically been a main driver of

Biratnagar's industrial growth and expansion. In 1991, the city had a total of 130,129 people. *See also* INDUSTRY.

BIRATNAGAR JUTE MILLS. Founded in 1936, it is the oldest jute factory and certainly one of the earliest large-scale manufacturing enterprises in Nepal. It manufactures a variety of jute products. *See also* INDUSTRY.

BIRENDRA, KING. *See* SHAH, BIRENDRA BIR BIKRAM.

BIRGANJ. Commercial and industrial center located close to the Indian border (*see* figures 2 and 4). Connected to **Kathmandu** via the **Tribhuvan Rajpath**, it is often regarded as a gateway city. Its industrial manufactures include matches, sugar, **agricultural** tools, and utensils. Birganj's commercial enterprises are heavily dominated by Indian merchants. Its 1991 population totaled 68,769.

BIRGANJ SUGAR FACTORY. Public enterprise established in 1964 with the aid of the former Soviet Union. The factory produces both sugar and liquors.

BIR HOSPITAL. Biggest and oldest hospital in Nepal located in the central part of **Kathmandu**. It was named after **Rana** Prime Minister Bir Shamsher because of his role in establishing this government hospital. Despite the fact that it is the national hospital of Nepal, its facilities are subpar and it is understaffed. It has, however, improved over the years. Because of its public (government) support, it is said to be relatively less expensive than other major hospitals in the **Kathmandu Valley**. It is always crowded.

BIRTA. Tax-free land grants made by kings and rulers as a reward or emolument to political supporters, military officers, and family members. Although it has a long history in the Nepali **land tenure** system, it was most abused during the **Rana** period. Despite its abolishment in 1959, it has left a profound blemish in the country's agrarian system.

BISKAT JATRA. Famous **Newari** festival observed on the Nepali New Year's day: 1 Baisakh. It is particularly observed in **Bhaktapur**. In the past, it used to be celebrated in **Pokhara** as well, but the tradition has basically disappeared. The festival was first introduced by King Jagatjyotir Malla of **Bhadgaun** (1614–1637).

BISTA, DAULAT BIKRAM (1926–). Author of several Nepali novels, he has received a number of literary awards for his contributions, including Sajha Puraskar in 1991 for the novel entitled *Anshu Tesai Chachalkinchha* (Tears Just Bubble). As a member of the **Tribhuvan University** faculty, Bista was elected president of the Sociological and Anthropological Association of Nepal in 1988 (1988–1991).

BISTA, DOR BAHADUR (1928–). A well-known anthropologist who has written several books. His 1967 book, *People of Nepal*, is highly acclaimed as a significant treatise on various **caste** and ethnic peoples of Nepal. It is fair to assert that Dor Bahadur Bista is by far the most recognized Nepali anthropologist overseas. He has visited America several times and given lectures on university campuses.

BISTA, KIRTI NIDHI (1927–). Former prime minister. Appointed by the king during the **Panchayat**, he served as prime minister at several different times between 1968 and 1978. Once a powerful figure in the Nepali political circle, he has become almost invisible in the post-**Panchayat** era, since 1990.

BISWAKARMA, BHUWAN SINGH. Adventurer. He is remembered as the first Nepali to reach Antarctica.

BIYOGI, GOVINDA (1933–). Noted journalist, publisher, and editor of a leftist weekly newspaper *Matribhumi*. He served as president of the Nepal Journalist Association during 1990–1992. In his capacity as editor of *Matribhumi*, he has served as a valuable outlet for leftist views and positions as well as a dissenting voice.

BODHISATTWA. One who is enlightened. It is a **Buddhist** term generally reserved to describe those who have attained **nirvana**—escape from earthly entrapments and, hence, from the cycle of births and rebirths.

BOHORA, AMRIT KUMAR (1949–). Leftist politician and member of the Unified Marxist-Leninist (UML) faction of the **Communist Party of Nepal.** Elected to the **House of Representatives** during the first parliamentary election in 1991, he was reelected in 1994, but not in 1999.

BOKSI. Witch. The concept of *boksi*, which is closely tied to witchcraft in Nepal's shamanistic tradition, is common throughout the country. Unlike **bhut**, which is gender neutral, *boksi* is always used to refer to females. The term is sometimes used in a derogatory manner against women. For instance, when a woman is called a *boksi*, it is demeaning and engenders a sense of rage or even hatred. *See also* BHUT.

BRAHMA. Hindu god of creation. One of the members of what can be called the Hindu trinity: Brahma, **Vishnu**, and **Shiva**. He is depicted as having four heads, facing all four directions (east, west, north, and south). This is symbolic of his role as the creator of the universe. Although central to the foundation of **Hinduism**, he is obscure; of the three he is the least visible one in the popular imagination of Hindu devotees, both philosophically and in terms of daily practice. Unlike his counterparts, he has no known cult following or groups.

BRAHMAN (BRAHMIN). Regarded as the highest **caste** in the Hindu caste system; traditionally associated with priesthood and learning. In Nepal, they are generically and commonly referred to as **Bahun**.

BRATABANDHA. *See* BARTAMAN.

BRITAIN-NEPAL RELATIONS. Nepal's relations with Great Britain span more than two centuries, dating back to its expansion in **India**. In terms of longevity of Nepal's foreign relations, India and **China** are the only two countries that surpass Britain. In many respects, however, unlike the Indian and Chinese relations with many dimensions, the British relations with Nepal were narrowly focused. In other words, the British colonial interest in Nepal can basically be traced to one single element that the country could offer: human resource, namely, its pool of soldiers to serve in their imperial army. As Sir Arthur Hirtzel, Undersecretary of State for India, openly admitted, "It is, after all, mainly because of the Gurkha (**Gorkha**) element in the Army that we value the friendship of Nepal."

It was during the **Anglo-Nepal War** (1814–1816) that the British discovered the inherent military value of the Gorkha element that

Hirtzel spoke of in such crude terms. The **Treaty of Sagauli**, signed in 1816, clearly gave the British an upper hand. Consequently, Britain not only relegated Nepal into a semicolony, but also embarked on a relentless campaign of recruiting Gorkha mercenaries to serve in its imperial army. But the campaign met with little success until the rise of the **Rana** clan to prominence.

In 1855, the British managed to initiate a convention whereby the successive Rana prime ministers sought unofficial confirmation from the British representative in Nepal prior to assuming the powers of their office. In addition to granting legitimacy to Rana autocracy, this semicolonial British precedent sanctioned the deployment of the coup d'etat as an instrument of usurping power, which happened occasionally during the Rana period. Furthermore, it placed the Rana prime minister in a position of utter obligation to the British.

The degree of Rana loyalty—or subservience as some claim—to the British was on full display during the Indian Sepoy mutiny of 1857, when Prime Minister **Jang Bahadur Rana** provided military assistance. In addition to dispatching 6,000 soldiers, Jang Bahadur personally marched with 9,000 troops to suppress the rebellion in support of the British. Heading a 15,000-strong army, he gave the British a crucial victory around the north Indian cities of Gorkhapur and Lucknow, a victory that proved decisive in terms of allowing them to consolidate their imperial hold on the subcontinent. As one official British statement noted, "by means of the Nepalese troops first sent to our relief he (Jang Bahadur) has... rendered [great service] to us in our utmost needs. We are unwilling to imagine the position in which we should now have been without this aid from the Maharaja—and still less the course which events might have taken."

That was not the end of unparalleled Rana loyalty to the British. During the First and Second World Wars, the British needed Gorkha mercenaries more than ever before to protect their global reach. Again, the Rana prime ministers came through by not only permitting the British to recruit unlimited numbers of Nepali youth, but actually mobilizing all the powers of their office to push those youth to join the British army. According to one British account, "Nepal denuded her **rice** fields and maize terraces, her high villages and **mountain** pastures to send forth her best. In all, some 160,000 were streamed down to the recruiting centres" during World War I. During World War II, Prime Minister **Chandra Shamsher Rana** "stripped his own country of virtually all its finest men," herding over 200,000 to join the British army. The hills were completely depleted of youth; the only ones left behind were the **women**, old men, cripples, and children. In addition, the prime minister sent almost 17,000 troopers from his own army. Yet the British demand continued to pour in. Unable to round up any more able bodies, Chandra Shamsher offered prisoners, an offer which the British quickly accepted.

Based on various historical accounts, it can be surmised that the relations between the two countries were lopsided in favor of Great Britain. It is true that the Ranas benefitted as well, but not Nepal. Between the two wars, nearly 45,000 young men of Nepal sacrificed their lives in the name of the British Empire, and 40,000 were incapacitated. In a surprising twist, what was once a mighty force, a venerable symbol of Britain's imperial glory, the number of Gorkha mercenaries in the British military has today dwindled to around 2,000.

In the post-Rana period, British relations with Nepal are largely reflected in their effort to offer development assistance. Although its influence in Nepal has apparently diminished, Britain still remains a leading **foreign aid** donor to the country. Over the past four decades, Britain has launched several development projects in Nepal, including rural development. *See also* BRITISH GORKHAS.

BRITISH GORKHAS (GURKHAS). Gorkha (Nepali) soldiers who are basically mercenaries. The British recruitment of Gorkha mercenaries began after the conclusion of the **Anglo-Nepal War** (1814–1816). The number of British Gorkhas drastically declined after **India**'s independence because a large number of them were transferred to the Indian military forces when the British departed from India. Although the British military establishment has currently reduced their Gorkha battalions to around 2,000 soldiers, they continue to recruit them on a periodic basis but unlike before, only in small numbers. Some of the ex-Gorkha servicemen are now hired as security guards in several Southeast Asian countries, e.g., Brunei, Malaysia, and Singapore. Hong Kong also has many of them within its territory despite its handover to the People's Republic of **China** in the late 1990s.

In the past few years, retired British Gorkha ex-servicemen and their association in Nepal have raised a serious issue with the British government over the extreme pension disparity between what they are paid versus what their British counterparts receive. They have vehemently argued that they should be paid at about the same par as their British counterparts, for they both served the British Empire equally and with the same conviction. In light of their logical and legitimate claims, the British government has agreed to raise their pensions to a level that is almost twice as much as the current amount. This decision has not, however, fully mitigated their concern and demand. See also BRITAIN-NEPAL RELATIONS; GORKHA.

BUDDHA. Source of **Buddhism** and son of Queen Mahamaya and King Suddhodhana, a Sakya (Shakya) king, who ruled the **Kapilvastu** region located in the central **Tarai** along the Nepal-India border (see figure 2). He was born in **Lumbini** in 563 B.C. In his book *The Wonder That Was India*, Basham notes that at birth Buddha stood upright, took seven strides, and spoke: "This is my last birth—henceforth there is no more birth for me." The boy was named Siddhartha Gautama (Gautam) at a ceremony on the fifth day from his birth. It was prophesied that he would become a Universal Emperor or a Universal Teacher.

He married his cousin Yasodhara. One morning when he was 29, the news came that his wife had given birth to a son. That very night he decided to renounce his princehood as he sneaked out of the palace in search of Truth. After years of wandering around, he decided one day to go into deep meditation and not to leave his seat until the riddle of suffering was solved. Finally, on the 49th day of his deep meditation, he discovered the Truth, the secret of sorrow. He had attained enlightenment. Siddhartha, once a **Hindu** prince, became a Buddha, the Enlightened One and the source of Buddhism. He was only 35 years old at that time. He spent the rest of his life going around and preaching his principles or setting in motion the "Wheel of the Law" or simply *Buddha Dharma* (Buddhism), the eternal path to **nirvana**—a state where one is free from human sorrow, suffering, and miseries resulting from earthly temptations and trappings. His end came at the advanced age of 80. Buddha informed his disciples of his imminent death. As he believed that one should not turn down what he or she is given, he ate a meal that was served to him when he was being entertained by a lay disciple. The meal included pork that apparently was spoiled. Soon after the meal, he fell sick and presumably died of food poisoning in a place called Kushinagar.

BUDDHA JAYANTI. This is a major festival for the followers of **Buddhism** and is celebrated with much enthusiasm throughout Nepal. The day of Buddha Jayanti falls on the full moon of the month of Baisakh (*see*

Nepali Calendar). It is the day to commemorate **Buddha**'s birth, attainment of knowledge, and death. Thus, it is a thrice-blessed day. Prayers are sung and the Buddhists offer worship in all the major Buddhist shrines such as **Swayambhu** (Swayambhunath) and **Baudhanath**. At Swayambhu, for example, millions of devout Buddhists gather from all over the world to chant prayers and to burn butter lamps. The next morning a giant figure of Lord Buddha is displayed to all the followers and hundreds of small shrines are visited and worshiped. Large groups of people parade through the streets praising the Lord and his teachings. Special flags, usually red, blue, yellow, and white can be seen flying high above all the Buddhist households.

BUDDHABHADRA (BUDDHAVATAM SAKYA). Buddhist teacher who visited **China** in the fourth century A.D. He is believed to have translated *Mahavaipulya Sutra*, a Buddhist text, into Chinese.

BUDDHISM. Buddhism, also known as Buddha dharma, has its origin in the teachings of the **Buddha** whose birth name was Siddhartha Gautama. The Four Noble Truths summarize Buddha Dharma (or Buddhism) as related to human miseries and suffering and the solution Buddha discovered for these problems associated with earthly life. The first truth says life is inherently imperfect and sorrowful, and that misery is not merely a result of occasional frustration of desire or misfortune, but is a quality permeating human experience. The second truth is that the cause of sorrow is desire (similar to maya in **Hinduism**), the emotional involvement with existence that leads one to undergo a cycle of births and rebirths through the operation of **karma**. In other words, it is the element called desire that tempts people to commit misdeeds (un-dharmic acts) which result in a series of rebirths. The third truth is that the sorrow can be ended only by eliminating desire. The fourth truth sets forth the Eightfold Path leading to elimination of desire, rebirth, and sorrow—in essence, **nirvana**, a state of bliss and enlightenment, a state in which the soul is free from desire and the cycle of rebirth.

BUDHA NILKANTHA. Shrine of sleeping **Vishnu** situated about eight kilometers north of **Kathmandu**. It has a stone image of reclining Vishnu on a carved black stone bed of the serpent deity, **Ananta Nag**, and it is situated in a small pond. It is a highly revered shrine where many **Hindus** visit and worship. The ruling king is prohibited from visiting this shrine.

The reason behind this prohibition is that King **Pratap Malla** was once advised in a dream that the royal visit there would result in the monarch's death. As a result, its replica Bala Narayana (another popular name for Vishnu) was built in **Balaju** to accommodate royal visits and worships. It is noted that Nilkantha is actually one of the various names of **Shiva** who is believed to have once drunk poison that turned his throat (*kantha*) dark blue (*nil*), hence Nilkantha.

BUDHATHOKI, BINA. Film and telefilm actress. She has performed in several movies produced in the early 1990s. She was quite popular among the Nepali youth during her heyday.

BUTTERFLIES. There are over 500 species of butterflies in Nepal. Within the **Kathmandu Valley, Godavari** is considered to be a rich area for butterflies. There is a small but significant butterfly museum on the campus of Prithvi Narayan College in **Pokhara**. The museum was initially established and funded by Dorothy Mierow, who worked as an American Peace Corps volunteer in Pokhara in the mid-1960s.

BUTWAL. Located at the intersection of the Mahendra and Siddhartha Rajmarga (highways), it is considered a gateway city as it lies at the transitional zone between the central hills and the **Tarai** (*see* figure 4). It is a relatively old town, largely settled by merchants from Tansen and **Baglung**. It is one of the very few towns in the Tarai where commercial domination by Indian merchants is significantly absent. In this sense, it is quite similar to Bhairahawa and **Narayanghat** (*see* figure 4). Historically, it served as a stopping point for central hill migrant workers returning from **India** during their leaves or upon retirement. Stories are told that it was also a place where returning migrants were ripped off by shady merchants and prostitutes. Today, with a total 1991 population of 34,243, it is a relatively thriving town that features a few factories. Its twin town across the Tinau River is called Khaseuli.

BUTWAL INDUSTRIAL DISTRICT. Industrial center in **Butwal** that was founded in 1975 with Indian assistance.

BYAS RISHI HIMAL. Himalayan mountain range in western Nepal, named after sage (*rishi*) Byas. The range is found between the Seti and

Mahakali Rivers and includes two principal peaks: Api Himal (7,132m) and Nampa Himal (6,757m).

BYATHIT (VYATHIT), KEDAR MAN (1914–1998). Litterateur and academician whose poems tend to portray imaginativeness and rebellion. Jailed for five years (1940–1945) for holding anti-**Rana** activities, he was actively involved in the 1950–1951 revolution. Author of many literary works, he has received several awards and served as vice-chancellor of the **Royal Nepal Academy** between 1969 and 1974. He remains a highly respected literary personality of Nepal.

C

CALENDAR. See NEPALI CALENDAR.

CARPET INDUSTRY. This is a major export **industry** of Nepal and it is growing. In 1999, carpets accounted for 35 percent of total exports, with a dollar value of $144.2 million. Although Nepal has a long history of carpet weaving, particularly in the hill and **mountain** regions, **Tibetan** refugees are credited with its commercialization and trade. Not surprisingly, therefore, the carpet industry is heavily controlled by Tibetan refugees. In recent years, the carpet industry of Nepal has come to rely on **child labor** for its production, despite the growing chorus of domestic and international voices against child labor abuse and exploitation. Two weaknesses of this industry are that it is highly dependent on imported raw materials on the production side and on **tourism** on the consumption front. It has experienced a major setback in recent months because of a precipitous decline in the volume of Western tourists visiting Nepal—a decline that is clearly attributed to both the terrible events of 11 September 2001 and the intensification of the ongoing **People's War**.

CASINO. One of the major outcomes associated with the growth and expansion of **tourism** in the **Kathmandu Valley** is the emergence of casino gambling as a principal tourist attraction. With four casinos operating, this capital city of Nepal now boasts its dubious status as the "Las Vegas of South Asia." In fact, this was a title that was bestowed upon this medieval city by Joe Manickavasagam of the **World Bank** that has financed some of the hotels. These casinos are set up in the city's four fanciest hotels, most of which are directly connected to the royal palace (family) in terms of ownership. All four casinos are managed by Richard Tuttle, who is locally known as the "American casino king of Nepal."

CASTE SYSTEM. Although hard to provide one universally acceptable definition, caste is generally viewed as a multifaceted status hierarchy that groups all members of society into specific caste categories. In all likelihood, the **Hindu** caste system is a bastardized version of the initial four broad, functional class divisions that resulted from the mixing of the migrant, seminomadic, and marauding bands of people from the great Eurasian steppe land (Central Asia to Poland)—who are collectively identified as the Aryans—with the local aboriginals of darker complexion. To be sure, there was already a class division when they entered **India**: the nobility called the *kshatra*, apparently the root of Kshatriya (*see* **Chhetri**) vs. the ordinary tribesmen called the *viś*, most likely the root of **Vaisya**. But, later, the class divisions expanded.

A. L. Basham argues that as the lighter-skinned migrant Aryan bands settled among the darker aboriginals or Dasas, they laid greater emphasis than before on blood purity and complexion. Not surprisingly, therefore, class divisions hardened and broadened based on both functional roles and *varna*, which in **Sanskrit** means "color" (in this case one's skin color). Since the Aryans had already assumed the position of power in society and were fairer in color, they placed themselves at the top of the class hierarchy. As a result, they relegated the darker-skinned Dasas to a lower place on the social scale, many of whom were **slaves**. (In fact, the word *dasa* or *das* was later adopted in Sanskrit to mean "slaves.") Dasas had found a place on the fringes of Aryan society, as did those Aryans who had intermarried with the Dasas and adopted their culture (mode of living). Thus, the so-called pure-blood Aryans lowered these groups on the social class hierarchy. Eventually, four broad functional classes were crystallized: the priest (**Brahman**), warrior (Kshatriya), peasant/trader (Vaisya), and serf (**Sudra**). Where the members of society belonged in this hierarchy was largely determined by blood purity or the degree of their pigmentation, which seems to have initially defined their functional roles and class status, that is, the lighter the skin color or *varna*, the higher the class status. Because of the importance of *varna* in the class division of Aryan society, it was closely associated with class; they were later seen as being synonymous. And this association was subsequently carried over to the four overarching caste divisions, which were directly forged from the initial four Aryan classes, each with its separate societal duties and distinctive way of life (cultural values).

According to Basham, use of castes to define the four Aryan class divisions has a fairly recent origin. He notes that when the Portugese came to India in the sixteenth century, they found the Hindu community divided into separate groups. They called those groups *castas*, which meant tribes or clans (consisting of people with similar features and cultural practices). Apparently, the Portugese descriptive term stuck, and the word was adopted with a slight adaptation—from *castas* to *castes*— to describe the four Hindu functional classes, perhaps much more rigidly than previously. Regardless of its terminological origin, India witnessed a remarkable proliferation of castes or subcastes in the eighteenth and nineteenth centuries, some of them obviously spilling over to Nepal. It was not uncommon for people to take on new castes strictly based on their occupations, thus inventing a new subcaste, affiliated with one of the four principal castes which remained intact. In Nepal, there are many subcastes that are directly tied to their professional occupations. Take, for example, Chitrakar (who draw paintings and art works; *chitra* = paintings) or Tamrakar (who make containers and vessels out of copper and brass; *tama* = copper). Both are subcastes of the **Newar** caste which, in turn, belongs to the Vaisya caste group.

Moreover, even though *varna* has never meant caste, its loose use as a synonym for the latter has continued to this day despite the fact that the early direct correlation between one's class position and *varna* is hardly applicable any more. There are plenty of high-caste people who are dark in complexion and low-caste people with relatively fair skin color. Nor does the strict correlation between caste and professional occupation hold in a traditional sense. Yet the caste identity, as signified by one's last name, remains an entrenched symbol of Hindu orthodoxy.

- Brahman: In terms of their functional roles, the Brahmans are designated as priests and scholars—transmitters of knowledge and interpreters of *shastras* and *sutras* (religious treatises and texts). The Nepali term commonly used for the Brahmans is **Bahun**. They are placed at the top of the Hindu caste hierarchy.
- Chhetri (Kshatriya): According to the caste code, their assigned roles and duties include acting as rulers and warriors and protecting citizens. Chhetri (Chetri) is the Nepali adaptation of Kshatriya. On the caste

hierarchical scale, they occupy the second rank from the top, just below the Brahmans.
- Vaisya: Their caste-prescribed duties are to act as merchants and traders, to engage in farming, or simply to fulfill the material needs of society and its citizens. In terms of social ranking, they are third.
- Sudra: They are the lowest caste group, considered to be polluted and, hence, treated as **untouchable** by the higher caste groups. Placed in the professional roles of serving as artisans and menial laborers, they are, nonetheless, integral to fulfilling societal production functions and material needs.

Within each group, there are many subcastes. According to the caste code instituted by King **Jayasthiti Malla** (reign: 1382–1395), the population of Nepal was divided into 64 subcastes. Although his caste codification generally remains intact, it is futile, in practice, to assume that the subcaste groups in the nation are limited to 64. It is, in fact, entirely plausible to argue that subcastes can be almost infinite as they are often arbitrary by-products of marriages between different caste and subcaste groups. Regardless of the number of various caste and subcaste groups, the caste system is a defining marker of Nepal's social system.

It is true that, given its Hindu ethos, the country's caste system finds its immediate application among its **Indo-Nepali** people, those who initially came from India and who are now the primary bearers of Hinduism. But by no means is it limited to them; it is imposed on virtually all members of society as they are all grouped into one of the four caste categories. Everybody has a preordained caste identity that stands out like a birthmark. Not surprisingly, therefore, the caste system's influence is widespread and far-reaching. Even the Muslims are technically categorized as polluted, thus situating them in the Sudra group of the Hindu caste hierarchy.

The Newars—regarded by most as the indigenous population of Nepal—have certainly adopted the caste system, along with their designation as members of the Vaisya caste. After all, they are the original traders and merchants of Nepal, who successfully extended their commercial domain all the way to **Tibet**. Despite this general adherence to the Hindu caste system, they do not strictly uphold the four divisions specified above. They have their own parallel castes and subcastes, with a distinct priestly group that is equivalent to the Hindu Brahmans. This is particularly true among those who lean more toward **Buddhism**, i.e., those who are generically called the Gubhaju. Similar to the Hindu system, each caste (*jati*) is regarded as an endogamous group as caste membership is both hereditary and permanent.

Although subjected to the Hindu caste system at large, the question of caste is less ingrained in **Tibeto-Nepali** communities, which usually follow the Tantric version of Buddhism, mixed with some aspects of Hinduism. Similar to the Newars, they, too, have generally accepted the prevailing caste system. Accordingly, they are loosely placed into the Vaisya caste. Nevertheless, the Tibeto-Nepalis tend to see themselves at a higher level than do the Indo-Nepalis and Newars. In addition, they share some similarities with the Newars' internal caste divisions. That is, the Tibeto-Nepali groups have their own internal social hierarchies, although rarely as rigidly delineated as that found among the Newars and Indo-Nepali population. For example, the **Thakalis** have their own caste-like hierarchies. At the top, there are four groups of equal status. Then below them are several groups whose social status is definitely lower than that of the four top-ranked Thakalis. Such hierarchical patterns and rankings are common among almost all other Tibeto-Nepali ethnic groups as well. In addition, they all have their own respective priests: the **Lamas**, who perform various rituals from birth to death. Many of these groups also follow many Hindu customs and practices.

At the core of the caste structure lies a rank order of values bound up in concepts of ritual status, purity, and pollution. It is, therefore, no surprise that the caste system is deployed to determine an individual's social behavior as well as societal obligations and expectations (which are often equated with acts of **dharma**). One's social, economic, religious, legal, and political activities are prescribed by sanctions that determine access to land, position of political power, and command of human labor. Within this constrictive system, wealth, power, privilege and social ranks normally tend to converge, as hereditary occupational role is a common feature. For example, the **Kamis**, who belong to the Sudra caste, are expected—in some cases even obligated—to fulfill their caste-based occupational duty, which is to produce and repair agricultural implements and iron utensils (i.e., all types of iron works). Yet it is pertinent to bear in mind that caste and caste roles are functionally significant only when viewed in a regional or local context and at a particular time, for the system has undergone significant transformation in recent years, both legally and in practice. Moreover, the assumed correlation between the caste hierarchy and the socioeconomic class hierarchy does not always hold, except perhaps in the case of the Sudra caste group. *See also* ETHNICITY; UNTOUCHABILITY.

CENTRE FOR ECONOMIC DEVELOPMENT AND ADMINISTRATION (CEDA). Research and training institute founded in 1969 with financial aid from the Ford Foundation as an integral part of its institution-building initiatives in Nepal. It is associated with **Tribhuvan University**. Since its inception, it has published many research reports and position papers on economic development and administration issues.

CENTRE FOR NEPAL AND ASIAN STUDIES (CNAS). A research-oriented institute founded in 1972 under **Tribhuvan University** for promoting graduate-level Nepal and Asian studies in the country. Its journal, *Contributions to Nepalese Studies*, is a major academic outlet of research. Within the Nepali academic circle, it is recognized as a major professional journal.

CHABAL (CHABIL). Buddhist *vihar*. Located in the northeastern part of **Kathmandu** and built in 250 B.C., it is flanked by ancient statues.

CHAINPUR. The headquarters of Bajhang district in far western Nepal. The name is also used for a relatively small **Newar** settlement, a commercial center in the district of Sankhuwasabha in eastern Nepal, that is renowned across the country for its production of traditional bronze utensils and products of unsurpassed quality.

CHAITYA. Small version of Buddhist mound or stupa. Found throughout the **Kathmandu Valley** and often used as reliquaries for the dead.

CHAKARI (CHAKADI). Seeking undeserved favors from those in high ranks or power by paying frequent visits and through flattery. In a way, it is a form of self-imposed servitude. *See also* APHNO MANCHHE; CHAMCHA.

CHAKARIBAD. (*Chakari* = servitude; *bad* = value system or principle.) Inherent practice of gaining favors through servitude. Rooted in a system of social and political paternalism, it is very popular across Nepal.

CHAKRAPATH. Known as the Ringroad, it goes around **Kathmandu** and **Patan**. It was built with the technical and financial assistance of the People's Republic of **China**.

CHALISE, CHAKRA PANI (1883–1958). Poet who composed Nepal's national anthem. His works include *Nepali Samchhipta Ramayana* and *Nepali Dictionary*.

CHAMAR. Plains caste (leather workers), equivalent to **Sarki** in the hills.

CHAMCHA. Literally, it means "spoon." But the word also has a deeper meaning as it is used as a metaphor to describe a person who acts like a mouthpiece (i.e., a political lackey) of a political leader to gain undue favors. *See also* CHAKARI.

CHAMCHABAD. Essentially the same as *Chakaribad*.

CHAND, DASHARATH (1903–1941). One of the four national political martyrs, he was killed by Prime Minister **Juddha Shamsher Rana** on 27 January 1941. He was a true patriot who sacrificed his life to rescue Nepal from **Rana** autocracy. The Shahid Gate of **Kathmandu**, established to honor the four martyrs, includes his statue. There is little doubt that he was one of the earliest anti-Rana activists who sowed the seeds of democracy in Nepal. He was a founding member of **Praja Parishad**, the first political party of Nepal, formed to overthrow the Rana regime and set Nepal on the path of democracy and progress. The Dasharath Stadium of Kathmandu is named after him.

CHAND, LOKENDRA BAHADUR (1939–). Politician and short story writer. During the **Panchayat** period, he served as prime minister from 1983 to 1985. He was also appointed prime minister in early 1990 when Prime Minister **Marichman Shrestha** was removed by King **Birendra Bir Bikram Shah** from his post. Chand remained in that office for 13 days until the Panchayat system came to an end, replaced by a multi-party democratic system. He rose to power to become prime minister in 1997, heading a coalition government of the right-wing **National Democratic Party** (Rastriya Prajatantra Party), Unified Marxist-Leninist (UML), and **Nepal Sadbhavana Party**. This time, his premiership lasted roughly seven months, from early March to early October. In early

October 2002, King **Gyanendra Bir Bikram Shah** sacked elected Prime Minister **Sher Bahadur Deuba** and his entire cabinet. Following this action, the king usurped executive powers and, on 11 October, chose Chand, a staunch royalist, to be Nepal's new prime minister. One notable development under his premiership is that the Maoist revolutionaries led by **Baburam Bhattarai** agreed to participate in peace negotiations to end the ongoing **People's War**. However, Chand resigned on 30 May 2003, as thousands rallied against the king and his suppressive political rule and practices, bringing fresh political uncertainty to Nepal (*see* Chronology).

CHANDRA GRAHAN. (*Chandra* = moon; *grahan* = eclipse.) It is widely treated as a ritualistic event occurring on the day of lunar eclipse. *Grahan* is generally believed to represent bad omens. Their observance is, thus, highlighted by fasting and ceremonial bathing in a holy river to appease the evil spirit, Rahu. Gifts of cloth, money, and salt are given to the sweeper **caste** at this time. *See also* SURYA GRAHAN.

CHANDRA JYOTI. Nepal's first electricity project located at **Pharping**, southeast of **Kathmandu**. It was built in 1911 by Prime Minister **Chandra Shamsher Rana** and named after him: Chandra + *jyoti* (light). It has a power generation capacity of 550kw.

CHANDRA NAHAR. Nepal's oldest irrigation canal in the eastern **Tarai** district of Saptari, built during the premiership of **Chandra Shamsher Rana** and named after him: Chandra + *nahar* (canal).

CHANGU NARAYAN. One of the ancient monuments. This holy **Hindu** site has become a favorite point of attraction for foreigners as well as local people. The Changu Narayan temple is on the way to Sankhu about 16 kilometers east of **Kathmandu** and 4 kilometers from **Bhaktapur**. The temple was constructed by a **Licchavi** king in 325 A.D., but the shrine itself has been there for a long time, going well beyond the time when the temple was erected.

CHARKHA. An elaborately carved spinning wheel, still to be found in use in some parts of the country. It is often considered a work of art as it involves intricate and elaborate woodcarving. In India, it was popularized by Gandhi as a symbol of self-reliance (*swabhalambi*) and promotion of national production and products (*swodeshi*). The message was to boycott

English textiles that had decimated the Indian textile industry and to reassert or reassert the national textile heritage which used to play a dominant role prior to the rise of the British textile industry following the industrial revolution. But the symbolic role or message of *charkha* failed catch on in Nepal.

CHAR KOSE JHADI. Twelve-kilometers-wide dense forests of the **Tarai** region. It was simply called the Tarai jungle. Because of its density and malarial infestation, this band of forests was deployed as a defensive barrier during the time of British rule in **India**. Prior to the early 1950s, attempts were made periodically to settle this region in order to increase Nepal's revenue base. Migrants from the bordering provinces of India were often encouraged to resettle in the region and bring its virgin lands under cultivation. Such resettlement attempts of the past were relatively insignificant, however, in terms of producing desired results. Finally, in the mid-1950s, a national policy was implemented with the aid of the **United States** Operations Mission (USOM) in Nepal to eradicate malaria from the region and open it up for land resettlement by hill migrants. It was declared an agricultural frontier of Nepal.

Since then, the region has seen massive resettlement by hill migrants, resulting in what is commonly labeled *paharization*. It is a politico-demographic process designed to create a hill population majority (domination) in the Tarai, a border region that is often treated by the country's central government as an internal colony. The Tarai and its non-hill population are generally viewed with suspicion because of their close geographical, cultural, and economic ties with India. Due to massive hill resettlement and both legal and illegal logging, much of the *char kose jhadi* has disappeared, and the official policy of land resettlement has been essentially halted.

CHATARA NAHAR. Famous irrigation canal in the eastern **Tarai** district of Sunsari. It drains water from the Sapta Kosi River. *See also* KOSI RIVER SYSTEM.

CHAUBISE. (*Chaubis* = 24.) This phrase is invariably used in the context of the 24 principalities—**Chaubise Rajya**—that ruled the Gandaki basin in central Nepal prior to Nepal's national unification that began after **Prithvi Narayan Shah**'s conquest of the three **Malla** kingdoms of the **Kathmandu Valley** in 1769. *See also* BAISE.

CHAUBISE RAJYA. Collective term applied to ministates (chiefdoms or fiefdoms) ruled by separate chieftains in the central region of Nepal drained by the **Gandaki River system**. Collectively, their territory generally spanned between the ***Baise Rajya*** in the Karnali basin in the west and the **Kathmandu Valley** to the east with their number prior to unification reaching up to 24 (*chaubis*), hence the name, ***chaubise***.

They were all eventually annexed to Nepal between 1786 and 1790, some by means of negotiations and others through their military defeats at the hands of the unification campaign forces, initially unleashed by **Prithvi Narayan Shah**. Because of the paucity of reliable records, Nepali historians have discovered that it is difficult to offer historically specific details and precise accounts of their territorial boundaries and administrative rules and status. But there is little doubt that some of them were quite prominent and relatively powerful, including, of course, the principality of **Gorkha**. The following names are frequently mentioned as constituting relatively autonomous territorial principalities:

1. Argha
2. Bhirkot
3. Dhor
4. Dhurkot
5. Gajarkot
6. Galkot
7. Garahun
8. Ghiring
9. Gorkha
10. Gulmi
11. Isam
12. Kaski
13. Khanchi
14. Lamjung
15. Musikot
16. Nuwakot
17. Paiyun
18. Palpa
19. Parbat (Malebam)
20. Pyuthan
21. Rising
22. Satahun
23. Tanahun
24. Tarki

Of these 24 *rajyas*, **Gorkha**, Kaski, **Palpa**, Lamjung, and Tanahun, presently exist as administrative districts, along with Gulmi, Parbat, and Pyuthan. Argha and Khanchi were later combined to create the district of Arghakhanchi and much of Nuwakot (west) now comprises the district of Syangja. *See also BAISE RAJYA.*

CHAUDHARI (CAUDHARY). Tax collector in the **Tarai** prior to the overthrow of the **Rana** regime in 1951. It is also a common surname in the Tarai.

CHAUDHARI, BINOD (1955–). Leading businessman and industrialist in Nepal. He has served as president of the Nepal Chambers of Commerce and Industries. He is the managing director of several commercial and industrial enterprises belonging to the Chaudhari group of industries including Pashupati Biscuits, Nepal Thai Foods, Champion Footwear, Goldstar Nepal, Arun Emporium, Apollo International, Nirvana Banaspati Udhyog, Megha Woollen Mills, and others.

CHAUDHARI, LUNAKARAN DAS (1922–). Businessman. He is also the founding chairman of several business and industrial enterprises belonging to the Chaudhari Group of Industries. In addition, he is a founding member of the Marwari Sewa Samiti, an ethnic organization in **Kathmandu** that is concerned with the welfare of the **Marwari** community.

CHAUDHARI, PARSHU NARAYAN (1928–). Politician from **Dang**, a western **Tarai** district (see figure 2). He began his career as a member of the **Nepali Congress Party**, but later joined the **Panchayat** system in 1981. Subsequently, he became minister of industries and commerce (1984–1985) and of education and culture (1988–1989). As an opportunist, he rejoined the Nepali Congress Party when the Panchayat system was abolished in 1990.

CHAUDHARI, SURENDRA PRASAD (1956–). Politician from the Parsa district in the central **Tarai** (see figure 2). As a member of the **Nepali Congress Party**, he was jailed for seven years during the **Panchayat** period. He has been elected to the **House of Representatives** in all three general **elections** (1991, 1994, and 1999) held since the return of democracy in 1990. In 1992, he was appointed assistant minister of commerce and supplies.

CHAUDHARI, TRIYUGI NARAYAN (1947–). Politician from the district of Nawalparasi in the central **Tarai** (see figure 2). Between 1990 and 1993 he was general secretary of the **Nepal Sadbhavana Party**, which generally espouses a **Hindu** fundamentalist view. He was elected to the **House of Representatives** in 1991.

CHAULAGAIN, KAMAL PRASAD (1955–). Leftist politician from the Ramechhap district (*see* figure 2). He began his political career as a member of the leftist All Nepal Free Student Union and the **Communist Party of Nepal.** He was elected to **House of Representatives** in 1991.

CHAURIGAI. The Nepali name of the yak (*Bos grunniens*), a stout and hairy animal raised in the mountainous areas. An important source of milk and meat in the **mountains**, they are also used to carry loads in high altitude areas and to extract yak wool out of which mountain dwellers make various items to wear.

CHAUTARA (CHAUTARI). A resting place shaded by at least one of the three religious trees called bar, pipal, or sami (or some combination), it is found along roads and trails throughout Nepal. It is deeply imbued with cultural and religious symbolism as well as social and environmental values. In the past, building *chautaras* was a time-honored and highly valued tradition as it was seen as a religious act to serve travelers and porters who might need to take some rest during their journeys. Embedded in this tradition was the profound belief that to serve people, especially those in need, is to serve God. In this sense, *chautaras* stood as a unique tradition and as an enduring feature of the cultural landscape of Nepal. They were often established by individuals, but also, sometimes, by villages as part of their communal efforts or community service. While they are still found, the tradition of building *chautaras* is rarely practiced any more. Due to road and urban expansions some of the chautaras have been demolished in some places.

CHAUWANNI KOTHI. It was the residence of the British mission in **Kathmandu** during the **Rana** period.

CHEMJONG, IMAN SINGH. Scholar of **Kirata** (Kirant; Kirati) **literature** and history. He has written books on Kirata history, language, and stories, including *Kirantko Veda* (The Veda of Kirata).

CHEPANG. Ethnic tribal group living in the Mahabharat range south west of **Kathmandu.** They are often associated with the nomadic way of life as they practice slash-and-burn **agriculture**. Fishing is also part of their livelihood.

CHHETRI (CHETRI). Nepali variation of the **Hindu** caste Kshatriya. According to the Hindu **caste system**, they are ranked second from the top on the caste hierarchy and are recognized as warriors and rulers. Initially concentrated in the lower hills following their migration to Nepal less than a 1,000 years ago, they are now scattered throughout Nepal. *See also* ETHNICITY.

CHHANG (CHANG). Home-brewed beer, usually made out of barley, millet, or **rice**. It is a **Sherpa** beverage that is also commonly used in almost all **Tibeto-Nepali** communities. Some call it *jand* (a Nepali term). It is a very popular drink in the hills and among the rural people. In most urban areas, it is being increasingly replaced—or displaced—by commercial beer, much of which is domestically produced through joint ventures.

CHILAM. Smoking pipe made from clay. About 10 to 12 centimeters in length, it is used to smoke tobacco and marijuana. It became popular in the 1960s when the Hippie movement was at its peak and when many Hippies flocked to Nepal in search of dope (**ganja**) and rustic tranquility. *See also* TOURISM.

CHILD LABOR. Nepal has ratified the **United Nations** Convention on the Rights of the Child. The government has stated its commitment to safeguarding the rights and interest of the children in Nepal. But little has happened beyond that as the exploitation and abuse of children continue unabated. There is enough evidence that the number of "street children" or *khate* (ragpickers) as they are collectively called, has greatly swelled over the past few years. According to one estimate, there were close to 11,000 *khates* in the three municipalities of **Kathmandu, Patan,** and **Bhaktapur** in 1994. Instead of finding remedies for the root causes of their numerical explosion, they are now summarily treated as street nuisances and criminals, as some of them have embarked on the path of organized pickpocketing, stealing, and intimidation. A local publication called *Voice of Child Workers* has done much to expose their problems and publicize their cause.

In addition to this dimension of child labor, many Nepali children—both boys and girls—are engaged in what is commonly called the informal **economy** or vending operations such as selling small quantities of goods (e.g., cigarettes, soda drinks, and snacks) along the sidewalks or shoe polishing to supplement family income. No matter how one views or defines it, child labor is historically, as well as presently, an integral part of growing up in Nepal. Unlike Western children, Nepali children have a very short childhood that is free of family responsibilities. Most children are put to work by the time they are six or seven years old, doing all sorts of work—from family chores such as looking after younger siblings, gathering firewood, and herding domestic animals to street vending. *See also* CARPET INDUSTRY; EDUCATION.

CHINA-NEPAL RELATIONS. The People's Republic of China (its autonomous region of **Tibet**) is the only nation, other than **India**, with which Nepal shares borders. Nepal's relations with China date back many centuries, at least to the **Licchavi period**, generally via Tibet. The first military encounter between the two countries occurred in the early 1790s when Nepal's adventurism in Tibet led China to intervene in support of Tibet. In 1792, they signed a treaty which favored China as Nepal was required to send a tribute-bearing mission to the former every five years as an indisputable symbol of Chinese political and cultural supremacy in the region. But beginning in 1908, Nepal unilaterally terminated tribute to China and later, in 1911, broke relations when Tibet drove the Chinese out. Consequently, the relations between the two countries were further strained.

Then came 1950 when China invaded Tibet. To Nepal, this event was at once threatening and sobering. In addition, it undermined the trade relations between Nepal and Tibet. Nepal was forced to reassess its diplomacy on both the southern and northern fronts. There was no doubt about Nepal's need to pursue a diplomatic balance between India and China as a matter of political sovereignty and survival. In 1955, Nepal restored its relations with China and exchanged resident ambassadors in 1960. They signed an agreement in 1961 to construct an all-weather highway from **Kathmandu** to Kodari at the Tibetan border with total Chinese assistance. Following its opening in 1967, this highway was renamed **Arniko Highway**. In reality, the highway is mostly symbolic as it has failed to yield any measurable economic benefits for Nepal.

In 1956, Nepal recognized China's sovereignty over Tibet and, in 1962, withdrew its ambassador from Tibet. Despite the warming ties between the two, Nepal reasserted its neutrality during the Indo-China War of

1962. Nonetheless, Nepal has a long-standing commitment to check anti-China activities in its soil. In 1974, the Nepali army successfully disarmed the Khampa rebels (exiled Tibetans), who were trained, armed, and financed by the **United States** government (through the CIA). They had been conducting cross-border raids into Tibet since the early 1960s from the Nepal side as well as marauding Nepali citizens in the northern region. That disarmament was highly appreciated by the Chinese. Furthermore, sensing Chinese displeasure, Nepal has also discouraged the Dalai Lama from entering its territory except once in 1981, when he was allowed to spend a day at **Lumbini**, the birthplace of Lord **Buddha**.

In short, however, Nepal's foreign policy has been of one balance, striving to maintain equal friendship with both China and India while trying to minimize its dependence on India. While China tacitly recognizes India's predominance in the region, it has neither hesitated to make its presence felt, nor shied away from expressing its long-range strategic interest. There is little doubt that China has carefully cultivated and promoted its influence in Nepal. As a result, since the reestablishment of its diplomatic link, the People's Republic of China has steadily increased its economic and technical assistance to Nepal to develop its industrial base by building various factories. But unlike India, China has not been seen to meddle in Nepal's internal affairs. To drive this point home, Chinese leaders have always been scrupulous in their dealings with Nepal, going all the way back to Prime Minister **Bishweswar Prasad (B. P.) Koirala** in 1959–1960. Yet the Chinese leaders have found it convenient to work with a stable institution of monarchy, while maintaining a stance in which the monarchy is viewed as a feudal anachronism. *See also* INDIA-NEPAL RELATIONS; INDUSTRY; JOINT BOUNDARY COMMISSION.

CHITRAKAR, AMAR (1920–1999). Self-taught sculptor. Born and raised in **Kathmandu**, Amar Chitrakar was responsible for creating many modern statues found in the different cities of the country, particularly within the Valley.

CHITTADHAR, HRIDAYA (1906–1981). He was a distinguished poet of **Newari** language. Born and raised in **Kathmandu**, his published works numbering three dozen have contributed much to elevate and enrich the Newari literature. Sweetness and simplicity are special traits of his writings. He served as founding president and patron of the Nepal

Bahasa Parishad (Nepal Language Association). He passed away on 21 May 1981.

CHITWAN. Central **Tarai** district in the **Narayani Zone** (*see* figures 2 and 3). Chitwan is a key producer of corn and mustard oil seeds. Once densely forested and mostly inhabited by the indigenous **Tharu** population, it symbolized the meaning and value of the *char kose jhadi* (dense forests) that was synonymous with the Tarai. Because its dense jungle environment was heavily infested with deadly malaria, Chitwan was routinely referred to as *kala pani* (poisoned water). So deadly was the malarial condition that not too many were expected to survive in Chitwan, especially in the summer when malaria would be at its peak. It was even used as a natural defensive barrier against the British incursion into Nepal—a sort of primitive biological warfare. Those who were found guilty of capital crimes, but could not be subjected to a death sentence (e.g., members of the **Bahun caste**) would be exiled into Chitwan under the assumption that they would die of malaria.

Today, Chitwan is a leading farming belt with a total population of 355,300 (1991) distributed over an area of 2,218 sq. km. It owes its current agricultural status mainly to the fact that it was the first Tarai district in the post-**Rana** period to be opened for planned land resettlement by hill migrants. Its **Rapti Valley**, fed by a relatively small river named Rapti (not the one in western Nepal with the same name), was opened in the mid-1950s as an integral part of Nepal's planned resettlement strategy that was directly associated with its first Five-Year Plan (1956–1961). The **United States** Operations Mission (USOM) based in **Kathmandu** (now USAID) was instrumental in financing and designing the resettlement strategy in Chitwan's Rapti Valley. The United States also financed a massive malaria eradication campaign in conjunction with the resettlement project. Subsequently, the campaign was expanded to cover all of Nepal below the altitude of approximately 1,200 meters, as those areas were either infested with or susceptible to malaria.

As the land resettlement reached its advanced phases, much of the thick jungle that gave Chitwan its dreadful reputation was destroyed to reclaim land for **agriculture**. Furthermore, the indigenous Tharus, who never practiced a system of private property ownership and land registry, lost much of their farmland to land hungry and unscrupulous hill migrants who literally usurped their land. Today Chitwan is thoroughly dominated by the *paharis* in all spheres of life: cultural, demographic, economic, and political. *See also* GURUNG, BAKHAN SINGH.

CHITWAN NATIONAL PARK. Nepal's oldest—and perhaps most popular—national park, situated in **Chitwan**. Established in 1973, it is particularly famous for wild elephants, tigers, and rhinoceroses. It does, however, contain many different types of wild animals. It is a major tourist attraction; organized tour groups are routinely taken to the park for tiger viewing and safari rides.

CHIURA. Flattened and dehydrated rice made out of boiled rice. *Chiura* is one of the most common food items in the **Newar** community, especially during ceremonies and feasts. No Newari feast or ceremony is complete without *chiura*, which is invariably consumed with some meat or vegetable dish, sometimes combined with *raksi*.

CHOMOLONGMA (QOMOLUNGMA). Sherpa and Tibetan name for **Mount Everest**. Its Chinese variant is: Zhumulangma.

CHORTEN. Mound or monument associated with **Buddhism**. It is a term generally used in the Lamaist or **Tibetan** Buddhist tradition, which essentially means a stupa. A *chorten* is believed to be created as a mound to commemorate the **Buddha**'s death or to represent the form of the contemplating Buddha.

CHOVAR. Popular settlement located in the southwest of **Kathmandu**. The temple of Lokeswor is situated in Chovar. Its narrow gorge, through which the **Bagmati River** flows, allowing the **Kathmandu Valley** to be drained, is said to have been cut open by Bodhisattva Manjusri in order to drain the lake from the Valley.

CHOWK. Courtyard, quadrangle.

CHURIA HILLS. Located along the northern ridges of the **Tarai** belt, Churia is a narrow range of low hills running east-west parallel to the **Mahabharata Lekh (Range)**, which constitutes the country's Hill Region. The Churia Hills, also known as the Siwalik Range, varies from 150 to 1,368 meters in altitude and are mainly composed of gravel or conglomerates of sand and limestone deposited by rivers from the **mountains**. They contain significant patches of commercially valuable forests.

CIVIL CODE. From a historical perspective, **Jayasthiti Malla** was the first king to institute a formal and elaborate civil code of religious and social conduct in Nepal. Since his code was drawn up with the help of five **Brahmans** from **India**, it was imbued with **Hindu** imprints. In fact, the legal and social code he instituted was directly intended to consolidate the country within the framework of orthodox **Hinduism**. Some of the distinctive features of his code included:

- In addition to the division of the population into the traditional four **castes** (based on *varna* or "color"), he created 64 subcastes and laid down detailed rules for intercaste marriage, dining, and drinking water.
- Introduction of the system of weights and measures for commercial or business transactions.
- Formal rules governing the use of pastures and irrigation water.

The impact of his civil code is clearly demonstrated by the fact that, to this day, the **Newars** of Nepal, particularly those in the **Kathmandu Valley**, rely on it, with only some minor adjustments. The next notable phase in the evolution of Nepali civil codes was associated with the first **Rana** prime minister, **Jang Bahadur Rana**, who implemented Muluki Ain which can roughly be translated to mean the national (*muluki*) laws (*ain*) or **constitution**. Following his return from a European tour in 1851, he commissioned leading administrators to codify the nation's legal system into a single body of laws. What resulted from Jang Bahadur's initiative was the relatively comprehensive Muluki Ain of 1854, which formalized administrative procedures and legal frameworks for interpreting civil and criminal matters, revenue collection, landlord-peasant relations, intercaste disputes, and family law.

CLOUDED LEOPARD. Called dhwanse (smokey) chituwa (leopard), these wild cats (*Neofelis nebulosa*) roam the highlands of Nepal. Since their number is believed to be very small, they were added to the list of endangered species.

COLOMBO PLAN. Founded in 1951 and named after Sri Lanka's capital city, Colombo, this organization is designed to coordinate and aid development of countries in Asia and the Pacific. It is headquartered in Colombo, and offers scholarships to qualified students from Asian and Pacific countries to study overseas. Nepal joined it in 1952. Included among the donor countries are: Australia, Canada, Great **Britain, India,** Japan, New Zealand, and the **United States.** Many Nepali students have received scholarships under this plan and obtained their higher (college) degrees in various fields from various countries within the plan.

COMMUNICATIONS. Nepal's communication (telecommunication) network is, by most standards, in its rudimentary phase, but certainly not in the dark ages. However, since the mid-1980s, the country has made significant strides in the communication sector, which can be divided into three broad mediums:

- Telephone: Domestically, most of the cities have telephone service. On the international front, Nepal's telecommunication network is now digitalized with fiber optic links to **India** and satellite links to other countries. For instance, the telephone connection between the **United States** and Nepal is direct and quite noise-free and reliable. Almost all localities in Nepal with telephone lines can make international calls.
- Satellite television: Television arrived in Nepal in the early 1980s. In its early days, **Nepal Television**'s broadcast was quite limited in terms of both time slots and topical coverage. Although its programs have greatly expanded since then, they are hardly the most popular ones, however. Satellite programs offered by foreign TV networks such as CNN, BBC, and those broadcast from India are the ones that tend to top viewing-preference charts in most households. In recent years, satellite dishes have become one of the most visible and prominent features of **Kathmandu**'s cultural landscape, often overshadowing ancient and ubiquitous temples.
- Internet: The Internet has arrived, and it is especially prevalent in urban areas. The whole world is accessible to those Nepalis who have Internet links, and anybody in the world can access Nepal from his or her bedroom instantly with the touch of a key. There are plenty of websites devoted to Nepal and based in Nepal, which offer all types data, information, and services related to the country. There are commercial Internet hubs—or so-called Internet cafes—where the tourists can access e-mails as well as surf the Internet. One can now

listen to radio broadcasts from Nepal and read Nepali newspapers on the Internet, including those published in Nepali.

From a policy perspective, it is noteworthy that the government has created the Nepal Telecommunication Authority, a regulatory body, to facilitate private sector participation and fair competition within the sector. The Nepal government plans to further develop this sector to augment the country's trade, **industry**, commerce, and **tourism**.

COMMUNIST PARTY OF NEPAL (CPN). Created in early 1949 as a revolutionary party, with the purpose of dethroning the **Rana** regime and forming a socialist state, the CPN has a relatively long and somewhat fractured history. **Puspa Lal Shrestha**, a highly charismatic leader, was the founding general secretary of the party. As an integral part of its anti-Rana struggle, its first declaration stated: "CPN is dedicated to activate, organize and lead the emerging struggle of the working people towards the victory. No terrorism and alluring propaganda can make it deviate from the track." Despite its unifying motto, the CPN underwent many changes in a manner similar to the **Nepali Congress Party** (NCP) due to philosophical and programmatic differences among party leaders and constant internal tussles for leadership positions. Consequently, those who quit the party organized their own factions and mini parties under the overarching ideology of Marxism. However, following its Fourth Congress in the late 1980s, the CPN began to develop a much more united and cohesive front than ever seen before.

During the 1990 anti-**Panchayat** and pro-democracy movement, the CPN decided to coordinate its efforts with the NCP. As part of this participation, the CPN under the leadership of **Madan Bhandari** (who was later killed) succeeded in unifying seven communist factions into what is now commonly identified as the Unified (also known as United) Marxist-Leninist (UML) party. It is now the largest CPN faction. As it won the largest numbers of Parliamentary seats in the 1994 general **elections**, it was able to form a national government with **Man Mohan Adhikari** as prime minister. In essence, the UML and most other factions of the Communist Party of Nepal have committed to the basic principles of democracy as a platform of political governance and rules. This is clearly verified by their ongoing participation in local/national elections and governance. From its humble and fractured beginning, the Communist Party of Nepal as a whole has come a long way to establish itself as a powerful force and voice in Nepali politics. A summary treatment of its history is available from its official website: www.cpnuml.org.

COMMUNITY FORESTRY. In Nepal, **forests** are not merely a source of timber, they are an integral part of agrarian life and sustenance. The primary source of fodder for animals, fuel wood, and other essential materials for rural residents, they are an indispensable bedrock of rural life and living. It is precisely because of this reason that forest resource sharing and management was viewed as a communal issue. That is, Nepal has a long history of communal management and stewardship of forests with proven records of their viability, sustainability, and effectiveness. However, the traditional system of community forestry suffered a deadly blow in 1956 when forests were nationalized. After this misguided nationalization, forest resources experienced rapid declines across the country. But, in the past couple of decades, the practice of community forestry has been introduced or revived in Nepal, interestingly as a Western invention. This is not surprising at all given the fact that virtually every community forestry project that has been undertaken in the country is initiated and funded by foreign donor agencies.

In its Western reincarnation, the concept is organized around what is called the Community Forestry User Group (CFUG)—a village level organization formed to manage forests handed over to it by the government. The Department of Forestry guides and facilitates the functioning of CFUGs. In addition, it offers technical assistance to CFUGs if and when needed. While there is evidence to suggest that the community forestry project has yielded some success in reviving forest resources, particularly in the hills, its results are far from being conclusive. As of 1997 almost 400,000 hectares of community forests were managed by various CFUGs in 59 districts. In 2001, the figure had increased to 750,000 hectares, and there were 10,000 CFUGs. The government plans to further increase the total number of community forests in the future, giving more control to local user groups with respect to their management. One notable aspect of this growing emphasis on community forestry in Nepal is that it has proven to be a reliable milk cow to attract **foreign aid**, much of which goes to the palace and to the pockets of political leaders, policymakers, and **elites**.

CONGRESS PARTY. *See* NEPALI CONGRESS PARTY.

CONSTITUTIONS. Not withstanding the Muluki Ain of 1854 (*see* **Civil Codes**), which was revised several times and which basically vested absolute power in the ruler (the **Rana** prime minister), Nepal's first major constitutional initiative was undertaken in 1947 by Padma Shamsher Rana, who was considered uncharacteristically liberal for a Rana prime minister. But the constitution itself was drafted in 1948 with the help of Indian advisers. It created a bicameral legislative body whose members were appointed by the Rana prime minister, and specified a **Panchayat** system of local governance at the village, town, and district levels. It also included certain fundamental rights and duties as well as the freedom of speech and of the press. Despite the incorporation of some reform measures, the constitution posed little threat to the prevailing autocratic Rana system.

Nonetheless the conservative Ranas were extremely unhappy with Padma Shamsher's constitutional initiative. Before it was passed and formally instituted, Padma Shamsher was forced out of office and the draft was suspended, thus rendering the constitution merely a draft, not a body of laws. In view of the gathering revolutionary rage against Rana autocracy, the draft was revived and implemented in September 1950 by Prime Minister **Mohan Shamsher Rana** to project the image of reform within the Rana system along democratic lines. What he hoped to achieve with that move was to dissipate the gathering anti-Rana rage. But the plan did not work. With the downfall of the Rana regime in February 1951, the constitution was nullified.

Then came the interim constitution of 1951 whose most notable feature was to reassert the **Shah** king's absolute executive, legislative, and judicial powers, which the Rana prime minister had usurped since the time of **Jang Bahadur Rana**. The king was free to appoint his advisory council at will until the constituent assembly was elected, with final authority resting with him to approve any legislative measures passed by his council. In its organic structure, the interim constitution was hardly any different from the Rana system. Although it was supposed to be only temporary, King **Tribhuvan Bir Bikram Shah** and his son King **Mahendra Bir Bikram Shah** could not resist holding on to it. However, under mounting pressure from those who had shed blood against the Rana regime and yearned for the dawn of democracy in Nepal, Mahendra was eventually forced to hold a national **election** to form a democratic government and to promulgate a new constitution, one that was firmly embedded in the fundamental principles of democracy.

In 1959, Mahendra, who was crowned in 1955 following his father's death, reluctantly granted a new constitution, a relatively democratic one as it was modeled on the constitutional systems of Great **Britain** and **India**. It confirmed a parliamentary system, including the **House of Representatives** that comprised 109 popularly elected members and was responsible for electing the prime minister to serve as the head of the government. However, the king was vested with the executive power and retained ultimate sovereignty, even though the document itself did not specify it explicitly. The constitution granted the king full power to scrap the parliamentary system and suspend the constitution under emergency conditions as he defined them. It was precisely this emergency power that Mahendra invoked in December 1960 to prematurely cut short the life of democracy some 15 months after the elected government of Prime Minister **Bishweswar Prasad (B. P.) Koirala** was inaugurated.

Once again, the king was the law of the land. Determined to formalize his absolute monarchy within a constitutional framework, Mahendra gave the country a new constitution in 1962. Known as the Panchayat constitution, it was carefully woven into what the king called the Panchayat system of governance, centered around the palace as the axis of absolute power. Both the Panchayat constitution and political system were disguised under what the king proclaimed as an indigenous framework of "guided democracy," one inherently rooted in and suited to the soil of Nepal. But the constitution was anything but democratic—guided or not. In reality, it was merely an instrument of legitimation of absolute monarchy, reminiscent of Rana autocracy.

In many respects, the new constitution was a revised version of the one that was formulated in 1948 during the reign of Padma Shamsher Rana. In fact, the system of Panchayat was almost literally lifted from that constitution as its basic format was replicated. One difference was that the framework was expanded from the local (village and town) and district levels of Panchayat to four tiers: local (village and town), district (*zilla*), zonal (***anchal***), and national (*rastriya*) Panchayats. In essence, the Panchayat constitution of 1962 vested complete constitutional power and authority in the king, who could suspend or amend it simply by royal proclamation.

Regardless of its content and orientation, it provided the framework for governance of Nepal and its citizens for nearly 30 years, notwithstanding occasional minor adjustments. When the Panchayat system suddenly disintegrated in 1990, the 1962 constitution was dismantled and later replaced by the democratic constitution of 1990, which was drafted and ratified under the interim democratic government headed by **Krishna Prasad Bhattarai** as prime minister. One fundamental feature of this constitution, which is largely based on the British parliamentary system, is that it has essentially eliminated the absolute power of the monarch, turning him into a constitutional one. It vests sovereignty in the people and grants them all democratic and **human rights**, including the freedom of thought, expression, and the **press**, all within the basic framework of the rule of law. In addition, it aims to establish an independent system of justice.

However, all these constitutional rights were suspended following the imposition of the state of emergency by the king on 26 November 2001 under the pretext of battling the Maoist movement (*see* **People's War**). The government has instituted nightly curfews since then, along with the banning of the freedom of assembly, expression, and the press. Since its first declaration, the state of emergency has been renewed twice, thus posing a grim threat to the whole framework of freedom and democracy. It is not clear when and if the state of emergency will be lifted. Since the **House of Representatives** has been dissolved, the emergency measures will continue at least until the next general election, which is scheduled to be held in mid-November 2002 to elect parliamentary members for the House. The constitutional fate of democracy may largely hinge on how the next House of Representatives handles the prevailing situation and on the response of the king as the commander in chief of the army.

COW. (*Gai* in Nepali.) National animal of Nepal. It is highly revered in **Hinduism** as a holy animal and mother figure. Nepal's legal codes prohibit killing of cows in any form and sale of beef. It is worshiped by Hindus as a personification of Goddess **Laxmi**. On various religious occasions and during certain rituals, cow dung and urine are used to purify houses and properties.

COOPERATIVES. Commonly known as *sajha sansthan* in Nepali, these are socioeconomic institutions. The Nepal government's Department of Cooperatives registers these bodies once they apply with a minimum deposit of 2,500 Nepalese rupees. At least 25 members are required to form a cooperative, which is authorized to accumulate savings and distribute credits in small areas. As soon as they are registered, they can start functioning as a financial institution or as a bank, but not necessarily required to do so. According to the Department of Cooperatives, there are 6,000 cooperatives registered in the country. Cooperatives have provided people in remote areas easy access to credit, especially for micro enterprises. One big problem with most of the cooperatives is that they are not operated by local citizens. As a result, the chances of abuse and misallocation of cooperative funds are relatively high. And there have indeed been reports of such abuses.

CRORE. Unit of measurement, used almost exclusively in the monetary context. One crore is equal to one hundred lakhs or ten million rupees.

D

DABUR NEPAL. Dabur Nepal produces Ayurvedic (homeopathic) medicines, usually made from plant extracts. Ayurvedic medicines, which have their roots in the Vedic tradition of **Hinduism**, have been used in Nepal for ages, both in crude and refined forms. What Dabur produces are considered refined and are sold in the open market and pharmacies, whereas the crude varieties serve as homemade concoctions and are normally prepared by individuals when they are needed. Once severely undercut by the penetration of Western medicines, this age-old medical practice is seeing a noticeable comeback and its resurgence has brought changes in the income of rural inhabitants of Nepal, as some are engaged in the production of medicinal plants. Dabur has set up, in recent years, three modern greenhouses and support facilities at Banepa with a capacity to produce three to four million medicinal plant saplings per annum in order to preserve and expand medicinal plants widely found in Nepal. Dabur has also established herbal farms in 11 districts of Nepal that occupy 50 hectares of land, where altogether one million medicinal plants are cultivated. *See also* HEALTH.

DAHAL, HOMA NATH (1941–). Journalist and politician, associated with the **Nepali Congress Party**. He is editor of *Rastrapukar*, a Nepali weekly that often promotes the party position. In 1990, he served as chairman of the Gorkhaptra Corporation, which publishes the country's oldest daily, the **Gorkhapatra**, and its English version, **The Rising Nepal**.

DAHAL, KHAGENDRA (1956–1974). Born in Okhaldhunga (*see* figure 2), he was a democratic fighter against the **Panchyat** system and was arrested when carrying explosive weapons into Nepal. He was killed near Nakhu Jail along with three other revolutionaries who were taken there under the pretext of transferring them to that jail.

DAHAL, LILANATH (1949–1974). Born in the Okhaldhunga district (*see* figure 2), he was passionately involved in anti-**Panchayat** activities. Inspired by **B. P. Koirala**, he came to Nepal from **India** to participate in the armed struggle against the Panchayat system in 1974. He was arrested and later shot dead near the Nakhu Jail the same year under the pretext of transferring him to that jail.

DAHAL, RAMNATH (1939–1972). Born in Tehrathum (*see* figure 2), Ramnath Dahal was a man of militant character. As an activist in the **Jhapa movement**, he organized local people against feudal oppression. He was arrested in 1972 and was implicated in the murder of Dharma Prasad Dhakal, a local landlord with considerable political influence. After being captured, he was taken to the Sukhani forest under the pretext of jail transfer and was murdered in cold blood along with four other activists in April 1972.

DAIBAGYA, JANANI DAS (1887–1980). A well-known choreographer who was responsible for the creation as well as performance of many ancient and traditional dances.

DAIRY DEVELOPMENT CORPORATION. Public firm engaged in the production and supply of milk and milk products. It was founded in 1952 and incorporated in 1969 under the Company Act of 1964.

DAKSHINKALI. Hindu religious/pilgrimage site within a small forest, southwest of **Kathmandu**. It has a famous temple of Goddess **Kali**, built by King **Pratap Malla**. It is one of the most popular temples for animal sacrifice, namely roosters, male ducks, and male goats. In general, Saturday is the day of worship and sacrifice. On any given Saturday, one can see a huge line of worshipers waiting for their turn. It is hardly unusual for worshipers to have to wait one to two hours in line. In addition to being a favorite religious site, it has emerged as one of the desired **tourist**

spots in the Valley, for it offers a living sight of the daily practice of **Hinduism** by the local people.

DAL. Lentils or pulses (commonly black, yellow, or red lentils); also soup made from them. It is normally eaten with boiled **rice** called *bhat*.

DAL-BHAT. A regular Nepali meal of **rice** and dal.

DALIT. Dalit is a generic term reserved for the untouchable **caste**. The term generally means the poor and oppressed people. As a caste group it includes all segments of the untouchables with various professional caste roles such as the **Chamar, Damai, Kami,** and **Sarki**. Although there does exist a Dalit association (**Dalit Sangha**), the term is less common in Nepal than it is in **India**. *See also* UNTOUCHABILITY.

DALIT SANGHA. Association of the oppressed, i.e., ex-untouchables.

DAMAI. Ex-untouchable professional **caste**; also referred to as Darji in certain communities. Traditionally, their caste-based occupation is tailoring. The institutionalized **Hindu** practice of caste **untouchability** (or caste pollution) was outlawed in 1963.

DANCE. *See* MUSIC AND DANCE.

DANDI BIYO. Old-fashioned Nepali sport, similar to cricket. It is played between two teams with one long and one short stick, generally in an open field. Once a very popular form of entertainment and socialization for local teenagers, it is basically extinct; it is rarely played these days.

DANG. Inner **Tarai** district in the **Rapti Zone**, with a 1991 population of 352,237, spread over an area of 2,555 sq km. Situated on the south side of the **Churia Hills** (Siwalik Range), its physiographic condition is quite similar to that of **Chitwan**. It is the primary domain of the **Danguria Tharus**, many of whom have relocated further west to Banke, Bardiya, and Kanchanpur districts within the Tarai (*see* figure 2).

DANGAURA THARU. Tharu people concentrated in **Dang**, Banke, and Kanchanpur districts. They are akin to other Tharu groups in different parts of the **Tarai**, including the **Chitwan** Tharus. Their major occupation is farming and they follow **Hinduism**.

DANPHE. Impeyjean pheasant. Found in mountainous areas, it is Nepal's national bird.

DANUWAR. Small ethnic group found in the low hills and in the **Tarai**.

DARAI. Small ethnic group similar to **Danuwar** concentrated in the inner **Tarai**.

DARJEELING. Town and district in West Bengal, adjacent to Nepal's eastern border with **India**. It was once a part of Nepal before it was ceded to British India by the **Treaty of Sagauli** (1816), following the **Anglo-Nepal War**. It has a large Nepali population and has long been a leading hub of Nepali **literature** and **music**, at times serving as an epicenter of new trends within Nepal. It also supplies a large pool of teachers for many of the private schools in **Kathmandu**.

DARNAL, RAM SHARAN (1937–). A musician and researcher who has been associated with the **Royal Nepal Academy** since 1959. He is also the author of several books and articles on Nepali folk **music** and musical instruments, e.g., *Nepali Sangeet Sadhak* (1981), *Sangeetko Bishtrit Avalokan* (1984), and *Sangeet Parikrama* (1981).

DAS, GYAN DIL (1821–1883). Born in eastern Nepal, Gyan Dil Das occupies an eminent place in Nepali **literature**, mainly because of his literary activism, for which the **Ranas** persecuted him. In other words, he used literature as a voice of revolution against the Ranas. As a result, he was exiled in **Darjeeling**. He was openly opposed to discrimination and Brahmanism.

DAS PRATHA. (*Das* = slave; *pratha* = tradition.) *See* SLAVERY.

DASHAIN. Also known as **Bijaya Dashami**, it is the most important and biggest **Hindu** festival which is celebrated throughout the country with great fanfare. It is also Nepal's longest holiday season when all government offices are closed for two weeks. It involves 10 (or 15) continuous days of festivities and worshiping, including massive male animal (e.g., buffaloes, goats, roosters, and ducks) sacrifices in commemoration of Goddess **Durga** for her victory over a marauding demon named Mahishura. During the festival, 100 buffalos are slaughtered inside the **Hanuman** Dhoka in **Kathmandu**. The whole courtyard is littered with a massive amount of blood. To some it is a gross, bloody scene, while for many Hindus it is simply an integral part of religious celebration. Regardless of one's outlook, however, buffalo slaughtering inside the Hanuman Dhoka is a scene to behold.

Because its arrival is always determined in accordance with the lunar calendar, the timing of this festival varies from year to year. Generally it falls in October, almost immediately after the **rice** harvest season is over. As a result, the period of celebration rarely conflicts with the farming tasks. During this festival, gifts are given. This is particularly true for children who receive new clothes and other gifts from their parents and seniors. On the 10th day, the head of the household blesses all family members by placing a red *tika* on their foreheads. Given the fact that there is so much social pressure on families to celebrate it with as much pomp and show as they can, many plunge into debt, often mortgaging their land and pawning their gold ornaments and other valuable possessions. Some never recuperate from it. That is why *Dashain* is often referred to as *dasha* (misery).

DASHARATH STADIUM. Nepal's oldest and largest sporting stadium located in **Kathmandu**. It was named after the martyr **Dasharath Chand**.

DATTATRAYA. Magnificent temple in the **Bhaktapur Durbar Square**. It was built in 1428 by King Yaksha Malla.

DAURA. Loose shirt-type garment. Also called *labeda*, it is mostly worn with *suruwal*. When paired together, they constitute the national dress for men.

DAURA-SURUWAL. Nepali national dress for men, often worn with the Nepali *topi* (cap). It is compulsory for government officials holding high ranking positions to wear this national dress during office hours.

DEEPAWALI. *See* TIHAR.

DEHRADUN. Part of **India** located in its northwestern region. Once a part of the Nepali territory, it was ceded to British India by the terms of the **Treaty of Sagauli** concluded in 1816. It is also a place where many well-off Nepali families send their children to boarding schools for English education.

DEMOCRACY DAY. Called the Rastriya Prajatantra Diwas in Nepali (i.e., national democracy day), it is the day when the **Rana** regime fell. Because of its historic significance, it is designated as a national holiday, observed on 7 Falgun (February; see **Nepali Calendar**). Throughout the country, people organize various programs, including processions in which students at all levels participate with significant fanfare. It was technically a day of liberation.

DESH **(DESA).** Nation, also connotes one's motherland. It is the opposite of *bidesh* (foreign land or country).

DESHI **(DESI).** For some, this word can be quite confusing, for it is used in two distinct contexts. In one sense, it usually means a native of the plains of **India**. In its vernacular use, however, the term often refers to anybody from India (or even to the **Tarai** residents of Indian origin). They are also called the *madhesi* because both words carry the same colloquial connotation. The second meaning of this word, on the other hand, is distinctly nationalistic as it is a synonym for the word *sowdeshi* (meaning anything pertaining or belonging to one's own nation). Both *deshi* and *sowdeshi* are used interchangeably, often to invoke (and provoke) a deep sense of patriotism in a manner that is identical to the popular American slogan of "Buy American." The opposite word of *deshi* is *bideshi* (foreigner or something foreign in origin). In fact, Mahatma Gandhi not only popularized the word *sowdeshi*, but actually deployed it as a powerful ideological weapon of nationalism during his anti-colonial "Quit India" movement against the British. One difference between *deshi* and *swodeshi* is that the former can be applied to both people and objects, whereas the latter is mostly used to denote something indigenous.

DEUKI. Also called Devadashi, a Deuki is a young unmarried **woman** offered to a religious shrine or temple as part of some religious act. She often serves as an attendant at the temple and is expected to remain celibate throughout her life. In reality, however, most Deukis are used as sex workers in their communities.

DEUBA, SHER BAHADUR (1946–). Longtime career politician from the Dadeldhura district, which is located in the far western hills of Nepal (*see* figure 2). He has spent much of his life advancing the political interest of the **Nepali Congress Party** (NCP), of which he is a high-ranking member. He has been active in Nepali Congress politics since his student days as president (1971–1973) of the Nepal Students' Union, a student wing of the party. As a political leader, he first came to national prominence in 1996 when he was voted by his party to head the Congress government. Within less than a year, he was forced to resign as prime minister. He rose to power once again in July 2001 when he replaced **Girija Prasad Koirala** as prime minister of the current Congress government. He assumed prime ministership for the second time with a commitment to end the ongoing **People's War** through negotiations. But he failed to achieve that goal in November 2001.

After that, Deuba adamantly refused to engage in a negotiated settlement with the Maoists. Instead, he set aside the fundamental democratic principle of his own party and openly supported King **Gyanendra Bir Bikram Shah**'s anti-democratic state of emergency measures, a situation which is pregnant with the potential to return monarchy to the position of absolute power which it enjoyed prior to 1990. In May 2002, he paid a state visit to President George W. Bush in the **United States** and Prime Minister Tony Blair in England to beg for military aid and other support to root out what he calls "Maoist terrorism." He played the "terrorism" card quite well with the ideological axis of the Bush and Blair administrations that are apparently flush with money and military hardware to support any government that promises to wage an all-out war against "terrorism," a much-dreaded word in today's global arena. Backed by Bush and Blair, Deuba was determined to crush the Maoist movement regardless of the enormous cost to human lives and to the **economy**.

In late May, when it became clear that he was going to lose the vote of confidence in the **House of Representatives,** Prime Minister Deuba asked King Gyanendra to dissolve Parliament so he could remain in power until the next **elections**. His action led to the split of the NCP into two factions, one controlled by himself and another by Girija Prasad Koirala. Subsequently, in mid-September, Nepal's election commission refused to recognize Deuba's breakaway faction as the official Nepali

Congress Party. That decision was a big setback for him as it severely undercut his faction's chances of doing well in the elections.
Nonetheless, Deuba did not stop his political maneuvering to prolong his power. On 3 October, the prime minister asked the king to postpone the elections scheduled for November 2002. Ironically, King Gyanendra seized the opportunity presented by Deuba's request to dismiss him, sack his entire cabinet, assume executive powers, and, at the same time, postpone the elections indefinitely—all with one short announcement on 4 October. Thus, Deuba was wittingly or unwittingly instrumental in what can be considered a palace-led abortion of Nepal's nascent democracy.

DEVANAGARI. Official script of the Nepali language as well as Hindi and **Sanskrit**.

DEVIGHAT HYDROELECTIC PLANT. Hydroelectric power station at Devighat which is located in the district of Nuwakot. Built in 1983 with **Indian** assistance, it has a capacity to generate 14,100 kilowatts of energy. Much of its capacity is utilized to supply electricity to the **Kathmandu Valley** where the demand appears steep.

DEVI, LEELA. First Nepali **woman** to receive a Ph.D. She received her degree in home economics in 1968 from Southern Illinois University in the **United States**.

DEVI, TARA (1945–). A popular female singer, she is associated with **Radio Nepal**. In many respects, she is a trailblazer who opened the door for many future female singers in Nepal. Her contribution to the field of Nepali **music** is undoubtedly significant and will continue to shine for many years to come. To this day, she is a household name in Nepal.

DEVKOTA, BACHASPATI (1944–). Leftist politician and activist. He began his career in 1958 and remained underground for several years. Charged with inciting anti-national and anti-king views, he was jailed for eight years during the **Panchayat** system.

DEVKOTA, GOVINDA PRASAD (1954–). Leading expert in the area of biogas technology, which has emerged as a viable source of energy in the country. Govinda Devkota is perhaps Nepal's best-known native biogas specialist. Along with various waste products, animal dung is being increasingly used to generate biogas in different parts of Nepal.

DEVKOTA, LAXMI PRASAD (1909–1959). One of the most versatile literary figures of modern Nepal and Nepali **literature**, he wrote epics, plays, poems, essays, short stories, and novels. In a relatively short space of 25 years of his literary career, he produced more than forty books. Many regard him as the father of modern poetry in Nepal. It is no wonder that he was bestowed with the honorific title of Maha Kabi (Great Poet). He was once a professor of English and, for a brief period, served as assistant minister for education during the **Panchayat** period. Devkota occasionally composed poems in English as well as translated English poems. *Muna Madan* (The Story of Muna), which is described as a *khanda kavya*, an episodic poem or mini epic, is perhaps his most famous literary work, and definitely the one he cherished most. On his death bed, he said no matter what happened to his other works, *Muna Madan* should be saved.

What one sees in Devkota is a reflection of the Romantic era in Nepali literature. As Michael Hutt, a well-known British scholar of Nepali literature, remarked, "[W]hen a truly great poet appears during an important phase in the development of a particular literature, the fortunes of that literature are changed forever." And Devkota was that great poet that changed the fortunes of Nepali literature. His place in the literature of Nepal is firmly secure as he remains a household name to this day. With the exception of **Bhanu Bhakta Acharya**, not many Nepali literary figures can match his stature and contributions.

DEVKOTA, RAJESWOR P. (1929–). Politician and novelist from the **Gorkha** district (*see* figure 2). He is a relatively obscure figure amongst both Nepali political leaders and literary figures despite the fact that he once served as deputy prime minister under the **Panchayat** system.

DEVKOTA, RHISHI (1944–1980). Born in a peasant family, Devkota was a communist revolutionary and a true adherent of Marxism. He was an unrepentant believer in the cause of class struggle, spending much of his time propagating his hardline Marxist views and anti-king stance. He was arrested and brutally killed in Sindhuli in 1980.

DHAKAL, BIRMANI (1947–). Politician from **Jhapa** (*see* figure 2). He began his long political career as a member of the Nepal Students' Union. As an ardent member of the **Nepali Congress Party** and the Upper House of the **Parliament**, he once served as minister of forest and soil conservation after 1990.

DHAKAL, NARAYAN (1953–). Leftist journalist and editor of *Drishti*, a weekly Nepali newspaper published in **Kathmandu**. He has used his newspaper as a media platform to promote leftist political views and agenda over the years.

DHAMI. Traditional healer and channel in Nepal's shamanistic system. In some cases, it is also a surname.

DHAMI, PREMSINGH (1952–1997). Uncompromising patriot from the district of Darchula (*see* figure 2). A central member of the **Communist Party of Nepal** (UML), Dhami adhered to Marxism and Leninism. Dhami was a theoretician of the party as demonstrated by his theoretical writings. He died in a jeep accident at Keureni in the Nuwakot district.

DHANGADHI-DADELDHURA ROAD. This is a highway in the far western hills of Nepal. About 140 kilometers long, it runs in a north-south direction, linking the districts of Dhangadhi and Dadeldhura (*see* figure 2). It is major feeder road, partly constructed with American assistance.

DHANGAR. Small ethnic group around **Janakpur**, largely dependent on farming. They generally follow **Hinduism** as their primary religion.

DHANKUTA. District in the **Kosi Zone**, with a population of 146,724 in 1991, distributed over an area of 891 sq. km. (*see* figure 2). It is well known for oranges and a medicinal herb called *chiraito*.

DHANKUTA INDUSTRIAL DISTRICT. Industrial area in **Dhankuta**. It was founded by the Nepal government in 1984.

DHANUSHA SAGAR. Holy pond in **Janakpur** where **Hindus** bathe.

DHARAHARA. Nepal's tallest monument located in the central district of **Kathmandu**. It is a Mugal-style minaret, first built in 1832 by Prime Minister **Bhimsen Thapa**. It is also called Bhimsen Stambha. It was later reconstructed and repaired following significant damage caused by a massive **earthquake** in the mid-1930s.

DHARAN. Commercial center and municipality in the district of Sunsari. It includes an industrial district. Until 1990, it also served as the eastern center of British **Gorkha** recruitment, particularly designed to recruit **Rais** and **Limbus**. It has a population of 68,173 (1991).

DHARAN INDUSTRIAL DISTRICT. Industrial area in **Dharan**. It was founded in 1975 with Indian aid. Products include polyethylene pipes.

DHARMA. It is a **Hindu** concept that is applied in **Buddhism** as well. Dharma can be loosely defined as religious acts and obligations that one is expected to perform. In other words, according to the Hindu belief system, individuals should play their proper role in society as prescribed by their dharma. In view of this belief, the **caste system** has incorporated it as a caste duty, simply because a person is born into a particular caste, whose traditional occupation is graded according to the degree of inherent caste purity and impurity. In other words, every caste has its own prescribed functional caste role or duty that its members are expected or even obligated to carry out. Logically then, one's caste role turns into his or her dharmic duty. The other side of the Hindu configuration of dharma is **karma** which is loosely defined as universal justice or outcome of dharmic acts.

DHARMA SHASTRA. Generic term of compilations of **Hindu** laws and codes of conduct ascribed to the legendary sage Manu.

DHARMSALA. Religious shelter. Some of these shelters are built near river banks (ghats) where dying **Hindus** are sometimes taken so they may expire in peace by a holy river, e.g., the **Bagmati River**.

DHARNI. Unit of Nepali weight measurement. One Dharni is roughly equal to 2.2 kilograms.

DHAULAGIRI. With a height of 8,167 meters, Dhaulagiri is the seventh highest **mountain** peak in the world. Located to the northwest of **Pokhara**, Dhaulagiri's crest stretches approximately 50 kilometers. The name of the **Dhaulagiri Zone** is derived from this peak, which is quite popular among mountaineers.

DHAULAGIRI ZONE. Named after the **Dhaulagiri** peak, it is located in the north central part of Nepal (see figure 3). It consists of four districts: **Mustang, Baglung,** Parbat, and Myagdi. In 1991, its population totaled 491,729 people, spread across 8,143 sq. km.

DHIGUR. System of financial pools organized by local people to raise capital. Members contribute an equal amount of money, usually on a monthly basis, and take turns to collect the total sum. Members' turns are decided on a lottery basis or through mutual agreements.

DHITAL, BHARAT PRASAD (1933–2002). An agroeconomist by training, he served as the first executive director of the **Agricultural Projects Services Centre** during 1975–1988 and vice chairman of the **National Planning Commission** from 1988 to 1990. For a long time he has acted as a leading voice of modernization patterned after the Western trajectory of development.

DHOBI. Professional **caste** group that does laundry cleaning. *See also* UNTOUCHABILITY.

DHORPATAN WILDLIFE RESERVE. Wildlife reserve covering 803 sq. km. around a place called Dhorpatan in the **Baglung** district (see figure 2). Known for thar, ratuwa (barking deer), bears, leopards, and other animals, the reserve extends into Rukum and Myagdi districts.

DHOTI. Traditional male garment in the **Tarai** and **India** worn exclusively by men. It is wrapped around the upper legs, but its length from the waist down varies considerably from place to place as well as from person to person, depending on their preference. Within Nepal, one can see individuals wearing dhotis outside of the Tarai.

DHOTIWALA. Technically, dhoti wearer, but the term is also used in a derogatory manner to denote those from the **Tarai** and from **India**.

DHUNGANA, DAMAN NATH (1942–). A politician and lawyer in Kathmandu who is a high-ranking member of the **Nepali Congress Party**. After the **Panchayat** system was abolished, he was appointed to served as a member of what was called the Constitution Recommendation Commission in 1990. Following his election to the **House of Representatives** in 1991, he was elected to be the first speaker of the House in the post-Panchayat era.

DHUNGANA, PUNYA PRABHADEVI (1924–). As a politician, she is an active advocate of **women's** causes. She was appointed to serve as president of the Nepal Women's Organization for four years (1971–1975) and of the International Women's Year Nepal Committee in 1975.

DIBYA UPADESH (UPADES). Collection of **Prithvi Narayan Shah's** reminiscences and guidelines (quotations) regarding national policies, politics, and economy, including trade and commerce.

DIPLOMATIC RELATIONS. Nepal's history reveals that its foreign relations date back to the **Licchavi period**. During that time, Nepal's contacts were mainly limited to **India, Tibet,** and **China**. The circle gradually expanded with the passage of time. As seen from the following list, Nepal has established diplomatic relationships with 100 countries in Africa, Asia, Europe, Latin America, and North America:

Country	Established	Country	Established
Afghanistan	1961	Brunei	1984
Albania	1968	Bulgaria	1968
Argentina	1962	Cambodia	1975
Armenia	1993	Canada	1965
Australia	1960	Chile	1962
Azerbaidzhan	1995	China	1955
Bahrain	1977	Colombia	1987
Bangladesh	1972	Costa Rica	1977
Belarus	1993	Croatia	1998
Belgium	1963	Cuba	1975
Bhutan	1983	Cyprus	1980
Bolivia	1987	Czech Republic	1960
Brazil	1976	Egypt	1975

Estonia	1992	Mozambique	1986
Ethiopia	1971	Myanmar	1960
Fiji	1986	Netherlands	1960
Finland	1974	New Zealand	1961
France	1949	Nigeria	1975
Gabon	1985	Oman	1977
Germany	1958	Pakistan	1960
Greece	1960	Peru	1976
Guyana	1994	Philippines	1960
Iceland	1981	Poland	1969
Indonesia	1960	Portugal	1976
India	1947	Romania	1968
Iran	1964	Russia	1989
Iraq	1968	Saudi Arabia	1977
Israel	1960	Seychelles	1986
Italy	1959	Singapore	1969
Japan	1956	Slovak Republic	1994
Jordan	1965	Slovenia	1997
Kenya	1975	Somalia	1984
Korea (North)	1974	South Africa	1994
Korea (South)	1974	Spain	1968
Kuwait	1972	Sri Lanka	1957
Kyrgyzstan	1993	Sweden	1960
Laos	1960	Switzerland	1959
Latvia	1992	Tanzania	1975
Lebanon	1963	Thailand	1960
Libya	1975	Tunisia	1984
Luxembourg	1975	Turkey	1962
Macedonia	1998	Ukraine	1993
Malaysia	1980	United Arab Emirates	1977
Maldives	1980	United Kingdom	1934
Malta	1983	United States	1951
Mauritius	1981	Vatican City	1983
Mexico	1975	Venezuela	1987
Moldova	1993	Vietnam	1975
Mongolia	1961	Yemen	1975
Morocco	1975		

DISTRICT DEVELOPMENT COMMITTEE. Composed of elected members at the district level, it is responsible for formulating district-level development policies. It was formed in 1990, following the end of the **Panchayat** system.

DISTRICT PANCHAYAT. Known as Zilla **Panchayat** in Nepali, it was one of the four administrative divisions during the Panchayat system (1962–1990). During the Panchayat time, the country was divided into a total of 75 districts, and they were retained intact as political administrative and electoral units to elect the members of the **House of Representatives** in the post-Panchayat period.

DIVAS, TULSI (1933–). Original name: Tulsi Prasad Joshi. He is a poet and scholar from the **Dhankuta** district in eastern Nepal (*see* figure 2). He is the author of a book on the Dhimal ethnic group and of *Nepali Lok Katha* (Nepali folklore).

DIXIT, KAMAL MANI ACHARYA (1929–). Essayist, literary critic, and poet. He is the author of several literary books. From 1965 until 1972, he was chairman of Sajha Prakashan, a leading Nepali book publisher based in **Kathmandu**. *See also* LITERATURE.

DIXIT, KEDAR MANI ACHARYA (1904–1992). Litterateur and travel writer. He has written many travel accounts, including his 1965 book, *Belayat Janda* (which roughly means "While Visiting England"). He was the founding president of Madan Puraskar Guthi (Madan Award Foundation), which was created to recognize literary achievements and contributions of Nepali authors. *See also* LITERATURE.

DIXIT, MADAN MANI (1923–). Novelist and journalist. His literary works include *Towards Mega-Hiroshima* and *Madhavi* (based on Vedic society). He was also the editor of *Samiksha* (*Samichhya*), a Nepali weekly that he started publishing in 1954. The newspaper was acclaimed for its critical analysis, pointed views, and journalistic sophistication. During the Cold War era, the paper was known to be supportive of the former Soviet position in international affairs. On the domestic front, it was highly critical of the **Panchayat** system. As a result, it was often banned. For a period of five years (1994–1999), Dixit was vice-chancellor of the

Royal Nepal Academy, a period which he now considers wasted years of his life. He spent 30 years working for the **Communist Party of Nepal**.

DOG'S DAY. *See* KUKUR TIHAR.

DOLPA. Located in the **Karnali Zone**, it is the largest and least-densely populated district of Nepal (*see* figure 2), with a 1991 population of 25,075, spread over an area of 7,889 sq. km. Although one of the most remote areas in the nation, it includes the **She-Phoksundo National Park**.

DOLPO. Generic term for the people inhabiting the Dolpo area in **Dolpa**. As part of their religious belief, they follow **Lamaism**, a variation of **Buddhism**. Polyandry is practiced to some extent among the Dolpos.

DOLPO VALLEY. Region in **Dolpa**. This is where the Phoksundo lake and the **She-Phoksundo National Park** are situated.

DOTI. District in the far western **Seti Zone** of Nepal (*see* figure 2), with a total 1991 population of 167,469, spread over an area of 2,023 sq. km. Located in the hills, Doti is believed to be one of the poorest districts in Nepal, in fact so poor that it resides at the core of a poverty metaphor which says, "*Gayo doti, khayo* **dhoti**." It literally means "if one goes to Doti, he will have to eat (or sell) his dhoti to survive."

DRINKING WATER CORPORATION. Public enterprise established in 1973 for supplying drinking water in cities, namely **Kathmandu** and **Patan**.

DUBO. Common grass (*Synodon dactylon*) having cultural and religious significance, especially among the **Hindus**. Regarded as immortal grass, dubo is used during certain ceremonies, especially during the of the elephant-headed god named **Ganesh**.

DUGAR, GYAN CHAND (1942–). Industrialist from **Biratnagar**. He is the managing director of several **industries** including the Hulas Metal Crafts company that produces stainless steel utensils, mostly for the domestic market.

DUGAR, KISHAN LAL (1943–). Industrialist and modern farmer from **Biratnagar**. He established solvent **industries**, a starboard factory, and rice mills in eastern Nepal.

DUGAR, TOLA RAM (1932–). Industrialist from **Morang**. Founder of several industrial and business concerns in **Biratnagar**. There is little doubt about his role in Nepal's **industrialization** and his prominent place among the leading industrialists in the country.

DURA. Small tribal group concentrated in Dura Danda, which is located in the district of Lamjung (*see* figure 2). They resemble the **Gurung** ethnic group in appearance. Their number is believed to be dwindling, perhaps down to just a few hundred.

DURBAR HIGH SCHOOL. Nepal's first high school, it is located in **Kathmandu**. It was founded by **Jang Bahadur Rana** in 1853 after his return from his European tour in 1851 to provide systematic or formal **education** to **Rana** children within a palace (*durbar*) setting. *See also* EDUCATION.

DURBAR SQUARE. Courtyard around a palace (*durbar*). Surrounded by various temples, statues, and quaint shops, it is a famous tourist spot in **Patan**. Although both **Kathmandu** and **Bhaktapur** have their own respective *durbar* squares, the **Patan Durbar Square** (or simply Durbar Square) is the one that is most commonly recognized in the parlance of **tourism** centered in the **Kathmandu Valley**.

DURGA. Mother goddess endowed with enormous power, who is similar to Goddess **Kali** in many respects. Some believe that they are two sisters, with Durga having a fair face and Kali a black face (*kali* literally means "a woman with a dark complexion"). Durga is the central deity of the **Dashain** festival which is celebrated by the **Hindus** with great pomp, devotion, and animal sacrifice.

DURGAM CHHETRA BIKAS SAMITI. Remote Areas Development Committee constituted for the development of Nepal's remote areas, especially its far western hills (*see* figure 2), which are considered to be the poorest districts in the country.

DWIBEDI, SURENDRA RAJ (1943–). A career journalist who once served as deputy chief editor of the *Gorkhapatra* (1990–1991). He is the chief editor of the children's monthly magazine, *Muna*, published by the **Gorkhapatra Corporation**.

E

EARTHQUAKES. In Nepali, it is called *bhukampa* (*bhu* = earth; *kampa* = quake; tremor.) Nepal has experienced many earthquakes. This is not extraordinary in light of the fact that the **mountains** are still growing because of the continuing northward tectonic thrust of the Indian subcontinent. It is believed that the draining of the lake hundreds of years ago in what is now the **Kathmandu Valley** was caused by an earthquake. Perhaps the most destructive tremor in recent times occurred in 1934 around 2 o'clock in the afternoon. Generally known as the Nepal-Bihar earthquake or *mahabhukampa* (great earthquake), it measured about eight on the Richter scale, with the shocks lasting two to three minutes. The number of people who were killed in the earthquake totaled 8,519 and a quarter of a million homes were destroyed. Many families had to live in tents set up at **Tundikhel**, an open space in the middle of **Kathmandu**. Many towns and villages were severely damaged. Because the Kathmandu Valley was the most developed (built-up) environment in the country, it suffered the greatest loss in terms of human casualties and property destruction. One interesting sidelight is that while many buildings were ruined and people killed, famous wooden temples were spared. Folk tales ascribe the salvation of the temples to various gods, particularly **Bhairav**.

EAST INDIA COMPANY. Originally a commercial firm set up in Great **Britain**, the company became a potent political power in its own right, at times indistinguishable from the British monarchy, especially in terms of its colonial impacts. The company's greatest influence in Nepal was felt during the late eighteenth and early nineteenth centuries. Conflicts between Nepal and company forces eventually led to the **Anglo-Nepal War**, the signing of the **Treaty of Sagauli** in 1816, and the subsequent establishment of the British residency in **Kathmandu**. In addition, the British were allowed to openly engage in massive recruitment of Nepali youth for the imperial army. *See also* BRITAIN-NEPAL RELATIONS; GORKHAS.

ECLIPSE. *See CHANDRA GRAHAN; SURYA GRAHAN.*

ECONOMY. According to a report released by the **World Bank** in 2002, with an annual per capita income of $220, Nepal is the twelfth poorest country in the world. Even within South Asia, a region with one of the lowest per capita incomes in the world, Nepal ranks toward the very bottom.

In 1999, the only year for which the Asian Development Bank has compiled Nepal's employment data, the country's labor force totaled 9.64 million people or 43 percent of the total population. Of the total labor force, **agriculture** employed 75 percent. Manufacturing and mining, on the other hand, employed barely 6 percent, whereas the service sector generated almost 18 percent of employment. Those who were unemployed constituted less than 2 percent of the labor force. However, this unemployment picture is distorted. According to a report prepared by the Asian Development Bank, Nepal suffered from 47 percent underemployment in 1999–2000. And for the same year, urban unemployment was as high as 7 percent, a figure which is believed to have deteriorated in 2001.

It is quite unlikely that this picture of employment structure has changed much since then. The agricultural sector (including **forests** and fisheries) contributed close to 39 percent of the national GDP in 2002. The service sector's share in the GDP was almost 40 percent and the rest came from **industry**. Within the service sector, **tourism** was a very important activity in terms of hard currency earnings. In addition, it was instrumental in the growth and expansion of the nation's two principal exports—**carpets** and **garments**, which are not only key to the industrial sector, but also are major hard-currency earners.

The relatively high rates of economic growth that started in the late 1990s continued in 2001 when Nepal's GDP grew 5 percent. Despite some good showing in recent years, by most accounts Nepal underwent a significant economic downturn in 2002, mainly because of increased attacks and counterattacks between the Nepali army and Maoist forces. Moreover, the annual economic growth rate over the last two decades has averaged hardly 2.5 percent. That is, economic growth barely kept pace with the country's population growth over the same period. It is, therefore, no surprise that the nation remained heavily dependent on **foreign aid**, with 58 percent of development expenditures in 2001 being financed by external loans and grants. Overall, foreign debts accounted for 47 percent of GDP, and the national budget deficit stood at 4.2 percent of GDP.

Much of Nepal's economic success during the 1990s resulted from macroeconomic stability and liberalization and **privatization**. The economy became much more open with increasing **foreign trade** fueling its growth—especially exports to both advanced countries and India (which accounts for 40 percent of total exports and imports). However, although growth increased and became more broad-based (*see* tables 5–7), this performance could not be sustained in the face of external economic shocks and internal political instability. The global economic slowdown starting in 2000 and worsening in the aftermath of 11 September 2001 has impacted Nepal's economy rather harshly; its key economic activities such as exports as well as hotel and **tourism** have taken a heavy beating.

Continued political instability in the country, with frequent government shuffling and reshuffling, has engendered an ongoing crisis of confidence and undermined the economy. In addition, recent escalation of violence resulting from the armed struggle between the army and Maoist forces (i.e., the **People's War**) has exacted a heavy toll from the economy that was already teetering at the margin. The situation is further aggravated by growing fiscal pressures. State revenue collections have fallen in recent months while expenditures and domestic borrowing have increased. As a result, the risk of fiscal instability is growing.

As indicated earlier, Nepal's export sector has witnessed a major setback. Both carpet and apparel (garment) exports declined in 2001 according to most news reports. What is more, the prospect of their immediate rebound looks quite dim because of the continued global economic slowdown that is affecting most advanced countries—the primary destinations of the country's relatively high-valued carpet and garment exports.

As a leading loan institution closely guiding Nepal's development process, the **World Bank** has come to the general conclusion that the country is at a crossroads regarding its development process. Medium-term growth prospects are under threat due to external shocks and slow implementation of reforms. Also, poor governance, rising insecurity, and political instability are greatly hindering human development and **poverty** reduction. The government has responded to these challenges by declaring a state of emergency and directly confronting the threat to security posed by Maoist insurgencies. But they have failed to yield any tangible results in terms of reversing the current economic course. How long the Nepali economy will remain entrenched in its present predicament is a big question that is hard to answer at this point with any degree of certainty.

Nepal's Basic Economic Indicators	Year
Nominal Gross Domestic Product by Sector (in billion/Nepali rupees)	Projected for 2002
Agriculture (plus fisheries and forestry)	164.9
Industry	92.7
Mining	(2.2)
Manufacturing	(40.9)
Electricity and water	(7.0)
Construction	(42.6)
Services	168.9
Transport and communications	(34.1)
Trade, restaurants, and hotels	(50.3)
Financial and real estate	(43.3)
Community and social services	(41.2)
Total GDP at factor cost	**426.5**
Percentage Share in Nominal GDP by Sector	
Agriculture	38.7
Industry	21.7
Services	39.6
GDP by Expenditure Components	Estimates for 2001
Consumption	343.6
Public	(41.7)
Private	(301.9)
Gross domestic investment	105.0
Gross fixed investment	(78.4)
Public	(31.3)
Private	(47.1)
Change in stock	(26.6)

Trade Balance	− 34.1
Exports	(95.9)
Imports	(130.0)

Source: World Bank (www.worldbank.org.np)

Labor Force (population in million)	1999
Employed	9.46
Agriculture	7.20
Manufacturing	0.55
Mining	0.01
Others (service and government)	1.70
Unemployed	0.18
Total	**9.64**

Central Government Finance (in million/Nepali rupees)	2001
Current Revenue	49,606.8
Taxes	38,770.8
Non-taxes	10,836.0
Current Expenditure (regular)	43,460.9
Current surplus/deficit	6,145.9
Capital Receipts	–
Capital Expenditure	39,763.9
Capital account surplus/deficit	−39,763.9
Net Lending	–
Overall surplus deficit	−33,618.0
Financing	
Domestic borrowing	7,000.0
Foreign borrowing	15,941.1
Foreign grants	9,677.2
Use of cash balance	999.7

Central Government Expenditure by Function	2001
General Public Services	8,112.0
Defense	3,867.2
Education	11,778.2
Health	3,682.2
Social Security/Welfare	3,633.9

| Housing/Amenities (drinking water/local development) | 7,822.4 |

Economic Services	26,308.8
Agriculture	(9,130.2)
Industry	(5,71.2)
Electricity, gas, and water	(7,929.9)
Transport and communications	(6,970.5)
Other economic services	(1,707.0)
Others	12,369.5

Source: Asian Development Bank (www.adb.org).

EDUCATION. Historically, the educational system of Nepal was based on what can be called the **Sanskritic** education, often carried out at some local **Bahun**'s home or in a local *pathsala*, a small schoolhouse, containing one or two rooms. Children sat on the mud floor—or, in some cases, on straw or bamboo mats—held their slate boards, faced the teacher, and mostly recited or wrote down what the teacher said. It was replete with a great deal of parroting. In many respects, education occurred in an informal setting and was limited to basics. Those with higher aspirations went to what could be essentially described as religious schools where they learned **Hindu** epics, **literature**, and philosophy—or simply *Vedanta*. Some sent their children to **India**, where one could not only receive a higher quality of education, but also advanced and formal degrees.

Perhaps the most important feature of the old educational system was that it was basically confined to the Bahuns and **Chhetris**. In essence, education was treated as a distinct **caste** privilege and monopoly or even duty, although some filtered down to the **Vaisyas**, namely, the upper-class **Newars**. Education was rarely viewed as a vehicle of national progress and prosperity or the upliftment of the masses. The **Sudras** were denied any form of education because of their caste status. They were not only seen as intellectually inferior, but their caste roles required no education—so no need to educate them.

Following the establishment of **Rana** autocracy in 1846, the old tradition of and perspective on education remained intact. In fact, the notion of education was given an oppressive ideological twist by the Ranas. As the Rana rulers feared an educated population, they were bent on limiting public access to education. They viewed education as a source of social consciousness and public agitation which, as their thinking went, would eventually lead to their own political destruction. The only interest that they demonstrated in education was the education of the Ranas.

The Ranas, however, did see the class benefit of the non-Sanskritic education for their children. Specifically, after his European tour in 1850–1851, **Jang Bahadur Rana** realized the importance of English in communication with the outside world. As a result, he chose to give his children an English education rather than the religiously oriented education in the Sanskritic tradition. In 1853, he brought two teachers from England and engaged them to hold classes for his and other Rana children in his palace. In addition, other teachers were recruited from Bengal, India, for his school, which was descriptively named the Durbar (palace) School. It was later renamed the **Durbar High School**. Jang Bahadur's action eventually tipped the balance in favor of English education. As time went on, the traditional Sanskritic education declined as its status was gradually reduced in the public eyes.

A temporary shift in the Rana education policy came in 1901, when Prime Minister Dev Shamsher Rana called for sweeping educational reforms. Relatively liberal in his civil outlook, he proposed a system of universal public primary education, using Nepali as the language of instruction and opening the Durbar High School to non-Rana children. So unpopular was Dev Shamsher's policy initiatives among the conservative faction of the Rana clan that he was deposed within a few months. His call for reforms did not entirely fall on deaf ears, however. A few Nepali-language primary schools scattered around the country remained open, and the policy of admitting a few middle- and low-caste children to the Durbar High School continued.

Before World War II, some English-medium middle and high schools were established in **Patan**, **Biratnagar**, and elsewhere, and a girls' high school was set up in **Kathmandu**. In rural areas, public respect (and demand) for education was rising, largely thanks to the influence of returning **Gorkha** soldiers, many of whom had learned to read and write while serving in the British army. Some retired soldiers began giving rudimentary education to the children of their villages. And education-minded members of the high-caste, **elite**, and wealthy families sent their children to India for higher academic or technical training. It was, in fact, many of those students who launched anti-Rana movements, provided revolutionary cadres, and finally launched an anti-Rana revolution.

The wind of education sweeping the nation was much too strong to resist, even for the hardcore Ranas. As a result, Prime Minister **Chandra Shamsher Rana** felt that he had no choice but to give in to the demands of the changing time. He finally decided to establish **Tri-Chandra College** in 1918 to offer higher education opportunities within the nation and named it after himself. But what is noteworthy is what he said during the inauguration of that first college. Chandra Shamsher lamented that with its opening he had laid the foundation for driving the ultimate death knell to Rana autocracy. He personally felt responsible for what he envisioned to be the inevitable downfall of the Rana rule. And, indeed, his words proved prophetic as the Rana political power structure crumbled 33 years after his memorable act.

In spite of this slowly opening opportunity, access to education was highly limited. Geographically, the few schools that existed in Nepal were mostly concentrated in the **Kathmandu Valley**. And, socially, it was accessible basically only to the rich and powerful. The fact that until 1944 the students in Nepal had to go to Bihar University in India to take their high school matriculation exams, called the School Leaving Certificate (SLC), meant only a handful of students could afford the cost. As a result, educational opportunities were naturally limited to the top socioeconomic strata, which constituted no more than 5 percent of the total national population. Furthermore, until 1957, Tri-Chandra College was the only college in the country for higher education. Even then, it offered only up to intermediate level studies or what is commonly called the IA degree, which is equivalent to the AA (associate) degree in the **United States**.

At the end of Rana rule in 1951, Nepal had merely 310 primary and middle schools, eleven high schools, one college, one normal school, and one technical school, but no university for graduate education. As of 1999, the country's educational profile was as follows:

Type of School	Number	Enrollment
Primary (1–5 grades)	26,226	3,780,314
Lower Secondary (6–8 grades)	7,232	915,649
Secondary (9–10 grades)	4,082	385,079
Higher Secondary (11–12 grades)	500	65,000
Undergraduate College (Year: 2000)	220	129,174
University (Master level; Year: 2000)	4	16,240

The figures in the last column for the first three grade levels reveal that roughly 70, 31, and 20 percent of the children in their respective age groups are enrolled in schools. The higher secondary education is a new concept in Nepal, introduced only a few years ago, largely to meet the college admissions standards in advanced countries, including the United States. So it is difficult to determine the extent of its impact at this point. With respect to postsecondary education, not even 1 percent of the population is enrolled in colleges and universities within the country. This figure on college education is somewhat misleading because it does not capture Nepali students attending colleges and universities in India, other South Asian countries, and those in North America and Europe. Although the data is scanty, the number of Nepali students studying abroad is significant. Nonetheless, the fact would not change much even with the inclusion of those studying in foreign countries. Most likely, the figure would still hover in the vicinity of 1 percent.

In addition to formal education revealed by the above figures, Nepal has a program for nonformal education for both adults and school-age children who are not enrolled in school. Adult literacy is, however, the primary focus of this program. During the 1992–1997 period, this program helped more than 930,000 adults acquire literacy, which is defined in Nepal as the ability to read, write, and perform simple arithmetic calculations.

In the early 1950s, the national literacy rate was merely 5 percent: 10 percent for males and 1 percent for females. Since then the literacy rate has certainly improved. Nepal's average literacy rate in 1997 was almost 53 percent: 70 percent for males and 38 percent for females. When these figures are viewed in isolation, the picture reveals that educational progress has occurred over the years. And, in a way, it certainly has. However, genuine progress cannot be measured simply in terms of numbers alone. Quality is equally important. It is precisely in the area of quality where the problem resides. Over the years, there has been a noticeable decline in the quality of education at all levels. To a large extent, this decline can be attributed to the general lack of qualified teachers and professors; many of those who are qualified exhibit little commitment to the mission of education. One of the key issues infecting Nepal's educational system is the low pay scale for teachers and professors. As a result, their morale is low, a reality that is rarely conducive to educational dedication.

Further aggravating this deplorable situation is the general absence of students' devotion to their education. Schools and colleges are frequently closed as students engage in *haritals* (protests) and boycott classes. Sometimes, professors also organize strikes. Some professors go on extended leave to join the ranks of freelancing consultants who make good money in the ever-expanding market of development consultancy. And cheating is rampant at all levels and everywhere in the country. In short, the education system of Nepal is in dire need of fundamental repairs, virtually in every respect. What is more the class disparity in education in terms of both access and quality continues unabated. That is, while the wealthy and powerful families send their children to boarding schools in India, the United States, Great **Britain**, and to other advanced countries to expand their educational frontiers, the poor and less wealthy are entrapped in the national educational system that is badly broken with few viable alternatives in sight. *See also* KATHMANDU UNIVERSITY; ST. XAVIER'S SCHOOL; TRIBHUVAN UNIVERSITY.

ELECTIONS. In the post-**Panchayat** period, three national elections have taken place under the supervision of the Election Commission. They were held in 1991, 1994, and 1999 to elect members of the **House of Representatives**. The political party-based election results are presented in the following table:

Political Parties	Total Number of Seats Won		
	1991	1994	1999
Nepali Congress Party	110	83	111
Communist Party (UML)	69	88	71
Other leftist factions	13	6	7
National Democratic Party	4	20	11
Nepal Sadbhavana Party	6	3	5
Independents	3	5	0
Other contesting parties	0	0	0
Total	205	205	205

ELECTORAL SYSTEM. The 1990 **constitution** provides for a bicameral legislature called **Parliament**. It consists of the **National Council** (Rastriya Sabha) and the **House of Representatives** (Pratinidhi Sabha). Also called the Upper House of Parliament, the National Council is comprised of 60 members, of whom 10 are nominated by the king. Of the remaining 50 council members, 35 (including at least three **women**) are elected by the House of Representatives, and 15 are elected by the electoral college. The National Council is a permanent body, but one-third of its members must retire every two years. Their term of service is for six years. Although it is called the Upper House, its legislative role and power is somewhat dwarfed by the House of Representatives, which is also known as the Lower House.

The normal term for the House of Representatives is five years unless it is dissolved earlier. The representatives are popularly elected from their respective constituencies. Each of the 75 administrative districts is allocated at least one electoral constituency, that is, at least one representative in the House. Depending on the total population, some districts have more electoral constituencies, although only those Nepali citizens who are 21 years of age and older are eligible to vote in local and national **elections**. The largest number of constituencies is allocated to **Kathmandu** and **Morang** districts—seven each. Altogether, the house has 205 representatives from 75 districts.

The House of Representatives is the primary legislative body. With a simple majority, it elects the prime minister who must be a member of the House and is invariably the leader of his or her party. In other words, whichever party wins the majority of the seats in the House forms the government under the leadership of its party-designated prime minister. In the event no party commands a clear majority in the House, a minority or coalition government is formed by the party that puts together a majority. In forming the cabinet, the prime minister must select members of the House or the National Council to serve as ministers. The House can bring down the prime minister and his cabinet at any time through a simple majority vote of no confidence. Similarly, the prime minister can dissolve the House at any time. In such a case, the fresh **elections** must be held within six months after the dissolution of the House to elect new representatives. *See also* CONSTITUTIONS.

ELECTRIC CURRENT SYSTEM. Nepal uses 220 volts A.C. Most of the cities have access to electricity, although they are often subjected to electric outage, rationing, and irregular current flows. As a result, most households use voltage regulators.

ELITE. No fixed definition exists for this term when used in the context of Nepal. It is often used to denote: the ruling elite, the political elite, or some other elite group, including the *buddhijibi* (intelligentsia) class. The "ruling elite" throughout history basically governed Nepal. Before the **Rana** regime, *bhardars* were the primary ruling elites aside from the royal families (*see* **Bhardari Sabha**). They generally came from a family of prominent *bhardari* clans, namely, Thapa, Basnyat, Pandey, and Kunwar clans. Following the usurpation of political power by **Jang Bahadur Rana** in 1846, the Ranas emerged as the epicenter of both political and ruling elites. Although many of these previous elite clans still have a strong hold on Nepal's political power structure, the centrality of ruling and political elitism has significantly diffused since 1990 when the democratic system was reintroduced. Since the system of governance is now based on the party structure, there seems to be no single elite family clan that has a tight grip on Nepali politics.

ENCROACHMENT OF HISTORICAL SITES. Many public spaces around temples, shrines, and other historical sites are openly occupied by those who can fight the system or who are powerful and connected to the political power structure. As a result, they have been converted into highly valuable private properties. Shopping complexes around Sundhara and the temple of **Pashupati** are some examples of growing encroachments of historical sites and public spaces. What is surprising is that the inclusion of the **Kathmandu Valley** in the UNESCO World Heritage List 21 years ago has done little to prevent this trend, which in fact become more intensified than ever before as the demand and value of land soars. Now some local government agencies have begun to publicly sell some of such spaces.

ETHNICITY. Ethnically, the population of Nepal can be broadly divided into three groups: Indigenous, **Tibeto-Nepali**, and **Indo-Nepali**.

- Indigenous: The indigenous people are generally scattered in small pockets. The two largest indigenous groups are the **Tharu** and the **Newar**. While the Tharus are traditionally found in the **Tarai**, the Newars are native to their ancient domain: the **Kathmandu Valley**. Historically a merchant group involved in trade, commerce, and craft production activities, many of them have, over the years, moved out of the Valley to settle in different parts of Nepal. In the process, they

have established urban centers or towns throughout the country, for instance, **Pokhara**, Tansen, **Baglung**, Bandipur, Dharan, Banepa, and **Chainpur** to name a few prominent ones. The Tharus, on the other hand, remain mostly confined to the Tarai and primarily engaged in farming.
- Tibeto-Nepali (Tibeto-Burman): Collectively, this group comprises the Nepalis of **Tibetan** and Mongolian origin. They too came to Nepal in different waves, dating back to the unrecorded period of Nepali history. Most likely, the first wave mainly consisted of the **Kiratas**. The second wave brought the various Tibeto-Nepali ethnic groups of central Nepal, e.g., the **Gurungs** and **Magars**. Finally, there was a third wave which included the **Dolpos** in northwestern Nepal and the **Sherpas** in the eastern hills. In all likelihood, this last group crossed the **Himalayas** only after **Tibet**'s conversion to **Buddhism** in the mid-seventh century.

   Geographically, the Tibeto-Nepalis are dispersed from east to west along the hill and **mountain** belts of Nepal. But their dispersal is quite distinct from that of the Indo-Nepalis; it occurs in concentrated patterns. Unlike the Indo-Nepalis who are divided along **caste** lines, the Tibeto-Nepalis are divided by distinct ethnic groups. Each ethnic group within the Tibeto-Nepali population has its own geographical domain with concentrated settlement communities. Altitudinally, some are found in the higher hills and mountains, including the **Trans-Himalayan** zone. Included among them are the Sherpas, **Thakalis**, **Bhotes**, and Mananges (native inhabitants of **Manang**). Some Tibeto-Nepali groups inhabit the mid-hill region, e.g., the Gurungs, Magars, and **Tamangs**. In terms of general east-west direction, the Sherpas, **Rais**, and **Limbus** are concentrated in the eastern hills, whereas the Gurungs, Magars, Thakalis, Bhotes, and Mananges occupy the central corridor of the country. In recent years, however, sizeable numbers of many ethnic groups have moved to urban centers and lowland areas to participate in businesses. For example, many Thakalis, Gurungs, and Mananges have relocated to major urban centers for business purposes.

   Some of the hill ethnic groups are renowned as martial tribes and are often referred to as the **Gorkhas** (Gurkhas) in the **British** military parlance. Prominent among these groups are the Rais, Limbus, Gurungs, and Magars whom the British fancied.

- Indo-Nepali (Indo-Aryan): They comprise the Nepalis of Indian origin. Despite the lack of concrete records, it is evident that the demographic relations between Nepal and **India** go way back. There are at least two Nepali historic figures who had extensive contacts with India and its various tribal kingdoms. They are: King **Janak**, who ruled Videh from its capital, Mithila (**Janakpur** area), and **Hindu** Prince **Siddhartha** (**Buddha**) whose father's kingdom was centered in **Kapilvastu**. In the case of King Janak, his daughter **Sita** was married to **Rama**, the hero of the *Ramayana* and the tribal king of Kosala (Kousala) in northern India. With those kingdoms situated at the northern edges of the subtropical Gangetic Plains and mostly oriented toward the south in terms of their geographical seamlessness and close cultural interaction, their direct influence into the hills to the north was probably limited or sporadic.

Regarding the numerical growth of Indo-Nepalis, their large-scale settlement in much of the hills and later in the Tarai, and their subsequent domination of Nepal, one can attribute to two relatively recent and discernible waves of Hindu immigrants from India. The first wave brought a large volume of Indian immigrants about a 1,000 years ago. It was this early wave that proved decisive in terms of laying the institutional foundation of what is now called modern Nepal as they shaped its cultural geography and framed its political and economic structure.

They moved to the Nepal hills to escape what they considered to be the tyrannical treatment of the Hindus by the invading Muslims and their subsequent rule of India. Those fleeing Indians included all castes, many being **Brahmans (Bahuns)** and Rajputs (**Chhetris**). Equipped with their formal literary tradition and agrarian mode of production, combined with a farming technology which was, in many respects, superior to the pastoral technology of the Tibeto-Nepali groups, they gradually took over the hills, thereby subordinating the local Tibeto-Nepali groups and their communal mode of production.

The two most dominant segments within this population group are Bahuns and Chhetris. They turned the hills into the political and cultural center of Nepal, with their domination reaching a peak when the country was consolidated under one flag after **Prithvi Narayan Shah**'s victory over the three **Malla** kingdoms of the Kathmandu Valley. Although the hills still remain their main geographical domain and power base, they are widely dispersed throughout the country.

Their presence is all too visible in every region, including the Tarai. It was these Indo-Nepalis who were the primary purveyors of Hinduism across Nepal. Known as the **pahari** or **parbate** (hill and mountain dwellers), these Nepalis, at the apex of which resides the royal family, generally control the political and administrative machineries of Nepal from the local to the national level.

In contrast to the first one, the second wave of Indo-Nepalis largely involved poor peasants and tenants who came to Nepal from the bordering Indian provinces of Bihar and Utter Pradesh as well as many from Bengal. They began to filter into Nepal after its unification in 1769 and mostly settled in the Tarai belt. Unlike the first wave, they arrived at different times and in small numbers, generally coinciding with agricultural land resettlement initiatives by the rulers of Nepal. As the various Nepali rulers attempted to develop agricultural land in the Tarai to augment their revenues but failed to lure the *paharis* to relocate, they offered incentives for Indian peasants and tenants to resettle in the Tarai. Sensing the opportunity to hold land, many relocated across the border to the Tarai.

Vernacularly known as the **madhesi**, they too are ardent Hindus like their *pahari* counterparts. Despite sharing the same religion and roots of their geographical origin (i.e., India), there is a sharp divide between the two. As the *paharis* have historically considered the *madhesis* to be less cultured, they tend to look down upon them. Such a sentiment is heightened by the fact that many *madhesis* are darker in complexion with their roots grounded in the north Indian peasantry and tenancy—a class of people often associated with serfdom and servitude. Compounding this perception is the sense of distrust of the *madhesis* on the part of the *paharis*, especially within the ruling circle. This distrust is deeply rooted in their suspicion that the *madhesis* have yet to be fully acculturated to Nepali nationalism like the *paharis*, meaning they have a much greater level of affinity toward India than loyalty to Nepal. As a result, the government's Tarai land resettlement scheme was, in part, motivated by a plan to *paharize* the Tarai by resettling the hill residents in the region. The idea was to create a demographic majority of the *paharis* in the Tarai, thus overwhelming the *madhesi* influence and imprints. While it is difficult to ascertain the extent to which the policy has achieved its intended objective, there is little doubt that the hill shadow has been cast in the Tarai through land resettlement and consequent population shifts from the hills.

Regardless of the regional integration (or domination) between the hills and the Tarai through ongoing demographic manipulation, together these two groups of Indo-Nepalis constitute the demographic majority in Nepal, thereby clearly overwhelming the political landscape and power structure of the country. On a regular basis, they have controlled more than 80 percent of the seats in the national cabinet as well as in the **House of Representatives**. With the exception of **Marichman Shrestha** in the late 1980s, the post of prime minister has been totally monopolized by the axis of Bahuns and Chhetris since the rise of the Shah dynasty in 1769. *See also* ART AND ARCHITECTURE; CHITWAN; RAPTI VALLEY DEVELOPMENT PROJECT.

F

FATHER MORAN (1906–1992). Father Moran first came to Nepal as a Christian missionary and later established a missionary school called **St. Xavier's School** at **Godavari**. His act made an English medium schooling system available to the rich and **elites** of Nepal without having to send their children overseas or to **India**. What was remarkable about it was that in a **Hindu** society rooted in strict Hindu codes, the school became instantly popular among the Hindu elites of Nepal, mainly because of its English medium and **British** standards. Although not intended, the school not only undercut Nepal's public **education**, but also further widened the educational class divide between the elite and the masses. Moran was also active in relief efforts for **Tibetan** refugees.

FESTIVALS. It is no exaggeration that Nepal is the land of festivals. One prominent Nepal website (www.nepalhomepage.com) lists some 35 festivals. What this number means is that on average, Nepal celebrates almost three festivals a month. Incidently, it is a conservative count in that it excludes many festivals that are either somewhat regional or local in nature. Many of the listed festivals are celebrated across the nation and by almost all groups, regardless of their **caste** and **ethnicity**. Included in this family of festivals are **Dashain, Gaijatra, Holi**, and **Tihar**. Then there are others, for example, **Baghjatra**, Ghodejatra, and Indrajatra, that are mostly observed by the **Newars**. The **Kathmandu Valley** alone has many festivals; most of them were instituted during the **Licchavi** and **Malla** periods. They are still celebrated with great fanfare, especially by the Valley Newars. On the other hand, there is also a festival like **Tij** that is observed almost exclusively by the **Bahun** and **Chhetri women** of Nepal. **Buddha jayanti** is by far the biggest and most important festival for **Buddhists**, and it is observed by many **Hindus** as well. Many of these festivals represent national holidays, with the Dashain and Tihar being the longest.

Needless to say, most Nepali festivals are intertwined with some aspects of Nepal's cultures and religions. Therefore, a festival means worshiping time for a particular god. For many, some festivals represent times for entertainment and socialization. This is a dimension of festivals that takes on greater meaning in remote areas where there are no movie theaters, nor TV and other entertainment avenues. Also important is the fact that, as religious events, festivals provide opportunities for family reunions and socialization. People from distant places visit relatives. During the Dashain time, for example, family members who might be away in **India** or other places, working as migrants, come home on leave to participate in the festival as a family affair. So, for a couple of weeks before the Dahsain, hill trails are dotted with ever eager migrants returning home and carrying gifts for the family and relatives, ready to share a precious moment of joy that every family reunion ushers in.

FIRANGI. Term used to describe foreigners, namely Europeans. *See also* GORE.

FLAG OF NEPAL. The Nepali flag is unique; it is a two-peaked banner, with the points extending outward. The triangular peaks representing the nation's **mountains** are red with blue borders and carry white emblems of the crescent moon (top triangle) and the 12-pointed sun (bottom triangle). While the moon is believed to signify the nation's peaceful outlook and existence, the sun is presumed to express its fiery determination to defend its nationhood.

FOOD. The most common diet in Nepal constitutes **dal-bhat** (bean or lentil soup and cooked **rice**), usually supplemented by *tarkari*, which is most often prepared out of some type of green or tuber vegetables. *Tarkari* can also be made out of meat or fish. In this sense, *tarkari* is both a dish and a process of preparation which involves using various spices, mainly cumin, coriander, garlic, ginger, onion, and hot pepper. Meat or fish dishes are not too common, especially in the poor and less well-off households; they are consumed only occasionally or during festivals. This norm does not hold true, however, with wealthy households, where meat or fish consumption is very frequent. The process of preparing most *tarkaris* is similar to that used in northern India.

With respect to Nepali diets, one group that clearly stands out is the **Newars** who are renowned for their cuisines. The Newari dishes are quite distinctive because of their sophistication and originality in terms of both preparation and varieties. In addition, many of their dishes are perhaps the only ones that are indigenous to Nepal and that deserve special attention. Most dishes are also quite exquisite in their tastes, particularly sweets and meat dishes. So well known are the Newari dishes that many of them have become national standards; they are served throughout Nepal, both geographically and ethnically. One of the dishes is called **momocha** or *momo* which is, in some way, similar to Chinese dumplings. Most likely, Newari merchants doing business in **Tibet** introduced it to the **Kathmandu Valley**. Besides *momocha*, other highly popular Newari dishes are *bhutan* (thoroughly fried animal organs such as intestines, lungs, and hearts), *chhwa-la* (similar to shish kebab; in Newari *chhwa* = grilled or cooked on fire; *la* = meat), and *kachi-la* (fresh raw meat tastefully marinated in spices; in Newari *kachi* = raw). While *bhutan* and *chhwa-la* can be made from any meat, *kachi-la* is restricted to buffalo and goat/sheep meat. *Momocha* is also usually made out of buffalo and goat meat. These dishes are widely served in local restaurants in the Kathmandu Valley. Although foreign dishes such as pizza have become popular on an occasional basis, they still have a way to go before they can compete with native Newari dishes on a sustained or day-to-day basis.

FOREIGN AID. It is fair to claim that foreign aid entered Nepal in 1951, following the overthrow of the **Rana** regime. Although **India** has historically been a leading donor nation, it is Western aid and agencies, especially from the **United States** and **World Bank**, that have become most influential in terms of setting Nepal's development direction and agenda. The very first package of American aid came in 1951, containing a mere sum of 22,000 rupees (or just a few thousand dollars). Of course, the amounts of aid from the United States and other Western countries continued to climb with the passage of time—all in the name of Nepal's economic development. For instance, when Nepal launched its first Five-Year Plan in 1956, it was almost entirely financed by foreign aid.

Although the share of foreign aid financing of development has diminished, it still remains high. Since the mid-1950s, the overall share of development financing through foreign aid—again mostly foreign debt now—has averaged 66 percent. In 2001, it stood at 58 percent. It is plausible to contend that no development project is possible without some form of foreign aid. Worse, as the nation's economic fate is inextricably predicated on foreign aid, it has generated a huge debt. Yet the economic picture clearly reveals that almost five decades of official development mission fueled by foreign aid has done little to alleviate **poverty**. In spite of this generally gloomy result, the amount of Nepal's foreign debt continues to soar, for instance, from $1,640 million in 1990 to $2,646 million in 1998. While it may seem like a tiny amount by international comparison, it is actually a huge burden for a poor and resourceless country like Nepal whose annual GNP is barely $5 billion.

In reality, what is called foreign aid is actually foreign debt. Initially, almost 100 percent of foreign aid to Nepal constituted outright grants regardless of the country of its origin. As such, foreign aid was free; there was no obligation to pay it back. These days, however, the picture has almost entirely reversed. In 1998, Nepal's GNP was nearly $5 billion. For the same year, its total foreign aid amounted to $2,960 million, including $2,646 million in foreign debt and around $314 million in grants from various countries. So 90 percent of the so-called foreign aid money was pure debt, and only 10 percent involved grants. What this means is that the amount of foreign debt represented around 50 percent of Nepal's GNP in that year. *See also* ECONOMY; PLANNING AND NATIONAL PLANS; POVERTY; UNITED STATES-NEPAL RELATIONS.

FOREIGN TRADE. Given the small size of its **economy**, Nepal's foreign trade is naturally modest. Historically, Nepal's trade relations were mainly limited to **India** and **Tibet**. During the **Licchavi** and **Malla** periods, Nepal's trade with Tibet was relatively robust, as many **Newar** merchants from the **Kathmandu Valley** had set up trading houses there. At one time, Nepal even minted coins for Tibet. Furthermore, the Valley served as a major entrepôt between Tibet and India, which gave an added boost to Nepal's foreign trade.

Nonetheless, in terms of the volume and regularity of trade, India was, no doubt, Nepal's primary trading partner, mainly dictated by their historical links and geographical positions. So, until the 1950s, over 90 percent of trade was conducted with India, a country which supplied, and continues to supply, the majority of basic goods, along with raw materials and machinery goods for Nepali **industries**. In addition to being almost the exclusive supplier of basic imports, India acted as the primary foreign market for most of Nepal's exports. But, in these trade relations, Nepal always experienced a huge trade deficit with India, a reality that still persists. In fact, Nepal's trade deficit with India has been growing.

In recent years, however, Nepal's foreign trade with India has been on the decline vis-à-vis other nations, mainly for exports (*see* tables 5 and 6). For example, in 2000, Nepal's exports to the **United States** totaled more than $220 million. India ranked second with a total export value of almost $173 million, followed by Germany which bought slightly over $90 million worth of Nepali products. Also included among the trading partners were Bangladesh, France, Great **Britain**, Italy, and Switzerland. However, with respect to Nepal's imports during the same year, India was, as usual, the largest partner, with a whopping share of almost 33 percent or $522 million. It was followed by the People's Republic of **China** (including Hong Kong), Argentina, and Singapore.

In total, Nepal's exports were worth almost $671 million, whereas its imports were valued at $1,620 million, thus resulting in a trade deficit of nearly a billion dollars (*see* table 6). While ready-made **garments** and **carpets** were Nepal's main exports, topping the list of imports were basic manufactures, machineries and transport equipment, and chemicals. One obvious reason why Nepal's export base is so small is because foreign direct investment is extremely low, totaling a mere $12 million in 1998. Despite its reasonable incentives for foreign investment and push for **privatization**, Nepal has yet to attract foreign companies to invest in the country. See *also* FOREIGN AID; TOURISM; TRANSPORTATION.

FOREST PRODUCT DISTRIBUTION COMMITTEE (FPDC). After the multiparty system was reinstituted in early 1990, the earlier system of the Forest Product Distribution Board was replaced by the Forest Products Distribution Committee (FPDC). The FPDC evaluates stock of forest products and makes decisions concerning the distribution of forest products: to the local people when emergency needs occur for forest products; to meet timber needs of government projects; and to satisfy constructional timber requirements. *See also* FORESTRY.

FORESTRY. "*Hariyo ban, Nepalko dhan*" (Emerald forests, Nepal's national wealth). This slogan was trumpeted across the nation in the 1960s almost like a choral song with many voices but the same note. It was popularized by King **Mahendra Bir Bikram Shah**. There was hardly a city in the country where one would not see at least one or two big green metal signboards with the slogan written in white letters as a quotation from the king. In **Kathmandu**, it was displayed in several strategic places where it was most visible. One simply could not miss them. The message was that Nepal was a land of bountiful, dense commercial forests. Since the hill forests had already been significantly reduced in size due to both landslides and land reclamation, the reference of the slogan was undeniably to the **Tarai** forests, popularly known as the *char kose jhadi*, a 12-kilometers-wide band of dense forests, straddling the Tarai belt all the way from east to west.

The slogan proved to be eerily prophetic, for it was indeed harnessed as a source of wealth (revenues). Many high-ranking government officials (including the palace and the **Panchayat** system) as well as commercial contractors profited from the Tarai forests immensely. Both legal and illegal logging, combined with land resettlement in the Tarai, reduced the amount of forests drastically. The thick canopy was gone by the early 1980s. In some parts of the Tarai, patches of once dense forests were turned into parched land with little vegetation left. Some of the parched land was later occupied by squatter settlers. Panchayat rulers routinely deployed forests and land resettlement, including the land that squatters had occupied, as a political instrument to gain political support for the system that had few other means to sustain itself.

Given this abuse, it was hardly surprising that the forested area of the country declined from 64 percent in the early 1960s to less than 40 percent by the mid-1970s. Many within the Nepal government's forest department actually believed the forest cover was probably no more than 35 percent. Currently, the forested area amounts to hardly 29 percent according to government claims. This includes almost 21,000 square kilometers of national parks, wildlife reserves and conservation areas, i.e., 14 percent of Nepal's total land area. As the situation reached a delicate point in the early 1980s, environmentalists from around the world sounded an alarm and poured money into Nepal to save its forested environment. Their concern was that deforestation in Nepal would cause massive landslides and consequent soil erosion, leading to a chain of environmental damage from the **Himalayas** down to the Bay of Bengal. What was painted was a grim picture as the whole scenario was treated as the "Himalayan Degradation Theory." Although such an alarmist view was blown out of proportion, the problem certainly existed. With the help of **foreign aid** and technical assistance, projects were launched to reforest some hill areas to slow down the process and degree of landslides and soil erosion. Several Western donors nations, including the United States, implemented **community forestry** as a novel approach to revive Nepal's forests.

What was interesting about the Western promotion of community forestry was that it was nothing new to Nepal. It was a traditional hallmark of Nepal's forest management system, especially in the hills, prior to the nationalization of forests in 1956. Irrespective of the origin of the concept of community forestry, forest nationalization proved to be disastrous as it undercut the communal foundation of community forestry, a system in which communities shared both the responsibility toward the stewardship of community forests and the much-needed resources provided by them. In other words, there existed an uncanny balance in the communal system of forest management. This was particularly true in the hills, where forests were generally scarce resources which are fundamental to the short-term survival and the long-range viability of the peasant ecology that involves farming, forestry, and animal husbandry. But forest nationalization changed all of that. Suddenly, what was once communally owned and managed became a common resource, a form of free good, to be had without sharing common responsibility toward its long-term sustainability.

There are signs that the country's forest resource base has relatively stabilized over the past few years, generally due to some reforestation and push for community forestry. The annual rate of forest coverage decline currently stands at slightly over 1 percent. Nevertheless, the pressure on forest resources continues to mount as the demands for commercial timbers, firewood, and fodder remain high. It is relevant to note that while the demand for commercial timbers is coming from the urban sector and wealthy people, the demand for firewood and fodder is primarily tied to rural areas and farming folks. Regardless, there is little doubt that as both legal and illegal commercial logging invariably results in mass forest clearing, it tends to cause large-scale forest deterioration, eventually reducing the amount of forests available for firewood and fodder.

Since the arrival of the multiparty system in 1990, the forest policy of Nepal has undergone some change. Specifically, the Forest Act of 1993 and the Forest Rules of 1995 were enacted; these laws classified forests into four principal types, not counting those with a religious designation.

They are: natural (national), community, leasehold, and private forests. However, with the exception of private forests, which mostly include trees grown on family farms, they belong to the state irrespective of their designation. Furthermore, in terms of amounts, private and leasehold (largely forests leased to private entrepreneurs or companies) are merely a fraction. In spite of the significant increase in the amount of community forests in recent years, the vast majority of the forest land in the country is directly controlled by the state and managed by the district forest office, thus perpetuating the spirit of nationalization intact. And most of the national forests are natural.

Nepal's natural forests can be broadly grouped into two categories on the basis of their vegetation types and ecological characteristics. The first category of forests is found in the Tarai and inner Tarai belt. These forests are comprised of hardwood trees, the most renowned being the storied **sal** (*Shorea robusta*) species, indigenous to South Asia. Elegantly tall and majestic looking, sal trees are rich in legends. They once covered the Tarai and formed the central core the famed *char kose jhadi*. Legend has it that sal timbers last a thousand years in the water and another thousand years outside the water. There is no doubt about their durability even when untreated. It is precisely because of their enduring qualities and reputation, they are much desired for both house construction and making furniture. In addition, they are widely used as electric and telephone posts and along railroad tracks. Also included in the family of commercial forests in this belt are **khair** (*Acacia catechu*) and **sisso** (*Delbergia sissoo*). In noticeable contrast to the Tarai's hardwood forests, the second category constitutes the softwood conifer forests of the high hills and **mountains** in the north. Mainly dominated by pine and fir species, these forest products are largely used for household purposes, including residential construction in the high hills and mountains. *See also* CHITWAN; RAPTI VALLEY DEVELOPMENT PROJECT.

G

GACHHADAR, BIJAYA KUMAR (1953–). An activist who began his political career as a member of the Nepal Students' Union and who was exiled for six years during the **Panchayat** period. Once the Panchayat system came to an end, he ran for **election** as a candidate of the **Nepali Congress Party** and was elected to the **House of Representa-**

tives from the Sunsari district in 1991. He served as minister of **communications** under Prime Minister **Girija Prasad Koirala**. He was reelected in the subsequent elections held in 1994 and 1999 from the same district.

GAIJATRA. Popular carnival-like festival widely celebrated throughout Nepal. During the celebration, families send a **cow** (*gai*) or a young man dressed as a cow to participate in the procession (*jatra*). The press enjoys tremendous freedom of satire, humor, and comedy, focused on politics and political personalities. First introduced by King Jagat Prakash Malla of **Bhadgaun**, it usually falls in August.

GAINE. Professional minstrel **caste** group or somebody from that group. Very small in number, they are mostly folk singers and mainly found in Kaski, particularly near the city of **Pokhara**. They are famous for melodious songs based on culture, legends, heroic deeds of great people, romance, and humor. They also play Nepal's typical stringed instrument, *sarangi*, which they make themselves. Their untouchable status was outlawed in 1963. *See also* DALIT; UNTOUCHABILITY.

GAJMER, RANJIT (1941–). Musician from **Darjeeling**. He is a well-recognized name within the movie-going young generation of Nepal as he served as **music** director for several Nepali movies produced in the 1980s and early 1990s.

GAJUREL, CHHABI LAL (1939–). Scientist and coauthor of a book on the traditional (indigenous) technology of Nepal. He once served as a professor at **Tribhuvan University**, but he is now retired.

GAJUREL, NARAYAN SHARMA (1943–). A well-known journalist who served as general manager of Sajha Prakashan (1977–1984) and general secretary of the Nepal Journalists Association (1972–1973).

GANDAK AGREEMENT. Agreement signed in 1959 between Nepal and **India** for the utilization of water of the **Narayani River**. At times, this agreement has proved to be a source of contentious debate in Nepal between the pro-India and anti-India political groups as well as between India and Nepal, partly because there is a sense running deep that India has been the primary beneficiary of the project, often at the expense of Nepal.

GANDAKI GORGE. Called *galchhi* in Nepali, this gorge is believed to be the deepest one in the world, with a depth of 6,967 meters. It is sandwiched between the **Annapurna** and **Dhaulagiri Mountains** in central Nepal and formed by the **Kali Gandaki** River.

GANDAKI RIVER SYSTEM. It is a river system in central Nepal, fed by seven Gandaki rivers, collectively called the Sapta (seven) Gandaki. They are: Budhi, Daruandi, Kali, Madi, Marsyangdi, Seti, and Trisuli (Trishuli). They all come together at a place called Devghat near the city of **Narayanghat** in **Chitwan** and become the **Narayani River** or the Sapta Gandaki.

GANDAKI ZONE. A zone located in central Nepal, it is named after the **Gandaki Rivers** (*see* figure 3). It consists of six districts: **Gorkha**, Kaski, Lamjung, **Manang**, Syangja, and Tanahun. Perhaps the most famous of these six districts is Gorkha from where **Prithvi Narayan Shah** rose to power. Inhabited by 1,262,694 people in 1991, it covers a total area of 12,275 sq. km.

GANESH (GANESA). Elephant-headed son of Lord **Shiva**. Ganesh is a very popular god as he is widely and regularly worshiped. He is often regarded as the god of wealth and success. His vehicle is the rat.

GANESH HIMAL RANGE. It is one of the subranges in the Greater **Himalayan Range** with many tall peaks, towering over 7,000 meters in height. It includes Ganesh Himal I or Yangra (7,429m), Ganesh Himal II (7,111m), Ganesh Himal III or Salsungo (7,110m), Ganesh Himal IV (7,052m), and Ganesh Himal V (6,986m). Magnetite ores are found in this range.

GANGETIC DOLPHIN. Elegant river dolphin (*Platanista gangetica*) found in the **Kosi**, **Karnali**, and **Narayani** Rivers. These dolphins called "sush" in Nepali are endangered due to netting and dam construction.

GANJA. Nepali word for marijuana. Hashish is extracted from marijuana plant resin. The term was popularized in the West by American and European hippies who flocked to Nepal in the 1960s and early 1970s in search of marijuana and tranquility from the stale suburban life they lived in America. The popularity of the word was further enhanced later by reggae singers of Jamaica, especially Bob Marley. In Nepal, one rarely smokes ganja by itself; it is normally mixed with tobacco. A short handmade clay pipe called *chilam* is the primary medium of smoking ganja in the country.

GARGI, VACHKANAVI. Famous female philosopher in King Janaka's court, who is believed to have challenged Yajnyavalkya, regarded as the greatest philosopher of his time. Her position in the court is frequently cited as a undeniable testament to Nepali **women**'s high social status as well as their intellectual attainment in ancient Nepal.

GARMENT INDUSTRY. Leading export **industry** of Nepal. In terms of its export value, it is close to the **carpet industry**. In 2000, Nepal's ready-made garment exports totaled $164 million, with the United States serving as its single biggest market, followed by European countries. It is an export-based growing industry. *See also* CHILD LABOR; ECONOMY; FOREIGN TRADE.

GARUDA. Hindu mythical bird of legendary proportions. With its head and wings resembling a giant eagle, it is regarded as the vehicle of Lord **Vishnu**. As a result, it is periodically worshiped by the Hindus. It is not uncommon for the Nepalis to utter "Garuda, Garuda" when they encounter a snake. Belief has it that the utterance of the word Garuda scares the snake away as the bird is viewed as a snake killer and eater. Its famous image lies in the **Patan Durbar Square**.

GAUCHAN, OM PRAKASH (1904–1991). Fondly known as "uncle" in **Baglung** (*see* figure 2), Gauchan established various schools and libraries in the district, including an English-medium school and a school for girls. He is both an entrepreneur and social worker, often mixing the two. For instance, opening schools is part of his social work. But, at the same time, it is entrepreneurial because private schools are money-making ventures.

GAUCHAN, OMKAR PRASAD (1935–). Politician from **Baglung** (*see* figure 2). He spent much of his political career during the **Panchayat** system as one of its advocates. Upon the rebirth of democracy in 1990, he freely participated in the 1991 general **election** and was elected to the **House of Representatives**, but not in the subsequent election in 1994.

GAUN PHARKA RASTRIYA ABHIYAN. *See* BACK-TO-THE-VILLAGE NATIONAL CAMPAIGN.

GAURIGHAT. Bathing and cremation **ghat** located at the bank of the **Bagmati**. In some respect, it is a religious site as it plays an important role in **Hindu** death rituals. As the Hindus believe in cremation, this is one of the most preferred cremation ghats in the Valley, precisely because it on the bank of the **Bagmati**.

GAUTAM, BAM DEV (1949–). Career politician born in Pyuthan (*see* figure 2). He has played a major role within the **Communist Party of Nepal** since his early years in politics. He was jailed for two years and remained underground for 19 years during the **Panchayat** era. He was elected to the **House of Representatives** from the Bardiya district during the parliamentary **elections** of 1991 and.1994.

GAUTAM, DHURBA CHANDRA (1944–). Nepali modern novelist. He has written many novels and plays, including one entitled *Jyaga* (1993) which focuses on Bhutanese refugees of Nepali origin. He is a professor of Nepali at **Tribhuvan University**.

GAUTAM, KASHI NATH (1926–1987). As an elected member of the **Nepali Congress Party**, he served as minister for health and local self-government when **B. P. Koirala** headed the first ever popularly elected government of Nepal as its prime minister (1959–1960).

GAUTAM, SHIVA RAJ (1943–). Leftist politician from the western **Tarai** district of **Dang** (*see* figure 2). As an activist and member of the **Communist Party of Nepal**, he was imprisoned for more than 10 years during the **Panchayat** period. Upon the rebirth of democracy in 1990, he was elected to the **Parliament** in 1991.

GAUTAM, SHREE PRASAD (1932–). A journalist who was editor in chief of the *Gorkhapatra* from 1990 to 1992. He also served as editor of *Madhuparka*, a highly acclaimed literary Nepali monthly published in **Kathmandu**.

GELUGPA GUMBA. Buddhist monastery near the **Baudhanath stupa** which is located in **Kathmandu**. It is a residential complex where the monks belonging to the virtuous order called Gelugpa live.

GHANTAGHAR. Nepal's first and biggest clock tower in **Kathmandu**. It was first built by Prime Minister Bir Shamsher Rana. When it was ruined during the massive **earthquake** of 1934, it was later rebuilt. It is situated on the **Tri-Chandra College** campus.

GHARELU SHILPAKALA BIKRI BHANDAR. Public corporation set up in 1966 to promote and sell Nepali handicraft products. In Nepali, it literally means a sales (*bikri*) depot (*bhandar*) for handicraft or cottage industry (*gharelu*) products (*shilpakala*).

GHARTI MAGAR, MOHAN BIKRAM. Politician with a Marxist bent. Born in Pyuthan (*see* figure 2), he is a founding member of the **Communist Party of Nepal**. A leader of the communist faction called Mashal, he boycotted the general **election** held in 1991. In essence, he expressed his opposition to the parliamentary system by boycotting the election.

GHAT. River embankment built with steps to provide relatively easy access to the river water. It is often associated with **Hindu** ritualistic bathing and cremation where funeral pyres are a common sight. *See also* ARYAGHAT; GAURIGHAT.

GHIMIRE, BISHNU BIBHU (1957–). Modern poet, literary journalist. He edited the literary monthly *Garima*. He was awarded the Pratibha Puraskar and Moti Puraskar (1988) for his literary contributions. His works include *Kathgharama Ubhiyera*.

GHIMIRE, LAXMAN PRASAD (1943–). Politician and civil engineer from Ramechhap (*see* figure 2). He was elected to the **House of Representatives** from the Ramechhap district in 1991 as a member of the **Nepali Congress Party** and became minister of water resources. In the 1994 election, he was defeated by his communist opponent. To this day, he remains an active member of his party.

GHIMIRE, MADHAV PRASAD (1919–). Distinguished poet from the western hill district of Lamjung (*see* figure 2). He has written many short epics and poetry volumes. He has been honored with life membership in the **Royal Nepal Academy** for his lifetime achievements and enormous contributions to enriching the field of Nepali **literature**.

GHIMIRE, NETRA (1946–1972). Born in Tehrathum (*see* figure 2), Netra Ghimire had a revolutionary career. He was one of the initiators (instigators) of what is known as the **Jhapa movement**. He was brutally murdered by the police at Sukhani along with **Ramnath Dahal** and others in April 1972 for his active participation in subversive activities.

GHIMIRE, SUPRABHA (1941–). A professor and democratic activist, she is associated with the English Department at the Padma Kanya College campus, the first women's college in the country. It is located in **Kathmandu**.

GHIMIRE, TULSI (1951–). Film director and scriptwriter. His movies often emphasize Nepali originality and style. He has directed many movies since the early 1980s.

GIDDHE CHHAPAKHANA. Nepal's first printing press, established in 1851 by Prime Minister **Jang Bahadur Rana** after his return from his European visit in early 1851.

GIRI, AGAM SINGH (1928–1970). Nepali poet from **Darjeeling**. He is particularly known for his juxtapositional writing style that is relatively distinct in Nepal; it captures the opposite forces (moments) of ecstasy and pain in human life.

GIRI, BANIRA (1946–). Novelist and poetess. Born in a small town near **Darjeeling**, she moved to **Kathmandu** with her parents when she was still a young girl. Her writings feature the lost art of history and finer sides of female sex and sexuality and often refer to the environment and society of Kathmandu. In addition, she was the first Nepali **woman** to earn a Ph.D. from **Tribhuvan University** in the field of Nepali **literature**, and has also authored several novels, including *Karagar* (The Prison, 1985) and *Nirbandha* (Unbound, 1986).

GIRI, PASHUPATI (1933–). Well-known industrialist from Siraha (*see* figure 2). He founded many factories producing hosiery, food, and plastic products. He served as chairman of the Federation of Nepalese Chambers of Commerce and Industry during 1973–1975.

GIRI, TULSI (1926–). Politician from the district of Siraha (*see* figure 2). Although he is generally regarded as a bright mind in Nepali politics, his political position was never grounded. He began his career as a member of the **Nepali Congress Party**, but spent much of his political life in the **Panchayat** system. During the **B. P. Koirala** government (1959–1960), Tulsi Giri served as a highly visible member of his cabinet. Following the 1960 **Palace Coup**, King **Mahendra Bir Bikram Shah** appointed Giri as chairman of the Council of Ministers (1960–1964) and later as prime minister (1975–1977). He was widely viewed in the Nepali political circle as a traitor because of his betrayal of B. P. Koirala.

GODAN (GAIDAN). Hindu ritual for gifting a **cow** to a **Brahman** or a priest with the belief of obtaining religious merit and crossing the mythological river Baitarni after death to reach heaven.

GODAVARI. Scenic village and forest, southeast of **Patan**. It includes a famous botanical garden of Nepal. It is also the site of Nepal's first formal English-medium school called the **St. Xavier's School** that was established and run by Christian missionaries. *See also* FATHER MORAN.

GOKARNA. Village, forested area, northeast of **Kathmandu**, on the bank of the **Bagmati River**. It features the temple of Gokarneswor and a park called Rajanikunja. It is believed to have been the Valley's capital of during the **Licchavi period**.

GOLCHHA, RAM LAL (1898–1983). Born in present day Bangladesh, Golchha came to Nepal in 1921. A decade later, he opened Nepal's first jute mill called the **Biratnagar Jute Mills** in 1931 and later the Raghupati Jute Mills in 1946. His contribution to Nepal's industrial development is considerable. In addition to his industrial contribution, he built the Golchha Eye Hospital in 1981.

GOLDEN PAGODA. Known in Nepali as the Hiranya Varna Mahavihar, the Golden Pagoda is located in **Patan**. It has a three-tiered, gilded roof and beautifully carved wooden windows and figures. Built in the twelfth century, it contains a magnificent golden **Buddha** and outsized **prayer**

wheel (not available to be seen by tourists) and other magnificent carvings and gold objects.

GOLDEN PHEASANT. Large golden bird (*Chrysolophus pictus*) found in the **mountains**. Adorned with a golden crest, its body is covered with hairlike feathers and orange and black markings.

GOMBA (GOMPA). Buddhist religious shrine, commonly seen in **Sherpa** villages and other mountainous areas where **Buddhism** and **Lamaism** are practiced. It is believed that the Thukchen Gomba of **Mustang** is the largest of all the Gombas found in Nepal.

GOPALA DYNASTY. Dynastic rulers in ancient Nepal. Few records are available about this dynasty and its institutional setup. It was a dynasty founded by **cow** (*go*, a **Sanskrit** variant of *gai*) herders or protectors (*pala*) that predated the **Kirata** dynasty in the **Kathmandu Valley**. Given their way of life, it is plausible to contend that the Gopala dynasty was a period marked by the pastoral mode of production and technology.

GORE. Descriptive term for white people from Europe and America. It literally means something that looks white. It is sometimes deployed as a derogatory term against Americans and Europeans. *See also* FIRANGI.

GORKHA. District in the **Gandaki Zone**, with a population of 252,524 in 1991, distributed over an area of 3,610 sq. km (*see* figures 2 and 3). Prior to unification, it was a principality (*see* **Chaubise Rajya**). It has a hill town with the same name. It is also a generic term applied to the people of Nepal in some parts of the world, especially in connection with its mercenary soldiers, the Gorkhas (or Gurkhas as the British called them with an Anglo Saxon tongue twist). As mercenaries, the Gorkhas were mostly recruited from the **Magar, Gurung, Limbu**, and **Rai** tribes. They were made famous by imperial **Britain** as they died in droves fighting to defend its empire across the globe during World War I and World War II.

GORKHA DAKSHINBAHU. Royal decoration medal instituted in 1895 by King Prithvi Bir Bikram Shah.

GORKHA DURBAR. Small hilltop palace in **Gorkha** (*see* figure 2). It housed the royal seat of the Shah kings of the Gorkha principality prior to national unification launched by **Prithvi Narayana Shah**, the land king of the House of Gorkha and the first **Shah** king of unified Nepal.

GORKHAKALI MANDIR. Famous temple of Goddess **Kali** situated at the top of a hill in the **Gorkha** district (*see* figure 2). Commonly known as **Manakamana**, it is one of the most popular temples where devout **Hindus** from all over Nepal come to worship. Animal sacrifices (male goats, roosters, and ducks) are an important feature of worship at this temple. Especially on Saturdays, one can observe a huge crowd waiting in line to worship at the temple. To accommodate older and weak folks, who previously had difficulty reaching the temple due to a long, relatively steep, and arduous climb from the base, a ropeway (cable car) has been installed to carry people to and from the temple, thus making it much more accessible than before. The only other Hindu temple that can match its reputation and the massive display of animal sacrifices is **Dakshinkali** located in the **Kathmandu Valley**.

GORKHAKALI RUBBER INDUSTRY. Rubber **industry** established as a public enterprise in the **Gorkha** district. Constructed with Chinese aid, production started in 1992.

GORKHALI. Person from **Gorkha** (*see* figure 2). It is also used generically sometimes to refer to the people of Nepal or to hill dwellers interchangeably with *pahari* (hill people) or *parbate* (mountain people). However, such a reference is hardly ever made in Nepal or by a Nepali person in a serious sense; it is sometimes uttered in **India** or by foreigners who possess only minimal historical and cultural knowledge of Nepal.

GORKHAPATRA. Oldest Nepali newspaper. It literally means "Gorkha paper" (*patra*). Originally it was a weekly whose publication began in 1901; it was launched by Prime Minister Dev Shamsher Rana whose unusually liberal views led to his early demise (*see* **Education**). It became a daily newspaper in 1966. As a government publication, however, the *Gorkhapatra* invariably functions as a mouthpiece of state policies and positions. This was especially true during the **Panchayat** system. In some respect, it can be called a royal palace newspaper. Even now it never fails to glorify the royal family whenever there is an opportunity to do so.

Regardless of its biases, there is little doubt about its contribution to the field of journalism in Nepal. It also played an important role in the development of Nepali **literature** during the early 1900s when it acted as an outlet for Nepali writers to publish their poems and stories. The English version of this daily newspaper is titled *The Rising Nepal*.

GORKHAPATRA CORPORATION. Public enterprise incorporated in 1963 to look after the publication, sales, and distribution of newspapers and magazines. Its publications include the *Gorkhapatra*, *The Rising Nepal*, the literary magazine *Madhuparka*, the youth magazine *Yuva Mancha*, and *Muna* for children.

GORKHA PARISHAD. Common designation of the Nepal Rastrabadi Gorkha Parishad (Nepal Nationalist Gorkha Council), a party formed in 1951 by a group of **Rana** revivalists. It is no longer in existence.

GOSAIKUNDA. Mountain lake in Rasuwa, situated at the altitude of 4,360m. Surrounded by ice-capped mountains, it is the main source of the Trishuli Gandaki River. Because of its religious connotation, it is one of the **Hindu** pilgrimages in Nepal.

GOTH. Shepherd's hut where domestic animals are kept. It is often used in the context of **mountain** transhumance, a practice that involves moving *goths* with animal herds (e.g., goats and sheep). It is a cyclical process as *goths* are moved to low hills and valleys during bitter winter months (November to January) and back to high mountains after the winter subsides.

GREAT BRITAIN. See BRITAIN-NEPAL RELATIONS.

GUHESWORI. Hindu temple center on the bank of the **Bagmati**, next to the temple of **Pashupati**. Enshrined here is a *kalash* (triangular-shaped water vase), which represents Goddess Parvati or Taleju or simply indicates a symbolic vaginal representation (*yoni*) of female procreation. It includes the Guheswori temple.

GUNDRUK. It is fermented, dehydrated vegetable, strictly indigenous to Nepal; it is rarely found in any other cultures, including its closest neighbor **India** unless imported. *Gundruk* is made from a variety of winter vegetables such as cabbage, mustard, cauliflower, or raddish greens. The greens are first slightly sundried, beaten down to extract juice, packed tightly in bamboo, wooden, or clay containers for several days until they are fermented (but not rotten), and then taken out and thoroughly dried in the sun. *Gundruk* can be mixed with other dishes or prepared as a separate dish. No matter how it is fixed, it is perhaps the most typical specialty of Nepal.

GUPHA. See BAHRA (BARHA).

GURAGAIN, GOPAL (1948–). Leftist politician from the **Dhankuta** district (*see* figure 2). A member of the **Communist Party of Nepal**, he served as a teacher for 18 years and participated in various leftist movements. He was elected to the **House of Representatives** in 1991. During the 1994 general elections, he lost his House seat to former Prime Minister **Surya Bahadur Thapa**, a **National Democratic Party** candidate.

GURKHA. See GORKHA.

GURUBACHARYA, NARAYAN GOPAL (1939–1990). Modern singer and highly popular. Popularly known as Narayan Gopal, he greatly contributed to popularizing modern Nepali **music**. He received many awards for his singing and musical contributions before his death, which many believe was greatly hastened by his heavy drinking and smoking habit. To this day, he is a household name as his songs still command a wide spectrum of the Nepali audience.

GURUNG. Ethnic group concentrated in the central and western hills of Nepal. They are one of the most recognized hill ethnic groups within the **Tibeto-Nepali** population, particularly for their martial qualities. As a result, the Gurungs were primary targets of recruits for the British **Gorkhas** or imperial army. They are also one of the largest Tibeto-Nepali groups in terms of their demographic size. *See also* ETHNICITY.

GURUNG, AMBAR (1935–). Modern musician. He began his career as a **music** teacher in **Darjeeling** and later moved to Nepal, as many other artists and literary figures of Nepali origin have done before and after him. He is associated with **Radio Nepal** and has received many awards for his music and musical contributions.

GURUNG, BAKHAN SINGH (1900–1982). Politician closely affiliated with the **Nepali Congress Party**. He was instrumental in opening up the **Rapti Valley** in **Chitwan** (*see* figure 2) for settlement, even before it was officially opened in a planned manner. He enticed and led a number of supporters from the central hills, mostly Congress Party members, to Chitwan and settled, thus creating a strong political base in the district.

GURUNG, GOPAL. Politician and founding president of the **Mongol National Organization**. He is an active advocate of the social welfare and civil rights of the Mongoloid people in Nepal. However, in some corners of Nepal, he is viewed as a divisive figure. As Gopal Gurung plays up his ethnic politics, his movement is seen by some as a threat to tiny Nepal's national unity, which the nation has managed to carefully navigate up to this point.

GURUNG, HARKA BAHADUR (1939–). Politician, policymaker, and scholar. He is one of the earliest Ph.D. degree recipients in geography and has authored several books and served in various high-ranking capacities within the government. He was head of the **National Planning Commission**, the development policymaking body in the country, for four years (1971–1975). He is now considered by many to be a Nepali statesman.

GURUNG, TUL BAHADUR (1958–). Leftist politician. He served as president (1987–1990) of the **All Nepal National Free Students' Union**. He was elected to the **Parliament** in 1991, representing the **Communist Party of Nepal**. He was reelected from the Kaski district (*see* figure 2) during the general **elections** held in 1994. Given its strong **Gurung** population base, Kaski has a long history of electing Gurungs to the Parliament, dating back to the very first such election of 1959.

GUTHI. Religious fund or association, a form of tax-free landholdings dedicated to religious purposes. It is also a clannish type of community institution found among the **Newars**.

GUTHI SANSTHAN. Public corporation founded in 1964 to look after the affairs of *guthi* institutions. It holds many traditional worshiping and festival events. Although this corporation was created only about 40 years ago, *guthi* as a religious, social, and cultural institution has a long history in Nepal, particularly in its **Kathmandu Valley.**

GYAWALI, SURYA BIKRAM (1898–1985). Born and educated in India, he made enormous contributions to the cause of Nepali language, literature, culture, and history. During his career he published several biographical books on various Nepali political figures, both in India and Nepal. In addition, he edited A *Concise Nepali Dictionary*, which is believed to have elevated Nepali as a language to a higher level.

H

HABRE. Local name of red pandas (*Ailurus fulgens*). They are found in the highland of Nepal and are regarded as rare and endangered species.

HANUMAN. Hindu monkey god. Devotee of Lord **Rama**, he is featured prominently in the famous **Hindu** epic called the *Ramayana*. He is worshiped by Hindus as a powerful symbol of faithfulness, strength, and courage and has his statue displayed at the gate leading to the courtyard of the *durbar* (palace) that once housed the Malla kings of **Kathmandu.** Built by King **Pratap Malla**, this palace gate (*dhoka*) is widely known as the Hanuman Dhoka. *See also* KATHMANDU DURBAR SQUARE.

HARITAL (HADITAL). Mass protest often associated with the practice of civil disobedience, although it is sometimes inflicted with violence often resulting from confrontations between police and protesters. It occurs quite frequently throughout Nepal, especially on college and university campuses. *See also* LATHI.

HEALTH CARE. Nepal's medical system or practices can be grouped into three categories. They are: home-based (including shamanistic or traditional healing); Ayurvedic (homeopathic); and modern (Western or allopathic). The home-based medical system is prevalent throughout Nepal; it is based on both herbal treatment and faith healing (i.e., shamanism or deity worship). *Dhami* and *jhankri* are common Nepali terms used to describe those who are shamans or who act as healers in the shamanistic tradition. There is hardly a community where one cannot find a *dhami* or *jhankri*. For the vast number of people in Nepal, use of locally available herbs and a shaman is the first line of health treatment. Despite the onslaught of modern medicines, this age-old home-based medical practice remains highly popular in Nepal's local as well as national health system. In the nation's countless remote areas, it is the only system available.

On the other hand, the Ayurvedic medical system has its foundation rooted in one of the four Vedic hymnal scriptures: the *Ayur (Yajur) Veda (Ayurveda)*, which literally means the doctrinal scriptures (*Veda*) of health or life (*Ayur*). Heavily reliant on drug compounds prepared out of medicinal herbs and other natural elements, this medical system has a long history in the health system of Nepal. The highest ranking Ayurvedic medical doctor in this system is called the *kabiraj (kaviraj)*, whose number in the country is believed to total 211. Many go to **India** to receive their formal Ayurvedic medical training. The next in the rank is called the *baidya (vaidya)*, and there are around 210 *baidyas* in the country. Despite its enduring history, the Ayurvedic healing network is relatively limited as it is often confined to urban centers. Moreover, it is largely a private sector initiative, encompassing a total of about 500 practitioners and 100 clinics.

Ayurveda is used throughout the Indian subcontinent as a foundational source of medical knowledge and practices. As Professor L. M. Singh has noted, its prevalence in the past is vividly reflected in the fact that its use in the country spanned from ordinary peasants to ornate palaces. Before the country was opened to the outside world in 1951, every **Rana** and **Shah** *durbar* and military outfit had an official *baidya* attached to them. When **Jang Bahadur Rana** went to England, his *baidya* accompanied him to look after his health as well as the health of his entourage. In 1928, the Rajkiya Ayurveda Vidyalaya (Royal Ayurveda Institute) was started in Naradevi, a small **Kathmandu** neighborhood, to train *baidyas* up to the Acharya level, equivalent to bachelor of the present day standards.

Following the advent of democracy and Nepal's subsequent entry into the modern world in 1951, efforts have focused on modernization and expansion of modern health services. Consequently, the Ayurvedic system of healing almost went into a coma, experiencing a period of sustained decline. Already confined to urban areas with a limited reach, the penetration of modern (Western) medical practices and medicines further dampened its desirability. In the last two decades, however, the Ayurvedic system has regained some of the ground it lost earlier. Although most of the Ayurvedic drugs are imported from India, **Dabur Nepal**, an affiliate of India's major Ayurvedic company called Dabur, has begun to produce some of them for the domestic market. In addition, the government of Nepal has begun to promote Ayurvedic tradition by supporting the production of herbal plants.

Application of modern medical practices is relatively new in Nepal. In practical terms, it is fair to assert that their systematic introduction to the Nepali masses only dates back to the early 1950s. It is true that a hospital with some modern medical practices did exist in Nepal: the **Bir Hospital**, which was established by Prime Minister Bir Shamsher Rana in the early 1890s. Until then, the only hospital in Kathmandu was the one within the British Residency. But these are little more than historical footnotes in terms of mass access to modern medicines and medical practices. Initially brought by Christian missionaries, the allopathic system of medical cure and delivery became available only after the demise of the Rana regime. The Christian missionaries set up hospitals in Nepal's different areas, including the Shanta Bhawan Hospital in the **Kathmandu Valley** and the Shining Hospital in **Pokhara** and **Palpa**. With these and other missionary hospitals acting as chief conduits, the modern medical system gained rapid popularity among the general populace, dwarfing the Ayurvedic system. In addition to preventive vaccinations of Nepali masses (children)—for example, against smallpox—the new health system was responsible for curative medicines.

Practice of the allopathic health system has grown tremendously since its early days in the 1950s. Today, it has a wide network in the country. In 1999, there were 83 public hospitals and about 50 private hospitals and clinics. In addition, 160 primary health care centers, 705 health posts, and almost 3,200 sub-health posts were reported. While these figures certainly represent some progress in the public health sector of Nepal, health care delivery is quite poor in terms of both its physical accessibility and quality. Most of the primary health care centers and health posts suffer from chronic shortages of medical personnel, necessary medicines, and medical facilities. Many of them exist only in name, as the assigned nurses or other medical staff are absent from their posts. As a result, they are closed and inaccessible. The nation has only 5,000 hospital beds, 923 medical doctors, and 4,700 nurses to serve some 23 million people. What is more, the hospitals, doctors, and nurses are concentrated in the capital city and a few other urban areas. Most of the rural areas still remain outside the reach of medical facilities and centers.

The following table provides some key indicators of public health status in Nepal. The table reflects the figures available in 1996 unless specified:

Public Health Indicators	Figures
Births with no prenatal care (%)	56
Births at home (%)	92
Births receiving no assistance from trained personnel (%)	90
Mean time to health facility by region (in minutes)	
Mountain	86
Hill	61
Tarai	40
Male HIV/AIDS cases (reported in 2000)	19,000
Female HIV/AIDS cases (reported in 2000)	11,000
Pregnant women with anemia (%)	63
Mean duration of breast-feeding (in months)	28
Women married by age 19 (%)	44
Married women giving birth by age 19 (%)	42
Neonatal mortality rate	50
Infant mortality rate	79
Child mortality rate (under age 5)	118

Neonatal tetanus, measles, acute respiratory tract infection, polio, tuberculosis (TB), and diarrhea are some of the principal killers of children in the underdeveloped world. They are also the major causes of disability. And Nepal is no exception. TB is quite prevalent despite a notable effort to curb it through child vaccination. In 1996, it was reported that over 75 percent of children aged 12–23 months had been vaccinated against TB, DPT, and polio. The number of children who had been vaccinated against measles stood at 57 percent.

In addition to these diseases, one chronic public health problem infecting Nepal is malnutrition, a problem which invariably magnifies other diseases as it results in a reduced level of natural immunity. It is obvious that malnutrition is a function of food shortages, along with necessary minerals, vitamins, and proteins. This problem has a debilitating effect on the poor and in the hill and **mountain** areas of the country where food deficits are quite common. Evidently, there is considerable malnutrition among Nepali children, with many of them trapped in a vicious cycle of malnutrition, poor health, and perpetual poverty. Nearly 50 percent of the children under three years of age are stunted, 11 percent wasted, and 47 percent underweight. Compounding this health problem are micronutrient deficiencies, e.g., vitamin A, iron, and iodine. It is no surprise that approximately 40 percent of the children between the ages of 6 and 11 suffer from goiter. Similarly, roughly 80 percent of them aged 6–48 months are diagnosed with anemia, resulting from iron deficiency. *See also* NEPAL LEPROSY ASSOCIATION; UNITED STATES-NEPAL RELATIONS

HELAMBU. Trekking resort in Sindhupalchok. Historically very well known as a place of beautiful girls, the **Rana** rulers acquired concubines from this village. It is also an important center of apple production in Nepal.

HETAUDA. One of the earlier industrial centers of Nepal. Located in the district of Makawanpur, it had a population of 54,072 in 1991. It is the major gateway to **Kathmandu** from the south.

HETAUDA INDUSTRIAL DISTRICT. Based in **Hetauda** in the central **Tarai**, it was set up with American aid. It produces various consumer goods. It also features a cement factory with a production capacity of 8,000 metric tons.

HETAUDA-KATHMANDU ROPEWAY. Nepal's only freight ropeway. It is a continuous cable carrying suspended loads (e.g., grains and construction materials). It was also the very first mechanical mode of long-distance freight **transportation**; prior to this, the movement of goods and products relied solely on humans and animal (donkeys and mules). Built in 1928, it was later replaced by the longer and larger cable, spanning 45 kilometers from **Hetauda** to **Kathmandu**. It carries up to 28 tons per hour with a maximum single load of one-half ton. In the absence of motorable roads, this ropeway was installed to allow the transport of heavy loads from **India** via **Birganj** and **Amlekhganj**. At one time, Nepal was exploring the possibility of constructing a series of ropeways in the middle hills to facilitate the transport of goods, but so far very little has happened. At any rate, although still used quite regularly, the transport value of this ropeway system diminished noticeably after the **Tribhuvan Rajpath** (highway) was constructed, linking Birganj to Kathmandu. *See also* GORKHAKALI.

HILLARY, SIR EDMUND (1919–). Mountain climber and explorer from New Zealand. Along with **Tenzing Norgay (Sherpa)**, Hillary is the first climber to successfully scale **Mount Everest**. They did it 50 years ago in 29 May 1953. Now that his mountaineering days are behind him, Sir Edmund Hillary devotes much of his time and energies to environmental causes and to humanitarian efforts on behalf of the Nepali people, particularly the **Sherpa** tribe with whom he has developed a close bond. Nepal celebrated the fiftieth anniversary of his first ascent of Everest by making Hillary an honorary Nepali citizen.

HILL REGION. One of the ecological regions of Nepal. It runs parallel to the **Himalayan Mountains** to the north and the **Tarai** region to the south. This is where the **Shah** dynasty rose. With the **Kathmandu Valley** centrally located in this region, the hills are definitely the political and cultural hearth of Nepal, although it is dependent on the Tarai for economic resources, namely grains. In short, Nepal's national identity is rooted here. The region is also the primary domain of the major segment of the Indo-Nepali population in the country. *See also* Introduction.

HIMALAYA. (*Him* = snow; *Alaya* = abode, collection.) It is a Sanskrit word, which means "snow-capped **mountains**." The Nepali variant of this word is *himal*. The central and major segment of the Himalayan Range, containing the majority of the 10 tallest peaks, passes through northern parts of Nepal and occupies almost 20 percent of the country's total land mass. It is this section of the country that is generally referred to as the Himalayan or mountain region, lying immediately to the north of the **Hill region**. From a geological perspective, these are considered some of the youngest mountains in the world, and are still growing in height. According to **Hindu** mythology, this is the land of gods, the land where they dwell and recreate. Towering over the whole region as a crest is none other than **Mount Everest**. *See* Introduction.

HIMALAYAN BANK LIMITED. Commercial bank founded in 1992 as a public company in a joint venture with the Habib Bank of Pakistan. It was created by **Himalaya Shamsher Rana**.

HIMAL CEMENT COMPANY. Public enterprise founded in 1974 and incorporated in 1976. It is located at **Chovar**.

HINAYANA. School of Buddhism advocating adherence to the principle of **ahimsa** (nonviolence). It literally means the Lesser Vehicle standing in contrast to **Mahayana** which means the Great Vehicle. Its followers are Theraveda Buddhists (the ancient ones) whose strongholds include Burma, Indonesia, Kampuchea (Cambodia), Laos, Sri Lanka, and Thailand. Monks following this school wear yellow robes.

HINDU. Observer of **Hinduism**; something pertaining to Hinduism.

HINDUISM. Hinduism is the oldest formal religion in the world. Unlike other major religions of the world such as Buddhism, Christianity, and Islam that are monotheistic in their respective belief systems, Hinduism is distinctly polytheistic with a pantheon of deities. At times, it appears that what Hinduism reveals is an uncanny functional division of gods and goddesses as they come with different functions and powers. But they are considered merely different manifestations of a single underlying divinity that is expressed as a Hindu triad comprising the religion's three major gods: **Brahma, Vishnu,** and **Shiva**. What they respectively personify are: creation, preservation, and destruction. This division of the universality of their functions is, however, somewhat technical as Vishnu and Shiva can both function as the protector and destroyer, depending on the particular context and the demand of time.

Hindus believe that the totality of existence, including God, man, and universe, is too vast to be contained within a single set of beliefs. One fundamental precept of Hinduism is that of **dharma**, loosely defined as religious acts and obligations. It holds that individuals should play their proper role in society as prescribed by their dharma. The **caste system** has been incorporated as an integral part of its social expression, as each person is born into a particular caste whose traditional occupation is graded according to the degree of inherent caste purity or impurity.

The other side of dharma is **karma** (universal justice; the outcome of dharmic or undharmic acts and duties). The belief is that the consequence of every good or bad action must be fully realized. In other words, one's dharmic act dictates his or her karmic manifestation and one's karmic act or outcome reflects his or her dharmic deeds and behavior. The two are, therefore, absolutely inseparable. Another basic concept is that of samsara, the transmigration of souls; rebirth is required by karma in order that the consequences of action be fulfilled. The role an individual must play throughout his or her life is fixed by his or her good and evil actions in previous existence. It is only when the individual soul sees beyond the veil of maya—illusion or the belief in the appearance of things—that it is able to realize its identity with the impersonal, transcendental reality (world soul) and then escape from the otherwise endless cycle of birth and rebirth to be absorbed into the world soul. This ultimate release is what the Hindus call *moksha*—a concept similar to **nirvana** in **Buddhism**.

Buddha, the founder of Buddhism, is regarded as the ninth **avatar** of Vishnu. Some Hindus regard Christ as the tenth avatar; others regard Kalkin (Kalki) as the final avatar who is yet to come to rescue the world from total abyss ushered in by the **Kali yuga** or aeon (not Goddess **Kali**), a redemptive conception of the world that has its parallel in the apocalyptic thinking in Christianity. According to Hindu cosmogony, we are actually currently undergoing the Kali yuga, the yuga marked by the confusion and conflicts of classes, the overthrow of established standards, the cessation of religious rites, and the subjugation by cruel and alien rulers. When seen in a cosmic context, the concept of avatar appears fundamental to Hinduism, as time is conceived in epochal terms. That is, every yuga represents a different time period with its own distinct character, configuration, and problem, demanding a different solution. What this means is that time is a changing concept and the change is constant in Hinduism.

In view of this universality of change as being constant and every new yuga being different than the previous one, a new avatar emerges as the demand of changing time: a new solution to a new problem. As a result, different avatars are believed to descend upon earth from time to time to restore peace and order, thus saving humanity from injustice and miseries or simply regenerating the orderly world. The Hindu view of the centrality of avatars in the unending universal cycle of creation, preservation, and destruction is, therefore, as much pure philosophy as it is religion. It is a profound concept equipped to capture the continuous decay and regeneration of the universe or humanity in general. *See also* MAHABHARATA.

HOLI. Festival of colors widely observed by **Hindus**. It is marked by joyful splashing of colored powders and liquids on friends, relatives, or almost anybody. This festival is invariably celebrated in the month of Falgun (February–March).

HOUSE OF REPRESENTATIVES. Known as the Pratinidhi Sabha in Nepali, it is the Lower House of **Parliament**, represented by 205 elected members from 75 districts in the country. It is the primary legislative body of the country. Whichever party manages to muster the majority of votes in the House of Representatives—whether through its own party majority or by means of forming a coalition of parties—forms the government and appoints the prime minister. In other words, the prime minister must be a member of the House of Representatives, whereas the cabinet ministers can be appointed (selected) from either the House of Representatives or the Upper House of Parliament (National Council).

As a general rule, the prime minister can dissolve the House before its five-year term expires. Under such circumstances, fresh **elections** are held within six months to elect a new House of Representatives. In fact, in May 2002, Prime Minister **Sher Bahadur Deuba** dissolved the House of Representatives elected in 1999 prior to the expiration of its term in 2004. And the new elections were scheduled to be held in November 2002. Just as the prime minister can dissolve the House at any time, the House can bring the ruling prime minister down at any time by passing a vote of no confidence with a simple majority. In the event the prime minister loses the vote of confidence, a new prime minister is elected through the process described above. *See also* CONSTITUTIONS; ELECTORAL SYSTEM.

HRIDAYA, CHITTADHAR (1906–1981). He was a distinguished poet of the **Newari** language—one of the best known in the **Kathmandu Valley**. His more than three dozen published works have played a prominent and enduring role in elevating and enriching the Newari language and **literature**, largely centered in the Kathmandu Valley.

HUKUM. Order, command, generally associated with the ruler's order. It has a distinct feudalistic or authoritarian connotation. Until 1990 the ruling monarch's *hukum* was the final word that superceded any other judgement, law, or rule.

HUMAN RIGHTS. Although Nepal has suffered human rights abuses throughout history, with the climax reached during the **Rana** period, the concept is relatively new, dating back to the late 1980s. It took off in the early 1990s, following the return of democracy. While it has many dimensions, the immediate application of the concept in Nepal is found in the arena of political freedom and killings. It is no surprise that the issue of human rights abuses has received heightened attention since the onset of the **People's War** in 1996.

Amnesty International has reported that unlawful killings, torture, disappearances, arbitrary arrests, and detention have been carried out by the police and army in the context of the People's War. On the other hand, the Maoist revolutionaries are responsible for some killings, hostage-taking, and torture, including the abduction of 69 police officers and two civilians in the Rolpa district on 13 July 2001. The human rights situation has sharply deteriorated since 1996, and it has gotten worse since the imposition of the state of emergency in late November 2001.

The state of emergency declared by King Gyanendra was accompanied by a Terrorist and Disruptive Activities Ordinance (TADO). They were followed by the suspension of several fundamental rights, including the right to **constitutional** remedy (apart from habeas corpus), the right to assembly, the right to freedom of thought and expression, and the right not to be held in preventive detention without sufficient grounds. Concerns were raised by many that the unspecific definition of "terrorist" would give the government a wide latitude of powers allowing for detainees to be held in preventive detention for up to 90 days, with an extension of up to 180 days on the consent of the home ministry—which is just a mere formality—and could lead to people being detained for expressing peaceful oppositional views on policy differences.

Shortly after the deployment of the state of emergency and TADO, the army was accused of extrajudicial executions, i.e., killing civilians during "cordon and search" operations and shootings from helicopters at alleged Maoists. In one incident at Bargadi, Dang district, on 28 November 2001, 11 farmers were shot dead by an army patrol. Even though some of them may have been sympathizers of the Maoist movement, eyewitnesses claimed that none of them were armed and that soldiers deliberately shot them.

Prior to the above abuse, there were, according to the report filed by Amnesty International, numerous cases of "disappearance" under police and army operations. Further evidence emerged that prisoners were held by police in secret detention. Over 5,000 people were held in unacknowledged detention by police and army, sometimes for several weeks. Sixteen students were arrested in **Kathmandu** in December 2000 and held in incommunicado detention for a month.

In March, the government published a list of 282 people who were held in custody for their alleged involvement in "terrorist activities" and 12 others said to have been held in solitary confinement. Among them was Ishwari Dahal whose whereabouts had been unknown since he was arrested in September 2000. The list contained only three of the 73 Maoists whose whereabouts the Maoist leadership had urged the government to clarify.

There were several reports of torture, including rape, by police. The army was also responsible for torture, including subjecting prisoners to mock executions. There have also been many cases of arbitrary arrest and detention. For example, the arrests on 6 June of Yubaraj Ghimire, editor in chief of the main Nepali newspaper *Kantipur*, and his colleagues, Binod Raj Gyawali and Kailash Sirohiya, were seen as a warning to the **media** to refrain from commenting adversely on the massacre of the royal family. Their arrests were connected with the publication in *Kantipur* of an opinion piece by **Baburam Bhattarai**, a Maoist leader, in which he accused **India** and the **United States** of being behind the royal massacre and urged army personnel not to support the new king. Amid widespread protests, they were released on bail on 15 June. The case against them was subsequently withdrawn.

Krishna Sen was rearrested soon after he was released from jail on 10 March on the order of the **Supreme Court**, including the chief justice, and "disappeared" for five days afterwards. He was released amid widespread protests. In addition, several human rights defenders and more than 30 journalists were among more than 5,000 people arrested by army and police.

As noted earlier, there have been visible human rights violations on the Maoist side as well. Several members of the **Nepali Congress Party** (NCP) and the **Communist Party of Nepal** (i.e. the Unified Marxist-Leninist faction) were killed by the Maoist forces. The abduction of civilians and police, and the linking of their release to certain conditions, became a prominent feature of the People's War. They were also responsible for the execution-style killing of 8 police officers who were among 28 who had surrendered to them at Toli, Dailekh district, on 7 April.

Mukti Prasad Sharma, president of the Pyuthan District Committee of the NCP and former member of **Parliament**, was abducted on 22 May from his home at Tikuri, Pyuthan district. The next day, *Jana Ahwan*, a weekly known to be supportive of the Maoists, reported that the Maoist leadership had demanded the release of five of its members in return for the release of Mukti Prasad Sharma. He was allowed to return home on 12 July. The next day, Lokendra Bista, one of the five Maoists who had been imprisoned since 1996, was released.

In short, there have been numerous human rights abuses on both the state (police and army) and Maoist sides. In the first eight months since the imposition of the state emergency, more than 2,500 deaths have been reported as a result of armed confrontations between the two sides. Most of those casualties involve innocent citizens killed by army firings under the guise of combating "Maoist terrorists." Many have been detained arbitrarily in the name of national security, including some journalists. **Press** freedom has eroded and dissenting voices have been systematically silenced.

According to Amnesty International, despite some isolated moves on the part of the government to provide redress to victims of human rights violations by its police and army, official accountability was widely lacking. Moreover, the effective functioning and activity of the National Human Rights Commission has been hampered. *See also* CONSTITUTIONS.

HYDROELECTRIC POWER. Nepal's hydroelectric power potential is second in the world only to that of Brazil. According to the statistics published by the electricity department, Nepal's estimated potential is 83 million kilowatts of electric power, mostly confined to the three principal river systems: 32 million kilowatts in the **Karnali** basin, 21 million kilowatts in the **Gandaki** basin, and 22 million kilowatts in the **Kosi** basin. Harnessing this potential is, however, an entirely different matter for many reasons. For example, first, there is the lack of necessary capital and technology to develop it. Second, market demand uncertainties are a serious concern even if capital could be raised to develop it. **India** is obviously the primary market, but Nepal's utterly dependent position in its relations with the country makes the demand market issue very volatile and unpredictable. Third, massive dam construction creates enormous environmental consequences, including substantial human displacement.

I

IDRISH, SHEKH (1926–1997). A politician from the Rautahat district, he was elected to the **House of Representative** in 1991 and then became minister of labor and social welfare. He was later reelected to the House of Representatives during the general **elections** in 1994. He is one of the very few Muslim leaders in the country. The fact that he was elected to the House of Representatives two times suggests that the **Hindu** animosity toward the Muslims—a reality so entrenched and so prevalent across the border in **India**—is hardly an issue in the country. In fact, Nepal has rarely experienced Hindu-Muslim clashes. His election, thus, reflects the nature of party politics in which one's party affiliation generally tends to blur politicians' personal attributes such as **caste** and **religion**.

IJARA. Revenue farming, a system under which revenue was collected —or sources of revenue exploited—by an individual under contract with the government. It was particularly common in the **Tarai**. This system of land management is believed to date back the early period of the **Shah dynasty**. It was introduced to generate revenues from the Tarai land by bringing it under cultivation. Since not too many hill residents at that time were willing to reclaim and resettle land in the Tarai because of extreme malarial infestation, the *ijara* system was implemented to attract settlers from across the border in north **India** to develop and cultivate land in the Tarai on a contract basis. In the contemporary parlance, it was essentially a form of **privatization** of the state's land revenue functions, a system that remained intact until 1951. *See also* CHITWAN.

ILAM. District in the **Mechi Zone** (*see* figure 2). According to the 1991 census, it is populated by a total of 229,429 people, distributed over an area of 1,703 sq. km. Located in the eastern hills of Nepal, close to the famous tea-growing region of **Darjeeling**, Ilam is a leading tea producer in Nepal. *See also* LEPCHA.

INDIA-NEPAL RELATIONS. Formal diplomatic relations between the two countries were established in June 1947. But informal relations are much deeper and historical, rooted in their geographical proximity and cultural ties and inheritance. These realities are vividly reflected in the fact that India and Nepal have shared an open border since time immemorial. Nonetheless, the fact that Nepal is enclosed by India on three sides means the country is inherently dependent on India. Not surprisingly, therefore, their relations have occasionally exhibited signs of strain and sometimes been tense.

Irrespective of its inherent uneasiness with this utter dependence, India tops the list of Nepal diplomatic relations with foreign nations, superceding even the People's Republic of China (see **China-Nepal Relations**). Although Nepal's diplomatic relations with the two countries are about even, China cannot compete with India at a broader level. The links with China are not as extensive and expansive as they are with India, largely due to Nepal's physiographic layout and orientation.

Naturally, therefore, India-Nepal relations are far more extensive and entrenched. This inevitability has been further reinforced by the fact that, historically, Nepal's cultural ties with India go much deeper than with any other country. The population flows between the two countries are constant as both sides have maintained an open border policy with respect to the cross-border movement of their citizens. Most importantly, it is the economic relations that make Nepal and India intrinsically intertwined. This is particularly true for Nepal for at least two primary reasons. First, virtually all basic necessities that it cannot produce within its borders come from India, for example, petroleum, kerosene, salt, spices, and many other essential products, including raw materials for much of its industrial production. Second, as indicated above, India has a formidable choke hold on Nepal's transit facilities. As a landlocked country, Nepal has no direct access to the sea. It cannot even use the port facility in Bangladesh as the two nations are separated by a narrow strip of land, about 20 kilometers wide, that falls within Indian territory.

Consequently, the country is almost totally dependent on India and its diplomatic whims. This suffocating dependency was nakedly exposed and exploited in 1989, when India imposed a yearlong economic embargo, closing all border entry points except two and allowing only the minimum amounts of basic necessities to enter Nepal. While the disagreement over the terms of the new Trade and Transit Treaty was outwardly evoked as the reason for the embargo, the underlying cause was rooted in the Nepali king's decision to purchase certain military armaments from China without prior consultation with India. Because India fully realizes Nepal's extreme vulnerability and dependency, it never ceases to cast its ominous shadow over the Nepali regime. It is precisely this "bully" attitude and behavior on the part of India that engenders a profound sense of resentment across Nepal.

But, at the same time, most Nepalis realize the position they are in; they know there is little they can do to change it fundamentally. When their frustration boils over, they tend to vent it out through anti-India demonstrations and protests, shouting a few nasty slogans in front of the Indian embassy and even boycotting, occasionally, Hindi movies or burning effigies of Indian leaders. In the end, the practical reality sets in, the steam of anger evaporates, life reverts to the normal routine, and most Nepalis grudgingly bite the hard bullet. And, of course, they resume watching Hindu movies which, ironically, always seem to act as a palliative for all social ills as well as diplomatic ill feelings toward India.

INDO-NEPALI. Nepali people of Indian origin. *See* CASTE SYSTEM; ETHNICITY.

INDRA CHOWK. Famous conjunction and central area in **Kathmandu**. Known for its ancient bazaar and temples, including **Akash Bhairav**, it is one of the liveliest neighborhoods in the city. Being located right next to **Asan Tol** further enhances its liveliness and attractions. For those who are seeking to buy colorful glass necklaces and bangles, this is the place to go. No visit to Kathmandu is complete without a visit to Indra Chowk and Asan Tol whether the visitor is a foreign **tourist** or a Nepali from outside the Valley. It is believed to be named after Indra, the **Hindu** god of rain and king of gods who rules from heaven (**Swarga**).

INDRA JATRA. Festival observed for eight days during the month of Bhadra in honor of God **Indra**. The celebration is marked by masked dances, pole erection, chariot processions, and feasting. It starts with the raising of a flag called Indra Dhwajothan. This is accompanied by the display of the mask of **Akash Bhairav**. In addition, a *lingam* (a phallic symbol) is erected.

INDRAYANI. Mother goddess also known as Luti Ajima (or Ajima). She is said to possess the power to cure children's diseases, especially dysentery. When used in a casual sense, this word simply means a rainbow.

INDUSTRIAL AREA MANAGEMENT LIMITED. Public enterprise established in 1988 for the management of industrial districts in the country. It operates the industrial districts in **Balaju, Butwal,** Dharan, **Nepalganj, Patan,** Rajbiraj, and Surkhet. *See also* INDUSTRY.

INDUSTRY. Nepal's industrial development is in its infancy. This does not, however, mean the country is totally void of industrial history. Historically, Nepal was not only self-sufficient agriculturally; it also used to be self-supporting industrially. There were two main reasons why the country was relatively self-sufficient and even modestly advanced in craft, commercial, and small-scale industrial activities. First, and ironically, the very geographical isolation and landlocked condition that now stands as a huge impediment to progress led to an economic system reliant on itself for its requirements. As **Badri Prasad Shrestha** points out, "Such forced isolation and self-reliance made people industrious and content with whatever they had or whatever they could produce to meet all their few simple needs of daily life."

Second, the protective measures deliberately undertaken by the early **Shah** rulers promoted domestic trade and safeguarded Nepal's industrial infrastructure against foreign intrusion and competition. One example of such measures was the protective trade policy adopted by **Prithvi Narayan Shah** with regard to foreign imports and foreign merchants' entrance into the country. His instructions were to prohibit the use of foreign products and to encourage domestic production by utilizing local resources, by training local producers, and by providing them with samples of foreign products. This way money would not flow out of the country. On the other hand, herbs, drugs, and other indigenous products could be exported to foreign countries to earn money.

Even **Jang Bahadur Rana** understood the meaning and importance of Prithvi Narayan's protective economic policy. Despite cultivating a friendly relationship with the British in **India**, he kept a vigilant eye on the trade relations with them. However, the situation changed gradually with the passage of time. The more the **Ranas** and members of the nobility came in touch with the British, the faster the economic measures taken by the previous rulers to protect domestic industries from foreign competition dissipated. That is, the later Rana rulers showed little regard for the protective advancement of the existing domestic industrial foundation. Their lack of interest in fostering domestic industries was partially attributed to their preference for British imports. But it was also equally related to their perceived fear that indigenous technical innovations and economic progress would foment an upheaval in the Rana social and political order, eventually dismantling their autocratic rule.

Furthermore, some of the Western habits and ways of life adopted and cherished by the Ranas and members of the nobility began to slowly permeate into the upper crust of the Nepali public. This encouraged large inflows of cheap goods which hit hard, for the first time, the traditional craft of the country. The problem was further exacerbated when the Ranas signed a trade treaty with Great **Britain** in 1923, permitting practically unlimited imports of British goods and commodities into the country. Consequently, the domestic industries were effectively rendered impotent against British imports, thus marking their gradual demise. For example, the later Rana policy wreaked havoc on the relatively flourishing textile or cloth-making cottage industry of Bandipur in Tanahun district and other places.

In the midst of continued erosion of Nepal's industrial foundation and fortunes came World War II, which put a brake on the downward slide. In a sense, then, it can be plausibly argued that the so-called modern industrial history of Nepal began with the war. In response to the demand for jute products created by the wartime **economy**, the **Biratnagar Jute Mills** was established in the mid-1930s in an eastern **Tarai** town called **Biratnagar** located next to the Indian border. So high was the wartime demand for various industrial products that it engendered investment enthusiasm among entrepreneurs and industrialists. Soon after the creation of jute mills, several other factories were established, almost all of them in the Tarai's border towns because of their proximity to British India—the primary market for Nepali products. Furthermore, since Indian capital was most actively involved in the country's wartime industrial surge, the Tarai proved to be the most attractive location thanks to its easy accessibility to Indian railheads along the border, cultural similarity with north India, and ready access to Indian labor.

Between 1936 and 1945, some 20 joint stock companies sprouted, manufacturing mostly agro- and forest-based products such as paper, soap, furniture, matches, sugar, textiles, cigarettes, and mustard oil. Prominent among them were Juddha Match Factory, Morang Sugar Mills, and Nepal Plywood and Bobbin Company. Also established was the Morang Electricity Supply Company. By the time the Rana autocracy ended in 1951, a total of 65 companies had been registered, with the vast majority of industrial capital as well as labor coming from India. As the number of companies increased, so did the number of companies going belly up, especially after the end of the war. Such a rise in the liquidation rate was not surprising, especially in view of the fact Nepal's industrial growth during the war period was mostly attributed to the demand imperatives of the war economy, which entailed large profit margins. It had little to do with long-range industrial foresight, managerial experiences, sustained capital reinvestment, domestic markets, and necessary infrastructural development.

Nevertheless, the war economy proved to be instrumental in laying Nepal's industrial foundation. Its manufacturing base has expanded since then, albeit at a sluggish pace. The growth of **tourism** over the past 30 years and the deliberate adoption of neoliberal economic policies or **privatization** since the early 1990s have given added impetus to industrial growth and expansion. During the 1995–1999 period, the industrial sector accounted for close to 20 percent of GDP, with almost one-half of it coming from manufacturing alone. In addition, the industrial sector's share of national employment was almost 10 percent. It is estimated that this sector has been growing at the rate 4–5 percent per annum, which is considerably higher than the annual growth rate of 2.3 percent registered by the **agriculture** sector during the same period.

Nepal's industrial sector can be broadly categorized into two major groups: domestically oriented and export-based. The first group of industries tends to be largely agro-based, meaning much of their raw material needs can be met domestically. Included in this group are **rice**, sugar, cotton, paper, timber, and oil mills, along with cigarette and match factories. Some of them produce tools, utensils, bricks, and leather products. Also significant in this group are those enterprises focused on the country's growing tourist sector and the urban middle class. Although the middle class comprises perhaps no more than 5 percent of the total population, it does represent 20–25 percent of the national disposable income. Particularly notable among these enterprises are the beverage industry (beer and soft-drink production joint ventures are among the fastest growing enterprises) and the handicraft industry for which Nepal is quite well known.

Within the export-based manufacturing group, perhaps the most widely recognized is the **carpet industry**. Nepal's handmade carpet production is slowly gaining a foothold in the international carpet market, particularly in Germany. The gradual rise of the carpet industry is owed mostly to **Tibetan** refugees on the production front and to Western tourists on the consumption side. Settled in the country since the early 1960s, Tibetans are the primary drivers of this industry. On average, carpets alone account for more than 35 percent of Nepal's total exports, followed by ready-made **garments** which contribute another 27 percent. However, in 1999, the two exports were almost equal in terms of dollar values, with carpets grossing $144.2 million and ready-made garments $142.6 million.

Besides capital, there are five principal issues with regard to the viability of Nepal's sustained industrial growth and expansion. First, as already noted, its domestic market is very small and weak, a situation that automatically constrains its dynamic industrial growth. Second, except for some domestically oriented industrial enterprises, the country generally lacks necessary resources to fulfill its raw material needs. Consequently, it is heavily dependent on raw material imports, particularly for its export industries. Moreover, the industrial sector, in general, relies on imported technological resources and capital equipment. Third, its **transportation** and social infrastructure is very cumbersome and often unreliable. The country is totally dependent on India for transit facilities or sea access, the main artery of commodity flows. Fourth, as a result of the above limitations, Nepal is hardly in a position to enjoy any competitive advantage—cost or quality—in a world where deepening globalization has greatly heightened competition. Finally, political instability and resultant periodic administrative changes as well as directional uncertainties regarding economic policies are totally antagonistic to continued industrial growth and advancements.

INHI (EENHEE). **Newar** custom of marrying young girls with a **bel** (wood apple) before their actual marriages. Since the bel fruit is believed to be immortal, Newar **women** never become widows—technically—even after their human husbands die.

INNER TARAI. Also referred to as the Dun Valley, the inner **Tarai** is a valley (depression) sandwiched between the southern slopes of the **Churia Hills** to the north and the Tarai belt to the south. It is usually hot and malarial, with a relatively low quality of soil. Unlike the Tarai that straddles all the way from the east to the west along the border, the inner Tarai is found in only certain areas. The three major inner Tarai valleys are found in the Tarai districts of **Chitwan, Dang,** and Udayapur.

ISLAM. Religion observed by Muslims. Although it is the third-largest faith in Nepal, its adherents total only 3.5 percent of the population and are mostly found in the **Tarai.** Their biggest concentration is found in the western border city of **Nepalganj.**

J

JAGIR. Form of **land tenure** or landholding. It was common before 1951 when it was abolished. *Jagir* lands, which were tax-free, were granted routinely to military officers as compensation for their military service. Such lands were also assigned to other high-ranking *jagirdars* (holders of *jagir*, which literally means "government jobs") for their service.

JANA ANDOLAN. Public (popular) uprising, often applied in a political or revolutionary context. It usually implies a sustained and organized protest against a regime. There have been several *jana* (people, public) *andolans* (revolt, uprising) in Nepal, the most successful and historical being the one in 1950–1951 that toppled the **Rana** rule and another in 1990 that brought down the **Panchayat** system. *See also* HARITAL; JHAPA MOVEMENT.

JANAI. Sacred thread put around the neck or wrapped around the wrist. Most **Brahmans** and high grade **Chhetris** wear it around their necks on a permanent basis to suggest their **caste** purity. They are called the **Tagadhari** (*taga* = string; *dhari* = wearer) and are supposed to refrain from the consumption of alcohol and certain meats and foods. Strict adherents of the Tagadhari codes do not consume meat; they even avoid garlic. On the other hand, the wrist *janai* is a temporary phenomenon, as it is worn during the Janai Purnima festival and by non-Tagadhari members of the population as well.

JANAJATI (JANA JATI). Ethnic community. The term is now commonly used to refer to various tribal and lower **caste** groups who generally fall outside the **Bahun-Chhetri** axis.

JANAK. Janak ruled the Mithila Kingdom, located in southeastern Nepal, around twelfth century B.C. The region where Mithila was situated was then known as Videha. King Janak was believed to be a great idealist and benevolent king who courted and patronized philosophers and great minds in his court. His daughter **Sita** was married to **Rama**, the king of Ayodhya in northern **India**, a city which now resides at the center of recent **Hindu-Muslim** bloodshed and tensions in the region.

JANAKPUR. Border town in the Janakpur Zone (*see* figure 4). It is named after King **Janak** and was once the capital of his ancient kingdom and a highly acclaimed center of **Hindu** philosophical learning and discussions. Because of its ties to **Janak** and **Sita**, Janakpur is seen by Hindus as a holy city and important pilgrimage center.

JANAKPUR CIGARETTE FACTORY. Public corporation established in 1964 with Soviet assistance. Located in Janakpur (*see* figure 4), it is the biggest cigarette factory in the country.

JANAKPUR ZONE. Zone in southeastern Nepal along the Indian border. Named after King **Janak** who ruled at the same time **Rama**, the hero of the famous Hindu epic ***Ramayana***, was believed to be the crown prince of Kosala (Kausala) in northern **India**, Janakpur has a historic significance in the popular imagination of Hindu devotees. This zone includes six districts—Dhanusha, Dolakha, Mahottari, Ramechhap, Sarlahi, and Sindhuli (*see* figures 2 and 3). Its areal size totals 9,669 sq. km., populated by 2,058,735 people in 1991. This is one of the few zones that mostly lies in the **Tarai**.

JANGALI. Its root word is *jangal*, which means "jungle or forested and unpopulated area." In its vernacular use, the word *jangali* is a reference to somebody or something that is wild. In other words, it is often used to refer to somebody as uncivilized or very backward, or who acts wild.

JANG BAHADUR. *See* RANA, JANG BAHADUR.

JANTA (JANTI). Wedding procession. Throughout Nepal, traditional weddings are normally preceded and followed by a procession between the bride's and the bridegroom's residences.

JATRA. Public gathering during certain publicly celebrated **festivals**. It usually involves feasting, singing, dancing, and public processions. Nepal has many annual *jatras*. Sometimes, the word *jatra* is used in the context of creating a public scene out of private matters, for instance, a husband berating his wife in public. *See also* MUSIC AND DANCE.

JAWALAKHEL. Popular place in **Patan**. It is one of the major centers of local **Tibetan carpet** shops. Additionally, it is known for housing the nation's only zoo and for the presence of **St. Xavier's School**, the first Christian missionary, private, and English-medium school in the country.

JHANGAR. Small minority tribe in Sunsari. They are a solitary people who share only minimal cultural similarities with other **Tarai** groups and observe a mixture of animism and **Hinduism**.

JHAPA. District in the **Mechi Zone** (*see* figure 2), with a 1991 population of 594,100 people, settled in an area comprised of 1,606 sq. km. It is one of the most densely populated and agriculturally productive districts in the nation. In the 1970s, it was the primary base of what was then labeled the **Jhapa movement,** which engendered a profound sense of fear throughout the rural landlord class in the eastern **Tarai** region.

JHAPA MOVEMENT. The decade of the 1970s witnessed a resurgence of an armed struggle staged by a group of young radical communists inspired by Maoist philosophy and the Naxalite movement in **India**. The movement was directed against King **Mahendra Bir Bikram Shah** and his oppressive **Panchayat** system. It came to be known as the Jhapa movement because it sprang up in the eastern **Tarai** district of **Jhapa**. Despite its thunderous beginning, it ended with a whimper. It was a fairly small movement aimed at first attacking and destroying what is commonly referred to as "the class enemy" in the communist lexicon. The Jhapa movement was accused of being responsible for murdering several landlords in cold blood in the mid-1970s. By the end of the 1970s, the movement had basically fizzled because of three primary setbacks:

- Death of Chairman Mao Zedong in 1976—the spiritual leader of the Jhapa movement—and the subsequent decline of Maoism in **China** as well as elsewhere.
- Suppression of the Naxalite movement by the Indian government, a situation which greatly undermined the chief external source of support for the Jhapa movement.
- Lack of internal support from the local peasants who feared the movement no less than their presumed class enemy: the landlords. The fear was fundamentally attributed to the senseless and reckless radicalism and random murder of a few landlords in the name of exterminating the class enemy.

JHARRA. Forced or free labor, regularly deployed by the state and abused by the high-ranking officials and military officers. The state routinely exacted *jharra* labor from peasants and ordinary citizens without compensation. It was most commonly used during Nepal's territorial expansion, which started with **Prithvi Narayan Shah** and lasted until the end of the **Anglo-Nepal War** (1814–1816). The system was also abused during the **Rana** period. Many times, the *jharra* workers were required to bring their own rations in addition to providing free labor, thus plunging the Nepali peasantry into a state of underdevelopment.

JHYAURE. Popular folk singing and dancing, particularly common in the hills, often accompanied by a Nepali drum called a *madal*. Because of its uniqueness combined with a simple musical style, it has gained a significant national following. *See also* MUSIC AND DANCE; THAPA, DHARMA RAJ.

JIMIDAR (JAMINDAR). Private person authorized by the government to collect taxes in designated areas, usually called a *mauja*. Similar to **ijara**, this system of *jimidars* (also known as the *jimidari* system) was exclusively applied in the **Tarai**, again as a source of state revenue. As part of the contract, *jimidars* were required to transmit a specified amount of taxes to the state, a situation which often resulted in an undue exploitation of local peasants. In terms of its initiation and prevalence, it is coterminous with the *ijara* system. And, the *jimidars* are, in some way, similar to the zamindars in Mogul **India**. *See also* CHITWAN; LAND REFORM.

JIMMAWAL. Headman or revenue collector, usually for irrigated and private lands. Similar to ***jimidars*** in status and roles, *jimmawals* were mostly deployed in the hills, especially in areas where the peasants and farmers lacked access to a state land tax office called **Mal Adda** in Nepali.

JOINT BOUNDARY COMMISSION (1961). Officially known as the Sino-Nepal Joint Commission, it was formed by Nepal and China to adjudicate the boundary dispute. Although the boundary treaty was signed between the two countries in 1961, the joint commission was set up to agree on questions regarding the alignment, location, and maintenance of demarcation markers. The most problematic feature of the discussion was the Chinese claim to **Mount Everest**, which was eventually resolved by declaring the peak as a symbol of friendship and healthy **China-Nepal relations**. However, the Nepalis continue to lay claim to the peak as being in their territory—and this has not been challenged—although it is pragmatically and tacitly recognized that the north face of Everest is within the Chinese territory. The accord reached by the commission and its findings were formally embodied in the Sino-Nepal Boundary Treaty of October 1961.

One notable reason why King **Mahendra Bir Bikram Shah** willingly signed the 1961 treaty—by some account the king was eager to sign it—was because he was a playing a diplomatic game of pitting the two antagonistic neighbors against each other for his benefit. In essence, by tilting a little more toward China on the diplomatic scale, he was sending a message to **India** not to lend support to the self-exiled anti-king forces domiciled in India. In the early 1960s, following the **palace coup** against the elected government of **B. P. Koirala**, many party activists and leaders fled the country and took residence in India as they had done during their anti-**Rana** struggle. Using India as their base, those forces had carried out anti-royal incursions in the early 1960s along the border areas, thereby posing a plausible threat to Mahendra's autocratic rule. So the king saw his close leaning toward China as a necessary diplomatic hedge against India in case it chose to actively support the rebellious forces as it had done during their anti-Rana movement.

JOMSOM. **Thakali** settlement toward the northern reaches of the **Kali Gandaki River**. It is also the headquarters of the **Mustang** district (*see* figure 2), one of the leading producers of apples and apricots in the country. It is the last major settlement before reaching a relatively small **Bhote** (Bhotia) settlement in a place called **Muktinath**, one of the most significant destinations of **Hindu** pilgrims. Jomsom is also well known for its production of hard liquor from apples and apricots, which have largely failed to find a reliable market due to transport constraints.

JOSHI, GOVINDA RAJ (1949–). Politician from the district of Tanahun (*see* figure 2). A member of the **Nepali Congress Party**, he was elected to the **House of Representatives** in 1991 and served as minister of education and culture. He was reelected to the House in the two subsequent general **elections** held in 1994 and 1999.

JOSHI, SATYA MOHAN (1921–). A scholar who has written several books on Nepal's history and culture. He is also highly regarded for his valuable contributions to **Newari literature**, mostly confined to the **Kathmandu Valley**. His works have earned Joshi several national awards.

JOSHI, SHIVA RAJ (1952–). Politician from the Surkhet district (*see* figure 2). A member of the **Nepali Congress Party**, he was elected to the **House of Representatives** in 1991 and served as assistant minister of works and transport. He was reelected in the subsequent general **elections** held in 1994 and 1999, both times representing the Congress party.

JUDICIAL SYSTEM. The **constitution** provides for a judicial system headed by the **Supreme Court**. In the country's three-tiered court echelons, the Supreme Court resides at the top. Its justices, including the chief justice, are appointed by the king, and the tenure of the chief justice is limited to seven years from the date of appointment. As the ultimate judicial authority, the Supreme Court has the power to issue writs and orders as well as inspect, supervise, and give directives to all subordinate courts and all other institutions that exercise judicial powers for the enforcement or guarantee of the basic rights provided by the constitution. It can declare a law void ab initio if it determines that the impugned law contravenes the provision of the constitution. Although it is a separate unit within Nepal's constitutional system, its independence has at times been questioned because of its close ties and loyalty to the king. Supreme Court justices can be impeached in the **House of Representatives** for reasons of incapacity, misbehavior, abuse of power, or mala fide acts while in office.

Below the Supreme Court are found two formal lower tiers of judicial administration: appellate and district courts. In addition, courts or tribunals may be formed for the purpose of hearing special cases. The judges of all these courts are appointed by the king on the recommendation of the judicial council, which is presided over by the chief justice of the Supreme Court. The council is responsible for making recommendations and advising on transfers, promotions, and disciplinary actions of the judges of appellate and district courts and other matters related to judicial administration.

An independent judiciary, unencumbered by the executive branch of the government and palace interference, is a stated goal of political parties and a constitutional provision. In reality, however, historical records of Nepal's judicial independence and impartiality are extremely muddy. Furthermore, the judicial system has historically suffered from the absence of expeditious verdicts. Although some progress has occurred since the demise of the **Panchayat** system, this historically tarnished institution has a long way to go before it can restore public faith and trust. It is no surprise, therefore, that the independence, integrity, and impartiality of the judiciary at all levels are persistently—and rightfully—questioned in the **press**. Its image has been marred by its own corrupt nature. The systemic abuse of the judiciary reached its apex during the **Rana** and Panchayat periods.

JYAPU. Distinctive **Newar** group in the **Kathmandu Valley**. Mostly engaged in agriculture, they are highly accomplished farmers whose level of productivity per unit of labor and land input matches almost any in the world. They are the main suppliers of vegetables in the Valley. The term sometimes carries a derogatory meaning when used against Newars. It is revulsive to most Newars.

JYOTI, MANI HARSHA (1917–1993). Industrialist from **Kathmandu**. He first started his business in Kalingpong, Sikkim, and later moved to Nepal. Prior to his death, he was closely associated with several social organizations in Nepal, including the Dharmodaya Sabha and Lumbini Development Trust.

K

KABADI (KAPARDI). Typical Nepali court game played between two teams. During the game, a player from one team runs across the opponent's court holding his breath until he safely returns to his own court. *Kabadi* competition is held at the national level. The All Nepal Kabadi Association was founded in 1977 to promote this sport.

KAINLA, BAIRAGI (1939–). Pen name of poet and writer Til Bikram Nembang. Born in the Panchthar district (*see* figure 2), Bairagi received the Sajha Puraskar (literary award) in 1974 for contributions to Nepali **literature**, particularly in the field of poetry. He is a founding member of the Nepali literary movement called Tesro Ayam (*tesro* = third; *ayam*

= dimension or wave), which got underway in 1963 with the publication of a literary journal with the same name in **Darjeeling**. What is distinctive about Tesro Ayam is that, unlike any other literary movement or trend in Nepal, it represented the first effort by a group of Nepali writers to advance a systematic theory about the nature and function of the literature they produced. In essence, for the first time in the history of Nepali literature, there was a deliberate articulation of self-conscious modernism.

KAJI. Ministerial level post in Nepal's administrative hierarchy, mainly practiced during the early **Shah** period before the emergence of the **Rana** rule in 1846. When applied in a vernacular sense as it often is, it takes on an informal honorific meaning which is similar to "sir." It implies somebody of high social stature. In some cases, it is also used as a first name.

KAKANI. Hilltop lookout point, 29 kilometers northwest of the city of **Kathmandu**. It is a popular tourist spot for Western tourists as it offers a panoramic view of the **Himalayas**, including the **Ganesh Himal**.

KAL BHAIRAV. One of 64 forms of **Bhairav** with a black-masked face. Projecting a fierce look, the four-meters tall statue stands in front of the **Hanuman Dhoka**. It was installed by King **Pratap Malla** (reign: 1641–1674) after its discovery during the excavation of Nagarjun. Kal Bhairav is believed to cause blood vomiting and, eventually, bring death to any person caught telling a lie.

KALI. Black-faced **Hindu** goddess, representing sakti or shakti (power, energy). Invariably seen riding a lion or tiger and wearing a garland of slain human skulls, Kali is definitely one of the most commonly worshiped and highly revered divine Hindu deities. At times, she is associated with certain Hindu cults.

KALI GANDAKI. Originating in the **Mustang** district, it is the longest river in the **Gandaki River system**, commonly known as the Sapta Gandaki or the Narayani. It is rich in **shaligram** (shiny black stone) that is used by Nepali goldsmiths to determine the quality of gold. The river also contains small amounts of gold along its course.

KALI YUGA. Kali here does not refer to Goddess **Kali**. In fact, they are even pronounced differently—a short "a" sound (as in b*a*lloon; Kali yuga) vs. a long "a" sound (as in c*a*rtoon; Goddess Kali or Kaali). **Hindus** believe we are at present in the Kali yuga, characterized by the rule of cruel and alien rulers. Some Hindus regard Kalkin (Kalki) as the final **avatar** who is yet to come to rescue the world from the Kali yuga or total abyss, a redemptive conception of the world that is similar to Christian apocalyptic thinking. When humanity reaches its lowest point, characterized by total chaos, self-destruction, and disintegration, when hopes turn into absolute despair and despair into devastation—as it is predicted to happen one day—Kalkin will arrive in the form of a man mounted on a white horse, with a flaming sword in his hand, to spare humanity from its irreversible demise. He will judge the wicked, reward the good, and restore the golden age. Many oppressed and deprived Hindus have taken the Kalkin avatar very seriously and long for his much awaited arrival just as fundamentalist Christians believe in and look forward to the second coming of Christ: the Messiah.

According to the deep-seated Hindu belief system, different avatars are believed to descend upon earth from time to time to restore peace, order, and justice, to save humanity from injustice and miseries. Time in this context is conceived in epochal terms or what the Hindus call yuga, which can be roughly defined as the period covering the influence and impact of a particular avatar or his period, e.g., the Treta yuga (**Rama**) and the Dwapara yuga (**Krishna**). To extend this logic embedded in **Hinduism**, the coming of the **Buddha** can be defined as the Buddha yuga, and of Jesus as the Christ yuga. *See also* MAHABHARATA.

KAMI. Blacksmith. They belong to the ex-untouchable (also sometimes referred to as **Dalit**) professional **caste** group, traditionally engaged in iron works, namely, farm implements and cooking utensils. They make those tools and utensils as well as repair them. Even though quite small in number, because of their professional role in Nepal's agrarian society, they are distributed throughout the country. Usually, one finds just a few Kami families in most agrarian communities to fulfill local needs. So, despite their low-caste status, they play a vital—even indispensable—role to this day in many hill communities where manufactured **agricultural** tools are not readily accessible. *See also* UNTOUCHABILITY.

KANCHANJANGA. Himalayan peak in the eastern mountain district of Taplejung. The prominent peak in this particular group of mountains is Kanchanjanga I (8,598m), the third-highest peak in the world. It is followed by Kanchanjanga South (8,476m) and Kanchanjanga West (8,402m).

KANTI CHILDREN'S HOSPITAL. This is the only children's hospital in the country. It was established in 1962.

KANYADAN. Gift (*dan*) of a virgin girl (*kanya*). Ironically, in the **Hindu** tradition, marrying away a young, virgin girl (daughter) to a man is regarded not only as the highest form of conjugation, but also a highly virtuous deed that presumably guarantees the girl's father a safe and secure passage to heaven upon death. One devotional Hindu text in which it is most glorified is *Swasthani*, which is recited every night in many households during the whole month of Magh (January–February). Recital normally takes place in a ceremonial setting where family members and neighbors gather.

KAPILVASTU (KAPILBASTU). District in the **Lumbini Zone** that has a 1991 total population of 371,778, settled over an area of 1,738 sq. km. (*see* figure 2). It is situated in the central **Tarai** along the Nepal-India border. Its fame is closely linked to the fact that this is where **Lumbini**, the birthplace of **Buddha**, is located. This is also the region where Buddha's Shakya dynasty ruled.

KARKI, CHETAN (1939–). With a degree in biology, he served as the area director of fishery development in **Pokhara** in the late 1960s. Even during his time as a fishery development officer, he was keenly interested in writing plays and directing high school drama shows. He later quit his job and switched his career to become a commercial screenwriter. In this capacity, he has been involved in several Nepali movies from the very early days of film production, dating back to the 1960s. He is closely affiliated with the Nepal Film Devolvement Cooperation.

KARMA. It is invariably defined and accepted as universal justice or the outcome of dharmic acts and duties. It is basically the other side of **dharma**. Hindus firmly believe that every good or bad action has its own consequence which must be realized as it is manifested in one's life. That is to say every dharmic act results in a karmic manifestation and, inherently, every karmic act or outcome reflects dharmic deeds and behavior. The two are, therefore, absolutely inseparable. See also HINDUISM.

KARMACHARI SANCHAYA KOSH. Public corporation set up to look after the employees' (*karmachari*) provident (*sanchaya*) fund (*kosh*). It was incorporated in 1962 and is similar in nature to the social security fund in the United States. However, its funding level is much lower. Even before they retire, employees can borrow money from the fund under certain circumstances, e.g., for house construction, business ventures, and medical treatment.

KARNALI RIVER SYSTEM. It constitutes the drainage system in western Nepal, sometimes called the Karnali drainage basin. This river system is formed by the three major rivers (tributaries): the Bheri, Karnali, and Seti (not the Seti Gandaki in central Nepal). They all join each other and become one single river before crossing the border into **India** where it is called the Ghagra, which later joins the Ganges on its way to the Bay of Bengal.

KARNALI ZONE. Nepal's largest and least populous zone. Named after the **Karnali River**, it comprises five districts: **Dolpa**, Humla, Jumla, Kalikot, and Mugu (*see* figures 2 and 3). Mostly straddling the western **mountain** region, its share of the country's total population is merely 261,246 (1991), scattered over an area of 21,351 sq. km. Its inclement climate and harsh terrain are two major impediments to extensive human habitation.

KASTHAMANDAP. *See* KATHMANDU.

KASTURI. Native name of musk deer (*Muschus muschiferus*). It is an endangered antelope species, inhabiting the rhododendron, juniper and birch forests in the hills and **mountains** of Nepal. Adult males possess musk pod or gland which secretes *kasturi* (musk) used in the production of perfume and medicines.

KATHMANDU. Kathmandu embodies many things. It is a district in the **Bagmati Zone** (*see* figures 2 and 3). With an area of only 395 sq. km., the district is crowded by more than 675,000 people (1991). It is an ancient city whose name used to symbolize the whole nation of Nepal, especially to those who lived outside the **Kathmandu Valley**. It is also the capital and largest city—the cradle of Nepal's cultural heritage and civilization, largely owing to its early urban growth ((*see* figure 4).

The name Kathmandu has an interesting origin. It was known as Kantipur until the early sixteenth century when the new name was given. Legend has it that one day during the rule of King Lakshminarasimha Malla (1617–1641), the tree of paradise called *kalpa briksha* (*briksha* = tree) visited the city in human disguise and mingled with the crowd in the midst of a festival procession. One of the spectators in the audience named Biset noticed the man-tree, grabbed him by the arm, and would not let him go until he promised to implant a duplicate tree big enough to provide sufficient timber to build a whole temple. Four days later, the keen spectator was granted an enormous sal tree which he felled to build a temple now called **Kasthamandap** in 1633. It is a two-storey **pagoda** flanked by the residential houses and the **Kathmandu Durbar Square**. The combined **Sanskrit** word *kasthamandap* (*kastha* = wood or wooden; *mandap* = pavilion) was later converted into a Nepali word *kathmando* (*kath* + *mando*) which carries the same meaning. It was then that Kantipur was renamed Kathmando: the city of wooden pavilion. When it is pronounced fast, the last letter "o" tends to give off an "u" sound. Therefore, the new name is written as Kathmandu.

Historically, Kathmandu's political centrality is unparalleled. In the **Licchavi** and **Malla periods**, it was a thriving urban commercial hub of Nepal, owing to both its internal dynamism and external status as a center of entrepôt trade between **Tibet** and **India**. It is Kathmandu that gives Nepal its political, cultural, and civilizational identity.

Since it is the capital city housing the central government, this is where Nepal's policies are formulated with respect to virtually every sphere of society, e.g., political, economic, social, and cultural. Also located in the city are several colleges, art institutions, museums, and many national organizations. The nation has only two universities: **Tribhuvan University** and **Kathmandu University**. They are both situated in the city. The city is adorned with countless ancient temples juxtaposed against equally countless satellite dishes and fancy hotels. Furthermore, it is home to the country's only international airport, linking Nepal to the world. It features countless foreign development agents and agencies, including diplomatic missions and a horde of **nongovernmental organizations**—or NGOs as they are simply called.

Kathmandu is a fascinating city, with one of its legs stuck in the medieval times and another floating in the twenty-first century. During the 1960s and early 1970s, it acted as an irresistible Mecca for Western hippies seeking **nirvana** in the Nepali *chilam* filled with omnipresent and dirt-cheap **ganja**. And one can now legitimately claim it to be a dirty bowl of **pollution**, casting a long shadow on its historical achievements against many odds and on its major industry: **tourism**. Its dense pollution, unfortunately, seems to be getting worse year after year because of the rapid growth in the number of motor vehicles, most of which are relatively old and run on diesel, with little emission control. Compounding Kathmandu's pollution problem are rapid population growth and its bowl-shaped valley location, with few natural outlets for air pollutants.

KATHMANDU DURBAR SQUARE. Complex filled with temples and a palace, including a courtyard, all surrounded by a multitude of packed houses. It is a wonderful **tourist** spot, where one visit fulfills several objectives as it is populated by many different shops in one complex. So, with one visit to the Square and its surroundings, tourists can have a reliable glimpse of Nepal's cultural heritage and history, artistic and architectural traditions and advancements, or simply the whole way of life represented and reflected in the countless artifacts found in this area. In particular, it is a vivid window to what or how much the **Newars**, the indigenous inhabitants of the **Kathmandu Valley** and the bearers and founders of Nepali civilization, achieved despite their lack of access to modern technology and tools. In short, with a huge part of culture and history preserved in its little capsule, the Kathmandu Durbar Square is a mirror image of what Nepal looked like a few hundred years ago and how it behaves and looks today.

KATHMANDU UNIVERSITY. Private university established in 1991. It is widely expected to act as a viable alternative to the country's national and public university called **Tribhuvan University**. Since it is still in its infancy, it is too early to assess its performance records in terms of achieving its goals. Nonetheless, expectations are quite high.

KATHMANDU VALLEY. Bowl-shaped valley surrounded by hills on all sides. There is enough geological evidence that it was once a lake surrounded by lush vegetation. Nepal's *Vamsavalis* (chronicles) inform that the Valley was made inhabitable by Bodhisattva Manjusri (Manjushri) who split the **mountain** with his sword to open a gorge in order to drain the lake. In all likelihood, however, what was described as the Manjusri miracle was caused by a massive **earthquake** as it opened a gap along the fault line, thus allowing the water to be drained. What runs through this gorge at **Chovar** today is the **Bagmati**, a famed river that must have once fed and filled the lake. The Valley contains three historical cities: **Kathmandu, Patan,** and **Bhaktapur (Bhadgaun)**, previously the three **Malla** kingdoms. Prior to its conquest by **Prithvi Narayan Shah**, the Kathmandu Valley was the sole personification of Nepal, as those living outside it invariably referred to it as Nepal. In fact, this reality prevailed as late as the early 1950s.

KAYASTHA, BADRI NATH (1945–). Born and raised in **Pokhara**, he received his Ph.D. in agronomy from Kansas State University. After his return to Nepal from the United States in the mid-1970s, he reentered the government's civil service sector as an agronomist. Later, he quit the government service to open a development consulting firm called No-Frills Development Consultants in the early-1980s, which he headed until 2002. He is now retired, although he still does some development consulting on a limited basis.

KAYASTHA, JAMUNA (1948–). A graduate of the Multipurpose High School in **Pokhara**, she was awarded a government scholarship to study in **India**. She received her B.Sc. degree in home economics from India's Baroda University. Currently an entrepreneur and social worker, she is the first Nepali woman to own and operate a vegetable seeds exporting business. In her dual roles, Kayastha is striving to empower **women** through micro enterprising, particularly in the field of high quality vegetable seeds production, a practice which is now gaining popularity because of its ability to generate cash incomes. From her base in **Patan**, she has established a network of contacts with seed producers throughout the country, including some families in remote areas like the far western hills and mountains. She is also an educator who has taught Nepali to many expatriates living in **Kathmandu** and Patan. In addition, she has entered the realm of faith healing, promoting it among both the local people and expatriates through various mediums of healing.

KC, ARJUN NARSHINGH (1948–). Member of the **Nepali Congress Party**. During the late-1960s, he was a student leader of the Congress party at the **Tribhuvan University**. Because of his oratorical ability, he was quite popular and influential. Later, in the 1980s, he left the banned Congress party and entered **Panchayat** politics. However, following the demise of the Panchayat system in early 1990, he rejoined the Congress party and ran for **election** under its party banner. He was elected to the **House of Representatives** from the Nuwakot district in the 1991 election. He retained his House seat in the 1994 election as well.

KEDIA, SHANKAR LAL (1926–). Industrialist from **Birganj**, a gateway city in the central **Tarai** (*see* figure 4). He is the founder of several industries such as the Indushankar Sugar Mills, Sunder Furniture, and Birganj Textile Industry. He has also contributed to the establishment of an eye hospital as well as several schools in different parts of Nepal. *See also* INDUSTRY.

KESHAR LIBRARY. Biggest private library in Nepal set up by Keshar Shamsher Rana. Handed over to the government in 1966, it includes an extensive collection of manuscripts, books, and other documents.

KHAIR. Its botanical name is *Acacia catechu* and it is commonly found in the riverine forests that are scattered in the **inner Tarai** and **Tarai** belts. *Catechu* from its bark is widely used throughout South Asia. Its paste is consumed throughout South Asia mixed with *pan*, a green heart-shaped leaf wrapped with several ingredients that acts as a stimulant.

KHANAL, BHAIYA (1953–). Zoologist and **butterfly** specialist. He is associated with **Tribhuvan University's Natural History Museum** and has once served as deputy coordinator of the International Council of Museums.

KHANAL, JHALA NATH (1950–). Member of the **Communist Party of Nepal**. He served as cabinet minister during the post-**Panchayat** interim government (1990–1991) and was later elected to the **House of Representatives** in 1991 and reelected in the 1994 general **elections** from the **Ilam** district (*see* figure 2), but not in 1999.

KHANAL, YADU NATH (1913–). Professor and diplomat. He has published books and articles on international affairs. He served as Nepali ambassador to **India** (1967–1971) and to the **United States** (1974–

1978). Still actively involved in Nepal's foreign policy issues, he is considered by most within the country as well as by those associated with Nepal to be a senior Nepali statesman. He is by far the most renowned international relations expert in the nation. His views are highly respected.

KHARPAN. Twin carrying baskets resembling a huge weighing scale. They are almost exclusively used by **Jyapu** farmers to transport their produce to the market. A Jyapu carrying a *kharpan*, a frequent scene in the **Kathmandu Valley**, is still an enduring symbol of the Jyapu culture steeped in farming.

KHASA (KHAS). Term applied to the people and language in Nepal's western hills, around the **Karnali** basin. It is also sometimes used to denote the **Chhetris**, especially low-grade Chhetris.

KHATIWADA, BIRODH (1960–). Member of the **Communist Party of Nepal.** He was elected to the **House of Representatives** from the Makwanpur district (*see* figure 2) during the 1991 general **elections**. He was elected again from the same district during the general elections held in 1994 and 1999. That is, he is one of the handful of **Parliament** members elected in all three national elections held so far since the demise of the **Panchayat** system in 1990.

KHET. Irrigated land good for **rice** growing. It is also commonly used to simply refer to crop land.

KHUKRI (KHUKURI). Famous curved Nepali knife used as a symbol of **Gorkha** soldiers. Quite typical of Nepal, they are made in the town of **Bhojpur** and come in many different sizes.

KHUMBU GLACIER. Major **Mount Everest** glacier.

KIJA PUJA. Newari term which means "brother's day festival" during which sisters bless their brothers by placing an auspicious *tika* (red mark) on their foreheads. The Nepali term for this is *bhai tika*. *See also* TIHAR.

KIPAT. Form of Nepal's **land tenure** arrangements. It essentially means communal land (ownership) that was particularly common in the **Rai** and **Limbu** ethnic communities. It was abolished in 1968.

KIRATA (KIRANT, KIRATI or KIRANTI). Generic term used to refer to the **Rai** and **Limbu** ethnic groups. In ancient times, they ruled the **Kathmandu Valley** for about 1,500 years, until the rise of the **Licchavi** rule. They are described in the *Mahabharata*, a renowned **Hindu** epic.

KIRTIPUR. Relatively small and quaint city in the **Kathmandu Valley**, dwarfed by **Kathmandu** and **Patan**. It was, however, used as a major staging point during **Prithvi Narayan Shah**'s military drive against the kingdom of Kathmandu. It is the site of **Tribhuvan University**.

KISAN (KISHAN). Peasant or farmer. It is a very popular term across South Asia.

KOIRALA, BISHWESWAR PRASAD (B. P.) (1914–1982). With his family roots based in **Biratnagar**, B. P.—as he was fondly called by both his friends and the general public—was raised and educated in Banaras, **India**. B. P. Koirala is one of the most prominent founders of the **Nepali Congress Party** (NCP), which has remained the largest party throughout the history of Nepal's party politics, with a brief hiatus in 1994 when the **Communist Party of Nepal** won more seats in the **House of Representatives**.

In addition to a degree from the Banaras Hindu University, he received a law degree from the Calcutta University in 1937 and practiced law for several years in **Darjeeling**, an Indian hill town, with a large concentration of Nepalis. While still a student in India, he was involved in the Indian nationalist movement, joining the Indian Congress Party in 1934. During World War II, he was interned by the British in Dhanbad for two years (1942–1944). Following his release, with Indian independence imminent, he set about trying to bring change to Nepal. After returning to his home town of Biratnagar to lead a labor demonstration, he was imprisoned in 1947–1948. A year later, he was arrested again, but was released after a 27-day hunger strike, when Prime Minister Jawaharlal Nehru of India intervened on his behalf.

B. P. Koirala's political career is a case history of Nepali politics, especially in the 1950s, thanks to both his political stance and stature. More than any leader (except for **Ganeshman Singh** who was almost beaten to death by the **Rana** police), he seemed to typify the spirit of the 1950 revolution. Not only did he exercise a prominent role in spearheading that popular revolution that toppled the Rana regime in early 1951, but his constant efforts to base the political decision-making process outside the royal palace and on the will of the people set him apart from most of his contemporaries. He envisioned the goals of the 1950 revolution far beyond the political exigencies of the time and was constantly reminding his colleagues and party workers about the vital necessity of translating these into economic and social realities. So, for him, bringing down the house of the Ranas was merely the first order of urgent business to open the door for materializing those economic and social realities he envisioned by giving the nation of Nepal and its citizens a chance to aspire and achieve. To this end, he chose the ideology of democratic socialism as his main political faith and path, although its practical attainment seemed like a daring dream.

In addition to his well-articulated ideology, B. P. possessed certain personal qualities to separate him from most other Nepali political leaders regardless of their party affiliations. Unlike others, he was first and foremost an internationalist who kept himself well informed of political developments in other countries through various mediums, including his membership in the Socialist International. His brand of Nepali nationalism was also different from theirs. Although he was proud of Nepal's past artistic and architectural achievements, to him, Nepal's glory was placed in the realm of the future rather than the ruins and remnants of the past.

Following the general **elections** in 1959 in which his Congress Party scored a solid victory, he formed Nepal's first democratic government. Consequently, he became Nepal's first elected prime minister. But his government was short-lived as **Mahendra Bir Bikram Shah** launched a swift palace coup against him and against nascent democracy in December 1960. He was jailed for several years and all the political parties were banned. B. P. Koirala was also a highly accomplished author whose contribution to Nepali **literature** is extensive and profound. Some of his novels and short stories are among the best and earliest works that Nepal has produced as parts of its literary heritage.

KOIRALA, GIRIJA PRASAD (1925–). The youngest brother of **B. P. Koirala,** Girija is perhaps the most controversial, self-centered, and divisive figure within the **Nepali Congress Party.** Nevertheless, when the Congress Party won the general **elections** in 1991, he became prime minister. After losing the vote of confidence in the **House of Representatives** in 1994, his party witnessed a stunning defeat by the **Communist**

Party of Nepal in the general election held in the same year, largely because of his failed policies and divisive politics. But he became prime minister again in 1998 and 2000, both times for short durations. In 2000, he successfully launched a disgraceful party coup against his own party's prime minister, **Krishna Prasad Bhattarai**, so he could become prime minister. Typical of all clannish politics, his rise to power is largely hinged on his blood ties to B. P. Koirala rather than his own inherent competence or leadership ability, something he miserably failed to demonstrate despite being given several chances. In July 2001, Koirala was ousted by **Sher Bahadur Deuba** during a bitter intra-party feud. In 2002, Girija Prasad was engaged in a running battle with Sher Bahadur Deuba, the ruling prime minister of his own party, a battle which resulted in a split of the Congress party between his and Deuba's factions.

KOIRALA, MATRIKA PRASAD (1911–1997). Founding member of the **Nepali Congress Party** which he once led as its president. He was appointed prime minister in November 1951 by King **Tribhuvan Bir Bikram Shah** following the resignation of Prime Minister **Mohan Shamsher Rana**. In this sense, he became the first non-**Rana** prime minister in the post-Rana period. King Tribhuvan's favorite politician, most political observers of Nepal viewed him as a diehard royalist who bitterly feuded with his half-brother **B. P. Koirala** over many issues, ranging from party politics and political ideology to foreign policy. He was expelled from the Congress party because of his differences with the party's mainstream position. Subsequently, he formed his own party called the National Democratic Party (now defunct). Appointed prime minister by King Tribhuvan once again in 1953, he was able to lead his party to form a new government, which lasted until February 1954. However, he was later reinstated to the Congress party in 1959 by B. P. Koirala and assigned to play a role within its working committee and parliamentary board.

But the bitterness did not go away. In early 1960, he published an article in a local paper, bitterly critical of the B. P. Koirala government's domestic as well as foreign policies. The Nepali press widely regarded his views as a grand betrayal. One newspaper went so far as to allege that Matrika Prasad's article was a shameless petition to King **Mahendra Bir Bikram Shah** either to take the reins and administration in his own hands or to call upon him (Matrika) to form a new government. It did not take too long for the king to exercise the first option, launching a swift **palace coup**.

KOIRALA, MOHAN (1926–). Although born into a relatively well-off Kathmandu family, he encountered hard times. As his family could no longer afford his college fees, he quit college so that he could work to support his family. He is one of the most respected poets within the country's literary circle as he continues to have a sizeable following amongst the young writers. Michael Hutt goes so far as to argue that he is the most significant poet to have emerged in Nepal since **Laxmi Prasad Devkota**. At the core of Mohan Koirala's poetry resides his commentary on the nation's social and political issues. His contribution to Nepali **literature**, however, goes beyond the richness and freshness of his poems, along with his willingness and ability to evolve with the changing times. As an emerging and young writer, he played a leading role in setting a new tone in the 1960s; he broke away completely from the traditional style of poetry that emphasized meters and rhythms, also referred to as *shloka* (stanza). As he wrote poems in free verse, he popularized what is called in Nepali *gadhya kavita* which literally means "prose poetry" or nonmetrical verse. The complexity of Mohan Koirala's poems often stood in sharp contrast to the simplicity of poems composed by **Bhupi Sherchan**, another highly popular poet among the young generation of writers.

KOIRALA, TARINI PARSAD (1922–1974). Novelist, short story writer, and **B. P. Koirala**'s brother. He wrote several novels, mostly within a Freudian framework. Although least political of all the Koirala clan, he served as Prime Minister B. P. Koirala's chief of staff during his short-lived government. He was, however, widely perceived as being corrupt, taking undue advantage of his brother's prime ministership.

KOSI PROJECT. Kosi River dam project constructed and operated by **India**. The project stemmed from the Indo-Nepal Agreement, signed on 25 April 1954. Approximately 90 percent of the irrigation water from the project is diverted to India, whereas Nepal paid much of the price as it suffered a significant loss of land due to dam construction.

KOSI RIVER SYSTEM. River system in eastern Nepal formed by the seven Kosi rivers, commonly known as the Sapta (seven) Kosi or simply

Kosi. These seven Kosis are: **Arun**, Bhote, Dudh, Likhu, Sun, Tama, and Tamar. Situated along the Kosi banks is the Kosi Tappu Wildlife Reserve, which contains many types of wild animals within its boundaries.

KOSI ZONE. Named after the **Kosi River**, this zone is comprised of six districts: **Bhojpur, Dhankuta, Morang**, Sankhuwasabha, Sunsari, and Tehrathum. It had a population of 1,730,932 people (1991) and covers an area of 9,669 sq. km. It is one of the most populous zones in the nation (see figure 3).

KOT PARBA. Courtyard massacre. Nepal's bloodiest courtyard massacre of 14 September 1846, one in which 29 leading *bhardars* (courtiers) were butchered by **Jang Bahadur Rana** (Kunwar) and his brothers. Basically, prominent nobles of all competing courtier factions were either wiped out or exiled, leaving Jang Bahadur fully in charge of court affairs and without any parallel to challenge his power and authority. Following the massacre, he was bestowed with the title of prime minister and commander in chief.

KRISHNA. Hindu deity. Believed to be the eighth incarnation of Lord **Vishnu**, Lord Krishna is the central character in the **Mahabharata**, a masterful **Hindu** epic and philosophical treatise, one in which he reveals to Arjuna (Arjun), a leading hero of the epic, his universal look, proclaiming that he is the Universe. In essence, he is everything and every act. There is some parallel between the circumstance under which he was born and rescued and that of Jesus. With a youthful look and black complexion, Krishna is also regularly depicted as a fun-loving playboy. He is recognized by many other names, for example, Gopal, Govinda, and Shyam, to mention a few. *See also* KALI YUGA.

KRISHNA MANDIR. Famous temple of Lord **Krishna**. Built in 1630 by King Siddhinarasingh Malla, it is located in the **Patan Durbar Square**. Patterned after the south Indian temple architectural style, it is dramatically different from the popular **pagoda** style that dominates Nepal's temple architecture. Krishna Mandir features a great colonnade and a fascinating and intricate series of carvings of battle scenes from the **Ramayana** and **Mahabharata** epics.

KSHATRIYA. *See* CHHETRI.

KUKUR TIHAR. Second day of the **Tihar** festival. It is the day of the dog (*kukur*) as the **Hindus** in Nepal honor the dog by offering it good food and putting a garland around its neck.

KUL. Clan (family clan). Since it directly reflects and represents one's family lineage (heritage), family adherence to its *kul* is an enduring tradition in Nepal specifically among higher-**caste** and upper-class families. Preserving the *kul* tradition is invariably regarded as a way of protecting the purity of one's family lineage (or caste status). This is one tradition that tends to bring various factions of the clan together at least on a temporary basis, as they are all expected to show their pride in the common clan root. *See also* KUL DEUTA.

KUL DEUTA (DEVATA). *Kul* or clan god, generally kept inside one's house and worshiped on a regular basis. It is a common tradition among many **caste** or **ethnic** groups to worship the clan god. It is believed that two primary reasons drive this Nepali tradition. First, it signifies honoring or taking pride in one's family clan lineage. Second, the worship is meant to please the clan god for the sake of family welfare in terms of both financial prosperity and good health.

KULEKHANI. Hydroelectric power plant built in Makwanpur. There are actually two plants: Kulekhani I completed in 1982 and Kulekhani II completed in 1986. They are a major source of electric power in the **Kathmandu Valley**.

KUMALE. Occupational **caste** of potters. It is a small minority group, often inhabiting river basins in the lowlands of Nepal.

KUMARI. It literally means "a virgin girl." This is a young living goddess who comes from the **Newar** group. For a young Newari girl to be selected as Kumari, she must be virgin, about 4–8 years old, and possess a flawless body and pass an excruciating test of endurance against fear and terror. There are several Kumaris throughout the **Kathmandu Valley**, but the main one is in **Kathmandu**. She lives in a house (*ghar*) called Kumari *ghar*, which is an ornate building with finely carved windows and wooden balconies, built in 1757 by King **Jayaprakash Malla**. Because of its artistic beauty and cultural importance, the Kumari *ghar* is one of the main attractions of the **Kathmandu Durbar Square**. Somewhat commercialized these days as a result of the growth of **tourism**, it is a common sight to see the Kumari peek out the window to grace Western tourists and other visitors alike. It is a historical royal tradition for the ruling monarch to pay an annual visit to the Kumari to seek her blessing.

Attendants are appointed to take care of the Kumari meticulously. The ruling Kumari is immediately dethroned at the first signs of menstruation or any form of bleeding, including cuts. Given the unfathomable degree of exaltation of virginity, there is a cultlike atmosphere surrounding the Kumari. Once dethroned—whether simply due to the natural biological transition into adulthood or for some other reasons—Kumaris are cursed with the burden of remaining unmarried, a situation that invariably leads to deviant forms of sexual practice, including **prostitution**. *See also* BAHRA.

KUNWAR, BIR BAL BHADRA (?–1823). Regarded as the hero of the historic battle of Khalanga during the **Anglo-Nepal War**. It is said that even the British forces paid him tribute for his unmatched bravery during the war.

KUNWAR, JANG BAHADUR. *See* RANA, JANG BAHADUR.

KUNWAR, UTTAM (1939–1982). A literary journalist who was the founding editor and publisher of *Ruprekha*, a leading Nepali literary journal that played a prominent role in enhancing the quality of Nepali **literature** in the 1960s and 1970s. He once served as vice-president of the Nepal Council of World Affairs.

KUSUNDA. Nomadic tribe, largely dependent on hunting. It is a vanishing tribe of Nepal. The Kusundas are usually found around the lower hills of **Gorkha** and Tanahun (*see* figure 2).

L

LAHURE. Often used as a descriptive and generic term to refer to Nepali sons from the hills serving in foreign armies, namely, the British and Indian armies—or who sent to *muglan* (distant lands) seeking employment opportunities to supplement family incomes. These days it is also applied to those Nepalis who go overseas to work and earn money. It is believed that the word was initially used to refer to those Nepalis who went to Lahore (Pakistan) in search of employment, including army service. Most likely, its origin dates back to the mid-nineteenth century.

LAKE RARA. Situated in Jumla at an altitude of more than 3,000 meters, it is the largest lake in Nepal. Graced by wild swans and other fowl and surrounded by pines and cedars, its beauty radiates throughout the valley.

LAKH. Unit of monetary measurement equal to 100,000.

LALI GURANS. Rhododendron (*gurans*) flowers with a brilliant red (*lal* or *lali*) color. Largely found in the highlands, it is Nepal's national flower. It is believed to have a medicinal value. Sometimes people add it to curried fish dishes, believing that it softens fish bones.

LALITPUR. District in the **Bagmati Zone** (*see* figure 2). With an area of merely 385 sq. km., it is one of the smallest districts in the country. Its population totaled 258, 474 in 1991. *See also* PATAN.

LAL MOHAR. Nepali coin equal to one rupee. It is also an authoritative document issued by the king granting certain rights to a subject, e.g., land ownership and tax relief. It literally means the red (*lal*) seal (*mohar*) stamped on the document.

LAMA. Priest in the **Buddhist** or **Lamaist** tradition of most ethnic groups in the hills and **mountains** of Nepal, along with **Tibet** and Bhutan.

LAMA, ARUNA (1945–1998). A famous musician, Aruna Lama was born in **Darjeeling**, a major hub of Nepali culture and **literature** in the West Bengal province of **India**. Popularly known as "the nightingale of the **Himalaya**," she played a prominent role in elevating Nepali **music** to a higher plateau. There is no dispute about her prominent place in Nepali music.

LAMA, NIRMAL (1929–2000). Born in **Darjeeling**, Nirmal Lama was a leftist leader and a leading intellectual political voice of Nepal. Nirmal was an ardent believer in the revolutionary principle of Marxism and Leninism. He was both feared and admired by the political establishment of Nepal because of his ability to provide a penetrating analysis of Nepali politics. Following the democratic revolution of 1990, he served on the Constitution Recommendation Commission.

LAMAISM. School of **Buddhism**, mainly observed in **Tibet** and in the highlands of Nepal. Religious performances are guided by **Lama** priests as they officiate rites and rituals as well as govern religious shrines and ceremonies. In some way, it is a mixture of **Tantrism** and **Buddhism**.

LAND REFORM. Known as *bhumi sudhar* in Nepali, the Land Reform Act of 1964 supposedly provided a comprehensive framework for land reforms to bring about positive change in the country's agrarian system. However, by most accounts the act did not produce much change in the peasants' or tenants' lot. Nor did it result in any agricultural development. Since most members of the landed class were fully aware of the nature and content of the Land Reform Act during its formulation, they took a preemptive action to circumvent its negative impact on their holdings. They parceled out their land holdings among family members in such a way that the family or individual landholding ceilings imposed by the law would have no repercussion on them. In other words, they would not have to forfeit any excess land to the government because they all fell below the ceilings specified in the act. See also ADHIYA; LAND TENURE.

LAND SETTLEMENT. See CHITWAN; ETHNICITY; FOREIGN AID; RAPTI VALLEY DEVELOPMENT PROJECT.

LAND TENURE. The question of land tenure in Nepal is so complicated it defies description. Historically, all lands belong to the State. But the reality is different as land is distributed in different forms. Aside from the state-owned land category called **raikar**, the three most common forms of land tenure in Nepal were: **birta**, **jagir**, and **kipat**. Additional categories included **guthi** and **ijara**. While one can still find *raikar* and *guthi* lands, other categories are no longer in use. The *birta* and *jagir* systems, the two land tenure provisions that led to widespread inequality in land distribution in the country, were abolished as part of **land reform**.

LANGTANG NATIONAL PARK. National park around the Langtang Himal. Established in 1976, its areal coverage extends into the Nuwakot, Rasuwa, and Sindhupalchok districts (*see* figure 2). The park includes

Gosaikunda Lake and different types of fauna such as snow leopards, musk deer, barking deer, red pandas, and **danphe**.

LANGUAGE. Nepali is categorized as an Indo-European language that is closely related to Hindi as they both share the same root that is **Sanskrit**. It has emerged as a "link language" or lingua franca of the Nepali diaspora—various Nepali communities found in such places as Assam, Banaras, **Darjeeling**, **Dehradun**, Patna, and Sikkim in India and in Bhutan and Myanmar (Burma). Because of its widespread use and the continued growth of Nepali **literature** in recent decades, the prestige of Nepali as a major South Asian language has increased considerably.

Within Nepal, it has long been used as a primary language of communication and official transaction. But it was only in 1958 that Nepali was formally declared to be Nepal's *rastra bhasa* (national language). Due to its national status and persistent push as the medium of public **education**, Nepali has become the most dominant language in the country, dwarfing virtually every other language. It has also been systematically used over the years as a primary instrument to foster and fortify national unity as well as Nepali nationalism (patriotism), that is, loyalty to the Crown. Consequently, Nepali is now spoken even among the various **Tibeto-Nepali** ethnic tribal groups and the **Tarai**-based **Indo-Nepalis** who are historically least acculturated to Nepali (*see* **Ethnicity**). There are still many remote pockets, however, where Nepali is rarely heard. This is especially true in communities straddling the border with **China**'s autonomous region of **Tibet**.

Other languages of Nepal with a substantial geographical and demographic coverage include: **Newari**, Maithili, Bhojpuri, **Tharu, Tamang, Gurung**, and many others. Regardless of the fact that some of them have their own literary traditions (e.g., Newari), they are all essentially ethnic languages in that they are chiefly confined to their specific host groups. For example, the Tamang language is rarely spoken outside the Tamang communities or by non-Tamang groups. Like Nepali, Maithili and Bhojpuri belong to the Indo-European family, whereas the mother tongues of the Tibeto-Nepali groups, including Newari, are derived from the Tibeto-Burman language family.

LATHI. Wooden or bamboo baton. It is used by policemen as a nonlethal weapon. The term is normally applied to a police *lathi* charge against public protesters and demonstrators as the first weapon of deterrence, especially during **haritals**.

LAXMI. Hindu goddess of wealth and prosperity and consort of Lord **Vishnu**. She is a central figure during the festival of **Tihar** as its third day is devoted to worshiping Laxmi, that is, Laxmi *puja*. She is also a symbol of beauty.

LEAST DEVELOPED COUNTRY (LDC). In 1971, when the **United Nations** identified 25 nations as "Least Developed Countries," Nepal was included in the group. More than three decades later, the number of LDCs has risen to 48 countries, and Nepal still remains toward the bottom of this totem pole of development. *See also* AGRICULTURE; PEOPLE'S WAR; POVERTY.

LEKH. Mountains or high altitude areas where vegetation is generally sparse because of its harsh climatic condition. It is often used as a summer pasture land by pastoralists who raise goats and sheep. *See also* MAHABHARAT LEKH.

LEPCHA. Minority ethnic group, generally concentrated in parts of **Ilam** and further east in Sikkim. Of Mongoloid origin, they speak Lapcha and generally observe **Lamaism**.

LHOMI. Small minority ethnic group around the **Arun Valley**. Akin to the **Sherpa**, they are also known as Kath **Bhote** whose religious belief system and practices are embedded in **Lamaism**.

LICCHAVI PERIOD (400–879 A.D.). Although the Licchavi period in the political history of Nepal actually began earlier than 400 A.D., some historians have used this as a starting point. That is because that is when Nepal moved on to the terra firma of history supported by epigraphic records. This dynastic period came to an end 879. It is often referred to as the "Golden Age" in the annals of Nepal, for this period was marked by many artistic and architectural developments in the **Kathmandu Valley** as well as commercial expansion into **Tibet**. In essence, Nepal owes a great deal to the Licchavi rulers for its cultural heritage and historical development. *See also* Introduction.

LIMBU. Mongoloid people belonging to the **Kirata** group. They observe their native religion influenced by **Hinduism** and worship village deities, ancestor gods (Mangena) and spirits. During the heyday of British imperialism, they were one of primary martial group targets of British mercenary recruitment as **Gorkhas.** They have historically been exploited by the **Bahun** and **Chhetri** families through deceits and treacheries. *See also* GURUNG, GOPAL.

LIMBUAN. Parts of the hills east of the **Arun River** where the **Limbus** had established their own separate medieval kingdom, annexed to modern Nepal in 1774. It was also known as the Pallo (further east) Kirat, one beyond the Majh (middle) Kirat.

LINGAM. Phallus or phallic symbol. It is a powerful **Shiva** symbol as some aspects of Lord Shiva are closely connected to sex and sexuality. This is particularly true in the Tantric tradition, which is quite popular and commonly practiced throughout Nepal in one form or another. It is precisely in the arena of **Tantrism** where various **Hindu** and **Buddhist** practices are fused. The heaviest concentration of erect *lingams* is found around the temple of **Pashupati** where **women,** particularly those who are married but childless, worship them in hopes of becoming pregnant.

LITERATURE. By definition, literature means a body of writings of a specific language, period, people, etc. In this sense, Nepali literature was in its embryonic phase until about the mid-1800s. It was limited to royal edicts and inscriptions. In addition, there were some Nepali translations of **Sanskrit** literature and royal biographies. Michael Hutt states that Suvananda Das was the first Nepali poet who composed verse in praise of **Prithvi Narayan Shah,** but his impact was nil. Other than these scattered examples, there were few that could be legitimately claimed as a body of literary writings until the emergence of **Bhanu Bhakta Acharya,** a **Bahun** from Tanahun, to whom Nepali literature owes its genesis.

The publication of Bhanu Bhakta's *Ramayana* was the linchpin in the development of Nepali as a literary language as well as in laying the foundation of Nepali literature. The literary current generated by Bhanu Bhakta was later reinforced by **Motiram Bhatta** through his organized efforts and activism to promote Nepali literature. Yet there was no reliable and regular outlet or forum for publishing one's work until 1901 when the *Gorkhapatra* was initiated. Although it was only a weekly publication back then, the *Gorkhapatra* became a valuable outlet for the publication of literary works, namely poems and stories. In 1913, **Chandra Shamsher Rana** created a publication committee to promote Nepali literature. Unfortunately, however, those attempts were tainted by tight government censorship of literary works. As the freedom of unfettered literary views and expression was muzzled, the development of Nepali literature as a creative valve was generally kept closed.

Not surprisingly, therefore, Nepal had to rely on external venues for its literary growth and development, most notably Banaras and **Darjeeling** in India. Relatively large numbers of Nepalis lived in these places, where the barometer of anti-**Rana** fever was already on the rise. As the sincere desire to produce and promote Nepali literature converged with the revolutionary voices of the time, several publications emanated from Nepali diasporic communities in India, for example, *Sundari* (The Beautiful, 1906), *Madhavi* (1908), *Gorkhali* (1916), and the *Nepali Sahitya Sammelan Patrika* (Nepali Literature Association Journal, 1932). Those publications served as invaluable vehicles of Nepali literary expressions. **Balakrishna Sama** was quoted as saying, "What Darjeeling thinks today, Nepal thinks tomorrow." In short, it was those diasporic communities in India that propelled the early development of Nepali literature as a coherent body of writing.

However, Nepali literature was confined in terms of its geographic and demographic reach, a situation which naturally put a limit on its growth and development. What was published in India was not readily accessible within Nepal. So, in effect, Nepal had to await the birth of **Kathmandu**'s first literary journal, the monthly *Sharada*, in 1934. Although published with the help of a subsidy from **Juddha Shamsher Rana**'s government, *Sharada* managed to avoid overt censorship. By the time its publication ceased in 1963, *Sharada* had fulfilled its mission of giving Nepali literature its own identity and shape, publishing roughly 200 poems by **Laxmi Prasad Devkota, Lekhnath Poudyal, Gopal Prasad Rimal**, Balakrishna Sama, and **Siddhi Charan Shrestha** alone, and numerous stories by **Bhavani Bhikshu, B. P. Koirala**, and many others. The little seed of Nepali literature that Bhanu Bhakta Acharya planted about a century ago had grown into a mature tree with distinct and flourishing branches.

It was during the *Sharada* era that the concept of modernity spread its roots and emerged as a central theme in Nepali literature. During this time Nepali literature gained vigor and became diverse, clearly going beyond the dominant realm of poetry to cover a wide territory of short stories, plays, and novels, mostly thanks to such writers as Bhikshu, Koirala, and **Parijat** who led the way. Nonetheless, it is the field of poetry that is most advanced and that constituted the richest genre of Nepali literature from the very outset. It is also the one that has undergone the most notable change since the days of Bhanu Bhakta Acharya.

In its compositional style, the early phase of Nepali poetry was dominated by classical Sanskrit meters. The style was referred to as *shloka* or stanza that is very strict in terms of composition. It was considered to be not only elitist because of its Sanskrit bias, but also outdated because of its restrictiveness. But it was the only form of poetry with which early Nepali poets were familiar, and, certainly, the simplicity of Acharya's *Ramayana* helped to retain its popularity. Poudyal, Sama, and Devkota —the three dominant writers during the early phase—continued to use it. Poudyal was a master of this style.

However, attempts to break the tight grip of the classical style in Nepali poetry were made in the 1920s and 1930s by none other than Devkota and Sama. Devkota began to deploy a less restrictive form of rhythms popular in Nepali folk songs, especially the *jhyaure* genre, whose melodic singing can be heard to this day throughout the hills. His attempt also signified a new direction in that it gave Nepali poetry its own identity quite distinct from the Sanskrit and Indian traditions. Sama made a determined effort to free Nepali poetry from the confines of conventional forms. A further push came in the 1940s from activist poets like Rimal who widely used free verse or what is commonly known in Nepal as *gadhya kavya* (prose poems).

Yet the clear break did not occur until the 1960s, the decade that brought the dawn of a new era in Nepali poetry. It took the growing popularity and persistence of poets like **Mohan Koirala**, Parijat, **Bhupi Sherchan, Bairagi Kainla, Banira Giri**, and others who repeatedly composed their poems in free verse. After 1960, the torch of this new departure was carried forward by the Kathmandu-based publication of a new literary journal called *Ruprekha* (Outline), which quickly became highly popular and which might have hastened the subsequent demise of *Sharada*.

To conclude, the decade of the 1960s not only spawned creative streams in all fields of Nepali literature, but also firmly grounded the current of modernity, at times giving birth to what Michael Hutt refers to as the "cult of obscurantism," one in which poems were full of obscure mythological references and imageries. It was during this period that the

Tesro Ayam (Third Dimension) movement, which got underway with the Darjeeling-based publication of a literary journal with the same name, left deep marks in Nepali poetry. The 1960s can thus be described as a defining moment in the history of Nepali literature as the decade continues to influence its direction to this day. Since then, Nepali literature as a whole has witnessed tremendous growth and expansion.

LIVING GODDESS. See KUMARI.

LOHANI, GOVINDA PRASAD (1928–). Economist and politician. He has written books on the Nepali **economy** and served as a member of the **National Planning Commission** and **National Development Council** (1972–1973).

LOHANI, PRAKASH CHANDRA (1944–). Economist and politician from Nuwakot (*see* figure 2). After obtaining his Ph.D. degree in Economics in the **United States**, he returned to Nepal in the late 1960s, and was active in economic research. He has authored several articles. He was minister of finance (1983–1986) and of housing and physical **planning** in 1988. Elected to the **House of Representatives** in 1991 and reelected in the general **elections** held in 1994, he briefly served as minister of foreign affairs in the mid-1990s. He belongs to the **National Democratic Party**.

LOK SEWA AYOG. See PUBLIC SERVICE COMMISSION.

LOPA. Minority people inhabiting the upper reaches of the **Kali Gandaki River** in the **Mustang** district. *See also* ETHNICITY.

LUMBINI. The birthplace of **Buddha**, located in the central **Tarai** district of Nepal. It has emerged as a leading pilgrim destination for both Nepali and international Buddhists, particularly those from Japan. Despite some attempts to develop this sanctuary of peace, Lumbini remains relatively inconspicuous in terms of its physical aura and attraction. *See also* BUDDHISM.

LUMBINI SUGAR MILLS. Public enterprise founded in 1982. It is located in **Butwal** and has a production capacity of 5,400 metric tons of sugar per year.

LUMBINI ZONE. Named after **Lumbini**, the birthplace of **Buddha**, it consists of six districts: Arghakhanchi, Gulmi, **Kapilvastu**, Nawalparasi, **Palpa**, and Rupandehi (*see* figures 2 and 3). Situated between the lower hills of Nepal and the Indian border, it has 1,997,501 people (1991) and covers an area of 8,975 sq. km.

LUNGI. Sarong-like cloth worn by males, particularly the plains people of the **Tarai** and immigrants from **India**. *See also DHOTI.*

M

MACHHAPUCHHRE. In English, it is called the fish-tail **mountain** because its peak, when seen from the side, looks like a fish tail, split into two halves. Situated right next to **Annapurna**, few **Himalayan** peaks capture one's imagination as much as this peak does. Although only 6,993 meters high, it is by far the most attractive Himalayan peak that Nepal has to offer foreign visitors and tourists seeking majestic mountain views; its beauty is truly striking and unsurpassed, especially when viewed against the backdrop of **Phewa Tal**, a popular lake in the city of **Pokhara** (*see* figure 4).

MACHHENDRA NATH TEMPLE. It is a beautiful **pagoda** covered with two-tiered bronze roofs. Set in the midst of a courtyard full of stupas and other relics, it is surrounded by houses and shops—with the end result that it takes some imagination to view the building in isolation. The temple is located in **Kathmandu**'s Machhendra Bahal.

MADAL. Indigenous drum instrument, invariably associated with Nepali folk **music**. It is relatively small in size and is usually hung around the waist while playing it.

MADHES (MADES). This terms refers to the northern expansion of the Gangetic Plain, meaning the northern edges of **India** and the **Tarai** region of Nepal. Linguistically, it is believed that the term actually means the middle region or territory (*maddhe* = middle; *desh* = region, nation). That is, it is a shortened or pronunciation-friendly version of the phrase *maddhe desh*. The Gangetic Plain and its vicinity are considered to be the midland between the southern flanks (India) and northern hills and **mountains** (Nepal) of the Indian subcontinent (*see* figure 1).

MADHESI (MADESI). Inhabitants of the **Tarai** region or north **India**. The term is sometimes applied in a derogatory manner against the Tarai and north Indian inhabitants to suggest that they are uncultured or uncivilized, relative to those occupying the hills. Such a negative connotation is mostly dependent on the tone rather than the use of the word itself. After all, the *madhesis* use it to describe themselves as such. In its vernacular use, it is simply descriptive of the regional and cultural identity of the Tarai dwellers who originally moved across the border to Nepal from the north Indian provinces of Bengal, Bihar, and Utter Pradesh.

MAGAR. Ethnic group within the family of the **Tibeto-Nepali** population mainly concentrated in the central and western hills. They are one of the martial groups highly prized by British **Gorkha** recruiters to serve in their imperial army. They are certainly one of the largest Tibeto-Nepali ethnic groups in terms of their numerical size.

MAHABHARATA. One of the greatest **Hindu** epics composed by the sage **Veda Vyasa**. It can be literally translated as the great (*maha*) battle or drama (*bharat[a]*, which is also the native name for India, perhaps called so to mean "the land of the great battle"). Containing more than 90,000 stanzas that narrate the great civil war in the Indian kingdom of Kuru or Kuruchhetra (present Delhi region), it is probably the longest single poem in the world's **literature**. It is a classic tale of power and greed, good and evil as it is a captivating story of brothers against brothers. It is in this great civil war tale that one can also find a colossal philosophical treatise whose depth and scope are rarely matched and which distinguishes the *Mahabharata* from other religious texts. As a result, it is considered to be more important than the other great Hindu epic, the **Ramayana**. *See also* HINDUISM; KALI YUGA

MAHABHARAT LEKH (RANGE). This chain of **mountains** running from west to east covers the entire middle section of the entire country. Sandwiched between the **Churia Hills** (Siwalik Range) and the **Himalayan** Range, it is also sometimes referred to as the Mid-hills of Nepal.

MAHAKALI ZONE. Situated along Nepal's western border with **India**, this zone comprises a total of four districts: three in the hills (Baitadi, Dadeldhura, and Darchula) and one in the Tarai (Kanchanpur). Its name is derived from the Mahakali River which flows along the border (*see* figure 3). Spread over an area of 6,989 sq. km., it had a total population of 664,800 in 1991.

MAHAT, RAM SHARAN (1951–). An economist by training, he is a member of the **Nepali Congress Party**. He was elected to the **House of Representatives** in 1991 and reelected in the two subsequent general elections held in 1994 and 1999. During the first administration of the **Girija Prasad Koirala** government, he served as finance minister and later as foreign minister. In the mid-1990s, he was found to have deposited thousands of dollars in a foreign bank account. As a result of that discovery, he was suspected to have gotten suddenly rich by taking bribes as finance minister. Whether true or not, there was some logical merit to the accusation in that he could not have possibly made all that money within such a short time in office with his meager salary as finance minister. A minister's annual salary barely approaches $5,000.

MAHAYANA. School of **Buddhism**. As it accepts changes to the original teachings to **Buddha**, it does not adhere to the principle of **ahimsa** which forms the foundation of the **Hinayana** branch. So eating meat among the Mahayana followers is common and normal. The Mahayana school of Buddhism projects a fundamental outlook of optimism, although it agrees in theory with the Hinayana school that the world is full of sorrow. According to its precepts, the world contains much good as well as evil, and there is help for all who seek it. In essence, every living being is a Bodhisattva capable of attaining **nirvana**. It flourished all over **India**, Mongolia, Korea, and **China**, and later reached Japan, where it was modified into Zen Buddhism.

MAHENDRA, KING. *See* SHAH, MAHENDRA BIR BIKRAM.

MAHENDRA RAJMARGA. Highway named after King **Mahendra**. Commonly called the East-West Highway (its initial name), it is 1,034 kilometers long, running across the **Tarai** belt from the **Mechi Zone** in the east to the **Mahakali Zone** in the west. It was built in sections, each of them being sponsored or constructed with foreign assistance from different countries, namely **India**, the former Soviet Union, the **United Kingdom**, and the **United States**.

MAINALI, CHANDRA PRAKASH (1953–). A member of the **Communist Party of Nepal** who was elected to the **Parliament** in 1991 from Jhapa (*see* figure 2). He was reelected from the same district during the general **elections** of 1994 when the Communist party won the largest number of seats in the **House of Representatives** and formed its minority government.

MAINALI, RADHA KRISHNA (1946–). A leftist politician who was jailed for 16 years during the **Panchayat** system. He was elected to the **House of Representatives** in 1991, representing the **Communist Party of Nepal**. He won his seat again from the district of **Jhapa** (*see* figure 2) in the general **elections** held in 1994. He remains an important figure of the Communist party.

MAITHALI. Language spoken in the eastern **Tarai**. Roughly 11 percent of the people in Nepal speak Maithili.

MAJHI. Technically it means fishermen or boatmen or both. They form a small ethnic group, usually scattered in the lowland areas, along river valleys. Traditionally, they are engaged in fishing and ferrying travelers across rivers in places where there are no bridges.

MAL ADDA (MAL). Land tax office. *See also* JIMMAWAL.

MALLA. Historic people and rulers of Nepal (**Kathmandu Valley**); they belonged to the **Newar** group. There is another group of Mallas, the Thakuri Malla in the western hills, namely in the **Karnali** basin. But the reference here is distinctly to the Kathmandu Valley's Mallas whose rule can be historically separated into two distinct phases: prior to the death of King Yaksha Malla and after his death.

According to historical accounts, the dynastic rule of the Mallas over the Valley started in 1200 A.D. with the rise of **Ari Malla** as its first king. Prior to King Yaksha Malla's death in 1482, the Mallas ruled the whole valley as one unified kingdom. The Malla dynasty enjoyed its heyday during the reign of **Jayasthiti Malla**, perhaps the most farsighted of all the Malla kings to rule the Valley. However, Yaksha Malla is also accorded high honor in historical accounts as it is claimed that under his regime, the Valley kingdom experienced great prosperity and power. He conquered Mithila (what was once ancient King **Janak**'s kingdom) and extended the kingdom's boundaries as far as Bengal in the southeast, the Ganges in the south, and Shekar Dzong in Tibet.

Despite his magnificent achievements, Yaksha Malla failed to leave behind an institutional framework of governance to keep the kingdom unified. With his death, the stage was set for the breakup of the Valley into three kingdoms—**Kathmandu, Patan,** and **Bhadgaun**—to be ruled separately by his three sons. As the kingdom was officially divided among his three sons, it laid the ultimate foundation for their eventual demise. The fact that they survived as separate kingdoms for nearly 300 years after the breakup is no testimony to their internal strength, however. Rather it was merely an indication of the absence of an external enemy powerful enough to tear them down.

In addition to being endowed with the Valley's very fertile land cultivated by productive Newar peasants, all three kingdoms derived much of their wealth and other resources from their central position in the Himalayan trade between **India** and **Tibet**. It was this wealth that they used not only to sustain themselves, but also to expand on the artistic and architectural foundation firmly laid by the **Licchavi** rulers. They built various monuments and temples during their reigns. During the second phase of the Malla period, the successive kings of the three kingdoms often competed against each other in their one-upmanship regarding such construction projects. It is, therefore, no surprise that the Malla kings left behind many monuments that now serve as some of the focal points of Valley **tourism**.

Suffering from chronic internecine warfare among themselves, they were all, nevertheless, severely weakened, thus making them highly vulnerable to both internal and external incursions. They were unable to defend themselves and protect their vital interests. In fact, so shaky was Patan's position vis-à-vis Bhadgaun's and Kathmandu's that it invited in the late 1760s the rising and territorially ambitious **Gorkha** king named **Prithvi Narayan** to intervene in the Valley's internal politics—an invitation which he eagerly accepted. Later, he was invited by Bhadgaun, which lent him friendship and provided him with critical support at a crucial period in his territorial campaign. Those invitations proved to be a gold mine for him as they facilitated his relatively swift conquest of the Valley in 1769. Specifically, what they offered opportunistic Prithvi Narayan was not only an invaluable picture of internal animosities and weaknesses of the brotherly kingdoms of the Valley, but also a close-up view of the Valley's layout to plan his military invasion and eventual victory over them. *See also* ART AND ARCHITECTURE.

MALLA, ARI. First **Malla** king (reign: 1200–1216).

MALLA, BASUDEV (1926–). Professor. Associated with **Tribhuvan University** from the very beginning of his professional career, he was instrumental in the creation of the Nepal Council of World Affairs (1955). He served as vice-chancellor of Tribhuvan University in 1990 and as ambassador to the People's Republic of **China** in 1991.

MALLA, BIJAYA (1925–). Novelist and poet. Son of Riddhi Bahadur Malla, the first editor of *Sharada* (a literary magazine that played a crucial role in the development of Nepali **literature**), Bijaya had an early beginning in the field of literature. He has written many Nepali novels and served as vice-chancellor of the **Royal Nepal Academy** (1989– 1990). His novels were quite popular in the 1960s. He is also known for his short stories.

MALLA, JAYAPRAKASH (?–1768). Last **Malla** (**Newar**) king of the kingdom of **Kathmandu**. According to historical accounts, he ruled with great fortitude and equanimity despite many internal dissensions, internecine disputes, and external attacks. He was widely regarded as a brave and benevolent king whose reign spanned from 1734 to1768. As a ruler, Jayaprakash was called upon to meet many challenges and adversities. Although he succeeded in overcoming many, he could not mount an effective counterattack against **Prithvi Narayan Shah**. In short, he presided over the final demise of the Malla kingdom.

MALLA, JAYASTHITI (1354–1395). By most accounts, he was the most farsighted of all the **Malla** rulers. He was the first ruler to institute elaborate social codes that still govern many aspects of Nepal's social and cultural life. His was definitely a period of bold policy initiatives and consolidation. His official reign extended from 1382 to 1395. His death not only left a big void, but sowed the seed of internal discontent and disintegration of his kingdom as his three sons were entrusted with the joint rulership of its territorial units—**Kathmandu, Patan,** and **Bhadga-**

un—which together formed the Valley kingdom. Exactly 100 years after Jayasthiti ascended the throne in 1382, the inevitable division of the Valley kingdom occurred in 1482, when its was officially divided among King Yaksha Malla's three sons. Jayasthiti had many temples built during his rule, thus advancing the artistic and architectural heritage of Nepal.

MALLA, KRISHNA BAM (1915–1983). Writer and high-ranking civil servant. He once served as chairman of Nepal's Public Service Commission and as ambassador to **India** (1972–1975). Although he was certainly a capable and highly regarded public servant, much of his contribution to public service was overshadowed by his affairs with his own niece.

MALLA PERIOD (1200–1769). See MALLA.

MALLA, PRATAP (reign: 1641–1674). Viewed as a powerful ruler of the kingdom of **Kathmandu**, he ruled for more than 30 years. He played an important role in elevating Nepal's artistic and architectural heritage as he had many monuments constructed for various reasons, including the **Hanuman** Dhoka and **Rani Pokhari**.

MALLA, RANAJIT (reign: 1722–1769). Last king of the kingdom of **Bhadgaun**, one of the three **Malla** kingdoms in the **Kathmandu Valley**. Following his defeat by **Prithvi Narayan Shah**, to whom he had lent his true friendship and much support during his campaign, Ranajit left Nepal and went to Kashi, **India**, where he died in 1771.

MANAKAMANA. Hilltop **pagoda** temple of Goddess **Kali** in **Gorkha** (see figure 2). Very popular among **Hindu** devotees, animal sacrifices are common at this temple. The word *manakamana* literally means "fulfillment of what one desires." In this sense, Manakamana is regarded as the goddess of wish fulfillment. See GORKHAKALI MANDIR.

MANANG. One of the districts in the **Gandaki Zone**. Bordering on the autonomous region of **Tibet**, it is one of Nepal's remote areas. Until about half a century ago, it had its own mini king who exercised control over Manang with some degree of autonomy. But that is no longer the case as it is, today, fully integrated into Nepal. Many Mananges have migrated to urban centers, namely **Kathmandu**, and are engaged in import-export trade. In essence, they have transformed their tradition of **Trans-Himalayan** trade across the border into Tibet, which is now basically defunct, to contemporary foreign trade. It has been quite common in recent years for many of them to use **Gurung** as their last name. With a population of 5,369 people in 1991, it is the least populous district in Nepal. It covers an area of 2,246 sq. km. (see figure 2).

MANDALA. Geographical representation of the universe containing images of deities or symbols in geometrical patterns of concentricals. In essence, it is cosmography, routinely depicted in **Tanka** paintings. In the center lies the **Buddha**.

MANDALE. This term is used to refer to pro-**Panchayat** advocates and absolute monarchists. In terms of their attitude and behavior, they are similar to cult followers.

MANDEVA (MANADEVA) I (reign: 464–505). Perhaps the most prominent ruler of the **Licchavi period**, whose rule ushered in an era of social transformation. Broad in his outlook, Mandeva was one of the very few truly benevolent kings Nepal has ever witnessed. One significant change Mandeva instituted was to put into circulation coins, thus introducing a monetary basis for economic transactions, a bedrock of social and economic transformation.

MANE. See PRAYER WHEEL.

MANJUSRI (MANJUSHRI). Bodhisattva epitomizing wisdom. Often with a book in one hand and a naked sword in another (meant to destroy errors or falsehood), Manjusri's primary role is to stimulate understanding. As a Bodhisattva (a form of demigod), he represents the **Mahayana** school of **Buddhism**, which projects a fundamental outlook of optimism, although it agrees in theory with the **Hinayana** school that the world is full of sorrow.

MANTRA. Religious formula or prayer. It technically means release or transcendence (*tra*) of mind (*man*). It is recited repeatedly, either silently or vocally. It is common in both the **Hindu** and **Buddhist** traditions of Nepal.

MANU. Legendary sage. He is believed to be the founder of the **caste system** and the author of *Manusmriti*, generally regarded as the first and most elaborate treatise on statecraft or how to govern through the social, political, and economic institutions of the State.

MAOIST MOVEMENT. *See* PEOPLE'S WAR.

MARSYANGDI HYDROELECTRICITY. Power generation plant at Anbu Khaireni in Tanahun. Completed in 1992, it has a capacity of 66,000 kilowatts.

MARTYRS' MEMORIAL. Popularly called Shahid Dhoka, it is a martyrs' memorial gate near **Tundikhel** in **Kathmandu**. Built and inaugurated in 1961, the gate houses the statues of Nepal's four national martyrs who sacrificed their lives for democracy: **Dasharath Chand, Dharma Bhakta Mathema, Shukra Raj Shastri,** and **Ganga Lal Shrestha.**

MARWARI (MARWADI). Originally from Rajasthan, **India**, Nepal's Marwaris still maintain strong business, cultural, and marital ties to their motherland. They are famous as merchants or business people and control a large portion of business in the **Kathmandu Valley** and in many of the **Tarai**'s border towns. In short, the term Marwari is invariably equated with merchants, and sometimes it even carries a negative connotation.

MASAL. Radical faction of the **Communist Party of Nepal.** It is a small faction that has its support base confined to the **Kathmandu Valley.** However, it is quite active in organizing effective mass protests in the Valley. Although it occasionally forms alliances with other factions of the Communist party, it generally operates on its own.

MASKEY, CHANDRA MAN SINGH (1900–1984). Born and raised in **Kathmandu**, he occupies a prominent place in Nepal's artistic field. He achieved excellence in the study of arts through his training abroad. In addition to painting, he had a speciality in artistic design of different architectural works in stone and molded sculpture.

MATAWALI (MATWALI). Generally the opposite of **Tagadhari**. It is a generic term applied to those **caste** groups that are customarily allowed to consume alcohol and meats, including chickens, pigs, and buffaloes. They are considered lesser castes in comparison to the high caste **Bahun** and **Chhetri** groups. They do not wear *janai* as the Tagadhari groups do.

MATHEMA, DHARMA BHAKTA (1909–1941). Martyr, one of the four murdered by Prime Minister **Juddha Shamsher Rana** because of his anti-**Rana** and pro-democracy activities and views. Prior to his death, he served as a physical fitness instructor of King **Tribhuvan**. He was executed in 1941.

MECHI ZONE. Nepal's easternmost zone, it includes four districts: **Jhapa**, **Ilam**, Panchthar, and Taplejung. Its total area of 8,196 sq. km. supported 1,119,422 people in 1991 (*see* figure 3).

MEDIA. The Nepali media can be divided into two major groups: print and electronic. While the print media includes mainly newspapers, radio and television form the core of the electronic media in Nepal. These days one may extend the boundary of the electronic media to include the Internet, which arrived in the country in the mid-1990s. It is, however, noted that its accessibility is extremely limited. Basically, because of its English medium, only the educated and well-to-do segments of the population can access it.

Until 1951, when **Radio Nepal** was established, the print media was the only one available in the country, the most widely circulated publication being the *Gorkhapatra* which, at that time, was a weekly publication controlled by the government. According to one account, access to the radio media was an element of luxury, a rare treat, that not too many could afford. That is, radios were a scarce commodity that only a handful of people possessed. During the **Rana** period, citizens were required to obtain a permit to legally own a radio. And those with radios had to tune in to radio broadcasts from **India**. But the situation changed dramatically following the demise of Rana autocracy. Then came television some 30 years after Radio Nepal was set up; in the early 1980s, state-owned **Nepal Television** was launched, thus inaugurating a new age of electronic media. Given this scenario, it is obvious that the media history of Nepal is fairly young.

Following the overthrow of the **Rana** regime, Nepal was suddenly thrust into the world of **press** freedom. As the press enjoyed freedom of expression, newspapers sprouted in **Kathmandu**, the epicenter of the

Nepali media. But the freedom of the press was short-lived as it was snatched away by King **Mahendra Bir Bikram Shah**, literally overnight, following his palace coup against the government of Prime Minister **B. P. Koirala** who was arrested and jailed. The king imposed various regulations to severely curtail the freedom of the press, including prepublication censorship. Newspapers could not be published without registration with the government. Those that had been registered would lose their publication permission if they failed to adhere to state regulations.

Even though there was no letup in the restrictive regulations issued by the government, the number of newspapers continued to grow with the passage of time. In 1962, King Mahendra's government started a news agency, **Rastriya Samachar Samiti**, to collect and distribute news about and within Nepal. The Samiti monopoly over news collection and distribution was yet another mechanism deployed by Mahendra to muzzle the press. In addition to the domestic newspapers, foreign publications containing critical news reports on King Mahendra and his autocratic policy and politics were either selectively confiscated or entirely banned from the country. King **Birendra Bir Bikram Shah** continued to pursue these restrictive measures throughout the **Panchayat** period.

Finally, in early 1990, following the restoration of democracy, the country witnessed the return of the freedom of the press. In actuality, during the pro-democracy movement of the early 1990s, the Nepali press openly defied restrictive measures to express its support of the movement which culminated in the end of the Panchayat system within a few months. Since its momentous revival, Nepal's press freedom experienced a momentary setback in November 1990 when two reporters were charged with slandering the royal family in print. Charges were later dismissed in December. Currently, more than 400 newspapers and periodicals are published in the country, including several national dailies such as the *Gorkhapatra* and its English version, **The Rising Nepal.** Two other popular dailies are *Kantipur* and its English twin, *The Kathmandu Post*. Although relatively new and privately owned, they compete head on with the *Gorkhapatra* and *The Rising Nepal*, both government publications. In total, the combined circulation of all Nepali newspapers is perhaps around 200,000 and is mostly bound to urban areas. This is a low figure, but one that is quite reflective of Nepal's huge rural population base and low literacy rate—a situation that is hardly conducive to fostering newspaper subscription and readership. To most rural Nepalis, perhaps the most viable and accessible source of news is radio broadcast.

Once again in late November 2001, the light of media freedom in the country was drastically dimmed, if not completely turned off. As King **Gyanendra Bir Bikram Shah** announced a state of emergency, the freedom of the press as well as assembly was severely constricted. The rights granted by the **constitution** have been suspended. Since then, the state of emergency has been renewed twice, the latest being announced on 27 May 2002. Journalists are routinely harassed, with many of them jailed without any charges. According to one report, more than 100 journalists have been detained, thus creating a climate of fear. They are, as reported by the Associated Press (Asia), "literally abducted by security forces and held incommunicado, without charge." With the increasing entrenchment of the state of emergency, dissenting views and voices are under attack. *See also* COMMUNICATIONS; EDUCATION.

MISHRA, BHADRAKALI (1921–?). He has had a long political career, participating in various democratic activities. He served as minister of transport in 1951 during the first post-**Rana** government appointed by King Tribhuvan and headed by **Matrika Prasad Koirala**.

MIYA, ALI (1921–?). He is a traditional musician and folksinger from **Pokhara**. He is known for many popular songs.

MIYA, KHALIL (1917–?). Muslim leader and member of the **Nepali Congress Party**. Also known as an Ayurvedic doctor, he was elected to the **House of Representatives** in 1991. His **election** is significant in that in a society dominated by **Hindus**, a Muslim was elected or can be elected. This suggests both the nature of party politics and the degree of religious tolerance in Nepal, at least compared to **India**, where animosities between Hindus and Muslims run deep.

MOHI. Legally recognized tenant. *See also* LAND REFORM.

MOMOCHA (MOMO). Popular **Newari** and **Sherpa** dish, consisting of chopped, marinated goat or buffalo meat wrapped in a small, thin piece of dough. In some cases, chicken meat is also used. It is usually steamed and is identical to Chinese dumplings.

MONGOL NATIONAL ORGANIZATION. Political group established in 1989 to promote the cause of the **Tibeto-Nepali** ethnic groups of Mongoloid origin. *See also* ETHNICITY; GURUNG, GOPAL.

MONSOON. The rhythm of life in Nepal is intrinsically intertwined with its physical environment. So geography is not merely a geological entity, it is an indicator of life deeply imbued with cultural meaning and rituals, social customs and values. Nowhere is this relationship more keenly demonstrated than in the annual cyclical drama of what is commonly known as the monsoon, a climatic phenomenon that forms the lifeblood of Nepal. The annual cycle of the monsoon evokes both fear and reverence. To Nepali farmers and peasants, the monsoon is their rain god who can be as richly nurturing as ravagingly punishing. It all depends on the timing of its arrival. During every **rice** planting season, farmers and peasants await its arrival with a sense of urgency and eagerness, with profound fears and high hopes.

As dependent as life is on the monsoon, its timely arrival is rarely assured to ensure the success of **agriculture**. As a result, entrenched dependence on a phenomenon as uncertain as the monsoon turns life into an annual wager for the millions of farmers whose survival hinges on farming. The situation is greatly magnified by the fact the monsoon is the principal source of water for countless peasants and farmers. Regular and reliable irrigation facilities are limited and those that exist are mostly concentrated in the **Tarai** where the task of canal construction is less arduous. Despite this paradoxical uncertainty, the monsoon does exhibit a discernible pattern of seasonality. To be specific, it can be divided into four phases which are: premonsoon (March to May), summer monsoon (June to August), postmonsoon (September to November), and winter monsoon (December to February).

However, in its life cycle, it is the summer monsoon, also known as the rainy season, that holds the greatest value in Nepal and throughout Asia, for it corresponds to the most important farming season of the year. Even though the arrival of the summer monsoon can vary by as much as a month, it normally reaches Nepal in early June and lingers until late August. This is the season when the celestial drama of life begins, featuring the interplay between the towering **Himalayan Mountains** and the monsoon clouds surging from the Bay of Bengal. As the snow-capped mountains and the moisture-laden clouds engage in their swirling annual tango, farmers and peasants are busy in the valleys and lowlands, furiously readying their fields for paddy planting. At every touch of the standing mountains, the restless monsoon clouds calm down, finally melting into rain particles and nourishing countless paddy fields down in the valleys and lowlands.

At the very first arrival of summer rains, the celebration of life begins for the multitude of masses as they express their reverence to the rain god with worships and offerings. The season of rice planting gets underway at a furious pace for the next three-to-four weeks, for they have to capture those precious moments of timely rains. The timing of planting plays a big role in the vitality of paddy crops. Everywhere the rains have come, life is busy like a swarm of bees collecting nectar at the peak of the spring. Farmers wake up at the rooster's first crow, pack their breakfast (often roasted corn or some type of homemade bread), collect their tools, and hit the roads on their way to the field, some to prepare the fields and others to plant rice seedlings. The task of taking care of babies and bringing lunch to the field is often left to children. The imperative of life in Nepal is a family enterprise. On the other hand, if the rain god fails to descend with nimbus clouds bearing rains, farmers fear for a life condemned to misery, and they begin to pray. The new crops of rice, the grain of life across monsoon Asia, will suffer, and the harvests will be reduced, adversely affecting millions of lives. Such is the fragility of life in Nepal, all dependent on one timely stroke of the mighty monsoon.

With the arrival of the rains, the extreme—and often unbearable—dry heat of the premonsoon yields to the humidity of the summer. After every rainfall, the temperature slightly cools off, thus making the evening and nightly temperatures more manageable. The plains and hills receive more than 70 percent of their annual precipitation during the summer monsoon. The amount of summer monsoon rain generally declines from southeast to northwest as the maritime wedge of air gradually becomes thinner and dryer.

Although the timely arrival of the summer monsoon is critical for farmers and peasants, it does not always represent an eternal blessing. Periodically, the monsoon turns violent, causing immense landslides and flooding. At times, human lives and livestock are lost, farmlands are washed away, and properties are destroyed (not to mention great difficulty in the movement of goods and people from one area to another). Besides these visible and measurable losses, day-to-day life becomes ruptured. As basic an act as daily cooking can be severely affected. Everything is so damp and soaked in rain that it is very difficult to find relatively dry firewood to cook food. Lighting a fire suddenly becomes a defiant challenge. As a result, a simple task of cooking that normally takes about an hour turns into a daunting chore. This situation is particularly precarious for the countless poor, for whom gathering firewood is a daily routine like securing food itself.

MORANG. District in the **Kosi Zone** (see figure 2). Its population in 1991 totaled more than 676,000, settled over an area of 1,855 sq. km. Located in the eastern **Tarai**, along the Indian border, Morang is perhaps the most industrial districts in Nepal, with the exception of **Kathmandu** and **Lalitpur**. Its industrial status is chiefly anchored to its largest city of **Biratnagar** (see figure 4) that features some of major manufacturing enterprises in the country.

MOUNTAINS. Nepal's high mountains constitute the **Himalayan** Range and are situated to the north of the **Mahabharat Lekh** or the Hill Region (see Introduction; figure 2). The 10 tallest mountain peaks of Nepal are as follows:

Name	Height in Meters
Mount Everest	8,848
Kanchanjanga	8,598
Lhotse	8,516
Makalu	8,463
Cho Oyu	8,201
Dhaulagiri	8,167
Manaslu	8,156
Annapurna I	8,078
Sisa Pangma	8,013
Annapurna II	7,937

MOUNT EVEREST. Called **Sagarmatha** (roof of the world) in Nepali and **Chomolongma** (the mother goddess of the snow) by the **Sherpas**, it forms Nepal's identity in the Western popular imagination. Situated in the northeastern part of the country along the border with **China**, it is a majestic peak, towering over all other Himalayan peaks. With the altitude of 8,850 meters (29,035 feet) above sea level, it is the highest summit in the world, imbued with legends and lore. To the Sherpas, it is a sacred land, the land of gods and goddesses and, of course, home to the ever illusive, "abominable" snowman, fondly called **Yeti**. Although it is no longer considered to be the formidable peak that it once was, it is still the ultimate dream of almost any serious **mountain** climber. It is no surprise, therefore, that it attracts many mountaineering expeditions from all over the world, no matter how intimidating and merciless it has proven to be. Over the years, it has consumed many climbers' lives.

Traditionally, as the people who live in its vicinity considered the mountain to be sacred, they refrained from scaling it before the early 1900s. This tradition changed with the arrival of Western mountaineers. In 1913, British explorer John Noel sneaked into **Tibet**, which was also closed at the time, and made a preliminary survey of the approaches to the peak from the north where the topography is less varied than on its southern side. Led by George Leigh Mallory, the British explored the north side in 1921. Mallory's expedition, and another that took place soon afterward, were unable to overcome strong winds, avalanches, and other hazards to reach the summit. In 1924 a third British expedition resulted in the disappearance of Mallory and a climbing companion while only 240 meters from the summit. More attempts were made throughout the 1930s and 1940s. Then, with the conquest of Tibet by China in the early 1950s, the region was closed to foreigners. As a result, the peak was approached from the Nepal side (south), starting with W. H. Tilman and C. Houston in 1950.

After several failed attempts, the peak was finally conquered on 29 May 1953 by an expedition team composed of John Hunt of **Britain**, **Edmund Hillary** from New Zealand, and **Tenzing Norgay (Sherpa)** of Nepal, as the latter two managed to reach the top of Mount Everest. Since then, Everest expeditions have become quite routine and the success rate as well as the number of tragedies have greatly increased. It is now a popular pilgrimage for a unique breed of people called mountain climbers. Since its first ascent by Hillary and Tenzing Norgay, more than 1,200 people have climbed Everest. Over the years, 175 people have died as a result of Everest expeditions and many of their bodies remain frozen on the mountain. On 29 May 2003, Nepal celebrated the fiftieth anniversary of its first successful conquest with street parades and by making Hillary an honorary citizen of Nepal. About 450 summiteers participated in the celebrations. *See also* TOURISM.

MUDRA SANGRHALAYA. Numismatics museum of Nepal, located in the **Hanuman Dhoka**. It houses a sizable collection (*sangrhalaya*) of Nepali and foreign coins (*mudra*), dating back to the **Licchavi period**.

MUKTINATH. Highly renowned **Hindu** shrine adorned with the three-roofed **pagoda** temple of Jwalamai, which contains a small eternal (constantly burning) flame (*jwala*) fed by natural gas underneath that issues through a fissure in the rock. Located about 4,000 meters from sea level, close to the **Tibetan** border, in the **Trans-Himalayan** district of **Mustang** (*see* figure 2), Muktinath is considered an important destination for Hindu pilgrims from different parts of Nepal and from **India** and **Tibet**.

MUKTI SENA. Liberation (*mukti*) army (*sena*). It was the military arm of the **Nepali Congress Party** that was deployed during the anti-**Rana** revolution of 1950–1951.

MULUKI AIN. *See* CIVIL CODE.

MULUKI KHANA. State treasury office during the **Rana Period**. It was created by Prime Minister **Jang Bahadur Rana**.

MUSALMAN. Muslim or Moslem; adherents of **Islam**. The term is used widely throughout Nepal.

MUSEUMS. Although Nepal is often considered a treasure trove of arts and artifacts, it has only a few museums. Moreover, its museums are quite poor in terms of both collections and maintenance. They sorely lack necessary funding, resources, technical support, and logistical facility to elevate their quality as well as collections. Some of the museums in Nepal include: **National Museum** in **Kathmandu**, National Brass and Bronze Museum in **Bhaktapur**, **Patan**'s National Bronze Art Museum, **National Metal Works Museum**, **National Wood Working Museum**, and **Natural History Museum**. *See also* ART AND ARCHITECTURE.

MUSIC AND DANCE. Music and dance are important aspects of Nepali cultural tradition. They are common virtually in every corner of Nepal, from east to west and north to south. It is not uncommon for visitors and tourists to see peasants—both men and **women**, old and young—singing mellifluous songs while working in the field or while on the way to or returning from the field after a long a day of work, as well as frolicking shepherds in their colorful garbs. They sing songs of pain and joy, loneliness and hardship of life, and sing on all occasions, almost spontaneously. Even soldiers returning home from abroad on vacation sing when they hit the hill trails leading to their villages. Singing is, for many, an essential part of Nepali life as it transcends all ethnic groups and geographic regions. It is a form of self entertainment and recreation.

While singing is often performed independently, dancing is usually accompanied by singing and playing certain musical instruments. Music and dance are quite common during certain **festivals**, festivities, and national holidays when they are performed in a well-organized and rehearsed fashion on stage or relatively spontaneously in open fields. Sometimes men and women dance separately and other times together, but rarely touching each other or holding hands. Most dances are folk dances, although Western disco clubs have penetrated the **elite** circle in **Kathmandu**. Music and dance performances used to be common in royal palaces as they used to patronize such artists, but they are now rare because videos, movies, and television have become their favorite means of entertainment and recreation. Here are some of the typical and traditional forms of Nepali music (singing); they are performed independently or accompanied by dancing during certain celebrations and entertainments. Not included in this short list is *kathak*, which is a classical dance of Indian origin, performed by both men and women with elaborate and delicate movements of hands, heads, and feet; it is accompanied by musical instruments such as **tabla** and sitar.

- *Bhailo*. It is group singing performed during the **Hindu** festival called **Tihar**. It is practiced by various ethnic and age groups both in the hills and the **Tarai**. The *bhailo* singing group goes from door to door, collecting donations.
- *Bhajan*. It is a typical **Newar** tradition that involves religious group singing, accompanied by various musical instruments. It is very rhythmic and repetitive and is usually conducted in the evening after dinner. Neighbors gather in a temple shelter on a fairly routine basis and sing for about an hour or two. It is also performed during certain clan-based **guthi** festivities or religious festivals. Although religious in nature, *bhajan* is not considered a prayer. It is on the decline, even in the **Kathmandu Valley**, where it had a strong following.

- **Bhote** *selo*. Also known in some quarters as **Tamang** *selo*, it is a popular form of singing and dancing that is particularly common among the Bhotes, Tamangs and **Sherpas** as well as other **Tibeto-Nepali** groups. It has received national recognition in recent years and is sometimes performed in Kathmandu's fancy hotels catering to Western tourists as part of their cultural shows.
- Dangali Vadi (Badi). The Vadis are a distinct group of people in the district of **Dang**; they are akin to the **Tharu**. Many of them have resettled around **Nepalganj**. They are professional singers and dancers who in the not-too-distant past led an itinerant life moving from place to place to earn their living by performing for public entertainment. Although the group itself was confined to a particular locality, their tradition was known in many parts of Nepal because of their occasional tours. However, this is now a dying tradition for three reasons. First, their already small number has dwindled further. Second, the Vadis now live a settled life and many of their women are engaged in **prostitution** in Nepalganj to earn their livelihood. Third, ubiquitous Hindi movies have rendered their traditional profession of singing and dancing archaic and obsolete.
- *Dohari*. It can be defined as a form of duet songs, usually sung by one male and one female who may be lovers or simply engaged in *dohari* singing to challenge each other. In Nepal, *dohari* is the only form of singing in which the two parties go back and forth as if they are debating or questioning and answering each other on an instant basis and in a melodic form. The format is highly unique in that it has no prewritten or composed songs to rely on; it is entirely instantaneous improvisation in terms of both content and melody. It invariably involves certain themes that may change over the course of singing, which can go on for several hours—nonstop. It is a total test of one's wits, composure, and endurance. There have been reported cases of *dohari* singing that have lasted two to three days, but they are rare. Most *doharis* last about an hour or so and are normally spontaneous, as they tend to be carried out during certain farming activities such as planting or weeding. It rarely involves any dancing or instrument. *Dohari* can be carried out face to face or across the field without seeing each other.
- **Gaine** songs. The Gaines are a minstrel group who instill into their songs topical themes in a poignant manner and a beautiful tone. They are renowned for their formal as well as informal singing in many parts

of the country. It always involves playing a *sarangi*, a stringed musical instrument which they make themselves.
- **Jhyaure**. Typical Nepali folk songs that are sometimes combined with dancing and a drum called a **madal**, which is indigenous to the hills. It is nationally recognized and has, in recent years, reached its peak in terms of popularity. It is a fixture with **Radio Nepal**. It is largely a hill-based musical form and is practiced by different ethnic groups. *Jhyaure* singing can be conducted in a group setting or individually.
- *Rodi*. It is a group singing tradition, largely confined to the **Gurung**. It is conducted after dinner in a common house where young men and women gather to sing together, sometimes all night long. It may involve dancing, but not often.
- **Tij**. Almost exclusive practiced by **Bahun** and **Chhetri** women, Tij too can be considered a form of Nepal's traditional music and dance; its celebration involves both. While the Tij songs are rhythmic, associated dances tend to be somewhat random with a great deal of hand and head movements. Since there is no prior arrangement or training for Tij dances, they are spontaneous and free of inhibition. In the course of celebration, women enjoy the freedom of making sarcastic remarks and fun of their husbands or men in general.

In recent years, however, Nepali music can simultaneously be seen as advanced and diluted. It has advanced in that it is now diversified, going beyond the confines of its traditional forms and incorporating new trends borrowed from outside sources, including Western music and musical instruments. So its field has greatly expanded in terms of both musical forms and formats. Both songs and singing have been modernized. At the same time, the new forms of Nepali music have superseded some of the traditional forms. The only forms that seemed to have survived the onslaught of modern musical trends are Bhote *selo*, Gaine, *jhyaure*, and *rodi*. In a way, these four have even thrived, partly because of modernization. Nowadays, they are presented as showcases of traditional Nepali music, much of it for Western tourist consumption. In other words, the growth of **tourism** has, in its own curious or even contradictory way, led to a noticeable revival of traditional **art and architecture**, music and dance—sometimes adulterated and other times in their authentic forms.

MUSTANG. District in the **Dhaulagiri Zone** (*see* figures 2 and 3). It had a population of 14,319 in 1991, scattered over an area of 3,673 sq. km.

As a district, it is the primary domain of the **Thakali** ethnic group, which belongs to the **Tibeto-Nepali** population. Two popular places in this district are the Thakali settlements of Marpha and **Jomsom**, both situated along the **Kali Gandaki** River. They are both well known for apple and apricot growing as well as for the production of liquor from these two types of fruits.

N

NAG (NAGA). Serpent deities worshiped by **Hindus** especially on Nag Panchami (essentially, "the day of the Nag"). They are believed to have powers to invoke rain or to inflict droughts and famines and to protect houses and buildings. Lord **Vishnu** is sometimes depicted sitting on the bed of Nags with their heads towering over Vishnu's head.

NAGAR PALIKA. Municipality, designated urban area. Prior to 1990, it was called Nagar (town) **Panchayat**. Since then, any settlement with a minimum population of 9,000 people is defined as a Nagar Palika.

NAGHRAD. Abode of snakes. According to the **Newari** mythological belief, the **Kathmandu Valley** filled with a lake was the Naghrad before it was drained.

NAMASTE (NAMASKAR). Customary greetings in Nepal. It is generally expressed at the time of meeting; rarely used at the time of separation (departure).

NAMCHE BAZAAR. Famous **Sherpa** village (3,480m) in Solokhumbu at the foothills of **Mount Everest**. Often used as a base, it is a major stop before the Everest ascent.

NARAHARI NATH, YOGI (1919–?). A scholar who has written several books, mostly involving historical accounts of Nepal. He is also seen by many as a key villain of democracy, a right-hand conspirator of King **Mahendra Bir Bikram Shah** who orchestrated the choking of nascent democracy in 1960 when he was routinely involved in inciting civil disturbances and chaos to taint the democratic government of **B. P. Koirala**. According to one report, in **Gorkha**, the ancestral home of

Mahendra, he put out a call, "inciting the people not to pay taxes and overthrow the government by violent and terrorist methods."

NARAK (NARAG; NARGA). Hindu concept of hell; mythical place inhabited by devils and demons ruled by Yamaraj, ironically known as the god of death. It is the opposite of **Swarga** (heaven).

NARAYANGHAT. Important and booming city in **Chitwan**, situated on the bank of the **Narayani River**. Its early growth is largely associated with the opening of the **Rapti Valley** for planned land resettlement in the mid-1960s. It now serves as a central node in Nepal's road transport network because of its links to **Kathmandu** and **Pokhara** in the hills and **Birganj, Butwal, Siddhartha Nagar**, and beyond in the **Tarai** (see figure 4). Initially, it was developed by the **Newar** migrants (merchants) from the hill town of Bandipur in Tanahun. To this day, the Newar merchants from Bandipur dominate the town's trade and commerce, although in recent years Indian merchants have begun to make some inroads. A major gateway to Kathmandu, it is one of the very few urban centers in the Tarai that is still largely dominated by Nepali businessmen. Most others are controlled by Indian merchants.

NARAYAN GOPAL. See GURUBACHARYA, NARAYAN GOPAL.

NARAYANI (RIVER). See GANDAKI RIVER SYSTEM.

NARAYANI ZONE. Named after the **Narayani River**, it is exclusively a **Tarai** zone consisting of five districts: Bara, **Chitwan**, Makwanpur, Parsa, and Rautahat (see figures 2 and 3). It has a total area of 8,313 sq. km. and supported 1,868,634 people in 1991.

NARENDRADEVA (reign: 643–679). Perhaps the last paramount ruler of the **Licchavi period**, whose reign was marked with many notable achievements, including those on the diplomatic front. Before he was crowned king, he fled the country and sought asylum in **Tibet** after his father was dethroned by his uncle. Later, with the help of Tibetan King Song-tsen Gampo, he regained his father's throne and became king. In many respects, he was the first king to recognize the full gravity of Nepal's tenuous geographical position of being squeezed between the two giants of Asia. According to a **Buddhist** legend, he retired to a monastery in his old age and died there.

NATARAJ. Dancing form of **Shiva,** often represented in various dancing postures. It is worshiped as a patron deity of classical dances. *See also* MUSIC AND DANCE.

NATIONAL ART GALLERY. Art gallery in the **Bhaktapur Durbar Square.** It houses a collection of intricate and symbolic paintings on scrolls as well as many other ancient art objects.

NATIONAL BIRD. *See* DANPHE.

NATIONAL CONSTRUCTION COMPANY OF NEPAL (NCCN). Founded in 1961 and incorporated in 1968, it is a public enterprise engaged in many contractual public works construction projects, including roads. *See also* INDUSTRY; TRANSPORTATION.

NATIONAL COUNCIL. Known as the **Rastriya Sabha** or the Upper House of **Parliament,** it has 60 members elected and nominated in accordance with the **constitution.** *See also* ELECTORAL SYSTEM.

NATIONAL DEMOCRATIC PARTY (NDP). Also known in Nepali as the Rastriya Prajatantra Party, it is a party of leaders and supporters of the now-defunct **Panchayat** system. It was formed by two hardcore royalists: **Lokendra Bahadur Chand** and **Surya Bahadur Thapa.** It has two factions: one led by Chand and another by Thapa (which seems to be the stronger of the two). As a right-wing party, its agenda favors the palace position and is supportive of absolute monarchy.

NATIONAL FLAG. *See* FLAG.

NATIONAL FLOWER. *See* LALI GURANS.

NATIONAL LANGUAGE. *See* LANGUAGE.

NATIONAL METAL WORKS MUSEUM. Museum located in the **Patan Durbar Square,** housing several metallic art pieces. Although established in 1962, it was opened to the public in 1969. Additionally, it contains archeological terra-cotta figurines and beads. *See also* ART AND ARCHITECTURE.

NATIONAL MUSEUM. Nepal's biggest and oldest **museum**, located at Chhauni, **Kathmandu**. Initially founded in 1928 as Silkhana, it was opened to the public a decade later in 1938. Its present name was given in 1967. It has an extensive collection of **art** objects, weapons, garments, costumes, and photographs.

NATIONAL PLANNING COMMISSION (NPC). Functioning as an advisory body, it is responsible for formulating and implementing national development plans and policies at all levels under the direction of the **Nepal Development Council**. In addition, it plays an advisory role with respect to the sectoral and geographical allocation of resources and acts as a central institution for guiding, monitoring, and evaluating development plans and programs and their implementation.

Until 1990, it was chaired by the king; it is now chaired by the prime minister and composed of one full-time vice-chairman, five members, and one member secretary. The chief secretary and finance secretary are its ex-officio members. The NPC is supported by the National Planning Commission Secretariat as its secretariat, which is assisted by regional offices located in each of the five development regions: eastern, central, western, mid-western and far-western. The Central Bureau of Statistics functions as its technical wing and is responsible for generating, processing, and disseminating data and information required for **planning** purposes. The NPC's functions, roles, and responsibilities are carried out with the support of eight divisions which are as follows:

- Macro-economic management
- Central monitoring and evaluation
- Plan and policy coordination
- **Poverty** alleviation and employment
- **Agriculture** and **land reforms**
- Water resources, electricity, and physical planning
- Human resources development
- Local development, **transport**, and environment

NATIONAL THEATER HALL. This is the hall where national cultural activities and functions are staged on various occasions, including national-level dance and drama competitions. Called Rastriya Nach Ghar (*Nachghar*) in Nepali, it is located in **Kathmandu**. *See also* ART AND ARCHITECTURE; MUSIC AND DANCE.

NATIONAL TRADING LIMITED. Public corporation established in 1962 and incorporated in 1964. It is mainly concerned with the trades of capital goods and luxury consumers goods such as motor vehicles. *See also* FOREIGN TRADE.

NATIONAL WOOD WORKING MUSEUM. This **Museum** is based in the **Bhaktapur Durbar Square**. Created in 1962, it was opened to the public in 1967. It houses many woodwork objects produced in Nepal, particularly those made in **Bhaktapur**. *See also* ART AND ARCHITECTURE.

NATURAL HISTORY MUSEUM. Museum of natural history, based in Chhauni, **Kathmandu**. Founded in 1975, this museum has a relatively extensive collection of plants and animals, found in Nepal and elsewhere. It is administered by **Tribhuvan University**.

NEMBANG, TIL BIKRAM. *See* KAINLA, BAIRAGI.

NEMUNI (NE MUNI). Legendary patron saint of the prehistoric period who appeared in the **Kathmandu Valley** as the protector (*pala*) of the land. So the origin of the name "Nepal" is rooted in his name: *Nepala* meaning "the land protected by Ne." Nepal is a condensed version of Nepala which, when pronounced in Nepali, carries a shorter sound as in Nepal. *See also* Introduction.

NEPAL AID GROUP. International committee of foreign donor agencies and nations interested in providing assistance for Nepal's economic development. *See also* FOREIGN AID.

NEPAL ASSOCIATION OF FINE ARTS (NAFA). This is the only such association in Nepal. It organizes art exhibitions, runs a gallery, and promotes fine arts and artists.

NEPAL ASSOCIATION OF TRAVEL AGENTS (NATA). As a trade association, it facilitates and promotes the interests of travel agents and agencies while, at the same time, insuring that they provide high quality service to **tourists** and travelers.

NEPAL BANK LIMITED. Nepal's first commercial **bank** established in 1937. It has branches throughout the kingdom and recently faced tremendous competition from many other private banks. See also PRIVATIZATION.

NEPAL BAR ASSOCIATION. Formed in 1962, it is a professional association of Nepali barristers and legal practitioners that is meant to not only protect and promote their interests, but also preserve the sanctity of what is called "due process" in the legal lexicon. See also CONSTITUTIONS; HUMAN RIGHTS; JUDICIAL SYSTEM; MEDIA.

NEPAL CHAMBER OF COMMERCE (NCC). As the self-descriptive name suggests, it is an association of commercial enterprises and businessmen. It was founded in 1950, and acts as an active advocate of business interests in the country. See also FOREIGN TRADE.

NEPAL CHILDREN'S ORGANIZATION. Organization dedicated to the welfare of Nepali children. It has been in existence since 1964. See also CHILD LABOR; HEALTH CARE; HUMAN RIGHTS; PROSTITUTION.

NEPAL DEVELOPMENT COUNCIL (NDC). In a message to the nation on 13 April 1972, King **Birendra Bir Bikram Shah** underlined the importance of a development council with a view to accelerating the pace of economic development in a manner consistent with the actual needs and aspirations of the people as reflected in national development plans. As a result, the National Development Council was born on 11 June 1972 under the king's chairmanship.

Following the restoration of the democratic system, the NDC was reorganized on 26 December 1991. Its aim is to provide opportunity for all geographical regions, social classes, and communities to contribute to the comprehensive development of Nepal as well as to give an institutional stability to the process of national development. Since its reorganization in 1990, it is now chaired by the ruling prime minister as opposed to the king, who used to be its designated chair. The council consists of representatives of various groups and communities from different walks of life. The major function of the council is to provide directives to the **National Planning Commission** on various development issues of local, regional, and national importance. In addition, the NDC also gives directives to the commission on the formulation of periodic and annual plans as well as on budgetary matters.

NEPAL ELECTRICITY AUTHORITY. Public authority formed in 1985 by the amalgamation of the Nepal Electricity Corporation and concerned governmental departments. it looks after the production, distribution, supply, and maintenance of electricity in the nation. Its forerunner Bijuli Adda was instituted in 1911 and incorporated as the Nepal Electricity Corporation in 1962.

NEPAL FOOD CORPORATION. Public enterprise established in 1974 to manage sales and supply of food grains in the country. *See also* AGRICULTURE.

NEPALGANJ. Border city, commercial center in Banke. With a 1991 population of 48,656, it is the largest city west of the **Gandaki** basin. Its features include a domestic airport and an industrial district built with **Indian** assistance. It has the largest concentration of **Muslims** in Nepal, where one wakes up every morning to a call to prayer.

NEPAL GOVERNMENT RAILWAYS. Nepal's first railway tracts were built from **Amlekhganj** to Raxaul, a small city in **India** right across the border from **Birganj** (*see* figure 4). Built in 1928, it is a narrow gauge system, covering a mere distance of 40 kilometers. But only less than 10 kilometers are currently used. Another 53-kilometers long railway was opened in 1937, linking a railhead in India. Since they are both poorly maintained, they are in dire need of repair. No additional tracts are likely to be built in the future. *See also* TRANSPORTATION.

NEPAL GRINDLAYS BANK LIMITED. Private bank. In existence since 1986, it is a joint venture between the Grindlays Bank of England and the **Nepal Bank Limited**. *See also* PRIVATIZATION.

NEPALI CALENDAR. Based on the lunar system, the Nepali calendar uses **Bikram Sambat** (B.S.) and is a little more than 56 years ahead of the Christian era. For instance, according to this system, 2000-2001 A.D. is 2057 (B.S.). The New Year begins in mid-April. Like the Julian system, there are 12 months, each month beginning around the middle of a Western month.

Nepali Months	Western Months
Baisakh	April–May
Jestha (Jeth)	May–June
Ashadh (Asar)	June–July
Shrawan (Sawan)	July–August
Bhadra (Bhadau)	August–September
Ashwin (Asoj)	September–October
Kartik	October–November
Marga (Mangsir)	November–December
Poush (Push)	December–January
Magh	January–February
Falgun (Fagun)	February–March
Chaitra (Chait)	March–April

NEPALI CONGRESS PARTY (NCP; NC). It is the largest political party of Nepal. Founded in January 1947, its immediate revolutionary intention was to dismantle **Rana** autocracy and establish democracy. Led by **B. P. Koirala**, the NCP was, indeed, instrumental in bringing down the Rana rule in 1951. Immediately following the fall of the Ranas, a transitional coalition government was formed between the Ranas and the NCP. Although it was headed by **Mohan Shamsher Rana** as prime minister, B. P. Koirala led the Congress faction as defense minister. A few months later, the NCP quit the coalition and the transitional government fell. Although the NCP was by far the most powerful and organized political party in the nation, it was given no opportunity by King **Tribhuvan Bir Bikram Shah** and later by King **Mahendra Bir Bikram Shah** to form subsequent governments until the general elections were finally held in 1959 to elect a government. As the NCP swept the elections, it was finally allowed to form a popular government headed by B. P. Koirala and to lead the nation. But 15 months later, the Congress government was overthrown by King Mahendra in a **palace coup**. And Koirala was jailed for several years.

After B. P. Koirala's death in 1982, **Ganeshman Singh** emerged as the primary voice of the party. Under his leadership, the NCP played a guiding role during the 1990 anti-**Panchayat** and pro-democracy movement that led to the sudden disintegration of the Panchayat system. It is not far-fetched to assert that B. P. and Ganeshman are essentially synonymous with the Nepali Congress Party. However, Ganeshman Singh chose not to lead the interim government in 1990; the task was given to another senior NCP leader, **Krishna Prasad Bhattarai**, who presided over the interim coalition government as prime minister and oversaw the drafting of the new **constitution** as well as the general **elections**.

In the elections of 1991, the NCP won the majority of contested **parliamentary** seats in the **House of Representatives**, thus giving it the sole right to form the new government, the first democratic government since the premature suffocation of infant democracy in 1960. It was led by **Girija Prasad Koirala** as its prime minister, but it was marred by intra-party squabbles. As it finally collapsed prior to the completion of its full term, the general elections were held in 1994 to elect another government; the NCP lost to the **Communist Party of Nepal** (CPN–UML). But, during the 1999 elections, it managed to win the majority of the House seats. As a result, the NCP was able to form the Congress government to lead the nation, this time under the prime ministership of Krishna Prasad Bhattarai. But Bhattarai was deposed within a year by Girija Prasad Koirala who lost his prime ministership to another Congress leader, **Sher Bahadur Deuba**, in 2001. In 2002, the Nepali Congress Party was split into two factions, one led by Koirala and another by Deuba. However, Nepal's Election Commission refused to recognize the Deuba faction as the official NCP, thus giving the Koirala faction a victory, in that it is the only one that can feature its official logo or name. The party has its own website to disseminate information about its history, leaders, and plans: www.nepalicongress.org.np.

NEPALI LANGUAGE. See LANGUAGE.

NEPALI LITERATURE. See LITERATURE.

NEPAL INDOSUEZ BANK LIMITED. Private bank. Set up in 1986, it is a joint venture between the Indosuez Bank of Paris and Nepal's **Rastriya Banijya Bank.** See also PRIVATIZATION.

NEPAL INDUSTRIAL DEVELOPMENT CORPORATION (NIDC). Public corporation established in 1957 to promote investments in Nepal's industrial sector. It has played a significant role the nation's industrial development since its inception. See also INDUSTRY.

NEPAL JOURNALISTS ASSOCIATION. Association of professional journalists founded in 1951. Its primary objectives are to protect and promote the freedom of the **press**, to enhance the role and quality of journalism in the country, and to ensure journalistic integrity in news coverage and reporting. See also HUMAN RIGHTS; MEDIA.

NEPAL LEPROSY ASSOCIATION. Association founded in 1971 to cure and control leprosy in Nepal. Leprosy has long been a serious problem in the country. Since it is a profound social stigma in that lepers are treated as social outcasts with whom nobody wants to come in contact, many hide the disease just to remain accepted in society. Those who are exposed often go into hiding in order to avoid public shame and humiliation. There are several leprosy treatment centers in the country. The association also tries to restore former lepers' acceptability in society through awareness efforts as well as to revive their confidence.

NEPAL LUBE OIL LIMITED. Public enterprise founded in 1984 for producing and distributing lubricants used in motor vehicles. It is based in **Amlekhganj**, Bara, and has a production capacity of 3,000 metric tons a year. See also PRIVATIZATION.

NEPAL, MADHAV KUMAR (1952–). Leader and current secretary general of the **Communist Party of Nepal** (CPN–UML) since 1990. Since the death of **Man Mohan Adhikari** in 1999, Madhav Nepal took over the leadership of the CPN–UML. He served as a member of the Constitution Recommendation Commission in 1990 and as deputy prime minister in 1994 during the Communist party government led by Prime Minister Man Mohan Adhikari. In the general **elections** held in 1999, he was elected to the **House of Representatives**. Given the fact that his party won the second-largest number of seats in the House he became the main opposition leader in the **Parliament** until its dissolution by Prime Minister **Sher Bahadur Deuba** in May 2002

NEPAL MEDICAL ASSOCIATION. Professional association of Nepali medical doctors. It was formed in 1950. Although one of its primary goals is to promote good health and universal **health care**, its efficacy is questionable. Its records of health reforms in Nepal are fuzzy at best.

NEPAL OIL CORPORATION (NOC). Public corporation established in 1971 for the sale and supply of petroleum and kerosene fuels. Since Nepal produces few petroleum products, its requirement is met with imports from **India**. And this corporation has a great deal of control over the mechanism of petroleum distribution in the country. *See also* PRIVATIZATION.

NEPAL PRAJA PARISHAD. *See* PRAJA PARISHAD.

NEPAL RAJPATRA. Gazettes issued by the government of Nepal 1951.

NEPAL RASTRA BANK. Established in April 1956, the Nepal Rastra Bank is the central bank of the country. At the time of its establishment, the monetary system of Nepal was quite traditional and characterized by a dual currency system whereby one could freely use both the Indian and Nepali rupees. Nepal has come a long way since those days. As the central bank, it has the sole right to issue currency notes and coins and is responsible for managing the country's foreign exchange reserves. In addition, it is in charge of developing Nepal's banking and financial system, rendering advice to the government on financial and economic matters, mobilizing capital, managing public debt, and regulating monetary and banking activities. *See also* BANKING.

NEPAL RED CROSS SOCIETY. Affiliated with the International Committee of the Red Cross, the Nepal Red Cross Society was founded in 1964 to promote the principles of humanity, unity, neutrality, and impartiality. With its size being relatively small and scope being limited, the organization is mostly involved in social service activities within the country. In fact, its day-to-day operation is generally confined to the **Kathmandu Valley** where it is located.

NEPAL SADBHAVANA PARTY (NSP). Political party, largely composed of the **Tarai** people of Indian descent. It is designed to promote and protect their interests. *See also* ELECTIONS.

NEPAL TEA DEVELOPMENT CORPORATION. Public enterprise established in 1967 for the production and distribution of Nepali tea. Although the amount of Nepal's tea production is quite limited, falling far short of its domestic demand, the country has directed its attention to exporting some of its tea. The far eastern district of **Ilam** is the main tea-growing area in Nepal, largely owing to its proximity to **Darjeeling**, a world renowned tea-growing district in **India**. A significant amount of Ilam's tea estate is owned by King **Gyanendra Bir Bikram Shah**. *See also* PRIVATIZATION.

NEPAL TELEVISION. Public corporation for broadcasting television in Nepal. It was founded in 1985. With the arrival of television, life in Nepal seems to have undergone some noticeable changes. During the first few years of its existence, Nepal Television's programmatic coverage was generally limited to news and some domestic issues. Once a week in the evening it broadcast some Hollywood shows. *Miami Vice*, one of the very first American shows to be broadcast on Nepal Television, became quite popular and revealed to Nepal a level of sexual explicitness that this prudish society had never seen before. And other such shows followed. As family members consisting of husbands and wives, sons and daughters, along with neighbors and their children gathered in the TV room almost every evening, silence descended upon them, displacing a casual social climate filled with an evening of laughter, chatter, and sharing news about communal events and farming. What is interesting to note about this sudden transformation is that in a society where even the mere mention of the word "sex" was taboo, transparent sexual scenes and themes became an integral part of regular TV diets. Although Nepal Television's programs have greatly expanded since its early days, they are hardly a match for satellite programs offered by CNN and BBC. Those broadcast from **India** are also popular in most households. *See also* COMMUNICATIONS; MEDIA; PRIVATIZATION; RADIO NEPAL.

NEPAL TRANSPORT CORPORATION (NTC). Public corporation created in 1964 to manage, regulate, and promote transport in the nation. It mostly covers public and ground **transportation**.

NEPAL WOMEN'S ASSOCIATION. Women's association advocating democracy and empowerment. It was established in 1949 under Mangala

Devi Singh's leadership and played an important role in the democratic movements of 1950–1951 and 1990.

NEWAR. Ethnic group indigenous to the **Kathmandu Valley**. It is no exaggeration that the Newars are the ones who give Nepal its identity because Nepal owes much of its civilizational, cultural, and commercial heritage to them. The Newars are thus the mirror of Nepal. They established Nepal's urban civilization and charted its institutional course, particularly dating back to the reign of **Jayasthiti Malla**, perhaps the most farsighted of all **Malla** (Newar) rulers of Nepal. Imagine for a moment the Kathmandu Valley without all those historical achievements meticulously carved onto its landscape by the Newars, achievements left behind as the living relics of the past. Nepal's **tourism**, a principal source of hard currencies and jobs, would have no charm to attract all those tourists. As such, the whole tourist **industry** is founded on the cultural history of the Newar.

Jayasthiti Malla who ruled for 13 years from 1382 to 1395 with great foresight, fortitude, and vision gave the Malla dynasty its vigor, vitality, and identity. To bring order to the system of governance and to establish uniformity (or standardization) of rules and laws, he instituted many legal and social codes. As a result, the country was consolidated under one set of rules. The fact that his codes still form the general basis for the way Nepali society operates is a clear testament to his foresight; they have passed the test of time (although one must admit that one of his codes, namely the formalization of **caste** rules, has scarred Nepali society; and is hardly a mark of modernity).

One of his most important achievements obviously was his ability to restore a considerable measure of order and stability throughout the land after a period of anarchy and to consolidate the Malla dynasty. As noted by some historians, he united the entire Valley and its environs under his rule, an accomplishment still remembered with pride by Nepalis, thus further fortifying the cradle of Nepali culture and civilization that the Newars had methodically grafted.

NIDHI, MAHENDRA NARAYAN (1923–1999). Senior leader as well as prominent member of the **Nepali Congress Party** from the very beginning. Nidhi took an active part in the 1950 revolution against the **Rana** regime and also during the pro-democracy movement in early 1990 that dismantled the **Panchayat** system. Nidhi was elected to the **House of Representatives** in the first democratic **election** of 1991.

NIRVANA. Buddhist concept of ultimate salvation—the state of bliss reached by the **Buddha**. Nirvana is believed to be a state neither of being nor annihilation. A. L. Basham remarks that it has no definite location, but it may be realized anywhere and at any time, while still in the flesh. The man or woman who finds it never again loses it, and when she or he dies she or he passes to this state for ever. To many, it is the final release from the cycle of birth and rebirth resulting from one's freedom from earthly trappings, the prime source of sorrow.

NONGOVERNMENTAL ORGANIZATION (NGO). NGOs are seen as the principal force in engendering and reinforcing what these establishments call the civil society which, as they claim, is a must to foster democracy and forge development. These days, NGOs come in all different forms and shapes and their numbers have multiplied exponentially across the world. It is believed that there about a hundred different international and several hundred national nongovernmental organization operating in Nepal. While international NGOs normally receive their funding or grants from their respective home governments, Nepali NGOs are funded by international NGOs working in the country. It is quite fashionable and profitable to set up local NGOs in Nepal under the pretext of redressing certain social, environmental, or development issues or taking on some popular cause as an effective avenue to raise free money for personal and family well-being. In fact, it has turned into a mini cottage industry. Here are some of the NGOs actively operating in Nepal: Action Aid; AIDS Public Awareness; Ama Milan Kendra; Amnesty International; Ananda Kuti Bihar; Andha Apanga Pravidhi Sheep; Britain-Nepal Medical Trust; CARE; Educate the Children; Friends of Disabled; Green Energy Mission; Lumbini Development Trust; Oxfam Nepal; Public Health Concern Trust; Save the Children; World Neighbors; and the World Wildlife Federation. There are also various church-based NGOs including the United Mission to Nepal, as well as business "clubs" like Lions Club and Rotary Club. *See also* FOREIGN AID; PRIVATIZATION; UNITED STATES-NEPAL RELATIONS; WORLD BANK.

NORGAY (SHERPA), TENZING (1914–1986). Tenzing Norgay was a **Sherpa** who accompanied Sir **Edmund Hillary** to the top of **Mount Everest** in 1953, thus becoming one of the first two successful climbers of this highest peak. He later moved to **India** and became an Indian citizen because of certain material benefits that India offered him. In India, he ran a mountaineering school, teaching aspiring climbers the art and science of **mountain** climbing. Yet, there is little doubt that he will always be recognized as Nepali because he was born and raised in Nepal. Moreover, having attained his fame in the country, Nepal still claims him as its native son. Despite his flight to India, Nepal seems to have expressed no bitterness toward him.

NYATAPOL. Tallest temple in Nepal based in **Bhaktapur**. Built in 1708 by King Bhupatindra Malla (reign: 1696–1722), it features a five-tiered roof tapering toward heaven. Interestingly, unlike most other temples in the **Kathmandu Valley**, it stands aloof; it is rarely visited by local worshipers. Only curious **tourists** seem enchanted by its sheer size and ornate design and arrangements, which include pairs of various gate guards sitting in front of the main entrance in ascending order, each with 10 times the strength of the figure immediately below.

O

OLI, KHADGA PRASAD (1952–). Central member of the **Communist Party of Nepal**. Arrested and imprisoned by the **Panchayat** regime (1973–1987), he was elected to the **House of Representatives** in 1991 from the eastern **Tarai** district of **Jhapa** (see figure 2). He was reelected in the general elections held in 1994 and 1999, thus making him one of the handful of parliamentarians elected in all three elections since the return of democracy.

OM (OUHM). Compound alphabet. The sacred syllable *Om* is perhaps the greatest of all **Hindu mantras** and certainly the most powerful yet simplest symbol of **Hinduism**. It is interpreted as *Aham Brahma Asmi* (I am the ultimate reality) as it contains the essence of the Vedas, pregnant with the utmost power and mystery. *Om* is much revered in the Yoga school of Hinduism as it gives insight into the sublime purity of the soul and, thus, aids meditation.

OM MANI PADME HUM. Sacred **Buddhist mantra** and incantation, especially in its **Lamaist** tradition. It is inscribed on stone tablets and prayer wheels. This mantra is recited as an integral part of the **Tibetan** and Lamaist prayers. This mantra is rendered into English as "hail to the jewel in the lotus."

OPEN BORDER. Nepal shares an open border with **India**. As a result, Nepali and Indian citizens can freely cross the border into each other's country without restriction. However, at the check points, they are not allowed to carry goods and products beyond certain amounts in values without paying custom duties. At times, both countries have raised the issue of closing the border to unrestricted movements of citizens between the two countries. But, in the meantime, it remains open to both sides.

P

PAGODA. Architectural style very common in Nepal and in East and Southeast Asia. The pagoda style is, in fact, said to be an exclusively Nepali contribution to **art and architecture**, and is closely associated with some forms of **Hinduism** and **Buddhism**. In Nepal, its origin is definitely traced to the **Newar**. It was a Newar, as the story goes, who built the famous white pagoda of Beijing (*see* **Aniko**). The pagoda forms an enduring cultural landscape of the **Kathmandu Valley** as it is dotted with countless pagoda temples that come in various sizes and with varying degrees of reputation. The structures are square-shaped and characterized by multitiered roofs of diminishing size, overshadowing a square; they are often raised onto step-block foundations. The effect is one of an upward cascade, wherein the building soars symbolically into the heavens. The foundations are made of bricks and stones and roof tiers may be constructed either of tiles, stones, or wood shingles. Ornate carvings of deities, geometric patterns, and iconographic motifs decorate the wooden trims of most pagodas. Some temples are adorned with many erotic wood carvings, showing various positions of human sexual copulation. This classic Newari architectural style evolved over a 2,000 year period, dating at least back to the **Licchavi period**, but attained its glory during the **Malla** period. **Bhaktapur's Nyatapol** temple is perhaps the finest and most striking example of the pagoda style architecture in Nepal. Another example is the temple of **Pashupati**, perhaps the holiest of all temples in the Valley, which is said to be the oldest pagoda temple in Asia.

PAHARI (PAHADI; PAHARIYA; PAHADIYA). Hill people; people from the hills (*pahar*). This term is sometimes used generically in **India** to denote all Nepali people. Depending on the tone and context, the term carries a derogatory connotation in India; it is a put-down, meaning the Nepalis are backward. This connotation has largely to do with the fact that the vast majority of hill migrants in India are involved in menial work or as *chaukidars* (watchmen). *See also* CASTE SYSTEM; ETHNICITY.

PALACE COUP. Coup launched by King **Mahendra Bir Bikram Shah** on 15 December 1960 against the popularly elected government of Prime Minister **Bishweswar Prasad Koirala**. It was this coup that prematurely aborted the infant democracy. *See also* PANCHAYAT.

PALACE MASSACRE. *See* ROYAL PALACE MASSACRE.

PALPA. District in the **Lumbini Zone** (*see* figure 2). It has a population of 236,238 (1991) and covers an area of 1,373 sq. km. The major town in Palpa is Tansen, a typical **Newari** town built on a hilltop. Located roughly halfway between **Pokhara** and **Siddhartha Nagar**, it is renowned all over Nepal for its hand production of bronze containers, particularly Nepali water vases. It is also well known for a Newari duck meat dish and highly potent *raksi* (home-brewed **rice** liquor that is similar to Japanese sake).

PANCHAYAT. In ancient times, the concept of panchayat was widely used as a community institution and process to resolve local issues and disputes. It means a public assembly comprised of five (*pancha*; *panch*) village elders or leaders. A *pancha* is a member of the Panchayat. In the early 1960s, King **Mahendra Bir Bikram Shah** incorporated this simple and time-honored concept and practice into his political doctrine as he instituted the Panchayat system as a fundamental framework to govern Nepal. It was layered into four tiers: *gaun/nagar* (village/town), *zilla* (district), *anchal* (zone), and *rastriya* (national) Panchayat.

Although Panchayat was heralded as a partyless system, a guided democracy inherently suitable to the Nepali soil and tradition, it was basically a one-party system, designed to serve the absolute power that he usurped from the people through a **palace coup** he launched against the popularly elected government of **Bishweswar Prasad Koirala** in 1960. Under this system, the king controlled all three branches of the government—executive, legislative, and judiciary—plus the military and civil service, the other two critical levers of governance. The Panchayat system was overthrown in early 1990 through a popular uprising called the Restoration of Democracy movement. *See also* CONSTITUTIONS; FORESTRY; *JANA ANDOLAN*; RAPTI VALLEY DEVELOPMENT PROJECT.

PANDAY, DEVENDRA RAJ (1939–). An economist, **human rights** activist, and scholar, Panday received his Ph.D. in Public and International Affairs from the University of Pittsburgh in Pennsylvania. He has served as secretary of finance during the **Panchayat** system and later as minister of finance in the interim government of Nepal (1990–1991). He is one of Nepal's internationally recognized intellectual personalities. Panday is currently associated with several civic organizations in Nepal and abroad and serves as a member of the Board of Directors of Transparency International in Berlin. He has authored many books and articles on Nepal and South Asia. He is highly regarded as a Nepali statesman.

PANDE (PANDAY; PANDEY), DAMODAR (1751–1804). Military officer during the unification campaign in the 1780s and 1790s. He was appointed **Kaji** (chief courtier) and was later executed in 1804. To this day, he remains one of Nepal's most prominent historical figures who evoke a profound sense of Nepali patriotism and nationalism.

PANDE, MINA (1952–). Served as president in the Students' Union at Padma Kanya Campus (women's college) in 1980. She actively participated in the democratic movement of 1990 and was elected to the **House of Representatives** in 1991.

PANDEY, KALU (1713–1757). Regarded in Nepali history as a symbol of valor and bravery, he was appointed **Kaji** (chief courtier) of King **Prithvi Narayan Shah** in 1743. In his post as Kaji, he was the king's right-hand man. Kalu Pandey was, however, beheaded at the age of 44 in 1757 during Prithvi Narayan's reign.

PANT, YADAV PRASAD (1928–). Economist and author. He served as governor of the **Nepal Rastra Bank** (1968–1973), ambassador to Japan (1975–1979), minister of finance (1981–1983), and minister of water resources (1986–1988). He has written several books on the **economy** of Nepal. He is regarded by many as a leading economist and authoritative voice on running the economy thanks to his theoretical grounding and practical experience spanning more than three decades.

PARBATE (PARBATIYA). Derived from the word *parbat* (**mountain**). It basically means the same as *pahari*, i.e., mountain or hill folks. *See also* ETHNICITY.

PARIJAT (1937–1993). *Parijat* in Nepali means "a species of jasmine with a special religious significance," and is the pen name for Bishnu Kumari Waiba, a **Tamang** woman who was born in **Darjeeling**, but later moved to Nepal. Although Parijat launched her literary career with Nepali poetry, she quickly became very famous as a novelist within the Nepali literary circle. Hers was a powerful and profound voice in Nepali **literature**. In addition to publishing books of poems, she wrote several novels. Occasionally, she also wrote short stories. She is one of the very few Nepali writers with a formal training in English literature; she earned an M.A. in English literature.

Regardless of the medium of her creative expression, the themes and philosophical outlooks of her works reveal her Marxist-feminist perspectives as well as her own personal experiences in life. She was partially paralyzed since her youth and never married. Her love affair ended in heartbreak, a situation which caused a period of severe depression. She is not only by far the most recognized female writer in Nepal, but also the most influential feminist voice within the Nepali literary circle.

PARLIAMENT. Parliament can be defined as a legislative body which consists of the **House of Representatives** and **National Council**. As the head of the state, the king's signature (assent) is required in order for the bills passed by the two houses to become formal laws. *See also* CONSTITUTIONS; ELECTORAL SYSTEM.

PARMA. Labor sharing or reciprocity. Instead of hiring wage workers, villagers exchange labor for labor during the planting and harvesting seasons. It is an enduring feature of Nepal's agrarian **economy** and social system as it is still common—and one that promotes community-level cooperation and mutual support.

PAROPAKAR SANSTHA. Organization founded in 1947 by Dayabir Singh Kansakar. It provides social services and runs a high school and a maternity hospital. In many respects, it serves as a Red Cross organization. Its activities are largely limited to the **Kathmandu Valley**.

PASHUPATI (PASHUPATINATH). Technically, it means the master (*pati*) of beasts (*pashu*). In the present context, Pashupati is another name for **Shiva**, one of the principal gods of the **Hindu** trinity, the other two being **Brahma** and **Vishnu**. While Shiva is regarded as the god of destruction, Brahma and Vishnu are, respectively, the gods of creation and protection. Located on the bank of the **Bagmati River** in **Kathmandu**, Pashupati is treated as one of the four major destinations of Hindu pilgrimage or Char Dham which every able Hindu is prescribed to visit during his or her lifetime. Every year, Hindus flock to visit Pashupati, especially during the festival called *Shiva Ratri* (the night of Shiva). Pashupati (also referred to as the temple of Pashupati) is a very popular destination for Hindu worshipers, both local and those from **India**. It is also a place where many young men and women go for the purpose of socialization or secret courtship and romance. White Europeans and Americans are not allowed to go inside the temple compound because, traditionally, they are identified as the *mlaksha* (polluted) who are placed in the same league as the **Muslims** and untouchable **castes**.

PASNI. **Hindu** ritual feeding **rice** to a baby for the first time, usually when the baby is five to six months old. The vast majority of babies are breast-fed until they are one year old or even older. But following *pasni*, the frequency of breast-feeding declines. *See also* BARTAMAN; SANYAS.

PATAN. Busy and crowded city; old name of **Lalitpur**, which is also an administrative district in the **Bagmati Zone** (*see* figures 2, 3, and 4). Situated to the south of **Kathmandu**, across from the **Bagmati River**, it is a historical city founded around 300 A.D. and filled with many ancient statues and monuments. A **Newar** city, Patan is a leading tourist attraction in the **Kathmandu Valley** and host of the **Bhoto Jatra** festival.

PATAN DURBAR SQUARE. Complex comprising a **Malla** palace, different prominent courtyards, artistically exquisite waterspouts, and temples, including **Krishna Mandir** (which is a famous non-**pagoda** or south Indian style temple). It is the most renowned of the three *durbar* squares in the **Kathmandu Valley**, the other two being found in **Bhaktapur** and **Kathmandu**.

PATAN INDUSTRIAL DISTRICT. One of the major industrial estates in Nepal. It is a leading producer of textiles, **carpets**, cable wires, metal handicrafts, **Tanka** paintings, and steel furniture. *See also* INDUSTRY.

PATI. A resting place along hill trails or in a village/town, constructed to serve travelers. It is usually built by an individual or family as a religious charity, representing a **dharmic** act to serve humanity as a form of service to God. *See also* CHAUTARA; HINDUISM.

PEOPLE'S WAR. It is a direct product of the Maoist movement that was organized by the Maoist faction of the **Communist Party of Nepal** (CPN–Maoist). First declared on 13 February 1996, with a series of attacks on several private and state entities in different parts of the country, the "People's War" is a revolutionary movement. It is led by three Maoist leaders: Puspa Kamal Dahal (alias Prachanda), **Baburam Bhattarai**, and Mohan Vaidya (alias Kiran). It is generally believed that its military wing called the People's Liberation Army comprises about 6,000 combatants and includes a significant number of rural **women** in its ranks. A report by Amnesty International and **Human Rights** Watch claims that they have also recruited a sizeable number of young boys and girls between 14 and 18 years old to join their guerilla army.

Regardless of the size and composition of their active guerilla forces, there is little dispute that their support base is much larger, mostly coming from rural peasants throughout the country. The fact that the Maoist movement has managed to maintain control over some 30 percent of the national territory is a clear demonstration of how widespread its support base is. Geographically, the epicenter of the movement is largely found in the western hills (namely around the districts of Pyuthan, Rolpa, Rukum, and Salyan) where it has set up its own quasi-administrative structure, often supplanting the state apparatus.

Within the three weeks following the onset of the People's War, the party distributed leaflets about the war activities in 65 of Nepal's 75 districts. Destruction and seizure of properties and punitive actions against local goons, police informers, and other enemy elements were carried out in three additional districts: Jajarkot and Sallyan in the west and Sindhupalchok in the east. During the first three weeks, the movement's radical actions were concentrated in nine districts, although propaganda activities were scattered throughout the country. Again, they were directed against those considered to be local "feudal tyrants and comprador and bureaucratic capitalists." In addition to a soft-drink bottling factory in **Kathmandu**, the only other entity with foreign affiliation that came under attack was the locally staffed field office of Save the Children, a **United States** nongovernmental organization based in **Gorkha**. There were no hostilities directed against foreigners or foreign entities directly run by foreigners.

The war is being waged in a typical guerilla warfare fashion: hit-and-run, advance-and-retreat as necessary. From the very outset, the party declared that "In the present condition of the balance of forces, the enemy wants to drag us into a decisive war, but on our part we want to avoid it and prolong the war. The enemy uses the strategy of attack, but we use the strategy of defense. The enemy wants to incite us, but we want to harass the enemy, tire him out and attack him at his weak points at the time and place of our convenience. . . . This path will unfold by making use of all forms of struggle in keeping with the historical stage of development of Nepal and principally, as we have been saying all along, according to the strategy of encircling the city from the countryside, with agrarian revolution as the axis and from the midst and in conjunction with the rural class struggle. . . . Our armed struggle will be conducted by relying on the labouring masses, particularly the poor peasants."

One notable feature of the ongoing People's War is that it is being fought most intensely in the western hills, including the districts in the **Rapti Zone** (*see* figure 3). Interestingly, this is the very zone where the USAID has implemented its largest development project in Nepal since the early 1980s (in fact, it is the largest such project in the country funded by a Western donor agency). At the core of the project lies its heavy emphasis on the promotion and adoption of commercial farming and other forms of micro-enterprising among small farmers, including the production of liquor from fruits such as apples. The fact that Rapti peasants are actively supporting the Maoist movement in the region in open defiance of the state and its police forces suggests that so-called development efforts undertaken by the USAID have polarized the communities and that they have further aggravated poor peasants' socioeconomic conditions, consequently inciting them to resort to violence or to fight back for their survival rights.

After more than five years of Maoist insurgency and its expansion, the government of Nepal decided to enter into negotiations to end the war in 2001 (see Chronology). In the meantime, emboldened by their seeming success and with their bargaining position strengthened, the leadership of the Maoist movement agreed to embark on the path of negotiated settlements. Aware that under the pretext of negotiations the state might be buying time to prepare for a massive offensive against the movement, the Maoist revolutionaries pursued a two-pronged strategy of their own throughout the long negotiation from August to November 2001.

During the talks, the Maoist proposed the formation of an interim government, drafting a new **constitution** and institutionalization of the republic as the minimum political solution to the problem of the country. The proposal was further toned down to the question of an interim government and the **election** of a constituent assembly, when the question of the direct proclamation of the republic threatened to short-circuit the talks prematurely. In all likelihood, the tragic events of 11 September 2001 adversely affected the ongoing negotiation as the government stance hardened. It appears that the heavily **foreign aid**-dependent government of Nepal headed by Prime Minister **Sher Bahadur Deuba** came under pressure from the George W. Bush administration to slam the door on negotiations and label the Maoists "terrorists." In view of the American willingness to lend military and other support, the government was no longer in any mood to compromise.

With the government position stiffened and hopes of ending the People's War doomed, the talks broke down in November. And both parties placed themselves on a warpath, with the state ready to crush the movement with American support and the Maoists equally intent on getting rid of the monarchy and establishing a socialist republic. It was the Maoists, however, who struck the first blow, unleashing their guerilla forces on 23 November—immediately after the sudden end of negotiations—with the biggest-ever and most successful attacks on the army barracks and police outposts in **Dang**, thus shattering "the halo of the so-called invincibility of the royal army."

In response, with the symbolic recommendation of Prime Minister Deuba, King **Gyanendra Bir Bikram Shah** declared a nationwide state of emergency on 26 November and openly deployed the royal army against the Maoist forces. Since then, the state of emergency has been renewed two times and endless rounds of offensives and counteroffensives have been launched by both sides. While the showdown between the two parties has occurred in different parts of the country, the most intense battles are being fought in western Nepal, the Maoist stronghold. With neither party gaining a clear upper hand, the two sides have reached a stalemate. But there is little doubt that this ongoing full-scale war has engulfed the whole country and cost over 2,500 human lives, mostly innocent civilians, since its intensification in November 2001. If the number of those killed prior to the state-of-emergency declaration is added, the figure surpasses 4,500 casualties (see Chronology).

In the meantime, the U.S. role in the Nepal government's decision to engage in an all-out military operation against the Maoists has become increasingly transparent. First, after the disengagement from the negotiation, the government has abandoned its treatment of the Maoist movement as a nagging internal rebellion, something not too far removed from the very tactics the ruling **Nepali Congress Party** itself had used during its anti-**Rana** movement in the late 1940s and 1950 and during its failed anti-**Mahendra** rebellion in the early 1960s (see **Rapti Valley Development Project**). In addition, the party was, if necessary, prepared to use similar tactics during its successful anti-**Panchayat** democratic movement in early 1990. In line with the Bush administration's definition of terrorism, the government pinned a "terrorist" label on the Maoists.

Second, as an immediate reward to the Deuba government for its hardline stance against the Maoist movement, U.S. Secretary of State Colin Powell paid an official visit to Nepal on 18 January 2002. In addition to holding talks with the king and the prime minister, Powell met with the army chief to discuss the military offensive against the Maoists. Subsequent to his visit, U.S. military advisors-cum-personnel went to Nepal to advise the armed forces. They were also active in scouring parts of Nepal currently controlled by the Maoist revolutionaries.

Third, not too long after Powell's visit, the government floated bounty offers of $64,000 per head for the capture or murder of Maoist supremo: Baburam Bhattarai, Puspa Kamal Dahal, Mohan Vaidya.

Fourth, the much expected big reward for the Deuba government came in April 2002 when President Bush announced a $20 million in military aid for Nepal in addition to sending other assistance and military advisers. Furthermore, Bush gave Deuba an opportunity to meet with him in the White House. It was an opportunity that Prime Minister

Deuba considered to be a moment of glory in his political career. Ironically, however, because of his willingness to go along with the American design and to closely cooperate with the palace in extending the state of emergency, he has been a source of split in the Nepali Congress Party. This is a development that will most likely lead to the defeat of his party in the upcoming general election to be held in November 2002 and to a coalition government, a government saddled with bickering, backbiting, and indecision. It will not only lead to the consolidation of the king's power and authority—and then to the demise of democracy—but also strengthen the Maoist position. In case democracy is derailed, it will be absolutely sardonic that it took place under the watch of Deuba who has fought for democracy all his political life.

Despite a relatively massive deployment and offensive, the royal army with its incomparable logistical advantage and sophisticated weapons has failed to strike a blow to the heart of the Maoists as the People's War continues to rage on. There is no question that from the Maoist viewpoint, the ongoing People's War has entered a new and higher stage in its evolution, a stage that is bound to further paralyze Nepal, a country already badly stricken with abject **poverty** and rapid economic deterioration. Furthermore, up to this phase in the People's War, the Maoist revolutionaries have deliberately limited their guerilla actions mostly to rural areas except for a few minor and sporadic hits in the capital city. There are two main reasons for this decision. First, from a strategic point of view, they have their strongest support base in rural areas where they feel that they have an advantage over the royal army. The longer the war goes on in rural areas and hills, the more demoralized and weaker the army will be. At that point, they can hit the army hard and then extend the war to the urban frontier where the weakened army will be less effective against the Maoists. Second, at this phase of the war, they want to minimize the damage to the **economy** and infrastructure. They are aware that sustained and organized attacks in urban areas and against foreign entities and infrastructure would rapidly destroy the economy.

Nonetheless, when and if the current state of equilibrium between the military and Maoists is broken, the People's War will transit into the next phase. In other words, that is when the Maoist revolution will have either gathered or lost steam vis-à-vis Nepal's royal army. In either case, the war will, in all likelihood, get uglier, extending its boundary to the urban territory, specifically the **Kathmandu Valley**, the heart of the royalty and royal army. In other words, it is unlikely that the People's

War will end any time soon. It is a frightening specter that is poised to haunt Nepal for many years to come.

In the midst of this dark scenario has suddenly appeared a ray of hope in January 2003 when both the Maoist revolutionaries and government have agreed to renew peace talks to end the bloody war. Although many differences remain between the two sides, they seem to have concluded that the raging war has been extremely costly in terms of human lives (over 7,200 dead) as well as economically for the poor nation of Nepal. *See also* Chronology; CONSTITUTIONS; MEDIA.

PHARPING. Popular hill village southeast of **Kathmandu**. Famous for pears, it is the site of **Chandrajyoti**, Nepal's first power plant.

PHEWA TAL. Famous lake in **Pokhara**. It is a major **tourist** attraction. In recent years, it has suffered greatly from **pollution**. It used to be a very popular picnic site for the young men and women of Pokhara, especially those enrolled in the city's high schools and college.

PIPAL. Sacred tree for Hindus (*Ficus religiosa*). It is worshiped widely. Almost every *chautara* in the country is adorned with a pipal tree, which also serves as an important source of fodder for domestic animals and of food for wild birds when its berries ripen.

PLANNING AND NATIONAL PLANS. Since 1956, Nepal has adopted planning as an institutional approach to development. As a centralized process of economic development and management, it is rooted in the assumption that the State is the most informed and balanced allocator of limited capital resources. Although socialistic in nature, it is, in essence, what some call "State capitalism." Since its inception, Nepal has implemented nine different plans as an integral part of its national policy of development, and is currently in the process of formulating and formalizing its tenth plan.

The **National Planning Commission**, which functions under the direction of the **National Development Council**, is almost entirely responsible for formulating development plans. In terms of gathering data necessary for planning and its performance, the Central Bureau of Statistics assists the commission. In addition, various ministries and the **Nepal Rastra Bank** are consulted and provide inputs. Although the commission develops plans, much of the direction and guidance for planning is provided by Western donor agencies such as USAID. No less important are the **World Bank** and Asian Development Bank. As major donors, they exercise a great deal of influence—and even control—over Nepal's planning process and priorities.

Funding for the early plans came almost 100 percent from external donor agencies. In recent years, the percentage of external financing has gone down, ranging from about 50 to 65 percent, with the rest supplied from internal revenues such as taxes and borrowing. The nature of external financing has, however, shifted significantly in the past two decades. For instance, the budgets for the first two plans were not only underwritten almost entirely through external sources, but they were based on outright grants that required no repayment. But these days as much as 90 percent of external aid is foreign debt (loans).

Despite almost five decades of development planning experience and effort, Nepal's records of performance remain questionable. First of all, almost 50 percent of the budget earmarked for the first two plans went unspent. The situation has certainly improved since then, but achievements are far from planned objectives and expectations. The two obvious illustrations of this distance between planning objectives and performance are found in the fields of **poverty** and **agriculture**. While poverty (i.e., the percentage of the population living in poverty) has increased over the years, agricultural productivity as measured in terms of yields per hectare of land cultivated has remained constant.

Plan	Plan Period
First Plan	1956–1960
Second Plan	1962–1965
Third Plan	1965–1970
Fourth Plan	1970–1975
Fifth Plan	1975–1980
Sixth Plan	1980–1985
Seventh Plan	1985–1990
Eighth Plan	1992–1997
Ninth Plan	1997–2002
Tenth Plan (draft phase)	2002–2007

See also FOREIGN AID; PRIVATIZATION; UNITED STATES-NEPAL RELATIONS.

POKHARA. A city nestled in a narrow central hill valley (see figure 4), it is perhaps the most preferred **tourist** destination outside the **Kathmandu Valley**, largely thanks to the fact that it is situated at the foothills of **Machhapuchhre** and **Annapurna**. Its attraction is further enhanced by the presence of **Phewa Tal** where their reflections dance in its gentle waves, a scene that is unparalleled in its beauty. It also owes its popularity to the earliest wave of Western tourists in Nepal: the hippies who came in the 1960s, mostly seeking dope and tranquility who found Pokhara, which back then was merely a small commercial center of less than 10,000 inhabitants, to be exquisitely charming and hospitable with plenty of cheap—or even free—**ganja**. It was also one of the first places in the country where some members of the initial group of American Peace Corps volunteers (1962) were stationed, including those in the Pokhara Multipurpose High School, the first high school in Nepal to incorporate vocational programs (agriculture, commerce, home economics, and trade & industry) with American aid. Located in a corner of the lake are the Nepali king's winter palace and a fancy tourist hotel.

POKHARA INDUSTRIAL DISTRICT. Established in 1974, various consumer goods are produced in this center. See also INDUSTRY; PRIVATIZATION.

POKHREL, CHHABILAL (1904–1999). A dedicated educator, he made significant contributions to modern **education** by opening schools and colleges in Dharan, **Dhankuta**, and other places.

POKHAREL, LILA MANI (1953–). A dedicated communist leader, he was elected to the **House of Representatives** from Sindhuli in 1991 (see figure 2). He ran again during the general **elections** of 1999 in the same district and won his seat in the House. A captivating orator, Lila Mani's views are rarely supportive of parliamentary democracy.

POLLUTION. In recent years, Nepal has come to recognize the problem of environmental pollution. Nowhere is the problem of pollution in Nepal more visible and serious than in the **Kathmandu Valley**. In 1992, Nepal signed the resolution passed by the **United Nations** Conference on Environment and Development held in Rio de Janeiro, Brazil. Moreover, it put environmental considerations in its eighth **plan** (1992–1997). Yet, as one International Union for Conservation of Nature (IUCN) report published in 1998 noted, so far very little real action has been directed toward environmental protection.

Environmental decay of the Kathmandu Valley is directly reflected in the quality of its air, land, and water. In other words, these are the three most visible aspects of pollution facing Nepal. Since they are intertwined, they combine to intensify their overall adverse impact on the Valley's environment. The quality of its air has deteriorated so much that some people in the Valley have begun to wear masks to protect themselves from the smog and dust. Contributing to this significant downturn in the air quality are carbon monoxide, sulphur dioxide, hydrogen sulfide, nitrous oxide, and lead.

For example, it was estimated that 18,000, 3,300, 1,660, and 275 tons of carbon monoxide, hydrocarbons, nitrous oxide, and sulphur dioxide, respectively, were being annually released into the Valley air in the early 1990s. In all likelihood, these volumes have gone up significantly since then. Investigation has also revealed a high level of lead content in dust and other particulate matters as a result of rapid growth in the numbers of motor vehicles, which are mostly of inferior quality using adulterated fuel products. Additionally, cement factories discharge into the air massive amounts of dust particles, thus magnifying the smog in the Valley. The whole problem is further exacerbated by the bowl-shaped physiographic formation of the Valley. Surrounded by **mountains**, the Kathmandu Valley resembles a huge fish bowl, almost like the city of Mexico, with few natural outlets to release its foul air. As a result, the pollutants generated in the Valley are entirely trapped within itself.

No less problematic is solid waste and water pollution. Solid waste pollution is evident from the heaps of trash and garbage, illegal dump sites, open landfills, and other exposed wastes, scattered throughout the Valley. Hospitals are estimated to contribute more than 700 tons of solid wastes per annum. Their wastes are composed of paper, glass, tin cans, injection needles, human wastes, blood or body fluids, along with hazardous materials such as corrosive acids, inflammable, and reactive and toxic substances.

Many times, solid wastes are dumped in the Valley's rivers, along with industrial effluence from factories, carpet washing, and leather processing. The discharge of untreated sewage into the rivers is also very common. No less problematic is the disposal of animal carcasses into those rivers whose volumes of water discharge has dramatically fallen over the years due to increased siltation and sedimentation, thus causing severe pollution. The problem of water pollution in the Valley is further compounded by the fact that all types of toxic elements are routinely dumped in the rivers. As a consequence of increasing air, land, and water pollution, the Valley's environment has suffered greatly in the past 25 years. The Valley is not the only polluted area, however. The same can also be said, to a greater or lesser extent, of other parts of Nepal. Even in small villages, problems of waste disposal exist although air and water pollution is often less acute. Another form of environmental degradation is deforestation. Even the once pristine **forests** are now suffering due to overcutting. Indeed, it has been noticed that on **Mount Everest** there is an embarrassing amount of trash, and most trekking trails, frequented by **tourists**, are littered with garbage.

POUDYAL (POUDEL; PAUDYAL), LEKHNATH (1884–1966). Poet. He was bestowed with the title Kabi (Kavi) Shiromani (the poet laureate). To this day, his works are quite popular and included in many books on Nepali **literature**. Perhaps his most famous poem, one that had a significant revolutionary impact on the political movement against the **Rana** regime, was "Pinjarako Suga" (A parrot in a cage). This poem has been interpreted in many different ways. To the anti-Rana revolutionaries of that time, however, it was uncannily symbolic of the fate of the people of Nepal under the Ranas as they were projected as a parrot (*suga*) imprisoned in the Rana cage (*pinjara*). According to Michael Hutt, Lekhnath Poudyal was the founding father of twentieth-century Nepali poetry. Often described as a traditionalist, he was particularly responsible for perfecting a classical style of Nepali verse.

POUDYAL, RAM CHANDRA (1941–). Central committee member of the **Nepali Congress Party** (NCP). Elected to the **House of Representatives** in 1991 from the central hill district of Tanahun (*see* figure 2), he became minister of local development in 1991 under the prime ministership of **Girija Prasad Koirala**. Later, in the mid-1990s, he served as deputy prime minister during an NCP government. He was reelected to the House during the general **elections** held in 1994 and 1999. Highly active in Nepali Congress politics from his student days, he is a noted theoretician of socialism and democracy.

POVERTY. With an annual per capita income of less than $250, Nepal is one of the poorest countries in the world (*see* **Least Developed Country**). Many attempts have been made to alleviate poverty in Nepal over the past five decades. From the very outset, many foreign countries, including the **United States** and other Western countries, have been directly involved in Nepal's development process and projects, all designed to improve the social and economic conditions of its citizens. Ironically, over the same period, the incidence of poverty in Nepal has climbed from about 40 percent in 1970 to nearly 60 percent in the early 1990s. And there is no sign of its abatement. What one witnesses in Nepal today is an entrenched landscape of poverty, virtually everywhere—in urban trenches as well as rural fringes. *See also* AGRICULTURE; FOREIGN AID; PLANNING AND NATIONAL PLANS; PRIVATIZATION.

PRACHANDA GORKHA. Episode involving the founding of a political party and organization in 1931 by several activists. As the plot to launch a bloody attack against the **Ranas** was revealed to the then Prime Minister Bhim Shamsher Rana, it was foiled. The activists behind the plot were arrested and imprisoned for life.

PRADHAN, AMRIT PRASAD (?–1966). Highly renowned scientist and educator. He founded the Public Science College in 1956, later renamed Amrit Science College after him. Located very close to the royal palace in **Kathmandu**, it was perhaps the best science college in the nation. Many graduates of this college went on to pursue further **education** or professional degrees in medicine and engineering—usually on national or foreign scholarships. It is no wonder that many of today's Nepali medical doctors and engineers have some affiliation to Amrit Science College and owe a debt to Amrit Prasad Pradhan. Sadly, however, once the pride and emblem of Nepal's energetic science education, the college is now in poor condition in terms of both facilities and maintenance. Its quality has taken a nosedive, and student discipline and commitment has hit its lowest point. During the pro-democracy revolution of 1990, some student activists were killed by the police on this campus. Amrit Prasad was killed in a plane crash over the Alps in Switzerland on 2 March 1966.

PRADHAN, HRIDAYA CHANDRA SINGH (1915–1959). Novelist and short story writer. Before his death in 1959, he wrote many novels, focusing on such themes as male chauvinism, vanity, and hollow pride. He also edited a Nepali literary magazine entitled *Sahitya Shrot* (1947–1949).

PRADHAN, MAHESH LAL (1942–). Businessman and industrialist. He founded textile and poultry **industries** in addition to launching several businesses in **Kathmandu**. During 1990–1992, he served as president of the Federation of Nepal Chambers of Commerce and Industries, and remains very active in the business community.

PRADHAN, NARAYAN DEVI (1953–). Well-known choreographer. She is a highly accomplished Nepali classical dancer who has greatly contributed to the development and promotion of classical **dance** in the country, especially in the **Kathmandu Valley**.

PRADHAN, PARAS MANI (1898–1986). Paras Mani Pradhan was a Nepali short story writer, lexicographer, linguistic, and biographer born in Banaras, **India**. He compiled a Nepali-English dictionary and wrote books on Nepali grammar and **literature**. He authored numerous books and edited a literary magazine called *Chandrika* while he was in India.

PRADHAN, PRACHANDA (1939–). Researcher and Nepal's leading authority in the field of public administration. He once served as director of the **Centre for Economic Development and Administration**, the first and perhaps the most genuine research organization in Nepal. He has written several books dealing with **planning** and development.

PRADHAN, PREM DHOJ (1938–). A modern singer who is associated with **Radio Nepal**. One of the most recognized voices in the Nepali **music** circle, he has sung several modern songs. He is often treated as one of the early trendsetters in terms of giving Nepali music a modern twist.

PRADHAN, SAHANA (1932–). Leading personality of the **Communist Party of Nepal** (CPN). She was married to **Puspa Lal Shrestha**, a prominent leader of the communist movement in Nepal. She joined the CPN in 1952. Following the second coming of democracy in 1990, she became cabinet minister (1990–1991) during the interim government and minister of **industry** and commerce (1994) during the Communist government headed by Prime Minister **Man Mohan Adhikari**. It is notable that unlike other Nepali **women**, she chose to retain her own maiden name after marriage instead of adopting her husband's family name as almost every woman in Nepal does.

PRAJA PARISHAD. (People's Council.) Nepal's first political party. In the beginning, it was a secret political society composed of some of the leading **Kathmandu** intellectuals. Included among its primary leaders were **Tanka Prasad Acharya, Dasharath Chand, Dharma Bhakta Mathema,** and others. Even King **Tribhuvan Bir Bikram Shah** was reported to be among its supporters. The nucleus of the Praja Parishad party was established as early as 1935. A general **election** of its officers was held in 1940, and Tanka Prasad Acharya was chosen as its first president. It was a comprehensive political party as it included in its fold a broad spectrum of Nepali **castes** and **ethnic groups**. From the very start, it was driven by the aim to dismantle the **Rana** regime and usher in democracy.

PRAJATANTRA. Democracy. *See also* DEMOCRACY DAY.

PRATINIDHI SABHA. *See* HOUSE OF REPRESENTATIVES.

PRAYER WHEEL. Called *mane* in **Tibetan**, prayer wheels are used by **Buddhists** as an integral part of their prayer. They are inscribed with the sacred **mantra** *om mani padme hum* and other prayers that become activated with a clockwise motion or revolution of the wheel.

PRESS. *See* MEDIA.

PRESS COUNCIL. Council founded in 1972 for the growth of healthy and clean press in Nepal. *See also* MEDIA; NEPAL JOURNALISTS ASSOCIATION.

PRITHVI JAYANTI. Birthday anniversary commemoration of King **Prithvi Narayan Shah**.

PRITHVI NARAYAN, KING. *See* SHAH, PRITHVI NARAYAN.

PRITHVI RAJMARGA. One of the few highways (*rajmarga*) running entirely in the hills—from **Kathmandu** to **Pokhara**. Covering a distance of 200 kilometers, it was built in the late 1960s with Chinese assistance. Initially called the Kathmandu-Pokhara Highway, it was later renamed Prithvi Rajmarga after **Prithvi Narayan Shah**.

PRIVATIZATION. Since the very dawn of development in the 1950s, **planning** as an institutional approach to economic engineering has dominated Nepal's economic scene. Although it is still popular, it has undergone some significant change in its policy focus and emphasis, especially since the return of democracy in 1990. Urged by the **United States** Agency for International Development (USAID) and **World Bank**, the two most powerful development agencies in the world in terms of development policy formulation and recommendation, planning has now increasingly emphasized economic privatization under the new banner of neoliberalism.

In addition to paving the path for political democratization in many previously undemocratic countries, the sudden downfall of the former Soviet Union signaled a massive wave of economic liberalization across the Third World in the 1990s. Nepal was no exception as it witnessed both. To be sure, Nepal was never a socialist state. Except for some major state-controlled basic industries and utilities, much of the **economy** was private, including the two fundamental sectors: retail and farming. Private ownership and independent businesses have always been an inseparable part of Nepal's economic fabric. So plans and planning mostly revolved around setting an agenda for national development within the framework of what can be called a guided economy. The focus was on the public sectors such as developing infrastructures, for example, **transport** networks, higher **education** and training, **agriculture**, as well as various **industries**.

Nevertheless, a definite shift in focus occurred after 1990. Swept by the rising tide of neoliberalism, the Nepal government, together with its **National Planning Commission**, made provision to relax state control of public industries, stressing privatization. Between 1991 and 1997, Nepal privatized more than 15 enterprises, including the **Bhrikuti Paper Mills**, Harisidhi Brick and Tile Factory, **Bansbari Leather and Shoe Factory, Balaju Textile Industry**, and **Agriculture Tools Factory**. The government has also agreed to privatize the **Nepal Tea Development Corporation**. Other state-run enterprises are under consideration for privatization. Included in the list are the Nepal Telecommunications Corporation, Butwal Power Company, **Nepal Bank, Salt Trading Corporation,** cement factories and others. To what extent state-owned enterprises are privatized in the future will largely be contingent on the government makeup. It is safe to assume that while the single party majority in **Parliament** will have a decisive impact on further privatization, coalition governments will most likely slow it down because of party-based disagreements over its merits as well as the absence of a focused economic agenda.

PROSTITUTION. Although prostitution is not new in Nepal, it was nothing like what one sees today. In the past, it was mostly a local phenomenon confined to local communities. Today, its tentacles are much deeper and wider. With the boom of **tourism** within the country and the growing demand for Nepali prostitutes in **India,** particularly in cities like Bombay, prostitution in Nepal is widespread and deeply entrenched. According to some accounts, each year roughly 7,000 Nepali girls, usually between the ages of 12 to 16, are taken to the sweat-drenched brothels of Bombay. Within the **Kathmandu Valley,** hotels are the primary conduits of the flesh trade and transactions involving young Nepali girls and women. As the specter of AIDS haunts the global centers of sex markets such as Bangkok, Saigon, and Manila, the frontier of global prostitution expands into countries like Nepal that are considered "virgin" territories, relatively free of AIDS. *See also* HEALTH CARE.

PUBLIC SERVICE COMMISSION. Constitutional body concerned with the general principles of civil service appointment, protection, and promotions.

PUNYA. Hindu acts and deeds of benevolence to assure religious merit and unhindered passage to heaven. The concept of *punya* is at the core of the Hindu belief and emphasis that having a son is critical not only to keep alive the family lineage or heritage, but also to deliver *punya* (clear passage) to the parents after they pass away. As the son performs the required religious rituals, including formal mourning (normally lasting one full year), he frees his dead parents' souls so that they can enter heaven.

PURANA. Narrative texts accepted as **Hindu** scriptures, filled with tales, legends, and some history. They consist of 18 books dealing with the creation of the universe, its destruction, the genealogy of gods and patriarchs. The Puranic Gods are **Brahma, Vishnu** and **Shiva**, who together constitute the Hindu trinity. *See also* HINDUISM.

PURNAGIRI DAM CONTROVERSY. Activists and leaders of the Unified Marxist-Leninist faction of the **Communist Party of Nepal** marched to **Tanakpur** in far western Nepal in 2000, where **India** is trying to construct a dam at Purnagiri across the border in a unilateral way. If constructed, the dam will submerge several villages on the Nepali side and displace at least 30,000 people residing in the Kanchanpur district. In addition to protesting, the Nepali activists threw survey instruments into the river. This incident led to a tense dispute and controversy between the two governments.

PYAKUREL, SINDHU NATH (1943–). A leftist politician and lawyer who served as advocate for 20 years and as secretary of the **Nepal Bar Association** (1982–1985). He became a member of the Upper House of **Parliament** in 1991.

R

RADIO NEPAL. First radio broadcasting station in the country, founded in 1951 and run by the government. It airs programs on short and medium waves. Initially, the transmission covered a duration of 4.5 hours through a 250-watt transmitter. These days, Radio Nepal transmits 19 hours of programs. On public holidays, there is an additional two hours. Over the years, Radio Nepal has strengthened its institutional capacity and diversified itself in terms of programming format, technical efficiency and nationwide coverage, largely in response to stiff competition from private radio stations such as HBC94 FM, Hits FM91.2, Kantipur FM96.1, Kath97.9 FM, and Makalu Radio. An FM channel covering the **Kathmandu Valley** and adjoining areas was started in 1995.

Radio Nepal features various programs such as documentaries, dramas, talk shows, interviews, **music**, and commentaries. Recognizing the citizen's right to be informed under a multiparty democracy, it attempts to provide informative, educational, and entertainment programs. That is, the major program highlights can be divided into three categories: **education** (religion, **literature**, science and technology, **agriculture**, **women**, **health** and sanitation, public health, and children and youth); entertainment (Nepali songs including various ethnic songs in different dialects and languages, Western music, Hindi songs, radio dramas, and comedy); and information (news, current affairs and analysis, reports, and **press** reviews). Compared to its role during the days of the **Panchayat** system, when it was used as the most accessible vehicle of propaganda, the mouthpiece of both the palace and Panchayat, its pro-regime tendency has been tempered since the reestablishment of democracy in early 1990. Nonetheless, as a state radio, it is still slanted in favor of the government stance, policies, and programs. Furthermore, it has become increasingly commercialized because of growing competition. Now accessible online (www.radio-nepal.com), the geographical reach of Radio Nepal has vastly increased since the mid-1990s. See also COMMUNICATIONS; MEDIA.

RAGHUPATI JUTE MILLS. Public enterprise based in **Biratnagar** and established in 1946. See also INDUSTRY; PRIVATIZATION.

RAHUL. Son of **Siddhartha Gautama** and **Yasodharma**. The name technically means "the cause of evil." He was so named by his father because Siddhartha believed his son would chain him to the trappings of earthly matters, thus keeping him from finding a solution to the humanity filled with grief, misery, and sorrow. Parents sometimes call their sons "rahu" when they cause undue troubles.

RAI. Well-known **Tibeto-Nepali** ethnic group, generally concentrated in the eastern hills of Nepal. Similar to the **Limbus**, they are members of the **Kirata** group. Because of their martial qualities, they were one of the highly prized hill tribes sought by British army recruiters for army service as **Gorkhas**.

RAI, ACHHA RASIK (1928–1952). Nepali novelist born in **India**. He is mostly known for his two novels *Lagan* and *Dovan*, both published posthumously in 1954.

RAI, ASHOK KUMAR (1957–). Member of the **Communist Party of Nepal**. He was elected to the **House of Representatives** from the Khotang district in 1991 (*see* figure 2). He was reelected to the House from the same district during the general elections held in 1994.

RAI, BALA BAHADUR (1920–). A member of the **Nepali Congress Party** who was elected to the **House of Representatives** from the hill district of Okhaldhunga in 1991 (*see* figure 2). Later he became minister of housing and physical **planning** during the first **Girija Prasad Koirala** government. He was reelected in 1994.

RAI, DIWAN SINGH (1927–1972). Member of the **Nepali Congress Party**, he was murdered in 1972 by **Panchayat** supporters. He was a member of **B. P. Koirala**'s cabinet as deputy minister of **forests, agriculture**, and food in 1959–1960.

RAIKAR. State-owned land. *See also* LAND TENURE.

RAITI. Landholding peasants subject to taxes.

RAJBANSI (RAJVAMSI). Ethnic group based in the eastern **Tarai**.

RAJBANSI, BIREN (1945–1972). Born in **Jhapa** (*see* figure 2), Biren Rajbansi was a revolutionary. He was arrested for his participation in a movement against the autocratic **Panchayat** system and was murdered by the police in **Ilam** in 1972, along with **Ramnath Dahal** and three others.

RAJBHANDARI, GEHENDRA BAHADUR (1923–?). Vocal supporter of the **Panchayat** system. He was appointed by King **Mahendra Bir Bikram Shah** to serve in various powerful and highly visible ministerial capacities, first as minister of home affairs in 1967 and later as minister of foreign affairs in 1969 and minister of finance in 1970. Because he occupied high positions, he was viewed as a powerful figure during the Panchayat period, especially prior to Mahendra's death.

RAJBHANDARI, PRADYUMNA LAL (1928–). He has spent much of his career in the civil service, working for the government in various capacities. He was appointed to serve as governor of the **Nepal Rastra Bank** in 1965. Later, in the 1980s, he served as chairman of the **Public**

Service Commission (1983–1989) and as member of the Constitution Recommendation Committee in 1990.

RAJ PARISHAD. King's council. Constitutional body represented by ex-officio members, including the prime minister, chief justice, speaker of the **House of Representatives**, and those nominated by the king. One primary function of this body is to determine accession to the throne of the heir apparent, especially if a clearly defined heir apparent is absent, as was the case following the **royal palace massacre** in June 2001. It used to be called Raj Sabha until 1990.

***RAKSHAS* (*RACHHESH*).** Demons. The term is sometimes used to refer to those who project or espouse evil motives either verbally or through their acts and deeds (i.e., demonic characters).

***RAKSHYA* (*RAKCHHYA*) *BANDHAN*.** Hindu custom of putting sacred threads around the wrists of men, **women**, and children on the day of Janai Purnima. *See also JANAI.*

RAKSI. Similar to Japanese *sake* in taste and texture, it is perhaps the most common and traditional alcoholic beverage in Nepal. Although it can be made from a variety of grains, **rice** and millet are the two most commonly used. Depending on the preparation, it comes in various levels of alcoholic content or strength. The **Newars** are considered to be some of the best *raksi* makers. Their best *raksi* can easily match some of the finest scotch in the West. Not too many people serve or drink *raksi* (and other alcoholic beverages) by itself, without some snacks, the most preferred being meat-based snacks. Unlike other types of commercially produced alcoholic beverages available in Nepal, *raksi* cannot be purchased in the open market. It is strictly confined to household-level production, often for family consumption. Some households also sell it to neighbors and friends to generate supplementary cash income, but such transactions are conducted discretely because of the restriction on its commercial production.

RAMA. Hero of the **Hindu** epic ***Ramayana***. He is believed to be the seventh incarnation of **Vishnu**. King of Ayodhya, Rama *rajya* (Rama's rule) is often regarded as the "Golden Age" of **India**. He was married to **Sita**, the daughter of King **Janak** who at that time ruled Mithila.

RAMAYANA. Perhaps the most influential and popular **Hindu** epic, it was written by Maharishi (great sage) Balmiki. As many other texts, the core of the moral story of *Ramayana* revolves around the eventual victory of the good (**Rama**) over the evil (Ravana): the virtues of being virtuous. In addition to many subplots, it is a story of the epic battle between Rama and his archenemy Ravana to rescue **Sita** whom Ravana had abducted to draw Rama into a decisive confrontation.

The enduring popularity of the *Ramayana* is mainly attributed to the simplicity of verses (stanzas) and plots. Unlike the **Mahabharata**, it is an epic for common folks who can easily relate to its themes. Its Nepali version was first composed by **Bhanu Bhakta Acharya.**

One side note about the *Ramayana*, like its counterpart *Mahabharata*, is that it offers some insight into the state of military technology in ancient India. If the descriptions of some of the arrows used during the battles detailed in the two epics are any indication of how far India was advanced in developing weapons of war, the weaponry system was quite sophisticated. For example, both epics mention arrows of fire (called *agni* arrow) that could ignite a ball of fire in the enemy camp, causing significant damage (it is perhaps no coincidence that some of India's missiles are named *agni*) and arrows that could rain gummy objects to immobilize enemies.

RANA. Honorific title associated with valor and bravery. It was bestowed upon Prime Minister **Jang Bahadur Kunwar** who later adopted it as his last name, thereby establishing the Rana clan as well as dynastic rule in Nepal (1846–1951).

RANA, BARUN SHAMSHER (1929–). Journalist. He served as editor of *The Rising Nepal* from 1965 to 1976. He later served as editor of the *Sunday Dispatch* (English weekly). His rise in the field of journalism in Nepal was often viewed within the **Kathmandu** circle with some suspicion because of his **Rana** family connection. Regardless of the factual basis of the general suspicion about his credentials, he appears to have rarely lent his vocal support to unbridled **press** freedom in Nepal.

RANA, CHANDRA SHAMSHER (1901–1929). As he deposed Prime Minister Dev Shamsher Rana, he became prime minister on 27 June 1901, the fifth **Rana** prime minister of Nepal. Chandra ruled until his death on 25 November 1929. In the annals of Nepal, it has been fairly customary to mention his abolition of **Sati** *pratha* (the practice of widow self-immolation) in 1920 and of *das pratha* (**slavery**) in 1924. He also opened the first college of Nepal named after himself: **Tri-Chandra College** in 1918. While laying its foundation, Chandra Shamsher reportedly uttered that with the opening of the college he had laid the foundation for the demise of his Rana family (hereditary) rule, but he could not help moving with the time.

RANA, DIAMOND SHAMSHER (1918–). Historical novelist, often focusing on themes related to **Rana** palace intrigues and deviant behaviors of which the general public had only vague knowledge, but to which Diamond Shamsher was close thanks to his Rana family connections. Much of what the public knew about such occurrences within the palace compounds was invariably based on heresies. He has written several novels.

RANA, GEHENDRA SHAMSHER. Acknowledged scientist. Based on popular accounts, he designed and made some of Nepal's first pistols and revolvers. He is also said to have experimented with steam engines and flying machines.

RANA, HIMALAYA SHAMSHER (1925–?). Economist. Born to a privileged family with a **Rana** name, he was chosen to serve as the first governor of **Nepal Rastra Bank** during the 1956–1960 period. He later founded Gorkha Brewery, Gorkha Bricks Factory, and the **Himalayan Bank Limited** in 1992 (named after himself with a slight twist).

RANA, JANG (JUNG) BAHADUR (reign: 1846–1877). Jang Bahadur established the **Rana** rule and relegated the **Shah** monarchy to a puppet role. Whether justified or not, few Nepali political leaders or prime ministers are remembered with the degree of disdain that is reserved for Jang Bahadur, perhaps because his rise to power was scripted in ruthless bloodshed. In terms of known records, the murderous course of history that Jang Bahadur Kunwar pursued began with his 1845 assassination of his own uncle, Prime Minister **Mathbar Singh Thapa**. This was followed by the **Kot Parba** of 1846, in which he and his brothers slaughtered 29 high-ranking courtiers in one fell sweep, thus exterminating virtually everybody who could potentially challenge his authority. Immediately following the massacre, he became prime minister, thereby setting in motion what later became known as the dynastic Rana rule. Jang Bahadur changed his surname from "Kunwar" to "Rana" after King Surendra bestowed upon him the honorific title of **Rana**. He ruled until he died in 1877. Two of his enduring contributions, if they can be described as such, are the implementation of Muluki Ain (**Civil Code**) and the establishment of what came to be known as the **Durbar High School**.

RANA, JUDDHA SHAMSHER (reign: 1932–1945). Perhaps the most ruthless of all **Rana** prime ministers with the exception of **Jang Bahadur**. He rose to power on 1 September 1932. Juddha Shamsher adamantly adhered to his ill-founded belief that a **constitutional** form of government was neither possible nor desirable for Nepal, a belief that King **Mahendra Bir Bikram Shah** later popularized. Juddha Shamsher is most remembered for his 1941 execution of those who are now honored as the four national martyrs (*shahid*): **Dasharath Chand, Dharma Bhakta Mathema, Shukra Raj Shastri,** and **Ganga Lal Shrestha**. He was one of the few Rana prime ministers to voluntarily relinquish his office. After his resignation on 29 November 1945, he moved to **Dehradun, India,** where he died on 20 November 1952.

RANA, MOHAN SHAMSHER (reign: 1948–1951). Very conservative in his policy, he is the last **Rana** prime minister. With the end of his prime ministership also came the inevitable demise of the Rana rule. He rose to power when Prime Minister Padma Shamsher Rana issued his letter of resignation on 30 April 1948. His reign was relatively short-lived, lasting until 12 November 1951. He once told **B. P. Koirala**, a revolutionary engaged in the anti-Rana movement, that to be a prime minister it must be written on one's forehead (Nepali expression, meaning one must be predestined to be a prime minister).

RANA, PASHUPATI SHAMSHER (1942–). Politician and economist. He served as director of the **Centre for Economic Development and Administration** from 1969 to 1973 and as minister of **Panchayat** and Local Development (1986–1988). He has published some research works and was elected to the **House of Representative** in 1991.

RANA PERIOD. Hereditary or dynastic rule of Rana prime ministers over a period of 105 years, from 1846 to 1951. It was a dark period in the history of Nepal as the country was economically bled white and sociopolitically oppressed by the Ranas who wielded absolute power in every respect and in every arena of society and life. *See also* Introduction.

Rana Prime Ministers	Regnal Years
Jang (Jung) Bahadur Rana	1846–1877
Ranoddip Singh Rana	1877–1885
Bir Shamsher Rana	1885–1901
Dev Shamsher Rana	1901 (5 May–22 June)
Chandra Shamsher Rana	1901–1929
Bhim Shamsher Rana	1929–1932
Juddha Shamsher Rana	1932–1945
Padma Shamsher Rana	1945–1948
Mohan Shamsher Rana	1948–1951

RANA, PUSKAR SHAMSHER (1901–1961). Short story writer and grammarian. Prior to his death, he published several works and edited an English-Nepali dictionary. In addition, he once served as editor of the ***Gorkhapatra***.

RANA, SUBARNA SHAMSHER (1909–1977). Industrialist and central figure of the **Nepali Congress Party**. As a relatively progressive **Rana**, he carefully navigated between his close affinity toward his Rana heritage and privileges and his pragmatic view of democracy. He was deputy prime minister and minister of finance as well as **planning** and development during the elected Congress government headed by **B. P. Koirala**. He was—curiously, one might add—the only member of Koirala's cabinet who was neither arrested nor imprisoned during the **palace coup** launched by King **Mahendra Bir Bikram Shah** on the fateful night of 15 December 1960. Subarna Shamsher was conveniently absent from the country. He had departed for Calcutta, **India**, three days before the coup. It was widely suspected that the king had carefully arranged his personal visit to Calcutta prior to the coup so he would not have to arrest and jail Subarna to whom he was related through matrimonial ties. It is, however, unknown to any reliable source or acknowledged historian of Nepal's entangled politics whether Subarna Shamsher had any clue about the imminent palace coup.

RANI POKHARI. Small manmade pond in **Kathmandu**, built by King **Pratap Malla** to console his queen after the death of their son. It is one of the most visible features of Kathmandu because of its central location and because of its proximity to the city's only public park called Ratna Park.

RANJITKAR, GHANASHYAM (1942–). Industrialist. He is managing director of Krishna Pauroti Udhyog (Krishna bakery), a pioneer bread and bakery enterprise in the nation. In addition, he is a **Newar** literary activist.

RANJITKAR, PARASMANI (1909–?). Artist, painter. He is famous for portraits made of threads. He has won awards for his contributions in the field of thread art. Although it is believed that he has expired, no record of whether he is dead or still alive could be unearthed at the time of this writing.

RAPTI INTEGRATED RURAL DEVELOPMENT PROJECT. As the name suggests, it is a rural development project launched by the **United States** Agency for International Development in 1980 in the **Rapti Zone** in western Nepal (*see* figure 3). It is the biggest-ever rural development undertaking in the nation. Ironically, however, it is precisely this area where the project has been implemented with great fanfare that now finds itself as the primary hub of the ongoing Maoist revolution or what is commonly called the **People's War**.

RAPTI VALLEY DEVELOPMENT PROJECT (RVDP). Successive **Shah** and **Rana** rulers had made many attempts prior to 1951 to settle **Chitwan** (*see* figure 2) and other parts of the **Tarai** with the *pahari* migrants, but with minimal success. In the mid-1950s, the policy of land settlement in the Tarai was resurrected as an integral part of Nepal's planned development, this time on a systematic basis and much larger scale. Unlike in the past, the renewed effort reflected a direct government involvement in terms of both **planning** and implementation. The impetus for the plan emanated from the 1954 massive floods and landslides that ravaged the central hills, causing enormous property damage and rendering many villagers landless. Plus, they created food shortages. Additionally, the new post-Rana government had other pressing elements to redress. For example, the popular revolution that kicked the

Ranas out of power in 1951 ushered in what may be characterized as "the revolution of rising expectations" among the general masses, comprised almost exclusively of peasants.

Under such circumstances, land colonization in the Tarai appeared to be the most logical and immediate measure to mitigate some of the severe consequences of natural disasters as well as agrarian problems. The stated broad objectives of the new Tarai settlement policy were to: *rehabilitate* natural disaster victims and landless hill migrants through their resettlement in the Tarai; *enhance* **agricultural** output by bringing more land under cultivation to tackle food shortages in the hills, specifically in the **Kathmandu Valley**; and *attain* a better regional human-land resource balance through population shifts from the hills to the Tarai, that is, to reduce population pressure in the hills. Not openly stated as an objective, but always rooted at the heart of the central government was to *paharize* the Tarai (i.e., to populate it with the *paharis* to create a hill demographic majority). The project was almost exclusively funded by the **United States**.

Chitwan's Rapti Valley was chosen as the site to launch the first Tarai land settlement project under the new policy. Because of its physical proximity to the Kathmandu Valley, Chitwan has always received attention from the central government for both political and economic reasons. Strategically speaking, Chitwan (along with the adjacent district of Makwanpur) is the heartland of Nepal. As a Tarai gateway to the Kathmandu Valley, the central government has considered Chitwan to be a very strategic district from a politico-geographical point of view. Hence, its control in whatever way possible is seen as a critical issue within the Nepali policymaking circle regardless of who rules the nation. In fact, when Makwanpur fell into the hands of the British forces during the **Anglo-Nepal War** of 1814–1816, the government of Nepal lost its confidence to contain them from marching on to the Kathmandu Valley, so it decided to surrender.

The centrality of Chitwan is still intact. Immediately following the overthrow of autocratic Rana rule in 1951, some political leaders saw Chitwan's virgin territory as an area in which to establish their strong political base. For example, **Bakhan Sing Gurung**, an important leader of the **Nepali Congress Party**, seized the opportunity, convincing a contingent of his central hill villagers (followers) to move to Chitwan with him and settle there permanently. Bakhan Sing was a pioneer who paved the path of frontier migration to Chitwan. However, the number of hill settlers remained relatively small until the Rapti Valley Development Project (RVDP) was launched in 1956 as an integral part of Nepal's first development plan (1956–1961). A malaria eradication program ensued in order to enhance its habitability by reducing the threat of malaria and to induce more hill migration. The RVDP was vested with full power to regulate land clearance and distribution in accordance with policy goals stated earlier. Approved applicants were given land, ranging from 4 **bighas** (1 *bigha* = 0.68 hectare) to as many as 100 *bighas* (68 hectares), although the official ceiling was set at 50 *bighas* under some rare circumstances. Altogether, 5,233 households were settled, and they were granted a total of 41,027 *bighas* of land in Chitwan.

By the time the RVDP came to an end in 1961, encroachment of public lands and forest fringes, and subsequent squatter settlement, had emerged as a common trend and a growing problem among hill migrants who were unable to receive land either through government grants or purchase. Then there were armed insurrections in 1961 carried out by the then outlawed Nepali Congress Party against the autocratic system of King **Mahendra Bir Bikram Shah**. The battle between the king's army and the Congress liberation forces of 1960 had deep effects in terms of intensifying the land encroachment movement in Chitwan. Even though the king had managed to repel the Congress rebels, he badly needed the support of the landless in order to maintain his firm hold in the district. The landless in the district took advantage of the king's weakened position and encroached on the public lands in Chitwan with greater vigor.

In order to gain the political support of Chitwan's rapidly growing landless masses, the majority of whom were sympathetic to the Congress cause, the king began to distribute land in small quantities to squatter settlers who had occupied public (common) land. In essence, the king had politicized the land to protect his **Panchayat** system. What the king's implicit policy of land politicization resulted in was more encroachment of public land in the district by both the landless and opportunists who took advantage of the situation. This unsavory process continued right through the early 1980s across Chitwan. *See also* ETHNICITY; FOREIGN AID; FORESTRY.

RAPTI ZONE. Named after the Rapti River in the **Karnali** basin, it had a population of 1,043,196 in 1991, distributed in its five districts: **Dang**,

Pyuthan, Rolpa, Rukum, and Salyan. Its total areal coverage extends over 10,482 sq. km. (*see* figures 2 and 3).

RARA NATIONAL PARK. Named after Rara Lake, which forms the central feature of this park, it is situated in the remote mountainous district of Mugu (*see* figure 2). This national park is a habitat for musk deer, ghoral, serow, red panda, and many other animals and birds, including blood pheasant and **danphe** (the national bird of Nepal).

RASTRA BHASA. National language. *See* LANGUAGE.

RASTRIYA ABHILEKHALAYA. Nepal's national archives. Founded in 1967, it houses archival records, including national treaties and agreements.

RASTRIYA BANIJYA BANK. Commercial bank established in 1966. With its branches distributed throughout the nation, it has played an important role since its inception in terms of making loans available for various commercial and industrial enterprises. However, because of the absence of viable and sufficient competition, loan terms are relatively high and the quality of service is poor, especially in rural and remote areas. It has joined the Indosuez Bank of Paris in a joint venture.

RASTRIYA BIMA SANSTHAN. Public insurance corporation. It was incorporated in 1968 and is located in **Kathmandu**. It is the first such company in the country and issues various types of life insurance to the general public as well as business enterprises.

RASTRIYA PRAJATANTRA DIWAS. *See* DEMOCRACY DAY

RASTRIYA PRAJATANTRA PARTY (RPP). Major political party. *See* NATIONAL DEMOCRATIC PARTY.

RASTRIYA SABHA. Upper House of **Parliament**. *See* NATIONAL COUNCIL.

RASTRIYA SAMACHAR SAMITI. National News Committee. It is the state news agency of Nepal and was founded in 1962 by King **Mahendra Bir Bikram Shah** as an integral part of his policy to control the freedom of the **press** by tightly controlling the mechanism of news collection and distribution in the country. *See also* MEDIA.

RATNA, NHUCHHE (1888–1950). Active in the anti-**Rana** movement, he was beaten to death in 1950 by the Rana police in **Kathmandu**. His death further fueled the revolutionary movement that was already raging across the country against Rana autocracy, thereby expediting its impending demise in early 1951.

RATNA RECORDING CORPORATION. Corporation for collection, recording, and development of Nepali **music** and songs. Founded in 1967, it is the first such entity in the country. It merged with **Nepal Television** in 1990.

RAUTE. Nomadic people in Nepal, mostly found in the **Tarai** and **inner Tarai**. They live in forests and hunt monkeys and deer.

RAYABANDI SYSTEM. It is a system in which anybody who builds an irrigation canal and provides irrigation water to newly reclaimed areas, namely the canal builder, would receive one-tenth of the land reclaimed free of charge. And the land would remain with the builder and his family, even in the event that the builder committed a capital crime. It was instituted to entice entrepreneurs to engage in private land and agricultural development activities. Since the end of the **Rana** regime, the system has basically become defunct.

RAYAMAJHI, KESHAR JUNG (1926–). A founding member of the **Communist Party of Nepal**, Rayamajhi was once considered to be a prominent figure of the party. He later bolted from the party over internal disputes and formed his own faction of the Communist party, generally following the line pursued by the former Soviet Union. He served as minister of general administration and **education** and culture during the interim government (1990–1991).

REGMI, DILLI RAMAN (1915–). Politician and scholar. However, he is recognized more for his scholarly achievements than political success. He is a distinguished Nepali historian who has written several authoritative books on Nepal. He was appointed minister of **education** and foreign affairs in 1954 and of home affairs in 1958–1959. His intellectual place in Nepali historiography is indisputable and unparalleled. From a Western perspective, one clear advantage that he had over other renowned Nepali historians is that he wrote his books in English, thus making them readily accessible to the Western audience.

REGMI, MAHESH CHANDRA. (1929–). Economic historian. One of the most recognized and distinguished Nepali scholars, he has written several definitive books on the economic history of Nepal, especially focusing on the **Rana** period. Few can match his published records and authoritative knowledge in this area. Mahesh Chandra is one of the handful of Nepali scholars whose works are equally familiar to both the Western audience and domestic readers.

RELIGION. Religion occupies an integral position in Nepali life and society. Most dominant and visible among the religious faiths is **Hinduism**. This is hardly surprising because Nepal is the only constitutionally declared Hindu state in the world. There is, however, a great deal of intermingling of Hindu and **Buddhist** beliefs in terms of daily practice and interactions. Many of the people regarded as Hindus could also be called Buddhists. The fact that **Hindus** worship at Buddhist temples and Buddhists worship at Hindu temples clearly explain why adherents of the two dominant groups in Nepal have never engaged in any overt religious conflicts. Because of such dual faith practices, the differences between Hindus and Buddhists have been, in general, subtle throughout the country's history.

However, according to the 1991 census, approximately 86 percent of the Nepali people identified themselves as Hindus. Buddhists and **Muslims** comprise less than 8 and 4 percent, respectively. The remainder follow other religions, including Christianity (*see* table 9). Although the followers of Christianity are very small in number, it does have a visible and active presence. The primacy of Hinduism in the census largely stems from its status as the national religion. When asked about their faith, people tend to mention Hinduism. This is particularly true among those who straddle with ease the religious fences between Hinduism and Buddhism.

The geographical distribution of religious groups reveals a preponderance of Hindus in virtually every region. In terms of broad geographical patterns, the lower hills are heavily influenced by Hinduism, whereas the upper hills and **Trans-Himalayan** areas are predominated by Buddhism.

Large pockets of Buddhists are also found in the eastern hills, the **Kathmandu Valley**, and the central **Tarai**; in each area about 10 percent of the people are Buddhist. Buddhism is relatively more common among the **Newar** and **Tibeto-Nepali** groups. On the other hand, **Bahuns** and **Chhetris** tend to be almost exclusively Hindus. Among the Tibeto-Nepali, those most influenced by Hinduism are the **Magars** and **Rais**. Hindu influence was less prominent among the **Bhote, Gurung, Limbu, Sherpa, Tamang,** and **Thakali** groups, who continue to employ Buddhist monks for their religious ceremonies.

RICE. When it comes to the place of rice in the social and cultural life of Nepal, the situation is no different than what is observed throughout **monsoon** Asia. Its preeminence is demonstrated not only in terms of its extensive cropping, but also through its use during many festivals and ceremonies from birth to death. It is an unmistakable symbol of Nepali culture and social status. Those who cannot afford rice on a daily basis are generally considered poor. If a family cannot afford to serve rice to guests, this becomes a source of shame. And those who can afford it consume it up to three times a day (including breakfast), but certainly for both lunch and dinner.

Rice comes in many different varieties in terms of quality, flavor, and shape. Out of rice are prepared many different dishes, especially in **Newar** communities. They also make drinks out of rice, namely *jand* (fermented rice mixed with water) and *raksi* (similar to Japanese *sake*). As a solid dish, boiled rice is the main dish and the most common form of consumption, followed by *chiura* (beaten or flat rice). However, in Nepal, rice is rarely consumed by itself; it is invariably mixed with some other dishes such as cooked **dal** (lentil), some vegetable dish, and/or chutney. If families can afford meat, it will be added. The higher the household economic position, the greater the variety and the number of side dishes to complement or enhance the taste of rice.

Given its prominent place in Nepali society and culture, it is no surprise at all that rice is the most important grain crop grown in the country. It constitutes more than 55 percent of the nation's total farm production. Because of its demanding cropping requirements (i.e., regular supply of water, humid and sunny condition, and flat planting beds), wet rice production is almost exclusively concentrated in the lowland areas of Nepal. As a result, it occupies some of the best or most fertile land surfaces in the country. *See also* AGRICULTURE; FOOD.

RIG (RG) VEDA. Oldest **Hindu** scripture. In many respects, its serves as the fundamental foundation and framework of **Hinduism** and Hindu social life.

RIJAL, NAGENDRA PRASAD (1927–). Politician and participant in the anti-**Rana** revolution of 1950–1951. In the early 1960s he entered **Panchayat** politics and was appointed minister of **forest** and **agriculture** in 1965. He was appointed prime minister (1973–1975 and 1986). He served as president of the World **Hindu** Organization in 1985.

RIMAL, GOPAL PRASAD (1918–1973). Born in **Kathmandu** in 1918, Gopal Prasad is believed to be the first Nepali poet to reject the use of meter, which was regarded as being too restrictive to promote the development of Nepali **literature**. Remembered as a revolutionary poet, Gopal Prasad Rimal was openly political, especially at a time when political activism drew the wrath of the **Rana** regime. As his voice of protest grew louder in his poems, the Rana government had him removed from his post as editor of *Sharada* only two months after being appointed, and later jailed him several times. As he deeply longed for a social awakening, he never hesitated to criticize the Rana regime in his poems, often phrased as pleas to a mother (i.e., Nepal) from her suffering children against the oppressor (i.e., the Ranas). Sadly, the powerful voice of change that Rimal's poetry represented suddenly fell silent after 1960 when he suffered from a severe form of mental disorder.

RIMAL, HARI PRASAD (1925–?). Actor and singer. He is recognized as the singer of the first song aired on **Radio Nepal** in 1951. He performed various roles in Nepali movies produced in the 1960s and early 1970s.

RISING NEPAL, THE. Leading English daily newspaper, published by the Gorkhapatra Corporation. It is essentially the English version of the *Gorkhapatra*. Until the publication of *The Kathmandu Post*, an English daily published in **Kathmandu**, *The Rising Nepal* was only daily English newspaper in the country with a nationwide circulation.

RODI GHAR. House (*ghar*) where *rodi* (collective singing) is performed. It is a time-honored tradition and institution in **Gurung** communities. Young men and women in the village—sometimes including those from surrounding villages—periodically gather at the *rodi ghar* after dinner and spend the night singing and socializing. Physical contacts and sexual expressions between opposite genders are normal during *rodi ghar* gatherings. See also MUSIC AND DANCE.

ROPANI. Unit of land measurement, especially in the hills. One *ropani* is equal to roughly 0.052 hectare.

ROYAL DRUGS LIMITED. Public enterprise for production and sales of pharmaceutical drugs. It was founded in 1972. Due to its limited production capacity, most of what it produces is consumed within the country. See also HEALTH CARE.

ROYAL KARNALI WILDLIFE RESERVE. Wildlife reserve based in Bardiya. It contains different types of wild animals. It is believed that many royal family members organize secret hunting trips for high-class Western tourists to this park and to the **Chitwan National Park** as part of their hotel business.

ROYAL NEPAL ACADEMY. Organization designed for the promotion and preservation of Nepali arts, **literature**, and culture. Founded in 1957, it regularly holds drama and poetry competitions.

ROYAL NEPAL ACADEMY FOR SCIENCE & TECHNOLOGY. Academy for the promotion of science and technology. Established in 1982, it conducts research on issues and topics related to science and technology. Despite its high-profile name, its records of research outputs and activities are fuzzy.

ROYAL NEPAL AIRLINES CORPORATION (RNAC). Public corporation that owns and operates Nepal's national air flights, both domestic and international. While there are several private airlines in Nepal to operate domestic flights, it is the only Nepali airline that has regularly scheduled international flights. It has direct flights to several cities in the world, for example, Bangkok, Delhi, Frankfurt, Hong Kong, London, Paris, and Singapore. Historically, it has suffered from mismanagement and losses. See also AIRLINES AND INTERNATIONAL AIR SERVICE; AIR SERVICE WITHIN NEPAL; TRANSPORTATION.

ROYAL NEPAL ARMY. Under his total command, the army is the right arm of the ruling king, whose key officer posts are stacked with his **Shah** and **Rana** relatives and supporters. It is, therefore, plausible to assert that it is his personal army, although, technically, it is the national army. It is currently engaged in a dog fight with the Maoist revolutionaries who have been waging the **People's War** since early 1996 to liberate Nepal from the institution of monarchy. Currently supported by the American George W. Bush administration in its global war against terrorism and the British government, the army has managed to acquire relatively sophisticated military hardware, including helicopters fitted for nighttime operations. Despite its superior military hardware and logistical advantage, the army has essentially reached a point of stalemate with the Maoists; it has neither gained nor lost ground vis-à-vis the Maoist insurgents. Since Nepal has no military conscription policy, recruitment for the army is voluntary. There is no air force.

ROYAL NEPAL FILMS CORPORATION. Public corporation set up in 1971 for the production, distribution, and promotion of Nepali films. Since its inception, it has produced several feature films. It was privatized in 1993.

ROYAL PALACE MASSACRE. In a most bizarre and bloody palace massacre, King **Birendra Bir Bikram Shah** and his immediate family were gunned down on 1 June 2001 by Crown Prince **Dipendra Bir Bikram Shah**, who was believed to have later shot himself. The massacre occurred in the royal dining room over family disputes concerning the crown prince's choice of his future bride. Since Dipendra was considered clinically alive, he was placed on life support. On 2 June, dying Dipendra was declared king. On 4 June, Dipendra was pronounced dead, thus paving the way for a new king. With no heirs surviving from Birendra's lineage, Dipendra's uncle **Gyanendra Bir Bikram Shah** was crowned king.

ROYAL SHUKLAPHANTA WILDLIFE RESERVE. Wildlife reserve in Kanchanpur. Founded in 1976, it contains many different types of wild animals, including tigers, elephants, and barking deer. It is home of the rare hispid hare. Avian fauna include peafowl, rock pigeon parrot, green pigeon, and many others. Among the reptilian fauna one finds pythons and gavials.

RUDRAKSHA. Sacred tree bearing hard nuts, also called *rudraksha*. These ripe beads are woven into garlands and worn by those who have renounced the world and who follow **Shiva**, commonly known as the *jogi* or *sadhu*.

RUPEE (Rs). Unit of Nepali currency. The term is also used for the Indian currency. In terms of its unit (not monetary) value, it is equal to one dollar. One rupee consists of 100 paisas.

S

SACRIFICE OF ANIMALS. Animal sacrifice is a common aspect of **Hindu** worships and rituals. It is routine within Nepal's **Tantric** and shamanistic traditions as well. However, it is pertinent to note that sacrifice involves only male animals. Popular sacrificial animals are goats, roosters, ducks, and buffaloes. While goats are used by all **caste** and **ethnic** groups, roosters, ducks, and buffaloes are confined to non-**Bahun** and non-**Chhetri** castes. *See also* DAKSHINKALI; GORKHAKALI MANDIR.

SADHU. Ascetic person, somebody who has renounced the earthly world. *See also* SANYAS.

SAGARMATHA. *See* MOUNT EVEREST.

SAGARMATHA NATIONAL PARK. World's highest national park in Solokhumbu. Included in its territorial bound is **Namche Bazaar**, flanked by **Mount Everest**. It contains among other animals **snow leopards**, flying squirrels, musk deer, red pandas, and, of course, the countless legendary tales of the famed **Yeti** without whose mythical or imagined presence the Park would not radiate the same aura of attraction and charm.

SAGARMATHA SATELLITE EARTH STATION. Nepal's satellite earth station based in **Kathmandu**. Built with British assistance and inaugurated in 1982, it has connection to INTELSAT–5, 36,000 kilometers above the Indian Ocean. It carries 60 channels and has greatly improved Nepal's **communications** with the world.

SAGARMATHA ZONE. Named after **Sagarmatha**, this zone consists of six districts (*see* figure 3). They are: Khotang, Okhaldhunga, Saptari, Siraha, Solokhumbu, and Udayapur (*see* figure 2). Its population in 1991 totaled 1,598,020, spread over an area of 10,591 sq. km. The **Sagarmatha National Park** is a major attraction of this zone.

SAGAULI, TREATY OF. Treaty signed in March 1816 between Nepal and British India (specifically the East India Company). It resulted from Nepal's surrender following what is commonly known as the **Anglo-Nepal War** (1814–1816). As dictated by the treaty, Nepal ceded around one-half of its territory to British India, eventually confining it to its current boundary.

SAINJU, MOHAN MAN, (1940–). A political scientist and royalist, he served as vice-chairman of the **National Planning Commission** from 1982 to 1988. After he received his Ph.D. degree from the University of North Carolina in the United States, he returned to Nepal and was recognized as an important figure within the **Panchayat** circle. He later served as ambassador to the United States (1988–1991).

ST. XAVIER'S SCHOOL. This is the first Christian missionary-run English-medium school in Nepal. With the exception of the **Durbar School**, few schools in the country have played as profound a role in changing the orientation and emphasis of **education** in Nepal as this one.

In January 1951, just days before the demise of Rana autocracy, Fr. Moran arrived in **Kathmandu** with Fr. Joseph Egan, the Chicago Province Provincial, to visit Godavari and make arrangements to open the school for Nepali boys. It was named St. Xavier's School. Later Frs. Frank Murphy and Ed Saxton came to join Fr. Moran. In late June 1951, 300 applicants were screened and 65 were admitted. With those 65 students, the school opened on 1 July 1951, at a time when the country was still celebrating the end of the **Rana** regime and the fresh dawn of democracy.

With Fr. Moran as its first principal, St. Xavier's was run as a private Christian boarding school. Joining the teaching staff in early 1952 was Fr. Downing, later followed by a chain of missionary priests. In May 1953, St. Xavier's School faced its first, but relatively minor, religious incident over the issue of taking an afternoon bath. Some boys refused to follow this rule, claiming that according to Hindu tradition it was forbidden to take a bath in the afternoon if the parents were still alive. A little more than a year later in September 1954, the missionaries expanded the school's operation, setting up a new one in Jawalakhel, **Patan**, about three kilometers from the central business district of Kathmandu.

The opening of St. Xavier's School in Jawalakhel was followed by the establishment of another missionary, English-medium school in February 1955 in the same locality. It was called St. Mary's School, exclusively designed to educate Nepali girls. On 15 February, it made its debut with 15 girls admitted. In many respects, it was a path-breaking social event as it was not only the first Christian missionary and English-medium school for girls; it was the first girls' school in the nation. The door for girls' education in the country had, thus, been opened.

These schools proved to be a mixed blessing, however, for Nepal's educational system. On the one hand, they elevated the importance of girls' education as well as set a new trend for modern education. The **elite** preference for English education was further heightened. Those missionary schools also embodied a sense of educational opening for those outside the immediate circle of Rana families and the elite class based in the Valley. They admitted some students from different parts of the country, thus broadening their geographical coverage. Yet those schools did little to tear down the existing class barrier. Instead, they played a role in reinforcing—and actually further widening—Nepal's educational class divide. Given their high costs, only the rich could afford to educate their children at those private schools. What is more the Nepali elite now had ready access to English education right in the nation. As a result, they were no longer totally reliant on India's English boarding schools to educate their children and were able to significantly reduce the costs of their education. Additionally, since those educated at St. Xavier's and St. Mary's were treated as educationally superior simply because of their English fluency, they automatically commanded a higher value. So, almost in every respect, children from the elite and wealthy families were endowed with better education and enjoyed an added advantage.

SAL. Tall tropical tree (*Shorea robusta*) with broad leaves; it belongs to the hardwood family. Because of its longevity (often described as lasting a thousand years), it is used in different construction projects and as telephone poles. It is mostly found in the **Tarai**, **inner Tarai**, and low hills. *See also* FORESTRY.

SALT TRADING CORPORATION. Public corporation established in 1973 to oversee salt trading and distribution. Nepal has no known salt mine. Until the early 1960s, much of the salt consumed in Nepal came from **Tibet**'s land salt mines. The sea salt imported from **India** was largely consumed in the **Tarai** region, but in the hills it was thought to be inferior to Tibetan salt, which commanded a relatively higher price. In the hills, sea salt was usually reserved for domestic animals, whereas Tibetan salt was used for people. Since trade with Tibet basically ended in the early 1960s, there is very little Tibetan salt imported into the country. Now it is all sea salt.

SAMA, BALAKRISHNA (1903–1981). A highly recognized literary figure, he introduced a new trend in Nepali **literature** by synthesizing oriental and Western philosophic and scientific thoughts. Because of his complex writing style, his plays were generally inaccessible to the public. As Michael Hutt puts it, Balakrishna was an intellectual whose knowledge of world culture brought austerity and eclecticism to his work. In many respects, his works set a new or modern trend in Nepali literature. Aside from his literary accomplishment, he is remembered most for defiance and rejection of his **Rana** heritage. Born Balakrishna Shamsher Rana, he changed his last name. Not only did he entirely remove the word Rana from his last name, he modified the word Shamsher to Sama in 1948. By adopting the name Sama—which literally means "equal"—he not only introduced a new surname, but was also showing his solidarity with the common citizens of the country.

SAMYUKTA BAM MORCHA. United left front of seven communist factions formed in 1989 in preparation for the democratic movement of 1990. This front decided to lend its support to the **Nepali Congress Party** in a nationwide movement to overthrow the **Panchayat** system and restore democracy. As a result of the joint efforts of the Congress party and the united left front, the movement succeeded in this goal.

SANGHA. Group-based organization. It also applies to organizations formed to promote particular religions.

SANSKRIT. Language used predominantly in **Hindu** religious treatises. As a classical language, its status is similar to that of Latin in that it acts as a source of several languages on the Indian subcontinent, but it is rarely used as a regular medium of communication. It is still taught at many institutions in **India** and Nepal, mainly because of its literary value. Both Hindi and Nepali languages are its direct descendants and use **Devanagari** scripts.

SANYAS. **Hindu** way of life; it is invariably associated with a state of life which entails renouncement of materialistic life or earthly things. It is an ascetic way of life, largely pursued by males (although female members of society are free to practice it). According to the classic Hindu conception of the human (mainly high-**caste** male) life cycle, one passes through four distinct phases from birth to death, not counting one's childhood. When a person puts behind his childhood after his investiture with the sacred thread called *janai*, he enters the first phase, one in which he leads a celibate and austere life as a student, supposedly living with his teacher in his ashram (home; place of quiet and frugal living or learning). Since this phase involves formal learning (**education**), it is called a *brahmacharin* (student) phase. Upon the completion of this phase, he returns home and assumes the *grihastha* (householder) phase, which entails family formation (*grihasthi*). He gets married, has children, raises them, and gets them married to ensure that his lineage continues. As he completes this *grihasthi* routine and approaches his advanced age, he transits into what is called the *banaprastha* (hermit) phase, usually living in the forest or by a river bank. By regular meditation and penance, he frees his soul from material objects and earthly temptation, at which point he enters the final phase: the state of *sanyas* (renouncement), thus leaving the hermitage and becoming a ***sanyasi*** (a homeless wanderer) of his own volition. *See also* BARTAMAN; TAGADHARI.

SANYASI. One who practices *sanyas* (homeless wanderer) of his own volition. The term is interchangeable with **sadhu** and **yogi** (*jogi*). It is also a surname in some cases. A female *sanyasi* is called *sanyasini* or *jogini*.

SAPKOTA, MAHANANDA (1896–1978). Linguist and educator. In addition to producing literary works, he established several schools at different places prior to his death.

SAPTA GANDAKI. *See* GANDAKI RIVER SYSTEM.

SAPTA KOSI. *See* KOSI RIVER SYSTEM.

SARASWATI (SARASWOTI). Wife of **Brahma**; goddess of learning, wisdom, and creative arts, including **music**. She is invariably shown with a book and a string musical instrument that resembles a sitar. Many students, along with their parents, worship Saraswati to help them with their learning and do well during exams.

SARDAR. Military official; chief. This term is also used to refer to a head porter, especially among the Sherpas who assist **mountain** climbers.

SARI. Long, loose garment worn by **women**. It is also part of the national dress for female government workers, especially for those occupying high-ranking positions. Although some Nepali women do wear other types of clothes, sari remains the most dominant form of female garment which is often worn with a matching blouse.

SARKI. Ex-untouchable professional **caste**; cobblers or leather workers. They also work as plowmen and carcass removers.

SATAR. Believed to be of Dravidian origin, they are mostly found in the **Jhapa** and **Morang** districts in the eastern **Tarai** (*see* figure 2). Akin to the **Tharu** in some respects, they usually rely on hunting, fishing, and some farming for their livelihood.

SATI. Custom of voluntary or involuntary immolation on one's husband's burning pyre. While some widows participated in it willingly, others were forced to do so. There were even scattered reports of widows being dragged to their dead husbands' funeral pyres. The practice was usually enforced among the high **caste** widows and widows of high-ranking officials. The cases of low-caste satis were scant. This **Hindu** practice was mainly instituted to prevent widows from remarrying or engaging in sexual relations, a form of action that was believed to prevent their dead husbands' entry to heaven as well as bring shame to their families. Although it was practiced until it was banned in 1920 under the premiership of **Chandra Shamsher Rana**, it did not seem to have gained wide popularity. Perhaps the most famous sati case in the country's history is that of Prime Minister **Bhimsen Thapa** whose wife sacrificed her life by burning herself on her husband's funeral pyre. Just before she killed herself she cursed the nation to be condemned to corrupt and despotic leadership—a curse that seems to haunt Nepal to this day.

SATSALKO KRANTI. Popular revolution (*kranti*) of the year 7 (*satsalko*). The year 7 (*sat*) refers to the Nepali year 2007, which corresponds to 1951 A.D. It was precisely this *kranti* that brought down the **Rana** regime in the month of Falgun (*see* **Nepali calendar**), allowing Nepal to emerge from the darkness of oppression to have a glimpse of democracy. As a national holiday, it is celebrated every year with some degree of fanfare that includes public processions and political speeches. *See also* DEMOCRACY DAY; PANCHAYAT; SHAH, MAHENDRA BIR BIKRAM.

SATYAGRAHA. Basically, a form of civil disobedience, often associated with nonviolent protests pioneered by Mahatma Gandhi. As a form of protest, it is sometimes accompanied by hunger strike (*annasan* in Nepali). During the pro-democracy movement of early 1990, *satyagraha* was practiced quite widely by various professional groups to express their support for the movement in defiance of the government. However, their stances of civil disobedience were rarely formally declared as such, and those groups did not go on hunger strike. It was also used in the late 1950s to protest King **Mahendra Bir Bikram Shah**'s tactics of delaying the promised general **elections** to elect the democratic government. One well-known case of *annasan* occurred in 1949 when **B. P. Koirala** deployed it for 27 days after Prime Minister **Mohan Shamsher Rana** jailed him for his anti-**Rana** activities.

SECURITY EXCHANGE CENTRE. Enterprise operating the Nepal stock exchange market which is in its infancy. Even though it was initially established in 1974, it is only recently that it has begun to gather some steam. In the 1990s, the government of Nepal launched a new economic policy initiative to promote **privatization** or market liberalization. This new policy generated a climate conducive to the operation of stock exchanges. However, it is too early to forecast how its future will unfold.

SENA SOUBHAGYA BHASKAR. Highest-ranking decoration medal awarded for military bravery.

SETI ZONE. Included in this zone are five districts: Achham, Bajhang, Bajura, **Doti**, and Kailali. Named after the Seti river in the **Karnali** basin, its 1991 population totaled 1,016,653, spread over an area of 12,550 sq. km. (*see* figures 2 and 3).

SHAH. *See* SHAH DYNASTY.

SHAH, BAHADUR (1757–1797). Son of **Prithvi Narayan Shah**. First imprisoned and then exiled by his elder brother, Pratap Singh, after being crowned king in January 1775. However, almost three years later, Pratap Singh was succeeded by his infant son **Rana Bahadur Shah** in November 1777. A few years later, Bahadur Shah served as the young king's regent (1785–1794). He was generally regarded as a highly capable regent.

SHAH, BIRENDRA BIR BIKRAM (1945–2001). Birendra was crowned following the death of his father, King **Mahendra Bir Bikram Shah**, and ruled for 18 years (1972–1990) under the institution of absolute monarchy and 11 years under the new system of **constitutional** monarchy. He was murdered by his own son, Crown Prince **Dipendra Bir Bikram Shah**, in a bloody **palace massacre** on 1 June 2001. Birendra was credited with his ability to preserve his father's **Panchayat** rule until 1990 and for finally dissolving it—although begrudgingly—to pave the way for the second dawn of democracy and constitutional rule. In essence, he saved the institution of monarchy from being rendered defunct. One of his first acts after assuming the throne in early 1972 was to establish the **Nepal Development Council** as an overarching national development policy body which is responsible for directing the **National Planning Commission**. He also actively supported the creation of the **South Asian Association of Regional Cooperation**. It was during his reign that Nepal suffered a yearlong **Indian** economic boycott in 1989, something that never occurred before and that played a role in the downfall of the Panchayat system.

SHAH, DIPENDRA BIR BIKRAM (1971–2001). Crown prince who killed his whole family, including father **Birendra Bir Bikram Shah**, on 1 June 2001. He later shot himself. While confined to his death bed, he was declared king on 2 June and, two days later, he died on 4 June.

SHAH, GYANENDRA BIR BIKRAM (1947–). Current king of Nepal. A younger brother of King **Birendra Bir Bikram Shah**, he became king by accident. When the former was killed, along with every member of his family, including murderous Crown Prince **Dipendra Bir Bikram Shah** (who shot himself), Gyanendra happened to be the next in line to climb to the throne. He became king on 4 June 2001, thus setting in motion a new Shah lineage. Incidently, he was crowned (declared) king once before at the age of two in November 1950 by Prime Minister **Mohan Shamsher Rana**. When King **Tribhuvan Bir Bikram Shah** fled the royal palace with his family, including Crown Prince **Mahendra Bir Bikram Shah**, in protest of **Rana** autocracy, his grandson Prince Gyanendra was left behind because he happened to be with his mother's Rana family at that time. Since the king's sudden asylum in the **Indian** Embassy posed a grave threat to the legitimacy of the Rana regime, Mohan Shamsher hastily crowned the young crown prince to be the next king, thus keeping the throne occupied. Because of that incident, it is believed that Gyanendra always privately claimed the throne to be his. Now it is indeed his. On 4 October 2002, King Gyanendra dismissed the elected government of Prime Minister **Sher Bahadur Deuba**, sacked his entire cabinet, and assumed executive powers (*see* Chronology). As a result, Nepal's infant democracy has, once again, been suffocated.

Before he occupied the throne, Gyanendra was widely known as one of the most corrupt members of the royal family. In a country buried in massive poverty, he is one of Nepal's richest persons who amassed his wealth from his extensive business involvement dating back to his days as a prince. For example, King Gyanendra owns luxury hotels, a sprawling tea garden in eastern Nepal (*see* **Ilam**), and gainful partnership with a cigarette factory. So far, he has steadfastly refused to make his tax returns public, thus conveying the impression that he has failed to pay taxes. It was widely reported that, as a prince, he never paid his utility bills. Furthermore, questions are being raised regarding funds routinely allocated to the palace from the national exchequer. Speakers at a public meeting held in **Kathmandu** pointedly questioned why the money for the palace was increased by more than three times, when the number of members of the royal family has actually decreased. In short, King Gyanendra has yet to demonstrate any sense of palace accountability, responsibility, and transparency and that he respects the rule of law.

SHAH, MAHENDRA BIR BIKRAM (1920–1972). Perhaps the most cunning of all the **Shah** rulers, he is mostly known for the **palace coup** he launched against the elected government of Prime Minister **B. P. Koirala** in 15 December 1960, a coup that killed Nepal's infant democracy. Suffering from intellectual insecurity and moral void, he saw his absolute monarchical power as a vindication of his authority. Following the coup, he instituted his own brand of political system which he called partyless **Panchayat** and guided democracy. It was essentially a one-party system under his total control. He ruled with an iron fist for almost 17 years, from 1955 until his death in early 1972. Perhaps one of his most creative policy initiatives from the development viewpoint was the **Back-to-the-Village National Campaign**, but by most accounts it failed miserably and it was later cancelled. One principal reason why his regime failed to lift Nepal from the dark veil of poverty is because he constantly shuffled and reshuffled his cabinet. This led to a total lack of policy continuity, focus, and certainty. No prime minister was allowed to develop any long-term roots to steer the country in any firm direction. As a result, both governance and bureaucracy (the fundamental bedrock of policy implementation and administrative cohesiveness) were run based on fear rather than firmness and fortitude. Mahendra died of a heart attack during a hunting trip in **Chitwan**, a famous royal hunting ground in the central **Tarai**. *See also* Introduction.

SHAH, PRITHVI NARAYAN (1722–1775). Initially king of **Gorkha**, a hill principality in central Nepal. One of the most farsighted kings that Nepal has ever witnessed, Prithvi Narayan is credited with the unification of Nepal as he set in motion the process of consolidation of mini states under one flag. It is said that his national unification campaign was partially driven by his determination to keep Nepal's territory from being incorporated into the expanding orbit of British control of the Indian subcontinent. With the conquest of the three **Malla** kingdoms of the **Kathmandu Valley**, a grand feat completed by 1769 with relative ease, his imperial ambition proved unstoppable. As a ruler of Nepal, semi-unified by the time of his death, his reign was, however, relatively short (1769–1775).

SHAH, RAM SAGAR (1899–1968). Born in 1899, Ram Sagar Shah was a torchbearer of education. He established various libraries and schools in the **Janakpur** area (*see* figure 4). In addition, he provided financial assistance to build the Ram Sworup College of Janakpur, named after his friend, Ram Sworup who also contributed to its construction.

SHAH, RANA BAHADUR (1775–1806). When his father passed away, he became king on 17 November 1777 at the age of two. His life was filled with sardonic drama. During a visit to **Pashupati**, he happened to see a beautiful young women (Kantimati), a widow who had come from

India to worship at the temple. Irresistibly attracted to her, he had her abducted and taken to the palace. After some time, he convinced her to marry him with a promise that he would allow her son to inherit the throne. Subsequently, he disinherited Ranodyot Shah, his legitimate heir to the throne, in favor of his other son from Kantimati. When Kantimati fell sick and her health deteriorated, she asked him to abdicate the throne and declare her son king, he obliged and left the throne in 1799. As his wife's health continued to slide downward, his behavior took a violent turn, actually reaching a point at which many thought he had gone crazy. At one point, he went into voluntary exile in Banaras (April 1800) and later returned to Nepal in March 1804 to seize the regency from his senior wife. He was assassinated by his half-brother, Sher Bahadur, on 25 April 1806.

SHAH, TRIBHUVAN BIR BIKRAM (1906–1955). The last **Shah** king under **Rana** autocracy, until 1951 he was essentially a figurehead. He is mostly remembered for his defiant stance against Rana autocracy as he fled the palace on 6 November 1950 and sought asylum in the Indian Embassy in **Kathmandu**. It was this daring move by Tribhuvan that provided a tremendous moral boost to the ongoing popular anti-Rana revolution, thereby hastening the demise of Rana autocracy which technically occurred on 15 February 1951. What is notable about this development, however, is that while the absolute Shah monarchy was firmly restored, it did little to foster democracy and bring about tangible social change in Nepal. He kept postponing his promise to hold general **elections** to establish a democratic government. He completely controlled the political and administrative machinery forming and dismissing his appointed government at will. Within a period of four years of his rule (1951–1955), he appointed four different governments. He died in Switzerland on 13 March 1955 during a visit for medical treatment. After his death, his son **Mahendra Bir Bikram Shah** behaved in the same manner. *See also* SHAH, GYANENDRA BIR BIKRAM.

SHAH DYNASTY (1769–). The Shah dynasty of Nepal began with the rise of **Prithvi Narayan Shah** as the king of Nepal after his army completed its sweep of the **Kathmandu Valley** kingdoms in 1769. The following is a chronological list of the Shah kings of Nepal:

Name	Regnal Year
Prithvi Narayan	1769–1775
Pratap Singh	1775–1777
Rana Bahadur	1777–1799
Girvana Yuddha Bikram	1799–1816
Rajendra Bikram	1816–1847
Surendra Bikram	1847–1881
Prithvi Bir Bikram	1881–1911
Tribhuvan Bir Bikram	1911–1955
Mahendra Bir Bikram	1955–1972
Birendra Bir Bikram	1972–2001
Dipendra Bir Bikram	2–4 June 2001
Gyanendra Bir Bikram	2001–present

SHAHA, RHISHIKESH (1925–2002). Politician, human rights activist, and scholar, diplomat. He has served as Nepal's representative to the United Nations (1956–1961), as minister of finance (1961–1962), and minister of foreign affairs (1962). In reality, however, he is most recognized for his scholarly works as he has published some of the definitive books on Nepal's political history.

SHAHID DIVAS. This is the day when the four national martyrs (*shahid*) are honored and memorialized. *See also* MARTYRS' MEMORIAL.

SHAKTI (SAKTI). Female form of divine energy, usually represented by Goddess **Kali, Durga,** or some other variations. Invariably regarded as the female version of **Shiva,** she is endowed with an unmatched power of both destruction and construction. The concept is sometimes associated with some kind of cult operation.

SHAKYA, KARNA (1943–). A **tourism** promotion activist, he is the founder of the Marco Polo Hotel (1993) of the **Kathmandu Valley.** In addition to his role as an entrepreneur, he is involved in cancer relief activities.

SHAKYA, MUNI BAHADUR (1942–). A well-known Nepali computer scientist who is given credit for developing the first computer script for **Devanagari** in 1984. The script has been vastly refined since then, and it can be downloaded from several Nepal-based web sites in order to access newspapers and magazines written in Nepali.

SHALIGRAM. Hard black stone (ammonite) found in the river beds of the **Kali Gandaki River**. It is basically a petrified black fossil shell. It is sometimes worshiped as a symbol of **Rama** (i.e., *Shalig + ram*; with the last letter "a" silenced) or **Vishnu**, both of whom have dark complexion when they are portrayed in prints and pictures. Many believe that some shaligrams contain gold. Virtually every goldsmith shop carries a few shaligram stones on which they rub the gold item (jewelry) to determine the degree of its purity (gold content).

SHAMASHUDDIN, INVASION OF. Invasion in 1349 by Bengal's Sultan Shamashuddin Ilyas into Nepal. It is said that he raided and looted as well as damaged **Pashupati** and **Swayambhu**.

SHARMA, PITAMBER. As a student in Nepal, he was actively involved in leftist politics. A graduate of Cornell University with a Ph.D. degree in Geography and Regional Planning, he served as a professor of geography at **Tribhuvan University**. Later, he was appointed to the Population Council in the early 1980s. He is currently associated with the International Centre for Integrated Mountain Development (ICIMOD), which is headquartered in **Kathmandu**.

SHARMA, SHREE BHADRA (1926–?). Politician from the central hill district of **Tanahu** (*see* figure 2). Once a high-ranking and popular member of the **Nepali Congress Party**, he later joined the **Panchayat** system and served as minister of general administration. While many other party activists who had participated in the Panchayat system rejoined the Congress party after democracy was restored, he failed to do so. He became instead secretary general of the Rastriya Janata Parishad party, which he helped to found in 1992.

SHARMA, TARA NATH. (1934–). Novelist and literary critic. He is perhaps the best-known literary critic of Nepal. He has published many books and received several awards. He has served as a visiting professor in the United States and editor in chief of *The Rising Nepal*. His pen name is Tana Sharma. He is definitely a prominent literary figure in the country who is equally versed in both English and Nepali.

SHASHI, BASU (1937–1992). Nepali poet and literary journalist. His actual name was Basudev Vaidya. He used the absurdity of the modern age as the main theme of his works. He was highly versed in the **Newari literature** as well. He wrote several books before he expired in 1992.

SHASTRI, DHUNDI RAJ (1940–). A member of the **Nepali Congress Party** since 1954, he was elected to the **House of Representatives** in 1991. He was later appointed minister of industries by Prime Minister **Girija Prasad Koirala** who headed the Congress government following the first democratic **elections** of 1991 in the post-**Panchayat** period. He was reelected during the general elections held in 1994.

SHASTRI, SHUKRA RAJ (1893–1941). He founded the Nepal Civil Rights Committee in 1937, with the aim of creating public awareness of the need for social reform. A teacher by profession, Shastri was highly influenced by Mahatma Gandhi whom he met in Calcutta. Arrested in November 1938 by the **Rana** government, he was hanged to death at the behest of Prime Minister **Juddha Shamsher Rana** on the night of 24 January 1941, along with **Dharma Bhakta Mathema**. *See also* MARTYRS' MEMORIAL.

SHE-GOMBA. Famous **Buddhist** monastery situated at the altitude of 4,878 meters in the western **mountain** district of **Dolpa**. Situated at the confluence of the Sebu and Hubalu streams, it includes a cluster of buildings ringed by *chortens*. It lies within the **She-Phoksundo National Park** boundary.

SHE-PHOKSUNDO NATIONAL PARK. In terms of areal coverage, it is Nepal's largest national park, with a span of 355 sq. km. Created in 1984, it extends into the **Dolpa** and Mugu districts (*see* figure 2). Found among the wild animals of this park are **snow leopards**, musk deer, yaks, and red pandas. More than 10,000 people living within and around the Park heavily depend on plant resources for their survival. Major impacts on **forest** resources are related to firewood and timber collection, grazing in high pastures, and collection of medicinal plants for trade. Dolpa is one of the major points of collection and trade of medicinal plants or herbs in the Karnali region. This activity is an important aspect of the **economy** in this area. Some of the important medicinal plants found in the park are: wanglax or panchaule (*Dactylorhiza hatagirea*), honglen or kutki (*Picrorhiza scrophulariiflora*), yartsagumbu (*Cordyceps sinensis*), sendu or darim (*Punica granatum*), ligadur (*Geranium pratense*), balu or sunpate (*Rhododendron anthopogen*), bashak (*Lagotis kunuwarensis*), wolmose (*Podophylllum hexandrum*), tsenduk/bikh (*Aconitum spicatum*), khurmong (*Taraxacum tibetanum*), and kyerwa (*Berberis aristata*).

SHERCHAN, AMIK (1943–). Leftist politician from **Chitwan**, a **Tarai** district (*see* figure 2), which is well known as one of the leading hotbeds of political activism. He was imprisoned for four years for his radical position and exiled for three more years during the **Panchayat** regime. He was elected to the **House of Representatives** in 1991. He lost his House seat in the subsequent **election** held in 1994.

SHERCHAN, BHUPENDRA (BHUPI) MAN (1936–1989). Popularly known as Bhupi Sherchan. A leftist in ideological orientation, he was a highly charismatic poet with a vibrant personality. He was extremely witty. His bitingly sarcastic and accessible style of poetry made him perhaps the most popular modern poet of Nepal, especially among the young generation. Bhupi Sherchan commanded respect across the political spectrum in a country where virtually everything is tainted with politics or political factionalism. He is keenly remembered for one political prank he meticulously staged in 1960 against his own brother Yogendra Man Sherchan who at that time was a deputy minister in the **B. P. Koirala** government led by the **Nepali Congress Party**, the arch rival of the **Communist Party of Nepal**. One night, he managed to remove the Congress party flag from his brother's residence and mounted in its place his Communist party flag.

SHERCHAN, DIWAKAR MAN (1950–). Politician and engineer. A member of the **Nepali Congress Party**, he was elected to the Upper House of **Parliament** in 1991 and later served as assistant minister for industries and labor under the Congress government headed by Prime Minister **Girija Prasad Koirala** (1991–1994).

SHERCHAN, YOGENDRA MAN (1933–1971). Born in the **Mustang** district, Yogendra Man was a very active member of the **Nepali Congress Party**. He served as deputy minister of **communications** in the very first Congress government headed by Prime Minister **B. P. Koirala**. Following the **palace coup** of December 1960, he was jailed along with Prime

Minister Koirala and many other Congress leaders. Some time after his release from the jail, the **Panchayat** forces murdered Yogendra Man in 1971.

SHERPA. People of Mongoloid origin, inhabiting the eastern foothills of the **Himalayas** around **Mount Everest**. They are believed to have migrated to Nepal from eastern **Tibet**. The word Sherpa is derived from the Tibetan language in which *shar* means "east" and *pa* means "people." They are recognized across the world as skilled **mountain** climbers. Thanks to their reputation, they have emerged as the primary support group for most mountain expeditions, often working as porters and guides. Mostly concentrated in the northeastern districts of Dolakha, Sindhupalchok, and Solokhumbu (*see* figure 2), the Sherpas normally follow **Lamaism**, along with shamanism, as part of their religious belief system. *See also* NORGAY (SHERPA), TENZING.

SHERPA, ANG DORJE. First Nepali (**Sherpa**) to reach the summit of **Mount Everest** without oxygen. He achieved this feat in 1978. Not too many Everest climbers have attempted or achieved it.

SHERPA, APA (1960–). He holds a record for scaling **Mount Everest** as he became the first climber to reach the top of Mount Everest for the thirteenth time. When he scaled the summit on 26 May 2003 as a member of a U.S. expedition—three days before the fiftieth anniversary of its first ascent on 29 May 1953—he improved his own enviable record of 12 successful climbs. *See also* HILLARY, SIR EDMUND; NORGAY (SHERPA), TENZING.

SHERPA, PASANG LHAMU (1960–1993). She is the first **woman** from Nepal to climb **Mount Everest**. Pasang Lhamu died at a tender age of 33 while returning to the base camp after reaching the summit.

SHERPA, SUNDARE (1956–1989). He successfully climbed **Mount Everest** five times between 1979 and 1988. He died in an accident in Solokhumbu in 1989.

SHERPA, TENZING NORGAY. *See* NORGAY (SHERPA), TENZING.

SHIVA (SIVA). **Hindu** god of destruction. One of the members of the **Hindu** trinity: **Brahma, Vishnu,** and Shiva. Like Vishnu, Shiva is widely followed and worshiped. Often presented in different forms and playing many different roles, he is perhaps the most dramatic and colorful of all the Hindu gods, with the possible exception of **Krishna.** He is simply many things to many people. He can be viewed as a symbol of sex, sometimes bordering on wildness (where **Tantrism** finds it roots), to a symbol of asceticism, total renouncement from sex and material life. He can shut the world out or let everything in. He may consume opium and drink poison to get high, totally oblivious to the world around him. He may dance like nobody can and entertain or he may entirely withdraw from the world and go into deep meditation. He is the ultimate metaphor of extremes. It is no surprise, therefore, that there are cult movements created around him.

SHIVALINGAM. Phallus emblem of **Shiva,** often found in combination with the vaginal emblem **Yoni.** It is widely worshiped, especially by those married women who have failed to conceive. They worship it, hoping to get pregnant and bear children. *See also* LINGAM; PASHUPATI.

SHRADDHA (SIDHA). **Hindu** ritual to pay homage to dead ancestors. It is observed every year on the day when the family member died. To carry out this ritual properly, a **Bahun** priest (Bahun *baje*) is invited to the house to perform the task. In return for his service, the Bahun *baje* receives certain items, usually food items, from the family. What they receive is called *sidha.*

SHREE KHANDA. Sandalwood (*Santalum album*) as well as paste made from it. This aromatic tree is regarded by **Hindus** as having religious significance. That is why on certain occasions paste (*chandan*) made from this tree is used to put a *tika* on one's forehead. Well-to-do Hindus take pride in cremating their dead family members with sandalwood.

SHRESTHA. High **Newar caste.** Sometimes lower caste Newars claimed to belong to the Shrestha lineage when they moved to a new place. In the Newar communities, it is a common surname.

SHRESTHA, BADRI PRASAD (1932–). Economist and scholar. He has written several books on the **economy** of Nepal and on economic planning. There is little doubt that he is a leading authority on the Nepali economy. Between 1975 and 1979, he was vice-chairman of the **National Planning Commission** and, later, member of the **National Development Council** (1986–1988). His views are highly recognized within Nepal as well as among the foreign development organizations there.

SHRESTHA, GANGA LAL (1918–1941). One of the four martyrs of Nepal who sacrificed their lives for democracy, he was an older brother of **Puspa Lal Shrestha**. A founding member of the nation's first political party—**Praja Parishad**—he was a highly popular revolutionary who fought against the oppressive **Rana** regime. He was executed by Prime Minister **Juddha Shamsher Rana** on 27 January 1941 for his anti-Rana stance and activities. What the Rana regime feared most about Ganga Lal was the fact that he had a large following within the **Newar** communities in the **Kathmandu Valley**, the central seat of the Rana government. Any mass movement among the Newars would pose a grave threat to their political survival because of their numerical strength and close proximity to the geographical base of Rana autocracy. *See also* MARTYRS' MEMORIAL.

SHRESTHA, GOPAL DAS (1901–1970). Noted journalist. He edited one of Nepal's first English daily newspapers called *The Commoner* published in **Kathmandu**. It was first published in 1956. Because of its anti-government position during the **Panchayat** period, when press freedom was extremely curtailed, the newspaper suffered as its publication was frequently banned. *See also* MEDIA.

SHRESTHA, GOPAL MAN (1947–). Politician and businessman from the Syangja district (*see* figure 2). He is a highly active member of the **Nepali Congress Party** in his district. Upon being elected to the **House of Representatives** in the 1991 general **elections**, he became minister of commerce in the first Congress cabinet headed by Prime Minister **Girija Prasad Koirala** (1991–1994). He was reelected to the House in the subsequent general election of 1994, but lost his district seat during the 1999 election to a candidate fielded by the **Communist Party of Nepal** (CPN–UML).

SHRESTHA, HIRANYA LAL (1941–). Political activist, journalist, and professor of political science. A noted orator and revolutionary, he spent 11 years in jail. He was elected to the **House of Representatives** from the Makwanpur district in the central **Tarai** in 1991 (*see* figure 2). As a nominee of the **Communist Party of Nepal** (CPN–UML), he was reelected from the same district in the 1994 general elections.

SHRESTHA, JUDDHA BAHADUR (1917–). Prominent industrialist and businessman from the Saptari district in the eastern **Tarai**. He was executive director of the **Biratnagar Jute Mills** (1956–1964), president of the Nepal Chamber of Commerce (1958), president of the Nepal Industry and Commerce Association (1967–1970), and executive director of the Morang Sugar Mill. In addition, Juddha Bahadur was appointed chairperson of the **Royal Nepal Airlines Corporation** in 1991. He has also authored articles on commerce and **industry** related topics.

SHRESTHA, KRISHNA BHAKTA (1940–). Journalist. He served as editor in chief of *The Rising Nepal*, *Madhuparka* and *Gorakhapatra* (1991–1993). Despite his journalistic achievements as editor in chief of two major dailies, his record of contribution to journalistic growth and advancement in the country remains fuzzy.

SHRESTHA, MARICHMAN SINGH (1942–). Politician from the hill district of Salyan. He began his political career as a leftist activist and schoolteacher. Since the end of the **Malla** rule in the **Kathmandu Valley** in 1769, no **Newar** had ever been appointed or elected to lead a government of Nepal. He is the first Newar to have risen to prime ministership (1986–1990), thus breaking the monopolistic grip on this post by the **Bahun-Chhetri** axis. Upon joining the **Panchayat** system, he emerged as a diehard royalist who, in his capacity as Panchayat prime minister, took extremely harsh measures against the pro-democracy movement and its participants in the early 1990s. As the movement intensified, King **Birendra Bir Bikram Shah** removed him as prime minister because of his failure to derail the movement and appointed **Lokendra Bahadur Chand** to serve as prime minister who also failed to reverse the course of the movement. Only 13 days later the Panchayat system collapsed. He appears to have deliberately kept his political profile low since the return of democracy.

SHRESTHA, MATHURA PRASAD (1936–). A physician and professor of medicine at the Teaching Hospital, he played a very active role in the pro-democracy movement of 1990, mobilizing medical personnel for humanitarian as well as political causes. He was appointed to serve as minister of health in the interim government (1990–1991). In addition, he is a leading **human rights** activist.

SHRESTHA, NATI KAJI (1925–). A popular singer and musician who is associated with **Radio Nepal**. He has recorded many songs and won several awards for his immense contribution to the enhancement and promotion of Nepali **music**.

SHRESTHA, PUSPA LAL (1924–1978). Initially from the hill district of Ramechhap, he was a popular face both within the **Kathmandu** circle and in Nepali politics. The husband of **Sahana Pradhan**, he was a fiery and charismatic leader of the **Communist Party of Nepal**, which he helped to found and diligently build. In some quarters of the **Kathmandu Valley**, his name still engenders a great deal of fond memories and reverence. Guided by his unyielding motto that the political party should be policy-oriented rather than personality-driven, Puspa Lal Shrestha fought hard against injustice and tyranny from the time he was a teenager. He passed away on 22 July 1978.

SHRESTHA, SIDDHI CHARAN (1912–1992). Born in Okhaldhunga on 22 May 1912, he was one of the most prominent literary figures in Nepal. He dedicated his entire life to epic writing and was known as Yuga Kavi (the poet of his time). A member of the first generation of modern Nepali poets, he grew up under **Rana** autocracy. His poetry often reflects the period of social turbulence under which he lived. He is regarded as a champion of both Nepali and **Newari** poetry and some three dozens of his works have been published. In addition to writing poetry, he also served as editor of the important monthly literary journal *Sharada* and of *Gorkhapatra*. He won several awards for his enormous contribution to Nepali **literature**.

SHRESTHA, TEK BAHADUR (1942–). Born in the town of **Pokhara**, he graduated from the town's first high school in the early 1960s. He was one of the very few early high school graduates of **Pokhara**, which at that time was basically a small bucolic commercial outpost in the central hills.

Upon graduation in first class, he received a scholarship to study at a university in **India** and earned his B.Sc. degree in **agriculture**. Following that he entered the civil service sector of the government of Nepal. He was later sent to study at Australian National University where he obtained a master's degree in agricultural economics. Climbing through the ranks, he has reached a secretariat level position within the government.

SHRESTHA, TULSI MEHER (1896–1978). He is a person of humble origins. Tulsi Meher entered the field of social service in 1926 by propagating the significance of **education**. He was trained by the late Mahatma Gandhi to spin and weave clothes at Sabarmati Ashram, **India**. He was the founder of Nepal Charkha Pracharak Gandhi Smarak Mahaguthi. This bachelor social worker was honored with the prestigious Nehru Award for International Understanding in 1977 in recognition of his tireless social service work.

SHRI (SHREE; SRI). Respectful form of addressing someone. In a way, it is similar to "Mr. or Mrs." in English.

SIDDHARTHA GAUTAMA. See BUDDHA.

SIDDHARTHA NAGAR. Commonly known as Bhairahawa and located in the Rupandehi district, it is one of earliest cities in the **Tarai** to be settled by hill migrants. Its history is similar to that of **Narayanghat** in that they were both predominantly settled, built, and dominated by hill migrants and at about the same time—in the mid 1950s. Even their climatic conditions are the same. One notable difference between the two is that while Bhairahawa was largely populated by **Newar** and **Thakali** merchants from **Pokhara**, **Narayanghat** was mainly inhabited by merchants from the dying hilltop town of Bandipur in Tanahun. The name was adopted from Siddhartha Gautama (*see* **Buddha**). Situated near the Indian border and featuring a domestic airport, it is a relatively vibrant town. In recent years, it has suffered somewhat because it was bypassed as a major point on the east-west highway. *See also* MAHENDRA RAJMARGA.

SIDDHARTHA RAJPATH. Highway between **Pokhara** and Sunauli at the Indian border. Nearly 190 kilometers long, it is one of the earliest highways in Nepal. It was completed in 1964 with Indian aid. Initially called **Pokhara**-Sunauli highway, it was later given its current name after Siddhartha Gautama (*see* **Buddha**).

SINDHULI, THE BATTLE OF. Battle fought in 1767 between **Prithvi Narayan Shah**'s army and the British troops that were sent to assist King **Jayaprakash Malla** against Prithvi Narayan's invasion of **Kathmandu**. It is reported that the British troops were repelled by the Gorkhali forces, thus neutralizing other potential British attempts to assist the **Malla** kingdoms and prevent them from succumbing to Prithvi Narayan's imperial ambitions.

SINDOOR (SINDUR). Vermillion flour used to make *tika* to place on one's forehead as a sign of blessing or during auspicious celebrations. If a Nepali woman sprinkles some dry *sindoor* at the front point of her hair partition, that symbolizes she is married and her husband is alive. It is an indispensable ingredient of any celebrative *puja* (worship). On the other hand, it is an absolute taboo in anything that involves mourning, for it is a symbol of joyous celebration,

SINGH, BHOGENDRA MAN (1931–1950). Revolutionary. He was shot dead by the police during the **Rana** regime when he organized a prison revolt inside the jail after being arrested during revolutionary struggles in 1950. His murder further fanned the fire already burning across the country against Rana autocracy, thus hastening its downfall in early 1951.

SINGH, GAJENDRA NARAYAN (1929–2000). Politician. He began his career as a member of the **Nepali Congress Party**. However, following the return of democracy in early 1990, he founded his own party called the **Nepal Sadbhavana Party** and became its founding president. He was elected to the **House of Representatives** from the Saptari district (*see* figure 2) during the 1991 general **elections**. He was reelected in the subsequent general election held in 1994.

SINGH, GANESHMAN (1915–1997). A true leader in every sense of the word and one of the greatest and boldest fighters for democracy that Nepal has ever seen, Ganeshman was almost beaten to death by the **Rana** regime for his anti-Rana activities. During the revolution of 1951, he played a paramount role as he was in charge of the **Birganj** front. Because Birganj was the most direct and critical route to take over **Kathmandu**, Ganeshman was entrusted by his **Nepali Congress Party** (NCP) with a major responsibility.

Although the NCP's success led to the demise of the Rana regime, it was not given the opportunity to form a government and organize national elections. When the party finally came to power in 1959 following its resounding victory in the general elections, Singh served as a full minister in **B. P. Koirala**'s short-lived government. But in 1960 King **Mahendra Bir Bikram Shah** overthrew the Koirala government and jailed Singh, along with Prime Minister Koirala for eight years. Then came 1990, when Ganeshman Singh led the pro-democracy revolution that brought down the **Panchayat** system. As a result, democracy was restored. However, when the interim government was formed after the downfall of the Panchayat raj, he chose not to serve as prime minister. Instead, he asked **Krishna Prasad Bhattarai**, a senior Congress leader, to head the interim government.

Singh is perhaps the only NCP leader who could match B. P. Koirala with regard to stature, respect, contribution, and name recognition. After Koirala's death, he was the embodiment of the Nepali Congress Party. Following the resurrection of democracy in 1990, he was called the supreme leader of the NCP and emerged as Nepal's elder statesman. For his tireless and lifelong dedication to the cause of democracy, he was honored with a U Thant Peace award in 1990 and United Nations Human Rights award in 1994. So far, he is the only Nepali to have received these awards.

SINGH, KHADGA MAN (1907–). Revolutionary against the **Rana** rule. He was arrested and imprisoned for 20 years (1930–1950), and was released when the Rana regime ended in 1951. He later served as ambassador to Pakistan, Iran, and Turkey.

SINGH, K. I. (1906–1982). Kunwar Indrajeet Singh, he was popularly known as Dr. K. I. Singh. He once served as prime minister for a period of four months in 1957. Generally a passionate advocate of democracy, he was a relatively wild or unpredictable political leader, somewhat impulsive in his action. K. I. Singh died of throat cancer in 1982. There is a small bridge in **Pokhara** built during his brief prime ministership that was named after him.

SINGH, MANGALA DEVI (1924–1996). Born in **Kathmandu** and married to **Ganeshman Singh**, she remained politically active, taking part in various activities. She played a role in founding the **Nepal Women's Association** based in Kathmandu.

SINGH, P. L. (1940–). Member of the **Nepali Congress Party** and son of **Ganeshman Singh**. As mayor of **Kathmandu**, the capital and largest city in the country, he is a relatively popular political figure in the country and certainly a highly visible personality within the party. His position is further enhanced by his family link to Ganeshman Singh, as his name is instantly recognized.

SINGH, RAMRAJA PRASAD (1936–). Although anti-**Panchayat** in his sentiment, Ramraja launched his political career as a member of the Rastriya Panchayat in 1971, namely as one of the four members of its graduate constituency—one that was composed of those with at least a bachelor's degree. He became a vocal critic of the system from within. Consequently, he was jailed and later released. Following his release, he went into self-exile in **India** in 1981. He was charged with the crime of masterminding a bombing operation in **Kathmandu** (including the royal palace). In 1987, he was actually prosecuted and sentenced to death in absentia. Following the overthrow of the Panchayat system, he was granted amnesty in 1991.

SINGHA DURBAR. Nepal's **Parliament** building built by **Chandra Shamsher Rana**. The biggest edifice in the country, originally containing 404 rooms, it once housed the entire ministries and secretariats, some of which are now housed in other buildings in order to accommodate their space needs.

SISSO. Large tropical tree (*Delbergia sisso*) abundant in riverine **forests** of the **Tarai**. It is a source of quality timber.

SITA (SEETA). Daughter of **Janak** married to **Rama** and heroine of the *Ramayana* epic. In a traditional sense, Sita is highly revered as an ideal woman, a symbol of chastity, fidelity, or *patibrata* (selfless and unquestioning devotion to one's husband). In fact, she has been declared as one of the national heroines of Nepal. In modern times, however, the same Sita is seen through an entirely different prism by those who espouse a women's liberation viewpoint. To them, Sita certainly deserves respect, but she is no heroine. She is rather a symbol and repressive justification of continued **Hindu** oppression of women, as any woman who fails to act like Sita is subject to vilification and condemnation.

SLAVERY. Known as *das pratha* (*das* = slave; *pratha* = tradition), it is not clear when the slavery system began in Nepal. In all likelihood, however, its origin in the nation dates back many centuries. Since slaves were regarded as **Sudras** during the formation of the **caste system** in **India**, a country which has historically influenced Nepal's cultural process and patterns, it is very likely that the *das pratha* was introduced to Nepal from India following the first wave of Indian immigrants about a 1,000 years ago (*see* **Ethnicity**).

Although one can find references to slavery throughout the hills of Nepal and among various ethnic groups, perhaps the total number of slaves never exceeded 100,000 at any given time. Nonetheless, the fact that Prime Minister **Bhimsen Thapa** attempted to abolish it as early as 1824 suggests that either the number was considered to be substantial enough or the issue was serious enough to raise concerns within his policy circle. In the meantime, what one can also surmise from his failure to emancipate slaves is that the entrenched pro-slavery forces were too powerful to overcome even for a dominant prime minister like Bhimsen Thapa, who wielded unparalleled power during his time. So the institution continued.

Historical accounts indicate that Nepal's slavery system was mostly tied to debt bondage rather being hereditary. As a result, the father could technically be free, but his sons (and daughters) would be held in slavery to work as domestic and field hands for their masters until the father paid back the debt. Even after the indebted individual died, his family members, namely those who could work (a source of productive labor), would be held responsible for the debt. In general, the amount of debt determined the number of family members held as slaves who could be bought, sold, or hired out for work.

There are many accounts of slaves fleeing the hills to gain freedom. To Prime Minister **Chandra Shamsher Rana**, who used the term "exodus" to describe the escape of slaves, the *das pratha* was not only a matter of humanitarian concerns. It was also an important national economic issue that needed to be addressed. In his successful 1924 appeal for the abolition of slavery in Nepal, Chandra Shamsher stated: "An exodus of population from whatever cause is a source of anxiety and much concern for the Government of the country. This institution of slavery is a fruitful source of such exodus and is much worse than the temporary absence of freemen in quest of remunerative employment abroad. . . . The absence of slaves, away in a foreign land, brings loss and trouble to their masters—loss because of the money value of the slave which has now to be written off, and trouble because the owner depended on the slave for the carrying on of his work. [I]t is curious that the masters . . . should feel abolition as a hardship and be under the apprehension that their everyday work will come to a standstill. Is it that the owners fear that with the abolition of the status of slavery the slaves themselves will vanish? This absurd idea requires only to be stated to be rejected. [S]laves are our own people and why should we be afraid of dislocation in work by abolishing the status?"

With this forceful and economically grounded call from Chandra Shamsher, the institution of slavery came to an end in 1924, exactly a 100 years after Bhimsen Thapa's attempt to retire it. In order to give emancipated slaves a new life, **Amlekhganj**, which literally means "a settlement (colony) of freed slaves," was set up in the central **Tarai**, quite removed from the hills, so that their former masters could not harass them due to geographical proximity. It was set up to resettle approximately 52,000 slaves freed in the early 1900s and was designed as an agricultural settlement in that new settlers would have access to sufficient land as a valuable resource base on which to build a new and economically viable life.

SMALL FARMERS DEVELOPMENT PROJECT. Project launched since 1975 by the **Agriculture Development Bank** to mobilize rural savings and investments in small farmers groups. How much this project has actually helped small farmers improve their economic lot and augment agricultural productivity remains unclear. *See also* AGRICULTURE.

SNOW LEOPARD. Called *him* (snow) *chituwa* (leopard) in Nepali, they are considered endangered. In Nepal, they are found in the **Rara, Shephoksundo, Langtang,** and **Sagarmatha National Parks.**

SOCIAL CLASSES AND STRATIFICATION. In terms of differences in wealth and access to political power, Nepal can be divided into: a small but powerful ruling elite class; a growing class of government officials, large landholders, and merchants; and a vast majority of peasants and workers. These divisions are descriptive, functional categories rather than social class entities based on the Marxist concept of the social relations of production. In a way, all three classes are a long continuum in Nepal's social structure.

Even though the peasant population as a whole faces similar economic and technological circumstances, it contains several strata in terms of landholdings, relative economic dependence, or social class status. Landholding is the primary determinant of one's economic position and social standing, however. While those with small or no landholdings are economically dependent and vulnerable, relatively large landholders both enjoy economic security and control local social institutions and political processes. The social, economic, and educational advantages of this segment make its members relatively homogeneous in terms of their shared interest. They generally aspire to achieve a middle or elite class status. Numerically, however, this group is quite small. Small landholders constitute the bulk of the rural population in Nepal—around 50 percent—followed by landless peasants.

The smallest and least diverse of the three social classes is the ruling elite, largely composed of high-**caste**, educated *paharis*, usually from the **Bahun** and **Chhetri** castes. Moreover, its number is relatively constant. Unlike this group, the second social class has witnessed a steady growth in its number. Its growth is largely attributed to the continued expansion of Nepali bureaucratic and development activities. In the absence of employment opportunities in the industrial and commercial sectors, the continued growth of bureaucracy has emerged as a path of least resistance to absorb an increasing number of the educated class. In addition, some growth in the service sector over the past 30 years has contributed to an increased pool of this class.

Since the early 1980s, many people with a college or university level **education**, namely those residing in the **Kathmandu Valley**, have discovered a second and lucrative employment outlet in the area of development consultancy. Because of the growing pressure on foreign donors to hire Nepali consultants for development feasibility and evaluation projects, development consulting firms and associated services have sprouted throughout the Valley and have been able to tap into a large pool of **foreign aid** money poured into the country. As a result, they have managed to generate a measurable number of jobs in the Valley. This opportunity has allowed many of the more educated to climb Nepal's socioeconomic ladder as they have attained a middle-class status. *See also* ETHNICITY.

SOUTH ASIAN ASSOCIATION FOR REGIONAL COOPERATION (SAARC). It was established when its charter was adopted on 8 December 1985 by Bangladesh, Bhutan, **India**, Maldives, Nepal, Pakistan, and Sri Lanka, which comprise its seven member nations. It is headquartered in **Kathmandu**, the capital city of Nepal.

SAARC is a regional association based on the consciousness that in an increasingly interdependent world, the objectives of peace, freedom, social justice, and economic prosperity are best achieved in the South Asian region by fostering mutual understanding, good neighborly relations and meaningful cooperation among the member states which are bound by ties of history, culture, and larger (regional) geography.

Founded on the five fundamental principles of sovereign equality, territorial integrity, political independence, noninterference in the internal affairs of other states, and mutual benefit, the main objectives of the SAARC charter are as follows:

- To promote the welfare of the peoples of South Asia and improve their quality of life.
- To accelerate South Asia's economic growth, social progress, and cultural development and to provide all individuals the opportunity to live in dignity and realize their full potential.
- To promote and strengthen collective self-reliance among the South Asian countries.
- To contribute to mutual trust, understanding, and appreciation of one another's problems.
- To promote active collaboration and mutual assistance in regional economic, social, cultural, technical, and scientific fields.
- To strengthen cooperation with other developing countries.
- To strengthen cooperation among themselves in international forums on matters of common interest.
- To cooperate with international and regional organizations with similar aims and purposes.

The eleventh SAARC summit meeting was held in Kathmandu on 6 January 2002 and was attended by the heads of state or government of all seven members. In the declaration of this summit meeting, they reaffirmed their commitment to regional cooperation through SAARC and underscored the importance of annual summit meetings to chart common strategies for the realization of the objectives and principles set out in its charter. In addition, they solemnly renewed their pledge to strengthen the association and make it more cohesive, result-oriented, and forward looking, by adopting clearly defined programs and effective implementation strategies in line with expectations. To give effect to the shared aspirations for a more prosperous South Asia, the leaders agreed to the vision of a phased and planned process eventually leading to a South Asian Economic Union.

Despite its lofty objectives and shared vision of a prosperous South Asia, SAARC has generally failed to live up to its promise. It has yet to harness its potential and exercise its regional significance. From the very outset, it has faced a major hurdle, the one associated with the lingering conflict and distrust between its two biggest members and arch rivals: India and Pakistan.

STHAPIT, CHINIYA KAJI (1937–1951). Martyr. He was killed during the post-**Rana** coalition government (1951) headed by Prime Minister **Mohan Shamsher Rana**. He was killed on 6 November 1951 when a gang of police fired on a student protest procession without any authorization from **B. P. Koirala** who, as the coalition government's minister of home affairs, was fully responsible for all internal security affairs and issues, including law and order. That tragic incident triggered a chain reaction in Nepal's volatile political landscape. On 10 November 1951, Koirala and other cabinet members of his **Nepali Congress Party** faction in the coalition resigned. This mass resignation severely undermined Prime Minister Mohan Shamsher's legitimacy and hold on power. Two days later on 12 November, Mohan Shamsher tendered his resignation, thus paving the way for King **Tribhuvan Bir Bikram Shah** to form a new government. In short, Chiniya Kaji's death hastened the inevitable dissolution of the unholy coalition between the two antagonistic forces: the Rana and Nepali Congress.

STILLER, LUDWIG F. Father Stiller came to Nepal as a missionary back in 1956 to teach at **St. Xavier's School** in Jawalkhel. He later became a Nepali citizen in 1969, earning his Ph.D. in history from **Tribhuvan University**. Because of his significant contribution to the historiography of Nepal through his writings, he is regarded by many as a leading historian of Nepal. His publications include *The Rise of the House of Gorkha* (1975) and *The Silent Cry* (1976), both published in Nepal.

STUPA. Funeral tumulus built by the recipients of the divided ashes of the **Buddha**. Some contend that originally the stupa began as an earthen burial mound which was revered by the local population, but the cult of the stupa was taken up by Buddhist adherents as **Ashok** built stupas in the Buddha's honor all over **India** and beyond, including Nepal. The two most famous stupas in Nepal are **Swayambhu** and **Baudhanath**.

Regardless of the original purpose behind its creation, the stupa has come to represent in Nepal a distinct, though simple, architectural style that is intimately associated with **Buddhism** and its offshoot **Lamaism**. It is a dome-shaped construction; standing on the dome is a relatively tall structure with a pointed top, symbolically soaring toward heaven. *See also* ART AND ARCHITECTURE.

SUDRA. Labor **caste**, often relegated to menial and dirty work. It is the lowest of the four caste groups that is treated as **untouchable**.

SUNDARI CHOWK. (*Sundari* = beautiful; *Chowk* = courtyard.) It is a famous courtyard in the **Patan Durbar Square**. In its center lies a sunken waterspout called Tusha Hiti, which is known for exquisitely carved, small images of various deities encircling it. The courtyard is flanked by finely carved wooden doors, windows, and roof struts.

SUNDARIJAL. Combination of Sundari (beautiful) plus *Jal* (water). It is a scenic place situated in the northeast corner of **Kathmandu**. It has a power plant built in 1934, with a peak capacity to generate 640 kilowatts of electricity, as well as a reservoir that supplies water to Kathmandu.

SUN KOSI HYDROELECTRIC PROJECT. Power plant in the Sun Kosi River at Lamosangu, with a capacity of 10,050 kilowatts. It was built in 1973 with Indian assistance.

SUNUWAR (SUNAR). Small professional **caste** group belonging to the **Sudra** caste. Traditionally, they are goldsmiths.

SUPREME COURT. Sarbocha (supreme) Adalat (court) in Nepal. In accordance with the **constitution** of 1990, it is a court of record with the power to impose punishment for contempt of itself or its lower courts. It has ordinary and extraordinary jurisdictions and the power to command writs such as habeas corpus, mandamus, prohibition, and quo warranto. It is headed by a chief justice who is appointed by the king. *See also* JUDICIAL SYSTEM.

SURUWAL. It is a pajama-like garment that covers the whole length of the legs from the waist down to the ankles. The basic difference between the two garments is that the *suruwal* is tapered in width. It is quite wide at the top and gradually narrows toward the ankles. This garment is invariably paired with *daura*. *See* DAURA-SURUWAL.

SURYA GRAHAN. Solar eclipse (*sun* = surya; *grahan* = eclipse.) It is a religious event observed on the day of the solar eclipse. *Grahan* is generally believed to represent bad omens. Their observance is, thus, highlighted by fasting and ceremonial bathing to fend off evil spirits. Gifts of such items as clothes, money, grains, and salt are given to the sweeper **caste** called the Pode (Pore) during the eclipse. Through this act of giving, the givers would transfer whatever bad outcome the eclipse brought to them to the Podes. In other words, the Podes would willingly bear other people's burden or curse of the eclipse. In fact, whenever an eclipse occurs, the Podes go from door to door in their neighborhoods, uttering "*grahan, grahan*" and collecting whatever they are offered. *See also* CHANDRA GRAHAN.

SWARGA (SWORGA). Heaven. In **Hindu** mythology, it is the place of benevolence, good deeds, happiness, and peace. It is the domain of gods ruled by **Indra**. The opposite of *swarga* is **Narak**.

SWARGA DWARI. Vedic *ashram* (shrine), hilltop pilgrimage center in Pyuthan. It essentially means the gateway to **swarga** (heaven). Precisely because of this Vedic or religious significance, many Hindus from both **India** and Nepal visit this place.

SWASTIKA. Auspicious symbol of well-being in both **Hinduism** and **Buddhism**. It is painted at places like the entrance of a house. It is said to have been derived from a wheel, reduced to four spokes at right angles to indicate the cardinal points. In terms of meaning and practice, it has no connection to the Nazi swastika symbol, although the two symbols exhibit a close resemblance. It is, however, possible that they both share an Aryan root.

SWAYAMBAR. Marriage ritual in which the bride and groom place ornate flower garlands around each other's neck. It is equivalent to an exchange of rings, vows, and kisses in Christian weddings.

SWAYAMBHU. It is a world renowned **Buddhist stupa** in **Kathmandu**. In addition to its enormous religious significance, it is a marvelous architectural piece with the colorful symbolic "Third Eye" (that is, inner eye, one that symbolizes enlightenment) embossed on all four sides of its top structure pointing toward heaven. Some two thousand years old, Swayambhu features the world's largest gilded image of the **Buddha**. The stupa is regarded as a symbol of world peace. Situated on a hilltop, with an approach of four hundred steps, it is also a religious complex adorned with a mosaic of small *chaityas* and **pagoda** temples. It is one of the holiest Buddhist pilgrimage centers in the world.

SYANGBOCHE. Sherpa village in Solokhumbu (*see* figure 2). It features the world's highest hotel—Hotel Everest View situated at the height of about 4,000 meters—and a famous monastery.

T

TABLA **(*TABALA*).** Classical drumlike musical instrument that is very popular throughout South Asia, including Nepal. This instrument is increasingly gaining popularity in the West as it has now been used in some new **music**.

TAGADHARI. Generic term used to refer to high-**caste Hindus**, namely **Bahuns** and **Chhetris**, who wear so-called sacred threads to suggest their caste purity by refraining from consuming alcohol and certain (in some cases all) meats that are considered polluting such as pig, chicken, and buffalo meats. In contemporary Nepal, however, the notion of Tagadhari is largely a matter of principle rather than practice. While Bahuns and Chhetris still wear sacred threads, not too many of them abstain from consuming alcohol and meats. So the historical correlation between caste purity and Tagadhari status as defined in terms of abstinence from alcohol and meat consumption is largely a matter of fiction that the Bahun-Chhetri axis has managed to perpetuate their dominant position in society. *See also* JANAI; MATAWALI.

TAMANG. One of the major hill tribes belonging to the **Tibeto-Nepali** segment of the population. Unlike the **Gurung, Limbu, Magar,** and **Rai** groups, the Tamangs were rarely treated as a martial tribe by the British **Gorkha** army recruiters; they seldom gave priority to this group in their recruitment efforts. From a religious perspective, they tend to follow **Lamaist Buddhism** as most other hill tribal groups of Mongoloid origin. *See also* ETHNICITY.

TAMANG, SHAMBHU (1956–). Mountain climber and guide. He is the first Nepali to climb **Mount Everest** from both the Nepali and Chinese sides. He is also believed to be the youngest climber to reach Mount Everest—at the age of 17 (1973).

TAMRAKAR, RAM KRISHNA (1943–). Politician and businessman from the Rupandehi district in the central **Tarai** (*see* figure 2). An active member of the **Nepali Congress Party**, he ran for a parliamentary seat in the 1991 general **elections** under the banner of his party and was elected to the **House of Representatives**. Subsequently, he was appointed to serve as minister of industries in the Congress government headed by **Girija Prasad Koirala** (1991–1994). He lost his House seat to a candidate fielded by the **Communist Party of Nepal** (UML) in the 1994 election, but regained it in the 1999 election.

TANAKPUR. Place or site of a hydroelectric project on the Mahakali River that flows along the border between Nepal and **India**. The Tanakpur project has been a source of political controversy in Nepal. *See* PURNAGIRI DAM CONTROVERSY.

TANKA (THANKA). Hanging scroll-type paintings based on traditional calligraphy called Paubha. It is a **Tibetan** style of religious painting on canvas, depicting various aspects of **Buddhism** and **Buddha**'s life and containing sexual symbolism, architectural structures, geometric diagrams, and others. It involves extremely intricate and detailed work, often associated with **Tantrism**. In Nepal, it is usually done by **Newar** artists and sold extensively in **Kathmandu** and **Patan**. **Asan Tol** is one of the prime locations for the sampling and purchase of Tanka paintings.

TANTRISM. Cult of belief in mystic mantras and magical spells. It is closely associated with some variations of **Buddhism** and **Hinduism** in Nepal. It involves worship as propitiation of deities, especially female divinities, as well as use of magic designs like Yantra (divine machine). **Vajra** or Bajra (thunderbolt) is a common instrument used in this tradition as a symbol of destruction of evil-doers.

TARA. Popular female divinity in **Vajrayana Buddhism** that exists in many forms, e.g., Harit Tara (green), Khadga Jogini (blue), Bhrikuti (yellow), and Kurukulla (red). In **Hinduism**, it is one of the forms of Goddess **Kali** or **Durga**. Linguistically, it means "star."

TARAI. Subtropical lowlands in southern Nepal; northern extension of the Gangetic Plain in **India**. A narrow strip of land containing 20 out of 75 administrative districts of Nepal, it stretches all the way from east to west along the border, running parallel to the Hill Region situated to its north. Because of its growing population and its status as the "granary" of Nepal, its political clout within the country is increasing. As the Tarai was considered the country's land frontier from the mid-1950s until the late-1970s, the government of Nepal launched its land resettlement policy in the region to settle hill migrants, starting with the **Rapti Valley Development Project** in the **Chitwan** district in 1956 (*see* figure 2). Although the policy of land resettlement has essentially been discontinued because of the fact that much of the available Tarai land has been used up, the *paharis* have continued to relocate to the Tarai in search of land. As a result, it has experienced the highest rate of population growth in the country since the mid-1950s.

TEMPLE CARVINGS. Wood and stone carvings, particularly those of a Tantric bent. Of particular interest are explicit depictions of various postures of human sexual intercourse. As such, they are a lively subject of discussions and comments among Westerners who happen to view them. It is not clear why such depictions are so common, particularly in the **Kathmandu Valley**. They do, however, indicate an interesting mix of art, architecture, and religion.

TEMPO. It is a three-wheeled motor vehicle widely used throughout the **Kathmandu Valley** and in the **Tarai** towns. It is a popular means of **transportation** that is relatively fast and carries up to six passengers at a time. In light of the Kathmandu Valley's growing air **pollution**, it has widely been viewed as a primary source. Attempts have been made to ban it from the Valley.

THAKALI. Relatively small in number and highly concentrated in the upper reaches of the **Kali Gandaki River**, they are perhaps the most enterprising of all the **Tibeto-Nepali** groups. The origin of the word Thakali is often traced to a river (*khola*) named Thakhola, which is a tributary of Kali Gandaki and flows through the geographical domain of this group. In other words, Thakali means "the inhabitants of Thakhola." Historically engaged in **Trans-Himalayan** trade, they have become settled merchants. In the past 40 years, they migrated to various urban centers throughout Nepal.

THAKUR, MAHANTA (1942–). As a member of the **Nepali Congress Party**, he was elected to the **House of Representatives** in 1991 from the Sarlahi district in the **Tarai** (*see* figure 2). He is one of the few members of the House to be elected in the two subsequent **elections** held in 1994 and 1999. He is also active with Amnesty International in Nepal.

THAKURI. Group of people belonging to the Indo-Nepali group, they are mostly concentrated in the western hills of Nepal. They belong to the **Chhetri caste** in terms of broad categorization.

THAPA, AMAR SINGH (1761–1816). Renowned military general in the early 1800s who played a key role in Nepal's continued campaign of territorial expansion. However, in 1814, a war broke out between the Nepali and East India (British) forces. Almost two years later, Nepal surrendered (*see* **Anglo-Nepal War**). After the surrender, the old general went to **Gosaikunda** under the pretext of retirement. According to some accounts, he secretly met with some Chinese officials to negotiate Chinese intervention against the British, but came back empty-handed. This true patriot of Nepal died on 16 August 1816.

THAPA, BHEKH BAHADUR (1937–). Economist and civil servant. He earned his Ph.D. degree from the **United States**, and was later selected to serve in various capacities within the government of Nepal. In the mid-1960s, he was appointed governor of the **Nepal Rastra Bank** (1966–1967), and later minister of finance (1974–1976). He was ambassador to the United States (1981–1985).

THAPA, BHIMSEN (1772–1839). Bhimsen Thapa, regarded as the first prime minister of Nepal, was the most prominent figure of the Thapa *bhardari* (courtier) clan of Nepal before the rise of the **Rana** rule in 1846. In his capacity as military general and prime minister, he controlled Nepal's political machinery for 31 years (1806–1837). During his long tenure, Nepal experienced both a dramatic rise and colossal fall as it made its most expansive territorial gains through military conquests and suffered its most humiliating military defeat. Following the signing of the **Treaty of Sagauli** in 1916, Nepal suddenly shrank as it lost about one-half of its territory (*see* **Anglo-Nepal War**).

Despite his political fame and fortunes, no national leader in the recorded history of Nepal was ever fated to the kind of gruesome and humiliating death that Bhimsen suffered. Subsequent to his removal from prime ministership, he was jailed. While in jail, unseemly rumors were passed to him, including one about his wife. He was told that his wife was paraded naked through the city's streets. Later, a ***khukri*** (Nepali knife) was strategically placed in his jail cell to entice him to commit suicide. Old, isolated, and disgraced, he slashed his own throat with the *khukri* to end his life. But the end was not so quick as he lingered for eight days in pain. He died a gruesome death with the final end coming on 28 July 1839. Even after his death, he was not given a proper funeral. Instead, his body was dismembered and the remains were scattered on river banks to be devoured by dogs and vultures. Following the **sati** custom, his wife burned herself to death on his funeral pyre. Before immolating herself she cursed Nepal to be forever subjected to corrupt, despotic, and mischievous leaders, a curse that later became known as the *satisarap* or *satishrap* (*sarap* or *shrap* = curse). The identical *sarap* is also believed to have been uttered during the **Malla** period by the sati wife of a Malla courtier named Bhim Malla.

THAPA, BISHWA BANDHU (1927–). Politician. He began his career as a member of the **Nepali Congress Party**. He was widely viewed as a key figure and rising star of the party. However, soon after the **palace coup** of 1960, he renounced his Congress party affiliation and openly embraced the **Panchayat** system, totally controlled by the king. For this, King **Mahendra Bir Bikram Shah** rewarded him by appointing him as minister of home in 1962 and as vice-chairman of the Council of Ministers in 1964. The king also appointed Bishwa Bandhu chairman of the **Back-to-the-Village National Campaign** of which he became a leading conceptual architect during its formative years.

THAPA, DHARMA RAJ (1924–?). Nepali lyrical poet, songwriter, and folksinger. Born and raised in **Pokhara**, he has published several collections of folk songs and poems from all corners and ethnic groups of Nepal and received several awards for his contributions. He is a highly recognized name within the Nepali **music** and literary circle. He is widely regarded as the Jhyaure Kabi, the poet (*kabi*) of folk songs and music (*jhyaure*), because he took a leading role in popularizing this genre of poetry and music in Nepal. He deserves a great deal of credit for the much-deserved rise of *jhyaure* music in the country.

THAPA, LAKHAN (?–1875). It is believed that he was the forerunner of political martyrdom in Nepal during the **Rana** period. He was killed for organizing a revolt in **Gorkha** against the extremism of Prime Minister **Jang Bahadur Rana**.

THAPA, MATHBAR SINGH (1798–1845). Renowned military officer and nephew of **Bhimsen Thapa**. He was instrumental in Nepal's territorial expansion in the west. He was removed from office and imprisoned during the purge of Bhimsen Thapa in July 1837. Upon his release from jail, he went to live in Simla. He returned to **Kathmandu** in April 1843 and was appointed prime minister and commander in chief on 26 December 1843. He resigned on 13 May 1844, but was reappointed in October 1844. He was assassinated on 17 May 1845 by his own nephew **Jang Bahadur Rana**.

THAPA, SURYA BAHADUR (1928–). A political personality who is no less known for his inability to pass a civil service exam than for his ability to survive in Nepal's volatile politics, specifically prior to the second coming of democracy in 1990. During that period he served as prime minister several times, starting with his first appointment by King **Mahendra Bir Bikram Shah** as chairman of the Council of Ministers (a post equivalent to prime ministership) in early 1964. He last served as prime minister between 1980 and 1984 during the **Panchayat** period. In addition, he served as prime minister in the post-1990 period when his right-wing **National Democratic Party** formed a coalition government which lasted less than a year (6 October 1997 to 11 April 1998). When Prime Minister **Lokendra Bahadur Chand** was compelled to resign, on 4 June 2003 King **Gyanendra Bir Bikram Shah** named Surya Bahadur Thapa—a hardcore royalist—as Nepal's new prime minister (*see* Chronology).

THAPATHALI, TREATY OF. Treaty signed between Nepal and **Tibet** on 24 March 1856, following the Nepal-Tibet War of 1854–1856, in Thapathali, a neighborhood in **Kathmandu**. As part of this treaty, Tibet agreed to pay Nepal an annual tribute in the amount of 10,000 rupees, along with the mutual exemption of customs and cooperation in case of attacks from a third country.

THAPA, YAGYA BAHADUR (1917–1978). Revolutionary affiliated with the military wing of the **Nepali Congress Party** in the 1970s when it was banned. A military strategist who planned to dethrone the monarchy in the late 1970s, he was arrested during his attempt to capture Okhaldhunga (*see* figure 2). He was later shot to death in a forest south of **Hetauda** in 1978.

THARU. Ancient tribal ethnic group found in the **Tarai** region. Skilled hunters and fishermen who live in a communal setting, they are believed to be indigenous to Nepal. Since the invasion of hill settlers, a process that began with the opening up of the **Tarai** in the 1950s, their mode of living has undergone enormous change. Their communal setup has been disrupted, as they were forced to lose much of their communal lands to unscrupulous migrants.

THIMI. Old, quaint town in the **Bhaktapur** district. Famous for **Newar** temples, arts and artifacts, and fairs. It is also the site of the Institute of **Education** where educational materials for schools are designed and published.

THULUNG, NARADMUNNI (1908–1990). One of the commanders in the 1950 revolution. He had laid a foundation of English education in **Bhojpur**. Under his leadership, the radio transmission technology was put to use for the first time in 1950.

TIBET. In Western imagination, Tibet is the land of ultimate Shangri-La, a place of mythical proportions popularized by James Hilton's *Lost Horizon* (1933), a novel which was later made into a movie with the same title (1937 and 1972). In reality, however, it is an entirely different country, a rugged and unforgiving land of 1,221,600 square kilometers in Central Asia. Given the fact that it is the world's tallest plateau with an average altitude of over 4,000 meters, it is often called the "roof of the world" with a population of nearly 6 million people. **China** annexed it in 1949 and, later, turned it into an autonomous region in 1965: Tibetan Autonomous Region (Xizang). Following its invasion, Tibet's theocratic leader Dalai Lama (born: Tenzin Gyatso) remained in the country until 1959 when he essentially fled to **India** where he now lives in Dharamsala, aptly known as "Little Lhasa," the seat of the Tibetan government-in-exile.

Stretched across the vast plateau, immediately to the north of the majestic **Himalayas**, Tibet is the only foreign territory—other than India—with which Nepal shares its border. As neighbors, the relationship between Nepal and Tibet go back many, many centuries. Popular legend has it that Nepali King Go Cha's daughter **Bhrikuti** was married to Song-tsen Gampo, the famous seventh-century king of Tibet. She played a big part in the diffusion of **Buddhism** to Tibet. During Song-tsen's rule, **Narendradeva** (reign: 643–679), a crown prince, fled Nepal and went to Tibet seeking asylum. Tibetan King Song-tsen Gampo later helped Narendradeva recover his father's throne. It is believed that Song-tsen wielded considerable influence in Nepal. And Tibet-Nepal relations had transformed **Kathmandu** into a cultural and commercial center and a bridge between South Asia and Central Asia.

Despite those early close relations and despite the presence of a sizeable number of Nepali merchants in Tibet, the two countries encountered periodic hostilities with each other. They fought wars, the last one being waged by Nepal in 1854, which lasted almost a year. In 1856, with the help of Chinese mediation, the two countries signed a treaty called the **Treaty of Thapathali**, which apparently favored Nepal as it gave Nepali merchants duty-free trade privileges. It also allowed Nepal to station a Nepali resident in Lhasa and forced Tibet to pay an annual tribute of 10,000 rupees to Nepal. In return, Nepal gave up territorial gains and agreed to aid Tibet militarily, if and when invaded by a foreign army.

Following the Chinese annexation in 1949, the trade relations between Nepal and Tibet subsided as China closed the border. Interestingly, however, even after China's invasion, the annual Tibetan tribute mission appeared regularly in Kathmandu as late as 1953. After that, China unilaterally annulled the provision of the 1856 treaty that it itself had helped to craft to resolve the Nepal-Tibet War of 1854. However, Nepal still has its consulate office in Lhasa, the capital of Tibet.

TIBETAN. People of **Tibet**; anything pertaining to Tibet. Nepal contains approximately 25,000 Tibetans, mostly concentrated in **Kathmandu** and **Pokhara**. They initially came to Nepal as refugees when they fled Tibet after the Chinese invasion, especially after its theocratic leader Dalai Lama left the country in 1959. They are heavily engaged in trade and commerce, specifically in carpet production and exports. Nepal owes much of its success in the **carpet industry** to its Tibetan communities. In addition, they have played a significant role in the rising popularity of the **Lamaist** version of **Buddhism** in Nepal. *See also* CHINA-NEPAL RELATIONS.

TIBETO-NEPALI. Nepali people of **Tibetan** and Mongoloid origin. *See* ETHNICITY.

TIHAR. Also called Deepawali or Diwali in some parts of the country, it is the second biggest and most important **Hindu festival** in Nepal. Tihar comes about a month after **Dashain**, generally in late October or early November. In a descriptive sense, some people call it the "Festival of Light," for one can see lights glowing virtually in every house after darkness descends in the evening. They place small oil lamps (or candles these days) around the houses, in entryways, and on windows. Businesses also follow the same practice. It is a marvelous sight as the burning lamps and candles light up the night. With lights defying the nightly darkness, the festival is celebrated over a period of three to five days, and involves honoring dogs (***kukur tihar*** or *khicha puja* in **Newari**) and worshiping Goddess **Laxmi** (Laxmi *puja*), along with **cows**. The festival culminates with the blessing of brothers (*bhai tika* or ***kija puja*** in Newari).

TIJ. Bahun and **Chhetri women**'s festival that occurs generally in late August or early September during which women first fast and later feast. As part of the festival, they participate in dance performances, combined with melancholic singing about their lives filled with troubles. Moreover, this is one of the rare occasions when they feel free and uninhibited to poke fun at their husbands and other males in general or even tell vulgar jokes about sexual behaviors. *See also* MUSIC AND DANCE.

TIKA. Mark placed on the forehead as part of religious worship, blessing or celebration. While the red *tika* always indicate an occasion of joy, other colors may suggest something else, including death rituals or honoring of dead ancestors. In such instances, it is yellow that is usually used, never red. While men rarely wear artificial *tika* made of some plastic object, it is very normal to see **women** with colorful artificial *tika* on the lower section of their foreheads

TIMBER CORPORATION OF NEPAL (TCN). It is a public corporation created in 1960 and incorporated in 1964 to manage timber production and supply in the country. Interestingly, this corporation which is located in **Hetauda** is believed to have played a major role in the massive destruction of the **Tarai** forests. It was marred with fraud and corruption. *See also* INDUSTRY; PRIVATIZATION.

TIWARI, BHIM NIDI (1912–1973). Well-known literary figure. He was proficient in almost all fields of Nepali **literature** such as play, short story, poetry, lyrics, essay, and novel. He contributed many works and was given several awards for his contributions.

TOL. Small neighborhoods in towns and cities. As town or urban centers were mostly associated with **Newar** settlements, the notion of *tol* is invariably linked to Newar communities. A town may have many *tols* depending on its size. *See also* ASAN TOL.

TOPI. Nepali cap worn by men. It is also part of the national dress for males. Its shape looks like a small **mountain** peak when folded and is made from a typical multipatterned and colored Nepali cloth called *dhaka* and from black, canvaslike hard cloth imported from **India**. *See also* DAURA-SURUWAL.

TOURISM. Although by no means an export **industry**, tourism is a major hard currency earner. In 1999, Nepal attracted almost half a million tourists from different countries (see table 8) who contributed more than 20 percent of foreign earnings or 3.6 percent of gross national product. From a historical perspective, Nepali tourism is quite new; its origin can be literally traced back to the late 1950s and early 1960s. Following Nepal's entry onto the world stage after 1951, **mountain** expedition teams from various countries arrived during the decade of the 1950s to climb various **Himalayan** peaks, a process that continues to this day. This early phase can be described as the *Peak* phase of tourism in Nepal, as it was associated with those who came to climb mountain peaks. It was soon followed by American Peace Corps volunteers, with the first group arriving in 1962, and hippies were right behind them, tracking their footsteps in search of marijuana and the mystic tranquility or **nirvana** that the East was presumed to possess. This second phase can be called the *Pot* phase because of its intrinsic link with dope.

Then came the decades of the 1970s and 1980s, a period of explosive growth of Western involvement in Nepal's economic development activities, all in the name of reducing **poverty**. **Foreign aid** projects mushroomed throughout the country and hordes of Western development experts and researchers found their way to Nepal. In addition to a rising number of tourists, the contingency of Western expatriates in the country experienced a dramatic upturn. All of these developments intensified demands for tourist services and activities. Seizing the investment opportunity, the **World Bank** and Asian Development Bank got into the act, financing the development of joint-venture tourist hotels. This third phase is what can labeled the *Poverty* phase of tourism growth in Nepal, as it was directly connected to Western development experts pouring into Nepal with the stated goal of curing Nepal's dire poverty. This was quickly followed by what can be called the *Poker* phase in the 1980s and 1990s as many came to gamble in the **casinos** of **Kathmandu**, often heralded as the Las Vegas of South Asia.

Irrespective of the various phases of tourism in Nepal, the outcome was a continuous growth and expansion of the tourist industry in the country. One notable feature of Nepali tourism is that it is heavily centered in the **Kathmandu Valley**. In recent years, attempts have been made to diversify it into other parts of the country. Ecotourism is growing in popularity. Those tourists who visit Nepal for trekking certainly leave the capital and follow the trekking trails. Yet, despite these trends, the vast segment of this industry is Valley-focused, mainly due to the fact that the majority of tourists are short-term visitors, normally for three to five days, often as an extension of their regional tour to, for example, **India** or some Southeast Asian countries. Consequently, the Valley's commercial **economy** has become heavily dependent on tourism, which is now suffering heavily from **pollution** and political chaos.

At no time was the vulnerability of this entrenched dependence on tourism more starkly exposed than in late 2001, following the tragic events of 11 September 2001. Every available evidence suggests that the number of tourists has declined dramatically since then. As a result, many Valley businesses catering to tourists have taken a nosedive in recent months. The problem was further exacerbated in late November 2001 when the state of emergency was declared. The Nepali army was unleashed with the intention of uprooting the Maoist rebels, waging what is called the **People's War** across the country. When and whether Nepali tourism will recover from these debacles remains a big question.

TRADE. See FOREIGN TRADE.

TRANS-HIMALAYAN RANGE. Also know as the inner **Himalayas**, it is the northern section of the Himalayan Range that extends toward the **Tibetan** (Xizang) Plateau. As it lies to the north of the Himalayas that block the rain-bearing **monsoon** clouds from the south, it is a rain-shadow belt that is generally arid and cold much of the year. As cultivation is very limited, the inhabitants of this belt mostly rely on animal herding (pastoralism) and Trans-Himalayan trade for their sustenance. *See also* Introduction.

TRANSPORTATION. Both historically and presently, the transportation system of Nepal has been poorly developed. Because of the absence of viable transport networks to link one part of the country to another, the **economy** of Nepal before 1951 could be characterized as a system of pocket economies or localized economies, largely isolated from each other in terms of regular interactions and transactions. Although Nepal has come a long way since the early 1950s, its transportation system still remains in a state of rudimentary development, in terms of both domestic movements of goods and products and global links. There are two immediate geographical elements that hinder Nepal's transport development. They are: mountainous physiography (which poses great difficulties for developing domestic networks of surface roads) and landlocked position (which impedes Nepal's direct access to sea transportation, a vital artery of global links). Currently, Nepal's transportation system can be divided into four modes:

- Trails: Historically, trails were the backbone of Nepal's transport networks. And they are still the most extensive, common, and accessible mode of transportation in the country. All of the **Trans-Himalayan** trade routes linking Nepal and **Tibet** were human and mule trails, as were the routes between Nepal and **India** until the early 1950s, excepting the **Hetauda-Kathmandu Ropeway** (1928) to carry cargos over the hills and valleys to the capital. Some of these trails have, in recent years, emerged as popular trekking routes for many foreign tourists, for example, the **Annapurana** trekking route in the central hills and the **Mount Everest** trekking route in the eastern hills.
- Roads: The first paved, motorable highway was built in 1956: the **Tribhuvan Rajpath** that connects Kathmandu with **Birganj**, a city located along the Nepal-India border in the central **Tarai**. Built with Indian aid and by Indian engineers, it is still an important highway in terms of trade and transit between the two countries. Before its construction, most of the goods and products coming from the Indian side to **Kathmandu** were carried by porters on their backs. In other parts of the country, both porters and mules or donkeys were deployed to haul freights, especially along the Trans-Himalayan trade routes. In fact, the first car to reach Kathmandu during the 1920s was manhandled through the numerous hills and valleys. Since that first highway, Nepal's road networks have increased. Currently, the country boasts over 13,000 kilometers of roads of which about 4,500 kilometers are paved, 3,500 kilometers graveled, and the rest fair weather. One noticeable characteristic of the road networks is that they are mostly concentrated in the Tarai and in certain nodal areas of the hills, the two most prominent points being Kathmandu and **Pokhara** (*see* figure 4). Among the paved roads are some of the major highways, including the **Mahendra Rajmarga** (East-West Highway), which spans the whole length of the Tarai from east to west. During the summer **monsoon** season, many of the roads passing through the hills are frequently hampered by landslides.
- Air services: Being a landlocked and mountainous country, airways are critical in Nepal's transportation system, domestically as well as inter-

nationally. Domestically, air transportation provides quick links to different parts of the country, including some areas inaccessible by motor vehicles. Small domestic airports are found in many parts of the country—from east to west and north to south as well as in some remote districts. Because of the emergence of private airline companies, the quality of domestic air service has vastly improved. Internationally, air transportation is more than an avenue of Nepal's direct link to countries beyond India; it is the umbilical chord of the tourist **industry**. Without it, there is little doubt that Nepal's **tourism** would flounder. Nepal's only international airport is situated in Kathmandu, and it is served by the **Royal Nepal Airlines** and foreign airlines.

- Ropeways and railways: These two are the least developed modes of transportation in Nepal, although they were the first mechanical modes of transport introduced in the country. The nation's first ropeway, which is 40 kilometers long, was, as noted above, built in 1928 to transport cargos to Kathmandu from **Hetauda** situated at the base of the **Churia Hills** and north of **Birganj**. The same year a railway line was constructed between **Amlekhganj** and Raxaul—40 kilometers long. But only less than 10 kilometers are currently used. Another 53-kilometers-long railway was opened in 1937, linking a railhead in India. They are poorly utilized and maintained. *See also* AIR SERVICE WITHIN NEPAL; AIRLINES AND INTERNATIONAL AIR SERVICE; COMMUNICATIONS; NEPAL GOVERNMENT RAILWAYS.

TRIBHUVAN INTERNATIONAL AIRPORT. Located in **Kathmandu**, it is the only international airport in Nepal. It is also the only airport serving the **Kathmandu Valley**. As such, all flights in and out of Nepal are directed to this airport. Similarly, all domestic flights from Kathmandu leave from here. Named after King **Tribhuvan Bir Bikram Shah**, it has only one runway equipped to accommodate jets. The first airplane landed in 1949 when it was basically a pasture field where the cows and buffaloes had to be driven away to facilitate plane landing. *See also* AIRLINES AND INTERNATIONAL AIR SERVICE; AIR SERVICE WITHIN NEPAL.

TRIBHUVAN, KING. *See* SHAH, TRIBHUVAN BIR BIKRAM.

TRIBHUVAN RAJPATH. Nepal's first highway linking **Kathmandu** with the border city of **Birganj** and then with **India**. Almost 190 kilometers long, it was built in 1956 with Indian aid to facilitate the movement of goods and products, mostly from India to Kathmandu. Later named after King **Tribhuvan Bir Bikram Shah**, this highway facilitated the movement of people both ways between India and Nepal. In recent years, its importance has waned to some extent due to the construction of a highway from Siddharthnagar to Bharatpur (**Narayanghat**) and then to Kathmandu (*see* figure 4).

TRIBHUVAN UNIVERSITY. Nepal's first and only public university. It was established in 1959 in honor of King **Tribhuvan Bir Bikram Shah**. It offers only graduate degrees, both Master's and Ph.D., but no undergraduate degrees. To be admitted to the university, one must have successfully completed an undergraduate degree. Nepal's higher public **education** system has two distinct layers. That is, higher education institutions designated as colleges are designed to offer undergraduate degrees, whereas the graduate degrees are pursued at those with the university designation. As a central authority of higher (college) education, Tribhuvan University is fully responsible for setting the degree standards and curricular requirements for all public colleges—or campuses as they are now called. Despite its status as the national university of Nepal, it is poorly equipped with low-level research facilities for the faculty.

TRI-CHANDRA COLLEGE. Nepal's first college founded in 1919 by Prime Minister **Chandra Shamsher Rana**. It is also the first college to offer college-level science **education** in the country. Until about the 1960s, college-level science education was extremely limited in the country. Those who wanted to pursue a higher degree in physical sciences to equip themselves for a further degree in engineering or medical studies would have to go to **Kathmandu** and enroll in either this college or Amrit Science College, which was the college of choice because of its better facilities and higher quality (*see* **Pradhan, Amrit Prasad**). Located in the heart of Kathmandu, the Tri-Chandra College was named after Chandra Shamsher Rana. One side note about this college is that, over the years, it has served as a barometer and hotbed of student politics in Nepal, sparking political protests and ideological contests throughout the

Valley and beyond. In the same vein, it is also marred by student protests and strikes, probably more so than most other campuses.

TRISULI HYDROELECTRIC PROJECT. Hydroelectric power plant on the Trisuli River. Located in the Nuwakot district and built with the assistance of **India**, it has an installed capacity of 21,000 kilowatts. Much of the electricity generated by this project is supplied to light up or power the **Kathmandu Valley**.

TULADHAR, PADMA RATNA (1940–). Leftist politician, journalist, and **human rights** activist from **Kathmandu**. During the 1991 general **elections**, he ran as a **Communist Party of Nepal** (CPN–UML) candidate and was elected to the **House of Representatives**. He won his seat again from Kathmandu during the 1994 election.

TULSI. Sacred herb plant belonging to the basil family. It is a religious plant that many **Hindu** families grow in the front yards of their houses, usually on a built-up mound. Hindus worship it.

TUNDIKHEL. Public open field in the middle of **Kathmandu**. Founded by Prime Minister **Bhimsen Thapa** in the early 1800s, it is a common ground where political parades and functions are held. Since there is no charge to use this space, vendors also use it freely to sell products in what is called in the social science parlance the "informal market." However, the informal market of Tundikhel is not only composed of small vendors, but also extends to herds of goats and sheep that villagers bring during certain times of the years to sell in Kathmandu.

U

UDAYAPUR CEMENT INDUSTRY. Public enterprise located in the eastern **Tarai** district of Udayapur (*see* figure 2). It is a leading producer of cement for domestic consumption. It was incorporated in 1987. *See also* INDUSTRY.

UNIFIED (UNITED) MARXIST-LENINIST (UML; CPN–UML). *See* COMMUNIST PARTY OF NEPAL.

UNITED NATIONS (UN). Nepal was admitted to the United Nations on 14 December 1955. Since joining the UN, Nepal has served as a member of its Security Council twice: in 1969–1970 and 1988–1989. In addition, Nepal has been a participant in the UN peacekeeping operations in Lebanon, Cambodia, and former Yugoslavia. The UN has played an important role in the arena of development and family planning since the 1950s, providing technical assistance as well as policy guidelines. Some of the UN or its specialized agencies that are active in Nepal are: Food and Agricultural Organization, United Nations Development Programme (UNDP), United Nations Population Fund, United Nations Educational Scientific and Cultural Organization, United Nations Children's Fund, and World Health Organization.

Another UN agency involved in Nepal's local development in recent years is the United Nations Capital Development Fund (UNCDF). Its basic motto is "investing with the poor," that is, reducing **poverty** through local development and microfinancing. Under this program, UNCDF has recently launched several small-scale projects such as lift irrigation, marketing infrastructure, and feeder roads. Additionally, it recently selected Nepal for the launching of a $5 million local development fund to promote decentralized **planning** and financing of rural development. The selection of Nepal was based on such criteria as government policies conducive to participatory development, the establishment of a multiparty system and efforts by the government to be more accountable to the population.

Furthermore, this UNCDF project will build upon the positive and encouraging results of UNDP's decentralization programs in Nepal. The objectives of this project are to assist in the management of local development and to forge partnerships with **nongovernmental organizations** (NGOs) and the private sector. Additionally, the project will initiate a process of social empowerment to organize local people into institutions of their own to take over decisions that affect their lives and to enhance democratic practices in the allocation and management of development resources.

UNITED STATES-NEPAL RELATIONS. The United States of America has been a leading supporter of Nepal for more than five decades. Initially, the diplomatic relations at the legation level were established in 1947 at about the same time the British left **India**, i.e., four years prior to the end of the **Rana** regime. In January 1951, the United States and

Nepal signed a general agreement for technical cooperation in New Delhi, India. The first project to be undertaken by the U.S. Operations Mission (USOM), predecessor for the U.S. Agency for International Development (USAID), involved a survey of Nepal's mineral resources by the U.S. Bureau of Mines. With that signing, the United States became the first bilateral **foreign aid** donor to Nepal.

In August 1951, the two nations raised the status of their diplomatic missions to the rank of embassy, although the ambassadorial residency was not set up until 1959 in either nation. In March 1952, former First Lady Eleanor Roosevelt visited Nepal during a world tour, and the U.S. Information Service opened a library in **Kathmandu** in June. In February 1956, USOM announced an economic grant of $2 million to Nepal. Technical cooperation projects focused on malaria eradication, community development, road construction in the **Rapti Valley** and teacher training. The teacher training program involved a contract with the University of Oregon to train 1,750 teachers and to establish a four-year teachers' college. Assistance provided for Rapti Valley development was intended to clear forests and make over 40,000 hectares (100,000 acres) of land available for **land settlement** and **agriculture**. Since then, roads, hospitals, schools, and drinking water systems have been built.

Much of the U.S. aid in the early years of its involvement in Nepal's development was channeled through USOM, which in the late 1950s was replaced by USAID whose initial project was to operate a joint program for cooperative services for **education** development. The project provided leadership and guidance for implementation of education programs across the country. The American Peace Corps program initiated by President John F. Kennedy began in 1962, and it is the only such program still operational in South Asia. Over a period of one-half century (1951–2001), U.S. aid to Nepal has totaled well over $500 million. Recently, the George W. Bush administration has approved an additional military aid package of $20 million to fight against what is labeled "terrorism," meaning the raging Maoist revolution that has gripped the nation for the past six years.

There is little doubt that USAID, together with the **World Bank**, has come to play a leading role in Nepal's development agenda and direction. In recent years, as part of its development involvement, USAID has focused on what it calls "five strategic objectives" that it believes are essential to Nepal's ability to offer a better life for its citizens. They are: agriculture and **forestry** development (through production and sales of forest and high-value products); health care and improvement; empowering **women**; hydropower development; and governance (democracy).

UNMATTA BHAIRAV. Erotic form of **Bhairav**. A famous temple of this Bhairav was set up by **Jayasthiti Malla** inside the **Pashupati** complex. Women suffering from menstrual problems tend to worship this Bhairav.

UNTOUCHABILITY. In the present context, this term simply refers to the untouchable or polluted **caste**. The complex distinction between the **Sudra** and untouchable castes that may exist in many parts of **India** is not that common in Nepal. The two are normally interchangeable, meaning a Sudra is untouchable and a member of the untouchable caste is a Sudra, although there certainly exist some groups such as **Dhobi** or washermen that may be technically placed in the Sudra group, but not necessarily untouchable. Commonly recognized among the Sudra or untouchable caste groups in the country are the **Damai, Kami**, Pode, **Sarki (Chamar)**, and **Sunwar** (Sunar).

At any rate, the notion of untouchability as practiced in Nepal's **Hindu** society simply means caste pollution. That is, if someone from a higher caste touches a person belonging to the untouchable or Sudra caste, that person becomes polluted. Under such circumstances, for the polluted person to become purified (i.e., to restore his/her caste purity), that individual must undergo a certain prescribed ritual. In many parts of Nepal, **Muslims** and white people (*mlaksha* as they were called) were treated as untouchable until the late 1940s. It is true that Prime Minister **Jang Bahadur Rana** (and other **Rana** prime ministers) had defied this long-held, absurd orthodox Hindu notion when he visited Europe and socialized with white people during his tour as well as in Nepal.

Yet, as late as the early 1900s the Rana rulers regarded the **Gorkhas**, soldiers serving in the British army, as polluted. The rationale (assumption) was that they had come in contact with Whites, Muslims, or some other unknown untouchable individuals. Although Whites were no longer being seen or treated as untouchables from the social and political perspectives, the cultural and religious stigma of their untouchability remained intact. As a result, upon return those Gorkha soldiers were required to undergo state-arranged mass de-polluting rituals for which they had to pay. The anachronistic notion of Whites' untouchability has not been completely erased from the pages of Hindu orthodoxy as they are still forbidden from entering many prominent Hindu temples, for instance, **Pashupati**.

The Hindu caste practice of untouchability and caste pollution as applied to domestic Sudra and untouchable caste groups was finally abolished in 1963. Nevertheless, it is still a common feature of Nepali society as it continues to hinder the ex-untouchables' social mobility and progress. In recent years, however, its practice has seen a visible decline in urban areas and new communities, specifically those settled by migrants in the **Tarai** where low-caste individuals may discretely adopt a new caste or where their caste status has blended with their migrant status to give a new dimension to their social identity in the new community. *See also* DALIT; ST. XAVIER SCHOOL.

UPADHYAYA, BISHWA NATH (1930–). A jurist and lawyer, he was appointed to serve as chairperson of the commission that was responsible for drafting a new **constitution** following the restoration of democracy and the parliamentary system of governance in 1990. Following that, he was appointed by the then King **Birendra Bir Bikram Shah** to serve as chief justice of the **Supreme Court**. His 1994 decision as chief justice of the Supreme Court to deny Prime Minister **Man Mohan Adhikari** the right to dissolve **Parliament** was generally viewed as unconstitutional. It was also interpreted as a decision that clearly favored the king's position, thus giving credence to the prevailing perception that Nepal's **judicial system** lacks integrity and public confidence.

UPRETY, DEVI PRASAD (1912–1992). Philanthropist. He was known for donating many hectares of land to various schools in **Jhapa** and Tehrathum. He was a social activist determined to elevate the status of ethnic minorities; he even discarded his holy thread (*see* **Janai** and **Tagadhari**). That was his way of protesting against **untouchability** or the **Hindu** code of **caste** pollution.

V

VAIDYA, GAJANANDA (1935–). Industrialist and businessman from **Kathmandu**. He is responsible for founding tea and automobiles companies. In addition, he has opened hotels in the **Kathmandu Valley** to serve tourists and travelers.

VAIDYA, KARUNAKAR (1917–1989). Scientist and writer. He wrote several books before his death in 1989. Included among his books is one on the **Buddhist** culture of the **Kathmandu Valley**. He earned several awards during his lifetime for his contributions.

VAISHNAV, SHYAM DAS (1924–?). Poet and short story writer. He has published several books and has received awards for his works. He was associated with **Radio Nepal** from its inception and worked there until 1969.

VAISYA. One of the four **Hindu caste** groups ranked third from the top. It is often associated with trade, commerce, or some other economic production activities that increase the wealth of a nation.

VAJRA (BAJRA). Thunderbolt associated with Tantric performances or rituals. Representing adamantine strength in the **Vajrayana** sect of **Buddhism**, it symbolizes male principles and power.

VAJRACHARYA, DAYANANDA (1945–). A professor of botany, he is associated with **Tribhuvan University**. He also served as a visiting professor in the **United States** (1982–1983) and rector of Tribhuvan University (1987–1990). He was appointed to serve as vice chancellor of the **Royal Nepal Academy of Science & Technology** in 2002.

VAJRACHARYA, KRISHNA RATNA. Scientist. He is regarded as the first Nepali person to develop a hand-operated printing press.

VAJRAYANA. "Diamond Way" as it is referred to. It is a popular form of Tantric **Buddhism** which incorporates parts of both **Lamaism** and **Newar Buddhism** called Mantrayana. Founded around the eighth century, it is believed to have originated as a subsect within the **Mahayana** school of Buddhism. Its name is derived from the divine instrument called **Vajra**, which is its sacred object. *See also* **TANTRISM**.

VAJRAYOGINI. Tantric female deity. She is widely worshiped in the Kathmandu Valley. She is often projected as holding a **Vajra** and a skull cup for drinking human blood. She wears a necklace of human skulls with one of her feet pressing down on demons. In essence, she appears to be the Tantric version of Goddess **Kali**.

VAMSAVALI (VAMSHAVALI). Collection of chronicles of Nepali rulers. They provide useful accounts of ancient and medieval history, mainly based on legends and lore, approximately covering the period between 600 B.C. to 450 A.D.

VARNA. This word literally means one's "color or complexion," but it is often used to mean **caste** group or status. This association is largely attributed to the fact that the caste hierarchy itself was initially based on complexion. That is, people were grouped into different castes and their caste roles on the basis of their skin color. Since the **Bahuns** and **Chhetris**, generally with fair skins and occupying high social positions in society, were in charge of assigning people into different castes and caste roles, they placed themselves at the top of the caste hierarchy and relegated others to the bottom. Those with the darkest color were placed in the **Sudra** group and assigned menial, dirty, or what was considered to be polluting work such as leather works, cleaning gutters and sewers, plowing, carcass removal, and sweeping streets. Essentially, their duty is to serve the three higher castes. So this simple word, when applied as a social concept laden with caste roles and realities, has a profound meaning and consequence in Nepali society. Simply put, for each person there was a place in society and a function to fulfill, with its own duties and rights—and all based on one's *varna*. *See also* HINDUISM.

VEDAS. Sacred, original religious texts of **Hinduism** containing hymns. Believed to have been composed between 1,500 and 900 B.C., they are divided into four volumes: **Rig Veda** (oldest religious text in the world), *Ayur (Yajur) Veda*, *Sama Veda*, and *Atharva Veda*. Together they serves as the basis of Hindu society, namely cults, doctrines, health, and metaphysics. The word *veda* literally means "knowledge, compiled, composed, and passed on by sage Vyasa (or **Veda Vyasa**)."

VEDA VYASA. Maharishi or great **Hindu** sage. Vyasa (around 1,500 B.C.) is credited as the author of various **Hindu** texts, e.g., the *Vedas*, *Puranas*, and **Mahabharata**, although they are believed to have been written, obviously, generations apart. It is not clear why such is the case. One possibility is that Vyasa might have established his school of learning, and those scholars who pursued the Vyasa school of thought and learning might have penned his name on the scripts they themselves composed in the tradition of Vyasa. Being the great sage that Vyasa was, they could have done this as a tribute to him for the profound tradition of learning that he had founded and left behind for generations to follow.

VIHAR (BIHAR). **Buddhist** religious shrines and residence of monks. It is also called Bahal or Baha, especially in **Newar** communities. There are several such shrines in **Kathmandu** and **Patan**. They usually have quadrangular bases, small windows, balconies, gilded and tiered roofs, platforms, and images of Buddhist deities.

VILLAGE DEVELOPMENT COMMITTEE. Body of representatives at the village level. They are vested with judicial and administrative authority and are responsible for formulating and implementing small development works at the village level. This new setup that was put in place following the restoration of democracy in 1990 is very similar to what was called Village **Panchayat** during the Panchayat system. At this point it is not clear about the efficacy of the Village Development Committee in terms of fostering rural development in the country.

VISHNU (BISHNU). **Hindu** god of protection. One of the members of the Hindu trinity: **Brahma**, Vishnu, and **Shiva**. Like Shiva, Vishnu is widely followed and worshiped. Often presented in different forms and playing many different roles, he incarnates himself in different forms (**avatars**) at different epochs (yuga). Vishnu's various avatars are believed to descend upon earth from time to time to restore peace, order, and justice, to save humanity from injustice and miseries. Time in this context is conceived in epochal terms or what the Hindus call yuga. Conceptually, therefore, Vishnu's divine role as a protector directly places him in the role of a destroyer, a role that he shares with Shiva. So, in the Hindu concept of cosmic configuration and tapestry, protection and destruction are inseparable. One cannot exist without the other, for they follow each other as cause-effect-cause in what may be called the cycle of the universal law. It is this cycle that perhaps explains the universal duality of good and evil or god and devil. *See also* HINDUISM.

W

WAGLE, CHIRANJIBI (1946–). High-ranking member of the **Nepali Congress Party**. He was elected to the **House of Representatives** in the first general **elections** held in 1991 and was appointed to serve as minister of supplies in the Congress government headed by **Girija Prasad Koirala** (1991–1994). Chiranjibi Wagle was reelected in the subsequent general elections held in 1994 and 1999. In the current government led by Prime Minister **Sher Bahadur Deuba**, he serves as minister of physical **planning** and works (2001–2002).

WANG HUEN-TSANG. Chinese traveler and pilgrim who arrived in Nepal in the seventh century A.D. In his travel diary, he described in detail the rule of **Amsuvarman**, along with his character as a ruler and person. His accounts are recorded in the Tang annals.

WEEKEND. Saturday is the weekend in Nepal. All offices are closed on this day. As for schools and colleges, they hold classes only for half a day on Friday. So, for students, the weekend is one-half day longer than it is for government employees.

WHEEL OF EXISTENCE. Wheel held by Mara, the Lord of Death. It is comprised of four concentric circles which represent: a stage of existence; those who are chained to life; the forces which keep the wheel turning; and the desire which keeps man chained.

WOMEN'S STATUS. The state of women's status in Nepal is one of absurdity as it represents a defiance of its **Hindu** norms and even its practice of worship and reverence. Nepal is the only constitutionally declared Hindu nation in the world. As such, it is technically governed by Hindu precepts and values. **Hinduism**, the oldest religion in the world, is also the only religion to offer equal status to women, at least in religious terms. In essence, it is sex neutral as its multitude of deities include a parade of goddesses who are no less powerful, no less revered or feared than their male counterparts; they are equal in status as well as in their overall roles in the cosmic configuration of the universe. These include **Kali**, **Durga**, **Laxmi**, and others.

Yet when it comes to the social status of women—the embodiment of one's mother, wife, and daughter—Nepal treats them as if they are male properties, born to serve their men at their pleasure and whims. This is the Hindu paradox—or what some call absurdity—that is hard to explain as it defies the fundamental tenet of Hinduism, both in theory and worship practice. For example, the practice of polygamy (which seems to be on the decline) was not only an indication of male fantasy; it was also directly linked to the fact that wives were viewed as free labor confined to one's own household and readily available. That is why it used to be common among males of landed families to have several wives as though they were material possessions.

The **United Nations** has defined the status of women in terms of their access to knowledge, economic resources, and political power, as well as their personal autonomy in the process of decision making. When Nepali women's status is analyzed in this light, the picture is generally gloomy. To be sure, Nepali women are not forced to live in the dark ages. Yet there is no denying that in this rigidly patriarchical society, women are regarded as subordinate to men, virtually in every facet of life and institutional setting. However, women's relative status varies from one ethnic group to another.

The status of women in **Tibeto-Nepali** communities is relatively better than that of **Bahun, Chhetri,** and **Newar** women. Also, women from the low-**caste** groups enjoy relatively more social autonomy and freedom of geographical mobility than the above three groups of women, for they are far less subjected to Hindu puritanical values. In addition, upper-class families used to restrict the geographical mobility of their unmarried daughters to protect their complexion (fair look) from being darkened by sun exposure. Lighter-skinned women are often seen as more desirable marriage partners than darker-skinned ones. Nonetheless, similar to the Confucian system, women's social status generally is directly associated with that of their men—that is, with the father as a daughter, with the husband as a wife, and with the son(s) as a mother.

Yet it is important to clarify that the universe of women's status in Nepal is, by no means, unidimensional or unidirectional. There are at least two distinct terrains of women's status: the public space and the domestic space. What was described above is a picture that generally captures the reality prevailing in the public space where women's status is quite diminutive. But, in the domestic space, the question of women's status takes on a significantly different dimension, one of greater assertiveness and complexity. In most households, the senior female member plays a commanding role by controlling resources, making crucial planting and harvesting decisions, and determining the family expenses and budget allocations.

Nepali wives are the managers of the domestic front. Nowhere is this more visible than in those communities where male outmigration is common, namely in the hills. While husbands join the ranks of migrants to earn cash income, virtually every decision-making task, not to mention the day-to-day chores, falls on wives. In a household consisting of different hierarchical echelons of female members, a mother-in-law normally exercises significant control over daughters-in-law, often more than she does on her own daughters. In fact, family tensions sometimes are directly tied to wives' influence on their husbands regarding family matters, often prompting married sons to separate from their parents and brothers. Separation allows wives to be not only free from the vise of their mothers-in-law and the shadow of other family members, but also to exercise greater leverage over their own family resources and affairs; they have less concern about their husbands giving more weight to their parents' decisions and wishes than their own.

On the whole, however, few would dispute that women's lives remain centered on their traditional roles, i.e., taking care of most household chores, fetching water and animal fodder, and doing farm work. Restrictions on their geographical mobility naturally limit their access to the market, employment, education, health care, and local services. Plus, malnutrition and **poverty** grip women hardest. The pattern is set from childhood. Female children usually are given less food than male children, especially when the family experiences food shortages, and yet are expected to work harder. Women usually work harder than men. One exception is that women from high-class families have maids to take care of most household chores and other menial work and, thus, work far less than women in lower socioeconomic brackets.

With respect to day-to-day operations, the economic contribution of women is substantial. But it is often devalued just like their social life as it largely goes unnoticed because their traditional role is taken for granted. Such diminished value of women and their work is often reflected at the broader institutional level. For instance, the economic contribution of their traditional work is seldom accounted for in any national income or economic calculations such as GDP. Furthermore, daughters are denied rights to family properties (namely land) unless they remain unmarried until they are 35 years old, the primary reason being that they become detached from their parental families upon marriage. Only thereafter can they claim a share (*amsa*) of family properties in amounts equal to their brothers' shares, for they are considered to have crossed the marriageable age. Daughters-in-law are entitled to their husbands' shares after they are widowed. When employed, their wages are substantially lower than those paid to men. In most rural areas, their employment outside the household is confined to planting, weeding, and harvesting. In urban areas, they are normally employed in domestic and traditional jobs. Within the government sector, they are often relegated to low ranks such as secretarial or clerical jobs. In the worst of cases, many women are forced into **prostitution.**

One tangible measure of women's status is **education.** Although the **constitution** offers women equal rights, many social, economic, and cultural factors impede girls' school enrollments. With high dropout rates, women's low education and illiteracy pose the biggest hindrance to enhancing equal opportunity and status for women. In short, they are caught in a vicious circle imposed by the nexus of patriarchical feudalism, Hindu orthodoxy, and poor family conditions. As their low status hampers their education, the lack of education, in turn, defines their status, placing them in a tenuous position. It is true that the female literacy rate has improved over the years, but their average educational attainment still falls far short of their male counterparts. Overall, women's status in Nepal seems lower than that in its neighboring South Asian countries, at least on the surface. That is, Bangladesh, **India,** Pakistan, and Sri Lanka have had women prime ministers—all elected in general **elections.** Nepal has yet to appoint a female minister to head a high-profile ministry such as finance, foreign affairs, or defense, let alone electing a woman prime minister. Given the current trend, it is highly unlikely that Nepal will see a woman head of the government any time soon.

WORLD BANK. Nepal joined the World Bank in 1961. The Bank has an office in the country and is a key actor in its development process. As a leading multilateral credit provider, the World Bank, in cooperation with the **United States** Agency for International Development, has played a prominent role in setting Nepal's development direction as well as agenda, especially since the late 1960s. In the 1990s, as the fashion of **privatization** caught on, the bank's role in Nepal reached a new height. In most cases, what the bank says goes; there is little debate. Currently, the World Bank is engaged in seven different categories of development projects with a total loan outlay of more than $240 million. These projects include: **agricultural** research and extension; basic and primary **education;** road development and maintenance; rural infrastructure development including water supply and sanitation; telecommunications reform; and transit and trade facilitation. Proposed projects mostly involve continued expansion of these ongoing projects.

Y

YAMARAJ. God of Death. According to the **Hindu** belief system, he is the one who decides weather a person is destined to **Swarga** (heaven) or **Narak** (hell), based on the records of that person's dharmic deeds during his or her lifetime.

YETI. Legendary abominable snowman. Described as a half-man half-ape creature living in the snow, Yeti's existence remains unverified from a scientific perspective. Concrete documentary evidence is as aloof as the famed Yeti itself. However, in the eyes of those native people (e.g., the **Sherpa**) who live in the general vicinity of the presumed habitat of the Yeti, there is little dispute about the existence of this legendary creature.

YOGA. **Hindu** practice involving total concentration upon something, for instance, meditation in order to establish an inner connection to the object of concentration. Often popularized in the West as a form of exercise based on prescribed postures and certain routine, yoga is, in principle, a mystical and ascetic practice, involving what can be loosely characterized as the total control of mind and body—that is, disciplining the mind and body to reach the realm of consciousness.

YOGI (*JOGI*). Technically, someone who practices **yoga**. In terms of its generic or vernacular application, it simply refers to a holy man, an ascetic person, one who has renounced the material world. The female version of this term is yogini (*jogini*). *See also* SADHU; SANYASI.

YOG MAYA. Legendary figure. Born in **Bhojpur** between 1860–1868, Yog Maya took a defiant stance against **caste** discrimination and the practice of **untouchability** in Nepal. Although she remains an obscure figure in the revolutionary history of Nepal, there is little doubt about her place in history. In view of her activism, she is considered one of the pioneers of the movement for **women**'s rights and equality. In fact, it is plausible to claim that in many respects, Yog Maya was a forerunner to today's feminism, a movement that has yet to emerge in Nepal. During her life she continuously raised her voice for good governance and is said to have made a deputation to Prime Minister **Juddha Shamsher Rana** to introduce tangible or meaningful reforms in the country. Disappointed at the deterioration of the rule of law and a general decay of society, she drowned herself in the **Arun River** in June 1941, along with her 68 disciples.

YONI. Platelike rimmed disk of stone, wood, or metal on which the *lingam* normally stands. It is, in essence, a vaginal symbol that is rarely found in isolation from the *lingam*. In all likelihood, their togetherness or mutual proximity represents the **Hindu** notion of male-female sexual conjoining and consequent biological production and reproduction. *See also* GUHESWORI; *SHIVALINGAM.*

YONJAN, GOPAL (1943–1997). Gopal Yonjan was one of the pioneers in the field of Nepali **music**. He was an accomplished flute player as well as songwriter. He worked as music director in many Nepali movies produced in the 1980s. His place in Nepali music is secure because of his many contributions and dedication to its expansion and elevation in terms of both popularity and quality.

Appendix

PRIME MINISTERS AND COUNCIL CHAIRMEN 1951–2002

Post-Rana Transition Period, 1951–1959[1]

Prime Minister or Council Chairman	Period
Mohan Shamsher Rana	Feb.–Nov. 1951
Matrika Prasad Koirala	Nov. 1951–Aug. 1952
Keshav Shamsher Rana (Royal Council Chief)	Aug. 1952–June 1953
Matrika Prasad Koirala	June 1953–Feb. 1954
Matrika Prasad Koirala	Mar. 1954–Ap. 1955
Gunja Man Singh (Royal Council Chief)	Ap. 1955–Jan. 1956
Tanka Prasad Acharya	Jan. 1956–July 1957
K. I. Singh	July–Nov. 1957
Subarna Shamsher Rana (Royal Council Chair)	Nov. 1957–May 1959

Democratic Period I, 1959–1960

Prime Minister	
B. P. Koirala	May 1959–Dec. 1960

Post-Palace Coup and Panchayat Period, 1960–1990[2]

Prime Minister or Council Chairman

Direct Rule by King Mahendra	Dec. 1960–July 1962
Tulsi Giri (Royal Council Vice Chair)	July 1962–Ap. 1963
Tulsi Giri (Royal Council Chair)	Ap. 1963–Jan. 1965
Surya Bahadur Thapa (Royal Council Chair)	Jan. 1965–Jan. 1966
Surya Bahadur Thapa (Royal Council Chair)	Aug. 1966–Jan. 1969
Kirtinidhi Bista	Ap. 1969–Ap. 1970
Direct Rule by King Mahendra	Ap. 1970–Ap. 1971
Kirtinidhi Bista	Ap. 1971–July 1973
Nagendra Prasad Rijal	July 1973–Dec. 1975
Tulsi Giri	Dec. 1975–Sep. 1977
Kirtinidhi Bista	Sep. 1977–June 1979
Surya Bahadur Thapa	June 1979–June 1980
Surya Bahadur Thapa	June 1980–May 1981
Surya Bahadur Thapa	May 1981–July 1983
Lokendra Bahadur Chand	July 1983–March 1986
Nagendra Prasad Rijal	Mar. 1986–June 1986
Marichman Singh Shrestha	June 1986–Ap. 1990
Lokendra Bahadur Chand	Ap. 1990

Post-Panchayat Democratic Period II, 1990–Present

Prime Minister

Krishna Prasad Bhattarai (Interim Coalition)	Ap. 1990–May 1991
Girija Prasad Koirala (Congress)	May 1991–Nov. 1994
Man Mohan Adhikari (Communist-UML)	Nov. 1994–Sep. 1995
Sher Bahadur Deuba (Congress–Coalition)	Sep. 1995–Mar. 1997
Lokendra Bahadur Chand (National Democratic–Coalition)	Mar.–Oct. 1997

Surya Bahadur Thapa (National Democratic–Coalition)	Oct. 1997–Ap. 1998
Girija Prasad Koirala (Congress)	Ap.–Dec. 1998
Girija Prasad Koirala (Congress–Coalition)	Dec. 1998–May 1999
Krishna Prasad Bhattarai (Congress)	May 1999–Mar. 2000
Girija Prasad Koirala (Congress)	Mar. 2000–July 2001
Sher Bahadur Deuba (Congress)	July 2001–October 2002
Lokendra Bahadur Chand (King-appointed under executive power)	Oct. 2002–May 2003
Surya Bahadur Thapa (King-appointed under executive power)	June 2003–Present

Notes

1. Compiled from Joshi and Rose, 1966.
2. Extracted mostly from www.nepalhomepage.com. Nepali months and years provided in the website were converted into English months and years. Due to the lack of access to old Nepali calendars dating back to the period covered here, all conversions have been approximated. As a result, it is possible that converted dates may be off slightly (just a few days), potentially pushing some beginning and ending months forward or back, but only in those cases in which dates were very close to either the beginning or the end of the corresponding months in the English calendar.

Glossary

Aama (Ama)	Mother; mother figure.
Abhiyan	Movement as in political or social movement.
Abikas	Opposite of *bikas*; lack of economic development.
Abikasi	Someone who is devoid of development mentality.
Adhikar	Rights; privileges.
Ain	Law; legal codes.
Anamol	Chaos; confusion; chaotic.
Andolan	Protest, uprising, rebellion.
Angrej	English man; White man.
Angreji	English.
Annasan	Fasting, particularly as a form of political protest.
Ashanti	Absence of peace; chaos; opposite of *shanti*.
Atma	Soul.
Awaj	Call or voice, used in a political movement context or in a regular sense.
Bajra	Thunderbolt; divine instrument.
Band	Shut down as part of social/political protest; shops are closed and surface transportation is halted.
Barga	Class as in social classes.
Barta	Fasting.
Batabaran	Environment such as physical, social, or political environment; overall condition.
Bazaar	Marketplace.
Bhardar	Courtiers; nobles.
Bhasa	Language.
Bhasan	Public lecture; political speech.
Bhatta	Beans (i.e., soy beans; black-eyed peas).

Bhranti	Chaos; confusion; disturbance.
Bhrastachar	Embezzlement; corruption.
Bhrastachari	Embezzler; corrupt.
Bhukampa	Earthquake.
Bides(h)	Foreign country; foreign land.
Bidesi	Foreigner.
Bikas	Economic development, progress.
Bikasi	Development-minded person; anything that leads to or promotes development.
Binas	Destruction; ruined.
Biswas(h)	Trust; belief; faith.
Boksi	Witch; somebody who practices witchcraft.
Byapar	Business; trade.
Byapari	Businessman.
Chakari	Ass kissing.
Chakaridar	Ass kisser.
Chal-Chalan	Tradition; routine acts.
Charesh	Hashish.
Chaukidar	Gatekeeper.
Das pratha	Slavery.
Desh	Nation, commonly used in a patriotic sense.
Deshbadi	Nationalist; patriot.
Dharti	Earth.
Dharti mata	Mother earth.
Dhatu	Minerals.
Durgam	Remote; isolated, invariably applied in a geographical context.
Durgam Chhetra	Remote area.
Gaun (Gaon)	Village.
Ghus	Bribe; bribery.
Grahan	Eclipse, e.g., *chandra* or *surya gragan* (lunar/solar eclipse).
Guru	Teacher, professor.
Himal	Himalaya; snow-capped mountain.
Jagirdar	Government employee.
Jamindar	Landlord.
Jana	People.
Jana andolan	People's revolution.
Janajati	Ethnic groups in general.

Janamat (jana mat)	Public polls; people's opinions.
Janata	People.
Jand	Home-brewed beer.
Jangal	Jungle, wild forests, or forested area.
Jangali	Wild; uncivilized.
Jatra	Procession associated with a religious festivity.
Jhilko	Sparks.
Jogi	Ascetic man.
Jogini	Ascetic woman.
Kanun	Law; rules
Karmachari	Government employee.
Karyakram	Program; agenda.
Ke garne?	What to do? Often expressed with a sense of resignation or helplessness.
Khate	Street children; ragpickers.
Khet	Relatively flat, wet lands where rice can be grown.
Kheti	Farming; harvest.
Kishan (Kisan)	Peasant, farmer.
Kranti	Revolution; massive uprising.
Krantikar(i)	Revolutionary.
Krishak	Farmer.
Lingam	Phallus.
Madal	Popular Nepali musical instrument (drum)
Maharaj(a)	King; great king; in Nepal, Rana prime ministers were called Maharaja.
Mahila	Woman.
Majdoor (Majdur)	Worker, laborer.
Mandir	Temple.
Mantra	Sacred formula used in prayer and incantation.
Mantri	Minister; somebody who holds a ministerial portfolio.
Momocha	Dumpling.
Mukti	Liberation.
Muluk	Nation.
Nagar	Town, city, municipality, or urban area.
Nagarik	Citizen.
Nagarikata	Citizenship.
Nagarpalika	Municipality.
Niyam	Law; rule.

Niyojan	Control.
Nyaya	Justice.
Pahar	Hills.
Pakhe	Uncivilized; someone unfamiliar to the urban way of life or urban culture.
Pakho	Dry, hillside lands where rice cultivation is usually difficult.
Parba	Event of some historical significance.
Parbat	Mountains; high hills.
Paribar	Family.
Paribar niyojan	Family planning.
Parishad	Council; assembly.
Parma	Labor sharing; labor exchange in rural areas.
Patra	Paper; newspaper.
Patrika	Newspaper.
Patrakar	News reporter.
Pradhan Mantri	Prime minister.
Praja	People; common people; citizen.
Pratinidhi	Parliament member; representative.
Prjatantra	Democracy.
Puja	Worship, invariably in honor of a god or goddess.
Pujari	Priest; one who performs *puja*.
Puraskar	Award.
Raj	Kingdom; rule.
Raja	King; ruler of a vassal principality.
Rajaniti	Politics; game (art) of politics.
Rajanitikar	Politician; someone who does or practices politics.
Rajnitigya	Political scientist; politician.
Rajya	Kingdom; a vassal principality.
Rastra	Nation.
Rastriya	National.
Rishi	Sage.
Sadhu	Hindu holy man; *jogi*.
Sahar	City.
Samaj	Society.
Samanata	Equality.
Sambidhan	Constitution.
Sammelan	Conference; meeting; gathering.
Samuha	Group; congregation.

Glossary

Sangathan	Organization; association.
Sarangi	Popular Nepali musical instrument (string).
Sarkar	Government; the State.
Sarkari	Related or belonging to government.
Sati pratha	Tradition of widow burning. No longer practiced.
Satyagraha	Passive resistance; disobedience.
Seto chhala	White skin (literally); often used to refer to a white man (woman) in a derogatory manner.
Shahid	Martyr.
Shanti	Peace.
Shiromani	Crown jewel.
Sidhanta	Principle; dogma; ideology.
Sukumbasi	Landless; landless settlers or squatters.
Swarthi	Someone who is selfish.
Tadi	Barren fields, usually found along riverbanks.
Tirtha	Pilgrimage.
Yojana	Plan; planning.
Yoni	Vagina; vaginal symbol.
Zilla	Administrative district.

Bibliography

This bibliography is a selective collection of writings on Nepal. Attempts have been made to represent as many aspects of Nepali life and society as possible. Moreover, the selection is also designed to represent Nepali and foreign scholars as well as their writings published in Nepal and overseas. In this endeavor, the current collection is tilted toward those publications that are written in English, mainly because of their linguistic accessibility to the readers of this volume. Additionally, they are much more readily available than those written in Nepali and other languages.

Historically, studies on Nepal—conducted by both Nepali and foreign scholars—have been limited, largely due to the fact that the country was isolated until the early 1950s. Furthermore, until fairly recently, much of the available literature on Nepal was focused on its cultural and historical aspects. This is generally true of works produced by Nepali and foreign scholars and authors. Dominated by anthropologists, the overall research focus on its cultural aspects still remains relatively strong. In recent years, however, especially since the early 1970s, national economic development issues have received a great deal of attention from both Nepali and foreign scholars. This is largely a result of the plethora of development projects that Nepal has witnessed in the past 30 years, projects initiated, financed, or undertaken by foreign agencies or those that have been launched with foreign loans. One lamentable feature of much of the development-related "research" output on Nepal is that it is mostly informational or factually oriented. This is particularly true of those studies produced in the country by development consultants, consulting agencies, and foreign agencies.

The works included in this volume are selected for various reasons. Some are classics in their fields as they have stood the test of time; they are bound to remain important for many years to come. It is no exaggeration that as they age, they gather more value thanks to their analytical insights and historical farsightedness. Some publications are less substantial and seemingly out-of-date in terms of informational contents; yet they act as relevant references in certain historical contexts. Some represent significant contributions to contemporary scholarship on Nepal, whereas others offer useful summaries and information on current problems and contemporary issues. Some works are included because they are usually the only sources of reference on particular topics and subjects. And many are left out because of the lack of their accessibility as well as space in the current volume.

To facilitate greater topical delineations of the entries in the volume, we have separated them into major subjects, largely based on research foci and orientations. The history section is grouped with politics and government and works on population are combined with those on society and culture; some of them are also mixed in the section on economy and development. After all, population cannot be isolated from economic and development issues. Simply expressed, some of the entries are cross-referenced or included in different sections, depending on their topical relevance.

For a panoramic view of Nepal, includes information on a range of topics, we recommend *Nepal and Bhutan: Country Studies* edited by Andrea Matles Savada. It is comprehensive, although some data are somewhat dated. Also valuable is Pradyumna Karan's *Nepal: A Himalayan Kingdom in Transition*. For information on issues related to geography and environmental issues, *Karnali under Stress* by Barry Bishop and *Himalaya* by David Zurick and P. P. Karan, are highly recommended. They are both extensive and reader-friendly, especially the *Himalaya*. For penetrating accounts of history and politics, we suggest the book by Bhuwan Joshi and Leo Rose, *Democratic Innovations in Nepal*. This book is a *must* for anybody who is interested in the political history of Nepal. Although its temporal coverage is somewhat limited, from a historical perspective it is a classic piece, one which is filled with unsurpassed insights into the nature of Nepali politics. One will also find Ludwig Stiller's *The Silent Cry* highly informative. A longtime foreign observer of Nepal and Nepali history, Stiller provides an interesting perspective on historical developments. Our recommended list also includes the volumes by Dilli Raman Regmi and Rishikesh Shaha, all cited in the section on "History, Politics, and Government."

For an informed analysis of people, society, and culture of Nepal, our choices are Lionel Caplan's *Land and Social Change in East Nepal*, William Fisher's *Fluid Boundaries*, Tom Fricke's *Himalayan Households*, Michael Hutt's *Himalayan Voices*, and Mary Slusser's *Nepal Mandala*, which serves as an excellent source of Nepali cultural history and traditions, with a particular focus on the Kathmandu Valley. The most systematic, sensible, and sound treatment of Nepal's contemporary economy and development is found in Devendra Panday's *Nepal's Failed Development*. As a leading authority, Panday offers an excellent and moving account of Nepal's development policy, performance, and problems based on the vast pool of his profound theoretical knowledge, empirical understanding, and personal involvement and experience. On the other hand, real-life stories of development are captured in Nanda Shrestha's *In the Name of Development*, focusing on such issues as drug abuse, prostitution, tourism, foreign aid dependency, Western cultural domination, and agrarian unrest. For a historical analysis of Nepal's economy during the Rana period, there are few books that can match *The State and Economic Surplus* by Mahesh Regmi. This book represents a masterful and insightful portrayal of the economic conditions and policies of Nepal during the Rana period.

As a final note to this clarification on the current bibliographic entries, it is pointed out that the ongoing Internet revolution has proven to be a great boon in the field of literature search, especially for books. Nowhere is this more true than in the cases of those who are endowed with infinite patience to click away on a computer keyboard and surf from one website to another. Websites like amazon.com, bn.com, and yahoo.com—just to name a few—have done wonders as they have revolutionized the whole notion of search and made the treacherous task of bibliographic search apparently manageable even to impatient souls. In the world of exploding websites, Nepal seems to have managed to keep pace as it has seen a massive proliferation of websites dealing with various facets of Nepali life and society. Literally, it has become difficult to keep track of all the Nepal-centered websites that have sprouted in recent years. The following is a limited list of websites on Nepal and they are chosen on the basis of the quality of their contents as well as their user friendliness.

NEPAL WEBSITES

www.nepalhomepage.com

This is perhaps the best and most comprehensive Nepal website, which provides information on virtually every topic related to the country— from politics and government to culture, business, economics, trade, and travel to popular culture and entertainment. It is also very user friendly as it is easy to navigate. In addition, it is an excellent source of current news and provides links to many other pertinent websites.

www.south-asia.com

This is also an excellent website and is quite comprehensive. Through this website, one can access the U.S. Embassy website, which provides valuable information to American tourists and travelers planning to visit Nepal, along with travel tips and alerts. Also included is information on the business climate, investment opportunities, and trade rules and regulations. The website for the U.S. Embassy in Nepal can be accessed quickly via www.south-asia.com/USA.

www.catmando.com

An excellent and comprehensive source of Nepal information on a variety of travel-related issues and topics, for example, hotels, airlines, tours, trekking, shopping, travel agencies, and a host of other useful and pertinent information.

www.visitnepal.com

An excellent site for tourists and travelers to Nepal. Plenty of good and valuable information.

MAJOR ENGLISH MEDIA

Daily Newspapers

The Kathmandu Post
The Rising Nepal

Weekly Newspapers

The Independent
Nepal Times
The People's Review

Spotlight
Sunday Dispatch
Sunday Post
The Telegraph

Magazines

Business Age
Himal South Asia
Kathmandu Post Book Review
Nepal Today
ShowBiz
Young Herald

Radio and Television

BBC Nepal (out of England)
Everest Radio Time–London (out of London)
Kantipur FM
Nepal Television
Radio Nepal
Sagarmatha Television (out of Washington, D.C.)

GENERAL

Acharya, Madhu R. *Nepal Encyclopedia: A Concise Encyclopedia of the Facts and Knowledge about the Kingdom of Nepal*. Kathmandu: Nepal Encyclopedia Foundation, 1994.

Acharya, Meena, and Lynn Bennett. *The Rural Women of Nepal: An Aggregate Analysis and Summary of Eight Village Studies*. Kathmandu: CEDA, 1981.

Adhikary, Dhruba. "Electric Cremation Sparks Row." *South China Morning Post* (27 November 2000).

Adhikary, Kamal R. "The Participation of the Magars in Nepalese Development." Ph.D. Dissertation, University of Texas–Austin, 1993.

Agrawal, Hem N. *Nepal: A Country Study in Constitutional Change*. New Delhi: Oxford and IBH, 1980.

Allan, Nigel J. R., ed. *Mountains at Risk*. New Delhi: Manohar Publications, 1995.

Allman, T. D. "Nepal: Changed for Good, for Bad, Forever." *National Geographic* 198 (2000): 96–117.

Andors, Ellen. "The Rodi: Female Associations among the Gurungs of Nepal." Ph.D. Dissertation, Columbia University, 1976.

Apte, Robert Z. *Three Kingdoms on the Roof of the World: Bhutan, Nepal, Laddakh*. Unknown, 2000 (amazon.com).

Armington, Stan. *Lonely Planet Trekking in the Nepal Himalaya* (8th Edition). Lonely Planet, 2001.

Aryal, Deepak K. *Nepal: Who's Who*. Kathmandu: Kathmandu School of Journalism, 1995.

Asian Development Bank (ADB). *Nepal*. www.adb.org

Association of Nepalis in America. *The Nepal Cookbook*. Ithaca, N.Y.: Snow Lion Publications, 1996.

Banister, Judith, and Shyam Thapa. *The Population Dynamics of Nepal*. Honolulu: East-West Center, 1981.

Baral, Lok Raj. "Nepal in 1987: Politics without Power." *Asian Survey* 28 (1988): 172–179.

———. *Nepal: Problems of Governance*. New Delhi: Konark Publishers, 1993.

Basham, A. L. *The Wonder That Was India*. New York: Grove Press, 1959.

Basnyat, Birendra B. "Nepal's Agricultural Sustainability and Intervention: Looking for New Directions." Ph.D. Dissertation, Wageningen University, 1995.

Bezruchka, Stephen. *Trekking in Nepal: A Traveler's Guide*. Seattle: Mountaineers Books, 1997.

Bhandari, Bishnu. "Landownership and Social Inequality in the Rural Tarai Area of Nepal." Ph.D. Dissertation, University of Wisconsin–Madison, 1985.

Bhattachan, Krishna B., and Chaitanya Mishra, eds. *Development Practices in Nepal*. Kathmandu: Department of Sociology and Anthropology, Tribhuvan University, 1997.

Bhattachan, Krishna B. et al. eds. *NGO, Civil Society, and Government in Nepal*. Kathmandu: FES, 2001.

Bhattarai, Baburam. *Nepal: A Marxist View*. Kathmandu: Jhilko Publications, 1990.

Bhattarai, Keshav. "Landownership and the Use of Forests in Bara District, Central Tarai Region of Nepal." Ph.D. Dissertation, Indiana University, 2001.

Bhattarai, Madan K. *Diplomatic History of Nepal: 1901–1929.* New Delhi: the author, 1990.
Bishop, Lila, and Barry C. Bishop. "Karnali: Roadless World of Western Nepal." *National Geographic* 140 (1971): 656–689.
Bista, Dor B. *People of Nepal.* Kathmandu: Ministry of Information and Broadcasting, 1967.
———. *Fatalism and Development: Nepal's Struggle for Modernization.* Calcutta: Orient Longman, 1991.
Bongartz, Heinz, and Dev Raj Dahal. *Development Studies: Self-Help Organizations, NGOs and Civil Society.* Kathmandu: NEFAS and FES, 1996.
Brown, Percy. *Picturesque Nepal.* London: Adam and Charles Black, 1912.
Brown, T. Louise. *The Challenge of Democracy in Nepal: A Political History.* London: Routledge, 1996.
Buchanan (Hamilton), Francis. *An Account of the Kingdom of Nepal and of the Territories Annexed to This Dominion by the House of Gorkha.* Edinburgh: Constable, 1819.
Burbank, Jon, ed. *Culture Shock!: Nepal.* Portland, Ore: Graphic Arts Center Publishing, 1992.
Caplan, Lionel. *Land and Social Change in East Nepal: A Study of Hindu Tribal Relations.* Berkeley: University of California Press, 1970.
———. *Administration and Politics in a Nepalese Town: The Study of District Capital and Its Environs.* London: Oxford University Press, 1975.
Central Bureau of Statistics (CBS). *Analysis of the 1991 Population Census.* Kathmandu: CBS, 1993.
———. *Statistical Year Book of Nepal.* Kathmandu: CBS, 1993.
———. *Statistical Year Book of Nepal.* Kathmandu: CBS, 2001.
Chadda, Maya. *Building Democracy in South Asia: India, Nepal, and Pakistan.* Boulder, Colo.: Lynne Rienner, 2001.
Chauhan, R. S. *Political Development in Nepal: 1950–1970.* Calcutta: World Press, 1970.
Clarke, G. E. "The Temple and Kinship among a Buddhist People of the Himalaya." D. Phil. Thesis, University of Oxford, 1980.
Coleman, M. E. The Tectonic Evolution of the Central Himalaya, Marsyangdi Valley, Nepal." Ph.D. Dissertation, Massachusetts Institute of Technology, 1996.
Conway, Dennis, Keshav Bhattarai, and Nanda R. Shrestha. "Population–Environment Relations at the Forested Frontier of Nepal: Tharu and Pahari Survival Strategies in Bardiya." *Applied Geography* 20 (2000): 221–242.

Coomaraswami, Anan.da K. "A Nepalese Tara" *Rupam* 6 (April 1921).
———. "A Tibeto-Nepalese Image of Maitreya" *Rupam* 11 (July 1922).
Cross, J. P. *The Call of Nepal*. London: New Millennium, 1996.
Dahal, Dev R. *Civil Society in Nepal: Opening the Ground for Questions*. Kathmandu: Centre for Development and Governance, 2001.
Dahal, Dilli Ram. "Is There Anything as 'Good Governance' in Nepal? Reflections on the Functioning of the Civil Society." In *Local Self Government in Nepal*, ed. Ganga B. Thapa. Kathmandu: POLSAN and FES, 1998.
Dahal, Madan Kumar, ed. *Impact of Globalization in Nepal*. Kathmandu: NEFAS and FES, 1998.
Dahal, Madan Kumar, et al. *Development Challenges for Nepal*. Kathmandu: NEFAS and FINNIDA, 1999.
Des Chene, Mary. "Relics of Empire: A Cultural History of the Gurkhas, 1815–1987." Ph.D. Dissertation, Stanford University, 1991.
———. "'We Women Must Try to Live': The Saga of Bhauju." *Studies in Nepali History and Society* 2 (1997): 125–172.
Douglas, Nik, and Penny Slinger. *The Erotic Sentiment: In the Paintings of India and Nepal*. Rochester, Vt.: Inner Traditions International, 1998.
Federation of Nepalese Chamber of Commerce and Industry (FNCCI). *Nepal and the World: A Statistical Profile, 1995*. Kathmandu: FNCCI, 1995.
Fisher, James F. "Education and Social Change in Nepal: An Anthropologist's Assessment." *Himalayan Research Bulletin* 10 (1990): 30–34.
Fisher, Robert J. *Indigenous Systems of Common Property Management in Nepal*. Honolulu: East-West Center, 1989.
Forum for Protection of Human Rights (FOPHUR). *Dawn of Democracy: People's Power in Nepal*. Kathmandu: FOPHUR, 1990.
Fürer-Haimendorf, Christoph von. *Himalayan Traders: Life in Highland Nepal*. London: John Murray, 1975.
Gaige, Frederick H. *Regionalism and National Unity in Nepal*. Berkeley: University of California, 1975.
Garver, John W. "China-India Rivalry in Nepal: The Clash over Chinese Arms Sales." *Asian Survey* 31 (1991): 323–347.
Ghimire, Krishna. *Forest or Farm? The Politics of Poverty and Land Hunger in Nepal*. New Delhi: Oxford University Press, 1992.
Gilmour, Donald. A., and Robert J. Fisher. *Villagers, Forests, and Foresters: The Philosophy, Process and Practice of Community Forestry in Nepal*. Kathmandu: Sahayogi Press, 1991.

Guneratne, Katharine Bjork. *In the Circle of the Dance: Notes of an Outsider in Nepal.* Ithaca, N.Y.: Cornell University Press, 1999.

Guneratne, Upali Arjun. "The Tharus of Chitwan: Ethnicity, Class and the State of Nepal." Ph.D. Dissertation, University of Chicago, 1994.

———. "The Tax Man Cometh: The Impact of Revenue Collection on Subsistence Strategies in Chitwan Tharu Society." *Studies in Nepali History and Society* 1 (1996): 5–36.

———. "Modernization, the State and the Construction of a Tharu Identity in Nepal." *Journal of Asian Studies* 57 (1998): 749–779.

Gurung, Ganesh Man. *Indigenous Peoples: Mobilization and Change.* Kathmandu: HISI Press, 1994.

Gurung, Harka. *Nepal: Dimensions of Development.* Kathmandu: Sahayogi Press, 1984.

———. *Regional Patterns of Migration in Nepal.* Honolulu: East-West Center, 1989.

———. *Nepal: Social Demography and Expressions.* Kathmandu: New Era, 1998.

Gyawali, Dipak. *Water in Nepal: An Interdisciplinary Look at Resource Uncertainties, Evolving Problems, and Future Prospects.* Honolulu: East-West Center, 1989.

———. "Buddhijibi: Intelligentsia Has No Clothes." *Himal* 7 (1994): 11–15.

———. "Are NGOs in Nepal Old Wine or New Bottle? A Cultural Theory Perspective on Nepal's Contested Terrain." In *NGO, Civil Society and Government in Nepal*, eds. Krishna B. Bhattachan, et al. Kathmandu: FES, 2001.

Hachhethu, Krishna. "Mass Movement in Nepal." *Contributions to Nepalese Studies* 17 (1990): 177–201.

———. "Transition to Democracy in Nepal: Negotiations behind Constitution Making, 1990." *Contributions to Nepalese Studies.* 21 (1994): 91–126.

Hagen, Toni. *Nepal: The Kingdom in the Himalayas.* Berne: Kummerly and Frey, 1961.

Hamal, Lakshman B. *Contemporary Nepal: Triumphs and Agonies of the Nepali People.* Varansi: Ganga Kaveri Publishing House, 1994.

Hays, Louis. "Educational Reform and Student Political Behavior in Nepal." *Asian Survey* 16 (1976): 752–769.

Herzog, Maurice, Janet Adam Smith, and Nea Morin (Translators). *Annapurna: The Epic Account of a Himalayan Conquest and Its Harrowing Aftermath.* New York: Lyons Press, 1997.

Hitchcock, John T. *Magars of Banyan Hill.* New York: Holt, Rinehart & Winston, 1966.

Hoftun, Martin, and William Raeper. *Spring Awakening: An Account of the 1990 Revolution in Nepal.* New Delhi: Penguin Books, 1992

Holmberg, David H. *Order in Paradox: Myth, Ritual, and Exchange among Nepal's Tamang.* Ithaca, N.Y.: Cornell University Press, 1989.

Husain, Asad. *British India's Relations with the Kingdom of Nepal.* London: Allen and Unwin, 1970.

Hutt, Michael. *Nepali: A National Language and Its Literature.* New Delhi: Sterling Publishers, 1988.

Hutt, Michael, ed. *Nepal in the Nineties: Versions of the Past, Visions of the Future.* New Delhi: Oxford University Press, 1994.

Iijima, Shigeru. "The Thakalis: Traditional and Modern." *Anthropological and Linguistic Studies of the Gandaki Area in Nepal.* Monumenta Serendica 10 (1982): 21–39.

Ives, Jack D., and Bruno Messerli. *The Himalayan Dilemma: Reconciling Development and Conservation.* New York: Routledge, 1989.

Jha, Sunil Kumar, Arene Sanderson, and Irene Sanderson. *The Simple Guide to Nepal: Customs & Etiquette.* Kent, Ohio: Paul Norbury Publications, 1998.

Jones, R. L. "Sanskritization in Eastern Nepal." *Ethnology* 15 (1976): 63–75.

Joshi, Bhuwan Lal, and Leo E. Rose. *Democratic Innovations in Nepal: A Case Study of Political Acculturation.* Berkeley: University of California Press, 1966.

Kamler, Kenneth. *Doctor on Everest: Emergency Medicine at the Top of the World—A Personal Account Including the 1996 Disaster.* Guilford, Conn.: Globe Pequot Press, 2000.

Kanel, K. R. "Farmer and Tree Linkages in the Tarai of Nepal." Ph.D. Dissertation, University of Minnesota, 1995.

Kansakar, Vidya V. S. "Population of Nepal." In *Nepal: Perspectives on Continuity and Change,* ed. Kamal P. Malla. Kathmandu: CNAS, 1989.

Karan, Pradyumna P. *Nepal: A Physical and Cultural Geography.* Lexington: University of Kentucky Press, 1960.

———. *Nepal: A Himalayan Kingdom in Transition.* Tokyo: United Nations University Press, 1996.

Karan, Pradyumna P., and Hiroshi Ishii. *Nepal: Development and Change in a Landlocked Himalayan Kingdom.* Tokyo: Tokyo University of Foreign Studies, 1994.

Kaushik, Pitambar. "Water Resources of Nepal: Key to Indo-Nepal Relations." *Water Nepal* 4 (1994): 275–281.
Khadka, Narayan. "The Political Economy of the Food Crisis in Nepal." *Asian Survey* 25 (1985): 943–962.
——. *Politics and Development in Nepal*. New Delhi: Nirala Publications, 1994.
Khanal, Yadu Nath. "Nepal in 1984: A Year of Complacence." *Asian Survey* 25 (1985): 180–186.
——. "Nepal in 1997: Political Stability Eludes." *Asian Survey* 38 (1998): 148–154.
Khatry, Prem K., ed. *Social Science in Nepal: Some Thoughts and Search for Direction*. Kathmandu: CNAS, 1997.
Kirkpatrick, Colonel. *An Account of the Kingdom of Nepaul, (being the Substance of Observations Made during a Mission to that Country in the Year 1793)*. New Delhi: Manjusri Publishing House, 1969 (Reprint of the 1811 edition).
Koirala, Niranjan. "Nepal in 1989: A Very Difficult Year." *Asian Survey* 30 (1990): 136–143.
Krakauer, Jon. *Into Thin Air: A Personal Account of the Mount Everest Disaster*. New York: Anchor Books, 1998.
Kramer, Sydelle A. *To the Top!: Climbing the World's Highest Mountain*. New York: Random House, 1993.
Kropp, Göran, and David Lagercrantz. *Ultimate High: My Everest Odyssey*. Los Angeles: Discovery Books, 1999.
Kumar, Satish. *Rana Polity in Nepal: Origin and Growth*. New York: Asia, 1967.
Levine, Nancy E. "Women's Work and Infant Feeding: A Case from Rural Nepal." *Ethnology* 27 (1988): 231–251.
Liechty, Mark. "Fashioning Modernity in Kathmandu: Mass Media, Consumer Culture, and the Middle Class in Nepal." Ph.D. Dissertation, University of Pennsylvania, 1994.
——. "Selective Exclusion: Foreigners, Foreign Goods, and Foreignness in Modern Nepali History." *Studies in Nepali History and Society* 2 (1997): 5–68.
Lohani, Mohan Prasad, ed. *Social Sciences in Nepal: Infrastructure and Programme Development*. Kathmandu: Institute of Humanities and Social Sciences, Tribhuvan University, 1984.

McDonaugh, C. "The Tharus of Dang: A Study of Social Organization, Myth and Ritual in West Nepal." Ph. D. Dissertation, University of Oxford, 1984.

McDougal, Charles. *Village and Household Economy in Far Western Nepal.* Kathmandu: Tribhuvan University Press, 1968.

MacFarlane, Alan. *Resources and Population: A Study of the Gurungs of Nepal.* Cambridge: Cambridge University Press, 1976.

Mahat, Tej B. S., David M. Griffin, and K. R. Shepherd. "Human Impact of Some Forests of the Middle Hills of Nepal: Forestry in the Context of the Traditional Resources of the State." *Mountain Research and Development* 6 (1986): 223–232.

Malla, Kamal P., ed. *Nepal: Perspectives on Continuity and Change.* Kathmandu: CNAS, 1989.

Maskay, Bishwa K. *Non-Governmental Organizations in Development: Search for a New Vision.* Kathmandu: Centre for Development and Governance, 1998.

Mathema, Padma. *Primary Health Care in Nepal.* Kathmandu: Vijaya Ram Mathema, 1987.

Messerschmidt, Donald A. *The Gurungs of Nepal: Conflict and Change in a Village Society.* Warminster, UK: Aris and Phillips, 1976.

Metz, John J. "Forest-Product Use in Upland Nepal." *Geographical Review* 80 (1990): 279–287.

Mierow, Dorothy. *This Beautiful Nepal.* Kathmandu: Sahayogi Press, 1981.

Mihaly, Eugene B. *Foreign Aid and Politics in Nepal.* New York: Oxford University Press, 1965.

Ministry of Health (MOH). *Country Health Profile: Nepal.* Kathmandu: MOH, 1988.

Mishra, Chaitanya. "New Predicament for Humanitarian Organizations." In *NGO, Civil Society, and Government in Nepal*, eds. Krishna B. Bhattachan, et al. Kathmandu: FES, 2001.

Mojumdar, Kanchamoy. *Nepal and the Indian Nationalist Movement.* Calcutta: Forma K. L. Mukhopadhyay, 1975.

Moore, Wendy. *Kathmandu: The Forbidden Valley.* New York: St. Martin's Press, 1990.

Nepal South Asia Centre (NESAC). *Nepal Human Development Report, 1998.* Kathmandu: 1998.

New Era. *An Evaluative Study of the Nepal Children's Organization.* Kathmandu: 1983.

Onta, Pratyoush. "The Politics of Bravery: A History of Nepali Nationalism." Ph.D. Dissertation, University of Pennsylvania, 1996.

Ortner, Sherry B. *Life and Death on Mt. Everest: Sherpas and Himalayan Mountaineering.* Princeton, N.J.: Princeton University Press, 2001.

Pal, Pratap Aditya, ed. *Art from India, Nepal, and Tibet: In the John and Berths Ford Collection.* London: Philip Wilson Publishers, 2001.

Panday, Devendra Raj. *Nepal's Failed Development: Reflections on the Missions and the Maladies.* Kathmandu: Nepal South Asia Centre, 1999.

——. *Corruption, Governance and International Cooperation.* Kathmandu: Transparency International Nepal, 2001.

Pandey, Rudra R., Kaisher Bahadur K. C., and Hugh B. Wood, eds. *Education in Nepal: Report of the National Education Planning Commission.* Kathmandu: College of Education, 1956.

Parker, Barbara. "Moral Economy, Political Economy, and the Culture of Entrepreneurship in Highland Nepal." *Ethnology* 27 (1988): 181–195.

Paudel, N. B. *Nepal Resettlement Company: An Introduction.* Pulchowk, Lalitpur: Nepal Resettlement Company, 1989.

Pettigrew, Judith. "Shamanic Dialogue: History, Representation and Landscape in Nepal." Ph.D. Dissertation, University of Cambridge, 1995.

Poffenberger, Mark. *Patterns of Change in the Nepal Himalaya.* New Delhi: Macmillan, 1980.

Poudel, R. "Farmers' Laws and Irrigation. Water Rights and Dispute Management in the Hills of Nepal." Ph. D. Dissertation, Wageningen University, 2000.

Rana, Pashupati S., and Dwarika Nath Dhungel, eds. *Contemporary Nepal.* New Delhi: Vikas Publishing House, 1998.

Rana, Pashupati S., and Kamal P. Malla, eds. *Nepal in Perspective.* Kathmandu: CEDA, 1973.

Rana, Pramod S. *Rana Intrigues.* Kathmandu: R. Rana, 1995.

Regmi, Mahesh C. *Landownership in Nepal.* Berkeley: University of California Press, 1976.

——. *Thatched Huts and Stucco Palaces: Peasants and Landlords in 19th-Century Nepal.* New Delhi: Vikas Publishing House, 1978.

Rose, Leo E. *Nepal: Strategy for Survival.* Berkeley: University of California Press, 1971.

Rose, Leo E., and J. T. Scholz. *Nepal: Profile of a Himalayan Kingdom.* New Delhi: Selectbook Service Syndicate, 1980.

Savada, Andrea Matles, ed. *Nepal and Bhutan: Country Studies* (Area Handbook Series). Washington, D.C.: Library of Congress.

Scot, Barbara J. *The Violet Shyness of Their Eyes: Notes from Nepal.* Corvallis, Ore.: Calyx Books, 1993.

Seddon, David. *Nepal: A State of Poverty.* New Delhi: Vikas Publishing House, 1987.

Shaha, Rishikesh. *Nepal and the World.* Kathmandu: Nepali Congress, 1955.

———. *Human Rights and Parliamentary Practices in Nepal.* Kathmandu: Development Research for a Democratic Nepal, 1995.

Shakya, Rabindra K. *Development Policies and Institutions and Their Impact on Sustainable Human Development.* Kathmandu: UNDP, 2000.

Sharma, Gopi Nath. "The Impact of Education during the Rana Period in Nepal." *Himalayan Research Bulletin* 10 (1990): 3–7.

Sharma, Jagdish. *Nepal: Struggle for Existence.* Kathmandu: Communications, 1986.

Sharma, Pitamber. *Urbanization in Nepal.* Honolulu: East-West Center, 1989.

Sharma, Prayag Raj. "The Land System of the Licchavis in Nepal." *Kailash* 10 (1983): 11–62.

Sharma, Shankar P. "Economics Education and Research Capacity in Nepal: An Agenda for Reform." In *Social Sciences in Nepal: Some Thoughts and Search for Direction*, ed. Prem K. Khatry. Kathmandu: CNAS, 1997.

Sharma, Subodh. "Biological Assessment of Water Quality in the Rivers of Nepal." Ph. D. Dissertation, University of Agriculture, Forestry and Renewable Natural Resources, Vienna, 1996.

Sharma, Udaya Raj. "Park-People Interactions in Royal Chitwan National Park, Nepal." Ph.D. Dissertation, University of Arizona, 1991.

Shrestha, Anand P., ed. *The Role of Civil Society in Democratization in Nepal.* Kathmandu: NEFAS and FES, 1998.

Shrestha, Badri P. *An Introduction to Nepalese Economy.* Kathmandu: Ratna Pustak Bhandar, 1981.

Shrestha, Badri P., and S. C. Jain. *Regional Development in Nepal: An Exercise in Reality.* New Delhi: Development Publishers, 1978.

Shrestha, Bihari K. *A Himalayan Enclave in Transition.* Kathmandu: ICIMOD, 1993.

Shrestha, Nanda R. "Human Relations and Primary Health Care Delivery in Rural Nepal: The Case of Deurali." *Professional Geographer* 40 (1988): 202–213.

———. "Frontier Settlement and Landlessness among Hill Migrants in Nepal Tarai." *Annals of the Association of American Geographers* 79 (1989): 370–389.
———. *Landlessness and Migration in Nepal*. Boulder, Colo: Westview Press, 1990.
———. "Nepali Labour and Global Capital: A Historical Perspective on Nepali Migration to India." *Arab World Geographer* 1 (1998): 60–78.
———. "The Environmental Degradation of Kathmandu: Losing Shangri-La?" *Education About Asia* 3 (1998): 11–18.
Shrestha, Nanda R., and Dennis Conway. "Ecopolitical Battles in the Tarai of Nepal: An Emerging Human and Environmental Crisis." *International Journal of Population Geography* 2 (1996): 313–331.
Shrestha, Nanda R., Raja Velu, and Dennis Conway. "Frontier Migration and Upward Mobility: The Case of Nepal." *Economic Development and Cultural Change* 41 (1993): 787–816.
Sierra Club. *Annapurna: A Woman's Place*. San Francisco: 1998.
Sill, Michael, and John Kirkby. *The Atlas of Nepal in the Modern World*. London: Earthscan Publications, 1991.
Singer, Jane C. *Gold Jewelry from Tibet and Nepal*. New York: Thames and Hudson, 1997.
Singh, Shiv B. *Indo-Nepal Relations: Discord and Harmony*. Varanasi: Ganga Kaveri Publishing House, 1994.
Skar, Harold O. *Development Aid to Nepal: Issues and Options in Energy, Health, Education, Democracy and Human Rights*. Copenhagen: NIAS, 1997.
Stevens, Stanley F. *Claiming the High Ground: Sherpas, Subsistence, and Environmental Change in the Highest Himalaya*. Berkeley: University of California Press, 1993.
Stiller, Ludwig F. *The Silent Cry*. Kathmandu: Sahayogi Prakashan, 1976.
———. *Nepal: Growth of a Nation*. Kathmandu: HRD Research Centre, 1993.
Stone, Linda. "Cultural Crossroads of Community Participation in Development: A Case from Nepal." *Human Organization* 48 (1989): 206–213.
Taylor-Ide, Daniel. *Something Hidden behind the Ranges: A Himalayan Quest*. San Francisco: Mercury House, 1995.
Thapa, Dharma Raj. *Chitwan Darpan*. Kathmandu: Nepal Rajakiya Prajna Pratisthan, 1993.

Thapa, Ganga B., ed. *Local Self-Government in Nepal*. Kathmandu: POL-SAN and FES, 1998.

Thapa, Poonam. "Socioeconomic Change and Rural Migration in Nepal: Individual and Households Relations." Ph.D. Dissertation, Indiana University, 1986.

Tucker, Francis I. S. *Gorkha: The Story of Gurkhas of Nepal*. London: Constable, 1957.

Turner, Ralph L. *A Comparative and Etymological Dictionary of the Nepali Language* (Reprint). New Delhi: Allied Publishers, 1980.

Upadhyay, Samrat. *Arresting God of Kathmandu*. Boston: Marriner Books, 2001.

Uprety, Hari. "Change of Policies in the Economic and Political Life of Nepal." *Nepali Political Science and Politics* 5 (1996): 79–90.

Uprety, Prem R. "The Economics of Buddhism: An Alternative Model for Community Development." *Contributions to Nepalese Studies* 23 (1996).

Vaidya, R. T., and B. R. Bajacharya, eds. *Nepal: International Perspec-tives*. New Delhi: Anmol, 1996.

Varughese, George. "Villagers, Bureaucrats, and Forests in Nepal: Designing Governance for a Complex Resource." Ph.D. Dissertation, Indiana University, 2000.

Varughese, George, and Elinor Ostrom. "The Contested Role of Heterogeneity in Collective Action: Some Evidence from Community Forestry in Nepal." *World Development* 29 (2001).

Wadhwa, D. N., and S. Mukhopadhyaya. *Nepal: Bibliography*. New Delhi: Sharada Publishing, 1991.

World Bank. *Nepal: Poverty and Incomes*. Washington, D.C.: World Bank, 1991.

——. *Country Assistance Strategy: Nepal, 1999–2001*. Washington, D.C.: World Bank, 1999.

——. *Development Challenges*. www.worldbank.org.np

Zaman, M. A. *Evaluation of Land Reform in Nepal*. Kathmandu: Ministry of Land Reform, 1973.

Zivetz, Laurie. *Private Enterprise and the State in Modern Nepal*. Madras: Oxford University Press, 1992.

Zurick, David, and P. P. Karan. *Himalaya: Life on the Edge of the World*. Baltimore, Md.: Johns Hopkins University Press, 1999.

GEOGRAPHY AND ENVIRONMENT

Adhikari, Ambika P., Bishnu Bhandari, and Bishwambher Pyakuryal, eds. *Environmental Economics in Nepal*. Kathmandu: IUCN, 1998.

Adhikari, Ambika P., Bishwambher Pyakuryal, and Jaklien Vlasblom, eds. *Environmental Economics in Nepal*. Kathmandu: IUCN, 1999.

Agricultural Projects Services Centre (APROSC). *Nepal Agriculture Perspective Plan*. Kathmandu: APROSC, 1995.

Agricultural Statistics Division (ASD). *Statistical Information of Nepalese Agriculture*. Kathmandu: Ministry of Agriculture, 1998.

Allan, Nigel J. R., G. W. Knapp, and C. Stadel, eds. *Human Impact on Mountains*. Totowa, N.J.: Rowman and Littlefield, 1988.

Amacher, G. S., W. F. Hyde, and K. R. Kanel. "Household Fuelwood Demand and Supply in Nepal's Tarai and Mid-Hills: Choice between Cash Outlays and Labour Opportunity." *World Development* 24 (1996): 1725–1736.

Anker, Conrad, and David Roberts. *The Lost Explorer: Finding Mallory on Mt. Everest*. New York: Simon and Schuster, 1999.

Asian Development Bank (ADB). *Ambient Air Quality Monitoring of the Kathmandu Valley*. Kathmandu: ADB-Nepal, 1999.

Axinn, Nancy W., and George H. Axinn. "The Human Dynamics of Natural Resource Systems." In *People and Participation in Sustainable Development: Understanding the Dynamics of Natural Resource Systems*, eds. Ganesh Shivakoti, et al. Rampur, Chitwan: Institute of Agriculture and Animal Science, 1996.

Bajracharya, Deepak. "Fuel, Food or Forest? Dilemmas in Nepali Village." *World Development* 11 (1983): 1057–1074.

Balla, Mohan K., Santosh Rayamajhi, and Narendra M. B. Pradhan. "Participatory Biodiversity Conservation in the South Asia Region." *Proceedings of Regional Networking Seminar and Second General Assembly*. Kathmandu: Forum of Natural Resource Managers, 2001.

Banskota, Mahesh, T. S. Papola, and J. Richter, eds. *Growth, Poverty Alleviation, and Sustainable Resource Management in the Mountain Areas of South Asia*. Kathmandu: ICIMOD, 2000.

Bastola, Tung S. "Agro-Biodiversity." In *A Compendium on the Environmental Statistics of Nepal*. Kathmandu: CBS, 1998.

Belbase, N. *The Implementation of Environmental Law in Nepal*. Kath-mandu: IUCN-Nepal, 1997.

Berreman, Gerald D. "Cultural Variability and Drift in the Himalayan Hills." *American Anthropologist* 62 (1960): 774–794.

Bhandari, Bishnu. *An Inventory of Nepal's Terai Wetlands*. Kathmandu: IUCN-Nepal, 1998.

Bhatta, Dibya Deo. *Natural History and Economic Botany of Nepal* (revised edition). New Delhi: Orient Longman, 1977.

Bhattarai, N. K. "Ethnobotanical Studies in Central Nepal: The Ceremonial Plant Foods." *Contributions to Nepalese Studies* 16 (1989): 35–41.

Bishop, Barry C. *Karnali under Stress: Livelihood Strategies and Seasonal Rhythms in a Changing Nepal Himalaya*. Chicago: University of Chicago, 1990.

Bishop, Naomi. "From Zomo to Yak: Change in a Sherpa Village." *Human Ecology* 17 (1989): 177–204.

———. *Himalayan Herders*. New York: Thompson International Publishing, 1998.

Bjønness, Inger Marie. "Animal Husbandry and Grazing: A Conservation and Management Problem in Sagarmatha (Mt. Everest) National Park, Nepal." *Norsk Geografisk Tidsskrift* 34 (1980): 59–76.

———. "Mountain Hazard Perception and Risk-Avoiding Strategies among the Sherpas of Khumbu Himal." *Mountain Research and Development* 6 (1986): 277–292.

Blaikie, Piers, and Harold Brookfield. *Land Degradation and Society*. London: Methuen, 1987.

Blaikie, Piers, John Cameron, and David Seddon. *Nepal in Crisis: Growth and Stagnation at the Periphery*. Oxford: Clarendon Press, 1980.

Blaikie, Piers, and S. Z. Sadeque. *Policy in High Places: Environment and Development in the Himalayan Region*. Kathmandu: ICIMOD, 2000.

Bolt, D. *Gurkhas*. London: Weidenfeld and Nicholson, 1967.

Bolton, M. *Royal Chitwan National Park Management Plan, 1975–1979*. Kathmandu: FAO-Nepal, 1975.

———. "New Parks and Reserves in Nepal." *Oryx* 13 (1977): 473–478.

Boukreev, Anatoli, and G. Westen DeWalt. *Climb: Tragic Ambitions on Everest*. New York: Tom Doherty Associates, 1998.

Brower, Barbara A. *Sherpa of Khumbu: People, Livestock, and Landscape*. New Delhi: Oxford University Press.

Bunting, B. W., M. N. Sherpa, and M. Wright. "Annapurna Conservation Area: Nepal's New Approach to Protected Area Management." In *Resistant Peoples and National Parks: Social Dilemmas and Strategies in*

International Conservation, eds. P. C. West and S. R. Brechin. Tucson: University of Arizona Press, 1991.

Burton, S., G. Kennedy, H. Schreier. "An Analysis of Land Use Options in Chitwan, Nepal." *Mountain Research and Development* 10 (1990): 73–87.

Burton, S., P. B. Shah, and H. Schreier. "Soil Degradation from Converting Forest Land into Agriculture in the Chitwan District of Nepal." *Mountain Research and Development* 9 (1989): 393–404.

Bustard, H. R. "Clutch Size, Incubation and Hatching Success of Gharial [*Gavialis gangeticus*–Gmelin] Eggs from Narayani River, Nepal, 1976–1978." *Journal of the Bombay Natural History Society* 77 (1980): 100–105.

Byers, Alton. "A Geomorphic Study of Man-Induced Soil Erosion in Sagarmatha (Mt. Everest), National Park, Khumbu, Nepal." *Mountain Research and Development* 6 (1986): 83–87.

Cameron, I. C. *Mountains of the Gods*. London: Century Publishing, 1984.

Carson, Brian. *The Land, the Farmer, and the Future: A Soil Fertility Management Strategy for Nepal*. Kathmandu: ICIMOD, 1992.

Carter, Andrew S., and Donald A. Gilmour. "Increase in Tree Cover on Private Farm Land in Nepal." *Mountain Research and Development* 9 (1989): 381–391.

Caughley, G. *Wildlife and Recreation in the Trisuli Watershed and Other Areas in Nepal* (Project Report No. 6). Kathmandu: Trisuli Watershed Development Project, 1969.

CBS. *National Sample Census of Agriculture, 1991*. Kathmandu: CBS, 1994.

———. *A Compendium on the Environmental Statistics of Nepal*. Kathmandu: CBS, 1998.

Chaturvedi, S. K. *Indo-Nepal Relations in Linkage Perspective*. New Delhi: B. R. Publishing, 1990.

Clarke, G. E. "A Helambu History." *Journal of the Nepal Research Centre* 4 (1980): 1–38.

Coburn, Broughton, David Breashears, and Tim Cahill. *Everest: Mountain without Mercy*. Washington, D.C.: National Geographic Society, 1997.

Community and Private Forestry Development (CPFD). *Community and Private Forestry Development*. Kathmandu: Department of Forest, 1999.

Conway, Dennis, Nanda Shrestha, and Keshav Bhattarai. "Population-Environment Relations at the Forested Frontier of Nepal: Tharu and Pahari Survival Strategies in Bardiya." *Applied Geography* 20 (2000): 221–242.

Dahal, Madan K., and Dev Raj Dahal. *Environment and Sustainable Development: Issues in Nepalese Perspective*. Kathmandu: NEFAS and FES, 1998.

Department of Agriculture (DOA). *Annual Report of Soil Science Programs, 1998*. Kathmandu: DOA, 1999.

Department of Forest Research and Survey (DFRS). *Forest and Shrub Cover of Nepal, 1994*. Kathmandu: DFRS, 1999.

Department of Health Services (DOHS). *Annual Report 1998*. Kathmandu: DOHS, 1999.

Department of Hydrology and Meteorology (DHM). *Information on TSP Concentrations in the Kathmandu Valley*. Kathmandu: DHM, 1999.

Department of Medicinal Plants (DMP). *Flora of Kathmandu*. Kathmandu: DMP, 1986.

Dignan, Tony, et al. "Land and Landlessness Among Rural-to-Rural Migrants in Nepal's Tarai Region." *International Regional Science Review* 12 (1989): 189–209.

Dinerstein, E. "Demography and Habitat Use by Greater One Horned Rhinoceros in Nepal." *Journal of Wildlife Management* 55 (1989): 40–411.

Economic and Social Commission for Asia and the Pacific (ESCAP). *Atlas of Mineral Resources of Nepal: Explanatory Brochure*. New York: ESCAP, 1993.

Edds, D. R. "The Fishes of Royal Chitwan National Park." *Journal of Natural History Museum* 10 (1986): 1–12.

Environment and Public Health Organisation (ENPHO). *A Report on Study on Reduction of Pollution and Waste in the Himal Cement Company Limited, Kathmandu, Nepal*. Kathmandu: ENPHO, 1999.

———. *Kathmandu City Looking through the Eyes of ENPHO*. Kathmandu: ENPHO, 2000.

Exo, S. "Local Resource Management in Nepal: Limitations and Prospects." *Mountain Research and Development* 10 (1990): 16–22.

Feldman, David, and A. Fournier. "Social Relations and Agricultural Production in Nepal's Tarai." *Journal of Peasant Studies* 3 (1976): 447–464.

Fisher, James F. *Sherpas: Reflections on Change in Himalayan Nepal*. Berkeley: University of California Press, 1990.

Fisher, Robert J. *Indigenous Systems of Common Property Forest Management in Nepal*. Honolulu: East-West Center, 1989.

Forest Management, Utilization and Development Project (FMUDP). *The Potential of the Natural Forests of the Tarai and the New Principles of Forest Management.* Kathmandu: FINNIDA, 1995.

Fox, J. M. "Livestock Ownership Patterns in Nepali Village." *Mountain Research and Development* 7 (1987):169–172.

———. "Forest Resources in a Nepali Village in 1980 and 1990: The Positive Influence of Population Growth." *Mountain Research and Development* 13 (1993): 89–98.

Fricke, Tom. *Himalayan Households: Tamang Demography and Domestic Processes.* New York: Columbia University Press, 1994.

Fürer-Haimendorf, Christoph von. *Asian Highland Societies in Anthropological Perspective.* New Delhi: Sterling Publishers, 1981.

———. *The Sherpas Transformed: Social Change in a Buddhist Society of Nepal.* New Delhi: Sterling Publishers, 1984.

Gammelgaard, Lene. *Climbing High: A Woman's Account of Surviving the Everest Tragedy.* Seattle: Seal Press, 1999.

Gilmour, Donald A. "Not Seeing the Trees for the Forest: A Reappraisal of the Deforestation Crisis in Two Hill Districts of Nepal." *Mountain Research and Development* 8 (1988): 343–350.

Gilmour, Donald A., and Robert J. Fisher. *Villagers, Forests, and Foresters: The Philosophy, Process and Practice of Community Forestry in Nepal.* Kathmandu: Sahayogi Press, 1991.

Gilmour, Donald A., and Michael C. Nurse. "Farmer Initiatives in Increasing Tree Cover in Central Nepal." *Mountain Research and Development* 11 (1991): 329–337.

Government of Nepal. "Private Forest (Nationalization) Act." *Nepal Rajpatra* 6 (1957): 5 February.

———. "Medicinal Plants of Nepal." *Bulletin of the Department of Medicinal Plants* 3 (1970).

———. "Wild Edible Plants of Nepal." *Bulletin of the Department of Medicinal Plants* 9 (1982).

———. *Agricultural Statistics of Nepal.* Kathmandu: Agricultural Statistical Division, 1983.

———. *Livestock Statistics of Nepal, 1984–1985.* Kathmandu: Agricultural Statistical Division, 1986.

Graner, E. "The Political Ecology of Community Forestry in Nepal." *Freiburger Studien Zur Geographischen Entwicklungsforschung.* Saarbrucken, 1997.

Griffin, David M. *Innocents abroad in the Forests of Nepal: An Account of Australian Aid to Nepalese Forestry*. Canberra: Australian National University, 1988.

Griffin, David M., K. R. Shepherd, and Tej B. S. Mahat. "Human Impacts on Some Forests of the Middle Hills of Nepal: Comparisons, Concept, and Some Policy Implications." *Mountain Research and Development* 8 (1988): 43–52.

Ground Water Resources Development Board (GWRDB). *Feasibility Report of Mahottari Deep Tubewell Irrigation Project*. Kathmandu: GWRDB, 1990.

Gurung, B. "The Perceived Environment as a System of Knowledge and Meaning: A Study of the Mewahnag Rai of Eastern Nepal." In *Nature Is Culture: Indigenous Knowledge of Socio-Cultural Aspects of Trees and Forests in Non-European Cultures*, ed. K. Seeland. London: Intermediate Technology Publication, 1997.

Gurung, Harka. *Vignettes of Nepal*. Kathmandu: Sajha Prkashan, 1980.

———. *Ecological Change in Nepal: A Native Interpretation*. Kathmandu: New ERA, 1981.

———. *Maps of Nepal: Inventory and Evaluation*. Bangkok: White Orchid Press, 1983.

Gurung, K. K., and Raj Singh. *Field Guide to the Mammals of the Indian Subcontinent: Where to Watch Mammals in India, Nepal, Bhutan, Bangladesh, Sri Lanka, and Pakistan*. San Diego: Academic Press, 1998.

Gurung, Sumitra M. "Human Perception of Mountain Hazards in the Kakani-Kathmandu Area." *Mountain Research and Development* 9 (1989): 353–364.

———. "Beyond the Myth of Eco-Crisis in Nepal: Local Responses to Pressure on Land in the Middle Hills." Ph.D. Dissertation. Honolulu: University of Hawaii, 1988.

Guthman, J. "Representing Crisis: The Theory of Himalayan Environmental Degradation and the Project of Development in Post-Rana Nepal." *Development and Change* 28 (1997): 45–69.

Gyawali, Dipak. *Water in Nepal: An Interdisciplinary Look at Resource Uncertainties, Evolving Problems, and Future Prospects*. Honolulu: East-West Environment and Policy Institute, 1989

———. "Troubled Politics of Himalayan Waters." *Himal* May–June, 1991.

———. "High Dams for Asia: Neo-Gandhian Maoists vs. Nehruvian Stalinists " *Himal* (March 1996).

Hagen, Toni. *Nepal: The Kingdom in the Himalayas.* Berne: Kummerly and Frey, 1961.

———. *Mount Everest: Formation, Population and Exploration of the Everest Region.* London: Oxford University Press, 1963.

Hara, H., and L. H. J. Williams. *An Enumeration of the Flowering Plants of Nepal* (Volume III). London: Trustees of British Museum (Natural History), 1978.

Hatley, T., and M. Thompson. "Rare Animals, Poor People, and Big Agencies: A Perspective on Biological Conservation and Rural Development in the Himalaya." *Mountain Research and Development* 5 (1985): 365–377.

Hellen, J. A. "Primary Health Care and the Epidemiological Transition in Nepal." In *Geographical Aspects of Health*, eds. Neil D. Blunden and John R. McGlashan. London: Academic Press, 1983.

Hemmleb, Jochen, Eric R. Simonson, and Larry A. Johnson. *Ghosts of Everest: The Search for Mallory and Irvine.* Seattle: Mountaineers Books, 1999.

Hillary, Sir Edmund. "Preserving a Mountain Heritage." *National Geographic* 161 (1982): 696–702.

Himal Power Limited (HPL). *Environmental Impact Assessment: Khimti Hydroelectricity Project Feasibility Study Report.* Kathmandu: 1993.

Hinrichsen, Don, et al. "Saving Sagarmatha." *Ambio* 11 (1983): 203–205.

Houghton, K. T., and R. Mendelsohn. "An Economic Analysis of Multiple-Use Forestry in Nepal." *Ambio* 25 (1996).

Howland, A. K., and P. Howland. *A Dictionary of the Common Forest and Farm Plants of Nepal.* Kathmandu: Forest Research and Information Centre, 1984.

Hulbert, I. A. R. "The Response of Ruddy Shelduck *Tadorna ferruginea* to Tourist Activity in the Royal Chitwan National Park of Nepal." *Biological Conservation* 52 (1990): 113–123.

International Centre for Integrated Mountain Development (ICIMOD). *Country Report on the Review of Institutional Capacities for Sustainable Mountain Agriculture Development.* Kathmandu: ICIMOD, 1995.

———. *GIS Database of Key Indicators of Sustainable Mountain Development in Nepal.* Kathmandu: ICIMOD, 1996.

———. *Energy Use in Mountain Areas: Trends and Patterns in China, India, Nepal and Pakistan.* Kathmandu: ICIMOD, 1999.

———. *Glaciers and Glacial Lakes of Nepal.* Kathmandu: ICIMOD, 2000.

———. *Nepal: State of the Environment 2001.* Kathmandu: ICIMOD, 2001.

International Union for the Conservation of Nature (IUCN-Nepal). *Environmental Impact Assessment of Upper Bhotekoshi Hydroelectric Project.* Kathmandu: IUCN, 1995.

Ives, Jack D., and Bruno Messerli. "Mountain Hazards Mapping in Nepal: Introduction to an Applied Mountain Research Project." *Mountain Research and Development* 1 (1981): 223–234.

———. *The Himalayan Dilemma: Reconciling Development and Conservation.* New York: Routledge, 1989.

Jackson, John A. *More Than Mountains.* London: Harrap, 1955.

Jenkins, Steve. *The Top of the World: Climbing Mount Everest.* Boston: Houghton Mifflin, 1999.

Jha, M. G., et al. *The Assessment of Groundwater Pollution in the Kathmandu Valley, Nepal.* Kathmandu: Department of Irrigation, 1997.

Johnson, K., E. A. Olson, and S. Manandhar. "Environmental Knowledge and Response to Natural Hazard in Mountainous Nepal." *Mountain Research and Development* 2 (1982): 175–188.

Joshi, A. R., and D. P. Joshi. "Endemic Plants of Nepal Himalaya: Conservation Status and Future Direction." *Mountain Environment and Development* 1 (1991).

Joshi, U. *Ensuring Food Safety in the Kathmandu Valley.* Kathmandu: ENPHO, 2000.

Kaddah, M. T. "Landform and Use and Characteristics of Some Soils in Nepal." *Soil Science* 104 (1967): 350–357.

Karan, Pradyumna P. *Nepal: A Physical and Cultural Geography.* Lexington: University of Kentucky Press, 1960.

———. "Land Use Reconnaissance in Nepal with Aero-Field Techniques and Photography." *Proceedings of the American Philosophical Society* 104 (1960): 172–187.

———. *Nepal: A Himalayan Kingdom in Transition.* Tokyo: United Nations University Press, 1996.

Karki, Madhav B. "The Rehabilitation of Forest Land in Nepal." *Nature and Resources* 27 (1991): 38–46.

Kleinn, C. *Forest Resource Inventories in Nepal: Status Quo, Needs, Recommendations.* Kathmandu: Forest Resource Information System Project, 1994.

Kunwar, U. K. *Ambient Air, Surface Water and Ground Water Quality Standards for the Kathmandu Valley.* Kathmandu: MOPE, 1999.

Laban, P. *Landslide Occurrence in Nepal*. Kathmandu: Integrated Watershed Management, Torrent Control and Land Use Development Project, 1979.

Lamjung Electricity Development Company. *Environmental Impact Assessment of Khudi Hydropower*. Kathmandu: 2001.

Land Resource Mapping Project. *Land Resource Mapping Project and Agricultural Forestry Report*. Kathmandu: Kenting Earth Science, 1986.

Lehmkuhl, J. F., R. K. Upreti, and U. R. Sharma. "National Parks and Local Development: Grasses and People in Royal Chitwan National Park, Nepal." *Environmental Conservation* 15 (1988): 143–148.

Liechty, Mark. "Kathmandu as Translocality: Multiple Places in a Nepali Space." In *Geography of Identity*, ed. Patricia Yaeger. Ann Arbor: University of Michigan, 1996.

Limbu, P. ed. *Mountains Forever*. Kathmandu: ICIMOD, 2001.

MacDonald, Alexander W. *Essays on the Ethnology of Nepal and South Asia*. Kathmandu: Ratna Pustak Bhandar, 1987.

McDougal, Charles. *The Kulunge Rai*. Kathmandu: Ratna Pustak Bhandar, 1979.

MacFarlane, Alan. *Resources and Population: A Study of the Gurungs of Nepal*. Cambridge: Cambridge University Press, 1976.

Mahat, Tej B. S. *Forest Farming Linkages in the Mountains*. Kathmandu: ICIMOD, 1987.

Majpuria, T. C., and I. Majpuria. *Sacred and Useful Plants and Trees of Nepal*. Kathmandu: 1978.

Malla, S. B. *Out-Reach Action Plan (Biodiversity and Bio-Technology) for the Department of Plant Resources*. Kathmandu: Department of Plant Resources, 1997.

Manandhar, A. *Status of Cleaner Production in Nepal*. Kathmandu: Ministry of Industry, 2000.

Manandhar, N. P. "Medical Plants Used by Chepang Tribes of Makawanpur District, Nepal." *Fitoteraparia* 60 (1989): 61–68.

Manandhar, S. *Gender Dimension of Eco-Crisis and Resource Management in Nepal*. Kathmandu: Mandala Book Point, 1994.

Manang Trade Link. *Environmental Impact Assessment of Lower Modi Hydroelectric Project*. Kathmandu: 2000.

March, Katherine. "Of People and Naks: The Meaning of High-Altitude Herding among Contemporary Solu Sherpas." *Contributions to Nepalese Studies* 4 (1977): 83–97.

Mason, Kenneth. *Abode of Snow: A History of Himalayan Exploration and Mountaineering*. London: Rupert Hart-Davis, 1955.
Messerchmidt, Donald A. "People and Resources in Nepal: Customary Resource Management System of the Upper Kali Gandaki." In *Proceedings of the Conference on Common Property Resource Management*. Washington, D.C.: National Academy Press, 1986.
Metz, John. "A Framework for Classifying Production Subsistence Types of Nepal." *Human Ecology* 17 (1989): 147–176.
——. "Conservation Practices at an Upper-Elevation Village of West Nepal." *Mountain Research and Development* 10 (1990): 7–15.
——. "A Reassessment of the Causes and Severity of Nepal's Environmental Crisis." *World Development* 19 (1991): 805–820.
Ministry of Agriculture (MOA). *Statistical Information on Nepalese Agriculture, 1998*. Kathmandu: MOA, 1999.
Ministry of Forest and Soil Conservation (MOFASC). *Master Plan for the Forestry Sector Nepal*. Kathmandu: MOFASC, 1988.
——. *Deforestation in the Tarai Districts, 1978–1990*. Kathmandu: MOFASC, 1994.
——. *Nepal Biodiversity Action Plan*. Kathmandu: MOFASC, 2000.
Ministry of Health (MOH). *Country Health Profile: Nepal*. Kathmandu: Policy, Planning, Monitoring and Supervision Division, 1988.
Ministry of Home Affairs (MOHA). *Loss of Lives by Disasters, 1983–1999*. Kathmandu: MOHA, 1999.
Ministry of Local Development (MLD). *Solid Waste Management National Policy*. Kathmandu: MLD, 1996.
Ministry of Population and Environment (MOPE). *Environmental Strategies and Policies for Industry, Forestry and Water Resource Sectors*. Kathmandu: MOPE, 1998.
——. *State of the Environment Report*. Kathmandu: MOPE, 2000.
Ministry of Water Resources (MOWAR). *Assessment of Water Resources and Water Demand by User Sectors in Nepal*. Kathmandu: MOWAR, 1999.
Mishra, Hemanta R. *Conservation in Khumbu: The Proposed Mt. Everest National Park: A Preliminary Report*. Kathmandu: Department of National Parks and Wildlife Conservation.
Mishra, S. B., and R. P. Kayastha. "Solid Waste Management." In *A Compendium on the Environmental Statistics of Nepal*. Kathmandu: CBS, 1998.

Miyoshi, Y. *Report on Industrial Pollution Control*. Kathmandu: Industrial Service Centre, 1987.

Muller-Boker, Ulrike. "Traditional Technology in the Kathmandu Valley: The Utilization of the Soils and Sediments." In *Change and Continuity: Studies in the Nepalese Culture of the Kathmandu Valley*, ed. S. Lienhard. Torino: Orientalia.Collana di Studi Orientali del CESMEO, 1996.

Nepal, S. K., and K. E. Weber. *Struggle for Existence: Park-People Conflict in the Royal Chitwan National Park*. Bangkok: HSD, 1993.

Nepal Agricultural Association. *Plant Genetic Resources Profiles Study*. Kathmandu: Nepal Agricultural Association, 1995.

Nepal Electricity Authority. *Annual Review of Electricity*. Kathmandu: Nepal Electricity Authority, 1999.

Nepal Water Supply Corporation. *Water Supply and Coverage in Urban Area of Nepal*. Kathmandu: Nepal Water Supply Corporation, 1999.

Netherlands Development Organization (SNV)-Nepal. *Final Report on the Biogas Support Programme*. Kathmandu: SNV, 1997.

Norgay, Jamling Tenzing (with B. Coburn). *Touching My Father's Soul: A Sherpa's Journey to the Top of Everest*. San Francisco: Harper, 2001.

Ortner, Sherry B. *High Religion: A Cultural and Political History of Sherpa Buddhism*. Princeton, N.J.: Princeton University Press, 1989.

Pant, K. P., and V. K. Pandey. Minimising Environmental Problems in Hill Agriculture of Nepal through Multi-Objective Farm Planning. *Indian Journal of Agricultural Economics* 54 (1999): 79–92.

Pant, S. D. *The Social Economy of the Himalaya*. London: Allen and Un-win, 1935.

Pfetzer, Mark, and Jack Galvin. *Within Reach: My Everest Story*. New York: Penguin Putnam Books, 1999.

Pig, Stacy. "Inventing Social Categories through Place: Social Representations and Development in Nepal." *Comparative Studies in Society and History* 34 (1992): 491–513.

Pohle, P. *Useful Plants of Manang District: A Contribution to the Ethno-botany of the Nepal-Himalaya*. Kathmandu: Nepal Research Centre, 1990.

Poudyal, K. *Forest Degradation and Environmental Problems in Chure* (in Nepali). Kathmandu: Nepal Forum of Environmental Journalists, 1991.

Pradhan, P. *Development of a GIS Database System for Refugee Programs in Eastern Nepal: Status of Environmental Conditions and Impacts Assessment*. Bangkok: UNEP, 1998.

Pradhan, H. B. A *Study on the Change in Forest Resources of the Koshi Hills in the Eastern Hill Districts*. Kathmandu: Nepal-U.K. Community Forestry Project, 2000.

Pratap, T., and H. R. Watson. "Sloping Agricultural Land Technology: A Regenerative Option for Sustainable Mountain Farming." Kathmandu: ICIMOD, 1994.

Rajbhandari, K. R., and R. Joshi. *Crop Weeds of Nepal*. Kathmandu: Natural History Society of Nepal, 1998.

Raut, Y. A *Handbook of Animal Husbandry*. Kathmandu: Department of Livestock Services, 1998.

Richard, C., K. Basnet, and J. P. Sah, eds. *Grassland Ecology and Management in Protected Areas of Nepal*. Kathmandu: ICIMOD, 2000.

Rijal, K., ed. *Renewable Energy Technologies: A Brighter Future: Policy Options for Mountain Communities in the HKH and Agenda for Action in Nepal*. Kathmandu: ICIMOD, 1998.

Rural Water Supply and Sanitation Project. *Report of Rural Water Supply and Sanitation Project*. Kathmandu: Department of Water Supply, 1999.

Scott, C. A., and M. F. Walter. "Local Knowledge and Conventional Soil Science Approaches to Erosional Processes in the Shivalik Himalaya." *Mountain Research and Development* 13 (1993): 61–72.

Shah, Devika, and T. B. Shrestha. *Biodiversity Databases of Nepal*. Kathmandu: IUCN-Nepal, 1996.

Shahi, B. B. "Restoration of Lost Biodiversity and Their Registration in Nepal." In *Institutionalizing Biodiversity Registration: Report of the National Workshop on Biodiversity Registration in Nepal*, eds. G. P. S. Ghimire, L. R. Sharma, and B. K. Uprety. Kathmandu: MOFASC, 2001.

Shakya, S. K. "Water Pollution in the Urban Rivers of Kathmandu, Nepal, A Case Study of Water Quality Assessment and Wastewater Treatment Requirements." Ph.D. Dissertation, Universität Für Boden Kulture, Austria, 2000.

Sharma, Pitamber. *Urbanization and Sustainable Development, Nepal Economic Policies for Sustainable Development*. Kathmandu: ADB-Nepal, 1992.

Shivakoti, Ganesh, et al., eds. *People and Participation in Sustainable Development: Understanding the Dynamics of Natural Resource Systems*. Rampur, Chitwan: Institute of Agriculture and Animal Science, 1996.

Shrestha, E. K. *Shallow Ground Water Resources of the Tarai*. Kathmandu: UNDP, 1992.

Shrestha, J. *An Enumeration of Fishes of Nepal.* Kathmandu: Biodiversity Profiles Project, 1995.

Shrestha, Nanda R. *Landlessness and Migration in Nepal.* Boulder, Colo.: Westview Press, 1990.

———. "The Environmental Degradation of Kathmandu: Losing Shangri-La?" *Education About Asia* 3 (1998): 11–18.

Shrestha, Nanda R., and Dennis Conway. *Forest Land, the State and the Rural Poor: Conflicts over Frontier Settlement in Contemporary Nepal.* Bloomington: Indiana Center on Global Changes and World Peace, Indiana University, 1992.

———. "Ecopolitical Battles in the Tarai of Nepal: An Emerging Human and Environmental Crisis." *International Journal of Population Geography* 2 (1996): 313–331.

Shrestha, R. R. "Graywater Treatment: An Option for Water Recycling." *Environment, A Journal of the Environment Ministry of Population and Environment* 5 (2000): 97–105.

Shrestha, T. B., and R. M. Joshi. *Rare, Endemic and Endangered Plants of Nepal.* Kathmandu: World Wildlife Fund-Nepal Program, 1996.

Stevens, Stanley F. *Claiming the High Ground: Sherpas, Subsistence, and Environmental Change in the Highest Himalaya.* Berkeley: University of California Press, 1993.

———, ed. *Conservation through Cultural Survival.* Washington, D.C.: Island Press, 1997.

Sthapit, K. H., and L. C. Tennyson. "Bio-Engineering Erosion Control in Nepal." *Conservation* (October–November 1991): 14–16.

Subedi, B. *Population and Environment in the Context of Sustainable Development in Nepal.* Kathmandu: CBS, 1995.

Tamang, D. *Indigenous Soil Fertility Management in the Hills of Nepal: Lessons from an East-West Transect.* Kathmandu: MOA, 1992.

Thapa G. B., and S. R. Devkota. *Managing Solid Waste in Metro Kathmandu.* Bangkok: Asian Institute of Technology, 1999.

Thapa, G. B., and K. E. Weber. "Statues and Management of Watersheds in the Upper Pokhara Valley, Nepal." *Environmental Management* 19 (1995): 497–513.

Thapa, V. K. T. *An Enumeration of Insects of Nepal.* Kathmandu: Biodiversity Profiles Project, 1995.

Thucker, P., and K. H. Gautam. *A Socioeconomic Study of Participatory Issues in Forest Management in the Tarai* (three parts). Kathmandu: FMUDP, 1994.

Tiwari, D. N. *Status of Environmental Economics Initiatives in Nepal*. Kathmandu: IUCN-Nepal, 1998.
Tulachan, P. M., and A. Neupane. *Livestock in Mixed Farming Systems of the Hindu Kush-Himalayas: Trends and Sustainability*. Kathmandu: ICIMOD, 1999.
Tulachan, P. M., M. A. M. Saleem, and J. Maki-Hokkonen, eds. *Contribution of Livestock to Mountain Livelihoods: Research and Development Issues*. Kathmandu: ICIMOD, 2000.
Tuladhar, B. *Hazardous Waste Management: Nepal Country Report*. Kathmandu: WHO, 1999.
———. *Private Sector Participation in Kathmandu's Solid Waste Management: A Status Report*. Kathmandu: Kathmandu Metropolitan City, 1999.
Tuladhar, R. M., and E. K. Shrestha. *Shallow Ground Water Resources of Tarai*. Kathmandu: UNDP, 1992.
United Nations Development Programme (UNDP). *Ecological Cooperation for Biodiversity Conservation in the Himalayas*. Kathmandu: UNDP, 1998.
Uprety, Batu K. *Nepal's National Report on Floral Diversity*. Colombo: South Asia Cooperative Environmental Programme, 1996.
———. *Natural Biodiversity and Environmental Statistics 1998: Nepal*. Kathmandu: World Wildlife Fund-Nepal Program, 1998.
Uprety, Prem R. "The Economics of Buddhism: An Alternative Model for Community Development." *Contributions to Nepalese Studies* 23 (1996).
Valli, Eric, and D. Summers. *Honey Hunters of Nepal*. New York: Harry N. Abrams, 1988.
———. *Caravans of the Himalaya*. Washington, D.C.: National Geographic Society, 2000.
Verghese, B. G., and R. Ramaswamy, eds. *Harnessing the Eastern Himalayan Rivers: Regional Cooperation in South Asia*. New Delhi: Konark Publishers, 1993.
Water and Energy Commission Secretariat. *Energy Synopsis Report, 1994*. Kathmandu: Water and Energy Commission Secretariat, 1996.
Weathers, Beck, and Stephen G. Michaud. *Left for Dead: My Journey Home from Everest*. New York: Dell Publishing Company, 2001.
Webster, Ed. *Snow in the Kingdom: My Storm Years on Everest*. Eldorado Springs, Colo.: Mountain Imagery, 2001.
World Bank. *Nepal: Public Resources Management in a Resource Scarce Economy*. Washington, D.C.: World Bank, 1992.

———. Country Assistance Strategy: Nepal, 1999–2001. Washington, D.C.: World Bank, 1999.
Yonzon, P. *Count Rhino 1994*. Kathmandu: World Wildlife Fund-Nepal Program, 1994.
Zurick, David. "Resource Needs and Land Stress in Rapti Zone, Nepal." *Professional Geographer* 40 (1988): 428–443.
———. "Traditional Knowledge and Conservation as a Basis for Development in a West Nepal Village." *Mountain Research and Development* 10 (1990): 23–33.
Zurick, David, and P. P. Karan. *Himalaya: Life on the Edge of the World*. Baltimore, Md.: Johns Hopkins University Press, 1999.

HISTORY, POLITICS, AND GOVERNMENT

Acharya, Baburam. "Rana Sahi ra Shadyantra" (Rana Rule and Conspiracy). *Sharada* 21 (2013 or 1957): 1–8.
———. "Bhimsen Thapa ko Patan" (The Downfall of Bhimsen Thapa). *Pragati* 2 (1957): 115–123.
———. *China ra Tibet Sita Nepal ko Sambandha* (Nepal's Relations with China and Tibet). Kathmandu: Jorganesh Press, 1958.
———. *Aba Yesto Kahilyai Nahos* (Let This Not Ever Happen Again). Kathmandu: Shri Krishna Acharya, 2055 (1998).
Adhikari, Krishna Kant. *Nepal under Jang Bahadur 1846–1877* (Volume I). Kathmandu: Buku, 1984.
Aditya, Anand. "Human Rights and Elections in Nepal." *Human Rights Year Book 2000*. Kathmandu: INSEC, 2000.
Adshead, Robin. *Gurkha: The Legendary Soldier*. Singapore: Asia Pacific Press, 1970.
Agarwal, Hem Narayan. *The Administrative System of Nepal: From Tradition to Modernity*. New Delhi: Vikas Publishing House, 1976.
Agrawal, Arun, Charla Britt, and Keshav Kanel. *Decentralization in Nepal: A Comparative Analysis*. Berkeley, Calif.: Institute for Contemporary Studies, 1999.
Aitchison, C. U. *A Collection of Treaties, Engagements, and Sanads Relating to India and Neighbouring Countries* (four volumes). Calcutta: Government of India Central Publication Branch, 1929.
Allen, Michael. *The Cult of Kumari: Virgin Worship in Nepal*. Kathmandu: University Press, 1975.

Amnesty International. *Nepal: A Pattern of Human Rights Violations.* London: Amnesty International, 1987.

———. *Violations in the Context of a Maoist 'People's War.'* London: Amnesty International, 1997.

Ballantine, Henry. *On India's Frontier or Nepal: The Gurkhas' Mysterious Land.* London: Redway, 1896.

Baraith, Roop Singh. *Transit Politics in South Asia: A Case Study of Nepal.* Jaipur, India: Aalekh, 1989.

Baral, Lok Raj. *Opposition Politics in Nepal.* Columbia, Mo.: South Asia Books, 1978.

Baral, Lok Raj, and Leo E. Rose. "Democratization and the Crisis of Governance in Nepal." In *Legitimacy and Conflict in South Asia*, eds. Subrata K. Mitra and Dietmar Rothermund. New Delhi: Manohar Publications, 1998.

Berreman, Gerald. *Hindus of the Himalayas.* Berkeley: University of California Press, 1963.

Bharati, Agehananda. *The Tantric Tradition.* London: Rider, 1965.

Bhasin, A. S. *Documents on Nepal's Relations with India and China (1946–1966).* Bombay: Academic Books, 1970.

Bhattacharjee, G. P. *India and the Politics of Modern Nepal.* Calcutta: Minerva Associates, 1970.

Bhattacharya, Benoytosh. *An Introduction to Buddhist Esoterism.* Varanasi: Chowkhamba, 1964.

Bhattarai, Baburam. *Nepal: A Marxist View.* Kathmandu: Jhilko Publications, 1990.

———. "Politico-Economic Rationale of People's War in Nepal." *The Worker* 4 (1998): 18–44.

Bishop, Edward. *Better to Die: The Story of the Gurkhas.* London: New English Library, 1976.

Bista, Dor Bahadur. *The People of Nepal.* Kathmandu: Department of Publicity, 1967.

Brown, T. Louise. *The Challenge to Democracy in Nepal: A Political History.* London: Routledge, 1996.

Burghart, Richard. "The Disappearance and Reappearance of Janakpur." *Kailash* 6 (1878): 257–284.

———. "The Formation of the Concept of Nation-State in Nepal." *Journal of Asian Studies* 44 (1984): 101–125.

Burghart, Richard, M. Ganeszle, J. Whelpton, and S. Wolf. "Private News Papers, Political Parties and Public Life in Nepal." *European Bulletin of Himalayan Research* 1 (1997): 3–15.

Cammann, Schuyler. *Trade through the Himalayas: The Early British Attempts to Open Tibet.* Princeton, N.J.: Princeton University Press, 1951.

Caplan, Lionel, *Land and Social Change in East Nepal: A Study of Hindu Tribal Relations.* London: Routledge, 1970.

———. "'Bravest of the Brave': Representations of 'The Gurkha' in British Military Writings." *Modern Asian Studies* 25 (1991): 571–597.

———. "From Tribe to Peasant? The Limbus and the Nepalese State." *Journal of Peasant Studies* 18 (1991): 305–321.

Chant, Christopher. *Gurkha: The Illustrated History of an Elite Fighting Force.* Dorset, UK: Blandford, 1985.

Chaturvedi, S. K. *Indo-Nepal Relations in Linkage Perspective.* New Delhi: B. R. Publishing, 1990.

Clarke, G. E. "A Helambu History." *Journal of the Nepal Research Centre* 4 (1980): 1–38.

Coburn, Broughton. *Nepali Aama: Portrait of a Nepalese Hill Woman.* Santa Barbara, Calif.: Ross-Erikson, 1981.

Comrade Parvati. "Women's Participation in People's War in Nepal." *The Worker* 5 (1999): 33–42.

Comrade Prachanda. "Two Momentous Years of Revolutionary Transformation." *The Worker* 4 (1998): 9–17.

———. "Third Turbulent Year of People's War: A General Review." *The Worker* 5 (1999): 15–25.

Dahal, Dev Raj. "Role of Political Education in the Democratization Process of Nepal." *Nepali Political Science and Politics* 5 (1996): 49–66.

———. "Geopolitics of Nepal: Survival Strategies of the Small States." In *The Political Economy of Small States*, ed. Anand Aditya. Kathmandu: NEFAS and FES, 1997.

———. *Civil Society in Nepal: Opening the Ground for Questions.* Kathmandu: Centre for Development and Governance, 2001.

Dahal, Dilli Ram. "Is There Anything as 'Good Governance' in Nepal? Reflections on the Functioning of the Civil Society." In *Local Self-Government in Nepal*, ed. Ganga B. Thapa. Kathmandu: POLSAN and FES, 1998.

Dahal, Madan K. *Constitutional and Political Development in Nepal.* Kathmandu: Ratna Pustak Bhandar, 2001.

Dammann, Nancy. *We Tried: Government Service in Nepal.* Sun City, Ariz.: Social Change Press, 1996.
Das, Rabindra K. *Nepal and Its Neighbors.* Banaras: Konark Publishers, 1986.
Davis, Hassoldt. *Nepal, Land of Mystery.* London: Robert Hale, 1942.
Des Chene, Mary. "Relics of Empire: A Cultural History of the Gurkhas, 1815–1987." Ph.D. Dissertation, Stanford University, 1991.
Dhanalaxmi, Ravuri. *British Attitude to Nepal's Relations with Tibet and China, 1814–1914.* Chandigarh: Bahri, 1981.
Egerton, Francis. *Journal of a Winter's Tour in India: With a Visit to the Court of Nepal* (two volumes). London: John Murray, 1852.
Elder, Joseph W., et al. *Planned Resettlement in Nepal's Tarai.* Kathmandu: CNAS, 1976.
Farwell, Byron. *The Gurkhas.* New York: Norton, 1984.
Fletcher, L. B., and D. F. Shan. *An Assessment of Food Aid as a Development Resource in Nepal.* Ann Arbor, Mich.: Community Systems Foundation, 1984.
Forum for Protection of Human Rights (FOPHUR). *FOPHUR & Pro-Democracy Movement.* Lalitpur, Nepal: FOPHUR, 1990.
Gaige, Frederick H. *Regionalism and National Unity in Nepal.* Berkeley: University of California Press, 1975.
Gauchan, S., and M. Vinding. "The History of the Thakali According to the Thakali Tradition." *Kailash* 5 (1977): 97–184.
Giuseppe, Father. "Account of the Kingdom of Nepal, 1768–1771." *Asiatic Researches* 2 (1901).
Glassner, M. I. *Access to the Sea for Developing Land-Locked States.* The Hague: Martin Nijhoff, 1970.
Gnoli, Raniero. *Nepalese Inscriptions in Gupta Characters.* Serie Orientale Roma X. Materials for the Study of Nepalese History and Culture No. 2. Rome: Istituto Itialiano per il Medio ed Estremo Oriente.
Goodall, Merill R. "Administrative Changes in Nepal." In *Asian Bureaucratic Systems Emergent from the British Imperial Tradition,* ed. Ralph Braibanti. Durham, N.C.: Duke University Press, 1966.
Goyal, Narendra. *The King and His Constitution: Observation and Commentary on the Constitution of the Kingdom of Nepal.* New Delhi: Nepal Trading Corporation, 1959.
Gurung, Harka. "Geographic Setting." In *Nepal: A Profile.* Kathmandu: Nepal Council of Applied Economic Research, 1970.

Gutschow, N., and Bernhard Kölver. *Bhaktapur: Ordered Space, Concepts and Functions in a Town of Nepal*. Wiesbaden: Kommissionsverlag Franz Steiner, 1975.

Gyawali, Suryabikram. *Nepali Birharu* (Nepali Heroes). Darjeeling: Nepal Sahitya Sammelan, 1956.

Hamilton, Francis (Buchanan). *An Account of the Kingdom of Nepal and of the Territories Annexed to This Dominion by the House of Gurkha*. Edinburgh: Constable, 1819.

Heck, Douglas. "Nepal in 1980: The Year of the Referendum." *Asian Survey* 21 (1981): 181–187.

Himal. "Nepalis in Foreign Uniform" (Special Issue). July–August 1991.

Himal South Asia (previously *Himal*). "Red Alert: Maoism in the Subcontinent." 10 (October 1997): 12–48.

Hitchcock, John T. *The Magars of Banyan Hill*. New York: Rinehart and Winston, 1966.

Hodgson, Brian Houghton. "On the Law and Legal Practice of Nepal, as Regards Familiar Intercourse between Hindu and Outcaste." *Journal of the Royal Asiatic Society of Great Britain and Ireland* 1 (1834): 45–56.

———. *Essays on the Languages, Literature, and Religion of Nepal and Tibet, Together with Further Papers on the Geography, Ethnology, and Commerce of Those Countries*. London: Trubner, 1874.

Höfer, Andras. *The Caste Hierarchy and the State in Nepal: A Study of the Muluki Ain of 1854*. Innsbruck: Universitätsverlag Wagner, 1979.

Hunter, William W. *Life of Brian Houghton Hodgson: British Resident at the Court of Nepal*. London: John Murray, 1896.

Husain, Asad. *British India's Relations with the Kingdom of Nepal*. London: Allen and Unwin, 1970.

Iijima, Shigeru. "Hinduization of a Himalayan Tribe in Nepal." *Kroeber Anthropological Papers* 29 (1963): 43–52.

———. "The Thakalis: Traditional and Modern." In *Anthropological and Linguistic Studies of the Gandaki Area in Nepal*. Tokyo: Tokyo University of Foreign Studies, 1982.

Indraji, Bhagavanlal. "Twenty-Three Inscriptions from Nepal with some Considerations on the Chronology of Nepal." Translated from Gujurati by G. Buhler, *Indian Antiquary* 9 (1880).

Jha, Shankar Kumar. *Indo-Nepal Relations*. New Delhi: Archives Books, 1989.

Joshi, Bhuwan Lal, and Leo E. Rose. *Democratic Innovations in Nepal: A Case Study of Political Acculturation.* Berkeley: University of California Press, 1966.

Joshi, Nanda L. *Evolution of Public Administration in Nepal.* Kathmandu: CEDA, 1973.

Kansakar, Vidya V. S. "History of Population Migration in Nepal." *Himalayan Review* 6 (1974): 58–68.

Kawatika, J. *Hill Magars and Their Neighbors.* Tokyo: Tokai University Press, 1974.

Khadka, Narayan. "The Crisis in Nepal-India Relations." *Journal of South Asian and Middle Eastern Studies* 15 (1991): 725–753.

———. "Politics and the Economy during Nepal's Partyless Panchayat System (1961–1990): A Study in Retrospect." *Asian Affairs* 25 (1994): 47–59.

———. "Factionalism in the Communist Movement in Nepal." *Pacific Affairs* 68 (1995): 55–76.

Khanal, Krishna P. *Constitution and Political Parties in Nepal.* Kathmandu: FES, 1997.

Khanal, Yadu N. "Nepal in 1984: A Year of Complacence." *Asian Survey* 25 (1985): 180–186.

———. *Essays in Nepal's Foreign Policy.* Kathmandu: Murari Upadhyay, 1988.

———. "Nepal in 1997: Political Stability Eludes." *Asian Survey* 38 (1998): 148–154.

Kirkpatrick, Colonel. *An Account of the Kingdom of Nepaul, (being the Substance of Observations Made during a Mission to that Country in the Year 1793).* New Delhi: Manjusri Publishing House, 1969 (Reprint of the 1811 edition).

Koirala, Niranjan. "Nepal in 1989: A Very Difficult Year." *Asian Survey* 25 (1990): 136–143.

Kölver, Bernhard, and Hemraj Sakya. *Documents from the Rudravarna-Mahavihara, Patan.* Sankt Augustin: VGH-Wissenschaftsverlag, 1985.

Korn, Wolfgang. *The Traditional Architecture of the Kathmandu Valley.* Kathmandu: Ratna Pustak Bhandar, 1976.

Kramrisch, Stella. *The Art of Nepal.* Philadelphia: Asia Society, 1964.

Krishnamurti, Y. G. *His Majesty King Mahendra Bir Bikram Shaha Deva: An Analytical Biography.* Bombay: Nityanand Society, no date.

Kumar, Dhruba, ed. *State, Leadership and Politics in Nepal.* Kathmandu: CNAS, 1995.

Kumar, Satish. *Rana Polity in Nepal: Origin and Growth*. Bombay: Asia Publishing House, 1967.
Landon, Perceval. *Nepal*. (two volumes). London: Constable, 1928.
Leonard, R. G. *Nepal and the Gurkhas*. London: Her Majesty's Stationary Office, 1965.
Levi, Sylvain. *Le Nepal* (three volumes). Paris: Ernest Leroux, 1905.
Levy, Robert I. *Mesocosm: Hinduism and the Organization of a Traditional Newar City in Nepal*. Berkeley: University of California Press, 1990.
Lindsay, Quentin W. *Democracy, Decentralization and Development in Nepal: Learning from Experience*. Kathmandu: UNDP, 1996.
Locke, John K. *Karunamaya: The Cult of Avalokitesvara-Matsyendranath in the Valley of Nepal*. Kathmandu: University Press, 1975.
———. *Buddhist Monasteries of Nepal*. Kathmandu: Sahayogi Press, 1985.
Mainali, Pramod. *Milestones of History* (Volume I). Kathmandu: Kanchan Printing Press, 2000
Majumdar, R. C. "The Eras of Nepal." *Journal of the Asiatic Society* 1 (1959): 47–49.
Malla, Kamal P. "Nepalavamsavali: A Complete Version of the Kaisher Vamsavali." *Contributions to Nepalese Studies* 12 (1985).
Malla, U. M. "Settlement Geography of Kathmandu Valley from 600 B.C. to 1000 A.D." *Geographical Journal of Nepal* 1 (1978): 28–36.
Markham, Clements R. *Narratives of the Mission of George Bogie to Tibet and of the Journey of Thomas Manning to Lhasa*. London: Trubner, 1879.
Maskay, Bishwa K. *Development Governance: Agenda for Action*. Kathmandu: Centre for Development and Governance, 2000.
Mihaly, Eugene B. *Foreign Aid and Politics in Nepal: A Case Study*. London: Oxford University Press, 1965.
Mikesell, Stephen. "Cotton on the Silk Road: Subjection of Labor to the Global Economy in the Shadow of Empire, or the Dialectic of a Merchant Community in Nepal." Ph.D. Dissertation, University of Wisconsin–Madison, 1988.
Misra, Shashi P. *B. P. Koirala: A Case Study in Third World Democratic Leadership*. Bhubaneswar, India: Konark Publishers, 1985.
Mitra, Debala. *Buddhist Monument*. Calcutta: Sahitya Samsad, 1971.
Mojumdar, Kanchanmoy. *Political Relations between India and Nepal (1877–1923)*. New Delhi: Munshiram Manoharlal, 1973.
———. *Anglo-Nepalese Relations in the Nineteenth Century*. Calcutta: Firma K. L. Mukhopadhyay. 1973.

———. *Nepal and the Indian Nationalist Movement*. Calcutta: Firma K. L. Mukhopadhyay, 1975.

Muni, S. D. *India and Nepal: A Changing Relationship*. New Delhi: Konark Publishers, 1992.

———. "India and Its Neighbours: Persisting Dilemmas and New Opportunities." *International Studies* 30 (1993): 189–206.

Nelson, D., et al. *A Reconnaissance Inventory of the Major Ecological Land Units and Their Watershed Condition in Nepal*. Kathmandu: Department of Soil and Water Conservation, 1980.

Nickson, R. A. "Democratization and the Growth of Communism in Nepal: A Peruvian Scenario in the Making." *Journal of Commonwealth and Comparative Politics* 30 (1992): 358–386.

Northey, W. Brook, and C. J. Morris. *The Gurkhas, Their Manners, Customs and Country*. London: John Lane, 1928.

Ojha, Durga P. "History of Land Settlement in Nepal Tarai." *Contributions to Nepalese Studies* 11 (1983): 21–44.

Okada, Ferdinand E. "Ritual Brotherhood: A Cohesive Factor in Nepalese Society." *Southwestern Journal of Anthropology* 13 (1957): 212–222.

Oldfield, H. Androse. *Sketches from Nepal* (two volumes). London: Allen, 1880.

Oli, Krishna P. *Conflict Resolution and Mediation in Natural Resource Management in Nepal*. Kathmandu: IUCN, 1998.

Oliphant, Laurence. *A Journey to Kathmandu, The Capital of Nepaul*. London: John Murray, 1852.

Onta, Pratyoush. "Creating a Brave Nepali Nation in British India: The Rhetoric of *Jati* Improvement, Rediscovery of Bhanubhakta, and the Writing of *Bir* History." *Studies in Nepali History and Society* 1 (1996): 37–76.

Pahari, Anup. "Ties That Bind: Gurkhas in History." *Himal* (July– August 1991): 6–12.

Panday, Devendra Raj. *Transparency in the Context of Good Governance in Nepal*. Lalitpur, Nepal: Nepal Administrative Staff College, 1998.

Parajuli, Ramjee P. *The Democratic Transition in Nepal*. Lanham, Md.: Rowman & Littlefield, 2000.

Paudel, Nayanath. *Bhasa Vamsavali* (Part I). Kathmandu: Nepal National Library, 2020 (1964).

Paudyal, Durga P. "Empowerment of the Rural Poor and Good Governance." Paper submitted at ESCAP, Bangkok, 2000.

Pemble, John. *The Invasion of Nepal: John Company at War*. Oxford: Clarendon Press, 1971.
Petech, Luciano. *Mediaeval History of Nepal (750–1482)*. Rome: Instituto Italiano per il Medio ed Estremo Oriente, 1984.
Pieper, J. "Three Cities of Nepal." In *Shelter, Sign and Symbol*, ed. Paul Oliver. London: Barrie and Jenkins, 1975.
Political Science Association of Nepal (POLSAN). *Political Parties and the Parliamentary Process in Nepal: A Study of the Transitional Phase*. Kathmandu: POLSAN, 1992.
———. *Good Governance as a Basis for Local Democracy in Nepal*. Kathmandu: POLSAN, 1999.
Powell, E. Alexander. *The Last Home of Mystery*. New York: Garden City Publishing, 1929.
Pradhan, Gajendra Mani. *Transit of Land-Locked Countries and Nepal*. New Delhi: Nirala Publications, 1990.
Pradhan, Kumar. *A History of Nepali Literature*. Sahitya Akademi, 1984.
———. *The Gorkha Conquest: The Process and Consequences of the Unification of Nepal with Particular Reference to Eastern Nepal*. Calcutta: Oxford University Press, 1991.
Prasad, Ishwari. *The Life and Times of Maharaja Juddha Shumsher Jang Bahadur Rana of Nepal*. New Delhi: Asia Publishing House, 1975.
Prinsep, Henry T. *A Narrative of the Political and Military Transactions of British India under the Administration of the Marquess of Hastings (1813–1818)*. London: John Murray, 1820.
Proksch, Andreas, ed. *Images of a Century: The Changing Townscapes of the Kathmandu Valley*. Kathmandu: GTZ, 1995.
Proudfoot, C. L. *Flash of the Khukri: History of the 3rd Gurkha Rifles, 1947 to 1980*. New Delhi: Vision Books, 1984.
Quigley, Declan. *The Interpretation of Caste*. Oxford: Clarendon Press, 1993.
———. "The Guthi Organizations of Dhulikhel Shresthas." *Kailash* 12 (1985): 5–26.
Rahul, Ram. "Making of Modern Nepal." *International Studies* 16 (1977): 1–15.
Raj, Prakash A. *Kathmandu and the Kingdom of Nepal* (13th edition). Kathmandu: Nabeen, 2000.
———. "National Integration or Destabilization in Nepal." *Economic and Political Weekly* 11 (1993): 30–33.
Ramakant. *Indo-Nepalese Relations 1816–1877*. New Delhi: S. Chand, 1968.

Rana, Chandra Shamsher. "An Appeal for the Abolition of Slavery (made on 28 November 1924)." *Himalayan Research Bulletin* 14 (1994): 1–2.

Rana, Padma. *Life of Maharaja Sir Jang Bahadur of Nepal*. Allahabad: Pioneer Press, 1909.

Rana, Pramod S. *Rana Nepal: An Insider's View*. Kathmandu: Sahayogi Press, 1978.

Reed, Horace B., and Marry I. Reed. *Nepal in Transition: Educational Innovation*. Pittsburgh: University of Pittsburgh Press, 1968.

Regmi, Dilli Raman. *A Century of Family Autocracy in Nepal*. Banaras: Nepali National Congress, 1950.

———. *Ancient Nepal*. Calcutta: Firma K. L. Mukhopadhyay, 1960.

———. *Modern Nepal: The Rise and Growth in the Eighteenth Century* (Volume I). Calcutta: Firma K. L. Mukhopadhyay, 1961.

———. *Medieval Nepal* (four volumes). Calcutta: Firma K. L. Mukhopadhyay, 1966.

———. *Modern Nepal: Expansion: Climax and Fall* (Volume II). Calcutta: Firma K. L. Mukhopadhyay, 1975.

———. *Inscriptions of Ancient Nepal* (three volumes). New Delhi: Abhinav Publications, 1983.

Regmi, Jagadish Chandra. *A Comprehensive Bibliography on the Ethnology and Anthropology of Nepal, including Sikkim, Darjeeling, and Kumaon*. Kathmandu: Office of the Nepal-Antiquary, 1976.

Regmi, Mahesh C. *Thatched Huts and Stucco Palaces: Peasants and Landlords in 19th-Century Nepal*. New Delhi: Vikas Publishing House, 1978.

———. *History of Nepal*. New Delhi: Low Price Publications, 1990.

———. *Kings and Political Leaders of the Gorkhali Empire: 1768–1814*. New Delhi: Orient Longman, 1995.

Regmi Research Series. "Land Regulations in Tarai Region, 1861." *Regmi Research Series* 1 (1969): 33–36.

Rose, Leo E. *Nepal: Government and Politics*. New Haven: Human Relations Area Files, 1956.

———. *Nepal: Strategy for Survival*. Berkeley: University of California Press, 1971.

Rose, Leo E., and Margaret W. Fisher. *England, India, Nepal, Tibet, and China, 1765–1958: A Synchronistic Table Showing the Succession of Heads of State and Other Political and Diplomatic Personages of Importance in These Countries, along with Nepali Tributary Missions to China, from the Mid-Eighteenth to the Mid-Twentieth Century*. Berkeley: University of California Press, 1959.

——. *The Politics of Nepal: Persistence and Change in an Asian Monarchy.* Ithaca, N.Y.: Cornell University Press, 1970.
Sanwal, B. D. *Nepal and the East India Company.* Bombay: Asia Publishing House, 1965.
Savada, Andrea M., ed. *Nepal and Bhutan: Country Studies* (Area Handbook Series). Washington, D.C.: Library of Congress, 1993.
Sever, Adrian. *Nepal under the Ranas.* New Delhi: Oxford and IBH Publishing, 1993.
Shaha, Rishikesh. *Nepal and the World.* Kathmandu: Naya Nepal Prakashan, 1962.
——. *Heroes and Builders of Nepal.* Calcutta: Oxford University Press, 1970.
——. *An Introduction to Nepal.* Kathmandu: Ratna Pustak Bhandar, 1975.
——. *Nepali Politics: Retrospect and Prospect.* New Delhi: Oxford University Press, 1978.
——. *Essays in the Practice of Government in Nepal.* New Delhi: Manohar Publications, 1982.
——. *Modern Nepal: A Political History: 1769–1955* (two volumes). Riverdale, Md.: Riverdale Company, 1990.
——. *Ancient and Medieval Nepal.* New Delhi: Manohar Publications, 1992.
——. *Human Rights and Parliamentary Practices in Nepal.* Kathmandu: Development Research for a Democratic Nepal, 1995.
Sharma, Balchandra. *Nepali Sahityako Itihas* (The History of Nepali Literature). Kathmandu: Nepal Rajkiya Prajna Pratisthan, 2039 (1984).
Sharma, Jana. *Democracy without Roots.* New Delhi: Book Faith, 1998.
Sharma, Kul Shekar. "Nepal in 1983: Another Year of Confusion and Lack of Direction." *Asian Survey* 24 (1984): 257–262.
Sharma, Prayag Raj. "The Land System of the Licchavis in Nepal." *Kailash* 10 (1983):11–62.
——. "How to Tend This Garden." *Himal* 5 (1992): 7–9.
Shastri, Hara Prasad. *A Catalogue of Palm Leaf and Selected Paper Manuscripts Belonging to the Darbar Library, Nepal* (two volumes). Calcutta: Baptist Mission Press, 1915.
Sheil-Small, D. *Green Shadows: A Gurkha Story.* London: Kimber, 1982.
Shrestha, Anand P., ed. *The Role of Civil Society in Democratization in Nepal.* Kathmandu: NEFAS and FES, 1998.
Shrestha, Bihari K. "Empowering People for Democracy and Development: A Critical Assessment of the Proposed Legislation on Local Self-Governance." In *Promoting Participatory Democracy in Nepal*, ed. Ganga B. Thapa. Kathmandu: POLSAN and FES, 1998.

Shrestha, Nanda R. *The Political Economy of Land, Landlessness and Migration in Nepal*. New Delhi: Nirala Publications, 2001.

Singh, Shiv Bahadur. *Indo-Nepal Relations: Discord and Harmony*. Varanasi: Ganga Kaveri Publishing House, 1994.

Slusser, Mary S. *Nepal Mandala: A Cultural Study of the Kathmandu Valley* (two volumes). Princeton, N.J.: Princeton University Press, 1982.

Smith, Thomas. *Narrative of a Five Years' Residence at Nepaul* (two volumes). London: Colburn, 1852.

Smythies, E. A. *Big Game Shooting in Nepal*. Calcutta: Thacker, Spink, 1942.

Snellgrove, David. *Buddhist Himalaya: Travels and Studies in Quest of the Origins and Nature of Tibetan Religion*. New York: Philosophical Library, 1958.

Sonntag, Selma K. "Ethnolinguistic Identity and Language Policy in Nepal." *Nationalism and Ethnic Politics* 1 (1995): 108–120.

Stiller, Ludwig F. *Prithvinarayan Shah in the Light of Dibya Upadesh*. Ranchi: Catholic Press, 1968.

———. *The Rise of the House of Gorkha: A Study in the Unification of Nepal*. New Delhi: Manjusri Publishing House, 1973.

———. *The Silent Cry: The People of Nepal (1816–1839)*. Kathmandu: Sahayogi Prakashan, 1976.

Stiller, Ludwig F., ed. *Letters from Kathmandu: The Kot Massacre*. Kathmandu: CNAS, 1981.

Subba, Tanka B. *Ethnicity, State and Development: A Case Study of Gorkhaland Movement in Darjeeling*. New Delhi: Vikas Publishing House, 1992.

Thapa, Ganga B., ed. *Local Self-Government in Nepal*. Kathmandu: POLSAN and FES, 1998.

———. *Promoting Participatory Democracy in Nepal*. Kathmandu: POLSAN and FES, 1998.

———. *Decentralization and Good Governance in Nepal*. Kathmandu: POLSAN and FES, 1999.

Tiwari, Chitra Krishna. "Domestic Determinants of Foreign Policy in South Asia: The Case of Nepal." *Journal of South Asian and Middle Eastern Studies* 10 (1987): 62–77.

Toffin, G., ed. *Man and His House in the Himalayas: Ecology of Nepal*. New Delhi: Sterling Publishers, 1991.

Tokyo University of Foreign Studies. *Anthropological and Linguistic Studies of the Gandaki Area in Nepal*. Tokyo: Tokyo University of Foreign Studies, 1982.

Tucci, Giuseppe. *Nepal: The Discovery of the Malla* (Translated from the Italian by Lovett Edwards). New York: E. P. Dutton, 1962.

———. *Preliminary Report on Two Scientific Expeditions in Nepal.* Rome: Istituto Italiano per il Medie Estremo Oriente, 1956.

Tuker, Francis Ivan Simms. *Gorkha: The Story of the Gurkhas of Nepal.* London: Constable, 1957.

———. *While Memory Serves.* London: Cassel, 1950.

Tyagi, Sushila. *Indo-Nepalese Relations, 1858–1914.* New Delhi: D. K. Publishing, 1974.

Upadhyay, Shailendra Kumar. *Tryst with Diplomacy.* New Delhi: Vikas Publishing House, 1991.

Upadhyaya, Shreeram Prasad. *Indo-Nepal Trade Relations: A Historical Analysis of Nepal's Trade with British India.* New Delhi: Nirala Publications, 1992.

Uprety, Hari. *Crisis of Governance: A Study of Political Economic Issues in Nepal.* Kathmandu: Centre for Governance and Development Studies, 1996.

Uprety, Prem R. *Political Awakening in Nepal.* New Delhi: Commonwealth Publishers, 1992.

Vaidya, T. R. *Prithvinarayan Shah: The Founder of Modern Nepal.* New Delhi: Anmol Publications, 1993.

Vannini, Fulgentius, O. F. M. *Christian Settlements in Nepal during the Eighteenth Century.* New Delhi: the author, 1977.

Walsh, E. H. "The Coinage of Nepal." *Journal of the Royal Asiatic Society of Great Britain and Ireland* (July 1908).

Weiner, Myron. "The Political Demography of Nepal." *Asian Survey* 13 (1973): 617–630.

Whelpton, John. *Jang Bahadur in Europe: The First Nepalese Mission to the West.* Kathmandu: Sahayogi Press, 1983.

———. *Kings, Soldiers and Priests: Nepalese Politics and the Rise of Jang Bahadur Rana, 1830–1857.* Delhi: Manohar Publications, 1991.

Wiesner, Ulrich. "Nepalese Temple Architecture: Its Characteristics and Its Relations to Indian Development." In *Studies in South Asian Culture*, ed. J. E. Van Lohuizen-de Leeuw. Leiden: E. J. Brill, 1978.

Worker, The. "The Historic Initiation and After" (Review of the People's War). 2 (June 1996): 4–9.

———. "Review of the Historic Initiation of the People's War and Future Strategy of the Party." 2 (June 1996): 15–18.

———. "One Year of People's War in Nepal: A Review." 3 (February 1997): 6–18.

———. "Document: Strategy and Tactics of Armed Struggle in Nepal." 3 (February 1997): 19–30.

———. "Experience of the People's War and Some Important Questions." 5 (October 1999): 8–14.

———. "State of the Historic Occasion of the Third Anniversary of the People's War." 5 (October 1999): 5–7.

———. "New Situation, New Opportunities and New Challenges." 7 (January 2002): 1–3.

Wright, Daniel. *Sketch of the Portion of the Country of Nepal Open to Europeans*. Calcutta: Office of the Superintendent of Government Printing, 1872.

———. *History of Nepal*. Cambridge: Cambridge University Press, 1879.

PEOPLE, SOCIETY, AND CULTURE

Acharya, Meena. *The Statistical Profile on Nepalese Women: An Update in the Policy Context*. Kathmandu: IIDS, 1994.

Adhikari, Ambika P. *Urban and Environmental Planning: Analysis, Policies and Proposals*. Kathmandu: IUCN, 1998.

Agarwal, Bina. *A Field of One's Own: Gender and Land Rights in South Asia*. Cambridge: Cambridge University Press, 1994.

Ahearn, Laura. "I Am Offering an Invitation to Love: New Patterns of Courtship in Nepal." Paper Presented at the 24th Annual Conference on South Asia, University of Wisconsin–Madison, 1995.

Allen, Michael. *The Cult of Kumari: Virgin Worship in Nepal*. Kathmandu: Mandala Book Point, 1975.

Allen, Michael, ed. *Anthropology of Nepal: Peoples, Problems and Processes*. Kathmandu: Mandala Book Point, 1994.

Allen, Nicholas J. "Approaches to Illness in the Nepalese Hills." In *Social Anthropology and Medicine*, ed. J. B. Loudon. London: Academic Press, 1976.

Amnesty International. *Nepal: A Pattern of Human Rights Violations*. London: Amnesty International, 1987.

Aryal, Deepak, Rabindra Regmi, and Nirmal Rimal, eds. *Nepal District Profile: A Districtwise Socioeconomic Profile of Nepal*. Kathmandu: National Research Institute, 1982.

Bajracharya, B. *Gender Issues in Nepalese Agriculture*. Kathmandu: Winrock International, 1994.

Bharati, Agehananda. *The Tantric Tradition*. London: Rider, 1965.

Bhattachan, Krishna, and Kailash N. Pyakuryal. "The Issue of National Integration in Nepal: An Ethno-Regional Approach." In *Emerging Ethnicity and Aspects of Community Adaptation*. Kathmandu: CNAS, 1996.

Bhattachan, Krishna, and Chaitanya Mishra, eds. *Developmental Practices in Nepal*. Kathmandu: Department of Sociology and Anthropology, Tribhuvan University, 1997.

Bhattacharya, Benoytosh. *An Introduction to Buddhist Esoterism*. Varanasi: Chowkhamba, 1964.

Bechert, Heinz. "The Original Buddha and Recent Buddha: A Preliminary Report on Buddhism in a Gurung Community." In *Change and Continuity: Studies in the Nepalese Culture*, ed. S. Lienhard. Turino: Orientalia, 1996.

Bennet, Lynn. *Dangerous Wives and Sacred Sisters: Social and Symbolic Roles of High-Caste Women in Nepal*. New York: Columbia University Press, 1983.

Berreman, Gerald D. *Hindus of the Himalayas*. Berkeley: University of California Press, 1972.

Bhandari, Bishnu. "Drug Abuse in Nepal: A Case Study of the Kathmandu Valley." Paper presented at the 18th annual conference on South Asia, University of Wisconsin–Madison, 1989.

Bishop, Barry C. *Karnali under Stress: Livelihood Strategies and Seasonal Rhythms in a Changing Nepal Himalaya*. Chicago: University of Chicago, 1990

Bishop, Naomi. *Himalayan Herders (Case Studies in Cultural Anthropology)*. New York: Thompson International Publishing, 1998.

Bista, Dor B. "The Forgotten People of Dang Valley." *Vasudha* 12 (1969): 10-14.

———. *Peoples of Nepal* (3rd edition). Kathmandu: Ratna Pustak Bhandar, 1976.

———. *Fatalism and Development in Nepal's Struggle for Modernization*. Calcutta: Orient Longman, 1991.

Bista, Dor B., et al. eds. *Anthropological and Linguistic Studies of the Gandaki Areas of Nepal*. Tokyo: Institute for the Study of Languages and Cultures of Asia and Africa, 1982.

Bughart, Richard. "The Political Culture of Panchayat Democracy." In *Nepal in the Nineties*, ed. Michael Hutt. New Delhi: Oxford University Press, 1994.

——. "The Category 'Hindu' in the Political Discourse of Nepal." In *The Conditions of Listening: Essays on Religion, History, and Politics in South Asia*, eds. C. J. Fuller and Jonathan Spencer. New Delhi: Oxford University Press, 1996.

Caplan, Lionel. *Land and Social Change in East Nepal: A Study of Hindu-Tribal Relations*. Berkeley: University of California Press, 1970.

——. "Tribes in the Ethnography of Nepal: Some Comments on a Debate." *Contributions to Nepalese Studies* 17 (1989): 129–145.

——. "'Bravest of the Brave': Representations of 'The Gurkha' in British Military Writings." *Modern Asian Studies* 25 (1991): 571–597.

——. "From Tribe to Peasant? The Limbus and the Nepalese State." *Journal of Peasant Studies* 18 (1991): 305–321.

CBS. *Population Monograph of Nepal*. Kathmandu: CBS, 1987.

——. *Statistical Year Book of Nepal*. Kathmandu: CBS, 2001.

Chauhan, R. S. *Society and State Building in Nepal: From Ancient Times to Mid-Twentieth Century*. New Delhi: Stosius, 1989.

Chemjong, I. S. *History and Culture of Kirat People*. Darjeeling: Tumeng Hang and Chandraw Hang, 1966.

Child Welfare Society (CWS). *Street Children: Our Failure*. Kathmandu: CWS, 1993.

Child Workers in Nepal (CWIN). "Street Kids in Kathmandu." *Voice of Child Workers* 5/6 (1989): 12–15.

——. *Lost Childhood: Survey Research on Street Children of Kathmandu*. Kathmandu: CWIN, 1990.

——. "Urban Domestic Child Labour in the Kathmandu Valley." *Voice of Child Workers* 23 (1994): 34–40.

Coburn, Broughton. *Nepali Aama: Portrait of a Nepalese Hill Woman*. Santa Barbara, Calif.: Ross-Erikson, 1981.

Conway, Dennis, and Nanda Shrestha. "Urban Growth and Urbanization in Least-Developed Countries: The Experience of Nepal, 1952–71." *Asian Profile* 8 (1980): 477–494.

Conway, Dennis, Keshav Bhattarai, and Nanda R. Shrestha. "Population–Environment Relations at the Forested Frontier of Nepal: Tharu and Pahari Survival Strategies in Bardiya." *Applied Geography* 20 (2000): 221–242.

Cox, Thomas. "Land Rights and Ethnic Conflict in Nepal." *Economic and Political Weekly* 25 (1990): 1318–1320.

Davis, Hassoldt. *Nepal: Land of Mystery*. London: Robert Hale, 1942.

Dahal, Dilli R. *An Ethnographic Study of Social Change among the Athpabariya Rai of Dhankuta*. Kathmandu: CNAS, 1985.

Dangal, D. R., and S. B. Gurung. "Ethnobotany of the Tharu Tribe of Chitwan District." *International Journal of Pharmacognosy*, 29 (1991): 203.

Davis, Hassoldt. *Nepal, Land of Mystery*. London: Robert Hale, 1942.

de Sales, Ann. "Wild Imaginings: French Anthropology in the Himalaya." *Himal* 8 (1995): 32–34.

Des Chene, Mary. "Ethnography in the Janjati-yug: Lessons from Reading Rodhi and Other Tamu Writings." *Studies in Nepali History and Society* 1 (1996): 97–162.

———. "'We Women Must Try to Live:' The Saga of Bhauju." *Studies in Nepali History and Society* 2 (1997): 125–172.

Devkota, Padam Lal. "Anthropological Perspective on Grassroots Development in Nepal." *Occasional Papers in Sociology and Anthropology* 4. Kathmandu: Department of Sociology and Anthropology, Tribhuvan University, 1994.

Dhakal, Suresh, et al. *Issues and Experiences: Kamaiya System, Kanara Andolan and Tharus in Bardiya*. Kathmandu: Society for Participatory Cultural Education, 2000.

Fisher, James F. "The Historical Development of Himalayan Anthropology." *Mountain Research and Development* 5 (1985): 99–111.

———. "Education and Social Change in Nepal: An Anthropologist's Assessment." *Himalayan Research Bulletin* 10 (1990): 30–34.

———. *Living Martyrs: Individuals and Revolution in Nepal*. New Delhi: Oxford University Press, 2000.

Fisher, William F. *Fluid Boundaries : Forming and Transforming Identity in Nepal*. New York: Columbia University Press, 2001.

Fricke, Tom. *Himalayan Households: Tamang Demography and Domestic Processes*. New York: Columbia University Press, 1994.

Fricke, Tom, A. Thornton, and Dilli R. Dahal. "Family Organization and the Wage Labor Transition in a Tamang Community of Nepal." *Human Ecology* 18 (1990): 283–313.

Fürer-Haimendorf, Christoph von. *Caste and Kin in Nepal, India and Ceylon: Anthropological Studies in Hindu-Buddhist Contact Zones*. London: Asia Publishing House, 1966.

Gajurel, C. L., and K. K. Vaidya. *Traditional Arts and Crafts of Nepal*. New Delhi: Asia Book, 1984.

Gellner, David N. "Language, Caste, Religion, and Territory: Newar Identity Ancient and Modern." *European Journal of Sociology* 27 (1986): 102–148.

———. "Hinduism, Tribalism, and the Position of Women: The Problem of Newar Identity." *Man* 26 (1991): 105–125.

———. *Monk, Householder, and Tantric Priests: Newar Buddhism and Its Hierarchy of Ritual*. Cambridge: Cambridge University Press, 1992.

———. *The Anthropology of Buddhism and Hinduism*. London: Oxford University Press, 2001.

Gellner, David N., Joanna Pfaff-Czarnecka, and John Whelpton, eds. *Nationalism and Ethnicity in a Hindu Kingdom: The Politics and Culture of Contemporary Nepal*. London: Routledge, 1997.

Gellner, David N., and Declan Quigley, eds. *Contested Hierarchies: A Collaborative Ethnography of Caste among the Newars of the Kathmandu Valley, Nepal*. Oxford: Clarendon Press, 1995.

Gilbert, Kate. "Women and Family Law in Modern Nepal: Statutory Rights and Social Implications." *Journal of International Law and Politics* 24 (1992): 729–758.

Glover, Warren W. *A Vocabulary of the Gurung Language*. Kathmandu: Summer Institute of Linguistics, Tribhuvan University, 1972.

Guneratne, Katharine Bjork. *In the Circle of the Dance: Notes of an Outsider in Nepal*. Ithaca, N.Y.: Cornell University Press, 1999.

Guneratne, Upali Arjun. "The Tharus of Chitwan: Ethnicity, Class and the State of Nepal." Ph.D. Dissertation, University of Chicago, 1994.

———. "The Tax Man Cometh: The Impact of Revenue Collection on Subsistence Strategies in Chitwan Tharu Society." *Studies in Nepali History and Society* 1 (1996): 5–36.

———. "Modernization, the State and the Construction of a Tharu Identity in Nepal." *Journal of Asian Studies* 57 (1998): 749–779.

Gurung, Ganesh Man. *Indigenous Peoples: Mobilization and Change*. Kathmandu: HISI Press, 1994.

Gurung, Harka. *Vignettes of Nepal*. Kathmandu: Sajha Prakashan, 1980.

———. *Nature and Culture: Random Reflections*. Kathmandu: Saroj Gurung, 1989.

———. *The Chepangs: A Study in Continuity and Change*. Kathmandu: New Era, 1989.

———. *Regional Patterns of Migration in Nepal*. Honolulu: East-West Center, 1989.

———. *Nepal: Social Demography and Expressions*. Kathmandu: New Era, 1998.

Gutschow, Niels, and Bernhard Kölver. *Bhaktapur: Ordered Space, Concepts and Functions in a Town of Nepal*. Wiesbaden: Kommissions-verlag Franz Steiner, 1975.

Gutschow, Niels, Bijay Basukala, and David N. Gellner. *The Nepalese Caitya: 1,500 Years of Buddhist Votive Architecture in the Kathmandu Valley*. Stuttgart: Edition Axel Menges, 1997.

Haddix, Kimber A., and Jit Bahadur Gurung. "'Excess Women:' Non-Marriage and Reproduction in Two Ethnic Tibetan Communities of Humla, Nepal." *Himalayan Research Bulletin* 14 (1999): 56–62.

Hasan, Amir. "The Occupational Pattern in a Terai Village." *Eastern Anthropologist* 22 (1969): 187–206.

Himal South Asia. "Orbital Junk" (Cover Story). 9 (September 1996): 12–28.

———. "Citizens and Cities" (Cover Story). 11 (August 1998): 11–32.

———. "The Price of Our Daughters" (Cover Story). 11 (October 1998): 12–31.

———. "Gods in Exile" (Cover Story). 12 (October 1999): 8–25.

Hitchcock, John T. *The Magars of Banyan Hill*. New York: Rinehart and Winston, 1966.

———. "An Additional Perspective on the Nepali Caste System." In *Himalayan Anthropology*, ed. J. T. Fisher. The Hague: Mouton, 1979.

Hodgson, Brian Houghton. "On the Law and Legal Practice of Nepal, as Regards Familiar Intercourse between Hindu and Outcaste." *Journal of the Royal Asiatic Society of Great Britain and Ireland* 1 (1834): 45–56.

———. *Essays on the Languages, Literature, and Religion of Nepal and Tibet, Together with Further Papers on the Geography, Ethnology, and Commerce of Those Countries*. London: Trubner, 1874.

Höfer, Andras. *The Caste Hierarchy and the State in Nepal: A Study of the Muluki Ain of 1854*. Innsbruck: Universitätsverlag Wagner, 1979.

———. *Tamang Ritual Texts: Preliminary Studies in the Folk-Religion of Ethnic Minority in Nepal*. Wiesbaden: Franz Steiner, 1981.

Hu, C. T. "Marriage by Exchange among the Tharu." *Eastern Anthropologist* 10 (1957): 116–129.

Hutt, Michael. *Modern Literary Nepali: An Introductory Reader*. New Delhi: Oxford University Press, 2000.

Hutt, Michael, ed. *Himalayan Voices : An Introduction to Modern Nepali Literature*. Berkeley: University of California Press, 1991.

Hutt, Michael, and Abhi Subedi. *Teach Yourself: Nepali*. New Delhi: McGraw Hill, 1999.

Hutt, Michael, et al. *Nepal: A Guide to the Art and Architecture of the Kathmandu Valley*. Boston: Shambhala Publications, 1994.

ICIMOD. *Mountain Tourism in Nepal: An Overview*. Kathmandu: ICIMOD, 1995.

Iijima, Shigeru. "Hinduization of a Himalayan Tribe in Nepal." *Kroeber Anthropological Papers* 29 (1963): 43–52.

———. "The Thakalis: Traditional and Modern." In *Anthropological and Linguistic Studies of the Gandaki Area in Nepal*. Tokyo: Tokyo University of Foreign Studies, 1982.

Integrated Development Systems (IDS). *Land Tenure System in Nepal*. Kathmandu: IDS, 1986.

International Child Year Committee. *International Child Year 1979: A Report*. Kathmandu: International Child Year Committee, 1979.

Ishii, Hiroshi. "Agricultural Labor Recruitment in a Parbate Village in Nepal." In *Anthropological and Linguistic Studies of the Gandaki Area of Nepal*. Tokyo: Tokyo University of Foreign Studies, 1982.

Jha, Hari Bansh. *The Terai Community and National Integration in Nepal*. Kathmandu: FES, 1993.

Joshi, D. D. "Women and Buffaloes in Nepal." *Asian Livestock* 9 (1984): 116–118.

Kansakar, Vidya V. S. "History of Population Migration in Nepal." *Himalayan Review* 6 (1974): 58–68.

Kaplan, Paul F., and Nanda R. Shrestha. "The Sukumbasi Movement in Nepal: The Fire from Below." *Journal of Contemporary Asia* 12 (1982): 75–88.

Karan, Pradyumna P. *Nepal: A Physical and Cultural Geography*. Lexington: University of Kentucky Press, 1960.

———. *Nepal: A Himalayan Kingdom in Transition*. Tokyo: United Nations University Press, 1996.

Kawatika, J. *Hill Magars and Their Neighbors*. Tokyo: Tokai University Press, 1974.

Korn, Wolfgang. *The Traditional Architecture of the Kathmandu Valley*. Kathmandu: Ratna Pustak Bhandar, 1976.

Kramrisch, Stella. *The Art of Nepal*. Philadelphia: Asia Society, 1964.

Krause, B. "Kinship, Hierarchy and Equality in North Western Nepal." *Contribution to Indian Studies* 14 (1980): 169–194.
Leal, D. *A Vocabulary of the Tharu Language*. Kathmandu: Summer Institute of Linguistics, Tribhuvan University, 1973.
Levy, Robert I. *Mesocosm: Hinduism and the Organization of a Traditional Newar City in Nepal*. Berkeley: University of California Press, 1990.
Liechty, Mark. "Paying for Modernity: Women and the Discourse of Freedom in Kathmandu." *Studies in Nepali History and Society* 1 (1996): 301–330.
——. "Selective Exclusion: Foreigners, Foreign Goods and Foreignness in Modern Nepali History." *Studies in Nepali History and Society* 2 (1997): 5–68.
Lienhard, S., ed. *Change and Continuity: Studies in the Nepalese Culture*. Turin: Orientalia, 1996.
Locke, John K. *Karunamaya: The Cult of Avalokitesvara-Matsyendranath in the Valley of Nepal*. Kathmandu: University Press, 1975.
——. *Buddhist Monasteries of Nepal*. Kathmandu: Sahayogi Press, 1985.
Macdonald, A. W., ed. *Essays on the Ethnology of Nepal and South Asia*. Kathmandu: Ratna Pustak Bhandar, 1983.
Macdonald, A. W., and A. Vergati Stahl. *Newar Art: Nepalese Art during the Malla Period*. New Delhi: Vikas Publishing House, 1979.
McDonaugh, C. "Losing Ground, Gaining Ground: Land and Change in a Tharu Community in Dang, West Nepal. In *Nationalism and Ethnicity in a Hindu Kingdom: The Politics and Culture of Contemporary Nepal*, eds. David N. Gellner, Joanna Pfaff-Czarnecka, and John Whelpton. Amsterdam: Routledge, 1997.
Manzardo, A. E. "Impression Management and Economic Growth: The Case of Thakali of Dhaulagiri Zone." *Kailash* 9 (1982): 45–60.
Manzardo, A. E., and K. P. Sharma. "Cost-Cutting, Caste and Community: A Look at Thakali Social Reform in Pokhara." *Contribution to Nepalese Studies* 2 (1975): 25–44.
Maskarinec, Gregory. *The Rulings of the Night: An Ethnography of Nepalese Shaman Oral Texts*. Madison: University of Wisconsin Press, 1995.
Michaels, A. "Widow Burning in Nepal." In *Nepal: Past and Present*, ed. G. Toffin. Paris: CNRS, 1993.
Morris, C. J. *The Gurkhas: An Ethnology*. New Delhi: B. R. Publishing, 1985.

Muller-Boker, Ulrike. "Spatial Organization of a Caste Society: The Example of the Newar of the Kathmandu Valley, Nepal." *Mountain Research and Development* 8 (1993): 23–31.

———. "Ethnobotanical Studies among the Chitwan Tharus." *Journal of the Nepal Research Centre* 9 (1993): 17–56.

Mumford, Stan. *Himalayan Dialogue: Tibetan Lamas and Gurung Shamans in Nepal.* Madison: University of Wisconsin Press, 1989.

Nag, M. B., N. F. White, and R. C. Poet. "An Anthropological Approach to the Study of the Economic Value of Children in Java and Nepal." *Current Anthropology* 19 (1978): 293–306.

Nakane, C. "A Plural Society in Sikkim: A Study of the Interrelations of Lepchas, Bhotias, and Nepalis." In *Caste and Kin in Nepal, India, and Ceylon*, ed. Christoph von Fürer-Haimendorf. London: Asia Publishing House, 1966.

Nepal South Asia Centre. *Nepal Human Development Report, 1998.* Kathmandu: 1998.

New ERA. *A Situation Analysis of Sex Work and Trafficking in Nepal with Reference to Children.* Kathmandu: New ERA, 1997.

Odegaard, S. E. "From Castes to Ethnic Group? Modernization and Forms of Social Identification among Tharus of the Nepalese Tarai." Ph.D. Dissertation, University of Oslo, 1997.

Ogura, Kiyoko. *Kathmandu Spring: The People's Movement of 1990.* Kathmandu: Himal Books, 2001.

Okada, Ferdinand E., and Nirmal Shamsher Rana. *The Child Beggars of Kathmandu.* Kathmandu: Department of Local Development, 1973.

O'Neill, T. "Peoples and Polity: Ethnography, Ethnicity and Identity in Nepal." *Contributions to Nepalese Studies* 21 (1994): 45–72.

Onta, Lazima. *Situation Analysis of Street Children in Nepal.* Kathmandu: Child Welfare Society, 1995.

Onta, Lazima, and Rachel Baker. *Nonformal Education for the Street Children in Kathmandu: A Report of Our Teaching Experiences.* Kathmandu: Child Welfare Society, 1995.

Onta, Pratyoush. "Anthropology Still Finding Its Feet: Anthropology in Nepal Struggles for a Unique Identity." *Himal* 5 (1992): 31–33.

———. "Activities in a 'Fossil State': Balakrishna Sama and the Improvisation of Nepali Identity." *Studies in Nepali History and Society* 2 (1997): 69–102.

Onta, Pratyoush, and Mary Des Chene. "Whither Scholarship on Nepal in the Nineties?" *Contributions to Nepalese Studies* 22 (1995): 213–223.

Onta-Bhatta, Lazima. "Street Children: Contested Identities and Universalizing Categories." *Studies in Nepali History and Society* 1 (1996): 163–200.
Pandey, Surendra. "The Vadi Community and Prostitution." *South Asia Bulletin* 13 (1993).
Parajuli, Buddhi Sagar. *Swasthani*. Kathmandu: Ratna Pustak Bhandar, 1972.
Parish, Steven M. *Moral Knowing in a Hindu Sacred City: An Exploration of Mind, Emotion, and Self*. New York: Columbia University Press, 1994.
Pettigrew, J., and Y. K. Tamu. "Tamu Shamanistic Possession (*khhlye khhaba*): Some Preliminary Ethnographic Observations." In *Anthropology of Nepal: People, Problems and Processes*, ed. Micheal Allen. Kathmandu: Mandala Book Point, 1994.
Pfaff-Czarnecka, Joanna. "State and Community: Changing Relations of Production after the 'Unification' of Nepal." In *Early State Economics*, eds. H. J. M. Claessen and P. van der Velde. New Brunswick, N.J.: Transaction Publishers, 1991.
———. "The Nepalese Durga Puja Festival or Displaying Military Supremacy on Ritual Occasions." In *Anthropology of Tibet and the Himalaya*, eds. C. Ramble and M. Brauen. Zurich: Ethnological Museum, 1993.
———. "Migration under Marginality Conditions: The Case of Bajhang." In *Rural-Urban Interlinkages: A Challenge for Development Cooperation*, eds. O. Schwank et al. Zurich: Infras, 1993.
Pigg, Stacey. "Inventing Social Categories through Space: Social Representations and Development in Nepal." *Comparative Studies in Society and Human* 34 (1992): 491–513.
Pokharel, Durga, and Anthony Willett. *Shadow over Shangri-La: A Woman's Quest for Freedom*. Washington, D.C.: Brassey's, 1996.
Poudyal, A. R. "Nepal: Ethnicity in Democracy." In *South Asia: Democracy and the Road Ahead*, Lok Raj Baral, ed. Kathmandu: POLSAN, 1992.
Powell, E. Alexander. *The Last Home of Mystery*. New York: Garden City Publishing, 1929.
Pradhan, Gauri. "Khate: The Street Survivors." *Voice of Child Workers* 19/20 (1993): 3–14.
Pradhan, H. D. "Social Economy in the Tarai (Tharus)." *Journal of the United Provinces Historical Society* 10 (1937): 59–76.
Proksch, Andreas, ed. *Images of a Century: The Changing Townscapes of the Kathmandu Valley*. Kathmandu: GTZ, 1995.

Quigley, Declan. *The Interpretation of Caste.* Oxford: Clarendon Press, 1993.
Raj, Prakash A. *Kathmandu and the Kingdom of Nepal* (13th edition). Kathmandu: Nabeen, 2000.
Ramble, C. "A Ritual of Political Unity in an Old Nepalese Kingdom." *Ancient Nepal* 130-133 (1993): 49–58.
Rogers, Paul, and John Aitchison. *Towards Sustainable Tourism in the Everest Region of Nepal.* Kathmandu: IUCN, 1998.
Sanday, John. *Monuments of the Kathmandu Valley.* Gemploux: UNESCO, 1979.
Seeland, K. "Sanskritisation and Environmental Perception among Tibeto-Burman Speaking Groups." In *Anthropology of Tibet and the Himalaya*, eds. C. Ramble and M. Brauen. Zurich: Ethnological Museum, 1993.
Shah, Saubhagya. "The Gospel Comes to the Hindu Kingdom." *Himal* 6 (1993): 35–40.
Sharma, Pitamber, ed. *Tourism for Local Community Development in Mountain Areas: Perspectives, Issues, and Guidelines.* Kathmandu: IUCN, 1995.
Sharma, Prayag Raj. "Values in the Doldrums: Does the West Meet the East in Nepal?" *European Journal of Sociology* 30 (1989): 3–21.
———. "Caste Societies in the State of Nepal: A Historical Perspective." In *Anthropology of Tibet and the Himalaya*, eds. C. Ramble and M. Brauen. Zurich: Ethnological Museum, 1993.
———. "Bahun in the Nepali State." *Himal* 7 (1994): 42–5.
Shrestha, Nanda R. "A Preliminary Report on Population Pressure and Land Resources in Nepal." *Journal of Developing Areas* 16 (1982): 197–212.
———. "Enchanted by the Mantra of Bikas: A Self-Reflective Perspective on Nepalese Elites and Development." *South Asia Bulletin* 13 (1993): 5–22.
———. *In the Name of Development: A Reflection on Nepal.* Lanham, Md.: University Press of America, 1997 (Kathmandu: Educational Enterprise, 1999, Nepal edition).
———. "A Personal View of Child Labor." *Education About Asia* 5 (2000): 47–49
———. *Nepal and Bangladesh: A Global Studies Handbook.* Denver, Colo.: ABC-CLIO, 2002.

Shrestha, Nanda R., and Dennis Conway. "Ecopolitical Battles in the Tarai of Nepal: An Emerging Human and Environmental Crisis." *International Journal of Population Geography* 2 (1996): 313–331.

———. "The Shadow Life of a Migrant's Wife." Unpublished manuscript, 1998.

Shrestha, Nanda R., Dennis Conway, and Keshav Bhattarai. "Population Pressure and Land Resources in Nepal: A Revisit, Twenty Years Later." *Journal of Developing Areas* 33 (1999): 245–268.

Singh, Ganesh Man. *Mero Kathaka Panaharu* (The Pages of My Story: Autobiographical Memoire). Kathmandu: Ayam Publication, 1998.

Singh, Mita. *Ba Sangaka Samjhanaka Chhenharu* (Moments of Memories with My Father Ganesh Man Singh). Kathmandu: the author, 1998.

Singh, Ramananda Prasad. *The Real Story of the Tharus*. Kathmandu: The Tharu Sanskriti, 1988.

Skar, Harold O. *Development Aid to Nepal: Issues and Options in Energy, Health, Education, Democracy and Human Rights*. Copenhagen: NIAS, 1997.

Slusser, Mary S. *Nepal Mandala: A Cultural Study of the Kathmandu Valley* (two volumes). Princeton, N.J.: Princeton University Press, 1982.

Snellgrove, David. *Four Lamas of Dolpo*. Kathmandu: Himalayan Book Sellers, 1992.

South Asia Partnership (SAP). *Capacity Building with Grassroots NGOs: Practical Techniques*. Kathmandu: SAP, 1991.

———. *People Centered Development Training: A Trainer's Guide Book*. Kathmandu: SAP, 1994.

Stone, Linda. "Cultural Crossroads of Community Participation in Development: A Case from Nepal." *Human Organization* 48 (1989): 206–213.

Takayama, R. *Economy of the Agro-Pastoral Tibetans in the Tarbo Region, N. W. Nepal Tarbo Ethnography No. 2*. Tokyo: Japanese Society of Ethnology, 1960.

Tamang, P. "Tamangs under the Shadow." *Himal* 5 (1992): 25–27.

Tokyo University of Foreign Studies. *Anthropological and Linguistic Studies of the Gandaki Area in Nepal*. Tokyo: Tokyo University of Foreign Studies, 1982.

Underprivileged Children's Educational Programme (UCEP). *A Case Study of Working Children Aged 8–14 Years in the Kathmandu Valley*. Kathmandu: UCEP, 1979.

Upadhyay, K. D. "A Socio-Economic Profile of the Porters in the Central Mid-Hills of Nepal." In *Occasional Papers in Sociology and Anthropology*, ed. S. Mikesell. Kathmandu: Department of Sociology and Anthropology, Tribhuvan University, 1990.

Upadhya, Shizu. "The Status of Women in Nepal—15 Years On." *Studies in Nepali History and Society* 1 (1996): 423–454.

Vansittart, Eden. "The Tribes, Clans and Castes of Nepal." *Journal of Asiatic Society of Bengal* 63 (1894): 213–249.

Wiesner, Ulrich. "Nepalese Temple Architecture: Its Characteristics and Its Relations to Indian Development." In *Studies in South Asian Culture*, ed. J. E. Van Lohuizen-de Leeuw. Leiden: E. J. Brill, 1978.

Zurick, David. "Adventure Travel and Sustainable Tourism in the Peripheral Economy of Nepal." *Annals of Association of American Geographers* 82 (1992): 608–628.

Zurick, David, and Nanda R. Shrestha. "Himalayan Dwellings: A Cultural-Environmental Perspective." In *Asia's Old Dwellings: Tradition, Resilience, and Change*, ed. Ronald Knapp. Hong Kong and New York: Oxford University Press, 2003.

ECONOMY AND DEVELOPMENT

Acharya, Keshav P. *A Review of Foreign Aid in Nepal*. Kathmandu: Citizen's Poverty Watch Forum.

Acharya, Keshav, and Karki Bharat. *Review of Recent Macroeconomic Policies in the Context of Their Effects on Poverty in Nepal*. Kathmandu: APROSC, 1996.

Acharya, Meena. *Statistical Profile of Nepalese Women: An Update in the Policy Context*. Kathmandu: IIDS, 1994.

———. "Globalization Process and the Nepalese Economy: Its Impact on Employment and Income." In *Impact of Globalization in Nepal*, ed. Madan K. Dahal. Kathmandu: NEFAS, 1998.

———. *Labor Market Development and Poverty in Nepal*. Kathmandu: FES, 2000.

Acharya, Meena, and Pushpa Acharya. *Gender Equality and Empowerment of Women: A Status Report*. Kathmandu: UNDP, 1997.

Acharya, Meena, and Lynn Bennett. *The Rural Women of Nepal: An Aggregate Analysis and Summary of Eight Village Studies*. Kathmandu: CEDA, 1981.

Agricultural Development Bank. *Small Farmer Development Program. Two Decades of Crusade Against Poverty*. Kathmandu: Agricultural Development Bank, 1996.

Asian Regional Team for Employment Production (ARTEP). *A Challenge to Nepal: Growth and Employment*. Bangkok: ARTEP, 1974.

Bagchi, D. K., et al. "Conceptual and Methodological Challenges in the Study of Livelihood Trajectories: Case Studies in Eastern India and Western Nepal." *Journal of International Development* 10 (1998): 453–468.

Bajracharya, Puskar, and Shankar Sharma. *Impact of Economic Liberalization in Nepal*. Kathmandu: IIDS, 1995.

Bhattarai, Baburam. *1998 and Political Economic Rational of People's War in Nepal*. Kathmandu: Utprek Publications, 1998.

Bishop, Naomi. "Circular Migration and Families: A Yolmo Sherpa Example." *South Asia Bulletin* 13 (1993): 59–66.

Bongartz, Heinz, and Dev Raj Dahal. *Development Studies: Self-Help Organizations, NGOs and Civil Society*. Kathmandu: NEFAS and FES, 1996.

CBS. *Annual Census of Manufacturing, 1990–1991*. Kathmandu: CBS, 1992.

———. *Nepal Living Standard Survey Report, 1996: Main Findings*. Kathmandu: CBS, 1997.

———. *Statistical Year Book of Nepal*. Kathmandu: CBS, 2001.

Chhetri, Ram B. "Rotating Credit Associations in Nepal: *Dhikuri* as Capital, Credit, Saving, and Investment." *Human Organization* 54 (1995): 449–454.

Cooke, P. A. "Intrahousehold Labor Allocation Responses to Environmental Goods Scarcity: A Case Study of the Hills of Nepal. *Economic Development and Cultural Change* 46 (1998): 807–830.

Dahal, Dev Raj. "Civil Society and Self-Governing Polity in Nepal." In *State, Leadership and Politics in Nepal*, ed. Dhruba Kumar. Kathmandu: CNAS, 1995.

———. "Towards Alternatives: Vision of Good Governance in Nepal." In *Good Governance in the New Millennium: The Path to a Strong Civil Society*. Kathmandu: SAP, 1999.

Dahal, Dev Raj, and Kishor Kumar Guru-Gharana, eds. *Development Strategy for Nepal*. Kathmandu: NEFAS and FES, 1996.

Dahal, Madan K., ed. *Future of Nepalese Economy*. Kathmandu: NEFAS and FES, 1993.

———. *Impact of Globalization in Nepal*. Kathmandu: NEFAS and FES, 1998.

Dixit, Kanak Mani. "Foreign Aid in Nepal: No Bang for the Buck." *Studies in Nepali History and Society* 2 (1997): 173–186.

———. "Lowly Labour in the Lowlands." *Himal* (January–February 1997).

Dixit, Praveen. *Economic Reform in Nepal: A Cursory Assessment*. College Park, Md.: Center for Institutional Reform and the Informal Sector, 1995.

Fisher, James F. *Trans-Himalayan Traders: Economy, Society, and Culture in Northwest Nepal*. Berkeley: University of California Press, 1986.

Fujikura, Tatsuro. "Technologies of Improvement, Locations of Culture: American Discourse of Democracy and 'Community Development' in Nepal." *Studies in Nepali History and Society* 1 (1996): 271–312.

Ghimire, Gopal, Lane Kinley, and Rabindra K Shakya. *Privatization in Nepal: An Independent Review of Privatization Programme*. Kathmandu: DFID, 2000.

Guru-Gharana, Kishor K. *Industrial Relations System in Nepal*. Kathmandu: NEFAS and FES, 1996.

Gurung, Harka. *Nepal: Dimensions of Development*. Kathmandu: Sahayogi Press, 1984.

Gyawali, Dipak. "A Fate Other Than Marginalisation." *Himal* 7 (1994): 11–21.

Himal. "Hill Poverty" (Special Issue). November–December 1990.

———. "Nepalis in Foreign Uniform" (Special Issue). July–August 1991.

Himal South Asia (previously *Himal*). "Collecting Orbital Junk" (Special Issue). June 1996.

ICIMOD. *Off-Farm Employment and Mountain Development*. Kathmandu: ICIMOD, 1992.

———. *Assessing the Potential of Market Towns in the Mountains: Case Studies from the Hindu Kush Himalayas*. Kathmandu: ICIMOD, 1996.

Integrated Development Systems (IDS). *Foreign Aid and Development in Nepal*. Kathmandu: IDS, 1983.

Ishii, Hiroshi. "Recent Economic Changes in a Newar Village." *Contributions to Nepalese Studies* 8 (1980): 157–179.

Jain, M. S. *Emergence of a New Aristocracy in Nepal (1837–58)*. Agra: Sri Ram Mehar, 1972.

Joshi, Bikas. "Diagnoses of the Nepali Economy: A Review of the Analysis of Economic Liberalization Policies in Nepal." *Studies in Nepali History and Society* 1 (1996): 231–246.

Kansakar, Vidya B. S. *Effectiveness of Planned Resettlement Programme in Nepal*. Kathmandu: CEDA, 1979.

Kaphley, K. P. *Nepal's Drive towards Export Promotion and Diversification: Perspective for Nepalese Economy*: Kathmandu: Ministry of Commerce, 2000.

Karan, Pradyumna P. *Nepal: A Himalayan Kingdom in Transition*. Tokyo: United Nations University Press, 1996.

Khadka, Narayan. *Foreign Aid and Foreign Policy: Major Powers and Nepal*. New Delhi: Vikas Publishing House, 1997.

Knall, B. "Economic Development, Participation and Decentralization in Nepal." *European Bulletin of Himalayan Research* 5 (1993): 26–29.

Koirala, G., et al. "Proposed Approach to Poverty Alleviation in Nepal." In *Poverty Alleviation and Human Development in Nepal*. Kathmandu: National Planning Commission, 1992.

Levine, Nancy E. "Webs of Dependence in Rural Nepal: Debt, Poverty and Depopulation in the Far Northwest." *Contribution to Nepalese Studies* 15 (1988): 213–246.

Lohani, Prakash C. "The Industrial Policy: The Problem Child of History." In *Nepal in Perspective*, eds. Pashupati S. Rana and Kamla P. Malla. Kathmandu: CEDA, 1973.

McDougal, Charles. *Village and Household Economy in Far Western Nepal*. Kathmandu: Tribhuvan University Press, 1968.

Maskay, Bishwa K. *Non-Governmental Organization in Development: Search for a Vision*. Kathmandu: Centre for Development and Governance, 1998.

Metz, John. "Development in Nepal: Investment in the Status Quo." *Geojournal* 35 (1995): 175–184.

Ministry of Finance (MOF). *Economic Survey*. Kathmandu: MOF, 1997.

———. *Economic Survey*. Kathmandu: MOF, 2000.

National Planning Commission (NPC). *First Five-Year Plan, 1956–1960*. Kathmandu: NPC, 1956.

———. *Second Plan, 1962–1965*. Kathmandu: NPC, 1962.

———. *Third Plan, 1965–1970*. Kathmandu: NPC, 1965.

———. *Fourth Plan, 1970–1975*. Kathmandu: NPC, 1970.

———. *Fifth Plan, 1975–1980*. Kathmandu: NPC, 1975.

———. *Sixth Plan, 1980–1985*. Kathmandu: NPC, 1980.

———. *Seventh Plan, 1985–1990*. Kathmandu: NPC, 1985.

———. *Nepal Basic Needs Programme*. Kathmandu: NPC, 1989.

———. *Eighth Plan, 1992-1997*. Kathmandu: NPC, 1992.

———. *Poverty Alleviation and Human Development in Nepal*. Kathmandu: NPC, 1992.

———. *The Revised GDP Series of Nepal at Current and Constant Prices.* Kathmandu: NPC, 1994.
———. *Ninth Plan, 1997–2002.* Kathmandu: NPC, 1997.
Nepal South Asia Centre. *Nepal Human Development Report.* Kathmandu: Nepal South Asia Centre, 1998.
Nepal Society for Applied Economics. *Review of the Implications of Minimum Fixed Capital Requirements for Foreign Investment in Nepal.* Kathmandu: Nepal Society for Applied Economics, 1995.
———. *Facts about Nepalese Economy, 1998.* Kathmandu: Nepal Society for Applied Economics, 1998.
Ojha, B. P. *Whither Nepalese Economy: Perspective for Nepalese Economy.* Kathmandu: Ministry of Commerce, 2000.
Ojha, Durga P., and Bihari K. Shrestha. *Impact Assessment of the Swabalamban Program in Dhading and Gorkha Districts.* Kathmandu: GTZ, 1996.
Panday, Devendra Raj. "Foreign Aid in Nepal's Development: An Overview." In *Foreign Aid and Development in Nepal.* Kathmandu: Integrated Development Systems, 1983.
———. "The Enigma of Aid." *Himal* (March-April 1992).
———. "Social Democracy in the Emerging World Order: Problems and Prospects for Nepal." *Contributions to Nepalese Studies* 23 (July 1997).
———. *Nepal's Failed Development: Reflections on the Missions and the Maladies.* Kathmandu: Nepal South Asia Centre, 1999.
———. "Matching Democracy and Development Policy Making in an Aid-Dependent Country: An Illustration from Nepal." *Harvard Asia Quarterly* (Winter 2000).
Pandey, Bikas. "Because It Is There: Foreign Money, Foreign Advice, and Arun III." *Himal* 8 (1995): 29–35.
———. "Local Benefits from Hydro Development." *Studies in Nepali History and Society* 1 (1996): 313–344.
Pandey, Tulsi Ram. *The Subsistence Farmers and Workers of Sunwal Village Panchayat, Nawalparasi District.* Kathmandu: USAID-GTZ-IDRC-Ford-Winrock Project, 1987.
Pradhan, Radhe S. *Industrialization in Nepal.* Delhi: NBO Publishers' Distributors, 1984.
Pyakuryal, Bishwambher, and Khem K. Dahal. *Import Substituting Industries in Nepal.* Kathmandu: Department of Economics, Tribhuvan University, 1989.

Rankin, Katherine. "Planning for Equity: Ethical Principles from Newar Representations of Finance." *Studies in Nepali History and Society* 1 (1996): 295–322.

Regmi, Govind Prasad. *Industrial Growth in Nepal: A Sectoral and Regional Analysis.* New Delhi: Oxford and IBH Publishing, 1994.

Regmi, Mahesh C. *Land Tenure and Taxation in Nepal* (four volumes). Berkeley: Institute of International Studies, University of California–Berkeley, 1963–1968.

———. *A Study in Nepali Economic History (1768–1846).* New Delhi: Manjusri Publishing House, 1971.

———. *Thatched Huts and Stucco Palaces: Peasants and Landlords in 19th-Century Nepal.* New Delhi: Vikas Publishing House, 1978.

———. *The State and Economic Surplus: Production, Trade, and Resource Mobilization in Early 19th-Century Nepal.* Banaras: Nath Publishing House, 1984.

———. *An Economic History of Nepal, 1846–1901.* Varanasi: Nath Publishing House, 1988.

Schroeder, R. J. "Himalayan Subsistence Systems: Indigenous Agriculture in Rural Nepal." *Mountain Research and Development* 5 (1985).

Schwartz, Moshe, and A. Paul Hare. *Foreign Experts and Unsustainable Development.* Burlington, Vt.: Ashgate, 2000.

Seddon, David. *Nepal: A State of Poverty.* New Delhi: Vikas Publishing House, 1987.

Seddon, David, ed. *Peasants and Workers in Nepal.* Warminster, UK: Aris and Phillips, 1979.

Seddon, David, J. Adhikari, and G. Gurung. *Foreign Labor Migration and the Remittance Economy of Nepal.* Report submitted to the Department for International Development, Great Britain, 1997.

Sharma, Gopi N. "The Impact of Education during the Rana Period in Nepal." *Himalayan Research Bulletin*, 10 (1990): 3–7.

Sharma, Gunanidhi. "Economic Liberalization in Nepal in the Context of Nepal-India Economic Cooperation." In *New Perspectives on India-Nepal Relations*, eds. Kalim Bahadur and Mahendra P. Lama. New Delhi: Anand Publications, 1995.

———. "Economic Aspect of Nepalese Foreign Policy." *Nepali Political Science and Politics* 6 & 7 (1998).

———. "The Economy of Nepal: A Macro-Economic Overview." In *Contemporary Nepal*, eds. Pashupati Shamsher Rana and Dwarika Dhungel. New Delhi: Vikas Publishing House, 1998.

Sharma, Gunanidhi, Navaraj Kandel, and Neelam K. Sharma. *Nepal: Missing Elements in the Development Thinking*. New Delhi: Nirala Publications, 2000.

Sharma, Gunanidhi, Hari Uprety, and Dev Raj Dahal, eds. *Debt Trap and Its Management in Nepal*. Kathmandu: NEFAS and FES, 1998.

Sharma, Kishor. *Trade Liberalisation and Manufacturing Performance in Developing Countries: New Evidences from Nepal*. Hauppauge, N.Y.: Nova Science Publishers, 1999.

Sharma, Robin. *Privatization: Lessons Learned*. Kathmandu: Mandira Sharma, 1995.

Shrestha, Ananda, ed. *The Role of Civil Society and Democratization in Nepal*. Kathmandu: NEFAS and FES. 1998.

Shrestha, Badri P. *An Introduction to Nepalese Economy*. Kathmandu: Ratna Pustak Bhandar, 1967.

———. "A Critique of Planning and Economic Development in Nepal." In *The Future of Nepalese Economy*, ed. Madan K. Dahal. Kathmandu: NEFAS and FES, 1993.

Shrestha, Bihari K. *A Himalayan Enclave in Transition*. Kathmandu: ICIMOD, 1993.

Shrestha, Nanda R. "The Political Economy of Economic Underdevelopment and External Migration in Nepal." *Political Geography Quarterly* 4 (1985): 289–306.

———. "A Postmodern View or Denial of Historical Integrity? The Poverty of Yapa's View of Poverty." *Annals of the Association of American Geographers* 87 (1997): 709–716.

———. *In the Name of Development: A Reflection on Nepal*. Lanham, Md.: University Press of America, 1997 (Kathmandu: Educational Enterprise, 1999, Nepal edition).

———. "A Personal View of Child Labor." *Education About Asia* 5 (2000): 47–49.

Shrestha, Nanda R., and Dennis Conway. "Issues in Population Pressure, Land Resettlement, and Development: The Case of Nepal." *Studies in Comparative International Development* 20 (1985): 55–82.

———. *Forest Land, the State, and the Rural Poor: Conflicts over Frontier Settlement in Contemporary Nepal*. Bloomington: Indiana Center on Global Change and World Peace, Indiana University, 1992.

———. "The Shadow Life of a Migrant's Wife." Unpublished manuscript, 1998.

Shrestha, Nanda R., and Truman A. Hartshorn. "A Neocapitalist Perspective on Third World Urbanization and Development." In *Urbanisation: Trends, Perspectives, and Challenges*, eds. Jaymala Diddee and Vimla Rangaswamy. Jaipur, India: Rawat Publications, 1993.

Shrestha, Saran H. *Economic Geography of Nepal*. Kathmandu: Educational Enterprise, 1986.

Skerry, Christa A., Kerry Moran, and Kay M. Calavan. *Four Decades of Development: The History of U.S. Assistance to Nepal, 1951-1991*. Kathmandu: USAID, 1991.

Timilsina, P. P., and B. P. Mahato. *Economic Development and Foreign Investment in Nepal: Issues and Perspectives*. Kathmandu: Nepal Society for Applied Economics, 2000.

Tuladhar, Bhushan. "Kathmandu's Garbage: Simple Solutions Going to Waste." *Studies in Nepali History and Society* 1 (1996): 365–394.

Uprety, Prem R. "The Economics of Buddhism: An Alternative Model for Community Development." *Contributions to Nepalese Studies* 23 (1996).

World Bank. *Nepal Fiscal Restructuring and Public Resource Management in the Nineties*. Washington, D.C.: World Bank, 1994.

———. *Nepal Poverty at the Time of the Twenty-First Century*. Washington, D.C.: World Bank, 1997.

———. *Country Assistance Strategy: Nepal, 1999-2001*. Washington, D.C.: World Bank, 1999.

Wright, Daniel. *Sketch of the Portion of the Country of Nepal Open to Europeans*. Calcutta: Office of the Superintendent of Government Printing, 1872.

Zivetz, Laurie. *Private Enterprise and the State in Modern Nepal*. New Delhi: Oxford University Press, 1992.

About the Authors

Nanda R. Shrestha was born and raised in Nepal. He graduated from the Pokhara Multipurpose High School in 1968 with a vocational concentration in trade and industry. After coming to the United States in early 1972, he earned his B.A. from Gustavus Adolphus College (Minnesota) and M.A. from Temple University (Pennsylvania). He then attended Indiana University where he obtained his Ph.D. in 1982 in geography with emphasis on population and development. He is currently professor of resource and cultural management in the School of Business & Industry at Florida A&M University (FAMU). Prior to joining the FAMU faculty he was an associate professor of geography at the University of Wisconsin–Whitewater (1985–1994) and lecturer at Georgia State University (1982–1985). In addition to his personal knowledge and experience, Professor Shrestha has conducted extensive field research in Nepal on several occasions as part of his two research grants from the National Science Foundation, as well as from the Ford and Rockefeller Foundations. He has published numerous articles in professional journals in the fields of geography and economic development, including: *World Development, Economic Development and Cultural Change, Annals of the Association of American Geographers, Journal of Contemporary Asia, International Journal of Population Geography, Journal of Developing Areas, Studies in Comparative International Development, Progress in Human Geography*, and *Political Geography Quarterly* (now *Journal of Political Geography*). In addition, he has published several books: *The Political Economy of Land, Landlessness, and Migration in Nepal* (2001; first published under the title, *Landlessness and Migration in Nepal*, Westview Press, 1990), *In the Name of Development: A Reflection on Nepal* (1997 and 1999), and *Nepal and Bangladesh: A Global Studies Handbook* (2002).

Keshav Bhattarai was born and raised in Nepal. He earned his B.A in Nepal and M.S. in forestry in England. In 2000, he received his Ph.D. degree from Indiana University where he studied geography with an environmental focus. Prior to coming to the United States in the mid-1990s, he worked as district forest officer for the government of Nepal. He has published articles in *Applied Geography*, *Journal of Developing Areas*, and *International Development Planning Review*. Currently, he is an associate professor of geography at Central Missouri State University.